America's Post-Christian Apocalypse

America's Post-Christian Apocalypse

How Secular Modernism Marginalized Christianity and
The Peril of Leaving God Behind at the End of the Age

Thomas R. Goehle

Alētheia Books

America's Post-Christian Apocalypse: How Secular Modernism Marginalized Christianity and The Peril of Leaving God Behind at the End of the Age

Copyright © 2015 Thomas R. Goehle

Scripture quotations are taken from the Holy Bible, English Standard Version® (ESV®). Copyright © 2001 by Crossway, a publishing ministry of Good News Publishers. Used by permission. All rights reserved. The author has added italics to Scripture quotations for emphasis.

ISBN-10: 0692397507
ISBN-13: 978-0692397503

Cover design by John Spain
johnspainart@gmail.com
Cover concept by Thomas R. Goehle

Author may be contacted at endtimeapocalypse@outlook.com

To Mom and Dad

Who always supported me in every way in every endeavor I undertook

Contents

Acknowledgments

I would like to thank my editor, Erin K. Brown, whose professionalism translated into numerous helpful recommendations that strengthened the manuscript. Erin persevered through a seemingly endless number of endnotes and general questions I posed. Like any good editor, Erin went on a mission to expunge all passive sentences. Any found in the text are a little rebellion I allowed myself.

I am also grateful to the following people who read various portions of the manuscript and offered helpful advice and encouragement. They were all instrumental in pushing the book over the finish line. My thanks go to Scott Brown, Betty Corbett, Sam Dold, Dale Engelhart, Carol Engle, Donald Ferguson, Elfriede Ferguson, John Gallo, Nicole Gallo, Paul Hensen, Anne Holmes, Anna Mae Jones, Nobby Kadohama, Bev Maurer, Betty Miles, Ernie Miles, Dorothy Miller, Bob Oliver, Dr. Robert H. Oliver, Diane Sharpe, Carolyn Sperl, Alex Stevens, Dr. Nick Yates, and Dr. Neil Yerkey.

Finally, I would like to thank Dr. Gordon Lewis, my former mentor at Denver Seminary, who offered invaluable guidance at the beginning of this project.

Introduction

The purpose of this book is to help the reader understand how the forces of secular modernism marginalized Christianity. Because Christianity no longer maintains the cultural authority it held in the past, we are now rapidly becoming a post-Christian nation. *America's Post-Christian Apocalypse* reveals how this happened and serves as a warning of the peril that lies ahead if we continue to leave God behind in our individual lives and as a nation.

This study goes deeper than the typical book on cultural criticism which spends chapter after chapter rehearsing various examples of societal deterioration the reader is already familiar with. Although we will certainly point out some areas of moral and societal decline, this book endeavors to be different in three ways.

First, we will trace the modern secular mentality back in time and uncover its historical origins. This will provide a richer understanding of how our contemporary (post)modern mind-set emerged, how it is playing out today, and how it pushed Christianity to the periphery of culture.

Second, rather than placing the blame for the marginalization of Christianity solely on the shoulders of secular modernists, I assert that Christians—both committed and uncommitted—must accept much of the blame for the disenfranchisement from Christianity in our culture. We will reveal, for example, how many professing Christians have accommodated secularism and the spirit of the age.

Third, instead of simply focusing on the present or the past, I look to the future to see how our folly of leaving God behind may play out in the light of the biblical apocalypse and the end of the age. This is imperative because the end time is looming closer every day.

In Chapter one we define key terms such as *secularism*, *modernism*, and *apocalypse*, as well as providing a broad historical overview of how

Christianity became marginalized in our country over the past hundred years.

In Chapter two, we will dig a little deeper into how the marginalization process takes place. I divide the agents of marginalization into two groups. The first group is composed of those "outside" of and, in some cases, opposed to Christianity. This includes agnostics and secular humanists, the latter of whom desire to see most vestiges of Christianity expunged from society. The second group is composed of those "inside" the Christian fold, which includes genuine Christians and practical atheists (nominal Christians).

Chapter three creates a historical context for understanding how Christianity became marginalized over time. We will go back in history and trace the roots of secular modernism, paying particular attention to the Enlightenment's role in Christianity's marginalization. Some of the philosophers we will look at include Ockham, Descartes, Hume, Kant, Hegel, Feuerbach, and Nietzsche.

In Chapter four we will observe how the Reformation, the two Great Awakenings, and Pietism all had a democratizing effect on Christianity in which "authority" shifted from ecclesiastical structures to the autonomy of the individual. This "autonomy" resulted in the privatization of religious belief and a smorgasbord approach to religion that is very much in evidence today. We will also examine how Protestant theologians, instead of resisting Enlightenment philosophy, accommodated modernism and retreated from its advance which resulted in a watered-down version of Christianity known as liberal Protestantism. Some of the theologians we will survey include Schleiermacher, Kierkegaard, Bultmann, Barth, Tillich, and a few others.

Modernism and the accommodationist approach to theology that followed in the wake of the Enlightenment produced what I call the "fruit of secularization" (autonomy, loss of Christian authority, and politically correct pluralism), which we will address in Chapter five.

Chapter six will continue to explore the fruit of the secularization process, which includes relativism, the loss of truth, and politically correct tolerance. I categorize these fruit under the auspices of postmodernism, which we will examine in some detail.

Chapter seven tells a fascinating story of how Christianity was marginalized after playing such an integral role in all the early colleges, notably Harvard and Yale. The liberal Protestant reformers, who were presidents at many of the colleges in the mid-nineteenth century, played a decisive role in modernizing and transforming those colleges into universities. The rise of science and big money were two significant factors in Christianity's disenfranchisement as the nineteenth century ended.

Chapter eight continues tracing the loss of Christian authority in higher education from the beginning of the twentieth century to the present. Today, Christianity is noticeable by its absence in our secular colleges and universities.

Chapters nine through eleven are the science chapters. We will examine the historical interaction between Christianity and natural philosophy (science), starting from the Middle Ages up to the time of Darwin. We'll become acquainted with natural philosophers which include Aquinas, Bacon, Galileo, Descartes, Newton, Boyle, and a few others. I dispel the myth that science and Christianity have always been at war.

Chapter ten explores Darwinism. We study Darwin in historical context noting factors other than science that went into his theory of evolution such as the Industrial Revolution and also the death of his daughter. We discard the myth that Christians were at war with Darwinism from the outset of the publishing of *On the Origin of Species*. The latter half of the chapter delves into what science really is and how it works, as well as examining its epistemological problems.

In Chapter eleven we look at how Darwin's theory affected the way science is practiced today. We note that the Scopes Monkey Trial solidified science as the accepted authority when it interfaces with Christianity. We examine the merits of two competing theories: whether life arose through matter plus time plus chance from lifeless matter (abiogenesis), or whether life came into existence as a result of an Intelligent Designer. We conclude that methodological naturalism has biased science in favor of atheism and abiogenesis.

We conclude Chapter eleven with a summary of all three science chapters, pointing out that no war existed between Christianity and science until methodological naturalism and naturalistic evolution took hold of science at the end of the nineteenth century. We note that naturalistic evolution is a competing worldview, which is why it is at war with Christianity today.

We look at the history of the public school system in Chapter twelve where we point out that Protestantism played a vital role in the nineteenth century when Bible reading in the classroom was a daily routine. After the turn of the century, secular humanists like John

Dewey steered students away from patriotism and traditional Christian morals and values. Today, progressive globalists attempt to instill their ideology of anti-Americanism and autonomous ethics such as values clarification into the children.

A good deal of the last half of the chapter is spent learning how psychology and the mental health professions have replaced parental authority. This coincides with the globalist and progressive agenda, which maintains that children should belong to the state. We also review the administering of drugs to school children under the dubious auspices of various contrived mental disorders.

Chapter thirteen examines cultural degradation which can be attributed in part to the fact that the Christian worldview is not being passed down to the generations coming up behind us. This, in turn, plays a role in the breakdown of the family, which results in more cultural degradation. Contributing factors also include a faulty notion of freedom, the influence of the media, and our love affair with the latest gadgets. We finish with a glance at the horror genre (Frankenstein, Dracula, and zombies) as a reflection of the Enlightenment project gone bad.

In Chapter fourteen we cover the very delicate subjects of homosexuality and abortion, which are presented in light of a biblical framework and done in a respectful manner. We dispel the myth that homosexuality is genetically predetermined. We note that the gay agenda is having a deleterious effect on the institution of marriage which is evident by the recent Supreme Court ruling on same-sex marriage.

In the second half of the chapter, we review the various ways abortion, just like the gay agenda, has had a harmful effect on the family and relationships in general. We bring to light something that society has heard little about since *Roe v. Wade*—women who have had an abortion are the second victims of this practice. The chapter concludes by offering hope for those who have had an abortion, as well as those practicing homosexuality.

Chapter fifteen looks at how our therapeutic culture has marginalized the Christian worldview. We note that Christianity in general, and evangelicalism particularly, has accommodated secular psychology over the past three decades. In the latter half of the chapter we revisit the pharmaceutical approach to psychiatry, questioning its efficacy. I argue that we are creating a society of functional zombies.

The final five chapters are an examination of the apocalypse that is unfolding as America rapidly becomes a post-Christian nation. Chapter sixteen involves an examination of how the global elites want to dominate humanity by setting up a one-world government in which those at the bottom ("unwashed masses") are corralled into a neo-feudal system. As we demonstrate, this may be accomplished by various "crises," whether real or contrived, which would expedite the implementation of the elites' malevolent agenda. We offer a cursory glance at various institutions such as the Federal Reserve, CFR, Trilateral Commission, etc., which have aided the globalists' agenda.

In Chapter seventeen we show the remarkable similarities between Nazi Germany and the totalitarian direction our country is currently moving toward. We uncover the history of the eugenics movement both in the United States and Germany, noting that the churches in both countries showed almost no resistance to eugenics or the Nazis, but instead supported them both. My conclusion is that presently our nation is susceptible to the same inclinations of being overrun by a totalitarian regime masquerading as a savior of sorts.

Chapter eighteen will tie together what we learned from the previous seventeen chapters and then place it within the framework of the book of Revelation (the Apocalypse). Because our country increasingly embraces secularism and leaves God behind, we are vulnerable to the lies and deceptions not only of the global elites but also the future Antichrist as well. We will look at how things that are trending today (RFID chips, surveillance, psychopharmacology, etc.) might play out in light of the biblical Apocalypse and Antichrist's kingdom.

In Chapter nineteen we will continue to look at the deceptions at the end of the age, noting two specific lies that will probably be in play at that time. In the first half of the chapter we will examine the similarities between transhumanists and New Age thinkers, many of whom hold to the lie that we can evolve and become "God." The latter half of the chapter is concerned with the coming "apostasy," when so-called Christians and practical atheists will fall away from the faith as they are deceived by the lies of the Antichrist, false doctrines, and what I label the "ecumenical push." Future Christians will suffer persecution during the time leading up to, and including, the "great tribulation" because of their unwavering stand that Jesus Christ is the only way to salvation.

We conclude the book in Chapter twenty by looking at how Jesus's *parousia* (coming) parallels the Jewish marriage customs. We will also examine the rapture of the church which is followed by the day of the Lord when God's judgment and wrath will be poured out on unbelievers who follow Antichrist and his counterfeit kingdom. The book concludes with demonstrating what true salvation involves and how following God's will for your life is the antidote to secularism.

It is my hope that *America's Post-Christian Apocalypse* explains how we lost our way and offers guidance on how to get our country back on the right track before it's too late.

Chapter 1

The Marginalization of Christianity: An Overview

The thesis of *America's Post-Christian Apocalypse* is that over the past century and a half secular (post)modernism has increasingly replaced Christianity as the hegemonic authority in our society. While it is true that our republic has been pluralistic, with different religious beliefs existing side by side, it is also the case that historically the Christian worldview, Protestant Christianity in particular, has provided the underpinning for our morals, values, and way of life in general. This is no longer the case.

With each passing generation, especially after the countercultural revolution, we became more and more a nation of practical atheists. What I mean by this is that while the majority of our populace gives lip service to a belief in God, most people go about their everyday lives as if God does not exist. The result is that as we move forward in time, secularism is progressively the default worldview in our society, not Christianity. In short, we are becoming a post-Christian nation.

In many ways, we are post-Christian already. One hardly needs to review the legal right to abortion, the negation of prayer, and the tossing of the Ten Commandments out of public schools as evidence that our nation no longer wants to acknowledge the God of the Bible. But in other ways we are not completely post-Christian just yet. For example, most people in our society still consider themselves Christians in some sense, even though many of these same people go about their daily lives without giving God a thought.

Leaving the God of the Bible behind as we move forward into the future is a clear and present danger to our nation and its people. Without mincing words, if we continue on our present godless course, our country is heading for disaster. Our culture is living on the spiritual and moral capital of Christianity that was passed down from previous

1

generations. This capital is almost entirely gone now. The foundation that Christianity once provided has crumbled. Without the Christian worldview underpinning our culture, and without repentance in our individual lives and our nation as a whole, we are moving inexorably toward a post-Christian apocalypse.

Anecdotal Evidence for Marginalization

I have watched the growing antipathy and disrespect for the Christian worldview over the course of my lifetime. Whether journalists, reporters, talk show hosts, anchors, television icons, television shows, or the movies, the media increasingly show their suspicion and often outright contempt for Christianity and its moral values.

In this regard, one thing that sticks out in my mind occurred a number of years ago on the TV show *Politically Incorrect*. The condescension directed at Christianity was blatant and, quite frankly, somewhat shocked me at the time. Hosted by Bill Maher, the show presented a debate-style format with two conservatives on one side and two liberals on the other side. It became obvious after watching the show that it was anything but politically incorrect. Maher, more often than not, seated a liberal in one of the chairs where a conservative should have been. Thus it was three liberals versus one lone conservative. Soon after Maher presented the topic, the three panelists holding the liberal position started hammering the conservative. Maher attempted to make the conservative look like a fool because all three liberal panelists took a contrary position.

If a Christian happened to garner enough courage to be on this show, Maher turned up the vitriol exponentially—something akin to throwing a Christian to the lions. The ridicule hurled from the three liberals, the studio audience, and Maher himself sent a clear message to the viewer of the show: Christians are backward thinking, closed-minded, and ignorant. I had never seen such open disdain of Christians on TV before. The show should have been entitled *Politically Correct*, because it was a centerpiece for denigrating Christian morals and values. Maher admitted, "I have hated the Church way before anyone else. I have been pounding religion for nine years on this show."[1]

I found it puzzling that liberals like Maher, who pride themselves on their high-mindedness and tolerance, displayed such a closed-minded and intolerant hatred of Christianity. More troubling to me at that time was why and when it became politically correct and entirely acceptable in our culture to denigrate Christian values and those who hold them. I saw a cultural paradigm shift occurring right before my eyes.

The disparaging of Christianity in such a blatant manner simply would not have happened twenty years prior to Maher's show. I used to watch *The Waltons* on prime-time television on Thursday nights back in the 1970s. *The Waltons* portrayed an era when both Christian values and family togetherness were something to be valued. Today it is hopelessly naïve to think this television show could occupy the same slot in the titillating prime-time lineup. How many current prime-time shows portray a traditional family upholding Christian values in today's world? The traditional family is denigrated at every turn today and has been redefined or replaced by the "modern family." Unfortunately, our television shows and movies are to a great extent a reflection of our cultural values.

Speaking of values, what happened to our morals and principles that used to be broadly "Christian"? Would anyone disagree that the moral bar is lowered with each passing generation? It's amazing to see what our politically correct society is willing to tolerate today. It wasn't that long ago that it would have been hard to imagine a group of women marching up and down the street, proclaiming the right to abortion on demand. Likewise, fifty or a hundred years ago it would have seemed preposterous to predict that two men or two women would be kissing each other in public and sharing marriage vows in this country. Everyone knew the difference between right and wrong back then. Those who didn't were reticent to march their anomalous behavior out in public. Why? Because back then most people in our country held to Christian morals and values, at least in principle. Not so today. Tolerance is king. Anything goes. We have no sense of moral accountability to God anymore. Everyone does what is right in their own eyes. Each passing generation witnesses a move further away from the Christian worldview and *toward* secularism as expressed by autonomy, moral relativism, the loss of truth, narcissism, and politically correct tolerance.

Our move away from Christianity is evidenced by Mr. Obama's declaration in 2007 that "Whatever we once were, we are no longer a Christian nation. At least not just. We are also a Jewish nation, a Muslim nation, and a Buddhist nation and a Hindu nation and a nation for non-believers."[2] Mr. Obama's assertion, combined with the increasing moral decadence and godlessness that we see all around us supports the fact that the United States is increasingly a post-Christian nation.

3

However, because a majority of people in our country still consider themselves Christian in some sense and therefore would disagree with Mr. Obama's statement points to the fact we are not as post-Christian as I predict we will be in the future. This is why I think it is fair to say that on the one hand, although we are *already* post-Christian in many ways, on the other hand, we are *becoming* more post-Christian with each passing day.

Christians are often their own worst enemies when it comes to allowing Christianity to be marginalized. This is exemplified, for example, when Larry King, on his old TV show *Larry King Live*, asked Christian leaders he had invited on his show seemingly innocent questions like "How could God allow that?" after a disaster like a tsunami, hurricane Katrina, or 9/11. King always asked this kind of question with a boyish golly-gee-whiz innocence, but in reality his not-so-innocent question was meant as an "I got you now" show stopper. Pitifully, almost without exception, Christians responded in a totally inadequate manner. In this way, Christians marginalize themselves by reinforcing the stereotypical view that the Christian worldview cannot address the toughest of questions and that Christians are therefore ignorant for believing in Christianity. If we cannot count on Christian leaders to answer tough questions, why should we be surprised that churches today are largely absent in the fight against secular (post)modernism?

Another problem is that an increasing percentage of Christians in each emerging generation are embracing the cultural zeitgeist rather than holding their ground against the onslaught of secularism. For example, in more and more ways we see little to distinguish the mind-set of present day Protestant churches from the culture at large. Even though most members and pastors won't admit it, a successful church is now measured in numbers (congregants and church membership). The larger the church, the more successful it is.

This is wrongheaded. Instead of shepherding the existing flock, many pastors today see their primary role as recruiting new people. This is done under the auspices of "making disciples." Rather than equipping the saints to *go out* into the world and proclaim the gospel to every creature, church leadership accommodates the cultural mind-set so that those in the world can come *into* the church and feel at home.

It seems to me that Protestantism in general and evangelicals particularly care more about what a visitor may think of the worship service than what God thinks of it. I'm troubled that we are increasingly treating our church services like a seminar. I think we've lost our sense of reverence. Taking coffee into the church service reminds me more of taking a college class rather than preparing oneself to worship the living God. Combine that attitude with the worship music, which in some cases borders on irreverence, and it becomes more difficult to draw the line between entertainment and worship.

I think this often superficial and sometimes worldly attitude with regard to "doing church" may be reflected in our increasingly shallow theology. So, for example, doctrinal verities that might make a newcomer feel uncomfortable are now in some cases baptized in the jargon of the latest motivational pop-psychology or watered down so they sound more "positive" and are more palatable. If I am right, then all of this may go a long way to explaining why we are a nation of biblical illiterates. (See Chapter two for more on this.) Immersing ourselves in the superficial will result in a superficial understanding of Christianity and God's Word. I think Christian leadership needs to reexamine its accommodative mind-set regarding the "contemporary" worship service lest we be swallowed whole by secular culture in the not too distant future.

We can see from the examples above that marginalization occurs in two major ways. The first component involves secular forces "outside" of and opposed to Christianity, which attempt to disparage Christianity and obliterate it completely from the public square. Or at least push the Christian worldview to the margins of culture. The other "outside" forces are modernism and postmodernism, which we will look at in Chapters five and six, respectively. These outside philosophical forces more often than not have a secularizing affect with regard to religion.

The second component of the marginalization process involves forces "inside" Christianity, that is, inside the Christian fold. This would include Christians, and those who consider themselves Christians, who have unwittingly aided the secularization process through accommodation and retreat. Many who are nominal Christians either attempt to adapt their Christian beliefs in some way to (post)modernism or retreat from secularism's advance. (We examine nominal Christianity in the next chapter.) Thus, both Christians and secularists play a part in how Christianity has lost its authoritative influence in our society.

A warfare analogy may be helpful to understand secularization. In war, when one country gains ground and finally conquers another country, it is said to have overtaken its foe. But from another perspective, it is equally fair to say that the conquered people retreated before the conquering foe. If we apply this analogy to secularization, it is clear that some who oppose Christianity would like to eliminate its cultural influence. It is also true that much of the secularization of our culture is due in large part to those inside the Christian fold who allow the secular worldview to have its way by either accommodating Christianity to the modern spirit of the age or retreating from secularization's advance.

Now is a good time to look at some key terms that will help us understand how the marginalization of Christianity occurs.

Definition of Key Terms

Secularism and the secularization process play a key role in the marginalization process, so let's start with a somewhat formal definition of these terms. The word *secular* comes from the Latin word *saeculum*, which means "time" or "age." Thus a person who is secular "is completely time bound, totally a child of his age, a creature of history, with no vision of eternity."[3] As far back as 1845, secularism was defined in terms of morality. As John W. Whitehead points out, a secular morality was based solely on the "well-being of mankind in the present life, to the exclusion of all considerations drawn from belief in God or in a future existence beyond death."[4] To be secular, then, is to be solely concerned with this present world—the here and now. Secular morals are not based on God or the Christian worldview.

Secularism is a worldview or ideology. Those holding to its more virulent form, ideological secularism (such as secular humanism), want to remove religion from the public square entirely.[5] If secularism is an ideology, then "secularization" may be defined as the sociological expression of this ideology being played out in society.[6] Secularization may be defined as the discernible, long-term,[7] historical process of secularism[8] where society frees itself from the authority of religion and "otherworldly" concerns and focuses solely on this world alone.[9] Steve Bruce claims that three changes take place during the secularization process. He lists these as "the decline of popular involvement with the churches; the decline in scope and influence of religious institutions; and the decline in the popularity and impact of religious beliefs."[10]

The warfare analogy that I used above to describe religion and secularization found literal expression around four centuries ago. The term *secularization* originally referred to land being taken away from ecclesiastical authorities during the Wars of Religion.[11] Today, it would be fair to say that the extent to which secularization is gaining a foothold in our culture is the same extent to which Christianity is losing ground. Berger puts it this way: "By secularization we mean the process by which sectors of society and culture are removed from the domination of religious institutions and symbols."[12]

Another concept that is closely related with secularization is *modernism*. This concept is important because a case can be made that the more "modern" a society becomes, the more secular it becomes. In its broadest form this is known as "secularization thesis."[13] There has been much conjecture pro and con along with a good deal of ink spilled over the merits of secularization thesis. Space does not permit unpacking this debate. For our purpose, secularization thesis is helpful in explaining the marginalization process. If the secularization thesis is true, then we would expect that as modernization increases (and post-modernism as well), so too would the marginalization of Christianity. This is what we will see as our study begins to unfold.

Modernity comes from the Latin *modernus*, which means "just now."[14] The reader will immediately notice the similarity between the word *modern* and the word *secular*. Both words are primarily concerned with "this present age" or "just now." Secularists' and modernists' primary focus is the here and now, not eternity or God.

John Dewey, one of the leading protagonists of modernity in the twentieth century, notes four characteristics of the modern era: 1) a loss of preoccupation with the supernatural and instead a focus on this world; 2) a loss of ecclesiastical authority and a turn to one's own experience and reflection for guidance in life; 3) a belief in progress; and 4) the experimental study of nature in order to gain technology for social progress.[15]

Modernism, in essence, involves a "desacralization" of the world where a more scientific orientation toward the cosmos replaces many of the traditional authorities.[16] Technology plays a role in this, because as technology advances, man starts to believe he can be his own savior. We will look at this in Chapter two when we examine secular humanism, and Chapter nineteen where we discuss transhumanism.

According to David Wells, modernism has constructed its own secular salvation history.[17] In other words, modernists have disenfranchised themselves from any religious constraints and placed their faith in humankind's ability, through science and technology, to advance without any divine guidance. Though they are not advocates of modernism themselves, Middleton and Walsh summarize modernism this way: "In the modern era we are our own saviors. And we effect our salvation in secular redemptive history through the ineluctable and inevitable march of progress. This is the heart of modernity's historical self-confidence."[18]

Christianity's Marginalization in Historical Context: A Brief Overview

Although Christianity was not established in any legal sense during the nineteenth century, it is fair to say that it was held in high esteem in our society. Protestant leaders helped build hospitals, orphanages, colleges, schools, youth camps, and publishing houses.[19] It was in this way that Protestantism exhibited a cultural supremacy over a broad sector of society.[20] In fact, as late as 1890, the U.S. Supreme Court ruled unanimously that if one takes "a view of American life as expressed by its laws, its business, its customs and its society, we find everywhere a clear recognition of the same truth . . . that this is a Christian nation."[21]

Modernism, Darwinism, and science, however, challenged the Christian cultural predominance in the late nineteenth century and into the twentieth century. So, for example, the aforementioned forces disenfranchised the Christian worldview from higher education by the end of the nineteenth century, which we will look at more closely in Chapters seven and eight.

Christian hegemony fared no better during the first quarter of the twentieth century. Phillip Hammond suggests that at certain moments in our history, the "disestablishment" of Christianity from culture became quite noticeable.[22] For example, during the period between the First World War and the Great Depression, a devastating impact on the country's morale diminished enthusiasm for evangelism.[23] The controversy between fundamentalists and modernists was in full swing during this time. The 1925 Scopes Monkey Trial exemplified this conflict, in which fundamentalism took a broadside, retreated, and thereafter adopted something of a bunker mentality.

The Scopes Monkey Trial marked an important point in the disestablishment of fundamentalist Christianity from culture. Antireligious journalists added fuel to the fire after the Scopes Trial by spewing epithets such as "meddlers" and "do-gooders" at the retreating fundamentalists.[24] As Christian Smith observes: "The old Protestant establishment moralizers and pastoral opinion makers were mostly swept aside in the 1920s by new cultural authorities in the social sciences, journalism, advertising, and Hollywood. By the 1920s, the old

Victorian struggles with religious doubt had finally been replaced with a distinct cultural sense, among social elites and beyond, of religion's mere irrelevance."[25]

Smith goes on to summarize the secularization process during the period between 1870 and 1930: "The secularization of the institutions of American public life did not happen by accident or happenstance. . . . Religion's historical marginalization in science, the universities, mass education, reform politics, and the media was a historical accomplishment, an achievement of specific groups of people, many of whom intended to marginalize religion."[26] Moreover, through a series of "campaigns" over a number of decades, secularization took place in the context of a struggle over power and authority in the political, cultural, and institutional structures.[27]

Even though Christianity lost some of its footing in the 1920s, one thing that average liberals and conservatives agreed on during that time was that religious values were universally applicable.[28] Most people back then believed that religion itself was a *collective* endeavor that required sustained social interaction and not mystical isolation.[29] In other words, a "good society" required people who were primarily accountable to God so that they would be equipped to act responsibly by upholding both moral and democratic values.[30] Unfortunately, whatever collective value Christianity had back then as the glue that held society together is lost today. Everyone today wants to be autonomous, a law unto themselves.

In the post–WWII era Civil Religion, which linked God and country, was very much in vogue and exemplified this collective value of Christianity. This was when Congress approved the motto "In God We Trust" to be added to the currency, and "under God" to the Pledge of Allegiance.[31] Religious belief appeared to regain some of its footing. Because the family played an important cultural role during the 1950s, church attendance peaked during this time.[32] This was the era when parents hauled a massive number of baby boomers to church. But this apparent religiosity belied a superficiality of religious belief that lay just under the surface.

During this time the typical American held to some orthodox Christian tenets such as the inspiration of the Bible, the Trinity, and some sense of the depravity of humankind. But for the average worshipper "religion was less a matter of theology than of simple experience."[33] A 1950 Gallup poll, for example, discovered the lack of theological depth. It showed that 53 percent of Americans could not name even one of the Gospels, and only 35 percent could name all four Gospels.[34] Only 34 percent of Americans could correctly identify who delivered the Sermon on the Mount.[35] When asked to rate the one hundred most significant events in human history, Americans ranked Columbus's discovery of America in first place. Unbelievably, Jesus's birth or crucifixion placed fourteenth.[36] In 1961, *Time* magazine described the Christianity of that time as "bland" and "homogenized," as if processed in a "suburban kitchen blender."[37] Moreover, the cracks in the foundation that started after the turn of the century were becoming even more evident during this time.

Much of what passed for orthodoxy was not much more than "nominal" Christianity ("Christian" in name only). According to Alan Wolfe, many people went to church on Sunday not out of inner conviction but rather because of "what their neighbors might think if they did not."[38] Will Herberg, in his classic book *Protestant-Catholic-Jew* written in 1955, describes a picture of religion at that time: "Christians flocking to church, yet forgetting all about Christ when it comes to naming the most significant events in history; men and women valuing the Bible as revelation . . . yet apparently seldom reading it themselves. Every aspect of contemporary religious life reflects this paradox— pervasive secularism amid mounting religiosity . . . America seems to be at once the most religious and the most secular of nations."[39] I believe this apparent contradiction of secular and religious belief was largely a product of nominal Christianity, which offered a thin veneer of Christian respectability but lacked much of the doctrinal orthodoxy and commitment needed to withstand the continual onslaught of secularism.

Higher education expanded greatly in the 1960s in order to meet the need for science and cutting-edge technology. This general trend in higher education, which continued thereafter,[40] had its own impact on religious belief. Whereas differences in religious beliefs prior to the 1950s were drawn either along denominational lines or between Catholics and Protestants, the new rise in education changed all that. A liberalizing attitude toward religion emerged and resulted in the separation of religious beliefs to some extent between the more educated and the less educated.[41] Those who were more educated tended to consider themselves more liberal with regard to their religious beliefs, while the less educated tended to consider themselves to be religious conservatives.[42] In fact, at that time one's level of education was the single most important predictor of one's position regarding social, moral, and political values.[43]

This liberalizing trend continued into the 1960s and 1970s and is another moment where a major disestablishment was occurring between Christianity and culture.[44] The "Me generation," with its emerging sexual revolution, declared that everyone was free to "do your own thing." This new commitment to individualism and personal autonomy spilled over into individual choices with regard to the "family and sexual sphere," such as abortion, sexual norms, family authority, etc.[45] Supreme Court cases such as *Roe v. Wade* demonstrated a decisive shift away from Christianity as a cultural authority and instead a move toward an emphasis on personal "autonomy" and individual "choice."[46] Thus, the culture shifted *away* from the collective good of religion and *toward* what was important for the individual alone.

It should come as no surprise that the emerging educational class, as noted above, was more liberal and tolerant on a wide variety of social issues, including legalized abortion and homosexuality.[47] Wade Clark Roof describes many of the baby boomers of this era as "a self-absorbed, narcissistic generation [which] abandoned theology in favor of psychology and self-help philosophies focused largely on their own individual wants and needs. They were born to be pleased, not to be saved."[48]

Moreover, an increasing percentage of the population considered religion an individual endeavor rather than something to be practiced by a community of believers.[49] Evidence of this was the burgeoning influx of Eastern religions with their individualistic meditation techniques. Individualism combined with the countercultural rebellion of the late '60s and early '70s to fuel the fire of autonomy. This rebellion, of course, resulted in the further loss of Christian cultural dominance when placed in the context of the liberalizing trend in education and court decisions that did not prove favorable to the Christian worldview.

All of this adds up to what Berger calls a loss of the "plausibility structure" of Christianity.[50] The plausibility structure functions somewhat like a paradigm or worldview. When the plausibility structure has a monopoly on society as a whole, it legitimizes much of society's core views about reality. As long as the plausibility structure stays intact, "all the important social processes within it serve to confirm and reconfirm the reality of this world."[51] As long as the plausibility structure is not challenged, it will be passed down from generation to generation and accepted as the normative way to view the world.[52] It is important to note that Christianity suffered a plausibility crisis during the countercultural revolution from which it has not recovered. The disestablishment of Christianity from culture continued and accelerated through to the present time.

Michael Novak explains that "it is usually the case that the first generation to reject religion continues to live from the internal capital they have inherited from belief and its inward practices. However, they have now made themselves incapable of passing on their inner beliefs and practices to their children. Thus their children grow up in an entirely different situation, and even more so do the children of their children. In this way, the loss of belief is not generally felt throughout society for at least three or possibly four generations."[53]

If Novak's argument is correct, we should expect Christianity would have lost much of its cultural authority now that we are two generations or so removed from the countercultural revolution. This is, in fact, just what we have seen. Previous generations have passed down an increasingly smaller percentage of the Christian worldview, and now we are becoming more post-Christian with each passing generation.

Wells summarizes our thoughts concerning secularism and the plausibility crisis that is occurring today with regard to Christianity: "Outside is a world that ignores what is most important to Christians and that is in fact now organizing itself on the basis of that rejection. Within the larger society, secularism seems natural because its context gives it plausibility; within that same society, Christian faith seems odd... The bias of our experience in the modern world tilts heavily against a perception that the Christian faith is true and equally heavily toward a perception that secularism is true."[54]

America's Post-Christian Apocalypse

The word *apocalypse* can help us understand what I argue in the coming pages. In its formal sense, *apocalypse* means to "uncover" or "reveal." In fact, the book of Revelation found in the Bible is known as the Apocalypse (from the Greek *apokalupsis*). The biblical Apocalypse is the Revelation that Jesus gave to His disciple John, who "reveals" events that will take place at the end of the age. So in the formal sense the word *apocalypse* means to uncover, to unveil, or to reveal.

This brings us to a few other uses of the word. I also want to use the term *apocalypse* in its less formal, more pedestrian sense. When most people use this term, they mean it in the sense of "catastrophe" or "cataclysm." People commonly use *apocalypse* as a synonym for "Armageddon" or some type of end-of-the-world devastation. So, for example, fans of the zombie genre often talk about a "zombie apocalypse." This is meant to refer to 1) some type of cataclysmic Armageddon-like event 2) that may take place now or in the future.

For the purposes of this book, I will be using *apocalypse* in all of its various meanings: 1) an "uncovering" or "revealing;" 2) a "cataclysmic" or "destructive" event that can take place now or at the end of the age; and also 3) the prophetic biblical book of Revelation, which reveals future events leading to the day of the Lord and Armageddon, where Jesus destroys the Antichrist's kingdom of evil.[55]

The lion's share of *America's Post-Christian Apocalypse* will involve revealing how our country is becoming post-Christian. As noted above, I argue that the Christian worldview is losing its hegemony because secular (post)modernism is destroying Christianity's plausibility structure. Moreover, the forces of secularism have pushed Christianity to the periphery of culture while simultaneously filling the vacuum left by the marginalization of Christianity.

In addition, I argue that the loss of Christianity's cultural authority is an ongoing catastrophe (apocalypse) that is taking place right now. Moreover, the disestablishment of Christianity from culture is a catastrophic process that is destroying our once great nation.

This brings us to the future sense of *apocalypse*. There are consequences for leaving God behind in our increasingly post-Christian culture. So, although the marginalization of Christianity is an apocalypse that is unfolding today, the destructiveness of this process will reveal itself for the real cataclysm that it is in the future. America's post-Christian apocalypse will result in the devastation of our nation as we move inexorably toward a loss of our national sovereignty and absorption into some type of New World Order (NWO) system.

With this in mind, the final chapters will place America's post-Christian apocalypse within the future prophetic framework of the biblical Apocalypse—the book of Revelation. The hope is that by being forewarned, the reader, and the younger generations coming up behind us, will be able to discern truth from falsehood and therefore avoid being sucked into the vortex of lies that will be part and parcel of Antichrist's phony kingdom.

Summary

It will be readily apparent as we move through our study that Christianity no longer maintains the authoritative status or cultural clout it once held. The forces of secularization, whether intentional or not, are pushing Christianity to the margins of culture. A growing percentage of people in our country are basing their lives on a secular worldview rather than the Christian worldview, even if they are unaware of it.

Secularists may range from those with an indifference to religion to those who are agnostic or openly atheistic. Secular humanists are the more virulent type of secularist and maintain a willful and vigorous opposition to Christianity. These people are not opposed to seeing most vestiges of the Christian worldview eradicated from culture. This is one way Christianity has been marginalized.

But Christians, and those who consider themselves Christians (but may not be), are also responsible for allowing Christianity to lose its cultural authority. Nominal Christians (practical atheists) live their daily lives as if God does not exist. These people offer no real resistance to the onslaught of secular (post)modernism.

Unfortunately, the culture is also capturing an increasing number of practicing Christians. Evidence for this may be seen in evangelicalism's approach to reaching the unsaved and the subordination of doctrine in some instances. This results in an increase in biblical illiteracy with each passing generation.

The bottom line is that the Christian worldview is rapidly losing its plausibility structure in our society as secularism continues to disestablish Christianity from culture. Secularism's sole concern with the here and now is rapidly becoming the default worldview of our culture. A greater percentage of people in each up-and-coming generation are ignoring God's existence. They don't give God or eternity a thought.

It may be fair to claim that our country is already post-Christian. But the disestablishment of Christianity is not as pervasive now as I predict it will be in the future. Many people today still consider themselves Christians in some sense. This is true of many baby boomers who, at least for a few more years, comprise the largest demographic group in our country. When the influence of the baby boomers gives way to the generations behind them, the marginalization of Christianity will be a *fait accompli*. Then we will truly be a post-Christian nation.

Chapter 2

Marginalization Through Secularism, Accommodation, and Retreat

In the previous chapter we looked at some key factors causing the marginalization of Christianity. We learned that secularism and modernism, in their broadest forms, are major components in this process. We also saw a brief overview of how secularization occurred in recent history.

In this chapter we will look at the various agents in the disenfranchisement of Christianity. For example, we will see that those "outside" (secularists) of the Christian camp are pushing Christianity to the periphery of culture. To understand secularism better, we will look at its most formal expression in our society known as "secular humanism."

We will also look at how Christianity is marginalized from the "inside." Moreover, "insiders" are those within the Christian fold—people who identify with Christian belief in some sense. We will note that though these people may identify with Christianity to a certain extent, many in this group unwittingly marginalize Christianity. This occurs through either 1) "accommodating" secularization by compromising Christian beliefs so those beliefs are acceptable to the modern age, or 2) "retreating" from the forces of secularism, which allows secularization to proceed unhindered. Insiders are often guilty of privatizing their Christian beliefs, which is really a form of retreat and makes it impossible for these beliefs to exert any influence or authority in culture.

I believe that both secularists (outsiders) and Christians (insiders) are responsible for the decline of Christian authority and influence in our culture. The end result is the emergence of the secular mind-set, which has increasingly taken Christianity's place as the default worldview in our country.

Group # 1: "Soft" Secularism
Let's begin by looking at forces outside the Christian worldview. The secularists in our first group are considered outside of Christianity

because they do not identify themselves as Christians in any way, shape, or form. Some hold an indifferent or agnostic view toward Christianity or religion in general.

Most of the citizens in this category are probably not willful instruments of secularization. These folks are secular in their thinking whether they are aware of it or not. This means that they simply are not religious people and don't give much thought to how their secular presuppositions affect their daily lives. If asked about religion, they would probably say something like, "I'm not very religious," or "I don't believe in religion." They are agnostics or atheists of some sort. They may not even be aware that they are secularists. People in this group comprise a "softer" brand of atheism. They simply do not affirm a conviction of religious belief or a faith in any gods at all.

These folks comprise part of the group known as the "unaffiliated," who account for up to 22 percent of the American population.[1] This statistic seems a little high to me, but more troubling is that one-third of those under thirty-three years of age are unaffiliated, which is the highest percentage in Pew's polling history.[2] This statistic supports one of my sub-theses: The older generations are not effectively passing down the Christian worldview to the younger generations. This trend is accelerating, which is why we are becoming a post-Christian nation.

Group #2: "Hard" Secularism

Our second group is also made up of those outside of the religious/Christian camp. They are "secularists," who are more *intentional* and *conscious* of their secularism. Those in this second category are philosophical secularists and atheists who have given philosophical thought to, and understand the consequences of, their secularism. They comprise a "harder" brand of atheism, which is more assertive in its denial in the existence of God or any other religious beliefs they consider unreasonable or superstitious.

Most secularists in this group believe the country would be better off if the Christian belief system was done away with. If they had their way, many of the traditional beliefs, moral absolutes, and values derived from Christianity would be swept from culture. As people of "reason," they believe they are providing a service to society by pointing out and attempting to discard anything in the public square that is founded on what they consider "faith." When this brand of secularism decides to bare its teeth, it can reveal a rather rabid form of atheism.

This militant brand of secularism is exemplified by professor of philosophy Thomas Nagel, who declared at one point in his career:

> I want atheism to be true and am made uneasy by the fact that some of the most intelligent and well-informed people I know are religious believers. It isn't that I don't believe in God and naturally, hope there is no God! I don't want there to be a God; I don't want the universe to be like that.[3]

This is not simply atheism. This is anti-theism. I thought that Nagel had backed off this position somewhat, but in his *Mind and Cosmos*, he reiterates that he has no *sensus divinitatis*, and he sees no divine purpose in the world. Concerning the existence of God, he wrote in a footnote, "I am not just unreceptive but strongly averse to the idea, as I have said elsewhere."[4]

Although we will map out the philosophical roots of secularism in the next chapter, for now it is worth noting that the likes of Marx, Nietzsche, and Freud all exemplified this more rebellious form of atheism.[5] All three men combined to exert a tremendous influence on thinking in the twentieth century and helped solidify a type of religious secularism known formally as "secular humanism." In 1961, the Supreme Court (*Torcaso v. Watkins*) declared that secular humanism is a "religion" that does not "teach what would generally be considered a belief in the existence of God."[6]

Two Humanist Manifestos were written in the last century, one in 1933 and another in 1973, which formally outlined the creed of these humanists. Some of the more notable signers of the Humanist Manifesto II were Isaac Asimov, Francis Crick, B. F. Skinner, Allen F. Guttmacher (president of Planned Parenthood Federation of America), and Betty Friedan, who founded the National Organization for Women.[7] Their call for a "world order" based on a transnational government caught my attention.[8] We will look at the implications for a New World Order in Chapter sixteen.

Drafted in 2003, Humanist Manifesto III boasts notable signers such as Richard Dawkins, Eugenie Scott, Oliver Stone, and former vice president Walter Mondale.[9] It goes without saying that these folks, along with their cohorts, have exerted a profound influence on culture and public opinion.

Paul Kurtz (1925–2012), one of the leading secular humanists in our country over the last four decades or so, laid out this belief system in a book entitled *In Defense of Secular Humanism*. Unlike most philosophers writing today whose prose seems bent on confusing the reader, Dr. Kurtz outlines the tenets of secular humanism in a clear and straightforward manner, for which he should be commended. For example, in no uncertain terms he proclaims, "We find insufficient evidence for belief in the existence of a supernatural. . . . As nontheists, we begin with humans not God, nature not deity." A few paragraphs later he states: "No deity will save us; we must save ourselves."[10]

Demonstrating the continuity of the secular belief system dating back to the first Manifesto, Kurtz notes that today, "humanists still believe that traditional theism, especially faith in the prayer-hearing God, assumed to love and care for persons, to hear and understand their prayers, and to be able to do something about them, is an unproved and outmoded faith."[11]

It follows that if there is no God, as Kurtz contends, then we humans are in charge; therefore, morality is autonomous, and individuals are a law unto themselves. Regarding this, Kurtz points out, "It is not obedience to a prescribed moral code that is the mark of the moral person but the flowering of the free personality."[12]

It is interesting that Kurtz chose the words *flowering* and *free*, because one cannot help but think back to the free-spirited "flower children" of the 1960s who exhorted everyone to "do your own thing." As we will see throughout our study, this emphasis on autonomy, or doing what is right in one's own eyes, is one of the fundamental moral axioms of secularism.

Ethics for the secularist, according to Kurtz, is "autonomous and situational, needing no theological or ideological sanction."[13] This, of course, holds serious implications for morality and law in our society. As an increasing number of laws are passed that support individual "rights" and autonomous "choice," the probability increases that the very concept of community will be threatened. If people do what is right in their own eyes, then anarchy may be on the horizon. This becomes more probable in the future when an economic disruption or pandemic of some sort occurs and all hell breaks loose.

What about the meaning of life? The answer to this question should provide another clue to the essence of secular humanism. Kurtz encourages us to "accept the facts that 'God is dead' (according to Nietzsche) and that we have no way of knowing that He exists or even whether this is a meaningful question. We should accept the facts that human existence is probably a random occurrence existing between two oblivions, that death is inevitable, and that there is thus a tragic aspect to our lives. A free thinker, too, is capable of stoic resignation."[14]

Kurtz paints a rather gloomy picture of our place in the cosmos indeed. If God is dead and humans are in charge, then it will come as no surprise that the central doctrine of secular humanism is that "value is relative to man."[15] This, then, is the essence of the secular worldview. God does not exist and there is no hope for a future because there is no hope in eternity. All secularists have is the here and now. Whatever value or meaning there is in life is up to autonomous individuals, who must find it for themselves.

Secular humanism gives scientific inquiry and the use of reason an inordinate amount of weight for cultivating intelligence and solving problems. Human intelligence, rather than divine guidance, provides humankind with a powerful antidote to Christianity, which is dismissed as one of many mythologies.[16]

Technology continues to provide convincing evidence for the secularist that humankind is capable of solving its own problems and finding its way in life. Secularists argue that science and technology will lead humankind out of the darkness of ignorance and superstitious belief. Unquestioned dogma may have offered sanctuary to religious adherents in the past, but modern society has moved beyond this false sense of security. Dogmatism of any variety violates the First Commandment of all liberal-secularist thinking: "Thou shalt be tolerant."

The appeal of the secular worldview is increasing in our society. In 1952 secularists accounted for only 2 percent of the population, but thirty years later, in 1982, this number reached 8 percent. The expansion of higher education that occurred in the 1960s and 1970s is the single most significant factor for this rise.[17] Those who identify as secularists rocketed to nearly 16 percent in 2002.[18] As we noted above, those who are unaffiliated with any religion hovers around 22 percent, so this number probably coincides with some of those who are secularists in our country.

Thus far we have identified secularism and its ideologues as a force that is outside of Christianity. We saw that the softer brand of secularism simply doesn't give religious belief much thought. However, the harder brand of secularism that we just looked at stands diametrically opposed to the Christian worldview and will contest it in every way in the public square.

Let's shift our focus and examine the marginalization process as it occurs "inside" Christianity, that is, by those who identify with Christianity in some way yet accommodate secularization or retreat from its advance. This occurs through Civil Religion and "practical atheism," which we will turn to now.

Religion American-Style: Civil Religion

Civil Religion is one way in which a shallow type of Christian belief is exemplified in our culture. We see Civil Religion in the use of religious symbols, ritual, and rhetoric, which are endorsed in public ceremony.[19] "So help me God" at a presidential inauguration is evidence of Civil Religion, as is "one nation under God" in the Pledge of Allegiance. It is also symbolized in words on our money: "In God We Trust." In short, Civil Religion is the marriage of God and country, or God and patriotism.

The idea of Civil Religion may be traced back to the founding of our country. It is the American myth that we are God's chosen people who are set apart to do good works in the world and to be a light to other nations.[20] It provides our country an identity as a God-fearing people who are proponents of religious liberty.[21] Civil Religion has traditionally supported the idea that we are a Christian nation. And since we are a Christian nation, we must be made up of Christians, right? Wrong. Civil Religion is not Christianity.

Robert Bellah, in his definitive essay "Civil Religion in America," argues that although Civil Religion shares much in common with Christianity and certainly reflected the founders' personal as well as public viewpoints, it is in no way specifically Christian. An example of this may be seen in George Washington's first inaugural address in 1789, when he stated in rather nebulous terms:

> No people can be bound to acknowledge and adore the Invisible Hand which conducts the affairs of man more than those of the United States. Every step by which we have advanced to the character of an independent nation seems to have been distinguished by some token of providential agency.[22]

Although Washington elsewhere spoke more specifically when referring to God and even to Jesus Christ, we can see in his quote an example of Civil Religion, which is a watered-down version of Christianity.

About a century and a half or so later, President Eisenhower echoed Washington's sentiments in terms of Civil Religion when he said, "Our government makes no sense unless it is founded in a deeply felt religious faith—and I don't care what it is."[23] This thoughtless statement demonstrates why Civil Religion cannot aid in stemming the tide of secular (post)modernism. It is too irresolute. By Eisenhower's logic might it be all right for the government to be founded on atheism? How about Devil worship? Apparently any religion goes, as far as Ike was concerned.

Moreover, even if Washington didn't come right out and mention the word *God* in his inaugural address, everyone at that time knew he was referring to the God of the Bible. But fast-forward to Eisenhower's statement, and we can see that Civil Religion today will end up taking the country down the slippery slope to believing any religion at all.

Even though Civil Religion is a weak, homogenized mixture of the Christian tradition and patriotism, it is still too much to stomach for some secularists. Atheist Michael Newdow, for example, attempted in 2000 to eliminate the words *under God* from the Pledge of Allegiance.[24] I found it interesting that Newdow would even think to do something like this today and then have the courage to follow through with it. I believe this kind of action supports my thesis: Christianity has lost a great deal of its cultural authority. Assertive secularists like Newdow follow in the footsteps of Nietzsche, who said, "If you see something slipping, push it." Today's secularists see the lofty edifice of Christian cultural authority teetering, and they want to knock it over completely, even if that edifice is just a watered-down version of Christianity in the form of Civil Religion.

I also found it interesting that Bill O'Reilly, on the Fox News Channel one evening, contradicted what Newdow proposed. I think it is fair to say that O'Reilly was aggravated with the extent to which Newdow had taken this issue, because O'Reilly said, "God is a philosophy!"[25] I believe the point O'Reilly was trying to make was that Newdow shouldn't have gone to all the trouble he did because God is *only* a "philosophy" with regard to the Pledge of Allegiance.

But is O'Reilly right? Is God merely a philosophy? No. From a Christian perspective, God is much more than a philosophy. God is the personal, living Creator and Sustainer of the universe. So from a strictly Christian view, O'Reilly is incorrect.

Here's the rub. Newdow takes the notion of God at face value, just like a Christian would. This is precisely why Newdow wants to eradicate God from the public square. O'Reilly, on the other hand, does just the opposite. He wants to keep God *in* the public square. But to do so, O'Reilly has to keep the concept of God below the enemy fire of atheists and under the safe cover of Civil Religion, where God is reduced to a philosophy. This is wrongheaded. If O'Reilly is going to tell secularists to cease fire because God is only a philosophy, then this watered-down God of Civil Religion is not worth defending anyway. In other words, if we are willing to accommodate the definition of God as a mere "philosophy," then secularists win outright, because we have reduced the living, personal God of the Bible to a mere concept. This is a form of accommodation.

It is not hard to predict that the wishy-washy brand of Christianity found in Civil Religion will not offer much resistance to secular pressure. In my judgment, wave after wave of secularism will prove to be too much, and any appellations to God found in the schools, on our money, and even prayer offered by Congress will sooner or later be too offensive to our politically correct, pluralistic mind-set.

This, of course, is already happening. Anything remotely or distinctively Christian is being swept out the door of the public arena. From my perspective, those who think they are Christians simply because they believe in the God of Civil Religion are mistaken and will offer no resistance to the agents of secular (post)modernism, which want to marginalize Christianity.

A quick example will make this clearer. Practically every hotel, motel, pancake house, billboard, and business store front displayed something like "God Bless America" or "In God We Trust," on signs and banners immediately following the 9/11 attack. But these references to God were shallow supplications that did not last long. Complacency and a general apathy toward God revealed the superficial Civil Religion of our country. God was quickly put back on the shelf a few weeks later when everything began to return to normal.

Group #3: Practical Atheists

There is little doubt that a large percentage of our population think of themselves as taking religion very seriously. And although most Americans feel that more religious influence is the best way to strengthen family values and moral behavior,[26] in reality there seems to be a vast disparity between the religious aspirations of the ordinary American and their real level of commitment. In other words, although most Americans consider themselves religious, this says nothing about the *quality* of their religiosity.[27]

Many who identify themselves as Christians suffer from a kind of religious doublethink. For some, Christianity is not practiced at all. For others, Christianity is practiced Sunday morning and then never leaves the friendly confines of the church building. People sing inspiring songs on Sunday morning, but their worship ends abruptly after the service with a trip home to watch football the rest of the day. There is nothing wrong with watching football. The problem is that Christian practice and belief is often confined to Sunday mornings, never to be seen or heard from until the following Sunday. Many folks have no personal devotional life. Religious commitment for many Americans is shallow at best.

How is it that the vast majority of people in our country identify with Christianity in some way—whether through the God of Civil Religion or in their personal beliefs—yet lack a commitment to the Christ of Christianity? The answer is that many people believe they are Christians when in many cases they are not.[28] In other words, much of what passes for Christianity in our country is nominal at best.

So what is nominal Christianity? A nominal Christian is someone who is a Christian in name only. It is someone who thinks he or she is a Christian but is not. Nominal Christianity has been defined by one observer as "a late stage of religion on the road to secularization."[29] Nominal Christians are not "practicing Christians." They are what I prefer to call "practical atheists."[30] I argue that a large percentage of people in our country who identify with Christianity are really practical atheists, which means that they practice something closer to atheism rather than Christianity.

I define a practical atheist as someone who gives lip service to a belief in God but goes about his or her daily life as if God does not exist. Practical atheists may have embraced Christianity at some point in their lives but have let that commitment lapse. Many other practical atheists have never committed themselves to God in any way. Yet if questioned in a poll, these folks will say they believe in the God of the Bible. You might see practical atheists attend church on Christmas Eve or Easter Sunday or even, on a good year, both holidays. Some might not attend church at all. They may remember to cross themselves at a wake or a funeral out of some old habit they learned as a youth. You might find some of them at your local coffee shop on Sunday morning, drinking a latte and reading the Sunday paper while their committed counterparts are driving past them on the way to church. Practical atheists may be found cracking open a "cold one" late Sunday morning as they prepare for football, never giving church a thought. Others promise themselves they will get to church next week. For some, a prayer may be thrown up once in a while if they encounter a personal problem. But, in general, practical atheists have no devotional life, and God plays no part in their decision making, whether large or small.

The point is that God is completely absent from their daily lives unless tragedy strikes, and then suddenly they might remember that they need God's help. Then He becomes the center of attention for a while. However, once the calamity has been resolved, God is put back on the shelf. In short, on the practical everyday level, this group lives like atheists. They don't give God a lick of thought. They live as if God does not exist.

Practical atheists may identify with, or even be sympathetic to, Christianity but instead have embraced the secular mind-set without even being aware of it. I think practical atheists comprise a far larger number of Americans than usually shows up in the polls. If I am right, this explains why the secularization process is marginalizing Christianity with the speed that it has over the past couple of generations—practical atheists are in no shape to either defend or promote the Christian worldview in the public setting because they are not committed to God in their private lives. Practical atheism may also help to explain why people give mixed signals regarding their religiosity and why our country seems to be both the most religious and at the same time the most secular nation on earth.[31]

Former Supreme Court nominee Robert Bork put it this way:

> The truth is that, despite the statistics on churchgoing, etc., the United States is a very secular nation that, for the most part, does not take religion seriously. Not only may the statistics overstate the religious reality—people may be telling pollsters what they think makes a good impression—but statistics say nothing of the quality or depth of American religious belief. It is increasingly clear that very few people who claim a religion could truthfully say that it informs their attitudes and significantly affects their behavior.[32]

Keith G. Meador corroborates my thoughts on practical atheism when he wrote the following:

It seems paradoxical to speak of American culture as secularized, for Americans profess their personal religious beliefs in study after study. Yet the governing institutions in which Americans live out their lives—business, education, entertainment, law, and medicine alike—bear little evidence of this faith.[33]

As we will see below, practical atheism not only demonstrates a shaky religious commitment but also the often confused and contradictory beliefs many people hold about Christianity.

Part of this confusion can be seen in the adoption/misperception of Christian terminology that Americans use to represent their religious beliefs. The media have picked up and popularized some of these terms. For example, it was only after Jimmy Carter proclaimed to be "born again" back in the 1970s that this theological tag became a household term. Before Carter became president, it was enough to simply say that one was a "Christian." Everyone knew what you meant by that term. Perhaps because committed believers at that time wanted to distinguish themselves from the "Jesus freaks" and the less committed, they began using the term *born again* to label themselves. The problem is that it didn't take long for this expression to catch on, and soon everyone claimed to be born again, whether they were or not.

The same thing happened with the term *evangelical.* Prior to George Bush 2.0 becoming president, radio, television commentators, and the print media rarely used this term. More often than not, they used *fundamentalist,* often in the pejorative sense to connote what they perceived in their minds as a right-wing conservative Christian who is closed-minded, somewhat uneducated, and intolerant. This changed after Bush came into office. The term *evangelical* largely replaced the word *fundamentalist,* especially in the media. Today, *evangelical* has become a household term like *born again.* It seems as though anyone who is not a Catholic but claims even the vaguest assent to Christianity and is politically conservative is labeled an evangelical. The problem is that the way it is used in the popular parlance results in the term not standing for anything anymore.

The use of these terms mirrors what we see taking place with practical atheism. Practical atheists may claim to be religious by labeling themselves with the latest Christian catchphrase, but most of them don't have the foggiest idea of what the terms *born again* or *evangelical* mean. This is borne out in the surveys and in the polls. Back at the turn of this century, almost 40 percent of Americans claimed to be born again.[34] This is ludicrous. A brief look at the data below shows that even though a large percentage of our population claims to be born again, these same people don't know or embrace the fundamental tenets of Christianity. Let's look at some statistical support for this.

An astonishing 82 percent of Americans feel that the most quoted verse in the Bible is "God helps those who help themselves." There is one small problem. This verse is not *in* the Bible. It was penned by Thomas Jefferson.[35] This is a classic example that people who claim to be Christians don't have a clue to what's in the Bible.

Here are some additional statistics. Keep in mind that 76 percent of US citizens identify themselves with some branch of Christianity,[36] and 72 percent of Americans say they are committed to Jesus Christ.[37]

Roughly 50 percent of those who describe themselves as Christians do not believe Satan exists; 33 percent believe Jesus sinned while He was on earth,[38] and only 43 percent of self-identified Christians firmly believe the Bible is accurate in all that it teaches.[39] Almost 50 percent of adults think that if they are good people and do enough good for others, they will make it to heaven. Roughly 40 percent of Americans think that it doesn't matter which religion an individual follows because all religions teach the same thing and "all people will experience the same outcome after death, regardless of their religious beliefs."[40] Even 25 percent of born-again Christians think that eventually everyone will be saved or accepted by God. Forty-percent of born-again Christians and 59 percent of adults in America think that Christians and Muslims worship the same God, even though both religions have different beliefs and names regarding God.[41] In fact, most Americans cannot identify any specific belief or attribute that distinguishes Christianity from other world religions.[42]

These statistics show that although 80 percent of Americans think they have a good grasp of the basic teachings of Christianity, they really don't. Americans, in general, and so-called Christians specifically, seem oblivious to the fact that what they believe about God and Christianity is not "Christian" at all. The Bible knowledge of most Americans, according to the Barna Group, is "astoundingly limited."[43] The data is convincing enough to conclude that we have become a nation of "biblical illiterates."[44]

The diminishing of the Christian worldview in our country is so apparent that William Bennett put it this way: "We have become the kind of society that civilized countries used to send missionaries to."[45] All of the above speaks more to the notion that many people who claim to be Christians are really practical atheists with little or no knowledge of the doctrines of Christianity.

Decline in Church Attendance and the Privatization of Religious Belief

Churchgoing also gives some insight into the overall direction Americans are moving regarding religious practice. While most polls suggest that churchgoing has remained constant, others show that religion in our country is moving in a less organized, more "private" direction.[46] One study, for example, showed that only 20 percent of Protestants and 28 percent of Catholics attend church on any given week.[47] Most statistics on church attendance show higher numbers, but sociologists, by and large, are aware of the fact that Americans overestimate their churchgoing.[48] The lack of biblical knowledge and adherence to fundamental doctrines, combined with declining church attendance demonstrates that we are becoming increasingly secular.[49]

From my perspective, this move *away* from organized religion— Christianity in particular—and the move *toward* the privatization of religious belief is extremely important. In fact, this shift represents one of the most significant changes in the recent history of Christendom.[50]

What exactly does it mean when someone privatizes his or her religious belief? "Privatization" may be defined as a religious belief that is personal and autonomous, not needing any approval by a religious authority. This, unfortunately, bears a striking resemblance to the kind of secular belief that atheist Paul Kurtz said needed no religious sanction.

Because the consumer mentality in our country is so pervasive, it should not be surprising that people treat the religious realm as a spiritual marketplace. In fact, 71 percent of adults in our country said that they are more likely to come up with their own set of religious beliefs rather than adhere to those by a particular church.[51] In other words, they pick and choose what they want to believe. In many cases the church is no longer needed. This group may be described as "believers but not belongers."[52]

Alan Wolfe explains why privatizing one's belief is becoming so pervasive in our culture when he wrote, "Americans are not comfortable being told what to do, even if, perhaps especially if, the teller is a supernatural force whose words are meant as commands."[53] This shying away from authority would seem to go double for young people. It appears that 82 percent of young adults under the age of twenty-five stated that they develop their own religious beliefs instead of embracing those held by a church.[54]

Another trend that coincides with the privatization of religious belief is the move *away* from being "religious" and *toward* being "spiritual." Religion holds negative connotations of being overbearing, rigid, cold, and formal—things that are usually associated with organizations like churches. Spirituality, on the other hand, gives the impression of freedom, flexibility, room for searching, and focuses more on personal experience.[55] When interviewed, a forty-four-year-old woman described the difference between spirituality and religion: "Spirituality is an inner feeling, an allowance of however you perceive it in your world, in your mind, and however it feels is okay." About religion she said, "Religion tells you what to do and when to do it . . . Lots of rules."[56]

A *Newsweek* article in 2005 demonstrated how Americans view the difference between religion and spirituality. While 79 percent of respondents to a poll said they were spiritual, 24 percent wanted to be considered "spiritual but not religious."[57] Religious authority is out. Spirituality and autonomy are in. Spirituality is more personal and offers more options. This directly correlates with the trend toward privatization of religious belief, which shies away from organized religion. Spirituality also meshes with the consumer mentality in our society where religion is reduced to an individual preference.

In their important book *Habits of the Heart*, Robert Bellah and company provide a stunning example of someone who adopted her private beliefs:

> Sheila Larson is a young nurse who has received a good deal of therapy and who describes her faith as "Sheilaism." She describes her faith this way: "I believe in God. I'm not a religious fanatic. I can't remember the last time I went to church. My faith has carried me a long way. It's Sheilaism. Just my own little voice."[58]

Sheila is a classic example of not only the privatization of religious belief but also of practical atheism. She believes in God but doesn't go to church. She has faith that has sustained her along the way, but that faith is in herself. Wuthnow astutely summarized this shift toward the privatization of belief when he wrote, "The religion practiced by an increasing number of Americans may be entirely of their own manufacture—a kind of eclectic synthesis of Christianity, popular psychology,

Reader's Digest folklore, and personal superstitions, all wrapped up in the anecdotes of the individual's biography."[59]

The main thesis of *Habits of the Heart* was to point out what Bellah and company see as the emergence of individualism in our culture, which they describe as "cancerous."[60] My concern with the acceleration toward rampant individualism and the privatization of religious belief is that it will further the compartmentalization of Christianity. If 76 percent of Americans claim an identity with Christianity yet don't know or don't care about the fundamental doctrines of Christianity, then combined with the privatization of their beliefs, the end result is a form of self-inflicted marginalization. Meanwhile, secularism fills the void that is left after Christianity's marginalization. Even if there is a shred of authentic doctrinal Christianity left after this privatizing process, the beliefs have no impact on culture but instead are kept sequestered and never expressed in the public realm.[61]

Boomers and Bobos

One group important to look at because it is so large by age-demographics is the baby boomers, those born between 1946 and 1964. The boomers are significant because, as we will see, they further exemplify what we illustrated above relating to shying away from organized religion and privatizing one's religious beliefs. The sheer number of boomers means they exert a good measure of influence in our society.

Let's take a look at the boomers' posture toward Christianity. Wade Clark Roof describes those in this group as "quest seeking," and having a "tourist mentality" pertaining to religion.[62] They want the freedom to explore their religious options but don't want to be tied down to any particular religion. Although they want to be able to search out different religions, they also want to be grounded. This means that they can't seem to get entirely free from their roots in traditional religion, which in most cases is some form of Christianity.

This cognitive dissonance between being grounded and yet fluid is evident in a forty-three-year-old boomer who practices "Christian yoga" as reported by *Newsweek*. Failing to see that "Christian yoga" is an oxymoron, she offers this simple explanation, "It gives me time alone with God . . . As a mom of two small kids, I don't get that—even in church."[63] I might suggest prayer and Bible study as a traditional way to spend time alone with God; but for boomers this appears rather stodgy and not as hip as something like yoga. Yoga gives one the sense of being "spiritual." Prayer and Bible study seem archaic and confining in comparison. Boomers want spirituality without accountability.

A prime example of this boomer "tourist" mentality is Tony Schwartz, who chronicled his search for wisdom in America in a book entitled *What Really Matters*. Schwartz's search took him through every psychological, esoteric, and New Age experience imaginable. His book is a veritable handbook on every strand of the human potential movement that has existed since the countercultural climate of the late 1960s. The disconcerting part, as I plowed through this painfully long book, is that he seems to find whatever he is searching for, only to find disappointment after disappointment as he trudges further along his never-ending journey. By his own admission, he still hasn't found what he's looking for.

Schwartz is the perfect example of Roof's prototypical "tourist" who wants to be "fluid" while still being "grounded" in his search for ultimate wisdom. Schwartz wrote, "Seeking the truth is sometimes painful and difficult, but it invariably makes me feel more authentic and more grounded. It's not truth in some absolute sense that I'm after. . . . What I'm most committed to is searching for my own truth."[64] Schwartz is important because his malformed idea of truth resembles what most Americans think of when they think of truth. For now, I might point out that there is no such thing as "personal truth." (We will look more closely at the concept of truth in Chapter six.)

A subgroup of the baby boomers is what David Brooks describes as "Bobos." Bobos is short for "bourgeois bohemians." These are the movers and shakers of the new information age elite. They are a combination of the bohemian radicals of the countercultural revolution of the '60s and '70s, and the bourgeois innovative yuppies of the 1980s. As the educated elite, they are basically running the country now as the "new establishment."[65] This seems rather hypocritical, because many of these bobos held "the establishment" in contempt back in the '60s.

Obviously, bobos are important for our purposes because, as people in positions of power, they can impact to a certain extent whether the secularization process will continue to take place. It appears that, like the boomers, bobos tread rather uneasily where traditional, organized religion is concerned. Brooks wonders whether bobos can have their freedom as well as their roots, which is precisely what the boomers are struggling with. Brooks asks the question, "Can you still worship God even if you take it upon yourself to decide that many of the Bible's teachings are wrong? . . . Can you establish ritual and order in your life if you are driven by an inner imperative to experiment constantly with new things?"[66] Brooks knows very well the spiritual struggle bobos deal with because he admits that he is a bobo.

It is very likely that many, if not most, of the bobos, like the garden-variety boomers, are practical atheists. Bobos are more concerned with power, wealth, and consumerism than they are with any commitment to the Christian worldview. They want to hold some of the traditional religious beliefs found in Christianity, but they are not willing to embrace doctrine that may cost them something, or hold beliefs that may appear intolerant.

If boomers and bobos continue to feel comfortable exploring all religious options, it is difficult to see how they will pass down anything of substance from the Christian worldview to their children and grandchildren. Brooks admits this: "The lack of age old rituals makes it very hard to pass your belief system on to your children. Organized religions have a set of stable ceremonies to guide and cultivate the spiritual lives of kids. Self religions do not."[67]

In short, if the boomers and bobos are searching for their own truth and discarding anything they don't like about Christianity, then how will the generations behind them know anything of true, authentic Christianity? Answer: they won't. This is precisely why Christianity is losing ground to (post)modernism with each passing generation. We are becoming a nation of practical atheists who are producing generation after generation of children who don't know God. Moreover, many children and grandchildren of Boomers and Bobos have not been exposed to anything resembling authentic Christianity.

George Barna provides a nice overall summary of the religiosity of this third group in our study, the practical atheists, when he argues that "the spirituality of Americans is Christian in name only. . . . We prefer choices to absolutes. We embrace preferences rather than truths. We seek comfort rather than growth. Faith must come on our own terms or we reject it. We have enthroned ourselves as the final arbiters of righteousness, the ultimate rulers of our own experience and destiny."[68]

I believe that this type of superficial religiosity will do nothing to stem the tide of secularization. It will allow for the unhindered marginalization of Christianity in our culture, which in this case is self-inflicted.

Group # 4: Committed Christians

Finally, we come to our fourth and final group: committed Christians. Of all the groups discussed so far, it is accurate to say that this group should provide the most resistance to the secularization process. However, even this group of authentic Christians is often susceptible to accommodating secularism and in some cases retreating from its onward advance. It appears, for example, that even genuine evangelicals suffer from many of the same maladies we witnessed with the boomers and bobos. This may be accounted for, in part, because many evangelicals *are* boomers and bobos. Let's briefly look at the evangelicals as exemplars of those *inside* the Christian camp.

Even though the popular definition of evangelicalism is very broad, Barna limits it to a much smaller sector than those who claim to be born again. Evangelicals meet the criteria of those who are born again—a personal commitment to Jesus Christ that is still important today, and a belief that they will go to heaven because they have confessed their sins and accepted Jesus Christ as their Savior. But in addition to those criteria, evangelicals also believe that "Jesus lived a sinless life; eternal salvation is only through grace not works; Christians have a personal responsibility to evangelize non-Christians, and Satan exists." By this restrictive definition, Barna concludes that only 7 to 8 percent of our populace is truly evangelical.[69] This means that, in reality, there are far fewer evangelicals than is popularly believed. This should not surprise us, because as I have been arguing, there are far more practical atheists around than we suspect. This is why we are becoming a post-Christian nation.

The problem is that not only are there fewer evangelicals and other so-called committed Christians around to hold back the secularization process, but evangelicals suffer from some of the same modernizing tendencies that affect practical atheists. For example, according to a Gallup poll, 88 percent of evangelicals agreed that "the Bible is the written word of God, accurate in all it teaches," yet 53 percent of evangelicals also believe that "there is no such thing as absolute truth."[70] This means that the traditional conviction by evangelicals, that God reveals *true* truth through His written Word no longer exists.[71] David Wells calls this loss of truth and accommodation of the gospel to relativism and the secular mind-set the "death rattle" of evangelical Christianity.[72]

It is a well-known fact that churches that upheld the truths of traditional fundamental Christianity gained membership since the 1950s while membership in the mainline Protestant churches declined.[73] In fact, proclaiming the unadulterated truth of Scripture used to be the strength of evangelical churches and the reason for their numerical growth. While there is numerical growth in these churches today, the reason for this in many cases, has less to do with adhering to God's Word, and more to do with accommodating the world.

If we no longer believe in absolute truth, then how long can Christianity be defended? How long can the secularizing process be impeded? The lack of a biblical worldview holds dire consequences for young people who go off to college and often lose their faith. This, in turn, makes it impossible for them to pass the Christian worldview down to their children.

Many committed believers are susceptible to the privatization problem. Christians are often squeamish about sharing their faith with nonbelievers for fear that they are not equipped to answer hard questions or that they will be looked at with suspicion and disdain. Like the less committed, evangelicals mistakenly believe that their Christian viewpoint should be kept to themselves and not trotted out into the public arena of culture or politics. As S. D. Graede observes:

> Sit down with a group of evangelicals these days and you will discover that they are petrified to express their faith. . . . But their reticence is not odd at all when we consider that one of our culture's deepest values is tolerance, and that value is embedded in a relativistic worldview. To assert truth in such an environment is blasphemy.[74]

This raises a question. How can Christians be the salt and light of our culture when they are afraid to share their faith and they are not committed to the truth of the Bible like they were in generations past?

In short, committed Christians in general, and evangelicals in particular, are part of the problem of what I see as self-marginalization. Self-marginalization occurs when Christians fall for the faulty notion of truth found in postmodernism and also when Christians privatize their faith and retreat from the public arena.

I have focused on evangelicals not because I believe they are the only committed Christians out there. Certainly fundamentalist Christians have demonstrated a commitment to resisting the spirit of the age when compared with their counterparts in Protestantism. Roman Catholics (notwithstanding my disagreement with them over more than a few fundamental doctrines) have also shown a commitment in some areas to restraining the forces of secularization, for example, with the abortion issue. But I will be dealing mostly with Protestantism in this study because it has been *the* cultural authority since the founding of our country.

Summary

I divided the population into four groups so we can get a better idea of how secularization is occurring. As we have seen, the loss of Christian authority and the rise of our post-Christian culture isn't occurring simply because of secularists. Yes, it is true that those like the secular humanists certainly want to push Christianity out of our culture and replace it with something more "reasonable," like secular modernism. But Christians and those who *think* they are Christians, in many ways have aided the secularization process.

People today, like many boomers, bobos, and Sheila, want to live by their own lights and are ready to discard any doctrine of Christianity that does not suit their fancy. This only serves to accommodate secularization. People like these are "Christian" in name only, and have no real commitment to Christ or the Christian worldview.

How can picking and choosing what one wants to believe from a spiritual smorgasbord of options be called Christianity? Holding beliefs contrary to Scripture or discarding Christian doctrines that don't mesh with political correctness doesn't make people Christians. It's far more likely that people like this are practical atheists who want to consider themselves Christians in some sense. In addition, an ill-defined belief in God that is then baptized in patriotism is Civil Religion, not Christianity.

The conclusion we can draw from all of this is that the commitment level of those who consider themselves Christians often resembles something a bit closer to practical atheism than we would like to admit. In addition, the biblical illiteracy demonstrated by most Americans means that the average person doesn't understand the basics of the Christian belief system anymore. It is difficult to see how this shallow understanding and commitment to Christianity will be able to withstand the continual barrage of modernism, postmodernism, and secularism.

Practical atheists may call themselves Christians as they have coffee and read the Sunday paper while lamenting the state of the economy. They may find the greed, consumerism, lawlessness, and general moral decay in our society rather disconcerting. But are

34

practical atheists, who don't give God a lick of thought, the kind of people who will stop the onslaught of secularism when they have no devotional life? Will they be able to slow down the march of postmodernism when, instead of darkening the door of their local church, they drink their lattes, take the kids to soccer, and prepare for a Sunday afternoon football party?

This is important because practical atheists are playing a major role in allowing the marginalizing of Christianity to occur because they are a much larger group than we suppose. Barna estimates that 40 percent of adults in our country may now be identified as "post-Christian."[75] How can 76 percent of our population claim to be Christian when 40 percent is post-Christian? I think a good share of the 40 percent who are "post-Christian" are really practical atheists who identify themselves as Christians but are really nominal Christians.

This is significant because practical atheists are far more likely (as a percentage) to partake of the fruit of secularization (autonomy, politically correct attitudes, moral relativism, narcissism, and so forth) than committed Christians. Practical atheists are more or less blind to the secularization process and will therefore accept it as a matter of course. Even if practical atheists sense something is wrong with culture, they are in no position to do anything about it, because they have built their vacillating worldview on the sinking sand of religious eclecticism and private belief.

Worse than this, their children will not be exposed to doctrinal Christianity in any way, shape, or form, and this process will be repeated with their own children. Thus, we can expect every generation behind the boomers to be increasingly post-Christian, and this is precisely what the statistics show.[76] Therefore, it is not difficult to predict that the marginalization of Christianity will continue as we move into the future. This is even more likely because the millennials (born between roughly 1980 and 2000) are soon to overtake the Boomers as the largest demographic group by age in the country. This may be part of the reason that those who identify with Christianity in our country has dropped ten points, to 76 percent, since I started researching and writing this book.

The two chapters outlined thus far described some of the key features in the marginalization process (Chapter one) and provided a broad overview of the primary agents that actualize this process (Chapter two). The next two chapters will explain how we arrived at our present situation by looking at the Enlightenment and the

Protestant Reformation as starting points, respectively. Going back in time and examining history will provide a clearer understanding of why Christianity is being displaced by the (post)modern secular worldview.

Chapter 3

The Enlightenment Project and the Demise of Christianity's Authority

History does not occur in a vacuum. Certain historical precedents have brought us to our present situation regarding the Christian worldview and its relationship to our culture. To gain a fuller understanding of how the marginalization of Christianity occurred we need to look back to the historical context. This will help us understand the secularizing process that is occurring today. We will look at various philosophers who contributed to the forming of modernism, because it is the modern/secular mind-set that began to erode the Christian worldview.

Thomas Aquinas (1225–1274) and the Medieval Synthesis
Unlike today, all learning and intellectual pursuits during the medieval period fell under the auspices of firmly established religious institutions.[1] Because Christendom was often threatened and invaded by those who rejected its religion, it was incumbent upon schoolmen like Thomas Aquinas, who was a Dominican Friar, philosopher, and theologian, to develop arguments that would persuade Christianity's opponents of its truth. Scholastic scholars like Aquinas worked and studied in natural philosophy and other disciplines to develop an apologetic that did not rely on biblical revelation, which would have been summarily dismissed by Christian antagonists.[2]

Unlike today, science and philosophy were not pitted against theology. In fact, during this time, scholars considered philosophy "the handmaiden of theology" because philosophy and theology worked in conjunction with each other to support the truth of Christianity. This is known as the "medieval synthesis." Please note that the rudimentary form of science at that time was not called "science" but "natural philosophy."

All scholastics like Aquinas, whatever their differences, believed that truth discovered by philosophy would not contradict the truth found by theology because God is the author of all existence.[3]

Moreover, the truth of "faith" and the truth of "reason" could never logically contradict each other. Reason and faith could both be used to pursue truth in a context such as "faith seeking understanding."[4] Reason and faith were not in separate compartments like they are today. This *medieval synthesis* between philosophy and theology, and likewise between reason and revelation, began to break down as the Renaissance began to blossom. Let's see how this happened.

William of Ockham (1280–1349)

William of Ockham was a key figure in the initial breakdown of the medieval synthesis of faith and reason. Ockham propagated doctrines that were contrary to church authority and fled his convent in 1328, barely escaping arrest. What was so subversive about Ockham's thought that he and his colleagues were in such danger?

Ockham held to "voluntarism," a doctrine that made God's sovereignty appear arbitrary and whimsical. According to Ockham, God's freedom is so radical that He could do anything except contradict himself.[5] For example, God could command us to hate Him rather than love Him. He is not bound by any of His previous commands, so He could change his mind at any time. There are no limits on God's will. It is His will alone that determines good and evil.[6] Anything could change as God saw fit.

All of this became very troubling for people because it made God's character capricious and incomprehensible. God could no longer be understood by the use of human reason. Anything that could be known about God could only be known by *faith* as revealed in Scripture. Ockham effectively undermined any rational foundations for faith. This, in essence, severed the medieval synthesis between faith and reason.[7]

For Ockham, reason and faith occupy different realms, and therefore they may contradict each other, though faith will always have priority over reason.[8] This split between faith and reason is very important for our purposes because it may be seen as the first step on the road to modern secularism.[9]

Another philosophical notion that Ockham is famous for is "nominalism." Because God can change His mind about anything, we have no unifying force for understanding the world. Ockham denied "universals." This means that he denied the reality of things like truth, morality, trees, apples, red, green, chairs, or tables. All of these things were traditionally regarded as "universals" because they provide a universal concept for everything in their particular category. But Ockham posited that these are only "names" (*nomos*) that we arbitrarily assign to these particulars because they seem to share the same characteristics. This rejection of universals is at the heart of nominalism. It has had a profound impact on the link between language and truth. It foreshadowed Wittgenstein and his "language games" in the early twentieth century, as well as adumbrating postmodernism, which we will examine in Chapter six.

The last thing worth noting about Ockham's thought is that it entailed the idea that the individual's "will" has priority over reason and gives meaning to an inexplicable world.[10] In other words, the individual "displaces" God as the center of the cosmos, because each person has to exercise his own will and determine meaning for himself. Why? Because God was too unpredictable and could not be trusted to provide a ground for understanding the world. This notion of an unpredictable God became even more entrenched after the devastation of the bubonic plague, known as the Black Death, which occurred during the middle of the 14th century. After this, many people no longer saw God as a source of comfort, but instead perceived Him as a terrifying God who was the source of anxiety and insecurity.[11]

However, shifting the focus of meaning by putting the emphasis on the individual didn't really solve the problem of trying to understand the cosmos. If God could change His mind so capriciously, then how was a person to understand anything at all? As Michael Buckley points out, "If the Eucharist looks like bread, and yet in Christian teaching is the body of Christ, who is to say that sense experience and even mathematical axioms cannot deceive?"[12] These radical doctrines of Ockham marked the beginning of modern intellectual skepticism. This is noteworthy because some Enlightenment thinkers used skepticism as a weapon against Christianity, which we will look at a little further below.

Ockham's nominalism, along with his radical concept of God, spelled the beginning of the end of the medieval synthesis between faith and reason and paved the way for the *via moderna*, the "modern way."[13] In fact, by the time of Martin Luther (1483-1546), only one university in Germany was not under the control of the nominalists.[14]

Two things are important to note here because they were the precursors to secular ideas that would later find traction in the Enlightenment. First, man began to displace God as the center of meaning. Second, the emphasis on human will foreshadowed the move toward atheistic humanism and Nietzsche's "will to power," which we will turn to a little later in the chapter.

Skepticism and the Thirty Years War (1618–1648)

The invention of the printing press (1439) was significant because it allowed lay people access to books, most notably the Bible. This led to rival interpretations of Scripture, which found footing in Martin Luther and the Protestant Reformation. The Council of Trent opposed Luther's reform movement at all costs.[15] This ultimately resulted in the Thirty Years War, which was one of the most devastating of any wars fought on European soil.

The deadlock on the battlefield had actually begun in the world of ideas. If the struggle between the Protestant Reformers and the Roman Catholic Counter-Reformers could not be resolved in the theological realm, then war unfortunately seemed inevitable. Only by grasping the severity of the Thirty Years War can we understand the quandary Europe was in. The intellectuals were urgent in their struggle to find a way out of the theological quagmire and the bloodshed that resulted from it. Skepticism and uncertainty were unacceptable if bloodshed was the only alternative.[16]

But it wasn't just the Catholics and Protestants who were fighting with one another. Protestants fought with one another over rival interpretations of Scripture. On top of this, a new threat from natural philosophy speculated that the earth revolved around the sun. This, of course, contradicted traditional church doctrine that stated that the sun and planets revolved around the earth. In short, nothing seemed to be certain. One wondered if anything could be known with assurance. If not, was war the only alternative?

René Descartes (1596–1650)

Enter René Descartes, the father of modern philosophy. Descartes spent most of his adult life during the Thirty Years War. He desperately wanted to put knowledge back on solid footing and overcome the intellectual skepticism that had built up momentum since Ockham. He also wanted to answer the atheists, whom he viewed as "ordinarily more arrogant than learned and judicious."[17]

To achieve the certainty of knowledge—the "clear and distinct ideas" that he was looking for—Descartes shifted the focus regarding the nature of knowledge from theology to philosophy. He made this important move for a reason. If Catholics and Protestants could not agree with one another, and Protestants themselves differed strenuously over doctrinal issues, how could theology alone be relied upon to solve men's problems? Maybe philosophy could come to the rescue.

This move can be seen in Descartes's *Meditations of First Philosophy*, in which he maintained that fundamental questions having to do with God and the soul "ought to be demonstrated by philosophical rather than theological argument."[18] Thus he reversed the medieval scholastic order; theology now became the handmaiden of philosophy.[19] This was a monumental shift in epistemology. Descartes wanted to find true knowledge, which was above history and not subject to a particular time and place, as was the case with historic Christianity.[20] Being a gifted mathematician, he felt that certainty of knowledge could be achieved only through arithmetic like geometry, where one thing is deduced from another.[21] Only this type of thinking could provide the certainty he was looking for.

Descartes wanted to find a self-evident premise—a foundation— from which all other truths could be derived. It had to be something irrefutable. After struggling with knowledge to the point of doubting his own existence, he decided that he couldn't really doubt his own existence because his doubt was proof *of* his existence. So he introduced his famous *Cogito ergo sum*, "I think, therefore I am." Descartes used this tautology as the foundation for his system of knowledge.

Whereas the scholastics started in the realm of nature to derive God's existence, Descartes found God, not in nature, but in the intellect. With God smuggled safely on board, there still remained the problem of His trustworthiness. Descartes answered the nominalists by maintaining that God would not deceive us. Although He *could* deceive us, to do so would mean that He has a moral defect. This cannot happen, because God is perfect.[22] God, for Descartes, was not the whimsical god of Ockham. Instead, God is the very underpinning for believing that our reason works properly.[23] Reason, in turn, is the essential heritage where truth was shared by the Divine and human mind.[24]

One cannot underestimate the power of reason that Descartes launched. Ernst Cassirer described its importance as an intellectual "force which guides the discovery and determination of truth."[25] But this "force," as Cassirer calls it, began to undermine tradition, authority, and revelation.[26] In fact, Descartes's ideas set in motion the entire project of the Enlightenment, which was a "flight from authority," according to Jeffrey Stout.[27] The new authority—reason—was used by many intellectuals to look down with skepticism on Christianity as the former authority.

To summarize so far, the monolithic epistemological authority found during the Middle Ages under the Roman Catholic Church began to crumble. There was the problem of competing authorities who disagreed with one another and never produced true knowledge (*scientia*) but only opinion.[28] Descartes originated the attempt by the lone individual, free from any authority, to launch out on his own and find truth for himself. Stout understands Descartes's impact this way: "One discovers truth in the privacy of subjective illumination, and this truth is underlined by a kind of self-certifying certainty. Community, tradition, authority: these have all started to give way to the individual, his inwardness, his autonomy."[29]

We saw in Chapter two how individuals today are moving away from organized religion and toward private spirituality. This type of thinking, at least in part, can be traced back to Descartes and the flight from authority, which occurred during the Enlightenment and blossomed during the Romantic era in the nineteenth century. This was the beginning of the notion today that each person must find truth for himself.[30] Moreover, Christianity loses its authority as the autonomous individual takes its place. This is the beginning of secular humanism.

Enlightenment Thought and Reason

We will now turn to some of the essential beliefs that exemplify Enlightenment thought. They are worth looking at because, as we just noted above, many of the fundamental tenets of the Enlightenment can be seen in our culture today.

I should note at the outset that no mass departure from Christian belief per se took place during this time. The *philosophes* (a French word designating the "family" of Enlightenment thinkers who were "international types" and secular men of letters[31]) took their religion seriously. But as their faith in reason's ability increased, many of the fundamentals of Christianity were called into question. James Byrne argues that "what the militant freethinkers of the Enlightenment provided was the intellectual weaponry which opened up the possibility of widespread disbelief."[32] Allan Bloom suggests that one of the political projects of the Enlightenment was to render old books like the Bible "undangerous."[33] Moreover, the intellectuals wanted to avoid the wars of religion.

The way in which reason began to undermine Christianity was subtle yet sure. Most philosophers at that time believed that Christianity was reasonable. Therefore it must be based on reasonable foundations. This was nothing new. Scholastics like Thomas Aquinas had shown this. But if Christianity is reasonable, the next logical step was to prove that every doctrinal belief must be reasonable. Reason now subtly took priority over revelation and became an autonomous authority. This in retrospect was momentous. Why? Because it didn't take long for skeptics to argue that some Christian beliefs did not meet the requirements of reason. The logical outcome was obvious. Those tenets of Christianity that contradicted reason should be discarded, because they were misleading or mistaken.[34]

Although they disagreed over many things, one thing that the intellectuals of that time shared was an aversion to superstition. They used reason to dissuade any irrational, superstitious imaginings. The problem for Christianity was that the *philosophes* discarded many of the distinctive doctrines, such as the Trinity, the divinity of Christ, and Original Sin, as untenable.[35] The Enlightenment philosophers wanted religion that was pure, simple, rational, common, and accessible to all humankind. They saw the fundamental doctrines of Christianity as having the potential to lead to more sectarian strife and bloodshed. They could no longer tolerate this.

In addition, the knowledge of other cultures that explorers like Columbus and da Gama discovered reinforced the emerging pluralistic mind-set. The Enlightenment thinkers were bitterly opposed to doctrines such as salvation through Christ alone, which constituted a "scandal of particularity." (The same disdain for Christianity among most intellectuals can be found today.) Enlightenment thinkers viewed Christianity, not as the one true religion, but one religion among many.[36] The special revelation of Christianity was not accessible to all cultures, and because of this it was rejected on moral grounds.[37] One can already see political correctness foreshadowed here. The exclusive truth claims of Christianity were rejected in favor of religious pluralism. (We will look at politically correct religious pluralism more closely in Chapter five.)

John Locke (1632–1704)

John Locke is famous for his work *The Reasonableness of Christianity* (1695), in which he defends Christianity on the grounds that it is reasonable. Locke also argued that whatever God has revealed must be true. But the *philosophes* challenged this assertion. As far as they were concerned, what counts as revelation must first be judged by reason; not just taken as authoritative because Christians claimed it to be so.

Unwittingly, by playing on the *philosophes'* playground where the rules were rigged, Locke began to compromise Christian doctrine. Unlike Descartes, Locke maintained that our knowledge comes through the senses not the intellect. In fact, Locke took a poke at Descartes when Locke stated that a person who doubted their own existence could hold that notion only until hunger set in and brought that person back to reality.[38] For Locke, the mind was a "blank slate" at birth.[39]

In part, Locke was trying to contradict the Christian doctrine that Enlightenment thinkers found particularly despicable: Original Sin and the depravity of man. If the mind was blank at birth, then it owed nothing to inheritance. Therefore Original Sin could not have been passed down from generation to generation as Christianity claimed. Instead, individuals were free to bring their ideas, conduct, and institutions in line with the natural order that God had created.[40]

Locke's attempt at defending Christianity was typical of those who wanted to hold on to Christianity with one hand and discard its fundamentals on the other.

Jean-Jacques Rousseau (1712–1778)

Jean-Jacques Rousseau explicitly rejected the doctrine of Original Sin. He held, instead, to the innate goodness and innocence of humanity.[41] Man was his own creator and deliverer in the ethical sense, not God.[42] Rousseau helped develop a new anthropology devoid of theology by tearing man away from the model of redemptive history found in the Bible.[43]

Rousseau is known as a forerunner of the Romantic movement. The individual could use his or her own experience as a criterion for judging truth in order to forge individual morality through the voice of conscience.[44] Much of the liberal mind-set today that holds a favorable view of humankind's inherent goodness can find its beginnings in Rousseau.

It doesn't take a keen observer to see that the Christian belief system was in trouble as philosophers either inadvertently or purposefully chipped away at the fundamentals. The Enlightenment intellectuals accepted reason as the be-all and end-all for attaining knowledge. One by one the essential doctrines of Christianity came under attack.

Advocates of Christianity during this time thought they were providing a defense by demonstrating the reasonableness of Christianity. But they played defense instead of offense. The defenders of Christianity were retreating when they should have been challenging the Enlightenment presuppositions instead. Leslie Newbigin notes that these "tactical retreats can—if repeated often enough—begin to look more like a rout."[45] That is exactly what happened.

In fact, Dennis Diderot, who was a vociferous opponent of Christianity at that time, bragged that religion was retreating as philosophy advanced.[46] It was precisely this advance of secular modernism that has put Christianity in retreat today.

Deism

As we have seen, some Enlightenment thinkers wanted to discard many particularly distinctive doctrines of Christianity because they were seen as going beyond what reason would allow. Two famous books at that time pointed this up. One year after Locke released his *The Reasonableness of Christianity*, John Toland published *Christianity Not Mysterious* (1697), which caused an uproar and was even burned in some places. The premise of Toland's book was that Christianity was only a naturalistic religion (nature is all that exists, not God) and therefore required no mysterious explanation at all.[47] Thirty years later, Matthew Tindal published his *Christianity as Old as Creation* (1730), which, like its predecessor, argued for a natural religion of reason while maintaining a bitter anticlericalism and a deep skepticism of the Bible.[48] Unlike Locke's book, which attempted to support Christianity's reasonableness, these latter two books did not place Christianity in a favorable light.

Many of Locke's contemporaries weren't ready to abandon Christianity like the two authors mentioned above. Even the most radical thinkers could see that the traditional role of the church as upholding morality benefited society. They had a difficult time believing that a strictly secular ethics could replace religion in this regard.[49] How then could opponents of Christianity maintain some of its moral precepts while abandoning its distinctive doctrines?

Enlightenment thinkers decided to develop a belief system that was universal and acceptable to all. They did this by removing doctrines unique to Christianity, which made the chances for sectarian strife and war less likely. Therefore, instead of embracing outright atheism, the intellectuals developed a hybrid, which was an admixture of Christianity devoid of its miraculous elements combined with a harmless notion of

God as understood from the study of nature.[50] In short, Deism was born.

Isaac Newton's (1642–1727) mechanistic model aided in this endeavor, because it showed that the universe operated according to fixed laws. This suggested to Enlightenment thinkers that there was a *design* to the cosmos. The Deists believed that God had fashioned the universe much like a watchmaker designs a watch. God wound up the universe like a watch and then let it run on its own, without any further assistance or interference from Him. In other words, Deists (from *Deus* for "God") believed that God was the Creator of the world, but denied that God took any further interest in human activity after the creation.[51]

Deism was a safer way to believe in God because it was devoid of any Christian doctrines that might cause war and strife. Although Deism never made it down to the pedestrian level of society in Europe, men such as Benjamin Franklin, Thomas Jefferson, Ethan Allen, and Thomas Paine carried Deism over to the founding of our country, where its influence can be seen, for example, in the writing of the Declaration of Independence.[52]

The Deist's cognitive dissonance regarding Christianity can be seen in the elderly Voltaire. In 1774 he and a companion made the arduous climb to the top of a hill where they were graced by a spectacular sunrise. Peter Gay relates the rest of this story: "Voltaire took off his hat, prostrated himself, and exclaimed: 'I believe! I believe in you! Powerful God, I believe!' Then he rose and added drily: 'As for monsieur the Son, and His Mother, that's a different story.'"[53]

David Hume (1711–1776)

David Hume is a hard man to pin down. Some commentators think he was an outright atheist. Others, in the minority, think Hume was a Deist of some sort, who merely poked fun at Christianity. Of one thing there is no doubt: Hume had a monumental impact on both the nature of knowledge and Christianity. In his well-known book *The Heavenly City of the Eighteenth Century Philosophers*, Carl Becker offers a nice observation on Hume's contribution. "It is as if, at high noon of the Enlightenment, at the hour of the siesta when everything seems so quiet and secure all about, one were suddenly aware of a short, sharp slipping of the foundations, a faint far-off tremor running underneath the solid ground of common sense."[54]

The far-off tremor that could be heard was the bomb Hume was dropping on the foundation of reason that was so prevalent at the time.

Hume ruthlessly attacked the supremacy of human reason as a way to gain true knowledge. For him, reason had distinct limits. Hume argued that many things people thought they knew could not be explained on the basis of either reason or experience. These things are not really *known* per se; rather, many of these pivotal beliefs are arrived at as a result of custom, habit, or instinct. Although we can't *know* many things in the technical sense, Hume felt it would be foolish to doubt them. Instead of trying to *prove* things in a way that the Rationalists (those that thought reason alone is the way to knowledge) like Descartes wanted to, we should accept many of our commonsensical beliefs because it is *natural* to do so.[55]

Hume's barrage also involved attacking the idea of miracles. Although he was careful not to specifically mention the Gospels, his attack on miracles included the Gospel miracles by association. For many people at the time, the occurrence of miracles, as attested by reason, was proof of the validity of Christianity. Hume argued against miracles, however, by stating that it was more probable that the person testifying to a miracle was either exaggerating or mistaken. He sought to cancel out the uniqueness of Christian miracles by pointing out that other religions attested to miracles as well.[56]

Hume attacked miracles by also claiming that in light of the uniformity of the laws of nature, it would be very difficult to show that the regularities of the natural world had ever been interfered with. This so-called scientific skepticism toward miracles is characteristic of the snubbing miracles receive today as well.[57] It is not that Hume believed miracles could not occur. It is that he thought it improbable that there was a reasonable ground for believing in them. In fact, the newly emerging science along with the mechanistic model of the universe increasingly seemed to demonstrate that there was less and less need for divine intervention of any sort.[58]

The damage that Hume did to the nature of knowledge and Christianity was considerable. In effect, he partitioned Christianity off into the realm of faith. For him, reason was powerless to convert anyone to the Christian belief system. He rejected rational knowledge of God and objective religious truth claims. Speculative matters like religion should be accepted on the basis of *faith* not reason.[59] Hume demolished the popular reliance on miracles for proof of Christianity's truth. Historian Bill Austin argues that Hume's ideas are "typical of the agnosticism of the modern secular man, and his part in producing that modern secular man is considerable."[60]

Immanuel Kant (1724–1804)

Immanuel Kant is arguably the most important philosophical figure in the Enlightenment period, if not all of modern Western thought since then. Kant's project offered a solution to the intellectual shambles that both philosophy and religion were left in because of Hume's skepticism. Empiricists like Locke and Hume had said that true knowledge ultimately came through the senses. On the other hand, Rationalists like Descartes maintained that true knowledge came through the intellect. Kant forged a middle path for understanding the world that required both the intellect and sense experience. Bryan Magee calls Kant's epistemological project "the most radical reconstruction of the theory of knowledge that anyone has ever carried out."[61] There is little doubt that we still feel the implications of Kant's epistemology today.

Against the Rationalists, Kant argued that thought without the content of experience does not produce knowledge. On the other hand, he discredited the Empiricists' claim that experience alone produces knowledge. Kant pointed out that if pure empiricism was correct, then there would be no categories with which to organize the data obtained from the sensible world.[62] This was precisely the problem with Ockham's nominalism. Kant ingeniously proposed that the mind was not passive, but active in evaluating the data of experience. The mind, for Kant, has cognitive forms that are *imposed on* and categorize the data of sense experience. In this way he combined the insight from both the Rationalists and the Empiricists.

Kant believed that the way we understand data is confined to the realm of *phenomena*—the experience of the world in the realm of space and time.[63] The phenomenal realm is the world as it *appears* to us. But herein lies a problem. How the world *appears* to us is different from how it exists independently of our experience of it.

As far as Kant was concerned, we can never have true knowledge of the world as it simply appears to us. This is because how we perceive the world of phenomena is different from how things really exist "in themselves," independent of our thought. Kant called this world of things as it truly exists the "noumenal" realm. This is the realm of true knowledge. However, humans have no access to the noumenon—how "things in themselves" really exist.

As noted above, for Kant, the way we understand the world is confined to *phenomena*, things as perceived by our mental faculties.[64] He believed the noumenon was a way to show that human knowledge could not go beyond the limits of the phenomenal realm of the senses.[65] This is what Kant addressed in his work entitled *Critique of Pure Reason* (1781). Reason had certain limits and could not obtain true knowledge, which existed only in the noumenal realm.

Of course, this posed problems for metaphysical concepts like God. God certainly cannot be perceived in the phenomenal world of everyday life. So for Kant, God resides in the noumenal realm. However, this is problematic for Christianity because it is as good as admitting that there can be no true knowledge of God's existence.

For Kant, religious belief can never count as true knowledge or be proved on rational grounds, like it could for the Deists.[66] But this was quite all right as far as Kant was concerned. He found it necessary to "deny knowledge in order to make room for faith."[67] Kant believed that faith and knowledge had nothing in common.[68] He effectively placed God in the compartment of the noumenal, where, in essence, nothing could be known of His existence.

Although Kant believed that the existence of God lay beyond the domain of pure reason, he wanted to preserve religious belief and put it on surer footing.[69] In his *Critique of Practical Reason* (1788), Kant argued that we live in a moral world because there seems to be a universal moral "oughtness" to the way we live. From this practical concern with morality Kant derived God's existence. Moreover, God's existence wasn't the foundation of morality as was traditionally thought. It was the other way around. The existence of morality (moral "oughtness") provided evidence that God really exists. For Kant, this was a "Copernican Revolution," because his philosophical thought reversed the previous order and placed man at the center of everything, including morality, and God at the periphery.[70]

Part of Kant's strategy here was to avoid the implications of the Newtonian worldview, where everything was part of the universal "machine." If everything operated according to fixed mechanical laws, then humans' freedom was in question, because they too were material beings and thus part of the deterministic laws of nature. So Kant argued that there must be a spiritual or transcendental realm in addition to the material world, otherwise it would be impossible for humans to have the ability to exercise their will and make moral choices. From this assumption of the spiritual, Kant posited the immortality of the soul and God's existence. Moral choice implied genuine freedom, something that was beyond material nature. For Kant, freedom meant "autonomy"; each individual was subject only to "laws imposed on oneself by oneself."[71] Thus, morality for Kant is not based on God's character or will. Rather, morality is discovered and grounded in humanity.

Moreover, a decisive move in Kant's thought made man the center of reality and morality. It is no longer how the world is given to us by God, but how *we* interpret that world that counts. It is no longer God's moral character that defines morality for humankind; it is each person's autonomous choice that defines what is moral. This is a decidedly anthropocentric shift. It is fair to say that much of the individualism, moral autonomy, and relativism that we witness in society today has its roots in Kant's project.

This whole notion of the phenomenal and noumenal realms resulted from Kant's radical theory of knowledge. Moreover, if we cannot truly know the everyday world as we experience it, how are we supposed to know spiritual things like God?

Critique of Kant's Project

But is Kant's radical skepticism regarding everyday experience justified? Francis Schaeffer thinks not. Against Kant, Schaeffer argues: "If a reasonable God made the world and has also made me, we are not surprised if He made the categories of the human mind to fit into the categories of the external world. Both are His Creation. There are categories in the external world, and there are categories of my mind. Should I be surprised if they fit?"[72]

Another problem with Kant's philosophy is that his notion of the noumenal realm is ultimately self-defeating. If nothing can be known about the noumenal realm, how does Kant know this, unless he is claiming to know something about the noumenal realm?

Kant felt he was doing a service for the Christian belief system by placing God in the noumenal realm, where the skeptics couldn't get at Him. In short, God's existence couldn't be proved, but it couldn't be disproved either. But this maneuver has cost Christianity dearly. God has now been completely partitioned off into the realm of faith. Kant's strategy of denying knowledge in order to make room for faith has left the general public today under the mistaken notion that Christian beliefs are based on faith without any foundation in reason. This is another example of how the medieval synthesis of faith and reason was severed.

Kant attempted to demonstrate the limits of reason. But his attempt at overcoming the skepticism of Hume simply left us with more uncertainty. Claiming that we cannot know the real world as we experience it has resulted in a radical skepticism that has seeped its way down into everyday life. The arrogantly held assumption today, especially among intellectuals, that skepticism and doubt are more "intellectually respectable" than some type of certainty have their roots in Kant and the Enlightenment.[73] The notion that everyone experiences the world differently and that truth is relative to each person can be credited in part to Kant. This perspectivalism is rampant in postmodernism and has damaged the notion of objective, absolute, and universal truth. The relativism of truth that is so prevalent today is evident in statements like "That's *your* truth, but it's not *my* truth," as if truth was a preference.

Kant stated that Hume woke him from his "dogmatic slumbers."[74] Perhaps it would have better to let him sleep. Kant's "accommodationist theology," as Garrett Green calls it, which was an attempt to "present Christianity in a form acceptable to the enlightened sensibility of modern people,"[75] has resulted in divorcing orthodox Christianity from any claims to truth. Unfortunately, like his predecessors who attempted to defend Christianity, Kant rejected the unique doctrines of Christianity found in special revelation. He gave assent instead to a universally accessible religion that did not derive from the incidents of history.[76] And finally, Kant's Copernican Revolution tipped morality upside down and made it relative and autonomous.

Summary of Enlightenment Thought

The Enlightenment era doesn't simply represent a historical period of time. It represents an entire ideology laden with assumptions, concepts, and values, that was emerging at the time—the modern worldview. This worldview transcended its own time period, and its impact can still be felt today. In short, the philosophical foundations that caused the pervasive secularization of Western civilization during the centuries that followed were laid in the Enlightenment era.[77]

The modern/secular worldview that began to take shape during this period can be summarized by much of what Enlightenment thinkers *rejected:* 1) superstition and prejudice in all forms; 2) ecclesiastical authoritarianism; 3) the burden of tradition; and 4) human depravity and an overly negative view of humankind.

Enlightenment thought may also be seen in some of the notions that most of the intellectuals *accepted:* 1) the light of reason to guide humankind into truth; 2) the use of reason to perfect the good life here and now instead of only the life beyond; 3) human progress and a utopian attitude based on the newly developing science and technology; 4) the notion that man is basically "good" and can be easily enlightened by the use of reason; and 5) a tolerant attitude for different religious beliefs and ways of life as long as they do not oppose what reason will allow.[78]

One of the most important developments during the Enlightenment era was the general loss of authority that Christianity held during the Middle Ages. In addition, reason and faith, which worked synergistically for scholastics like Aquinas, were now placed in separate compartments. Any aspects of Christianity that were not found to be reasonable were to be done away with. As Peter Gay puts it, "No one had thought that Christianity might give way to rationalism until Christians tried to prove Christianity was reasonable."[79] Michael Buckley summarizes the demise of Christianity during this time: "Religion protested that it could not speak for itself, that only philosophy could argue for it. Philosophy spoke, and its final word was no. In failing to assert its own competence, in commissioning philosophy with its defense, religion shaped its own eventual negation."[80]

Nineteenth Century Philosophers: A Snapshot

As we bring this chapter to a close, we must briefly touch on a few philosophers who were influenced by Enlightenment thought and in turn have influenced modern thinking today.

One philosopher who followed Kant is Wilhelm Friedrich Hegel (1770–1831). He is an extremely difficult philosopher to understand. For our purposes, the most important point about his philosophy is how he changed the concept of truth. Before Hegel, truth was based in "antithesis." Thus if I claim that God exists and someone else claims that God doesn't exist, then logically one of us would be wrong. Hegel changed this linear and logical notion of truth. His philosophy of history provides us with an example of how he changed the traditional concept of truth.

Hegel maintained that to truly understand something, you had to see how it relates to the whole. He saw an overall unity to history because history, in turn, was a reflection of ultimate reality, which he labeled the "Absolute." This Absolute he identified as "Spirit" or "Mind." All of history was moving toward the goal of the Absolute, yet because each thing is only a part of the Absolute, its truth is only partial and incomplete.[81] For Hegel, everything in history (science, religion, people, ideas, institutions, etc.) is in constant flux. Everything is part and parcel of a dialectic process, which is really the Absolute working itself out in history.[82]

Hegel was a dialectical thinker, which means that for him, the unfolding of history occurred as a "thesis" (which only represented partial truth). Its opposite, "antithesis," confronted thesis. The conflict of thesis and antithesis resolves itself not by simply rejecting the one that is false but by retaining and rejecting some elements of both. Truth is no longer absolute but rather a "synthesis" of the thesis and antithesis. The synthesis then becomes a new thesis and the whole process starts over again. Hegel changed the world when he relativized truth.[83] His new concept of truth, which does not follow the laws of logic, is strikingly similar to the postmodern concept of truth. Today, truth is relative. Everyone has their own truth.

Hegel used a lot of religious-sounding language in his philosophy. Although there is some indication that he returned to orthodox Lutheranism in his mature thought,[84] he had an adverse effect on Christianity and the notion of truth. He stated in his lectures that "The Christian religion is the religion of truth" but quickly added "but if by 'the truth of the Christian religion' we mean that it is historically accurate, this is not what is intended here."[85]

For Hegel, Christianity can at most be only partial truth because it is based in history as a product of faith communities which produced the Gospels. His ideas led to the formation of modern biblical criticism taught at the Tubingen School of Divinity. Biblical criticism may be credited as the single most destructive force for undermining Protestant Christianity in the nineteenth century. When challenged by a student that what he said bore little resemblance to reality, Hegel replied, "So much the worse for reality."[86]

Ludwig Feuerbach (1804–1872) agreed with Hegel that there was an inseparable connection between religion and the prevailing ideas of each age, but he rejected Hegel's view that religion was a rational endeavor. Religion, for Feuerbach, was merely a reflection of human desires and fears.[87]

Feuerbach believed that God did not make man is His image; it was man who had made God in his image. Philosophers in the past who talked about God were really talking about man. Theology and philosophy were self-deceiving endeavors to the extent that they promoted the "otherworldly" instead of focusing man's attention on legitimate human problems and needs. Genuine political reform would not occur until atheism displaced Christianity. Feuerbach maintained that "we must replace the love of God by the love of man as the only true religion . . . the fate of mankind depends not on a being outside it and above it, but on mankind itself."[88] This is basically secular humanism.

Karl Marx (1818–1883) spent a good deal of time in England during the Industrial Revolution where he learned to blame capitalism for the substandard living and working conditions in which a large portion of society found itself. Marx wanted to develop a philosophy that would demonstrate the inherent fallacies and harmful effects of capitalism and religion (especially Christianity).

Marx accepted and then adapted Hegel's dialectical philosophy concerning history. Marx, however, rejected the spiritual aspects of Hegel's theory like the Absolute, and instead employed Feuerbach's materialism in its place. The result was a philosophy called "dialectical materialism." Marx reduced all of humankind's problems to economics. Borrowing from Hegel's dialectic, Marx perceived that the dominant force of capitalism (thesis) becomes so oppressive that a class struggle occurs, followed by a revolution (antithesis), which results in the formation of a classless society (synthesis).[89]

Marx is best viewed as a humanist.[90] He agreed with Feuerbach that humans are merely material beings, and thus he denied the existence of God. Marx believed that religion is used by the wealthy to keep the oppressed focused on the life to come, as if their suffering prepared them in some way. Christians used other doctrines like Original Sin and predestination to help the oppressed feel comfortable with their place in life.[91] Marx believed people were willing to embrace religions because they were "alienated" in this life and lost the hope of salvation in the here and now. Marx called religion "the opium of the people."[92]

Friedrich Nietzsche (1844–1900), like his predecessors, had a monumental impact on much of the cultural mind-set in evidence today. In the area of knowledge, we noted that Descartes had grounded the ability to grasp truth in the guarantee that God would not deceive. Nietzsche took the opposite tack. All of life for him was based on deception and different points of view.[93] For Nietzsche, there was no such thing as bare facts that come to us uninterpreted. What we think of as truth is really our personal interpretation *imposed* on our experience. Therefore, truth is really each person's perspective.[94] One can see Kant's influence here.

Nietzsche believed that some interpretations are incorrect and even dangerous. The Christian religion is one of those false interpretations. Christianity is appealing to people because it gives hope to the weak and an overall meaning to life. But Nietzsche despised the idea that the weak should be accommodated. He felt that pity and weakness thwarted the laws of evolution, where only the fit had a right to survive. Nature has no place for the weak. Instead the natural inclination for all of life was the "will to power." For the individual, this means the power to impose one's will and interpretation on others.[95] Nietzsche saw Christianity as contradicting the will to power because it is fundamentally about sacrificing freedom, pride, and self. Christianity is also about the supreme sacrifice, which was Jesus's death on the cross.

Nietzsche is famous for his proclamation that "God is dead." By this he means that the idea of God is dead as far as having any significant cultural impact. Unlike other atheists who were still trying to find meaning in life through concepts like truth and goodness, Nietzsche sounded a clarion call to follow his declaration to its logical conclusion. The death of God leads to nihilism. In other words, no order or ultimate meaning can be found. Life is meaningless.[96]

It should not surprise us that the damage Nietzsche inflicted on truth, God, and the meaning of life would also have an unfavorable effect on morality. Nietzsche proclaimed that for a nonreligious person like himself, there is no distinction between good and evil. Christianity endorsed moral values to unite the natural slaves against the hero. For Nietzsche, the hero is the one who is willing to strike out on his own and exercise his autonomy and power.[97] He labeled this extraordinary individual the "superman,"[98] or more literally, the "overman" (*übermensch*).

Christianity, with its slave morality that invokes pity and weakness, must be rejected in favor of the dominant and strong Nietzschean man who is able to "will his own desire as a law unto himself."[99] It is worth pointing out that although Nietzsche was by no means a nationalist or an anti-Semite, the Nazis implemented Nietzschean phrases like "will to power" and "superman." They considered him the representative voice for their philosophy.[100]

Summary

This chapter provided a historical context for understanding some of the philosophical ideas that have made their way to us today. Significant thinkers affected the overall stream of thought, particularly beginning in the Enlightenment era. Many of the ways we think today were formed during this period when the modern worldview began to displace Christianity.

The major problem for Christianity, beginning with Ockham and then gaining steam as one approached the Enlightenment era, was primarily a loss of authority. Western European Christendom, which was a monolithic entity during the Middle Ages, fractured after the Reformation. This loss of Christian authority made it easier for non-Christian ideology to make inroads into philosophical thinking. This modern/secular thought has entrenched itself in the West ever since, and has made its way down to the culture at large in America today.

When you hear someone say, "You can't prove Christianity is true," or something like, "Faith is a personal thing," think back to the Enlightenment. Descartes made the move toward the "personal" with his *cogito*. Hume and Kant put faith and reason into separate compartments. This has affected our thinking today. People nowadays, especially liberal elites and secular humanists, feel that Christians *ipso facto* have no reasonable grounds for defending their belief system. This is because the widely held assumption today is that religion falls under the guise of faith, while things like science fall under the domain of reason and empiricism (facts and knowledge).

The divorce of reason and faith has resulted in a relativized attitude toward truth. Much of the credit for this faulty way of thinking about truth and religion may be laid at the feet of Hume, Kant, Ockham, and Nietzsche, as well as those who picked up their philosophy and ran with it.

The emphasis on the individual and much of the narcissistic attitude seen today found its beginnings in thinkers like Rousseau and Nietzsche. Descartes may have placed humans at the center of the cosmos, but Rousseau elevated human nature by proclaiming the natural goodness of each person who is untainted by Original Sin. The widely held notion today that people are innately good and simply need more education or therapy when they do something morally evil is a particularly Enlightenment concept. Those on the left have swallowed this hook, line, and sinker. Rehab not repentance seems to be the motto today. Besides, as the thinking goes, who is to say what is good or evil anyway? "Don't force your moral values on me" is the watchword these days.

Much of this moral autonomy may be traced back to the loss of Christian authority in culture. Kant's Copernican Revolution exacerbated this because he grounded moral imperatives in humanity, not

God. If God does not exist or is no longer relevant (Nietzsche) or He can't be trusted (Ockham), then people will have to decide what is right and wrong for themselves. Each individual must displace God as the center of the cosmos and impose his own will on the fabric of life (Nietzsche).

In short, the flight from authority, which provides the overarching framework for understanding the Enlightenment, resulted in autonomy and an emphasis on the "self," which became more pronounced as time moved on. Theology handed the reins of authority over to philosophy, and philosophy undercut theology and then handed authority over to the individual. The Enlightenment displaced God as the focal point for understanding reality, knowledge, and morals. Man, freed from the tutelage of revelation, became the be-all and end-all, and now today the know-it-all as he takes God's place at the center of the universe. The rise of the autonomous self, accountable to no one, is a theme we will see played out again and again as we move through our study.

In this chapter we saw an overview of how modern secularism surfaced from the realm of the philosophers. It is certainly the case that the Enlightenment philosophers had an impact on how secularism is replacing Christianity today as the hegemonic force in our culture. But that is only half the story. In the next chapter, we'll turn our attention to Christians and theologians who, like their philosophical predecessors, unwittingly opened the door and accommodated modern/secular thinking.

Chapter 4

How Liberal Protestantism Accommodated Secular Modernism

In the last chapter we saw how Christianity began to lose its authority in the world of ideas. Philosophers, many of whom considered themselves Christians, proposed theories of knowledge based on reason divorced from revelation. They discarded many of the fundamental doctrines of orthodoxy and tried to adapt Christianity to the latest epistemological crisis. Philosophical thought began replacing Christian revelation as the point of departure for understanding theology, the nature of knowledge, and reality.

In this chapter we will again take a step back in history where, in this case, we will look at Protestantism. The basic argument in this chapter is that the liberal strand of Protestantism, instead of resisting Enlightenment modernism, began accommodating/retreating from its advance with each successive generation. Protestantism will be our major focal point because it was this brand of Christianity that colonists brought over to our country and has remained, until recently, the hegemonic religious force in our culture.

As we will see, one part of the accommodation process revolves around the move toward the autonomy of the individual. With regard to theology, this meant a move on the part of each person *away* from "rational" religion, which was dry and detached, and a move *toward* the "experiential" and emotional aspects of faith. Pietism led one thread of this type of Christianity. Another strand involved the democratization of religious belief and autonomous individualism, which paralleled the American Revolution. Democratization enhanced the accommodation process during the nineteenth century, because each individual became the arbiter of his own faith.

In the latter half of the nineteenth century, liberal Protestantism which came from Germany, compromised and undermined orthodox Protestantism. Liberal Protestant theologians molded key Christian dogmas so that they would conform to the modern mind-set. Most of these liberal theologians were troubled that Christian doctrines seemed backward when compared with science and modernism. For others, the fact that Christianity claimed to be the one true religion was particularly disturbing.

By the middle of the twentieth century, the accommodation process inflicted a great deal of damage on the fundamental doctrines of Protestantism by redefining them as "myths" or discarding them altogether, leaving a neutered and inoffensive version of Christianity in the liberal Protestant camp. By the 1960s, radical theologians wondered aloud whether the word *God* really meant anything at all. Let's begin to unpack some of this.

The Reformation and the Founding

The Protestant Reformation of the sixteenth century represented a rejection of Roman Catholic authority. Martin Luther and others believed that Scripture alone (*sola scriptura*) was the sole authority for Christians in matters of faith and doctrine. The Protestant reformers also undermined Catholic authority by advocating the doctrine of the "priesthood of all believers," which in essence meant that all Christians have equal access to God (without the need for the Church or a priest) based on the merit of faith in Jesus Christ alone. This undermined the hierarchical structure and authority of traditional Roman Catholicism. This is one way that tradition and authority began to give way to the autonomy of the individual.[1]

The printing press, which had come into existence the previous century, exposed an increasing number of laypeople to readable translations of the Bible. This reinforced autonomy as well, because individuals no longer had to rely on the authority of the clergy for interpreting Scripture. The plethora of Bibles also resulted in a multiplicity of denominations in Protestantism because of varying interpretations of Scripture.

Luther's insistence that the Church was not needed for the priesthood, sacraments, or other traditions, gave Protestants a skeptical attitude toward the ecclesiastical hierarchy and other Catholic traditions. This attitude played itself out, for example, in an effort to purify the Church of England of any vestiges of Roman Catholicism. But as time wore on, these efforts fell short, and therefore a group of Puritans made their way to the New World in 1630 to establish a "city on a hill," which would be a beacon to the rest of the world and to England.[2]

What would later become the United States turned out to be the first society founded mainly by Protestants rather than Catholics.

North America offered something akin to a cultural version of Locke's "blank slate" in that a pluralism of nationalities and religious groups made their way to the newly founded colonies.[3]

The Great Awakening and the American Revolution

The rejection of ecclesiastical authority that began in Europe continued in the new territory. Whereas the Puritans had initially set up a united commonwealth of state and religion, proponents of the religious revival known as the Great Awakening called into question this union a century later in the 1730s and 1740s.[4] Before the Awakening, people had strict ties only to their own denominations. But the itinerant preachers who traveled from town to town changed all that by addressing each person as a unique individual, regardless of their religious affiliation.

Led by men like John Wesley and George Whitefield, the Great Awakening focused on the need for each individual to have a genuine relationship with Jesus Christ. Honoring one's church membership or merely adhering to dry, intellectual doctrine was not enough. The gospel called for a change of heart, a "new birth," which must occur on the individual level. Jonathan Edwards stated that "Our people do not so much need to have their heads stored, as to have their hearts touched."[5] The Great Awakening epitomized a reaction against the formal, arid rationalism that had been so much a part of the Enlightenment.

Traveling evangelists encouraged common folk to perform Christian duties on their own. The evangelists also convinced parishioners that it was perfectly acceptable to leave their churches. This was an extremely radical proposition at that time. The negative attitude displayed by itinerant evangelists toward the clergy, or any church authority for that matter, pointed to a change in the social hierarchy. In short, it represented a major incentive to a more democratic way of life. The Awakening was not only a populist movement per se; it was the first "truly national event."[6] In fact, historian Harry Stout called George Whitefield America's "first modern celebrity."[7]

The Awakening called three things into question: 1) the entire Puritan notion of the relationship between church and society; 2) the aristocratic posture and pretensions of the clergy; and 3) any churches that maintained strong ties with Europe, the most important of which was the Church of England.[8] The suspicious attitude toward authority, engendered by the Awakening, actually laid some of the groundwork for the American Revolution and thus set the tone for American society during that era.[9] In fact, noted historian Sydney Ahlstrom claims that a source of strength for the Revolution could be found in the "religious substratum which was always Nonconformist and Dissenting."[10]

Once the hunger for revolt against England came to the forefront of politics, the converts of the Awakening got carried away and co-opted into this patriotic fervor that came to a head in the American Revolution.[11] What should have been a time of genuine regeneration in much of Protestantism as a result of the Awakening soon became an example of how Christianity became overly enmeshed in the cultural attitude of the time. In short, the fires of revival died out as the Revolution was fanned into flame.

The Second Great Awakening, which occurred soon after the Revolution, started the fires of revival once again. The assault on political authority during the Revolutionary era translated into a democratizing process for Christianity as it developed in the early republic and into the nineteenth century. This democratizing inclination in the post-Revolutionary era found expression in the explosion of Methodist and Baptist churches, both products of the Second Awakening. By the middle of the nineteenth century, these two denominations accounted for two-thirds of church members in the country,[12] replacing the traditional Presbyterians, Congregationalists, and Episcopalians which had been the largest. The black church also grew out of the revivalism of this period. That black preachers aspired successfully to "the sacred desk" was significant evidence that Christianity was being democratized.[13]

Like the first Great Awakening, the traveling preachers of the Second Awakening played an indispensable role in spreading the gospel during the nineteenth century. In 1800 only 9 percent of the population lived west of the colonies, but by the beginning of the Civil War, 51 percent of the population comprised the Western territories.[14] The Methodist circuit riders thoroughly covered the new Western region. Their Baptist counterparts relied on "farm preachers" to multiply Christian ranks in these areas as well.[15]

The circuit riders had a legendary reputation for living in the saddle, working for little pay (if any), battling the elements, and often dying young from the hardship. During particularly adverse weather conditions, there was a saying that went something like this: "There's nobody out tonight but crows and Methodist preachers."[16] It was this monumental effort by the circuit riders and lay preachers that made evangelicalism the hegemonic religious force in our nation.[17]

The advent of the mass print media also aided in the evangelistic efforts. With fervor, traveling evangelists expedited the proliferation of pamphlets, books, spiritual songs, and tracts. Printed material that traditionally was the reserve of educated gentlemen or clergy subsequently fell into the hands of laypeople.[18] This in turn supported the autonomous nature of American culture. Everyone was free to exercise his or her private judgment regarding new information.

Pietism was another movement, besides the Awakenings, that emphasized the individual as the sole authority in deciding religious matters. Pietism was a reaction to the formal rationalism of the Enlightenment. It can also be understood as a movement in its own right that focused on each individual's religious feeling, piety, and purity of life.[19] Pietism focused on making religious experience deeply personal.[20] It originated in German Lutheranism and also found expression in Wesley's Methodism and revivals like the Great Awakenings.

For Pietism, the Bible was no longer adequate like it was for those in the Protestant Reformation who held to *sola scriptura*. Subjective religious experience took the Bible's place as the authority for discerning truth in this brand of Protestantism.

We can summarize so far by noting that what began in the Reformation continued and emerged in various historical ways that affected both the founding of our country and Protestantism. This includes 1) a revolt against religious authority, 2) autonomy of the individual in matters of interpretation, and 3) a democratization of information that supported a pluralistic frame of mind.

The leveling of authority that began in the Reformation carried over into the new democracy as each individual exercised his or her autonomy in political and religious matters. There was a move *away* from formal religion and *toward* individual spirituality. This autonomous spirituality, however, ultimately had a role in undermining the authority of Scripture.

We will now turn to the liberal theologians who played a part in accommodating Christianity to culture.

Friedrich Schleiermacher (1768–1834)

Motivated by the desire to resurrect religion among the intellectual class which had fallen by the wayside during the Enlightenment, Friedrich Schleiermacher argued that the authority of Scripture, miracles, and proofs of God were not in the realm of reason. Rather, the essence of religion was "feeling," not rational proofs.[21] In short, religion for Schleiermacher was a theology of "experience."[22] Against both rationalism and formal orthodoxy he maintained that awareness of one's consciousness of God—what he called the "feeling of absolute dependence"—was the true heart of religion.

Schleiermacher is known as the father of liberal Protestantism. Like his predecessors in the Enlightenment, Schleiermacher reduced many of the orthodox doctrines and beliefs in Christianity to natural religion. For example, he argued that passages describing God's act of creating the universe are not to be taken literally but rather should be interpreted to express the Christian's understanding that all things depend on God.[23] Or take Jesus as another example. Jesus is not the divine son of God, who was born of the virgin birth. Rather, Jesus had a supreme sense of God-consciousness, which He inspired in others.[24] Moreover, Jesus should be viewed simply as a pioneer in morals and ethics. For Schleiermacher, Jesus's humanity was emphasized to the neglect of His divinity.

Schleiermacher followed the Enlightenment ambition of embracing only religion that was universal in nature. Schleiermacher felt that the existence of religions other than Christianity was not a problem because they too have their own God-consciousness. There may be doctrinal disparities between other religions and Christianity, but underneath they all share a common experience.[25] Doctrinal differences don't matter anyway, because religion is based on the individual's personal experience. One can see the influence of Kant here, as well as Pietism, where Christianity is partitioned off into the realm of personal experience and faith.

Ironically, by trying to save Christianity from the Enlightenment critics and Christianity's "cultured despisers," Schleiermacher did more harm than good. Peter Berger calls Schleiermacher's attempt to rescue Christianity "an immense bargaining process with secular thought."[26] Schleiermacher compromised many fundamental Christian beliefs to make them compatible with natural religion. Natural religion, of course, means that God is just a part of nature, or He doesn't exist at all.

The irony is that instead of defending Christianity against its critics, Schleiermacher embraced the same naturalistic presuppositions that Enlightenment philosophers did and thus made the same fundamental mistake they made: he accommodated modernist thinking. This spelled disaster for the Christian belief system. Moreover, much of the compromising and accommodation found in Schleiermacher's thought is found in liberal theology even today. Let's take a look at liberal theology and see how it marginalized Christianity.

Liberal Theology

The word *liberal* came into regular use in the English language by the 1830s to refer to values associated with political liberty, certainty of progress, the virtue of toleration, and the merits of reason. Protestant theologians attempted to use liberal theology to modernize Christianity by bringing it up-to-date with recent advancements in philosophical, scientific, social, and historical studies.[27] In many ways it was a continuation of the Enlightenment use of reason to judge the merits of theology. A thread of Romanticism and Pietism also ran through liberal theology, which was a reaction *against* rationalism.

In keeping with the virtue of tolerance, liberal theologians desired to include all religions as equally meritorious. They therefore frowned on the particularity and exclusiveness of Christianity as expressed in scriptural revelation. Liberal theologians found proof of God in religious experience, not revelation. Truth in religion is judged by whether it makes the world a better place.[28] Whether the purported revelation is true or not is of secondary concern. Thus an emphasis in liberal theology on pragmatism and ethics took priority over doctrinal veracity. This was disastrous for orthodox Christianity where, of course, truth is the ultimate concern.

One of the particulars of Christianity that liberal theologians denied was the doctrine of Original Sin. As far as liberal theologians were concerned, nothing is fundamentally wrong with human nature. People simply needed to be educated and to follow the ethical standard of Jesus.[29] These progressive ideas are still reflected today in liberals' endorsement of "more education" as a panacea for humankind's ills.

It follows logically that this high view of man leads liberal theologians of that time to believe in the inevitability of progress. In short, liberal theologians rejected the radical transcendence of God that Deists held. Deists thought God wound up the world like a clock and then left it to run on its own while He roamed to some other part of the universe.

Against this, liberal theologians emphasized the *immanence* of God, which coincided with Hegel's idealistic vision of history. For Hegel, the world was inherently rational. God was working *in* the world by means of history so that the rational would overcome the irrational. This provided the optimism for liberal theologians that the kingdom of God could be set up on earth as history progressed toward Hegel's notion of the Absolute.[30]

Of course, from a traditional Christian perspective, this notion that God may be found *in* history comes dangerously close to some sort of panentheism, in which God becomes indistinguishable from the world or the historical process itself. Transcendental Idealism, which came out of Romanticism, added to this faulty notion because it made it difficult to distinguish between God and nature. Many liberal theologians during this time felt that God was so closely related to the world that He had no need to intervene in its affairs. To suggest that God needs to intervene from time to time in human history by performing miracles fails to see that He achieved what He set out to do at the original ordering of creation.[31]

Different historical components occurring in the latter half of the nineteenth century greatly influenced liberal Protestantism's faith in progress. The Industrial Revolution gave confidence that humankind was progressing technologically. Darwin's theory of evolution provided the assurance that humans were evolving. Bourgeois capitalism was beginning to triumph during the latter part of the nineteenth and early twentieth century. All of these social components provided a plausibility structure for the liberal Protestant worldview.[32] Even the average Bible-reading churchgoer could see God's hand and divine purpose in setting up His coming kingdom.[33] Progress seemed inevitable on all fronts.

This man-centered and progressive aspect of liberal theology can be seen in the Social Gospel movement which was a reaction against the pietistic emphasis on each individual at the expense of the community at large. Those in the Social Gospel movement felt that the kingdom of God was not meant as an eschatological end time event. They thought instead that a society on earth could be inaugurated in the here and now, when people lived like brothers in harmony with love and justice.[34] Thus, this theology contained a utopian aspect.

Liberal theology's social and ethical concerns birthed the Social Gospel movement. Walter Rauschenbusch (1868–1918) coined the term *Social Gospel.* It reflected the practical aspects of liberal theology, many of which were outlined in 1900 by Adolf von Harnack in his book *What Is Christianity?* The essence of liberal Protestantism from a Social Gospel perspective could be seen in three central tenets: the fatherhood of God, the brotherhood of man, and the immeasurable value of the human soul.[35]

It is clear then that theological emphases at this time revolved around humanity, not God. The Enlightenment had instilled in humanity the ability to solve its own problems by the light of reason not religious authority. Liberal theologians simply substituted religious experience in place of reason for understanding God. They envisioned the Almighty not as a fire-breathing, holy God who opposed humanity's every move but, rather, as the loving Father of all humanity, while Jesus served as our human brother. It was apparent to liberal theologians that God was working in history and everything was progressing as it should.

The problem with all of this is that the liberal Protestant theologians had begun bargaining with modernism. As urbanization, industrialization, and progress began to take hold of culture in the latter half of the nineteenth century, Christian beliefs started to seem somewhat archaic.[36] Alister McGrath argues that the most distinguishing element of liberal Protestantism during this era may be its "accommodationism," that is, "its insistence that traditional Christian doctrines should be restated or reinterpreted in order to render them harmonious with the spirit of the age."[37] This is exactly the point of this chapter—that liberals inside the Christian fold have a history of accommodating and then retreating from the forces of modern secularism.

Ernst Troeltsch (1865–1923) and Biblical Criticism

An often overlooked theologian who exemplifies liberal theology during that time was Ernst Troeltsch. He belonged to the History of Religions School, a group of scholars who compared Christianity's origin and development with other religions. Troeltsch emerged at a time when biblical criticism, as a school of thought, was a force to be reckoned with in German theological circles.

Troeltsch rejected what he labeled the older "absolutist" or "dogmatic" approach to Christianity in which the Bible was used as the sole authority like it was in the Reformation. He denied the distinction between natural and supernatural revelation, allowing him to endorse all religions as somehow equal.[38] Thus, he rejected Hegel's concept that Christianity was the "absolute religion" and supported the idea of religious pluralism instead. Troeltsch stated in no uncertain terms: "Indeed, the very thought of setting forth any one historical religion as complete and final, capable of supplanting all others, seem to us open to serious criticism and doubt."[39] For Troeltsch, there is no essence of Christianity found only in the doctrines and the authority of Scripture.

Rather, Christianity changes as it moves along in history and will continue to do so.[40] In this sense Christianity *is* its history and therefore is no different from any of the other religions.

When reading through some of Troeltsch's work, I got the impression that he wanted to uphold the uniqueness and supremacy of Christianity, but he couldn't quite bring himself to do so. He seemed to be aware of his inability because of the historical method he adopted. In fact, he went so far as to write, "Give the historical method an inch and it will take a mile. From a strictly orthodox standpoint, therefore, it seems to bear a certain similarity to the devil."[41] One wonders, then, why he continued to use this method.

Troeltsch is important for two reasons. First, he exemplifies the reticence which liberal theologians of his time had in declaring Christianity to be the one true religion. The general attitude then was that given the plurality of religions, how dare someone claim one particular religion is the only true one? But second, his notion that there is no essence to Christianity—that it somehow changes over time—seems to follow logically for those who cannot bring themselves to believe in Christianity's unchangeable truth (Jesus), who was revealed at a particular time in history.

This attitude of compromise exists today as well. For example, not too long ago John Shelby Spong wrote a book entitled *Christianity Must Change or Die*. When you see declarations like this, you know that men like Troeltsch have had an impact on today's thinking and that liberal theology is still alive and well. Liberal theologians want to retreat from proclaiming the absolute truth of Christianity. Instead they attempt to adapt Christian fundamentals to modern culture so that Christianity can somehow stay afloat in today's (post)modern world.

Because liberal theologians at that time did not believe in the miracle-working Christ of the Gospels, they decided to search for the "historical Jesus." They believed that the Christ portrayed in the Gospels was somehow different from what the human Jesus was like in real life. Liberal Protestant theologians not only used the latest historico-critical method but viewed their analysis through modernism, which disallowed Jesus's divinity and His miracles. One can see the influence of the Enlightenment project here.

This search lasted most of the nineteenth century with one theologian after another making a claim to construct the real Jesus of history. Albert Schweitzer compiled this historic search in his famous book *The Quest of the Historical Jesus* (1906). Schweitzer's conclusion was that each theologian simply created Jesus in his own image.[42] In fact, Catholic theologian George Tyrrell argued a few years after Schweitzer's book came out that the attempted reconstruction of the historical Jesus was little more than "the reflection of a liberal Protestant face, seen at the bottom of a deep well."[43]

Why is this important? It is apparent that as the Bible continued to lose its authority to the forces of biblical criticism, it also lost its right to speak for itself. It was being pushed, pulled, and tugged this way and that. As noted above, the problem is that much of the historico-critical methodology that liberal Protestants applied to Scripture was seen through the lens of modernism, which then read back its naturalistic presuppositions into the text. A worldview in which God is not allowed to intervene in history doesn't look much like Christianity. We are left with a Jesus who performed no miracles, a Jesus who did not rise from the dead, and a Jesus who certainly was not divine. We are left without a Christ and, therefore, without "Christianity."

Nevertheless, the march of liberal Protestantism continued and peaked just prior to World War I. This advance did not go unnoticed. There was a backlash against liberal theology by conservative theologians who were both inside and outside the liberal camp.

Soren Kierkegaard (1813–1855)

The next two theologians who follow chronologically in our stream of history after Troeltsch are Bultmann and Barth. However, to understand their ideas better we will briefly backtrack and introduce Kierkegaard, the father of Christian existentialism.

Soren Kierkegaard, like his counterparts in America, reacted against the pretensions of the church and people who belonged to it (his church was in Denmark). He felt that many people were nominal Christians at best and non-Christians at worst. If he were alive today, I envision him telling Protestants that just because they go to church on Sunday and hear God's Word preached does not mean that they are Christians. Likewise, he would tell Catholics that just because they were baptized into the Catholic Church and take the Eucharist on Sunday does not make them Christians.

Kierkegaard rejected Hegel's version of Christianity, which emphasized the collective and the rational. For Kierkegaard, the idea that Christianity conformed to reason, which Hegel and the Enlightenment thinkers believed, was sheer folly. For God to become a man in Jesus was paradoxical, not reasonable. To try to make this and other absurd doctrines into some kind of coherent synthesis of truth (as Hegel had done) was ridiculous in Kierkegaard's mind. Each individual instead should embrace the paradoxes of Christianity.[44] But because embracing a paradox is not reasonable, it must involve a "leap of faith."

Hegel's system saw salvation in a collective sense with everything progressing toward the Absolute Spirit in history. Kierkegaard instead maintained that salvation was an individual matter. A person's very existence is determined by his act of choosing or making a commitment.[45] For Kierkegaard there was a "yawning qualitative abyss" between the sinner and God.[46] Therefore, just because a person belonged to a church did not mean he or she automatically obtained salvation. Salvation occurs when an individual takes a leap of faith and commits himself to the absurdity of Christianity without any proof fostered by reason. William E. Hordern summarized Kierkegaard's thought: "Faith does not mean for Kierkegaard the believing of doctrines that cannot be proved; it means the giving or commitment of one's whole life. . . . Those Christians who try to hide in the Church as respectable persons are seeking a halfway house, but they are greater enemies of Christ than the atheist."[47]

Two things stand out in Kierkegaard's thought that relate to our thesis. First, to his credit, I think Kierkegaard would have railed against the practical atheists today who identify with Christianity in some way but won't make a true commitment to Christ. Second, we see in Kierkegaard a radical compartmentalization of both faith and reason that has become detrimental to the Christian worldview. For Kierkegaard, most of the doctrines of Christianity are so contrary to reason that it requires a blind leap of faith to accept them. Unlike the Enlightenment thinkers before him and the liberal theologians after him who rejected doctrines of Christianity that weren't considered reasonable, Kierkegaard simply wanted people to take a leap of faith and embrace them anyway. On this point Kierkegaard was wrong. One's faith *can* be reasonable.

Rudolf Bultmann (1884–1976)
Rudolf Bultmann followed in Kierkegaard's footsteps by taking up the latter's existentialist emphasis on inner commitment. Bultmann believed the uncertainty of historical knowledge should not be the ground for something as important as Christianity. Thus, he divorced Christianity from history, attempting to rescue it, just as his predecessors in the Enlightenment era and liberal Protestantism had done.

His rescue attempt involved "demythologizing" all parts of the Bible. He viewed a myth as anything that contradicted the modern worldview, which included the miracles found in the Bible.[48] Because Bultmann was a modernist, references to Jesus walking on the water, casting out demons, or rising from the dead had to be explained by natural means. Interestingly, Bultmann's ideas coincided with the rise of methodological naturalism in the realm of science, which we will look at in Chapters ten and eleven. As Bultmann stated, "A historical fact which involves a resurrection from the dead is utterly inconceivable."[49] He also maintained, "It is impossible to use the electric light and the wireless and to avail ourselves of modern medical and surgical discoveries, and at the same time to believe in the New Testament world of spirits and miracles."[50]

For Bultmann, the Gospel accounts of miracles were an embarrassment in light of modern science and technology. He wanted to strip away all of the miraculous elements of Christianity (the "husk") so that the true message (the "kernel") would remain.[51] In true existentialist fashion, Bultmann's primary concern was not history but how the faith message of the early church could impact people today in their existential here and now. What matters is not whether Jesus really rose from the dead in the *past*, but how He meets people in their *present* experiences today. For Bultmann, it is the Christ of *faith* that one must believe in, not the historical Jesus.

Bultmann followed in the paths of thinkers like Hume, Kant, and Kierkegaard. Bultmann divorced scriptural revelation from history and placed it in the realm of faith. But can Jesus's resurrection mean anything for us today if He did not really rise from the dead in the past? The apostle Paul certainly did not think so. Paul stated in no uncertain terms, "But if there is no resurrection of the dead, then not even Christ has been raised. And if Christ has not been raised, then our preaching is in vain and your faith is in vain" (1 Cor. 15:13–14).

If Bultmann wanted to dispense with all the miraculous elements in Christianity, he should have had the intellectual honesty to admit that he was no longer defending Christianity. Just because Bultmann and those like him baptized their made-up religions with Christian terminology does not make their religions Christian. They should admit that they are "promoting a new product," according to Ronald Nash.[52]

Karl Barth (1886–1968)

Like that of Bultmann, our consideration of Karl Barth will be extremely cursory compared with the weight of impact he had on twentieth-century theology. Barth's neoorthodoxy was a self-conscious rejection of the liberal theology he studied in his early years. Barth first became disillusioned with the liberal theologians when he saw one after another (such as Harnack) support the aggressive war policy of Kaiser Wilhelm in 1914. The liberal theologians failed him again when they couldn't muster the intestinal fortitude to stand against Hitler.[53] Barth's "crisis theology" was a response to liberal theology's faulty optimism regarding humankind's inevitable progress. The two World Wars and the Great Depression shattered liberal Protestantism's naïve optimism, so Barth attempted to redirect their theology back to a more orthodox position. Thus his theology is known as "neoorthodoxy."

Liberal Protestantism's starting point had been human experience. For Barth, this would not do. Following Kierkegaard's lead, Barth held that God was "Wholly Other." Barth was trying to distinguish God from the perception of those influenced by Romanticism and Transcendentalism who felt that God was an immanent part of nature.

Barth believed man's efforts to reach God are futile, because humankind is tainted with sin. It is God who must take the initiative and reach out to man. Moreover, Barth adopted what Richard Wightman Fox describes as a "dismissive posture toward secular culture, toward the human sciences that Troeltsch and other liberals had viewed as indispensable foundations of theology itself."[54]

Theology for Barth started from above, not below. Although Barth rejected the natural theology of the Enlightenment and the liberal Protestant theologians, unfortunately he did not distance himself as much as he may have thought from biblical criticism and modern thought.[55] Barth's attempt to overcome the historicism of men like Troeltsch fell short of the mark. Because Barth was so enmeshed in liberal thinking, he could not bring himself to admit that the Bible *is* revelation. Instead, Barth considered the Bible only a fallible testimony to how God revealed Himself in history.

Furthermore, Barth denied propositional revelation. That is, he denied that God could convey truth about Himself in sentences like those found in the Bible. Barth believed that God can convey Himself through His Word. Nevertheless, the Bible is not the Word of God until it is appropriated by the believer. It is only then that the Bible *becomes* the Word of God.[56] This reflects the existentialist, man-centered emphasis we saw in Kierkegaard. For Barth, Scripture had lost its objective authority, because for it to count as revelation it must be combined with an individual's faith. Whether or not Scripture is really a record of accurate history was of secondary concern for Barth.

We see in Barth and Bultmann the predicament of modern man. They want to believe in Christianity, but they don't want to look foolish by accepting that God works miracles in history. The evidence of miracles in the Bible was disconcerting to them because miracles go against modern sensibilities. Bultmann's way around this was to label anything in Scripture that did not line up with the modern worldview a myth. In this way a person could claim to be a Christian and continue to use Christian terminology and symbols, even though he or she doesn't believe the fundamentals anymore. But of course, this is really a form of atheism or humanism, not Christianity.

Barth's way of escaping historicism and biblical criticism was to pull a Kantian maneuver. He kept God high above the radar where the biblical critics couldn't get at Him. God is Wholly Other and exists in the noumenal realm, where He is safe from biblical criticism. But the problem is that God is so totally transcendent that He has no real contact in history.[57] Miracles can't occur, because the universe is a closed system and God is not allowed to perforate our space-time realm. But this is perfectly fine for Barth, because God still meets us in our existential situation today through His Word. Our job is to meet Him in a Kierkegaardian leap of faith. Some have seen Barth as the first postmodern theologian. As Albert Mohler Jr. warns, "What the postmodernists find most attractive in Barth, the evangelicals may find most dangerous."[58]

Klaus Bockmuehl summarizes the theology of Barth and Bultmann by arguing that they removed God from "the danger zone of philosophical debate" so that their theology would "comply with the theoretical, so-called scientific demands of a modern secular world view which allows no room for divine interference in this world. The result was . . . the unreality of God—a factual, if not nominal atheism."[59]

Fundamentalism

The fundamentalist movement started in the early 1900s as a reaction to modernism in both theology and culture. Fundamentalists didn't simply lie down while the secularizing of the faith was taking place. They fought back and were militant in their adversity to the modern assumptions of liberal Protestant theology.[60] Their rebellious attitude is highlighted by George Marsden, who wryly notes, "A fundamentalist is an evangelical who is angry about something."[61]

While liberal theologians saw themselves as *salvaging* the faith, fundamentalists saw the liberal efforts as *subverting* the faith. Fundamentalists did not view themselves as trying to correct liberal Protestantism from the inside like Bultmann had tried to do. Rather, fundamentalists considered themselves completely outside the liberal camp. Moreover, fundamentalists viewed the liberal theologians' efforts to adapt important doctrines of Christianity to modernism a "sell-out."[62]

A series of books published between 1910 and 1915 entitled *The Fundamentals* gave the movement its name while garnering its first major attempt to defend the supernatural/orthodox claims of Scripture. Unfortunately, what was gained by making *The Fundamentals* accessible to the general public (300,000 copies) was lost in scholarly prestige. In other words, the books were more popular than they were a scholarly struggle with modernism.[63]

A notable exception to this questionable scholarship was fundamentalist J. Gresham Machen, who took the liberals to task in his classic work *Christianity and Liberalism* (1923).[64] In his book Machen states:

> Despite the liberal use of traditional phraseology modern liberalism not only is a different religion from Christianity but belongs in a totally different class of religions . . . In trying to remove from Christianity everything that could possibly be objected to in the name of science, in trying to bribe off the enemy by those concessions which the enemy most desires, the apologist has really abandoned what he started out to defend.[65]

Machen understood perfectly that liberal theologians bowed down to modernism in every conceivable way.

Both science and evolutionary theory had gained momentum ever since the advent of Darwin's *Origin of the Species* (1859), and they both played a part in undermining the authority of Scripture through the latter part of the nineteenth century and right into the twentieth century. This was not lost on the fundamentalists. The legality of teaching evolution in a public school came to the country's attention in the famous Scopes Monkey Trial (1925). The trial epitomized the fundamentalist/modernist controversy at that time. This is where the so-called "warfare" between science and religion came to a head.

Space does not permit going into details of the trial, but suffice it to say that evolutionary theory and science came out on top. Science was perceived as authoritative. To put it bluntly, the fundamentalists were obliterated in the court of public opinion. Notions like the "inerrancy of Scripture" and "literal interpretation," which were long held by the fundamentalists, looked ignorant and backward in the public's mind compared with the authority of science. Because of the Scopes Trial debacle, many conservative Protestants silently discontinued their support of the fundamentalist movement, afraid of being embarrassed by their alliance with it.[66]

I mention the Scopes Trial because its impact can still be felt today. The trial epitomized much of society's perception of conservative Protestant Christianity. How? First, the myth in today's culture that conservative Christians are ignorant, intolerant, and militant became popular as a result of the Scopes Trial. Second, the trial resulted in a loss of authority of the Bible. Scripture today is regarded with some suspicion at best and as an outmoded mythical tale at worst when compared with modern science and all of its advances in technology. People today who take the Bible literally in any sense are equated with those who still believe the earth is flat. Third, the Scopes Trial solidified the popular belief in our culture that Christians are somehow opposed to science, or threatened by it. While there may have been some validity for using the term *warfare* as an appropriate metaphor between fundamentalists and science back then,[67] this conflict has more moving parts than most people are aware. But unfortunately this myth of the warfare between Christianity and science has entrenched itself in the cultural mind-set since the Scopes Trial. For now, suffice it to say that there wasn't any warfare between science and Christianity until after methodological naturalism became the modus operandi for doing science in the late nineteen century. We will flesh out this warfare myth in the science chapters.

After the Scopes Trial, the fundamentalists lost their national prominence. They began to pull out of the mainline Protestant churches, especially the northern branches of the Baptist and Presbyterian churches where there were doctrinal differences. They subsequently formed what Robert Wuthnow describes as "a rigidly patriarchal and puritanical subculture of their own."[68] In short, the fundamentalists adopted an "us versus them" mentality and withdrew into their own world. Critics at the time may have been hopeful that these products of rural, backwoods culture, as they viewed them, would disappear. But, in fact, they were realigning and would reemerge with their evangelical counterparts a few decades later.[69]

Liberal Theology after 1930

Though science and Enlightenment modernism were established as the authorities in epistemological matters during the first part of the twentieth century, the two World Wars and the Great Depression put a major dent in modernist aspirations of an inevitable utopia. In short, the World Wars and the Holocaust were wake-up calls for liberal theologians and secularists. The wars made the unreserved optimism in modern secularism's inevitable progress seem hollow and superficial.[70]

Moreover, theologians in the liberal camp were beginning to understand that the fundamentalists were right about one thing: mankind is sinful. Two theologians who came to terms with this were the Niebuhr brothers, both of whom followed in the line of Troeltsch. (H. Richard Niebuhr wrote his doctoral dissertation on Troeltsch at Yale.[71]) Both Niebuhrs are usually placed in the neoorthodox camp along with Barth, even though Reinhold Niebuhr battled Barth throughout his entire career.[72] Though they probably wouldn't have considered themselves either neoorthodox or liberal theologians, the Niebuhrs are important because they, along with Paul Tillich, kept liberal theology moving forward from the 1930s into the 1950s.

Both brothers considered themselves moderns and embraced reason, science, and biblical scholarship (following Troeltsch), which, of course, distanced them from their contemporaries, the fundamentalists.[73] They argued that revelation should be taken seriously but not literally. As they saw it, this was the mistake of the fundamentalists—taking the myths of Scripture literally, which got them into a confrontation with science over evolution theory.

Reinhold used the term *myth* to describe something that deceives but still conveys truth that can't be adequately expressed in any other form. Because God is radically transcendent (following Barth), nothing will ever adequately describe our relationship to Him. The Bible employed myths to give us an understanding of God's dealings with man. So, for example, Adam and Eve were not really the first man and woman in history but a myth that describes "the situation of every man and woman." The doctrine of Original Sin does not mean that Adam's guilt was passed down into the human race but that man naturally claims for himself things in the world that are not as objectively important as his desires warrant.[74]

The use of "myth" and "symbols" became very popular as liberal theologians attempted to hold on to Christianity with one hand and modernism with the other. This can be seen in the following example. I have an old copy of Paul Tillich's book *Dynamics of Faith* (1957). On the back cover you can find Reinhold Niebuhr's blurb describing how great Tillich's book is, calling it "A little classic."[75]

Inside the book, Tillich attempts to enlighten the reader on what the word *God* really means. Tillich's contorted logic is evident when he states: "God is the fundamental symbol for what concerns us ultimately. Again it would be completely wrong to ask: So God is nothing but a symbol? Because the next question has to be: A symbol for what? And the answer would be: For God! God is a symbol for God."[76] This ridiculous mumbo jumbo calls to mind Francis Schaeffer's critique of the liberal theologians' use of symbols: "To the new theology, the usefulness of a symbol is in direct proportion to its obscurity."[77]

Lest Tillich's readers be disconcerted with his circular logic, on the very next page of his book he takes another stab at trying to answer the question of whether God really exists: "Here again it would be meaningless to ask whether one or another of the figures in which an ultimate concern is symbolized does 'exist.' If 'existence' refers to something which can be found within the whole of reality, no divine being exists."[78] Ah, there we have it. God does not really exist. Tillich is really an atheist masquerading as a Christian.

It is my contention that the theological assertions Tillich made are nothing more than disingenuous gobbledygook masquerading as profundity. Tillich and other liberal theologians hide behind symbols, otherwise they would have to admit that they don't believe God exists. Those in academic circles heralded Tillich as a first-rate theologian. But in reality he was nothing more than an exemplar of the blind leading the blind.

As neoorthodoxy and liberal theology both ran out of gas in the middle of the century, notions like existential commitment, myth, and symbols finally took their toll by obscuring biblical revelation and orthodox doctrine to the point where theologians in the 1960s began practicing what one observer described as "Christian secularism."[79] Harvey Cox and "radical theologians" like Paul Van Buren and Thomas J.J. Altizer ruled out anything that contradicted the modern scientific worldview. Theologians like Van Buren pretended they could not understand what the word *God* meant anymore. They acted as if they were so far above it all. They threw up their hands in resignation and de-clared that the whole idea of God must be given up entirely. As Van Buren said, "We do not know 'what' God is" and furthermore "we cannot understand how the word 'God' is being used."[80] God is dead for these theologians (following Nietzsche).

The irony is that these radical theologians argued that even though God was dead to the modern world, it was still possible to be a Chris-tian. How? According to Van Buren, statements about God are really descriptions about a "Christian way of life" that shapes one's attitudes, behavior, and relationships.[81] Really? God is just a "Christian way of life?"

This has a peculiar similarity to Bill O'Reilly's notion we saw back in Chapter two, that "God is a philosophy." Apparently, God is not the personal Creator and Sustainer of the universe anymore. Rather, for the radical theologians He is merely a philosophy representing the Christian way of life. From my perspective, to call oneself a Christian theologian, like the radical theologians did, when you don't believe that God exists is like calling yourself a "Christian atheist."[82] It is a ridiculously confounding and oxymoronic attempt to accommodate Christianity to atheism.

The Mainline and Evangelical Churches

As we noted above, the fundamentalists in large part withdrew from the organized churches after 1925. This left the mainline churches in the hands of those who embraced liberal Protestant theology. The fol-lowing are considered the mainline Protestant churches today: Ameri-can Baptist Churches (in the USA), the Christian Church (Disciples of Christ), the Presbyterian Church (USA), the United Methodist Church, the United Church of Christ, the Evangelical Lutheran Church in America, and the Episcopal Church.[83]

I mention the mainline churches because they represent a brand of Christianity today that has to a greater or lesser extent been captured by the secular/modernist mind-set. Not only did the mainline churches soak up liberal theology, but their politics leaned to the left also. Dur-ing the 1950s and 1960s, these churches began to define themselves more in relation to cultural issues rather than with orthodox doctrine, which they discarded with each passing generation.[84] So, for example, one is far more likely to find politically correct attitudes in these churches than one would find in an evangelical church (at the time of this writing).

Embracing the theology of liberal Protestantism, however, has come with a cost for these mainline churches. Peter Augustine Lawler points this out: "The general rule, we now know, is that the more liberal or progressive a church becomes, the more members it loses. It is quite understandable that if their church implies that the Bible consists of nothing but symbols to be appropriated by the spirit of liberalism, then most believers will say the hell with it."[85]

Why go to church if you can receive the same message from those in culture, like your friends, your hair stylist, your psychotherapist, or the liberal news media? Mainline Protestant churches often downplay doctrinal Christianity to the extent that there is no distinction between their message and the cultural milieu. Peter Berger goes so far as to describe these mainline Protestant churches as "schools for secularity."[86] H. Richard Niebuhr offers a blistering attack of the politically correct "Christianity" of liberal theology: "A God without wrath brought men without sin into a kingdom without judgment through the ministration of a Christ without a cross."[87] The mainline churches, in many cases, embraced this wishy-washy brand of Christianity.

These churches lost the hegemony they once had and therefore marginalized themselves to the point where one observer argues that they should no longer be called "mainline churches" but instead should be called "sideline churches."[88] Steve Bruce points out that they cannot offer "any pressing reason why an atheist should accept their religious beliefs."[89]

Unfortunately, many evangelical churches today are heading in the same direction as the mainline churches. With each passing year evangelicalism increasingly accommodates the culture at large. The most obvious example of this is the "contemporary" church service where "super-fun-rock-bands," as one observer describes them, can be found in an increasing number of evangelical churches leading the praise and worship.[90] There was no problem back in the '80s and '90s when instruments like drums or guitars were brought into Protestant churches, because back then they were played with reverence. Today, however, the music is often indistinguishable from rock music. We're told not to worry because it's the words that count—the music is just a neutral medium. I wonder, however, if many evangelical churches (and Protestant churches in general) haven't crossed the line from worship to entertainment.

The mentality today is that if you want to bring people in, you have to give them what they want. However, it is my contention that if you are willing to bend over backward to give people what they want in the *music* part of the service, it is only a matter of time before you also tickle their ears in the *preaching* part of the service as well.

As we saw in Chapter two, statistics are already showing how evangelicals are compromising the fundamentals of the faith or discarding them altogether with each passing generation. Combine this with the fact that Christian philosophers and liberal theologians have been accommodating fundamental doctrines to secular modernism since the Enlightenment and it is no wonder we are becoming a post-Christian nation.

I predict the accommodation process will become more acute in the future under a more oppressive government or globalist New World Order, which will not put up with "extremist" and "intolerant" religions like Christianity. If you think this can't happen, then note that openly gay Houston mayor Annise Parker issued subpoenas to five local pastors who had sermons dealing with homosexuality, gender identity, or the mayor herself.[91] Christians who don't accommodate the PC-tolerant mind-set will be silenced completely through new laws regarding hate speech.

Summary

This chapter pointed out the most important ways theologians who were influenced by Enlightenment presuppositions compromised Christianity. The marginalization of Christianity we saw in this chapter was an inside job. In other words, Protestant Christianity sowed the seeds of its own destruction, called the "gravedigger hypothesis."[92] Os Guinness describes what has happened: "Christianity contributed to the rise of the modern world; the modern world, in turn, has undermined Christianity; Christianity has become its own gravedigger."[93]

Liberal theology as promulgated by the German theologians made its way over to our country through the universities and began to erode orthodox Christian doctrine. These theologians made the same mistake as did the philosophers of the Enlightenment. Instead of challenging the naturalistic presuppositions emerging because of science, they opted instead to embrace secular modernity and to redefine Christianity in terms of naturalism.[94] Biblical criticism also arose in the middle to latter half of the nineteenth century which undermined scriptural authority as well. All the miraculous elements of the Bible were compromised or discarded in order to make Christianity more amenable to the modern scientific way of thinking.

Although they attempted to battle the forces of liberal Protestantism and the authority of science during the first quarter of last century with some success, the fundamentalists retreated after they inherited the wind at the Scopes Monkey trial. Liberal theology continued to influence Protestantism after this time, primarily through the mainline churches. Liberal theologians used myths and symbols to obscure the fact that they did not believe the fundamental, historical doctrines of Christianity any longer. The radical theologians who came after the liberal theologians realized that "God" cannot be a symbol for God; so they gave up on the notion that any meaningful discussion could be forthcoming regarding God. They decided, therefore, to reduce God to a way of life.

In addition to the impact of the liberal theologians, we looked at many historical precedents that are responsible for the state of Christianity today. The Reformation, the American Revolution, the Great Awakenings, Romanticism, and Pietism all contributed to the autonomy of the individual. The first settlers in our country came over to be free of religious constraints. People today still aspire to freedom in religious matters. But unfortunately, this freedom (autonomy) has resulted in an increasing rejection of Christianity with each passing generation. People nowadays want to make up their own religion on their own terms, just like the liberal theologians did. All of this has led to what we are up against today as summarized by historian Steve Bruce:

> Religion used to be about the divine and our relationship to it. God was held to be a real force external to us. The Bible was his revealed word. Miracles actually occurred. Christ was the son of God and died for our sins. Heaven and hell were real places. Gradually over the last hundred years a quite different interpretation of these things has affected much of mainstream Christianity. God is no longer seen as an actual person but as some sort of vague power or our own consciences. The Bible is no longer the word of God but a historical book with some useful ethical and moral guidelines for living. Miracles are explained away; either they did not really happen or they were natural phenomena [misunderstood] by ignorant peasants. Christ is no longer the Son of God but an exemplary prophet and teacher. Heaven and hell cease to be real places and become psychological states.[95]

If evangelicalism goes the way of liberal theology (and the mainline churches), it won't be long before nothing resembling true biblical

Christianity is left in our country, except perhaps those fundamentalists who are holding their ground against the cultural zeitgeist. The inclination for evangelical Christianity (and Protestantism in general) to accommodate and retreat will be more likely as Christians increasingly become primary targets of harassment in the future from advocates of political correctness and also from the powers that be. True Christians, in the not too distant future, will have a difficult time getting along in our increasingly post-Christian nation.

The Fruit of Secular Modernism: Autonomy, Loss of Christian Authority, and PC Pluralism

The two previous chapters provided us with a historical background for understanding the how and why of the secularization process. Now we will look at the consequences of the onward march of modernization that has occurred since the time of the Reformation and the Enlightenment. Moreover, modernism has produced noticeable features (fruit) that are present in our culture today.

To put it another way, the fruit of modern secularism that has blossomed in our society did not materialize out of thin air. Rather, its predominance is the result of what has occurred over the last three centuries or so. In a metaphorical sense, we might look at modernism as a seed brought over from Europe, which began to take root in the United States after the middle of the nineteenth century. That seed has grown into a full-blown tree that has grown deep roots and has borne much fruit. It is to this fruit—the predominant features of secular modernism—that we will turn our attention to now.

The Loss of Authority and the Rise of Autonomy

Two of the most salient features of the secularization process today are the loss of Christian authority in our culture combined with the rise of autonomy. In short, the Christian worldview no longer holds the cultural clout it once held. Fifty or a hundred years ago most everyone appealed to the Christian worldview as a commonly shared belief system upon which our culture rested. This is no longer the case. People in ever increasing numbers nowadays don't care much about what the church, the Bible, pastors, or priests have to say when it comes to how to run their daily lives. They want to make up their own minds.

Each individual today wants to live his or her own life free of the constraints of some external authority such as Christianity and its teachings. Each person now decides for him- or herself what is true, and what is right or wrong. This is autonomy. In essence, each person is a law unto himself (*auto,* "self"; *nomos,* "law"). People today reject external authority. They look inward, not outward, for guidance in their lives. Christianity is out. Autonomy is in. In the new secular worldview, individuals are accountable to no one but themselves.

The loss of authority and the rise of autonomy go hand in hand. As people become more autonomous in their lives, the more they will dispense with authority. No one today wants to be told what to do, how to think, or have any external constraints placed upon them. People today want to be free to do their own thing. Autonomy and the loss of authority are the firstfruits of secularism in our increasingly post-Christian culture.

As we saw in the previous chapter, the religious thread of autonomy began at the time of the Reformation when Protestants challenged Roman Catholic authority. The move toward autonomy may be seen in the Reformers' proclamation that each individual could interpret Scripture by his own light and that salvation could be attained by each person without the authority of the Church.

Of course, this thread of autonomy found its way to the Puritans, who broke free from the authority of the Church of England and charted their own course over in the New World. However, even the Puritans themselves and others who established churches in the colonies became the object of suspicion. We saw that the traveling evangelists of the two Great Awakenings undermined the ecclesiastical establishment thus initiating their own "flight from authority" (to borrow Jeffrey Stout's phrase). The evangelists encouraged the common folk to exercise their own private judgment regarding religious matters, thus putting them on an equal footing with the educated clergy at the time. Pietism, which we also noted in the last chapter, certainly encouraged the move toward autonomy by emphasizing feelings and religious experiences rather than doctrine as the overriding authority in people's lives.

The other thread of autonomy can be traced back to the Enlightenment period. The Enlightenment thinkers challenged the authority of biblical revelation and replaced it with reason. Philosophers like Descartes brought reason to the forefront by asserting that each individual should venture out on his own using the force of reason to gain the certainty of knowledge. With reason replacing biblical authority, it wasn't long until the Christian belief system came under fire, even if it was misguided friendly fire at first with the likes of Locke attempting to prove the reasonableness of Christianity. As we saw, this was a costly tactical error.

Many Enlightenment thinkers were not as favorable to Christianity as Locke was. Many of the *philosophes* wanted to do away with the fundamental doctrines of Christianity that seemed like unreasonable, superstitious nonsense. In their minds, this was the cause of division and wars. Because of this attitude, autonomous reason began judging Christianity, not the other way around. Simply put, theology handed the reins of authority over to philosophy, and philosophy, in turn, undercut Christianity's authority and then handed that authority over to the individual's use of reason. This autonomy can be seen in Thomas Paine's statement: "I do not believe in the creed professed by the Jewish Church, by the Roman Church, by the Greek Church, by the Turkish Church, by the Protestant Church, nor by any Church I know of. My mind is my own church."[1]

While the Romantic movement in the nineteenth century emphasized feeling and intuition as tools to free individuals from their bondage and ignorance, the one thing Romanticism held in common with the Enlightenment was the focus on the self.[2] This thread of autonomy and free thinking has been carried down to the present day. It is evidenced by the statement of our friend Sheila Larson, whom we met in Chapter two, when she said: "My faith has carried me a long way. It's Sheilaism. Just my own little voice."[3]

We also saw in Chapter two that religion is out. Spirituality is in. This privatization of religious faith falls right in step with an increase in individualism that has resulted from autonomy. Religion, as an external authority, holds too many constraints on the individual. Spirituality, on the other hand, frees the individual from external authority. God is either put on a shelf or dispensed with altogether. This allows people the freedom to be their own authority in religious matters.

What Autonomy Means Today

Certainly even the casual observer of culture can see that one of the values most highly cherished today is freedom.[4] And, of course, in and of itself there is nothing wrong with aspiring to freedom. The problem, as I see it, is that freedom detached from God, truth, love, goodness, and moral absolutes—soon degenerates into an unhealthy autonomy. It is an autonomy that by definition wants to go its own way.

The fruit of autonomy is evident in culture today from three philosophical points of view. First, regarding the nature of reality (ontology), we see an ever increasing rejection of God. We are becoming a nation of practical atheists who give God a thought only during times of crisis. We want to tread our own path, and we don't want God obstructing our way. If God is not outright rejected, then it is fair to say that He doesn't carry any authority in the lives of the average practical atheist. People simply don't need God anymore. They want Him out of the way so they can exercise their autonomy more fully. Jean-Paul Sartre put it this way: "The best way to conceive of the fundamental project of human reality is to say that man is the being whose project is to be God."[5] People today want to be the god of their own lives.

The second philosophical way we can look at autonomy concerns the nature of knowledge (epistemology). Here we see that the Bible no longer holds authority in people's lives. People no longer believe the Bible is true and look upon it with suspicion at best and disdain at worst. Eyebrows lift at the mention of the word *Bible*. One can't be expected to believe that an outmoded relic written 2,000-plus years ago can hold any relevance for the sophisticated, technologically advanced individual in today's modern world.

To associate oneself in any way with the Bible nowadays is to invite an immediate intellectual demotion. People are under the impression that science alone gives us knowledge. The Bible is relegated to the compartment of faith. The reader will recall that Hume and Kant are partly responsible for this. Autonomous reason has replaced Scripture. People today feel that we have figured out everything scientifically, psychologically, and technologically because we are reasonable people. A commonly held viewpoint today is that we don't need to ascribe authority to an outmoded piece of work like the Bible anymore.

Much of this attitude can be traced to the liberal Protestants who gave up on the authority of Scripture in the last quarter of the nineteenth century. The Bible, according to this group, can no longer be considered inerrant. And if the Bible is no longer inerrant, it can no longer be considered inspired. And if the Bible can no longer be considered inspired, then it has lost its authority. This is the path liberal theologians and mainline churches have trod, and evangelicals have started in this direction also. The statistics we reviewed in Chapter two are evidence of evangelicalism's slide toward the rejection of biblical authority. Make no mistake, the loss of scriptural authority is the death knell for authentic Christianity.

The third philosophical perspective regarding autonomy is in the realm of moral values (ethics). It seems that in matters of moral authority, an increasing number of people today find comfort in being accountable to no one but themselves. We live in a society where moral authority is found solely in the individual. Each person lives autonomously by his or her own lights. Right and wrong are relative to each individual. Public schools particularly teach this to young children. They've taught the last two generations to clarify their own values. The psychotherapeutic environment has further engendered values clarification, which has created an unfathomable narcissism heretofore unheard of.

Best-selling author and New Age guru Deepak Chopra (Deep-Pockets)[6] epitomizes the over-the-top, self-absorbed, narcissistic attitude we see today. He offers the following phony wisdom: "In reality, we are divinity in disguise . . . True success is therefore the experience of the miraculous. It is the unfolding of the divinity within us."[7] It follows from Chopra's logic that if each of us is god, then we are accountable to no one but ourselves. Elsewhere Deep-Pockets offers this moral advice: "At the moment you consciously make a choice, pay attention to your body and ask your body, 'If I make this choice, what happens?' If your body sends a message of comfort, that's the right choice."[8] Can you imagine parents offering this type of advice to their hormone-charged teenagers? This advice is reminiscent of the Me generation's slogan, "If it feels good, do it." Christian morals are out. Countercultural narcissism is in. Deep-Pockets Chopra represents the hedonism and narcissism so prevalent in society. Biblical morals play little, if any, conscious part in the lives of individuals today.

Moreover, we live in a society where modern humans have emancipated themselves from traditional mores derived from the Christian worldview. Things that were unthinkable a few generations ago are commonplace today. Abortion on demand and gays demanding equal status regarding marriage are two of the more notable examples that our moral values have been tipped upside down. Forty-three percent of our population says that they rely on no outside authority when deciding matters of right and wrong. Only three in ten people consider Scripture an ultimate authority in matters concerning truth.[9] These stats support those who believe we are already a post-Christian nation.

Moral authority that used to be based on the Bible is a thing of the past. This portends disaster, because autonomy comes with a price. That price is the loss of community. How can we be a people of common values and purpose if we no longer share a common moral underpinning because each person is his or her own moral authority?

David Wells notes: "The modern children of the Enlightenment have themselves taken God's place. It is to ourselves that we are now accountable."[10] If the highest good for our community is sacrificed at the altar of personal preference, then the very idea of community itself is threatened.

Politically Correct Pluralism

Besides autonomy and the loss of Christian authority, another fruit of secularism that is evident today is "politically correct pluralism."

But before we get to that, let's define a general form of pluralism known as "cultural pluralism." Cultural pluralism is the idea that our society is made up of different peoples, cultures, and lifestyles.[11] This means that people from different backgrounds and beliefs exist side by side in a society in which each has a voice and can still be tolerant of one another. The incredible foresight of the Founders set in motion the foundation of our pluralistic republic.

For our concerns, a second type of pluralism, which is an extension of cultural pluralism, is what may be described as "religious pluralism." Religious pluralism naturally flows out of cultural pluralism, because it is only natural that a diverse people would have different religious beliefs and philosophies.

Now that we know what religious pluralism is, how would we go about defining politically correct (PC) pluralism? Well, it is one thing to admit that many different religious or philosophical beliefs exist like they do in our country. But there is a problem with PC pluralism. PC pluralism leads to the mistaken conclusion that just because many different belief systems exist in our culture also means they are all equal.

I would argue that they *are* all equal in that they have a right to exist in our pluralistic/tolerant society. But just because they exist does not mean they are all of equal merit regarding whether they are true or not. In other words, PC religious pluralism, especially as espoused by academia, confuses the *existence* of a religious belief with its *truth*. Just because many different philosophical and religious beliefs exist does not mean that they are all true. Moreover, PC pluralism comes into play when the tacit acceptance of multiculturalism overextends itself.

PC pluralism is a widespread and faulty notion that is evident in our culture today. It stems from what Harold Netland and Keith Johnson call the "pluralist intuition," which is the assumption that it is hard to believe that large numbers of people who are morally sincere and intelligent can be wrong about their religious beliefs.[12] Therefore, to speak in terms of one religion being true and another false is off limits in today's PC society.

People today believe religion is a private matter, and each person is entitled to have a faith of his or her own.[13] No problem there. The problem arises when people think that just because they believe in a religion means that their particular religion must be true. This is not the case. Often what happens is that PC pluralism glosses over differences between religious beliefs by viewing them as different perceptions of the same truth. In our politically correct society, it is simply easier on one's conscience to believe that perhaps everyone is worshiping the same divine being but in different ways. In short, it is more convenient.[14]

Moreover, both on the pedestrian level and in the halls of academia, there is a growing consensus that *all* religions are legitimate ways of responding to the same divine reality.[15] All roads lead to God, as the old saying goes, and to think that a particular religion like Christianity is the only way to God is anathema. Instead, the way to salvation is present in its own way in each religion, according to PC pluralistic thinking. People today, in increasing numbers, think it is simply arrogant and intolerant to maintain that a single religion holds the key to salvation.[16] So, for example, Jesus might be the Savior for Christians, but He certainly cannot be considered the Savior for all of humankind.[17] Each religion has its own way to salvation, according to the PC pluralistic approach.

What I have stated above demonstrates that the pluralist mind-set has taken on an imperialistic attitude in our culture.[18] As Richard John Neuhaus stated, "Pluralism is a jealous god. . . . Pluralism, relativity, secularization—all come to be much of a piece."[19] PC religious pluralism, as a fruit of secularization, relativizes all religions by making them qualitatively equal. It overemphasizes the commonalities between religions and undervalues their differences.[20] But all religions are not the same, and to say so is to display an ignorance of different religions and their exclusive ways of defining who God is and the purpose of life.[21]

Nothing is wrong with the plurality we see regarding matters of "taste," such as social manners, art, food, sport, hobbies, or whatever. These are all a matter of preference. When preference or matters of taste are involved, pluralism is welcomed as an inherent part of our diverse society.[22] However, when matters of truth are involved, then PC pluralism is unacceptable. Truth is not a matter of preference. Truth corresponds with the way things really are. And the way things really are (reality) applies to everyone equally and universally. There is no room for preference or diversity regarding matters of truth. Truth is universal, absolute, and objective, as we will see in the next chapter.

The problem today is that most people forget that religion in general, and Christianity in particular, is not simply a preference. Religious belief is supposed to be about truth. PC pluralism, however, has left people with the impression that because so many religions exist, they all must somehow be equal regarding the truth. This is because people conflate the religion's right to exist with the idea that it must be true. But just because many religions exist (pluralism) does not mean they are all true.

Prior to the countercultural revolution, the vast majority of people in our country would have appealed to Christianity as the one true religion. Today, however, even so-called Christians are tentative to do so. With so many religious options on the table, to say that Christianity is true while claiming that other religions are false is politically incorrect at best and judgmental at worst. In today's PC world, all people are viewed as God's children.[23]

The problem with communicating the gospel in our pluralistic society today is that it soon disappears.[24] Appealing to the Bible to support one's position may have worked two or three generations ago. But today it is met with the question "Why should I believe the Bible?"[25] In short, the person on the street is confronted with so many religious options that Christianity is no longer taken as authoritatively true like it was in years past. Christianity has lost its authority. The pluralistic consciousness has put Christianity in a credibility crisis.[26] Rather than being authoritative in matters of life, Christianity is lost in a sea of pluralism. It is regarded as merely a personal choice for its adherents but carries no authority beyond that.[27]

Peter Berger points to the option that faces Christianity today regarding pluralism. He says that Christianity can either accommodate itself to the present situation and "play the pluralistic game of religious free enterprise" by changing itself according to "consumer demands," or it can refuse to accommodate pluralism, and instead maintain and profess its traditional beliefs.[28] From my vantage point, I think many Christians and churches have chosen to accommodate Christianity to fit the PC pluralistic way of thinking.

Many so-called Christians don't believe half the things Christians a few generations ago used to believe about the fundamentals of

Christianity. For example, many nominal Christians no longer think the Bible is trustworthy. On the other hand, Christians who *do* hold their ground today are regarded with suspicion by a watching world that doesn't regard Christianity or the Bible as authoritative. According to Berger, all of this exemplifies the "crisis of the church" in contemporary culture.[29]

Harold Netland concludes our thoughts on the connection between pluralism and the marginalization of Christianity when he states the following:

> The ideology of pluralism did not suddenly appear out of nowhere. Rather, the cumulative influences of the disestablishment of Christianity in Western societies, the increased marginalization of traditional religion in modern life, a deepening skepticism about the claims of orthodox Christianity, and the existential awareness of cultural and religious diversity engendered by globalization work together to erode confidence in the truth of Christian faith in favor of more pluralistic alternatives.[30]

Summary

As the process of secularization continues its onward march, it is producing noticeable fruit. Specifically, we noted three modern fruits that are becoming more pronounced as the Christian worldview is displaced. The rise of autonomy is in evidence today as more and more people look inward for guidance rather than from an external religious authority like Christianity. Unfortunately, it follows logically that as autonomy increases, Christianity loses its authority in people's lives. A synergistic effect can be seen as the loss of Christian authority reinforces autonomy, which in turn reinforces the loss of Christian authority in our culture.

These two factors are likewise reinforced by a third factor, the rise of pluralism, especially regarding religion. As we noted, nothing is wrong with cultural pluralism in which many diverse tastes, ways of life, religions, etc., are present in society today. The problem lies with assuming that what is true of cultural pluralism can then be transferred over to the realm of religious pluralism regarding truth claims. Just because we have many religions and belief systems in our country, which all have an equal right to exist, does not mean they are all equal when it comes to their truth claims.

But this is precisely the mistaken notion that is gaining traction in our society. We are becoming more pluralistic with each passing generation. As the celebration of diversity and multiculturalism becomes more commonplace, it is only natural for people to mistakenly transfer this attitude over to religion. But just because we can celebrate each person's right to hold his or her religious belief does *not* logically carry over to mean that each religion is true. To believe this is to water down the exclusive claims of each religion in general and Christianity in particular. In essence, Christianity loses the authority it once held in our culture as its truth claims are lost in a sea of religious and cultural pluralism. This is due in large part to the Bible losing its authority to a smorgasbord mentality in which people pick and choose what beliefs they are comfortable with.

PC pluralism, autonomy, and the loss of Christian authority all reinforce one another in a vicious circle. Where in generations past the Christian worldview was authoritative in our country because the vast majority of our people were on the same page, today this is not the case. Instead, the pluralism of religious beliefs provides cover and legitimacy for those who want to exercise their autonomy and believe something besides Christianity. The exercise of autonomy by individuals ensures that Christianity will lose more and more of its authority in our culture. These two fruits, in turn, are reinforced by the pluralistic mind-set, which engenders the notion that Christianity is only one of many options to choose from.

We don't want to confuse correlation with causation, but I think it is fair to say that the three fruits of secular modernism work in tandem to marginalize Christianity's place in our culture.

I would now like to turn the reader's attention to more fruit that the secularization process has yielded, which we will look at in the next chapter.

Chapter 6

The Fruit of Postmodernism: The Loss of Truth, Relativism, and PC Tolerance

As we continue to observe the secularization process, we will examine three more fruits in this chapter: 1) the loss of truth; 2) relativism; and 3) politically correct tolerance, all of which I am placing under the heading of postmodernism. These three fruits could just as easily be placed with those in the previous chapter. I have chosen to place them here because they represent a more nuanced transition from modernism to postmodernism that is taking place.

As I see it, the Enlightenment brought about a macro shift in thinking that affected Christianity, both then and now. As we saw in the previous chapter, the loss of authority combined with the rise of autonomy and pluralism are part of the secularization process that can be traced back to the Reformation and the Enlightenment era. Skepticism toward religious authority combined with the autonomy of reason began to prevail as an epistemological shift took place as to how truth and knowledge could be acquired.

One thing that separates what took place at the beginning of the modern era and what is taking place now is how people regard truth and knowledge of the world. Back then, knowledge was considered objective; whereas, now it is seen in a much more nebulous light. In short, this shift in knowledge and truth distinguishes the modern period as it began in the Enlightenment from what is taking place today as we transition epistemologically to a more postmodern outlook.

Most of the books one reads today concerning philosophical and religious issues make much ado about postmodernism. Postmodernism is all the rage now, and the term is tossed around with reckless abandon as it is credited and blamed for just about everything under the sun. Quite frankly, in many ways I think the whole concept of postmodernism is a bit overblown and overused. Analysts employ the term because it is fashionable to do so, and it makes them look cosmopolitan and trendy. Nevertheless, I don't think we are nearly as postmodern as most pundits today would have us believe. Having said that, the one area where I think we *are* increasingly postmodern, as I noted above, is in the realm of epistemology, that is, the realm of knowledge and truth. With this in mind, it would serve us well to take a brief look at the new postmodern hermeneutic, which has had a significant impact on truth, knowledge, and the Christian worldview.

Postmodern Hermeneutics: A Matter of Interpretation

Many consider Friedrich Nietzsche, whom we mentioned in an earlier chapter, to be the first truly postmodern thinker. The reader will recall that Nietzsche proclaimed the death of God, by which he meant that the Christian influence on Western culture was waning as time wore on. Of course, Nietzsche's assertion supports the overall thesis of *America's Post-Christian Apocalypse*, and in this I believe he was prescient.

According to Nietzsche, the "will to power" should fill the vacuum left by the death of God. This means that each individual must strike out on his own, apart from anything transcendent, and forge his own values.[1] Thus, the authority and truth of Christianity diminishes for each individual. Why? Because the autonomy of each person "blossoms" (to borrow Paul Kurtz's term) as each person exercises his or her volition without any regard for God. This is exactly what we see happening today, as was demonstrated in the previous chapter.

But more important for this chapter is Nietzsche's take on truth and knowledge. Nietzsche rejected the Enlightenment assumption of an objective world that one could unveil to find knowledge such as that produced by science. Instead, he fostered the idea that objective knowledge was fiction. Each person constructed one's world from his or her own perspective.[2] Nietzsche believed that truth and knowledge are illusions we construct for ourselves by the language we use.[3] Fast-forward to the flower-children era.

I mentioned in a previous chapter how the Me generation liberals of the 1960s have contributed to the narcissism and autonomy we are seeing today. But it was not only in the United States that the student movement gave birth to some of the secularism that is playing out. During the 1960s, France was marked by political angst in which worker and student uprisings fell just short of overthrowing the government. Subsequently, a readjustment in thinking took place among the intellectuals, along with an increasing interest in alternative philosophies, such as feminism, phenomenology, nihilism, and Western Marxism. A criticism of Western philosophy and culture linked these philosophies together.[4] And this brings us to a French intellectual who was influenced by these revolts and is considered a true Nietzschean.

Michel Foucault (1926–1984), along with a host of other French philosophers, like their predecessors in the Enlightenment, led the charge in a new way of thinking: the postmodern way. (It should be noted that Foucault would have disavowed himself of any labels such as "poststructuralist" or "postmodernist.") Whereas Descartes was interested in trying to provide a firm foundation for objective knowledge, Foucault and contemporary postmodernists followed Nietzsche's lead and discarded the Enlightenment project as naïve.

The French student uprising of 1968 heavily impacted Foucault, and he subsequently became preoccupied with the notion of power and how it related to language. Foucault believed that there was no neutral way of looking at history. People interpret history the way they want to in order to legitimize structures that are in place at that time. Language is used to *construct* truth rather than to *represent* the truth of the world around us. Language is used to validate and manipulate anything that sustains the system of power that one wants in place.[5] It was from this way of thinking that a radical new way of looking at language emerged.

The traditional view of language—that it conveys a single authoritarian message—was increasingly viewed with suspicion and skepticism. Roland Barthes (1915–1980) posited the idea that one should no longer look at a text as if it has only one meaning intended by the author. Rather, each text may have multiple meanings, because each reader will have his or her personal perspective on it. Thus, for Barthes, the death of the author must give way to the birth of the reader.[6] The reader or listener of a text or speech becomes the focal point and discerns whatever meaning he or she wants, regardless of what the author of the text intended.

Jacques Derrida (1930-2004), a contemporary of Barthes, gave a famous speech at Johns Hopkins University in 1966, which took Western academia by storm. For Derrida, all people use language to convey their own interpretations of reality. None of these interpretations, however, are objectively true. Like Barthes, Derrida maintained that what matters is not the verbal or written text itself, but rather how one subjectively *interprets* it. A text will have as many interpretations as there are people interpreting it.

Traditionally, of course, this is considered absurd. Common sense informs us that when we read or hear something, we should decipher what the *author* of the book, article, or speech is trying to convey. But not for postmodernists like Derrida. In this way Derrida became a pluralist regarding hermeneutics. For him, language is the tool we use to *construct* reality, and each *interpretation* of this construction is just as valid as any other.

What is important in postmodern hermeneutics is not what is *intended* by the author of the text but how the listener or reader interprets the text. As David Harvey wrote in his classic book *The Condition of Postmodernity*, "It is vain to try and master a text because the perpetual interweaving of texts and meanings is beyond our control."[7] This is the essence of postmodern hermeneutics. Just let whatever you hear or read mean whatever you want it to. Interpret a text whichever way you see fit and that will be the "true" meaning of it, regardless of what the author intended. Let's flesh this out a bit further.

Derrida led a movement that is now known as "deconstruction." According to Derrida, the deconstructionist scrutinizes a text thoroughly enough to see the implicit contradictions in it. Any claim to truth that is found in a text, if examined hard enough, will be seen to contradict itself. This shows that the text was *constructed*. Finding these contradictions demonstrates the attempt by the author to manipulate the reader, because the purpose of writing texts is to exercise power.[8] It is the job of the scholar to "deconstruct" the meaning of language however it is used in order to dismantle the hold that it may have on our thoughts and actions.[9]

In fact, a text, according to Derrida, cannot possibly have only one meaning but *must* have a variety of meanings, all of which are valid concerning the multiplicity of people interpreting the text. The value of the text is in letting it express the meaning each person takes from it.[10]

It should be noted that as deconstruction gained more steam, everything began to be viewed as a "text," not just the written word. A piece of music or a work of art . . . even the whole world may be viewed as a text. All of these texts have various meanings, which do not have to agree with one another.[11]

All of this boils down to one thing: traditional hermeneutics was turned upside down. According to postmodernists, language and meaning are socially constructed and therefore everything becomes a matter of personal perspective. How the reader, listener, or receiver of the text *interprets* the text is what is important, not what the author intends.[12] This is basically autonomy applied to hermeneutics.

The very same fruit of secularization that we witnessed in the previous chapter has come home to roost in postmodern hermeneutics.

We have a loss of authority because the authority of the author is diminished. Then we have the autonomy of the individual, which replaces the author's authority, because each individual reader "author's" their own interpretations of a text. Finally, we end up with a pluralism of different interpretations, all supposedly of equal value, even though they may contradict one another.

All of this is not without implications for Christianity. Derrida and his cronies don't want to be saddled with overarching worldviews (what they refer to as "metanarratives") like Christianity. And, of course, the Christian metanarrative is found in a text: the Bible. According to postmodernists, these grand myths must be rejected because their "secretly terroristic function" is to provide the illusion of a totalizing view of the world that is applicable to everyone.[13] As Marcuss Honeysett explains, "For the deconstructionist the idea of God *revealing* truth is the ultimate evil to be fought because revelation limits creative thinking. It is seen as the greatest tool of oppression."[14] In fact, this "incredulity toward metanarratives" is the very essence of postmodernism, according to Jean-Francois Lyotard.[15]

Modernism, which emerged from the Enlightenment, upheld the notion of objectivity. Christianity, under modernist thinking, was still capable of providing a foundation for understanding the world if Christian beliefs could be found to be reasonable. Postmodernists, however, frown on the idea of objectivity. They reject the idea that worldviews like Christianity can provide an overarching framework for understanding the world, because everything, according to the postmodernist, is *subjective*, not objective. This means that metanarratives, such as Christianity, are historically and culturally conditioned. As we move into the postmodern era, postmodernists encourage everyone to leave behind outmoded frameworks like Christianity in order to understand reality because metanarratives like Christianity have lost their legitimacy.[16]

For the postmodernist, individuals construct their own world relative to the society in which they live. The postmodern era marks the end of the illusion that there is only one correct worldview, like Christianity.[17] Interpretation replaces knowledge. Interpretation is relative to each individual and is culturally conditioned. Reason, which was the *sine qua non* of Enlightenment modernism, is considered by many postmodernists just a tool of domination.[18]

This postmodern way of thinking holds serious consequences for the concept of truth. And how we view truth has its own implications for how we interpret the world we live in and how we go about living our lives. The diminishing value of truth is reason for great concern and is, in my estimation, the single most important problem facing us today.

If there is no truth, how will our generation and those in the future decide what morals and values should be upheld in our society? But more germane for our thesis, if there is no truth to be found today, there is no reason to pay any particular attention to Christianity, which claims to proclaim the truth regarding the living and true God. Christianity's truth claims will simply end up having no authority in our culture. This is precisely what has happened. In fact, the primary thesis of *America's Post-Christian Apocalypse* is that Christianity has lost its authority in our culture and has subsequently been marginalized. This is why the concept of truth is so important. It is to this we will now turn our attention.

Tolerance and Truth: PC Tolerance as the Supreme Cultural Value

It is part and parcel in our increasingly postmodern world that no one has a monopoly on truth.[19] As the postmodern worldview gains traction in our culture, metanarratives like Christianity, which purport to be the truth, are increasingly regarded with contempt. The PC pluralism of religious beliefs in our society today makes the truth claims of Christianity impossible to assert without appearing arrogant and intolerant.

We saw in Chapter five how PC pluralism happens. PC pluralism claims that all belief systems not only have a right to exist but are *somehow equal* regarding their truth claims. This makes it easier to believe that no one worldview can claim superiority over all the others. Since all belief systems are equal by the mere fact of their existence, they all must be tolerated. So, for example, if a Christian was to say that his belief system is true and that other belief systems must logically be false (where they disagree with Christianity on fundamental points) is to commit the unpardonable sin in our society. Questioning or rejecting the *content* of someone's belief is quite often confused with *rejecting* the person himself,[20] and this is considered politically incorrect and socially unacceptable.

Nothing infuriates people more in our culture than for someone to come along and say that his or her beliefs are the truth and that these same beliefs universally apply to everyone. For example, to say that Christianity is true and that Islam, Hinduism, and Buddhism are all false in their fundamental tenets is to invite the severest form of criticism and censor. It may have been acceptable in generations past in our society to claim that Christianity is the truth and that everyone on the planet should become Christians, but it is not acceptable to claim that today. We are not all on the same page anymore. As D.A. Carson has pointed out, philosophical pluralism in evidence today has certain "rules" to follow, the most important of which is that no one is allowed to make exclusive truth claims.[21]

It is simply not tolerant in today's PC world to claim that someone's truth is universal. An increasing number of people in our culture, although giving lip service to belief in the God of the Bible, find it unacceptable that *any* religion or worldview, even Christianity, should be considered universally true for everyone. But as Alister McGrath points out, "To allow criteria as 'tolerance' and 'openness' to be given greater weight than 'truth' is quite simply, a mark of intellectual shallowness and moral irresponsibility. The first, and most fundamental, of all questions must be: is it true?"[22]

I want to be clear about one thing. There is nothing wrong with living in a free country where a pluralism of religious beliefs is allowed to exist side by side without government interference. Pluralism is not a bad thing. It allows people to be exposed to a diversity of beliefs and then to decide for themselves which beliefs they want to embrace. I do not want to live in a theocracy of any sort or a totalitarian regime (which we will get to later). The problem is that pluralism should celebrate the diversity of beliefs among us, yet PC pluralism ends up doing just the opposite.

As it manifests itself today, PC pluralism becomes a law unto itself and it devolves into PC tolerance. This type of tolerance takes its cue from PC pluralism in that all belief systems and worldviews are somehow equal in merit and therefore must be tolerated. That is, all belief systems *except* Christianity. Once someone goes so far as to make exclusive truth claims such as "the God of the Bible is the only true God," then Christianity is not tolerated in our society. In an ironic twist, PC tolerance, which should be all-inclusive, *excludes* Christianity for making exclusive truth claims. In this way, PC tolerance is not tolerance at all. It is intolerance. This is especially noticeable in our public schools and universities where PC attitudes prevail.

PC tolerance promotes freedom of belief like abortion rights, homosexuality, and other PC beliefs but does not tolerate the Christian viewpoint that claims these things are morally wrong. Choosing abortion may be acceptable for you. Believing Hinduism may be true for someone else. Even Christianity is somewhat acceptable to the PC tolerant mind-set so long as someone does not say that Christianity must be true for everyone. The minute Christians overstep this line and claim that the Christian worldview is true and applies to everyone universally is the minute Christianity is not PC and is marginalized. To marginalize Christianity for its exclusive truth claims is not tolerance, but intolerance and hypocrisy.

Look at what has happened. Back in the Enlightenment, the concept of truth still mattered. Christianity was denigrated because the truth it purported seemed like superstitious nonsense to the Enlightenment mind-set. During the Scopes Monkey Trial, Christians were disparaged again. This time the charge was that the fundamentalists' beliefs were "ignorant," according to the modern scientific way of thinking. In both of these instances, however, the major problem the intelligentsia had with Christians is that they were wrong in what they believed. In other words, the beliefs Christians held were not *objectively* true. Truth was the primary concern at that time.

But a key shift has taken place today. The question of Christianity's truth has become secondary, because, from a postmodern approach, a subjective perspective is the criterion for truth. The major charge leveled at Christians today from a postmodern/PC mentality is not that Christians do not possess objective truth, but rather that they are intolerant. When Christians make claims like "Jesus is the only way to salvation," this is viewed as intolerance at its worst. How can Jesus be the only way to salvation when there are so many religions? Very few people in today's PC world believe that exclusive truth claims like this could or should apply to everyone.

No one cares if Christianity itself is true. People today only care if you are tolerant. PC tolerance has replaced truth as the supreme value in our society. The First Commandment of the Bible has been replaced by the First Commandment of secular postmodernism: Thou shalt be tolerant.

This raises some questions. How can Christianity flourish in a culture where to share the gospel is increasingly viewed as "imposing" one's beliefs on another? How will Christianity survive when the morals it espouses will increasingly apply only to a diminishing minority while the next generations progressively embrace autonomous ethics instead? If Christians and those claiming to be Christians (practical atheists) feel timid about sharing the Christian worldview with others, how will true Christianity survive in its truth-telling, unadulterated form? Will Christians succumb to the temptation to accommodate culture and water down the gospel? Haven't the statistics in Chapter two shown that this is already occurring?

Relativism and the Loss of Truth

Of all the fruit of the secularization process I see occurring as time unfolds, the one that holds the most severe consequences for us as a society is this loss of truth. PC tolerance is making it extremely difficult for a true concept of truth to survive in our present culture. The *philosophes* of the Enlightenment period may have questioned the best means for arriving at truth. But today this same epistemological quest has led to a questioning of the very notion of truth itself. This is the result of modernism transitioning into postmodernism.

In the late 1980s, Allan Bloom wrote a difficult and famous book about what was occurring in American higher education. The oft-quoted first line of his book *The Closing of the American Mind* is truer today than it was when he first wrote it: "There is one thing a professor can be absolutely certain of: almost every student entering the university believes or says he believes that truth is relative."[23] Almost twenty years later, Ben Shapiro wrote a book describing his experience at Stanford University and his disappointment with American higher education in general. He decries what he sees as a left-wing, liberal agenda being used to indoctrinate America's college students. One of his professors taught, (in Shapiro's own words) that "there is no such thing as capital-T Truth. There is no right and wrong, no good and evil . . . We must always remember that we are subjective beings, and as such, all of our values are subjective."[24]

If there ever was a place where postmodern relativism runs rampant it is in American higher education. We will trace in the next chapter how Christianity lost its authority in our colleges and among the intelligentsia. For now it is enough to note that what is commonplace in the university setting today has seeped down to the pedestrian level. Moreover, both academically and on the popular level, "truth" is increasingly regarded with suspicion and ambivalence.[25] Truth is out. Relativism is in.

In the old days we might have heard questions like "Which religion is true?" or "Is the Bible true?" or "Which God is the true God?" In the postmodern world the more pressing question is something akin to Pontius Pilate's query to Jesus, "What is truth?" And

101

the postmodern answer is that truth is no longer objective, universal, and absolute. Rather, truth is relative to individuals and societies. The end result of this type of thinking is PC pluralism and PC tolerance.

How did we arrive at this way of thinking where the entire concept of truth has changed so dramatically? It is simple. It is the result of fear. PC tolerance has become the premiere value in our culture. People are scared to death to appear intolerant. Ask yourself—are people today more afraid of being wrong, or are they more afraid of being intolerant? Answer: People are much more afraid of being considered intolerant, because intolerance is associated with bigotry and ignorance. People feel that it is ignorant and intolerant to assume that *your* truth applies to them. Your truth is your truth, and my truth is my truth. If you try to push your truth on me, you are being intolerant, which is breaking the First Commandment in our culture. Intolerance is the unpardonable sin in our PC society today.

When we see sophomoric notions bandied about, like "Your truth is your truth, and my truth is my truth," it is because people today assume that truth is relative. The relativity of truth is considered a fundamental axiom in our cultural mind-set today. But is this true? Is truth really relative? Let's examine this for a moment.

The phrase *truth is relative* is meant to apply to everyone. But wait a minute. If truth really *is* relative, then that statement is not true; it is relative. Look at it another way. If that statement (*truth is relative*) is really relative, then there is no reason to pay attention to it because it may not apply to me, because it is relative. How can truth be relative and at the same time apply to me and everyone else? But worse than that, how can "truth is relative" be true and relative at the same time? It cannot. But if the statement "truth is relative" is not true, then truth is *not* relative and therefore that statement is false. Therefore there is no reason to pay attention to it.

Put simply, the statement *truth is relative* is self-stultifying. It is self-referentially inconsistent and slits its own throat. It refutes itself. This is the problem with relativism in general. It always contradicts itself. It is like saying that I cannot communicate with you by writing. But I just did. A person who says that truth is relative is asking you to believe that what he is saying about truth is relative. But if what he is saying about truth is relative, and not universally true, why pay attention to that statement at all? He may as well say, "Don't pay attention to me when I say 'truth is relative,' because that statement is relative anyway and, therefore, may not be true."

The reason this self-contradictory notion of truth has gotten such a hold in our society today is because people are afraid of truth. They are afraid that if they say something is true in the absolute universal sense, then the implication is that it must apply to whomever they are saying it to, and this is considered arrogant and intolerant. This is why truth has devolved into this widely held belief that "It may be true for you but not for me." Or the ubiquitous notion that "My truth is my truth, and your truth is your truth," as if truth were something subjective. G. K. Chesterton was prescient concerning this fear of truth when he wrote, "We are on the road to producing a race of men too mentally modest to believe in the multiplication table. We are in danger of seeing philosophers who doubt the law of gravity as being a mere fancy of their own."[26]

Truth, today, is often mistaken for "opinion" or "preference."[27] In the realm of opinion, if I said, "Chocolate is better than vanilla," this may be true for me and not for you, because there is no logical contradiction here. We are not talking about logical truth in this instance, only a matter of opinion or a matter of preference. However, if I were to say, "God exists," this could not be true for me and not for you without there being a logical contradiction. If God really exists, then He exists for both of us, regardless of what either one of us thinks. This is how the law of noncontradiction works, which is one of the laws of logical thought.[28] Without the laws of logic, all rational discourse ceases.

Without getting too technical, if a propositional statement such as "God exists" corresponds with reality, then that statement is true. So if I say, "God exists," and, in fact, God really does exist, then my proposition or statement is true, because it corresponds with reality. This is the correspondence theory of truth. If you were to say that "God does not exist" when, in fact, God really does exist, then your belief as expressed in that proposition is false, no matter how sincerely you hold to that belief. The law of noncontradiction holds that A cannot be both A and non-A. In other words, a statement or proposition cannot be both true and false at the same time and in the same manner. Or to use our example, God cannot both exist and not exist at the same time and in the same manner.[29]

All of this rests on the assumption that reality exists independent of how we think of it. In its most general form, this is known as "realism."[30] Postmodern thought, however, is often antirealistic. It assumes that because there are so many perspectives from which to view something, it somehow follows that there is no objective reality.[31] From the postmodern perspective, when you read the "text" of the world, what you find true for you may differ from what I find true for me. This is postmodern hermeneutics applied to reality. This is perfectly in line with much of what we see today in academia and among the intelligentsia where "doubt" is more intellectually respectable than assenting to universal truths.[32] It is an amazingly phony sense of humility that allows people in academia to hold such a Kantian view of reality, which is ultimately unknowable and dependent on how each person perceives it. Unfortunately, this faulty epistemology has trickled down to the person on the street.

The pragmatic theory of truth seems to be the most popular view of truth today. According to the pragmatic theory of truth, as long as what a person believes "works" for him or her, then what he or she believes must be true. As far as pragmatic truth goes, the crucial test is not whether a person's beliefs correspond with reality, but rather if those beliefs work or are useful for that person. This is often heard in the expression today, "It works for me!" So, for example, if atheism works for someone, then atheism must be true, even if God really exists. Or if I say that Christianity is true, people take it to mean that Christianity is one way of life that has worked for me, but another religion might just as easily work for someone else. This way of thinking is often a cause of the relativism that is evident in PC pluralism.[33]

Postmodernism is the total and unequivocal privatization of truth. It reduces truth to a matter of personal belief or opinion. It is saying that if I *believe* something, it must be true. As long as it works for me or as long as I find this belief useful, then it is true. Your truth is your truth, and my truth is my truth. The way things really are doesn't matter from the postmodern perspective. The only thing that matters is if the person believes something and it works for him or her. It is autonomy applied to truth.

Truth, from the postmodern mind-set, is not something to be found. It is something to be *created* or constructed by each autonomous person. Individuals create their own realities. It is a reality that is useful or convenient for them, regardless of true reality, which is God-given and totally independent of how we may perceive it. This notion of truth is summarized by Tony Schwartz: "It's not truth in some absolute sense that I'm after. . . . What I'm most committed to is searching for my own truth."[34]

It follows then, that as far as religious belief is concerned, if a certain religion or religious belief brings the adherents comfort or they find it useful in some way, then for those devotees that particular religion or religious belief must be true,[35] even if the fundamental truth claims of that religion don't line up with reality. Of course, this type of thinking really has nothing to do with truth per se, it is really about preference.

Upholding a True Notion of Truth

The problem with pragmatic truth is that it is not truth at all. Just because a person believes something does not mean it is true. You may believe with all of your heart that the law of gravity does not apply to you. But it does. You may believe that two plus two equals seven. But you would be wrong. That faulty belief does not correspond to reality; therefore, it is false. The postmodern way of thinking about truth mistakenly conflates belief and truth. In addition, it takes both opinion and preference and elevates them to the status of truth.

Confusing belief and truth, as if they were both one and the same, is simply wrongheaded. As Douglas Groothuis has pointed out, attempting to judge truth by one's beliefs "begs the question of whether our beliefs are true or false in the first place."[36] If there is no standard of truth separate from our beliefs, we would never have any reason to change our minds, because all beliefs would be self-referential.[37]

Think about it for a moment. If there was no *true* truth (to borrow Francis Schaeffer's phrase)[38] to be found, there would be no scientific enterprise to carry out. It is only because the falsification process weeds out bad theories—the ones that don't correspond to reality—that we have progress in science in the first place. If truth was subjective, science would not exist. If scientists, or ordinary people, for that matter, never questioned their beliefs, no progress would be made, because there would never be any reason to change one's mind.

It comes as no surprise that truth is ill-received in today's world. People want to run from the truth, hide from the truth, and reject the truth. If all else fails, they attempt to relativize the truth, as if the truth is something you can mold to fit how you think.

All of this discussion about truth leads to an important consideration regarding the marginalization of Christianity. Jesus Christ claimed to be the Truth. He did not only claim to make known the truth. He claimed to *be* the Truth, with a capital T. The first two human beings ran away from God after exercising their autonomy. Why, then, should it surprise us that people today run away from, reject, or relativize Christianity and Jesus Christ? Human beings have been running away from God since Adam and Eve. Should it surprise us then that human beings in today's world are repelled by the truth of Christianity and Jesus Christ, who claimed to be the Truth?

As we have seen in the last two chapters, people want to be their own autonomous authorities, and they don't want anyone telling them how to live, even if that person happens to be the Author and Creator of the universe. So, for example, people want to "read" Jesus or "interpret" Jesus whatever way *they* want to, not by what He claimed for Himself. They want to reject or relativize Jesus's claim to be God by saying that He was just a great moral teacher. Some want to discard Him altogether. In the long run, these are just more ways of rejecting The Truth and leaving God behind.

Summary

Secularization has borne fruit in our culture. The loss of Christian cultural authority, relativism, the loss of truth, autonomy, PC pluralism, and PC tolerance are all byproducts of the secularization process.

It is amazing how these concepts function in our increasingly post-Christian world; they are so intertwined that they end up reinforcing one another. They all logically fall into place like a stack of dominoes. Autonomy results in a rejection of authority. With the loss of Christian authority, everyone becomes their own autonomous masters in the matters of morals and life. The endgame is a pluralism of belief systems and worldviews, each authored by autonomous individuals.

The mistake we have made regarding accepting the faulty notion of PC pluralism in our society involves logic. Just because different religions exist does not make it logically necessary that they are all true. This is a fundamental error. Just because someone believes something, and that belief is allowed in a tolerant society, doesn't logically mean that the belief is necessarily true.

Nevertheless, this is our plight in society today. PC tolerance has usurped truth in our pluralistic culture. It is considered uncouth at best and dangerous at worst for someone to claim that a particular religion or worldview is true and therefore applies to everyone. I would venture to say that even if one could *prove* somehow that Christianity is true, people would still find it distasteful to claim that it should therefore be embraced by everyone. Embracing Jesus in this day and age is just too costly. It's much easier to simply believe in your own "truth"—as long as it works for you.

People simply don't care about the truth anymore. There is no time to ruminate about the weightier matters of life in our fast-paced secular society. Everyone has their heads stuck in the latest gadget. Real truth is out. Tolerance is king, and this will become more entrenched with each passing generation. Peace and security, the outgrowths of tolerance, is what people will care about most in the future. As long as people are not bothered by others and can keep their heads glued to the latest technological innovation, then all is well. Truth will be found by what the latest technology disgorges and people swallow. The people in the future will be so mesmerized by technological advances that they will embrace any so-called "truth" that emerges from the pit of the Information Age. A phony Christ in the future could call fire down from heaven using the latest technological wizardry while calling himself "God," and the sheeple will accept this as truth, as long as it works for them. (We will look at "end of the age" scenarios in the final chapters.)

The loss of truth has dire consequences for our nation. A society that tolerates beliefs as if they were all meritorious has no moral direction or foundation. It is rudderless. How can a society survive when it has no common values and everyone is a law unto himself? How can there be such things as right and wrong and laws that apply to everyone when truth is relative? If truth is relative to each individual, then how can a particular law apply to someone who doesn't like it? If each person is a law unto himself, how do we justify any laws? It is not overly dramatic to suggest that as autonomy replaces truth, it becomes more probable that anarchy may be on the horizon.

The Christian worldview was the hegemonic glue that held our society together. We were all, for the most part, on the same page just three or four generations ago. This is no longer the case. Especially after the counterculture revolution, Christianity lost much of its cultural authority. Secularism is replacing Christianity as the default worldview in our culture. If the fruit of the secularization process—autonomy, relativism, and PC tolerance—are allowed too much leash, truth will disintegrate and there will be no glue to hold society together. If truth can be reduced to a matter of preference, then so can morals. Without the moral underpinning of Christianity, we are heading toward a secular/atheistic/evolutionary world in which the survival of the fittest will be the moral law of the land. This is something to consider in light of the probability that another economic collapse is on the way or even a pandemic or war of some sort, in which case all hell will break loose.

Chapter 7

The Decline of Christianity in Higher Education: Founding–1900

The next two chapters will tell the important, interesting, and tragic story of how progressives in higher education marginalized the Christian worldview during the last hundred and fifty years. This is important because we need to understand how and why those in academia, both yesterday and today, came to accept the presuppositions of secular (post)modernism which they are now tragically inculcating in the younger generations.

The Early Years
American higher education began with Harvard, which was founded in 1636.[1] It is an amazing fact that only six years after confronting the wilderness in Massachusetts, the Puritans began the first college to provide what they considered a foundational part of the civilization process.[2] Harvard College looked for young men who were spiritually and intellectually qualified to carry on the principles upon which society should be based. Because the Puritans followed the Calvinist model, which emphasized the sacred character of all areas of life, they viewed higher education as a way to prepare young men for service not only as clergymen but for other professions as well. The first college laws of 1646 at Harvard stated that "Every one shall consider the main End of his life and studies, to know God and Jesus Christ which is Eternal life."[3] Students at Harvard were expected to devote themselves to private prayer and to reading Bible passages twice a day.

The Puritans who started Harvard were not uneducated, narrow-minded individuals one might suppose. It would surprise most to learn that almost all of Harvard's founders received their education at either Cambridge or Oxford.[4] Their classical education served them well, and they passed this down to their students.

Unlike today where a clear distinction lies between faculty and administration, there was no distinction back then. Each faculty member functioned as a jack-of-all-trades by teaching whatever needed to be taught and by being proficient in all areas of study. The college president was the only administrator, and yet he often taught as well.[5] In fact, he was considered the most influential teacher on the faculty and taught the senior course in moral philosophy, which was the pinnacle of the students' education. Moral philosophy consummated the entire course of study. It applied Protestant morality to law, history, economics, etc., to support the idea that any area of learning, if done correctly, reinforced the truth of Christianity.[6]

In the context of Harvard's perceived theological decline,[7] Yale was founded in 1701. The school promised to protect the faith of the fathers as Harvard had done initially.[8] Yale's goal was that "Every student shall consider the main end of his study to wit to know God in Jesus Christ and answerably to lead a Godly sober life."[9] Those at Yale perceived Harvard as falling away from its orthodox Calvinism early on in the 1700s as well as exuding a somewhat liberal spirit, which was damaging to maintaining a holy character.[10] Therefore, Yale was bound and determined to instill in its students the traditional Puritan ideals of the time. In reality, both Harvard and Yale had much in common. They both were conservative and traditional, compared with the new revivalism that emerged by the middle of the eighteenth century.

Revivalism was fanned into flame across the country in the 1740s epitomized by New Lights like George Whitefield. New Light revivalists felt that they had a direct experience with God—an "awakening," if you will. Their critics labeled them "Enthusiasts." This pejorative term meant that some Enthusiasts claimed to be guided directly by the Spirit of God. They preached without having obtained a classical education. Those at Harvard perceived this New Light revivalism as a direct threat to their social authority.[11]

The hostility between the New Lights and the Old Lights, the latter of which were skeptical of experience and instead preferred the stability of an established clergy, can be seen in Whitefield's trip to New England in 1744. Unlike his previous trip, Whitefield received no invitation to Harvard this time and subsequently labeled that institution "godless Harvard."[12] Harvard, on the other hand, called Whitefield "an uncharitable, censorious, and slanderous Man" and labeled him an Enthusiast for good measure. Harvard and Yale were not disposed toward Mr. Whitefield, because upon return from his first visit to both institutions a few years earlier, he reported in one of his published journals that both schools "were not far superior" in piety to the universities in

England. This insult got legs because Whitefield considered Oxford and Cambridge "Seminaries of Paganism." This did not sit well, to say the least, with Yale and Harvard.[13]

Like its counterpart Harvard, Yale attempted to resist the revivalism of the New Lights. In fact, in 1744 two students were expelled because while at home for vacation they attended a New Light revival service led by a lay preacher rather than attending the traditional Old Light church in their town.[14] Yale officials said the offense was in violation of the "law of God, colony, and college."[15] The godly standards that colleges set back then were very high, to say the least. The institutions were founded so that they could produce godly young men with character, equipped to serve their fellow citizens in the ministry or other vocations like law or medicine.

Unlike Harvard and Yale, Princeton (1746), along with other colleges, was founded as a result of revivalism and embraced the New Light enthusiasm while refuting charges that they were against learning and that their clergymen were illiterate.[16] Other colleges that started as a result of the Great Awakening were Brown (1764); Rutgers (1766); Providence (1765), founded by Baptists; and also Dartmouth (1769), which the Congregationalists of New England founded.[17]

The revivals had an inestimable impact on the formation of these colleges. The influence of the revivals continued well into the first half of the nineteenth century. Because they did not come around that often, the revivals that were particularly powerful caused classes to be cancelled for many days as students and faculty gave themselves over to prayer and renewal. By the turn of the century, even Yale succumbed to the New Light influence. In 1802 after President Timothy Dwight preached a series of sermons, an unexpected revival broke out in which a third of the students claimed conversion.[18]

One can only imagine what would happen today if the president of Harvard preached a sermon at a commencement speech or some important event, encouraging students to know God and His Son Jesus Christ. There might be an outpouring of some sort, but it would not be an outpouring of the Holy Spirit. More likely, there would be an outburst of wrath by the students, faculty, board, alumni, and media, accompanied by weeping and gnashing of teeth. Instead of a revival, more likely riots would ensue.

I cite these examples of the early college days only to show how thoroughly unabashed their Christianity was back then. They made no bones about the fact that they were Christian. Christianity played a foundational and active role in all that the early colleges represented. This is in total contrast to the secular nature of our colleges and universities today.

The Antebellum College: Common Sense Philosophy and Classicism

As we mentioned in Chapter four, the American Revolution was a synthesis of Protestantism and Enlightenment ideals. Just as Protestants had liberated themselves from the Roman Catholic hierarchy in an earlier century, Protestants subsequently intended to liberate themselves from the tyranny of England as well. Foremost in the revolutionary agenda was that the new political entity should be built on a moral foundation while at the same time promoting freedom and progress.[19] Moreover, revolutionary ideals were grounded in universal *self-evident* and common sense principles upon which all could agree.[20] This is seen in our Declaration of Independence: "We hold these truths to be self-evident."[21] This horizontal man-centered way of determining the truth of things is, of course, a product of the Enlightenment, which we looked at in Chapter three.

Thomas Reid (1710–1796) promoted this type of philosophy, known as Common Sense Realism. It borrowed from Enlightenment philosopher John Locke's assertion that God has given everyone sufficient faculties to understand how to deal with their daily concerns. This Common Sense approach was extremely fashionable and favorable to the general population, who liked to consider America a common sense country.[22] By 1830, Common Sense philosophy had infiltrated every area of intellectual thinking.[23] The crux of Reid's philosophy was that self-evident truths found in nature could provide a firm foundation for constructing all knowledge.[24] This assumption was based upon the notion that truth found in the natural world (God's Book of Nature) would confirm the truths of Christianity in the Bible (God's revelatory book).[25]

Reid's philosophy was pervasive and appealed to many people because it was non-sectarian. It didn't depend on a particular denominational perspective. Rather, the principles of rational, self-evident common sense were shared by everyone and perceived as scientific and moral as well. As George Marsden puts it, in post-Revolutionary America "it was a widely shared article of faith that science, common sense, morality, and true religion were firmly allied."[26] Common Sense philosophy triumphed in the short run because it allowed everyone to maintain their traditional Christian beliefs without appealing directly to the

Bible. It dovetailed with what college moral philosophy courses taught and, therefore, was conducive to producing a moral citizen, which was obviously good for society.[27]

No conflict existed between science and religion at this point, although it is fair to say that natural law and reason were beginning to ascend while the supernatural was just beginning its authoritative decline.[28] Nevertheless, Scripture was still authoritative at this point. Science showed the works of God as the handmaiden of religion and a "useful tool" in the college setting.[29] Moreover, those in the colleges believed that truth found in God's Book of Nature corroborated truth found in Scripture.

The reader will recall that Locke took this same man-centered approach in his short work entitled *The Reasonableness of Christianity*. Christianity is reasonable, ergo it must be true. This bottom-up way of verifying Christianity's truth is extremely dangerous, as we saw in Chapter three. It basically says to look at Christianity through the lens of science or common sense. There is nothing to hide. In fact, those at that time made common sense and science the criteria for determining whether or not Christianity is true.

The problem, of course, occurs when the findings of science no longer confirm the truths of the Bible. This is precisely what happened in the latter part of the nineteenth century. By placing the validity of the Christian worldview in the shifting sands of science and common sense, Christian orthodoxy subsequently found itself in a precarious position.[30] Because those in intellectual circles inadvertently played this dangerous game of accommodation, they found themselves retreating and handing over intellectual and cultural authority to science in the latter part of the century. I point this out because Common Sense philosophy was pervasive at the time, and Christians in higher education unwittingly embraced it. They made exactly the same mistake as their counterparts in the Enlightenment era.

Common Sense Realism, therefore, is one way that Christians in the college setting began to allow orthodox Christianity to lose its footing. Nevertheless, before the Civil War, orthodoxy still held sway. Many of the old-time professors were still clergymen who felt it their duty to pass on the Christian worldview to their students. In fact, as late as 1868, seven out of ten faculty members at Princeton were Presbyterian ministers.[31] The vast majority of college presidents (nine out of ten) in the antebellum era were clergymen.[32] Indeed, in the antebellum era the overwhelming majority of colleges in America were founded by churches. This was a time when the colleges were a religious undertaking as well as a public service, therefore the church and state often worked together. Taxes from the state or the community often supported these colleges.[33]

Classicism remained the foundational curriculum for the colleges because it was widely held that timeless values of the past could be propagated to future generations of students who could grasp these by reason alone (like Common Sense Realism).[34] In this endeavor, professors believed they were the custodians of tradition. They took very seriously their role and obligation to teach not just facts but to integrate all knowledge into the meaning of life.[35]

Christianity still was very much a part of the entirety of college life in the antebellum era. In 1830, one-third of graduates from Princeton, Harvard, and Yale went on to enter the ministry. In 1876, that number would drop to one in thirteen.[36] Daily chapel services were still mandatory for many schools during the first half of the century. Just to cite a few examples, the University of Illinois required chapel every day, and twice a day at Michigan and Yale.[37] At Indiana the students met before classes every day for Scripture reading and prayer.[38] Look at what a graduate of Wisconsin university said about her experience there: "I shall never forget my first evening in South Hall and the sweet, impressive voice of the Preceptress as she led the kneeling girls in prayer."[39]

In 1844, Julian M. Sturtevant echoed the same type of Christian dedication as he wrote to a friend in the midst of his struggle with whether or not he should accept the position of president of Illinois College: "May the Lord give me wisdom. . . . If I am to be placed at the head of this College, may he pour out upon [me] his spirit till I am fully qualified for the holy and responsible work—to be wise, to be firm, to be humble, to shed over this College the holy influence of piety and to lead the successive generations of students to Christ."[40] I think it is safe to say that leading students to Christ is not high on the list of priorities for secular college presidents today. In fact, putting this on one's resume would most likely disqualify anyone seeking this type of appointment in today's politically correct climate.

It should be noted that many of the colleges in the Midwest, like the ones just mentioned, were land-grant colleges resulting from the Morrill Act of 1862. These new "state colleges" provided an alternative to the liberal arts college. The common folk viewed the land-grant colleges as democratizing American higher education because the colleges gave the farmer, for example, an opportunity at higher education for the first time. This opportunity was synonymous with the American way.[41] Though not neglecting the traditional classical curriculum, these schools emphasized the applied sciences like agricultural science and engineering, which would improve the agrarian society while at the same time helping it to transition into the emerging Industrial Age. Though nonsectarian, many of these schools were founded as Protestant institutions where the president and faculty were clergy, and daily chapel was the norm.[42]

The rise of the land-grant colleges is important because these new institutions helped lead the way out of the agrarian past and into the future of industrialization and urbanization. These colleges represent the slow but gradual move away from classical learning and toward specialization. Moreover, learning classical knowledge like rhetoric, Latin, Greek, and moral philosophy were not going to help the new industrialized economy along. But a concomitant result of this loss of classicism was that Christianity, which played an essential role in the classical curriculum, would lose its authoritative place in higher education as well. Religious control of the colleges, which was associated with classicism, began to seem amateurish compared with specialization, professionalization, and science, which began their ascent.[43]

The Reformers

The rise of the land-grant colleges was a demonstrable manifestation of the change in higher education taking place in the middle of the nineteenth century. But the rumblings of reform had been going on for decades. Much of what was happening in the nineteenth century revolved around the battle between the reformers—those who wanted to follow the German model and turn colleges into research universities—and the traditionalists, who wanted to retain the basic classical tradition of the old-school colleges.

One such mid-century reformer was Francis Wayland, the president of Brown University and a New England Baptist. Wayland was typical of those who used the Common Sense philosophy of the time, which, as we saw, combined both revelation and science to find truth. He felt that science could discover the laws of the Creator. One law that concerned him was the law of the market. Of particular concern for Wayland was that the traditional classical model of the colleges no longer seemed to be in a natural relationship with the ever diversifying economy. While he had no problem with clergy controlling the colleges, he could not see how a classical education, which benefited only a few professionals—those going into law, medicine, or the ministry—could be relevant to the new economy. Many colleges, at that time were supported artificially with scholarships. He wanted to see colleges that could support themselves on the bottom line by serving the emerging technological needs of society.[44]

Another figure who had an impact on university reform was Henry P. Tappan, the president of the University of Michigan from 1852 to 1863, often referred to as the "John the Baptist" of the age of the American university because of the path he attempted to blaze.[45] Tappan was one of the first reformers to study in Germany, where he became enamored with the German model of the university. Throughout the nineteenth century, any scholar worth his salt had spent at least some time studying in Germany's graduate schools.[46] The difference between America's old-school colleges and Germany's universities was that the latter emphasized scientific research, elective courses, and laboratory study.[47]

The most important notion that Tappan embraced while in Germany was that one should be considered a professional in his own field. For Tappan this translated into a person's literary and scientific qualifications. This newfangled notion collided with the traditional goal of colleges, which was to produce young men of Christian character who would then serve the community in some capacity. As far as Tappan was concerned, the traditional goals of the college were outmoded. He didn't care what Christian sect or political party a person belonged to. If they weren't qualified as a professional, they were of "no account" in his opinion.[48]

Tappan had an aristocratic way about him and many considered him an elitist. He displayed this highbrow attitude, in part, with his habit of taking wine with his meals, which he picked up from his German intellectual colleagues.[49] This rubbed some people the wrong way. For example, he made this highbrow comment: "Of all mere human institutions there are none so important and mighty in their influences as Universities; because, when rightly constituted, they are made up of the most enlightened, and the choicest spirits of our race."[50] His elitist attitude did not endear him to some people. Because his pretensions and ill-begotten attempts at reform irritated the very conservative board of regents,[51] Tappan was dismissed in 1863, whereupon he went back to Germany and had wine with his meals.

Another major figure in the reform movement was Charles W. Eliot, who served as Harvard's president for forty years beginning in 1869. It was during this time, in the post–Civil War era, that the transformation from colleges into universities began to accelerate, and Eliot was right there, along with a few others, leading the charge. But many people did not see the changes Eliot wanted as something positive. Because of this, as Frederick Rudolph notes, Harvard became the "bad boy" of American higher education.[52]

Eliot, like many of his contemporaries, spent a great deal of time in Germany. He desperately wanted the American colleges to embrace the German ideal, which he felt would better serve the needs of American higher education and the country as well. He saw religion, especially the denominationalism of the colleges, as impeding progress toward this goal. Eliot was opposed to the normal practice of selecting ministers to be the heads of colleges and universities.[53] He believed denominationalism made theology offensive, because it made ministers adhere to absolute creedal tenets. In addition, it would not allow students to judge theology freely in the scientific spirit. If religion was true, Eliot argued, it would thrive in the university setting where freedom and open inquiry reigned. Therefore, he was a vigorous opponent of "dogmatic theology" and sectarianism. One observer at that time concurred: "The notion that the Christian Church is to monopolize and manipulate education . . . is antique for our time and for all time."[54]

As an aside, I found it interesting that although Eliot was one of the leading reformers of the era, his ambitious notions for innovation didn't extend to the area of sports. He opposed football and attempted to do away with it, though his effort was unsuccessful. He was also opposed to basketball, hockey, and baseball, which he felt were not clean sports. When he was informed one year that the baseball team did well because the pitcher had a good curveball, he uttered, "I understand that a curve ball [*sic*] is thrown with a deliberate attempt to deceive. Surely this is not an ability we should want to foster at Harvard."[55]

The German Ideal and the Rise of Science

The model for higher education in America today cannot be properly understood without looking at how it was imported from Germany. Germany fostered two types of academic freedom. *Lernfreiheit* was the freedom of the students to choose their own courses of study. This is where the reformers in America got the idea for instituting "elective" courses. The second type of academic freedom in Germany was *Lehrfreiheit*, which meant the professors had the freedom to do research and teach in an atmosphere free from censorship or limitations.[56] The emphasis on doing research and becoming a professional and specialist in one's own field came from this concept.

Although the aforementioned terms are important, to really understand the emergence of the modern research ideal we must look at the German concept of *Bildung*. This concept provided the overall philosophical framework for understanding education in Germany.

Bildung can be translated "education," but perhaps the term should more accurately be understood as "formation" or "development."[57] The term *Bildung* can be traced back to the German Pietistic movement, whereby a devout Christian would ideally cultivate (*Bildung*) his talents and way of living according to the image of God.[58] The German philosopher Hegel used *Bildung* (education) to denote the dialectical process of one's interrelationship (struggle) with the world. Later it was similarly understood as the process of training and socialization of an individual. *Bildung* stressed the uniqueness of each person in light of a self-transformative process whereby the individual assessed and cultivated his talents in order to develop distinct gifts for the betterment of society.[59]

It's accurate to view *Bildung* as a "secularized expression" of the Christian belief in the sanctity of each individual. The cultivation of a person's talents becomes a moral responsibility in some sense in order to benefit all of humanity. *Bildung* gave the academic specialist and the research ideal a "spiritual dignity" and a "redemptive significance" because the goals of scholarship embodied "the highest spiritual values of the civilization."[60]

This way of understanding *Bildung* elevated specialization to a virtue. In essence, the research specialist understood his place in the long tradition of work that was previously done in his area of study. He considered his vocation as contributing new knowledge toward the advancement of learning in that particular field. In this way the specialist was more of a "steward" with some sense of duty for gaining new knowledge.[61] This was in sharp contrast to the antebellum classicism in which every student learned basically the same thing, and graduate level work was confined to the divinity schools that sprang up as part of some of the colleges in that era.

The rise of elective courses of study coincided with the disillusionment and growing discomfort with the classical core curriculum.

This put the philosophy of *Bildung* into action. Choosing electives put students in the "center of the educational universe" by giving them power to choose at least some of their own courses of study.[62] *Bildung* found additional reinforcement in the romantic notion of individual expression versus the forces of tradition.[63] By allowing specific departments of knowledge and scholarly interests to burgeon, the rise of the elective principle played a substantive role in the transformation of the college into the university.[64]

It is hard to underestimate the impact the German ideal had on the American model of higher education. Reformers like Eliot couldn't implement the transition from colleges to universities fast enough. The research ideal imported from Germany represented the move toward professionalization and the emergence of a line of demarcation between graduate and undergraduate education in America. The rise of the "professional," symbolized by the PhD—the first of which Yale awarded in 1861[65]—marked the emergence of the universities, which began to thrive after 1870.

Research and the scientific method went hand in hand as essential parts of the university. Researchers, the thinking went, made better instructors because they stayed up-to-date in their respective fields. In addition, researchers were more qualified to teach scientific methods because their knowledge was more precise.[66] The reformers embraced progressivist science, which was held in high esteem, because it added new knowledge through original research. But just as important as adding new knowledge was training the students to become "investigators." The reformers didn't want students simply inculcated with knowledge, as was the case under the old classical model. Instead, they wanted to train students to think scientifically, because the reformers considered the search for truth the highest purpose of the university. By training their charges to become investigators, the students would then be able to serve society through research, using the highest form of mental prowess.[67]

Daniel Coit Gilman and Andrew Dickson White

Daniel Coit Gilman, who accepted the offer as the first president of Johns Hopkins University in 1875, exemplified the new emphasis on science, research, and specialization. In fact, under Gilman, Johns Hopkins became the first American graduate university modeled after the German ideal.[68] Johns Hopkins provides a good representation of the transitional stage from the old-time college to the newly minted university with its innovative philosophy of education. For reformers like Gilman, science and the research ideal would lead the way.

As far as the reformers were concerned, science wasn't simply a body of knowledge but a tool for *acquiring* new knowledge. Therefore, it was singularly equipped to lead the universities in the increasingly complex and tumultuous world resulting from the Civil War, the Industrial Revolution, and the rise of evolutionary theory.[69] Traditional Christian education was pushed to the periphery of university curricula. Knowledge became fragmented into various specialized fields of study as science and the research ideal began their authoritative ascent.[70] It was during this time that the Christian worldview took a broadside from Darwin's new theory, although the real damage wasn't recognized until much later.

In spite of the move toward professionalism and science, we need to keep the reform efforts in perspective. Many of the men who headed the colleges after the Civil War were still Christians, or at least committed theists with Protestant leanings. Like many others at that time, they thought that Christianity could be united with any scientific findings that surfaced. Many even thought that Darwin's theory could be reconciled with scriptural revelation. Gilman, for example, certainly did not see science and Christianity at war.

Christianity's authority may have been teetering a bit, but it wasn't in full retreat just yet. In fact, though an avid reformer, Gilman acknowledged that scientific discoveries divulged a plan that was "incomprehensible" without "belief in one living and true God."[71] Most reformers like Gilman thought that the new age of science would vindicate Christian truth while fostering intellectual and moral integrity. In this way the reformers still maintained some traditional concern with the virtues and morals associated with the classical education. Moreover, if modern science corroborated the truths of Christianity, then the spiritual and religious influence of the university was evident.[72] In this way science could be seen as something other than promoting the secular.

Gilman's invitation of Thomas Henry Huxley at Johns Hopkins's inaugural solidified the avant-garde reputation of the school. Huxley was a legendary agnostic as well as being known as "Darwin's Bulldog" for his tenacious apology for Darwinism, as evidenced in his famous debate with Samuel Wilberforce in 1860.[73]

Because Huxley's invitation to Johns Hopkins was so controversial, I think it points out how strongly Gilman felt about the advancement of knowledge, science, and open inquiry at any cost. Yet at the same time he remained sensitive to the concerns of those who were not comfortable with the changes that were taking place. When a group of students wanted to purchase a bust of Darwin, Gilman put his imprimatur on the idea but suggested that it might be a good idea to surround Darwin's bust with busts of scientists who weren't so controversial.[74] This demonstrates that, although Gilman was strenuous in his advancement of science, he still respected the tradition that was ingrained in him in the antebellum era. Gilman's audacious invitation of Huxley was important in retrospect: science's status was rising in comparison to Christianity. Christianity was losing its authority as it gave way to the new paradigm shift.[75] Pretty soon there wouldn't be a need for Darwin's bust to hide among the others.

Gilman's attempt at keeping the peace between traditional Christian concerns and science represents that stage in retreat in which the Christian worldview, unbeknownst to its supposed advocates, was actually losing ground to the secular mind-set. As Marsden and Longfield assert, Gilman "strove to baptize the new learning's commitment to research with the mist of traditional Protestant concerns."[76] In other words, Gilman was holding on to his Protestant theism with one hand while attempting to accommodate it to science and the cultural zeitgeist with the other.

Gilman and Johns Hopkins University represent the accommodative process that we see over and over again. During the Enlightenment era, Christianity was acceptable as long as it was found to be reasonable. When it wasn't found reasonable, it lost its authority. In the latter part of the nineteenth century, the criterion became whether Christianity's scriptural claims could square with scientific findings. When it appeared that science contradicted biblical revelation, science came out on top and orthodox Christianity retreated.

Frederick Rudolph summarized what was taking place at Johns Hopkins: "For the acceptance of revealed religious truth the new university in Baltimore substituted a search for scientific truth. For preparation for life in the next world it substituted a search for an understanding of this world."[77] Of course, Rudolph's assessment describes the secularization process to a tee. Secularism is concerned with the here and now—this world, this age—to the exclusion of anything eternal. Perhaps then it is not surprising that Johns Hopkins is often recognized as the first "secular" American university.[78]

By the end of the century, some of those who sided with the authority of science became much bolder in their hostility toward sectarianism and dogmatic theology. One such man was Andrew Dickson White, a friend of Gilman. White was a former protégé of Henry Tappan, who brought White to Michigan to teach in 1857 and perhaps to share wine with him during his meals. White saw firsthand how sectarian attacks drummed Tappan out of Michigan, and this left a bitter taste in his mouth that would last his entire career.[79]

White shared some common goals with the independently wealthy Ezra Cornell. Through the aid of the Morrill Land Grant Act of 1862 Cornell University was born with White becoming its first president in 1868.[80] White had no problem with Cornell being considered a Christian institution, but he most assuredly did not wish to condone in any way the sectarianism that had thrown his mentor Tappan out of Michigan. White made no secret that he was dead set against sectarianism and what he described as "outworn creeds and noxious dogmas."[81] His watered-down version of Christianity seemed to be some admixture of generic theism and a preview of the Social Gospel that would become prevalent in the near future. White claimed to believe in a "higher power" that was inclined toward benevolence regarding human affairs.[82]

Notwithstanding his attempt to display Cornell as a Christian institution, White received more than a bit of public criticism from those predisposed to traditional orthodoxy. Nevertheless, White was prepared to forge ahead, making it clear in his inaugural address that "We will labor to make this a Christian institution—a sectarian institution it may never be."[83] In defense of Cornell being Christian, White pointed to the chapel services that were held daily and to the work of the Young Men's Christian Association (YMCA), which he encouraged.[84] Thus, even in the latter half of the nineteenth century, the reformers still needed to recognize Christianity, at least in a nominal way.

One cannot talk about White without mentioning the two-volume tour de force he published in 1896 entitled *A History of the Warfare of Science with Theology in Christendom*. White's problem, as he outlined it, was not with "religion" per se but with theology. As far as he was concerned, science had conquered "Dogmatic theology" but would go "hand-in-hand with Religion," which he defined as recognition of a "Power in the universe . . . which makes for righteousness."[85]

Thus it is evident by the turn of the century that science had entrenched itself enough in the cultural mind-set that White felt comfortable launching a direct assault on orthodox Christianity, specifically targeting fundamental doctrines, such as the Fall of humanity, creation accounts, and miracles, while advocating the superiority of science in providing alternative explanations.[86] White's two-volume masterwork did a great deal to solidify the common assumption with us today that Christianity and science are at war with each other. The intellectuals at the turn of the century supported this myth by attaching a negative connotation to the word *dogma* while painting a picture of science as "open," "tolerant," and "progressive."[87] They associated freedom with tolerance and maintained that modern religion, not older forms of Christian dogma, demonstrated the new scientific spirit.[88]

What was happening here was simple. The progressives considered the fundamental doctrines of Christianity outmoded in light of science. These reformers used terms such as *theology, dogma,* or *dogmatic theology* in a pejorative way. On the other hand, they accepted plain-vanilla "religion" because it had a generic, inoffensive connotation, and one could define it as one wished. So, for example, under the auspices of religion, God is reduced to a benevolent higher power, who provides some moral foundation for humans to live by. Jesus is demoted to a great moral teacher. Miracles are explained away. As long as the intellectual elite could get rid of dogmatic theology, religion had nothing to fear and could blossom in the light of science.[89]

White fell over himself in his antipathy toward dogmatic theology. In his Annual Report dated 1885, he made the following absurd statement: "Even error honestly arrived at will do more for religion and for science, than truth merely asserted dogmatically."[90] Really? So, presumably, if I very honestly arrived at the conclusion that two plus two equals six, supposedly this would be more helpful than someone who stated dogmatically that two plus two equals four? This nonsense is akin to what we discussed in the previous chapter about truth and tolerance. The problem, as I see it, is that if notions like these are bandied about long enough, sooner or later they gain validity and trickle down to the public at large. And that is what has happened in our society.

For example, as we noted in Chapter six, tolerance today is held in higher esteem than truth. People today find it easier to side with someone who is tolerant, even if that someone's assertions are false. No one today seems to be much concerned with the truth, because the truth can limit people's autonomy and people don't want that. Sometimes it seems as though everything is tolerated *but* the truth. Tolerance, even tolerating error, is more politically correct and acceptable than truth stated dogmatically.

On a more general note, commonly held assumptions that float around today, such as Christians are too dogmatic in their beliefs, or Christianity and science are at war, or truth is relative, all started somewhere. The material I have presented in this chapter and in previous ones provides a glimpse as to how these ideas, some of which originated in the Enlightenment, were carried through in various forms into the latter part of the nineteenth century and have made their way down to us today. But I digress. Let's continue to see how Christianity was compromised in the latter half of the nineteenth century.

German Philosophy and Liberal Theology

Besides the rise of science and the research ideal, other factors during the latter half of the nineteenth century were aiding and abetting the displacement of traditional Christianity in higher education. One of these factors, theological liberalism, we discussed at some length in Chapter four. Let's tie in what we learned there with what we know was occurring in higher education at this time. As you will recall, liberal theologians were modernists in the sense that they wanted to bring Christianity up to speed with the modern era. The reformers and others who had done graduate work in Germany picked up liberal theology from their German professors across the pond and brought it back to the states, where it proliferated in the latter decades of the nineteenth century.[91]

Because the original German liberal scholars were products of the Enlightenment, it is not surprising that, like their philosophical progenitors, they frowned on the uniqueness and particularity of Christianity. In short, the German liberal theologians considered all religions to be equal. Doctrines unique to Christianity like Original Sin, the resurrection of Jesus, and anything miraculous, they denied as unreasonable. They focused instead on the ethical value of Christianity. As we noted in Chapter four, the liberal theologians saw biblical criticism and science as good reasons to discard most of the traditional/fundamental doctrines of Christianity because they believed the modern worldview had eclipsed those dogmas.[92]

Many students who did their postgraduate work in Germany lost their faith because they imbibed the liberal theology over there. Yale sociologist William Graham Sumner was one such student. Although he was brought up in a staunch Calvinist family, Sumner began to drift

124

into agnosticism and then became outright critical of traditional Christianity after studying at the University of Gottingen. He recalled it this way: "I never consciously gave up a religious faith." Later he stated, "It was as if I had put my beliefs into a drawer, and when I opened it up there was nothing there at all."[93]

Many like Sumner who were influenced by liberal theologians and the biblical criticism of the time found themselves in the new research universities and nondenominational divinity schools where they attempted to integrate religion into modern life. Their goal was to make nondogmatic Christianity relevant to the modern world, and they felt that moral idealism combined with modern science could engender a compelling progressive vision.[94]

Ernst Troeltsch, whom we already met, exemplifies the retreat from orthodox Christianity and the bargaining process that liberal theologians embraced as the nineteenth century came to a close. Troeltsch dismissed out of hand the dogmatic approach to Christianity, which relied on Scripture as the sole authority. He did not see Christianity as superior to other religions. He claimed that there was no "essence" to Christianity found in traditional doctrines. How could there be? Christianity, he argued, changes as it moves along in history. In fact, Troeltsch believed the historical process (which Christianity is part of) *is* Christianity. This meshed with Hegel's historical idealism we noted in Chapter three.

These ideas were easy for those in higher education to swallow hook, line, and sinker. They were already disenchanted with the idea of defending or embracing a traditional brand of Christianity, which held to fundamental doctrines that seemed outmoded and static. Liberals and reformers were already connecting the dots between evolution and progress and their own ideas about religion. For them, religion should progress just as everything else was progressing. As Charles Eliot stated, "Religion is not a fixed thing, but a fluent thing."[95]

Troeltsch's notion that Christianity changes as it flows through history supported this kind of thinking. Hegel's utopian idealism, whereby history is moving toward its culmination in the Absolute (God), also underpinned the idea that everything was in some sort of progressive flux. Thus Troeltsch's, Hegel's, and others' misguided concepts about Christianity worked synergistically with evolutionary theory to undermine the timeless, unique, and universal truth of Christianity that had been traditionally taught as part of the classical curriculum.

Moreover, liberal thinking held that traditional dogmatic Christianity could not survive the scrutiny of science or biblical criticism, the latter of which treated the Bible as any other book. From the liberal point of view, biblical criticism was doing Christianity a service by purifying the Bible of all its supposed errors. As far as the reformers and liberal theologians were concerned, the Bible should be open to continual inquiry like any other scientific theories. The process of identifying problems with Scripture might seem harmful at first, but in the long run would yield new beliefs that would prove more satisfactory than the old dogmatic ones. After all, it only made sense that the way people in Bible times (mis)perceived things was problematic in the light of the modern era.[96]

Modernist liberals, in spite of their ill-begotten cogitations, pictured themselves as protectors of Christianity. By distinguishing dogmatic theology from religion, they were able to dispense with traditional dogma while upholding the promise of a broad form of religion that wasn't hampered by theological sectarianism and outdated orthodoxy.[97] It wasn't so much that they were against Christianity per se; it was just that they didn't want anything to impede the quest for truth. According to their way of thinking, the distinctive, sectarian dogma that defined Christianity, weighed it down. Science nullified these doctrines.

Science Becomes the Authority at the Turn of the Century

By the end of the nineteenth century, truth was defined as something that only science could validate.[98] Revelation as an authority was out. Science was in. Frederick Rudolf noted, for example, that science laboratories and libraries were overshadowing the chapel in the new dispensation.[99] Following this line of thought, Van A. Harvey wrote, "Because the ethos of the university was scientific and hostile to everything that did not lend itself to rational adjudication, theology was necessarily pushed to the margins of intellectual life."[100]

As we noted above, the Bible was treated as any other book—just a cultural product now.[101] Those in higher education referred to it as "literature."[102] Stripped of its distinctive elements and lumped in with religion, Christianity's value was not in its truth claims any longer but instead in its moral, emotional, psychological, and poetical value.[103] The thinking went that students would respect religion once they saw that it was studied scientifically and shown to play an important role in the modern scientific culture. But this backfired. Reformers, though they tried to integrate their liberal version of Protestantism into modern intellectual life, actually ended up marginalizing Christianity[104] because religious views of any sort were considered irrelevant in light of scientific truth.

Moreover, in an effort to accommodate Christianity to the modern scientific era, liberals in higher education attempted to cordon off religion into its own realm, which was the same Kantian play we saw take place during the Enlightenment. As the reader will recall from Chapter three, Kant partitioned off God into the noumenal realm, where the Enlightenment skeptics couldn't get at Him. This was Kant's way of protecting Christian "faith." The academic reformers did the same thing. The reformers and liberal theologians attempted to protect Christianity by stripping it of its fundamental doctrines and then hiding it in with religion, where its value became solely ethical, moral, and psychological. But by doing so, the modernist liberals stripped Christianity of not only its truth claims but also its cultural authority. It was difficult for Christianity to make any claims to authority when science, the new authority, studied it like a specimen.

With few remaining to defend it in its own right, a watered-down version of Christianity found itself in a rather tenuous position in higher education by the end of the century. With dogma and theology discarded, Christianity, or what was left of it, became disguised within the new discipline called "religious studies." Religious studies emerged in a wasteland somewhere between the department of humanities and the social sciences. It didn't exactly fit in with either, although it maintained loose affiliations with both disciplines.[105] Nevertheless, religious studies became a way that students could study religion in a neutral fashion.[106] Thus, traditional Christianity became lost in a petri dish of religion, where it could be plucked out and studied as a curiosity from a bygone era.

Since the Christian religion could no longer survive as a fact, it had to survive as something that promoted value. Another new field of study, the psychology of religion, came to the aid of religion in this regard. Those in this field were not concerned with whether religion was true or not. They did not address questions about God's existence and other fundamental doctrines, for they simply were not germane anymore. The supernatural was outside the purview of this discipline; therefore, it was not the duty of those in this field to make those kinds of judgments. If religion yielded any truth, it was poetical truth not scientific truth. Those in this field were concerned with demonstrating religion's inspirational value, not its intellectual value.[107]

William James's *The Varieties of Religious Experience*, published in 1902, was an instant success and helped put the psychology of religion on the map by garnering the attention of intellectuals and the public alike. James applied evolutionary standards to test what he called "saintliness" to determine if the religious life should be pursued as some kind of ideal. His conclusion was that, indeed, religion was essential both for individual survival and the improvement of society.[108]

How fortunate for religion that it received the stamp of approval from the nascent psychology. One wonders what religion's fate would have been if it hadn't received James's imprimatur in light of what Edwin Starbuck proclaimed in his book, *Psychology of Religion* (1899), in which he wrote, "Science has conquered one field after another, until now it is entering the most complex, the most inaccessible, and, the most sacred domain—that of religion."[109] It seems as though, from Starbuck's point of view, science went around like a roaring lion seeking whatever it could devour, and religion was its last conquest.

It is not an exaggeration to state that science had indeed become the authority on just about everything under the sun by the turn of the century. Science assumed its hegemony by knocking Christianity off its pedestal and neutering it (with the help of biblical criticism) to the point where it had to masquerade as a garden-variety religion in order to be accepted.

It was at the turn of the century that academia largely abandoned Christianity's fundamental truth claims because it appeared that an attempt to reconcile them with science was becoming too embarrassing or too costly. One gets the impression that it simply wasn't worth the effort any longer. It was easier to mix Christianity in with religion and cordon it off into its own little world, where no one would have to deal with its supernatural truth claims. Neutered of its dogmatic theology, Christianity's ethical benefits to society were promoted instead.

Summary

The material we've covered in this chapter demonstrates how some of the philosophical notions that came from the Enlightenment were passed down to the German liberal theologians and then eventually found their way to those who taught in higher education. This illustrates that the way Christianity is marginalized today does not result from ideas that just popped out of thin air, but rather have traceable historical precedents.

Chapter 8

Christian Disenfranchisement in Higher Education: 1900–Present

By the latter part of the nineteenth century, considerable opposition was building against denominational control of the colleges and universities. Specialization, professionalism, and a progressive view of knowledge, which science afforded, continued to play a major role with how the demise of Christianity in higher education took place. Protestant denominations, which heretofore had controlled much of the goings-on in their respective colleges, lost much of their control by the latter part of the nineteenth century and into the early part of the twentieth century. A short synopsis of how this occurred is as follows.

Loss of Denominational Control and Big Money

To the reformers' dismay, church-sponsored denominational institutions were likely to hire like-minded educators from their own denominations to fill teaching positions. Progressives and reformers considered this problematic for two reasons. First, denominational Protestants, in some cases, were more resistant to advances in scientific knowledge. The reformers believed this could stultify the advancement of intellectual progress. Second, hiring professors from one's own denomination meant that the most qualified scholars would not always receive the post.[1] This gave the impression that some colleges were more concerned with denominational orthodoxy than with the advancement of knowledge. The progressives considered this particularly odious in light of the specialization and professionalization of the academy. They wanted a clear line of distinction drawn between those who had the authority to teach a particular subject and those who did not.[2] Clearly, as far as the progressives were concerned, colleges and the classical curriculum were for amateurs, whereas the university was meant for professionals.

In the leading universities and a growing number of colleges as well, faculties and curricula were divided by subject matter and had separate departments. This made it easier for the department heads to exercise autonomy over the hiring and promotion of members within their particular departments. In light of this, those in higher education who did not make a unique contribution in a specific field were viewed as unqualified as an expert. They were not "professionals."[3] Therefore, old-school educators who wanted to cling tenaciously to orthodox Christianity and what was left of classical curriculum were unlikely to gain a position in the research universities.[4] They seemed amateurish in comparison to the professional, who increasingly held a PhD and had done some original research as a specialist in his field. It was becoming obvious that "the days were numbered" for colleges that wanted to become universities and still maintain their denominational ties.[5]

Another difficulty that made it harder for denominations to maintain their affiliation is that economic concerns and big money were squeezing them out. With the industrialization of the country came the rise of corporate capitalism, and this in turn produced immense pools of wealth for certain individuals. Some of these folks were disposed to philanthropic endeavors, which found its way to the universities. Johns Hopkins, John D. Rockefeller (the University of Chicago), Leland Stanford (Stanford University), and many other like-minded, wealthy industrialists gave the impression that by supporting university reform, they would be helping the nation and the economy.

Their goal was to promote scientific research based on the new German model of specialization and secular scholarship, which would become the national standard for higher education. Technical knowledge and those professionals who were trained in areas such as engineering, finance, management, advertising, and material sciences served corporate capitalism. The classically educated gentleman who was a product of the old-fashioned Christian moral order was no longer needed.[6]

The Carnegie Foundation was one such philanthropic institution set up with the express purpose of promoting the aforementioned goal of standardizing higher education. Carnegie handed over the responsibility of determining the criteria for disseminating the funds to Henry Smith Pritchett, president of MIT and close friend of Charles Eliot, the latter who served as chair of the foundation in 1905.[7] Pritchett made it very clear that the funds were available only to institutions that had no explicit denominational affiliations. Pritchett argued that denominational control of higher education led to subpar standards and just plain bad education. He also felt that if denominations wanted to control a college, they should pay for it instead of asking for public support. Perhaps his strongest argument was reminding everyone of how much money was available through the foundation.[8] Rather than standing up to the big money and demonstrating integrity and commitment to denominational orthodoxy and their students, at least fifteen schools severed ties with their denominations immediately. In this way, corporate capitalism undercut the last vestiges of Christianity's formal ties with higher education.[9]

Why did these denominational schools give up so easily? Robert Benne believes that in the end it was a crisis of faith: "Deep down, both church leaders and faculty members no longer believed the Christian faith to be comprehensive, unsurpassable, and central. Other sources of inspiration, knowledge, and moral guidance slowly displaced Christianity. In that context, secularization was simply the natural next step."[10]

Not everyone caved in. At least not right away. For example, Syracuse University, although claiming in 1872 to be nonsectarian, was a well-known Methodist university. James Day, who became chancellor in 1894, was a successful Methodist preacher from New York City with a reputation for rubbing shoulders with the wealthy. Apparently he believed he could handle Pritchett, who kept rejecting Syracuse's eligibility for money because of their Methodist trustees, along with other concerns that suggested denominational control.

After numerous attempts to overcome Pritchett's rejections regarding denominationalism, Day couldn't take it anymore. Day's denunciation of Pritchett and his foundation is as follows:

> Other colleges may do as they please. If they wish to crawl in the dirt for such a price, that is their privilege. But no university can teach young people lofty ideals of manhood and forget its self-respect and honor or sell its loyalty and faith for money that Judas flung away when in remorse he went out and hung himself. It is an insult for such a proposition to be made to a Christian institution, "The Money perish with thee," is the only answer to it.[11]

Day's obstinate attitude didn't last long, however. He really wanted to run a Methodist institution, but his dream was to build a "great university." His balancing act consisted of telling those outside of his jurisdiction that Syracuse was nonsectarian while suggesting to those on the inside, like his dean, for example, that the faculty didn't have enough percentage of Methodists.

The issue finally came to a head in 1919 when he decided to bring the New York State College of Forestry to the Syracuse institution. After being denied funding on the grounds that Syracuse was "sectarian," Day opted to amend the charter so that only a minority of board members could be elected by the Methodist conferences. Day's compromise worked and the school received the funding.[12]

Day received much criticism in the latter part of his career. One outspoken critic was the author Upton Sinclair, who thought Day was a hypocrite for hobnobbing with big shots like the president of Standard Oil (who happened to be on the board of the university) while at the same time firing people for trivial offenses like endorsing Sunday baseball or deviating from minor points of orthodox doctrine.[13] Day shouldn't have worried though. He was in good company. Upton Sinclair described the average modern university president as "the most universal faker and the most variegated prevaricator that has yet appeared in the civilized world."[14]

After the turn of the century, it became obvious, even in the public realm, that the secularizing trend in higher education had gained momentum. In 1909 the editors of *Cosmopolitan* summarized the findings of one of their journalists who visited various campuses. He interviewed professors and sat in their classes to ascertain what they were teaching. It caused quite a stir when the editors noted that in hundreds of classrooms, professors daily taught the following:

> The home as an institution is doomed; that there are no absolute evils; that immorality is simply an act in contravention of society's accepted standards; that democracy is a failure and the Declaration of Independence only spectacular rhetoric; that the change from one religion to another is like getting a new hat; that moral precepts are passing shibboleths; that conceptions of right and wrong are as unstable as styles of dress . . . and that there can be and are holier alliances without the marriage bond than within it.[15]

A survey of college catalogues between 1910 and 1920 showed a decline of more than 50 percent in the number of colleges that thought higher education should include religious aims. In addition, much of the faculty in higher education was showing an alarming disregard and even hostility toward religious questions and issues. In fact, by 1916 one study showed that nearly 90 percent of sociologists, biologists, and psychologists doubted the existence of God.[16]

How did the colleges go from Christian institutions in the middle of the previous century to secularized universities in such a relatively short time? Answer: there was an exponential growth in the number of undergraduates, graduate students, and professors after 1870 who collectively formed a self-conscious critical mass of elite educated people who had imbibed secular Enlightenment philosophy. In short, they were ready to willfully "marginalize the cultural authority of the Protestant establishment and secularize America's public institutions."[17]

Science, Social Gospel, and Sociology

After the turn of the century, it was apparent that the attempt by Christians to retain some sense of clout in higher education by accommodating secular impulses had failed. Christian authority had been neutralized. Professionalization was extinguishing classical curriculum. Big money severed denominational influence in many cases. Christians found themselves on the sidelines of academia, watching the game.

Science was no longer in need of Christianity's approval for anything. After usurping Christianity's authority, secular advocates of science went as far as they could in disengaging science from Christianity and its outdated beliefs. Science, which in the past had aided Christianity in understanding God's Book of Nature, had now become a worldview in and of itself.[18] By the turn of the century, science had taken over Christianity's role for providing a comprehensive paradigm for integrating the facts of existence. The Christian worldview was pushed aside after trying to accommodate the new kid on the block.

Biblical Christians readily admitted the power of science to answer many questions. What worried them was that science was becoming the guiding authority in *every* area of life, which had been Christianity's role traditionally. After conceding so much ground to science, many felt that there was still one safe haven where science could not claim to be authoritative: the moral and ethical realm. If Christianity was going to be stuck in its little cordoned off space, at least it could still provide authority in that area of life.[19]

Perhaps not by coincidence this hope occurred at the same time liberal theologians were emphasizing the Social Gospel, which supported the view that true Christianity was not so much about doctrine but rather about helping others. Liberal theologians, moreover, attempted to reduce Christianity to moral and social issues. For them, setting up the kingdom of God meant meeting the needs of humanity. They believed that this emphasis had gotten lost, in part, because of the Industrial Revolution and urbanization.

Champions of the Social Gospel wanted to bridge the gap between religious and secular forces during the first half of the twentieth century.[20] This, as we have seen previously, was part of the accommodation process that liberal theologians practiced since the Enlightenment. Having given up on the totalizing vision Christianity had provided in the past, liberal theologians and the Social Gospel movement focused mainly on social and ethical concerns.

But supporters of science would not concede that science couldn't offer any guidance in the ethical realm. Moreover, they were not willing to allow the one little patch of ground that Christians so desperately wanted to retain. As far as advocates of science were concerned, science was all encompassing. It could answer questions and provide guidance in any realm, even the ethical realm. The new science of society, known as sociology, was an example of this attitude.

Sociology began as a rather ill-defined and nebulous enterprise consisting of individuals who aspired to be authorities and provide knowledge concerning all aspects of society. Sociologists were lured by the advantages of status that the professionalization of higher education afforded. To bolster importance in what they embarked upon, they needed to remove some obstacles that could hinder the perception that they indeed had something to offer.[21]

As noted above, Christians were trying to hold their ground in the realm of ethics, and those in the Social Gospel movement were demonstrating in real-life ways that they were genuinely concerned with helping others. The new sociologists felt threatened by these amateurs whom they felt were barging into their territory. After all, *they* were the experts. Never mind that it was not at all clear at this point what a sociologist was, what they were supposed to do,[22] or what they needed to demonstrate that qualified them as "scientists" of society. As far as sociologists were concerned, individual needs should be subordinated to group needs so that culture could evolve. Thus, sociologists combined science and moral concerns to better society through social harmony. Scientific disciplines like sociology were morally significant because they could provide a framework for socially accepted standards of behavior.[23]

It is important to notice that sociologists marginalized Christianity because they were unsympathetic toward traditional Christian classical education, which they viewed as outmoded. They attempted to discredit their amateur counterparts who were involved in helping their fellow citizens through churches and voluntary associations.[24] Though most sociologists had been raised in religious families, many, if not most, discarded their faith and became antagonistic toward religion, though they masked this somewhat in public. Christian Smith describes sociologists of that time: "These were not men who accidentally slighted religion. These were skeptical Enlightenment atheologians, personally devoted apostles of secularization."[25]

The reformers in higher education eagerly embraced the social sciences, even before it was clear that these disciplines provided any real value to educational knowledge—a testament to the effectiveness with which the social sciences represented themselves as instruments of moral progress.[26]

John Dewey (1859–1952) and the Intellectual Gospel

The notion that science was the answer to all of life's problems may be described as the "intellectual gospel." The intellectual gospel appealed to both liberals and freethinkers of Protestant origin. Progressive advocates of this view borrowed words and imagery from Christianity and then applied them to an enormously idealistic view of science. The famous agnostic Thomas Henry Huxley, whom we mentioned in the previous chapter, symbolized this worship of science, which replaced Christianity as a thing of the past.[27]

The intellectual gospel evoked Christian imagery and promoted the idea that science was a religious endeavor in and of itself. For example, David Hollinger points out that Herbert Spencer called devotion to science "a tacit worship." One American zoologist described the laboratory as a "sanctuary where nothing profane should be tolerated." Woodrow Wilson held an image of science as something akin to a nun working at her prayers.[28] And finally, Hollinger points out that G. Stanley Hall, president of the newly established Clark University, "considered the spirit of 'research' as the modern voice of 'the Holy Ghost.'"[29] It is not an exaggeration to say that the intellectual gospel was a secularized version of Christianity at the turn of the twentieth century. Promoters of science, under the auspices of the intellectual gospel, were claiming religious authority for science.

A major figure of the intellectual gospel during the early 1900s was John Dewey. Dewey was a monumental figure in the modern progressive movement. He had a tremendous impact on many institutions (like the public school system) and ways of thinking throughout the entire first half of the twentieth century. Dewey's personal life is an example of what we have seen regarding the marginalization of Christianity in the academy. This is because the same process of accommodation, then compromise, then rejection of Christianity happened in his own life.

Dewey's mother was a Calvinist, so we know that he received at least some traditional Christian influence as a child. In fact, he was a member of his local Congregationalist church and even taught Sunday school there in his younger days. Dewey received his PhD from Johns Hopkins University and went on to teach at the University of Michigan. He was enamored with Hegel's philosophy, which he felt, in its essential features, was identical to the doctrinal teachings of Christianity.[30]

But by the time he was thirty-three years old, he denied that Christianity was unique in any way, whether historical, theoretical, or moral, when compared with other belief systems. Dewey believed Christianity was just another religion. In good Hegelian fashion, he defined Christianity as "the continuously unfolding, never ceasing discovery of the meaning of life."[31] Clearly, Dewey was wandering astray of any conventional understanding of Christianity that he had as a young adult.

We mentioned in Chapter two that Civil Religion is the conjoining of God and country. Dewey's philosophy was a precursor of this in that he joined Christianity with democracy. If the intellectual gospel proclaimed science as supreme, then faith in democracy was another gospel Dewey promulgated. Dewey borrowed Christian language to promote his new gospel of American idealism. He borrowed terms like "the kingdom of God" and "the brotherhood of man," which were popular concepts in the Social Gospel movement. For Dewey, it was not the individual who was so important but social relationships in the context of democracy that was paramount. Dewey argued, "It is in democracy that the incarnation of God in man becomes a living, present thing."[32] Of course, this is rubbish. Against Dewey, the orthodox understanding is that Jesus Christ, not democracy, is the incarnation of God in human flesh. Liberal modernists like Dewey love to baptize their secular ideas with Christian terminology to make them appear "Christian" and thus more palatable for the lay public.

Dewey offered ridiculous assertions like the one above because his new gospel denied anything supernatural. His democratic idealism served as a substitute for the Christian gospel.[33] In fact, in his book *A*

Common Faith, a series of lectures he gave at Yale, Dewey rejected supernaturalism outright.[34] In 1894 Dewey went to serve at the University of Chicago, where he let his church membership drop.[35]

Over the years his rejection of Christianity solidified. By 1908, Dewey and fellow colleague James H. Tufts published an influential book entitled *Ethics* that went through twenty-five printings by 1932. As I have been pointing out, the intellectual gospel proclaimed scientific dominance, even in the moral realm. Dewey and Tuft's book went a long way in supporting this view. In their work, Dewey and Tufts decoupled religion and morality by claiming that ethics should be understood in terms of nature and society. Moreover, they claimed that ethics is naturalistic and should fall under the auspices of secular fields of study like biology and the social sciences, which provide important resources for moral guidance.[36]

The university system that wanted to claim it provided some moral guidance heartily embraced Dewey and Tufts's work. The naturalistic mores proposed by *Ethics* provided a basis for a "scientific" morality. Their book went a long way in providing support for the notion that science had marginalized religion.[37]

In an effort to completely free themselves not only from ecclesiastical control but also from political and economic control, educators in the university system began to form a coalition that would ensure academic freedom. As we learned in the previous chapter, *Lehrfreiheit* allowed the unfettered pursuit of knowledge and the ability of the professor to offer his opinions, whether in journals or speeches, outside of the university setting without fear of reprisal from his university. In this way the common folk could rest assured that those in the universities were free of corrupt influences in their pursuit of scientific knowledge. Progressives wanted the university to be perceived as a public trust where scholars worked for society rather than merely as employees of the university.[38]

With this in mind, elite educators founded the American Association of University Professors (AAUP) in 1915. Not surprisingly, the association elected John Dewey as its first president. A report on Academic Freedom and Tenure, issued by the AAUP at the end of the first year, made it clear that one of their goals was to see that the university system and the elite professoriate assisted in guiding democracy by providing a check against tyranny and public opinion, which was often irrational.[39] (This was within the context of World War I.)

They also had in mind to insist that if institutions of higher education under denominational control wanted to propagandize, this was acceptable so long as those institutions admitted their bias up front and acknowledged that they did not serve the public but their own private interests. It was the opinion of the committee that it would be better if denominational institutions of higher learning became increasingly rare.[40] In fact, in their founding report in 1915, they noted that "the chief menace to academic freedom was ecclesiastical."[41] In short, these elites wanted to compartmentalize religion while promoting science as the authority in culture.[42]

A famous study at the time showed that the elite professoriate—men like Dewey who were a part of the AAUP—were more likely to be skeptical of religious truth claims than were their fellow garden-variety academics. The crème de la crème professoriate were also more likely to believe that scientific viewpoints formed the basis for discovering the highest good for culture while also believing that traditional religion had an adverse effect on "the common good."[43]

Membership in the elite community of the AAUP was by nomination only. Some of the qualifications necessary for admission into this elite club were full professorship, recognized scholarship, and scientific productivity. Those who gained admission then in turn nominated those from their own universities and disciplines,[44] which further marginalized any Christian influence.

In summary, to stay on solid ground, universities produced experts who would serve the public trust in their various fields in order to guide democracy. With tenure assuring their academic freedom, the arrival of the modern academic man was complete.[45] Middleton and Walsh put it this way:

> Dewey's modern 'man' . . . is self-assured and in control of his own destiny. This man knows what he knows and he knows it with certainty because he knows it scientifically. He needs no authority outside himself because he is autonomous, a law or authority unto himself. And he certainly needs no salvation outside of himself. Once he has liberated himself from past authorities and superstitions all he needs is the courage to follow his reason.[46]

This "modern" attitude held by professors like Dewey trickled down and reflected in the students' attitudes as well. J. Gresham Machen, a first-class theologian who taught at Princeton Seminary between 1915 and 1929, gives us a peek into the university environment during this time when he wrote:

> The trouble with the university students of the present day, from the point of view of evangelical Christianity, is not that they are too original, but that they are not half original enough. They go on in the same routine way, following their leaders like a flock of sheep, repeating the same stock phrases with little knowledge of what they mean, swallowing whole whatever professors choose to give them—and all the time imagining that they are bold, bad, independent young men, merely because they abuse what everybody else is abusing, namely, the religion that is founded upon Christ.[47]

The Chapel Service and Decline of Protestant Influence

Even though Christian hegemony was coming to an end by the latter half of the nineteenth century, it did not mean that every vestige of Christianity had been wiped away. After all, during that time, the reformers considered themselves Christians. At least they had to put a good face on it. They had no problem with retaining some Christian influence in the college and university settings, as long as it wasn't at the expense of science. Chapel services were a small way colleges and universities retained some remnant of traditional Christian influence. But even this didn't last much longer.

Compulsory chapel services were still the norm in the 1890s for almost all state universities.[48] At the University of Chicago, students criticized the chapel services for not being religious enough in 1904. The students were right. In general, the chapel services had become watered-down versions of Christianity that emphasized ethical sentiments like "clean living" and upstanding citizenship rather than doctrine. They became a secularized adaptation of conventional religion.[49] This appeal to the ethical dimension of Christianity, rather than doctrine, coincided with the Social Gospel movement and also with the need to be nonsectarian. Simple prayers and songs often replaced sermons altogether to avoid focus on denominational differences.[50]

By the 1920s, chapel services were becoming a thing of the past. Many educators and students wanted to dispense with the mandatory aspect of chapel, because they claimed that it was an insult to religion. They felt that by making chapel services voluntary, rather than mandatory, a more genuine atmosphere of true spirituality would prevail.[51] Of course, this is akin to telling your children that they don't have to go to church on Sunday if they don't want to. You know what the result is going to be: no one is going to go. For example, in 1923 the senior class at Yale voted to abolish mandatory Sunday service and weekday worship. Their rationale was that by making chapel voluntary it would improve the "religious quality" of the services for those who cared to attend, which would then represent a "sincere" gathering.[52] Compulsory chapel ended at Yale in 1926.[53]

The extinguishing of the chapel service followed the same pattern we have seen repeatedly in our study of the marginalization process: accommodation, compromise, and retreat. Robert Benne summarizes the plight of the chapel service and where it is today:

> First the "religious" content of the required period was mixed with more secular presentations. Then chapel attendance was required only for a portion of days during the week or term. Then it became voluntary, and with that was often dislodged from its 'public' position. . . . For many schools such an arrangement has become burdensome to sustain for the small number of attendees, and it has disappeared completely as a weekly event. It may live on as an ornament for important events, but it is no longer part of the collegiate way of life.[54]

While mandatory chapel services had been the norm as late as the 1890s, by 1939 only one-quarter of state universities held even voluntary chapel services.[55] I think it is fair to say that the chapel service to-day—for those who still have it—is not exactly the center of culture for university students.

The decline of the chapel service is one example that by the 1920s, Protestant cultural authority was in "shambles," and not only in higher education. Cultural influences like the social sciences, journalism, and Hollywood had displaced Protestant hegemony by the time of the Great Depression.[56] In academia, student volunteer organizations, like the YMCA, campus chaplains, and religious studies, carried out much of the work that Protestants needed to do in academia.[57] The educators relied more and more on extracurricular activities for nurturing the students' religious needs which pointed out the functional difference between science and religion, and between the intellectual and the devotional.[58]

Many, if not a majority, of the students demonstrated an indifference toward Christianity, and some an outright antipathy toward it. James Bissett Pratt of Williams College, who taught the history of religions, describes in 1923 how the attitude of college young people toward Christianity had changed over the previous few decades. "Their grandfathers believed the Creed; their fathers a little doubted the Creed; they have never read it."[59]

Resurgence During Mid-Twentieth Century

As noted above, the "religious studies" program, at least in some small way, was Protestants' attempt at retaining some sense of Christianity in the academic setting.[60] By the 1920s, this was about all they had left, notwithstanding the extracurricular activities like the YMCA and campus chaplains. Protestant educators intended religious studies to help keep the younger churchgoers "from leaving the faith."[61]

From the start, religious studies had a rather tenuous existence, owing in part to questions surrounding its methodology. Because it was not as professional as other disciplines in the academic setting, religious studies became associated with other pseudo-scientific endeavors like the social sciences and the humanities.[62] For Protestants to retain a place in the academy through the religious studies department, they were forced to acknowledge that they would no longer have the overarching authority they held in the olden times with the classical curriculum. In return, they were still considered experts in their field of biblical studies, theology, ethics, and so forth.[63] Actually, this was nothing new. It was just a continuation of the status quo.

During the 1930s religious studies found more stable footing largely because religion in general was finding a more essential role regarding societal concerns. This is because the First World War raised serious questions about the moral foundations and religious underpinnings of Western civilization.[64] This paralleled the unease of many who thought that the forces of secularization had left religion insufficiently represented in academic curricula. Critics of academia were waking up to the fact that the university had become too secularized, too "this worldly."[65]

Some felt that the university's preoccupation with the intellectual gospel made it responsible, at least in part, for the political and economic threats to liberal democracy because it did not instill the values necessary for a healthy society.[66] Others felt that the displacement of classical curriculum by elective courses was the primary reason for the loss of moral purpose. Some critics had seen as early as a decade previously that higher education had disintegrated into a multitude of disparate parts with no overall philosophy of life.[67] They wondered how different subjects could be taught in the university without any reference to religious or moral presuppositions.[68]

If Western civilization was in a state of moral decay, then science and specialization in the university were hardly going to provide the antidote to the cultural and spiritual crisis that were symptomatic of this moral malaise. To provide one example, the American professoriate prior to World War I became disillusioned, to say the least, at what they saw as the abandonment of the scientific stance by their fellow professors in the German universities. Many American academicians had studied in Germany, and it became particularly distressing to see the German professors defend Germany when, according to the American professors, the German professors were so obviously on the wrong side of the issue. This raised a question: If the universities on both sides of the pond were led by science, which was supposedly objective, then how did they end up on opposite sides of the debate?[69] How could they both claim the moral high ground? Was science really leading the way to objective moral conclusions?

The result of all of this was that after World War II, it was apparent that the notion of inevitable progress led by science was a misplaced assumption. It was clear that applied science could be used for good *or* evil. The invention of the atom bomb provided one such example. The idea that science, without any moral underpinning, could somehow lead to a utopian society seemed naïve in retrospect. This was not lost on those in higher education.

With the fate of Western civilization hanging in the balance after the wars, religious studies found relevance as Protestants and others in academia supported the idea that a Christian worldview could provide the "larger significance" for all the subjects being taught in higher education rather than simply dispensing information *about* those subjects.[70] The result was a surge in the number of religion departments and courses in religion designed to train religious leaders and, at least to some extent, encourage religious faith.[71] Because of the ubiquitous discontent with overspecialization, scientism, and materialistic presuppositions, religious studies moved from a "ragtag discipline" to a position of more academic esteem.[72]

It was during this time that religious studies were grouped with the humanities. Those in academia believed that religious studies, as an ethical concern, could work in conjunction with the humanities to exemplify the moral agenda of the university in modern culture.[73]

Educators at this time did not find fault with religious studies, because this discipline helped professors integrate values, which aided in the understanding of Western civilization and culture. Courses on the Old and New Testaments, church history, systematic theology, Christian ethics, and comparative religions filled the religion departments.[74] As D.G. Hart wrote, "After two world wars, economic depression, and constant fears of atomic weapons, many observers thought the university might very well use a little 'lift' from divine sources."[75]

Reinhold Niebuhr, a professor of applied Christianity at Union Theological Seminary, epitomizes Protestant Christianity's return to the good graces of academia and society when he found himself on the cover of *Time* magazine in 1948, which was the first time ever for a theologian.[76] Niebuhr accomplished this feat because he was able to convey in a palatable way to both academia and the American public the notion of society marred by sin and its consequences. This, of course, was in the historical context of the World Wars and totalitarian regimes. Rejecting the naïve optimism of liberal theologians from whom he got his start, Niebuhr's Christian "realism" brought a sober perspective to the liberals' optimistic view of humanity.

Niebuhr had immense influence on public life during the 1940s and 1950s, which bolstered the legitimacy of religious studies in the university up until the 1960s. People experienced a revival of religious faith, whether expressed in evangelicalism with the emergence of Billy Graham's ministry, for example, or evidenced in the proliferation of mainline Protestant churches. The fact that educators who taught undergraduates could appeal to the uniqueness of Hebrew and Christian Scriptures, which only a couple of decades previously would have invited the charge of sectarianism, is noteworthy.[77]

Thus, after the two World Wars, religious studies found its niche in the academy. Colleges and universities welcomed this area of study as an addition to the scholarly and scientific work already being done in other fields of study. But its acceptance was conditional. As long as religion contributed to the well-being of students and society, then it naturally supported the preservation of democracy and Western civilization, which the academy at that time found beneficial.[78]

Protestant Disenfranchisement after 1965

After 1965, the reasons for Protestant influence in higher education once again came into question. Times were "a changing," as Bob Dylan noted, and the countercultural revolution and the Vietnam War were foisted upon the nation. With these changes, the cultural reasons for promoting Protestant concerns in higher education were simply not there anymore. Piggybacking on the humanities department no longer worked for religious studies programs because many in academic circles questioned the rationale of Protestantism's underpinning of democracy.[79] Once again Christianity became disenfranchised as it had been in the latter half of the nineteenth century. For it to be considered a legitimate academic endeavor like other disciplines, religious studies needed to be more specialized and scientific with its own methods of research, scholarly journals, and professional associations.[80]

In light of this, the failure of the Protestant strategy for promoting a longer term agenda became apparent.[81] Protestant religion had morphed into Civil Religion, thus identifying itself too closely with the well-being of the nation and Western civilization instead of validating its existence through forming its own specialized area of research and systematizing its work during the era of its resurgence.[82] Educators tossed religious studies around, increasingly categorizing it as a social science rather than placing it with the humanities. Fewer instructors with clerical training were being hired. Rather, those with scientific credentials were employed. Even though those in the American Academy of Religion had their own technical language that gave the impression that religious studies was scientific,[83] this did nothing to foster any sense of Protestant orthodoxy once it had lost its footing.

In fact, charges of sectarianism reemerged as the free pass that Protestantism had received after the two World Wars began to wear off. To avoid the accusation that Protestantism held a privileged position, higher education increasingly offered non-Christian religions as courses of study.[84] These courses, along with study of the history of religions, emerged because interest in understanding other cultures became popular.[85] Thus, pluralism was not only accepted but promoted by the university as a normative role for the religion departments.[86] But this led down the slippery slope to what Will Herberg at the time called "ideological secularism."

For example, at the University of Chicago Divinity School in 1966, Langdon Gilkey noted: "The younger men don't even raise the issue of the Virgin Birth or Original Sin. They're discussing the existence of God. And if there's no God, you don't have to argue about any of the other doctrines."[87] Moreover, the "nonsectarianism" of the nineteenth century had morphed into the "nonreligious" of the mid-twentieth century.[88] (Today, God's nonexistence saturates almost all departments in the secular universities.[89])

By the 1970s, religion was recognized in large part as just a multicultural study as the "rhetoric of diversity" began to gain a foothold.[90] This shows that the prevailing mind-set after World War II continued to foster an openness to pluralism. Protestant influence declined because it was considered too exclusive

The same holds true today. D.G. Hart wrote, "Protestants now recognize that the truths of their religion once thought to have universal significance, are simply one patch on the colorful quilt of world religions." He sees this in part as "the triumph of Enlightenment categories in efforts to study religion."[91] Professor Allan Bloom also sees "traces of the Enlightenment's political project." In short, the Bible may be taught only as literature so that it may be rendered "undangerous." Bloom sardonically notes that a professor taking the Bible at its word "might rock the boat and start the religious wars all over again."[92]

That Hart and Bloom trace the marginalization process back to the Enlightenment supports my previous assertion that ideas that have found their way down to us today didn't pop up out of thin air. They started somewhere. This is precisely why we traced the marginalization of Christianity back to the Enlightenment and the Reformation. We will complete this chapter by looking at the contemporary situation of the university in which Christianity no longer plays any role.

Christianity's Disenfranchisement from the University

In addition to noting how the Enlightenment project and liberal theology aided in the marginalization of Christianity in higher education, we can now tie in as well some of the fruit of secularization I mentioned in Chapters five and six.

No one would question that PC pluralism, diversity, and multiculturalism are embedded in the fabric of the university setting today, whether in the teaching staff or as part of the various disciplines. The need for diversity is an unquestioned assumption in the university system today. But rather than true intellectual diversity, what we have is an inordinate number of educators who hold liberal political views. These include, of course, those who are sympathetic to gay, feminist, Marxist, PC multiculturalism, and postmodern values. A Harvard Divinity School graduate maintained that diversity in higher education could be defined as a gathering of as many of the left-minded as possible.[93] In fact, George Will noticed that professors who were officially registered in 2002 for both political parties lined up this way at their respective institutions:

Cornell: 166 liberals, 6 conservatives
Stanford: 151 liberals, 17 conservatives
Colorado: 116 liberals, 5 conservatives
UCLA: 141 liberals, 9 conservatives.[94]

That doesn't look like diversity to me. But it *is* statistically significant. The problem seems to be that while diversity in academia may extend to race, ethnicity, and sexual preference, it does not extend to thought. It follows that conservative belief systems, which include the Christian worldview, are looked upon with supercilious derision because they do not fit the PC liberal bias on our campuses. This PC atmosphere is often implemented through intimidation tactics like speech codes.[95]

Because open-mindedness and lack of conviction is correlated with intellectual sophistication,[96] belief in the Christian God does not sit well on campus because it is too exclusive. Christianity, at best, is just another religion. At worst, liberal progressives hold it in contempt because of its definitive and exclusive truth claims. In short, Christianity is "relativized, trivialized, marginalized."[97]

Many students had faith before they arrived on campus but then lost it through a slow PC erosion process. The default worldviews of naturalism, PC pluralism, and diversity wear away their Christian beliefs until slowly but surely it is "emptied of its contents."[98] Ben Shapiro puts it this way in his book, *Brainwashed*:

> Higher education undermines religion, not because knowledge inherently threatens religion, but because professors wish for religion to be undermined. As role models and teachers for their students, professors openly proclaim their atheism. They discard organized religion as foolishness, except for Islam, which they enshrine. They teach that science and religion must come into conflict, and that when they do, science is assuredly correct. The universities discriminate against religious Christians and Jews; their tolerance extends only to non-Judeo-Christian cultures. . . . God is no longer welcome on campus.[99]

While declarations of faith might be rare on campus, when Christians make them, they are frequently met with opposition.[100] At Yuba

College in California in 2008, a student faced expulsion for distributing Christian literature without having a school permit. The campus police told him that he could be arrested for violating school policy. And at the California College of Alameda, another student was caught in the act of praying. She was interceding for one of her professors who had become ill at Christmastime. Although the ill professor had no problem with the girl praying for her, another professor did. The latter reported her to the administration, which accused her of "disruptive or insulting behavior" and "persistent abuse" of college employees. She also faced possible expulsion for her behavior.[101]

The political bias of the faculty, combined with forced political correctness prompted one observer to suggest that the university somewhat resembles an "indoctrination center."[102] Many are afraid to express their faith in this type of setting. One undergraduate at Yale back in the 1990s, who described himself as a born-again Christian, felt marginalized because of what he described as an assault by the "rationality of the sciences" on Christian doctrine. Therefore, he kept his faith to himself and described his plight as a "ghettoized" Christian. When consulting with the college chaplain over this matter, he learned that the chaplain was sapped of any spiritual vitality and felt that his duty was only to promote a "healthy tolerance" of Christianity.[103] As one Harvard professor put it, "we are committed to nothing" in the university setting.[104] This is a recipe for nihilism if there ever was one.

I have always contended that nihilism will logically lead to moral decadence. If there is no ultimate meaning to life, how can there be morals? If life has no meaning, why would anyone care about morals anyway, even if morality could somehow exist under a nihilistic paradigm? If God is dead and everything is permissible, as Sartre concluded from Dostoyevsky's *The Brothers Karamazov*, then it follows that where the Christian worldview is absent, we should find moral decay. This decay is not only evident in society, but the absence of Christian morality is exactly what we find in higher education as well.

Ben Shapiro provides a plethora of examples of wrongheaded ethical thinking in the university system. I will cite just a few of the more despicable examples from his book, noted above. At the time of this writing, these illustrations were way beyond the pale of what is considered traditional mores. Perhaps fifty years from now they will be mainstream.

Professor Harris Mirkin of the University of Missouri thinks that there needs to be more discussion regarding what he labels "intergenerational sex," which presently is defined as pedophilia. Mirkin acknowledges that Americans today consider intergenerational sex to be evil but points out that it has been permissible (or even obligatory) in other cultures and in history. Professor Bruce Rind of Temple concurs in a study he published for the American Psychological Association in which he concluded that the deleterious effects of a child-victim of pedophilia were "neither pervasive nor typically intense."[105]

Shapiro points out a couple of professors who happen to think that sex with animals (bestiality) is acceptable. Peter Singer of Princeton notes that many times a dog will greet a stranger in its house by grabbing the stranger's leg and rubbing against it. Singer condones the bestiality argument by noting that "not everyone objects to being used by her or his dog in this way, and occasionally mutually satisfying activities may develop."[106]

Marjorie Garber, a professor at Harvard, describes real-life cases of bestiality in a chapter entitled "Sex and the Single Dog" from her book *Dog Love*. She enumerates the "long and honorable history" of animal contacts."[107] I think it's safe to assume that the aforementioned professors will not be holding a Bible study on campus on Sunday evenings. It's not politically correct to teach college students a dangerous thing like the Bible, but it's perfectly acceptable for professors to uphold the merits of bestiality and pedophilia.

Today's students have found some diversions as well. A *Time* magazine article in 2005 reported that the Hamilton College coed streaking team inspired Princeton students to form a similar squad. Apparently Princeton's Nude Olympics was banned six years previously.

And at Brown University, some gay and lesbian students were attempting to create sexual tension-free zones by being allowed to room with members of the opposite sex.[108] I don't think we'll see these kids at the mid-week prayer meeting (if there even is one). Some universities today are even offering bachelor's degrees in LGBT studies and it may not be long before they offer doctorates.

William Kilpatrick notes in *Christianity, Islam, and Atheism* (p.7) that many universities today are attempting to ban Christian student organizations while at the same time accommodating Muslim students by installing footbaths in the washrooms.

I cited these examples to show just how far higher education has divorced itself from the Christian worldview and the morals that underpin it. It's amazing to think that young men could get thrown out of college back in the Founding era just for attending a non-sanctioned church service. And now pedophilia, bestiality, and gay and lesbian "tension-free zones" are advocated by some professors and students alike. With the complete disestablishment of Christianity in higher education, PC attitudes and mores have run amok.

Conclusion and Summary

Higher education today is completely different from what the early Puritans of Harvard and Yale attempted to accomplish at the founding of those two institutions. I think the Puritans would be rolling over in their graves if they could see what has become of the colleges and universities today. The intention of the early founders of these colleges was to equip young men to be the finest Christians possible—men of character—and then to send them into the community to serve the public as ministers and teachers, or in law or medicine.

The faculty of these early institutions took very seriously their obligation not just to teach facts, but to integrate all knowledge into the meaning of life. They cared about the students' souls back then, and it would not have occurred to them to leave the question of life's meaning for the students to answer on their own.[109] The Christian worldview was the centerpiece for the entire curriculum, and everything the student learned was meant to reinforce the truth of Christianity. Thus, at Harvard the ultimate goal was that "Every one shall consider the main End of his life and studies, to know God and Jesus Christ which is Eternal life." This statement is totally anathema in today's university. The professors of today don't believe they have the duty or the right to guide the students in the search for the meaning of life, and they most certainly don't want anything to do with Christianity.

The acceleration of the marginalization process began with the reformers, who imported the German model for education. The concept of *Bildung* aided in the process of dismantling the old classical curriculum in which the Christian worldview was of central importance. *Bildung* elevated specialization to a virtue. With the implementation of other educational concepts, like *Lehrfreiheit* and *Lernfreiheit*, the overall vision of the classical curriculum came apart and with it the totalizing vision of the Christian worldview, which had played such a central role in higher education. Specialization and the PhD program in the emerging universities displaced the classical Christian education, which seemed antiquated and amateurish by comparison.

Many of the reformers embraced liberal Protestantism, which was simply a wishy-washy version of Protestant Christianity. Science, as the new authority, also displaced Christianity during the latter half of the nineteenth century. Therefore, both liberal Protestantism and science combined with the new German model of specialization, marking the beginning of the end of Christianity's central role in higher education.

Furthering Christianity's decline at the turn of the century was the big-money interests. These elites were intent on marginalizing what they called "dogmatic" or "sectarian" Protestantism. They were averse to throwing their money at schools where denominationalism still held sway. Big money and reformers neutered Protestant Christianity and classified this brand of theology under the discipline of "religious studies," which was tossed back and forth between the social sciences and the humanities departments.

During the middle of the twentieth century, religious studies made a comeback as a result of the two World Wars, which had made it apparent that science was not nearly as authoritative as everyone had thought it to be. Moreover, progress based on science was not inevitable. With this in mind, religious studies found itself back in the game. Religious studies brought value and perspective to other subjects and provided an underpinning for Western civilization. But resurgence of this watered-down version of Christianity didn't last long.

The Me generation radicals of the '60s and '70s opposed whatever was left of Christianity in the colleges and universities. PC religious pluralism, multiculturalism, and PC tolerance are ubiquitous forces that have gained the upper hand since the countercultural revolution, and these forces have worked together in an attempt to do away completely with authentic Christianity. The left-leaning bias of professors certainly does nothing but promote disdain for Christianity, which the liberals view as an intolerant religion because of its exclusive truth claims.

The result of all this is that higher education has become devoid of anything resembling the authority and respect the Christian worldview held at the time of the inauguration of schools like Harvard and Yale. In short, Christianity is no longer welcome on campus in any institutional sense. Instead, the fruit of secularization—PC tolerance, PC pluralism, relativism, and autonomy—constitute the PC worldview in higher education today. Unfortunately, this is what higher education is presently instilling in the young people.

Chapter 9

Are Christianity and Science at War?

Let's begin our three chapters on science with a historical review of Christianity's interaction with science. What we call "science" today was not known as science when it first began. During the Middle Ages until the early part of the nineteenth century, science was known as "natural philosophy." In the medieval universities founded between AD 1200 and 1500, natural philosophy was taught at the undergraduate level. Even though natural philosophy and theology maintained separate realms in the medieval university, theology underpinned natural philosophy, just as theology initially underpinned American higher education many centuries later.

Initially, natural philosophy studied phenomena like change and motion, first causes of nature, generation and corruption, and the motion of celestial bodies, among other things. All of these held implications for theology, such as God's creation, the evidence of design in the world, the immortality of the human soul, and so forth. For example, the study of change held implications for the Eucharist. Did the bread and wine actually become the body of Christ? Other questions, such as the causes of things in nature, led to the investigation into the Divine creation of the world.[1] Therefore, the early universities considered natural philosophy a legitimate form of study.[2]

We saw in Chapter three that Thomas Aquinas (1225–1274) was a monumental figure during the Middle Ages. Aquinas synthesized the newfound works of Aristotle (384-322 BC) with Christianity in what is known as Scholasticism. This aided in the emergence of natural philosophy in the thirteenth century.

Aquinas believed there was a limit to what Aristotle and his metaphysic could do to help understand God and the world. Reason could take one only so far and, therefore, it must be subordinate to faith and revelation.[3] The natural sciences should never be an end in and of themselves. They were useful as long as they stayed subordinate to theological purposes. This is referred to as the "handmaiden formula." The handmaiden formula was first employed by a predecessor of Aquinas named Augustine (354–430), who, like Aquinas, was a monumental figure in Christendom. The handmaiden formula was the motivating force behind the study of natural philosophy during the early Middle Ages and beyond.[4] In the handmaiden formula, Aquinas joined together faith (Christianity) and reason (Aristotle) to better understand the world.

Aristotelian natural philosophy tried to understand the *purpose* behind what was being studied. Once the purpose (Form) was understood, then other properties could be deduced from it. Aristotelian natural philosophy did not lend itself to experimentation (as practiced in modern science) because it emphasized the rational purposes of the Forms. The acceptance of Aristotelian rationalism was not universal. The troubling part for some was that the concept of Forms seemed to limit God's creative abilities, as if He were somehow limited by them because they were already inherent in nature.[5]

William of Ockham (1280–1349), whom we also met in Chapter three, rejected the notion that Forms were inherent in nature. For Ockham, the structure of the universe was not rationally necessary, as Aristotle had thought, but was totally contingent upon God's commands, which were imposed outside of nature.[6] Because God's will was the final cause of all things and because His will was arbitrary and thus subject to change, one must give up the teleological prospects of Aristotelian natural philosophy. For Ockham, all claims to scientific knowledge were *contingent* rather than necessary, (contrary to Aristotelianism with its Forms). For the voluntarists, the natural philosopher should no longer look for the *why* of something, but rather *how* something worked, because *why* something existed was subject to God's will and thus changeable. To find out *how* something worked involved testing. This was an early move toward modern science.[7]

There were other considerations revolving around Aristotelian natural philosophy that were troublesome when compared with Christian theology. In Aristotle's world the universe was eternal. This, of course, clashed with the doctrine that God had created the universe. Aristotle believed nature was a closed system of causes that operated deterministically. This posed a problem for those who believed God is providential and can intervene in His creation anytime He desires. Additionally, the Aristotelian position made it difficult to view the soul as something eternal and separate from the body. The extreme rationalism with which Aristotelianism came packaged, if taken to its logical conclusion, collided with biblical revelation as a source of truth and threatened to make "reason" the sole criterion of truth for both philosophy and theology.[8]

Because of these factors, we might expect that the religious authorities of the time would have wanted to stifle this type of thought. In some cases this proved to be true. For example, the University of Paris banned Aristotle's works on the natural sciences in the faculty of Arts in the years 1210 and 1215, although the ban did not extend beyond Paris. This ban was local, not a monolithic pronouncement offered *ex cathedra* for all times and places. Many scholars defended Aristotle's works because of its "extraordinary explanatory power."[9] Besides, a student back then was free to go to another university and study Aristotle's natural philosophy there.

This ban was later rescinded. By 1255 all of Aristotle's works were part of the syllabus for students taking their Bachelor's or Master's degrees at the University of Paris, which was one of the most prestigious universities at that time.[10] The point here is that a diversity of scholarly opinions existed regarding matters of natural philosophy and how Christian theology should accommodate it. It varied from place to place and scholar to scholar.[11]

When I was growing up, we were taught that much of the time between the six and fifteenth centuries was known as the Dark Ages because knowledge was not increasing. The underlying and not so subtle assumption was that the Church held up progress with its backward views. The Galileo affair, which we will look at next, epitomized this. Fortunately, this myth has been largely dispensed with, as recent scholarship has shed new light on the time period we are looking at. In fact, as Michael H. Shank explains, "If the medieval church had intended to discourage or suppress science, it certainly made a colossal mistake in tolerating—to say nothing of supporting—the university."[12]

The Medieval Church actively supported the sixty or so universities that had sprung up in Europe by the year 1500, and roughly 30 percent of the curriculum had to do with the natural world.[13] It is erroneous to believe that the Church was against all the new classical learning that scholars like Aquinas integrated with the Christian worldview.

Francis Bacon (1561–1626) was another important figure not enamored with Aristotelian natural philosophy because of its preconceived notions of how nature worked.[14] He thought that attempting to project human reason onto God's mind was not

153

warranted, and, therefore, he distrusted any *a priori* assumptions about the mind and the world.[15] This foreshadowed Locke's notion of *tabula rasa*, in which the mind is a blank slate at birth and all knowledge must come from the empirical realm. Many refer to Bacon as one of the first modern "scientists" because he shifted the epistemological emphasis from the preconceived rationalism of Aristotle to the experimental *method* of empirical investigation and inductive reasoning.[16]

A theological concern, namely, the Fall of Adam and Eve, motivated Bacon. On the surface, this seems preposterous. How could someone who was in good measure responsible for bringing about the beginning of modern science be concerned with something as theological as the Fall? The answer can be traced back to Augustine's thoughts on the subject.

Augustine believed that one of the consequences of Adam's sin was not only that Adam lapsed morally but that his sin thrust the entire human race into epistemological confusion and ignorance. Subsequently, people had a tendency to confuse error with truth.[17] In addition, Augustine also thought that the corruption of the cosmos meant that the natural world "does not make good on its promises, it is a liar and deceiver."[18] The idea that nature was rather opaque and mysterious for those trying to garner knowledge from it was common among Bacon and his peers.[19]

For Bacon, man's innocence could be restored only through grace. However, man's *dominion* over the planet could be partially restored through his ability to gain knowledge of nature, which had been lost at the Fall. In this way the Fall provided a reason for a more aggressive form of experimental study than had been the case under Aristotelianism.[20] Bacon's motivation was noble in the sense that he wanted to use the nascent science as a tool to overcome the adverse effects of the Fall and alleviate human suffering.[21] Important to note is the fact that attempting to use science to improve the lives of humanity marks the advent of technology.

One of the reasons Bacon is considered the first "scientist" was his desire to limit his quest in the understanding of nature to secondary causes—what we now consider "natural laws." According to Bacon, it would have seemed fruitless to try to discern every instance of God's intervention in nature through miracles when compared with natural laws. Attempting to find miracles at every turn could only add to confusion, and, therefore, Bacon warned against unwarranted influence of religion over natural philosophy. But on the other hand, he cautioned against the new science speculating beyond the bounds of the empirical realm and making overarching metaphysical claims. Bacon advised that one should practice the new scientific method with humility and self-denial, lest it play into one's fallen nature and lead to arrogance and undue ambition.[22]

Unfortunately, Bacon's concerns regarding the interface between his new science and Christianity have been ignored. Bacon never envisioned that his new method in natural philosophy would ever be divorced from Christianity.[23] But this is precisely what has occurred with "methodological naturalism." This is the scientific method used today that, by definition, excludes anything supernatural *a priori*.

The exponential technological advances that are occurring today without any regard to moral or ethical considerations is another example of ignoring Bacon's concern—that Christianity and science should never be divorced. I would argue, for example, that the full-steam-ahead approach involving the genetic manipulation of humans, with a disproportionate consideration of moral concerns in many cases, displays scientific arrogance. This is not the type of humility Bacon championed. It is hard to imagine that rearranging human genes without any theological consideration is what Bacon had in mind when he envisioned his new method as helping humanity recoup what was lost at the Fall. Bacon wanted to ensure that science was free from the erroneous influence of those who may have misinterpreted Scripture and who then attempted to foist those misconceptions into the study of science. But he never intended science to be totally divorced from the Christian worldview.

The Galileo Affair

By the end of the Middle Ages, the search for secondary causes (natural laws) had become more commonplace for Christian scholars. Bacon's contemporary, Galileo Galilei (1564–1642), was an avid promoter of this new philosophy of investigating natural causes. The common folk, on the other hand, were in the habit of assigning miracles to many events where they were not warranted.[24] Natural philosophers wanted to distance themselves from that practice.

Galileo sought true knowledge, known as *scientia*. One arrived at *scientia* by meeting one of two criteria: 1) necessary (logical) truths, or 2) demonstration. *Scientia* was to be contrasted with *opinio*, which was not true knowledge but merely beliefs that resulted from rumination or arguments. Galileo wanted knowledge (*scientia*) that was certain and based on demonstration, not *opinio*, which was based on the approval of the authorities and thus was only probable, not certain.[25] Much of the so-called "knowledge" from the Aristotelian position was really only *opinio*.

Galileo read the universe through the lens of mathematics.[26] This alone provided the type of knowledge Galileo was looking for. He rejected Aristotelian philosophy, with its idealistic metaphysic of Forms, and replaced it with the demonstrable certainty of mathematics. Galileo believed mathematical relations were real and were instilled by the Divine Mind in the creation of the universe. Even though our thoughts fall short of God's thoughts, what we do know mathematically, we know as certainly as God knows, and therein is true knowledge.[27]

Galileo, an interesting and rather obstinate man, seemed to have a somewhat rebellious streak in him. The University of Pisa docked Galileo's pay because he refused to wear the appropriate academic ceremonial dress at all times. Galileo felt that the pretentious dress hid a person's true character and hindered one's walking and working.[28] One of Galileo's contemporaries observed that when he was engaged in a debate, Galileo would make his adversaries look ridiculous by reinforcing their arguments with powerful evidence only to subsequently crush them completely.[29] Galileo's rebellious streak is important to note because it played a part in his interaction with church authorities and colleagues.

Galileo was a contemporary of Johannes Kepler, the Christian astronomer (1571–1630). Kepler was a Lutheran while Galileo was a Roman Catholic. Kepler believed that "God created the cosmos upon the basis of the divinely inspired laws of geometry."[30] Likewise Galileo described his own discoveries using the telescope as "first being illuminated by divine grace."[31] Neither natural philosopher had a problem with giving God the glory for their work. They remained lifelong friends through their correspondence. Both men agreed that mathematics and geometry were an inherent part of the universe. While Kepler was the greatest astronomer of the sixteenth century, Galileo is known as the father of experimental physics.

The invention of the telescope enamored Galileo, so he made one of his own. He discovered that Jupiter had moons that orbited around in what we would describe today as a miniature solar system. The importance of this discovery was that it demonstrated something besides the earth to be the center of various motions in the sky. The other important discovery was sunspots. If the sun revolved around the earth, then why did the sunspots change the angle of their paths on an annual cycle rather than a daily one?[32]

The Aristotelian natural philosophers had accepted the Ptolemaic system in which the earth was the center of the universe where everything revolved around it. But Galileo's discoveries convinced him that the Aristotelian cosmos needed to be rejected in favor of the Copernican system.

The rejection of the Aristotelian system was no small matter, because it had dominated intellectual life in the universities for hundreds of years. Thus it was the academics that had a vested interest in maintaining the Aristotelian worldview more than those in religious circles, the latter of which supported Galileo's findings in many instances.[33] Many Aristotelian scholars refused to look through Galileo's telescope, thinking it must be a trick of some sort. They were not about to repeal centuries of knowledge based on some mysterious gadget. Besides, Galileo was a mathematician, which placed him on the bottom of the pecking order in the university, while the natural philosophers were at the top.[34]

Galileo refused to let the establishment stifle him, so he left the university system and found employment as a court philosopher. He was now able to unleash his polemical assault from a distance through his publications, which his university opponents found sarcastic and insulting. But since they could not beat him in the realm of argument, and they could not suppress him through academic pressure, they resorted to trying to silence him through creating theological trouble. To catch the attention of Church authorities, they claimed that his assertions contradicted the Bible.[35]

In historical context, one cannot underestimate how entrenched the Aristotelian mind-set was during this time. Some churchmen saw the whole Aristotelian cosmology as providing an "overall vision of moral and social life." Any challenges to the Aristotelian framework were thus viewed as dangerous because they might threaten morality itself.[36] Viewed in this way, Galileo's teachings were a serious threat to the status quo.

This whole matter was all the more problematic because the Church had just recommitted itself to Aristotelianism in response to the Protestant Reformers. Moreover, the Reformation made the Church much more sensitive to any perceived theological dangers that could lead ordinary Catholics astray and challenge Church authority.

Galileo always maintained that because God was the Author of the Book of Nature and the Bible, the two of them, if interpreted correctly, should never be in conflict. So far, so good. But the problem, as Galileo saw it, was that God used figurative language in some cases to accommodate the common, uneducated folk. For Galileo, the truths of revelation did not represent the same demonstrative certainty that the new natural philosophy did when describing nature.[37] The reason for this, as he famously stated, is that "The Bible teaches how to go to heaven, not how the heavens go."[38] The conclusion of all this in Galileo's own words: "In disputes about natural phenomena one must begin not with the authority of scriptural passages but with sensory experience and necessary demonstration."[39]

This line of thinking got Galileo in trouble for two reasons. First, it allowed the findings of the new science to stand alone, requiring no appeal to the higher authority of theology.[40] In other words, no longer was natural philosophy the handmaiden of theology. Second, the Council of Trent in 1546 had limited the interpretation of Scripture to only the bishops and councils of the Church. They did this in an attempt to undermine the Protestants' assertions that each person had the right to interpret Scripture without the need for the Church's authority or tradition. The Church at the Council of Trent also moved toward a more literal interpretation of Scripture, which Galileo's accommodationist approach to Scripture contradicted.[41]

In his *Letter to Grand Duchess Christina*, which circulated widely though privately in 1615, Galileo argued that Scripture should be interpreted in consonance with the Copernican theory. This was brought to the attention of the Inquisition, which pointed out that no one was allowed to interpret Scripture contrary to what the Church Fathers agreed upon. Besides, Galileo was not trained as a theologian or a Scripture scholar, so he was not competent to judge in this particular area as far as the authorities were concerned. As a lay member of the Church, he was therefore at risk of violating the sanction regarding the interpretation of Scripture.[42]

This whole situation became especially acute after a papal commission decided that the Copernican cosmology was erroneous and placed this work on the Index of Prohibited Books, although it had escaped that fate for over a half a century. The pope instructed Cardinal Bellarmine to inform Galileo that he was not to embrace, defend, or teach Copernicanism under threat of prison (although there is some doubt among scholars whether Galileo was really threatened with imprisonment).[43] Bellarmine happened to agree with Galileo that if the Copernican position could be proven, then the Church would have to consider reinterpreting Scripture in light of it. But Galileo had not proven it in the formal sense. There was no getting around that. Note that in spite of this formal ban, members of the Jesuit Order taught the Copernican theory as a hypothesis in their colleges during the seventeenth and eighteenth centuries.[44] So we have examples in Bellarmine and the Jesuits that demonstrate that the Church did not stand in unison in attempting to suppress scientific progress.

Galileo met Maffeo Barberini, who was interested in natural philosophy, and the two became friends. In 1623 Barberini became the pope under the title of Urban VIII. The following year the two of them had six meetings in which they discussed the relative merits of the Ptolemaic and the Copernican systems. Galileo wrote *Dialogue Concerning the Two Chief World Systems*, the title having been proposed by Urban VIII himself. The book was to be published with two provisos. The pope wanted to make sure that what Galileo proposed in his discussion was kept at the level of hypothesis and also that he would defer to the Church's authority in theological matters. Galileo seemed to accept these conditions, but as he neared the book's completion, he had problems getting it approved by the Roman licensor.[45]

Galileo sidestepped this problem by having the book approved in Florence. The book got Galileo into trouble for a number of reasons. First, it clearly was not a balanced assessment of the two systems, and, in spite of disclaimers, it was evident that it was meant to support the Copernican system. Second, it was written in Italian rather than Latin, the latter of which was traditional for this type of scholarly work. Galileo did this, of course, to reach the widest audience possible, including the common folk. But this was precisely what the papacy did not want because it reached unsophisticated readers who might be swept away from the faith. This was due to their inability to separate good arguments from bad ones with regard to Galileo's Copernican claims and his unwarranted biblical interpretations. But the most egregious thing Galileo did was to place the pope's arguments throughout the book in the mouth of a character by the name of Simplicio, which meant "simpleton" in Italian. Calling the pope, and supposedly your friend, a simpleton is not going to get you too far.

One can hardly blame the pope for taking action in this matter. He was made to look a fool by his friend.[46] The pope appointed a commission. During the investigation they found a document from

1616 which proved that Galileo was personally served an injunction against holding or teaching Copernicanism. Although other alleged violations were at stake, they were moot in light of Galileo's ignoring the 1616 injunction. That is what ultimately sealed his fate.

Although he probably could have received a lighter sentence, Galileo didn't do himself any favors by enraging Urban VIII, who felt personally betrayed. On top of this, Galileo had a run-in with some of the Jesuits who earlier in his career had treated him as a celebrity. By issuing a harsher sentence, the pope placated some of the more prominent Jesuits whom Galileo had crushed in later debates over sunspots and comets.[47]

Certainly, as we mentioned above, the Catholic Church did not want to give in to the Protestants, many of whom accepted Copernicus's heliocentric worldview. Church authorities felt that opening the door to reinterpreting the cosmos by accepting a sun-centered system might also open the door to reinterpreting Scripture in general, which was already occurring among the Protestant Reformers, much to the Church's dismay. The Church's commitment to the Aristotelian paradigm would not allow for this, and Galileo's ignoring the injunction hindered the Church's mission of trying to maintain its authority and to bring Protestants of the Reformation back into the fold.[48]

At the conclusion of the trial on June 22, 1633, Galileo was forced to read an oath denouncing his teachings on the Copernican system. He was never held in prison, even during the trial, and he was never tortured.[49] He was, however, after some negotiations, confined to house arrest for the remainder of his life. He passed away within a few days of Isaac Newton's birth in 1642.[50]

The Galileo affair is entrenched in popular culture as a classic example of science and Christianity at war, otherwise known as the "warfare thesis" or the "conflict thesis." But as we can see, this is too simplistic a version of what took place, and it ignores the broader context of what really occurred, which was that the new natural philosophers and mathematicians challenged the Aristotelian paradigm. It also ignores the role that Galileo played in exacerbating his own problems by antagonizing the university establishment, the Catholic Church, and the pope.

Many observers now feel that Galileo didn't remain silent because he truly wanted the Catholic Church, the pope, and parishioners to see the truth of the Copernican system.[51] In other words, he was trying to uphold the reputation of Catholic scholarship, and he didn't want outsiders to think that there were no Catholics who understood and appreciated the Copernican system.[52] Thus, Galileo did not intentionally contradict the Church. Rather, he tried to help it maintain its reputation.

As Gary B. Ferngren points out, the irony of the whole matter is that if Copernicus's book had been published either one hundred years earlier or one hundred years later, the entire affair probably would not have happened. But since his book was published in 1543, just as the Reformation was gaining traction and the Counter Reformation was just beginning, all the players were in place by 1616 for the Galileo affair to occur.[53] But the point to remember is that the Church and science were not at war. That is an erroneous myth that has been handed down to us today.

The Mechanistic World

By the late seventeenth century, natural philosophy had transitioned into mechanistic physics. The basic proposal was that nature operated according to regular mechanical principles known as "natural laws" that could be expressed in mathematical terms.[54] Noteworthy is that many Christians supported this worldview and encouraged it along.

René Descartes (1596–1650), whom we met in Chapter three, was not only an advocate of the mechanistic system, he may be credited with the first modern mechanical worldview, which he based on analytical geometry.[55] The reader will recall that Descartes desired knowledge (*scientia*), which he felt could be based only in mathematics if it was to provide certainty, because the senses could not be trusted (the "moving" sun being one example). He wanted to eliminate any unexplained or occult conceptions from his natural philosophy. In fact, he would not allow anyone to know his date of birth because he did not want anyone casting a horoscope for him.[56] He also did away with Aristotle's Forms and their semi-spiritual nature as well. He instead opened up a whole new realm that made room for what later would be called "scientific explanations," which played a foundational role in the formation of modern science.[57]

Descartes maintained that God instituted mathematical laws in the same way that a king ordains laws in his own realm.[58] Descartes was a devout Catholic who received his education at a Jesuit college. Voltaire noted at the time that Descartes was driven from his native France because of his rejection of Aristotelian philosophy held by the Schoolmen in the universities and "the prejudices of popular superstition."[59] Descartes followed Galileo's trial and because of it delayed the publishing of his own book, which supported the Copernican system.[60] For Descartes, all knowledge depended first on knowing that God existed. As he wrote in his *Meditations*, "Man cannot achieve correct knowledge of natural things so long as he does not know God."[61]

By the late seventeenth century, the mechanistic worldview was firmly entrenched. Descartes viewed the universe mechanically because he witnessed sophisticated machinery in his own world such as clocks, pumps, and fountains, which seemed to mimic the way nature operated.[62] The common people picked up on Descartes's uber-obsession with looking at everything as though it was a machine, which included animals. In 1690, for example, one French woman was heard to say, "Please do not bring a dog for Pauline, we want only rational creatures here, and belonging to the sect we belong to we refuse to burden ourselves with these machines."[63] This may seem somewhat comical to us. But Descartes wanted to draw a distinction between matter and spirit. His animal-as-machine contention was meant to demonstrate that humans (as opposed to animals) had souls and that man also had dominion and privilege over nature, which referred back to the book of Genesis.[64]

Marin Mersenne (1588–1648) wanted to defend the Catholic priesthood from the accusations of Protestants who denied the miracles that Catholics claimed. Moreover, Protestants accused Catholics of using so-called miracles as a vehicle to convert people. Mersenne believed shoring up the difference between the natural order and the genuinely miraculous would be doing his Church a service. Showing how God normally chose to act through secondary causes in nature could make identifying a genuine miracle easier. Mersenne felt that the regular ordering of natural laws was an expression of the Divine Will.[65]

Robert Boyle (1627–1691), an extremely devout Protestant, once stated that he did not take an ordination because he did not want to be accused of bias when he spoke about God's hand in nature.[66] He saw the practice of natural philosophy as an act of worship and used it to combat what he saw as pagan notions that attributed semi-divine powers to nature and thus detracted from Divine purpose in the world.[67]

He picked up on the clockwork metaphor, like Descartes. He maintained that the knowledge found by natural philosophy supported Christian revelation. But whereas Descartes warned against trying to discern God's design in nature, Boyle rejected this by pointing out that the eye, for example, was a wonderful machination contrived by God with the obvious purpose that it allowed a person sight.[68] Boyle argued that empirical/natural philosophy was an ally of religion, even though the two were separated by different methodologies.[69] Thus he held a complementary view between the new science and Christianity.

Of course the monumental figure during the culmination of the scientific revolution was Isaac Newton (1642–1727). Like his predecessors, Newton rejected the Aristotelian worldview. In Newton's case this rejection was because Aristotle, and much of antiquity, drew such a fine distinction between the *heavens* and the *earth*. Aristotelianism perceived the heavens as immutable and perfect, in which the stars and moons and planets revolved in eternal circles around the earth. The earth, on the other hand, was supposedly the locus of change and corruption.

But in his *Principia*, Newton argued that the earth and the heavens were not different realms but part of the same realm. He believed that the entire universe was governed by the same natural laws of gravity and motion. He later developed the calculus that demonstrated mathematically the phenomena he was observing.[70] He desired to explain all of natural phenomena in terms of mathematical mechanics.[71]

Newton saw, in the way the universe worked, evidence for a Being outside of the natural order, which was both living and intelligent. By deducing causes from effects, it was possible to arrive at the first cause: God. Newton maintained that the business of a natural philosopher should be to inquire as to the attributes of God and His relationship to His world.[72]

Newton's theology could never be divorced from his natural philosophy. He saw in the law of gravity a God who had chosen to rule the world not by overbearing acts of power but through secondary causes—the laws of nature. Newton saw more evidence of God's handiwork in the design of the eye with all of its sophistication, and he asked rhetorically whether chance could have designed such a thing.[73] He was also acutely concerned with God's activity in human history and did an extraordinary amount of research and wrote voluminous works showing that biblical prophecies had been fulfilled.[74]

In spite of his doctrinal differences with the Anglican Church, he took his theology seriously. Newton's doctrinal beliefs were wide of the mark compared with orthodox Christian theology. He did not believe that Jesus was the second person of the Trinity who had come to earth in the Incarnation. Rather, Newton held to some form of Arianism, which meant that as the earthly Christ, Jesus was a created being and always subordinate to God. He did not believe in the Trinity, which he considered an abomination. This was problematic for him because to hold the Lucasian chair at Cambridge, orthodoxy was required and thus ordination for him was impossible. Nevertheless, some strings were pulled for Newton. The rules were changed so that a dispensation could be given to whoever held the Lucasian chair, thus dispensing with the requirement for ordination.

Newton understood the tenuous situation he was in going forward, and other than revealing his theological position to some of his close followers, it appears that he carefully guarded his heretical ideas. Denying the Trinity was not a safe position to hold in late seventeenth century England, as all public servants were required to believe in this doctrine.[75] He also maintained repugnance for the Catholic Church in which, interestingly, he identified the 1,260 year reign of Antichrist with the years of papal dominion in his interpretation of Revelation 12:6.[76]

Much of Newton's motivation for studying biblical prophecy was to defend against the mechanistic worldview of his day as epitomized in Deism, which held that God had wound up the universe like a clock and then allowed it to run on its own while He wandered off to some other part of the universe. Newton rejected Deism and its clockwork universe, which he believed would lead to materialism. Why? Because Newton believed that the deistic mentality would render God superfluous once the universe was set into motion. It turns out that he was right. Newton correctly surmised that his successors would view the mechanistic worldview as self-complete and thus autonomous.[77] Methodological naturalism, which is how science is practiced today, is the result of science divorced from God. Newton predicted this correctly.

Against the Deists, the fulfillment of biblical prophecies, which Newton worked so hard on, were meant to demonstrate that God was still active in the world. Unfortunately, to make Newton more palatable to the Enlightenment frame of mind, Voltaire emptied Newton's work of its religious content. This, combined with Newton keeping his theological views close to the vest, gives us the picture of Newton that has been handed down to us today as a great natural philosopher but totally devoid of religious and apologetic concerns (which subsequent historians found embarrassing in a person of Newton's stature).[78] It is a well-known fact today that Newton spent an extraordinary amount of time studying biblical prophecy.

As noted above, Newton's fear that God would be dispensed with was realized. Enlightenment rationalism made reason the be-all and end-all for epistemological concerns. The new mathematics, which was viewed as "the crown of human reason," provided certainty for the new scientific knowledge.[79] As the world came to be regarded as a machine, the need for God's providence was significantly diminished to the point that it was not needed at all—just as Newton predicted. Alister McGrath notes that one of the ironies of the religious thought of the eighteenth century is the way Newton's law-like universe "was initially interpreted as supportive of the Christian understanding of God, yet within a generation was seen as rendering such a concept unnecessary." Elsewhere McGrath states: "By the end of the eighteenth century, it seemed to many that Newton's system actually led to atheism or agnosticism, rather than to faith."[80]

Revisiting Hume and Kant

David Hume (1711–1776), whom we met in Chapter three, was an Empiricist and therefore he believed that knowledge could be apprehended only in the empirical realm of experience. This means that a hypothesis (the particular) is made from information collected from data (the general). Science is based on this inductive method. However, Hume came to realize that one could not prove anything from the inductive method with certainty.

His thinking went like this: if every time over a number of occurrences I observe that a swan is white, and I observe this hundreds of times without exception, then it seems safe to conclude that all swans are white. But Hume realized that this inductive method was faulty. What happened if you suddenly observed a black swan? And even if you didn't, how could you prove that in every single instance in the universe all swans are white? You can't. Therefore the inductive method can lead to knowledge that is only tentative or probable, not certain. Because we cannot make an infinite number of observations, we can never prove anything absolutely.

In addition, the inductive method can lead to faulty inferences. For example, just because events often seem correlated does not necessarily mean that one event is the *cause* of the other. Just because A is correlated with B does not mean that A necessarily *caused* B. Trying to prove universal truths that were apprehended from a finite number of observations is a non-logical leap of faith. For Hume, deriving concepts like natural laws or causal relations from sense data is erroneous. The inductive method can tell us only about human *expectations* about the data, not true conclusions about the way the real world works.[81]

On top of this, the inductive method at its core is not scientific, because one cannot conclude that the inductive method works on the basis of science. Rather, doing science is a leap of faith because the scientist takes it on *faith* that the observable world is rational and law-like and that science is therefore possible. Moreover, *that* conclusion (the universe is rational and law-like) cannot be drawn *from* science; rather, it is the starting point *of* science, otherwise the scientific enterprise would not get off the ground. It is circular logic to claim that the inductive method (science) is based on the findings in the empirical realm (science). As Bryan Magee observes, "That the whole of science, of all things, should rest on foundations whose validity it is impossible to demonstrate has been found uniquely embarrassing."[82]

Hume attacked Christianity as well. He did not believe in miracles (though he never tried to disprove them). He argued that belief in miracles, as well as many other beliefs, was based on habit, instinct, and custom. As far as "causes" were concerned, Hume did not believe that ascribing infinite characteristics such as omnipotence, omniscience, or Divinity to a supposed Uncaused Cause of the universe was justified. Moreover, he did not think it was correct to assign infinite powers to the cause of the universe, which itself was finite.

Hume also believed that Christians gave God an inordinate amount of credit for the beneficial things of nature. But why then didn't they assign blame to God for the pain and evil in the world as well? Generally speaking, Hume's problem with natural philosophers was that they assumed the existence of the Divine when they claimed to be proving it.[83] Just as science can't be proved by doing science, Hume maintained that doing natural philosophy deals with the finite, and one cannot draw conclusions about the infinite from the finite. Hume was a forerunner of those philosophers and theologians who divorced faith and knowledge.[84]

Immanuel Kant (1724–1804), whom we also met, attempted to answer the charges that Hume had brought against science and Christianity. Newton's accomplishments of discovering natural laws and employing mathematics to demonstrate those laws impressed Kant. But it seemed equally clear to Kant that Hume's criticisms concerning science held merit as well. Kant's project involved trying to come to terms with what appeared to be intelligible in nature, like Newton's laws, when there was no way to prove them (Hume).

Let's review what we learned back in Chapter three. Kant said that the world of nature appears intelligible to us because our minds impose order on nature. Moreover, the mind's mental grid imposes organization on the sense data it perceives. This makes it *appear* to us as if there are natural laws when, in fact, there is no way of knowing if those laws are really inherent *in* nature itself. It may simply be our minds ordering the world for us. For Kant, the world of perception—the world where it *appears* there are natural laws—is the realm of *phenomena*. The world as it really exists is the *noumena*, where no true knowledge can obtained because it exists independently of our experience. In short, how the world appears to us is different from how it exists independently of our experience of it. Thus Kant started his own Copernican Revolution, because man's mind was placed in the center of the universe and "created" the world that it perceived. God was no longer the Lawgiver of the universe as per Newton. Rather, after Kant, there could be no genuine knowledge of God because He exists in the noumenal realm, which we can know nothing about.

Part of Kant's strategy was to avoid the implications of the Newtonian worldview in which everything was part of the universal machine. A cosmos that ran like a machine would not allow for human freedom. If humans were material beings and thus part of the deterministic laws of the universe, then humans could not have the ability to exercise their will or make moral choices. So Kant proposed that there must be a spiritual or "transcendental" realm (the noumenon) where morality existed, which obviously couldn't be proved from the scientific "phenomenal" realm. God existed in this noumenal realm. Morality and God's existence could never be proven, but it was perfectly fine in Kant's view to make room for faith in these things.

The problem with this move is that it divorced science and faith. Science would subsequently deal in the phenomenal realm—the realm of sense experience of how things appear to us. God, however, does not exist in the phenomenal realm of everyday experience. Rather, Kant believed God exists in the noumenal realm, which is out of bounds for science. This leads to the logical conclusion that we can have no true knowledge of God's existence.

This compartmentalization of science and Christianity is exactly what we see today. Scientists say there is no proof of God's existence. When asked what would constitute proof, scientists claim that no criteria is available for proving God's existence, because God, if He exists, does not reside in the realm of nature where we can find Him. So God, in essence, is defined out of existence by most scientists today. This can be traced directly back to Kant, who divorced faith and knowledge. Kant may have thought he was performing a service for Christianity by placing God in the noumenal realm where the Enlightenment skeptics couldn't get at Him, but the results over the long haul have been disastrous for the view that science and Christianity are complementary. It would take only another hundred years for the handmaiden formula to completely breakdown.

Although Hume and Kant caused serious damage to the relationship between science and Christianity, the assumption (under the auspices of Common Sense Realism) that the truths found in God's Book of Nature confirmed what was found in the Bible still held for a while. Thus, in Britain and the American universities, the design argument and the handmaiden formula still held sway until the middle of the nineteenth century, notwithstanding the charges of Hume.[85] However, by the end of the nineteenth century, the relationship between science and Christianity in many respects rested on tenuous grounds. Moreover, if Hume and Kant rolled the grenades in, then Darwinism rolled in with the tanks. It was post-Darwin that the real conflict between science and Christianity evolved.

With this in mind, let's take a look at Darwinism and see the effect it had on science and Christianity. We will delay summarizing what we learned so far until the end of Chapter ten. For now, suffice it to say that up until the late nineteenth century, no war existed between science and Christianity.

Chapter 10

Darwinism, Evolution, and How Science Works

As I have stated repeatedly, ideas don't just pop out of thin air. There is a history behind them, a *sitz im leben* in which we can discern the historical context behind the ideas. Darwinism is no exception. Some scientists who preceded Charles Darwin (1809–1882) laid the groundwork for his work *On the Origin of Species* (1859). Let's take a look at a few of them.

Precursors to Darwin's Theory

Charles Lyell (1797–1875) is known as the father of modern geology for his work *Principles of Geology* (1830). The main argument he put forth in his multivolume work is that "the present is the key to the past," which James Hutton, who preceded Lyell, labeled "uniformitarianism."[1] Lyell posited that minute changes occurred over very long periods of time in the geological record. Furthermore, the forces that can be observed today were likewise present in the enormous expanse of time in the past, and, therefore, what we can perceive today should be our guide in understanding the past. Lyell believed that if geology was to be truly scientific, it needed to disengage itself from biblical teachings and teleology.[2] Lyell put it this way in a letter to a friend:

> I conceived the idea five or six years ago, that if ever the Mosaic chronology could be set down without giving offence, it would be in an historic sketch. . . . If we don't irritate, which I fear that we may . . . we shall carry all with us. If you don't triumph over them, but compliment the liberality and candour of the present age, the bishops and enlightened saints will join us in despising both the ancient and modern physico-theologians.[3]

A couple things are worth noting here. First, uniformitarianism flew in the face of the Genesis account. A literal interpretation of Scripture supported "catastrophism," which meant that there was not a uniform set of causes that flowed from the past to the present, Noah's flood being the prime example. Second, Lyell's historical geology undermined biblical chronology, because if uniformitarianism is true, then the earth was much older than the human history recorded in Genesis.[4]

None of this fazed Lyell, who, as Cornelius Hunter points out, had "faith" that uniformitarianism is true, because uniformitarianism was not a conclusion but a presupposition without which science could not proceed.[5] Lyell stated: "The philosopher at last becomes convinced of the undeviating uniformity of secondary causes, and *guided by his faith in this principle* he determines the probability of accounts transmitted to him of former occurrences."[6] (Emphasis mine.) As we saw in the previous paragraph, Lyell wanted to use his faith in uniformitarianism to undermine Christians' belief in the Bible.

Darwin applied Lyell's principle to biology. The small changes in species that could be observed in the present could be extrapolated to conclude that large changes could occur over longer periods of time.[7] This became part of Darwin's theory, known as "descent with modification," and explains how present species evolved from earlier species. Today, when we refer to "evolution," we are really referring to *macro*evolution in which large changes take place as one species evolves into another. This is to be contrasted with *micro*evolution in which minor adaptations occur within the *same* species. As Daniel Dennett points out, if Darwin hadn't come up with a mechanism to explain how evolution occurred, he might not have had the motivation to bring together all the evidence that it really took place.[8] So how did Darwin come up with a mechanism in nature that would explain the modification of species? He imported important components from Thomas Malthus and Herbert Spencer.

Thomas Malthus (1766–1834) published a work in 1798 entitled *An Essay on the Principle of Population.* Malthus was concerned with the number of displaced people and paupers of his time. He saw this as a result of the advances of industrialization and the severe famines that were taking place. He calculated that the rate of population growth would overrun the available resources needed for survival. He proposed that to keep the population in balance with the food supply, nature would eliminate the poor and inept because they were not as fit as their contemporaries. Therefore, in the struggle for survival, the strong would survive and the weak would perish.[9]

In the struggle for survival, nature would favor those species or organisms more fit or adaptable to their environments and those that survived long enough to pass on their adaptive characteristics to their offspring. Those not fit for survival would die before passing on their traits. Herbert Spencer (1820–1903) called this the "survival of the fittest." Darwin picked up on this idea, and now he had the mechanism nature used to "select" those species that would survive and thrive, which he labeled "natural selection." By the 1870s, most scientists and educated people had embraced some form of evolution.[10]

Other historical factors going on at the time appealed to Darwin's theory. In his book *Algeny*, Jeremy Rifkin makes a compelling case for why Darwinism came to be accepted at that time: Darwin's life coincided with the same span of time that marked the Industrial Revolution. In essence, Darwin transferred the mechanical metaphor of the universe to the realm of biology.[11]

As we saw in the previous chapter, one of Newton's concerns was that the mechanical model would lead to the universe being viewed as running on its own with no need for God. His fear was realized during the Enlightenment. We saw how out of control the mechanistic model got when even animals were thought of as machines. Rifkin argues that the mechanical model led to a total "desacralization of all forms of life during the ensuing Industrial Age."[12]

With this in mind, it seemed natural to Darwin that living organisms could be viewed as machines as well. The traditional view had been that God had created each species intact as a special unit. Each species fit a mold that God had designed it for and could not escape from. But Darwin, picking up on the mechanistic model, began to view living things as lifeless, inanimate parts that nature could arrange or assemble in any number of ways. A divine Craftsman who had a preconceived design in mind had not created plants and animals; instead, nature had assembled them like a machine that is put together piece by piece.[13]

People embraced Darwin's theory because it revealed in nature what people saw around them in everyday life in factories where the Industrial Revolution was taking place. As Rifkin points out, it seems more than coincidental that wherever industrial capitalism sprang up so did evolutionary theory.[14]

Many others have noticed the same thing. Oswald Spengler, a noted historian, posited that Darwin's theory was simply "the application of economics to biology."[15] Bertrand Russell pointed out that "Darwin's theory was essentially an extension to the animal and vegetable world of laissez-faire economics, and was suggested by Malthus's theory of population."[16] Karl Marx claimed that Darwinism served as "a basis in natural science for the class struggle in history." Marx was so thrilled with the implications of evolution for socialism that he wanted to dedicate *Das Kapital* to him, though Darwin declined.[17] Marx's comrade Engels called Darwin's teaching a "conjurer's trick" that was a combination of Hobbes's doctrine, bourgeois economic doctrine of competition, and Malthus's theory of population that was transferred from society to nature and then back to history. As Rifkin points out, this coincidence with the Industrial Revolution should have been enough to discredit Darwin's theory. It didn't because, in Rifkin's words, it "provided the best cosmological defense of industrialism available."[18]

Keeping in mind that there was mass unemployment, hostility, hunger, and despair in England where Darwin formed his theory, Rifkin summarizes his views:

> Darwin constructed a theory of nature that, in its every particular, reinforced the operating assumptions of the industrial order. In so doing, he provided something much more valuable than a mere theory of nature. Darwin gave industrial man and woman the assurance they needed to prevail against any nagging doubts they might have regarding the correctness of their behavior. His theory confirmed what they so anxiously wanted to believe: that the way they were organizing their existence was indeed "harmonious" with the natural order of things. Darwin's cosmology sanctioned an entire age of history. Convinced that their own behavior was in consort with the workings of nature, industrial man and woman were armed with the ultimate justification they needed to continue their relentless exploitation of the environment and their fellow human beings without ever having to stop for even a moment to reflect on the consequences of their actions.[19]

Darwin's Theodicy

It is important to mention some other factors in the life of Charles Darwin that many historians of science argue also played a part in the development of his theory. Most people are not aware that Darwin started out as a Bible believer, who at one point in his life wanted to become a country clergyman. His wife, Emma, was a devout believer and his father supported Darwin's decision to join the clergy.

Remember, natural theology, where God's Providence could be evidenced in the Book of Nature, was very much a part of science in the early part of the nineteenth century. William Paley's (1743–1805) watchmaker design argument, which was a part of the natural theology circulating at the time, immensely impressed Darwin. Paley's argument was basically that if you stumbled upon a watch, you wouldn't assume it was a part of nature, but rather that it was designed, and thus you could infer a designer of the watch. While initially Darwin bought Paley's argument, later in his life he came to reject it, along with Christianity. What caused this shift in attitude and how might it have affected his theory of evolution?

While Paley's argument from design accounted for God's beneficence in nature, Darwin could not reconcile this with the cruelty he saw as well. Darwin thought it was incongruous that a good and omnipotent God would design things like ants that make slaves, or parasites that torture their hosts, or a cat that plays with mice.[20]

But it went well beyond this. While the death of his father took a major toll on him, the death of his favorite daughter, Annie, who was only ten years old, proved to be too much. The doctrine of eternal punishment was especially troublesome for Darwin, who stated in his *Autobiography* that he gradually came to disbelieve Christianity, and he couldn't see how anyone would wish it to be true, because "the text seems to show that the men who do not believe, and this would include my Father, Brother and almost all my best friends, will be everlastingly punished. And this is a damnable doctrine."[21] In short, Darwin became an undogmatic atheist whose beliefs, in his own words, were a "simple muddle" and his "judgement often fluctuates."[22] By his own admission, Darwin gave up on Christianity when was he was forty years old, and yet, to spare the feelings of believers in his family, especially his wife, Darwin refused to speak against Christianity.[23]

Clearly, Darwin could not reconcile himself to all the suffering he saw in the world. The design argument, which previously had seemed so convincing to him, lost its weight in his mind. Instead, natural selection provided a theodicy for him, which, in essence, was a way for God to be separated from all the evil and suffering in the world.

Darwin employed the mechanistic metaphor of the universe, popularized in the previous century, so that God was seen as operating through secondary causes. Thus, evil and suffering existed because of natural causes, not directly because of God. In Darwin's own words: "The very old argument from the existence of suffering against the existence of an intelligent First Cause seems to me a strong one, and the abundant presence of suffering agrees well with the view that all organic beings have been developed through variation and natural selection."[24] Cornelius G. Hunter sums up Darwin's thoughts by stating that God "had to be distanced from the apparent failings of his creation."[25] But separating God from His creation meant that it was only a matter of time before God could be dispensed with altogether.

I think Darwin's theory was a watershed moment in the history of science because, although unintentional, it did indeed distance God from His creation. Before Darwin, natural theology allowed God in the equation as the Author of the Book of Nature. The universe was an open system under this way of thinking. God had designed the universe with a purpose. But Darwinism implied that nature was purposeless and run by secondary causes, because God, like the clockwork Deist, had no immediate or direct impact on nature any longer.

Christians at the time did not see this monumental metaphysical shift taking place. So they followed the pattern I have posited as how marginalization occurs. They *accommodated* Darwinism. Then they *retreated* (they got their noses bloodied in the Scopes Monkey Trial). Moreover, in the latter half of the nineteenth century Christians simply did not see that a naturalistic worldview (atheism) was the logical result of distancing God from nature.[26] Today, science has no place for God at all.

Continuing this line of thought then, many scientists, evolutionists, and Christians today think that the war between Christians and evolutionists accelerated right after Darwin published his *On the Origin of Species*. But they are wrong. No warfare was going on between evolution and Christianity in the latter half of the nineteenth century. We already saw in Chapter seven, for example, how the universities increasingly accepted science as the new authority in many ways. Most people, however, are unaware of the fact that Protestantism also accommodated various forms of Darwinism during the latter half of that century.

In fact, David N. Livingstone's *Darwin's Forgotten Defenders* shows how many evangelicals incorporated variations of Darwin's theory of evolution into their worldviews.[27] B.B. Warfield, a famous Princeton theologian, and James McCosh, the president of Princeton who arrived in 1868, were, for example, both self-admitted Darwinians. One of the staunchest advocates of Darwinism was the evangelical Asa Gray, a Harvard botanist, who was impressed with the progress of the physical sciences during his time. He stated: "The business of science is with the course of Nature, not with interruptions of it, which must rest on their own special evidence."[28] One can see the clear move toward naturalism in science here.

American geologist William North Rice, who was a Methodist and a Darwinist, also confirmed naturalism: "It is the aim of science to narrow the domain of the supernatural by bringing all phenomena within the scope of natural laws and secondary causes."[29] Thus, not only were Protestants embracing Darwinism, but they allowed science, aided by the new Darwinian worldview, to shift toward a scientific naturalism, which had no need of God like the former natural theology did.

One notable exception in the Protestant camp was Charles Hodge, who wrote a famous book entitled *What Is Darwinism?* (1873). His conclusion was that Darwinism is atheism, but not for the reason one might think. Hodge believed in evolution, but he made a distinction between evolution and Darwinism. Hodge rejected Darwinism because it denied teleology. That is, Hodge took issue with the rejection of providential design, which Darwin had replaced with natural selection. If Darwin would leave no room for God, then, strictly speaking, Darwinism was atheism. Hodge had no problem accepting the notion that a plant or animal evolved from earlier forms as long as God guided the designing process.[30]

Asa Gray, although accepting evolutionary theory, had the same problem as Hodge. These men did not want to give up on the watchmaker design paradigm that had been so much a part of natural theology earlier in the century. But Providential design clashed with natural selection, which was supposedly a blind, purposeless process. Darwin confided to Gray that it was not his intention to write atheistically, although he admitted that he did not see the evidence of design that Gray did.[31] Darwin confessed later in his life, however, that he lamented leaving the door open for readers of *Origin* to believe that a Creator was behind evolution. In a private correspondence to botanist J.D. Hooker, Darwin said that he regretted having "truckled" to public opinion by using the term *creation* in the second edition of *Origin*, when what he really meant was "appeared by some wholly unknown process."[32]

Let's take a step back for a moment and point out a couple of things. First, for the most part, no warfare was going on at that time, with battle lines drawn, between Darwinism and Christianity. Most Christians and theists attempted to incorporate some type of evolutionary theory into their belief systems. Darwin seemed to go out of his way not to offend Christian sensibilities at that time, so much so that he compromised what he really wanted to convey regarding his own theory, as we just noted. This leads to the second point. Darwin's reticence concerning offending average readers, who considered themselves Christians, means that Christianity still retained its cultural authority in England at that time, and we know it did in America as well.

Of course, the thesis of this book is that Christianity has lost its cultural authority over time. Fast-forward to the present: The common assumption today is that the Christian worldview and science, as generally viewed by scientists and those in lay society, have absolutely nothing in common. Most scientists want it that way. Because of how the media frames things in magazine articles and other news outlets, the public has the impression that science and Christianity are often at war and that the Christian worldview should stay out of science's business. As we have shown above, this has not been the case for much of science's history, nor was it the case right after *Origin* came out.

Though the accommodation process may be laid at the feet of Christians and theists, a small group of non-Christians near the end of the nineteenth century did, in fact, represent the warfare thesis in that they were *intent* on extricating science from the clutches of the Christian worldview. Although men like Darwin were content with trying to remove science from supernatural influence while leaving religion intact, antireligious men, such as the zoologist T.H. Huxley and physicist John Tyndall, led a new charge of philosophers and scientists who wanted to eradicate the authority of religion altogether. Their goal was not only to separate science from religion (Huxley labeled this project "scientific naturalism") but to use science as a weapon to secularize society.[33]

John William Draper's *History of the Conflict Between Religion and Science* (1874) and Andrew Dickson White's *History of the Warfare of Science with Theology in Christendom* (1896) certainly helped bolster the idea that Christianity and science were at war, although to be fair, White's contention was not that religion and science were at war, only *theology* and science were. It didn't matter. In the public's mind, both books solidified the warfare view.

By the early part of the twentieth century it was a commonly accepted principle that for science to be truly scientific, it must ban any considerations that involved religion. Even scientists who were fervent Christians dared not appeal to the supernatural realm when practicing science. Moreover, science was becoming the authority in American culture by the turn of the century.

Darwin helped naturalism become the *sine qua non* for the scientific endeavor. Materialistic explanations for humanity's origin and culture had become ubiquitous. In 1916 only 17 percent of well-known American biologists believed in God. By 1919, one observer claimed that science was necessarily materialistic and asserted that "we are all materialists now."[34]

Blaise Pascal (1623–1662) predicted that those who attempted to find God in nature apart from Christ would end up in atheism or Deism.[35] This proved to be true for many scientists after the turn of the nineteenth century. Darwin's mechanism of natural selection inflicted severe damage to the theistic design argument that had been such a part of natural theology. Science had come a long way from being the handmaiden of theology. After Darwin, naturalistic explanations were the only ones considered worthy of acceptance. As John G. West argues, "Darwin helped transform materialism from a fantastic tale told by a few thinkers on the fringe of society to a hallowed scientific principle enshrined at the heart of modern science."[36]

Evolution Today: A Scientific Theory or a Worldview?

I would argue that the theory of evolution has become much more than a scientific theory in our society today. It has become a fact. One can't get five or six pages into a book (even a fiction book) or more than a few paragraphs into a magazine article without evolution being mentioned as a presupposition. The evolutionary worldview has replaced the Christian worldview in many ways.

While God and the creation account, along with the Ten Commandments, have been banished from our public schools, evolution is allowed to be taught under the umbrella of science. The biblical account of creation is not allowed to be taught alongside evolution because the biblical account of creation is not considered a "fact" but "religion," and it is not fair to force Christianity on the young folks. Evolution is considered "science" and thus "neutral." Therefore it is allowed to be taught as a scientific theory, assuming that teachers present it fairly. John G. West summarizes this: "The contemporary debate over evolution is the largely unargued presumption that the critics of evolution must be motivated by religion, whereas defenders of evolution are supposedly the disinterested pursuers of truth."[37]

It is clear, especially in the classroom, that the Christian worldview has been marginalized while evolutionary theory is allowed to stand. We saw in the higher education chapters how the Christian worldview slowly receded in the universities as science became authoritative. We can see now how this has filtered down through the years to the public school classroom, as well as society in general.

Just questioning or, God forbid, doubting evolution in polite conversation is enough to earn one looks of scorn. *You don't believe in evolution? Oh, I get it, you are one of those ignorant conservative-type Christians who don't believe in science.* Bring up Adam and Eve as being specially created by God and thus an alternative to inorganic origins of life and you will be given up for lost, completely ignorant and uneducated. It has been my experience that the more education one has, the more likely the evolutionary worldview is viewed as a "given." This may be because evolution is presupposed at all levels of schooling; thus, the further one is educated, the more exposure to the evolutionary worldview one receives.

Inorganic origins, as fantastically implausible as it is, seems more scientific than believing God created Adam and Eve, which seems to modern ears a simple fairy tale. Given a choice between believing that God, or instead, matter plus time plus chance, created the first two human beings, I think the average educated person today dismisses the biblical account although he or she probably does not quite accept inorganic origins either. (I think in the future, *panspermia*—the notion that extraterrestrials seeded our planet will gain widespread acceptability.)

Many have accepted theistic evolution as a middle ground between the two positions. From that vantage point, God set in motion natural selection or perhaps guided the evolutionary process in some way. From my perspective this is simply more accommodation. In the future I think theistic evolution will give way as well. As each generation passes, an increasing percentage of people will accept naturalistic evolution and dispense with the Creator completely. This is how the marginalization process has taken place in other areas we have already looked at.

At this point a critic may argue that evolution technically does not address origins of life issues. Rather, it addresses only the theory that life as we know it emerged from a common ancestor that evolved over long periods of time through natural selection and serendipitous genetic mutation. Thus the question of inorganic origins, and God's part in evolution, or Adam and Eve for that matter, is moot. But this is not true. As chemist Henry H. Bauer (non-Christian) notes: "Context indicates that when evolution is asserted to be a fact, not a theory, the view actually being pushed includes that of common origin, *ultimate inorganic ancestry*, and modification through nonpurposive mechanisms: a set of beliefs that goes far beyond the mountain of fact that is actually there."[38] (Emphasis mine.)

Moreover, evolution, as understood today, has become much more than a scientific theory. It has become an entire worldview with something to say about origins, man, morality, and purpose. Because it has overgrown the discipline of science and become a worldview, the theory of evolution often contradicts what the Christian worldview has to say about many of the same things; therefore, from my perspective, the two are in genuine conflict.

Ex-Christian and prolific evolutionary advocate Michael Ruse, who testified in court in 1982 against a creationist statute, admits as much where he is cited by Nancy Murphy: "Evolution came into being as a kind of secular ideology, an explicit substitute for Christianity." And elsewhere: "Evolution is a religion. This was true of evolution in the beginning, and it is true of evolution still today."[39]

That is quite a statement by a noted evolutionist. Perhaps many in the evolutionary camp would not agree with Ruse's statement. But I think there is a lot of truth in it, which is troubling in light of the fact that evolution has gone well beyond the bounds of science and holds a massive amount of authority in our culture. We have already shown that Darwin, at least in no small measure, had a theodicy in mind when he constructed his theory. But a theodicy is not science. It is a philosophical defense of God against the problem of evil. This, combined with what we demonstrated about evolution mimicking the Industrial Revolution, should give one pause regarding the merits of evolutionary theory.

Even those in the evolutionary camp have had serious concerns with the theory. Most of the problems associated with evolution have come from those working in the scientific disciplines such as biology, paleontology, or biochemistry, for example. But the difficulties related with the theory don't seem to deter most of these scientists from their adherence to it. Although in-house fighting may arise among evolutionists about various components of the theory, these are ignored the moment criticism from the creationist camp emerges. Moreover, when criticism of evolutionary theory occurs, suddenly evolutionists come together and tow the party line.[40] This in itself lends credence to Ruse's statement that evolution has become a "religion," and this is especially the case for those in the field of biology. If this is true, then it is no wonder that scientists still cling to evolution, even though much of the evidence points against it. It is much more difficult to give up religion than a scientific theory. A religion is what people live by. Science on the other hand, by definition, simply describes the way nature is.

One in-house fight started when Harvard professor Stephen Jay Gould, a noted expert who wrote many books on the subject, pointed out that the fossil record doesn't correspond with gradual adaptation over long periods of time. The Cambrian Explosion, as it came to be known, shows that the fossil species went from simple to complex forms of life abruptly, without apparent ancestors. Gould called the fossil record an "embarrassment . . . that seems to show so little of evolution directly."[41] The logical conclusion from this is that either evolution did not happen slowly or something is wrong with the fossil record, such as missing fossils that have not been discovered.[42]

Another explanation is that evolution has never occurred, which is why the evidence for it doesn't show up in the fossil record. From this perspective, the fossil record supports the biblical account in which God created things "after their own kind," intact and without need for evolution. But this view can't be allowed a foot in the door. So Gould along with Niles Eldredge, a paleontologist and curator of the American Museum of Natural History, came to the rescue in 1972 when they proposed that even though evolution moved along gradually for the most part, this gradualism was interrupted (punctuated) occasionally by fits and starts. This would explain why the fossil record demonstrated such sudden abrupt changes. This is known as "punctuated equilibrium."[43] For many outside of the evolutionary camp, this proposal seems awfully convenient. No matter what evidence comes along, evolutionary theory seems capable of "adapting" to it.

Even zoologist Richard Dawkins, rabid apologist for Darwinian evolution, takes issue with punctuated equilibrium, because he thinks that without the gradualism of evolution, we are left with a miracle, which for him is no explanation at all.[44] In other words, Dawkins wants to stick more closely to the traditional theory as proposed by Darwin. Nevertheless, Dawkins is puzzled by the fossil evidence because, as he notes: "It is as though they were just planted there, without any evolutionary history."[45] Even agnostic Michael Denton, in his famous book *Evolution: A Theory in Crisis*, notes that Darwin himself saw that the crucial connecting links in the fossil record were missing, which points against his own theory of gradual evolution.[46]

Denton's work caused a firestorm and was met with derision from the evolutionary crowd because he questioned the macroevolutionary theory and found it wanting. Denton believed there is no plausible way to reconstruct Darwin's theory of continuous development of the species through natural selection and random mutation, either by thought experiment or empirical evidence.[47] Denton, nevertheless, holds to evolution. Interestingly, those who would soon pioneer the Intelligent Design movement read his book. They saw the obvious cracks in the evolutionary armor.

In addition to the fact that evolutionary theory has suffered from some dubious proposals like "punk eek" (punctuated equilibrium), some high ranking members in the evolutionary camp have made startling admissions involving problems with the theory itself. Colin Patterson, a senior paleontologist for the British museum of Natural History, gave a speech to fellow scientists in 1981 when he lamented that after studying evolutionary theory for twenty years, he suddenly realized one day that he knew nothing certain about it. So he questioned his colleagues about this and asked them to give him just one concrete thing that they knew with certainty about the theory. He said he was met with silence. In this same address, he said, "I think many people in this room would acknowledge that during the last few years, if you had thought about it at all, you have experienced a shift from evolution as knowledge to evolution as faith. I know that it's true of me and I think it is true of a good many of you here. . . . Evolution not only conveys no knowledge but seems somehow to convey antiknowledge."[48] This is quite an admission.

Concerning the origin of life, some prominent scientists have also found it more faith-based than evidential. Look at what Nobel laureate Harold Urey had to say: "All of us who study the origin of life find that the more we look into it, the more we feel that it is too complex to have evolved anywhere. We all believe as an article of faith that life evolved from dead matter on this planet. It is just that its complexity is so great it is hard for us to imagine that it did."[49]

The famous agnostic astronomer Carl Sagan put it this way: "Today it is far easier to believe that organisms arose spontaneously on the earth than to try to account for them in any other way. Nevertheless, this still is a statement of faith rather than of demonstrable scientific fact. Scientists have only sketchy notions of how this evolution occurred."[50]

The point to take away here is that the evidence for evolution and abiogenesis—the latter of which is the notion that life evolved somehow from inorganic matter—is not altogether scientific. For many it is taken on "faith" from the evolutionary worldview. (We will take a look at the evidence for abiogenesis and Intelligent Design in the next chapter.)

This raises a question. Is evolutionary theory really based on science, or is it based on something less than strictly science? The scientists quoted above seem to suggest that evolutionary theory has a bit more of a religious or philosophical quality to it than many would care to admit. Many scientists hold to the theory of evolution as if it were a religion built on the metaphysic of naturalism, and thus there is no need for God. As far as whether or not it meets the criteria of "scientific," perhaps it might be wise to step back and define what we mean by *science*. This should help clear up some of the confusion about what exactly science is and what it is not, which directly bears, for example, on why Intelligent Design cannot even be mentioned in the public school classrooms as an alternative hypothesis to evolution.

What Science Is and How It Works Today

Science involves the systematic observation of natural occurrences in order to collect data about these occurrences so that laws and principles stemming from the data may be formulated.[51] In essence, science deals with what is quantifiable.[52] In addition, I think many scientists would also agree, à la Karl Popper, that hypotheses and theories should be falsifiable. On a more mundane level, I think everyone knows that science, as traditionally understood, deals with the natural world (the empirical realm of the five senses), where scientists make measurements, collect data, propose hypotheses, and form theories.

But I believe the average person also holds some misconceptions about science. Often when we think of science, we picture someone dressed in a lab coat, standing in a laboratory, and making precise measurements of some sort. But as Henry H. Bauer points out, this is a popular myth.[53] For example, Watson and Crick, who discovered the structure of the DNA molecule, did so by data acquired from other scientists, other labs, and journals. And Darwin's own theory as promoted in *Origin* falls more under the genre of "historical science," because he was attempting to ascertain the past, like a detective, by drawing together evidence in the present. As Stephen C. Meyer argues, Darwin's theory contains "neither a single mathematical equation nor any report of original experimental research."[54]

Thus, in reality, the scientific method varies from discipline to discipline. Much more is going on than a lonely scientist slaving away in his laboratory. Many times scientists who tested things in the laboratory were not the ones who came up with the original idea. This is entirely appropriate because it eliminates bias from the results, which otherwise might lean in favor of those who originally proposed the hypothesis.[55]

Another myth about science that is embedded in the popular mind-set is that science is the *best* way, or even perhaps the *only* way, to acquire knowledge. When, for example, in the course of argument, someone says, "Well, science says," or "This is backed by science," these statements are meant to be argument stoppers. In other words, science is considered by the populace to be The Authority concerning attaining knowledge. But is science the only way to gain knowledge? Can science really tell us all we need to know? The short answer is science is an extremely important method of acquiring knowledge, but it is not the be-all and end-all for attaining knowledge. Let's unpack this further so we can better understand what science is today and how it interacts with the Christian worldview.

Keep in mind two branches of philosophy that are important for helping us to understand science: metaphysics and epistemology. Metaphysics deals with reality. Epistemology, on the other hand, deals with how we acquire knowledge *of* reality. So science would thus fall under the category of epistemology. Metaphysics and epistemology are needed to help us understand what science is and what scientists' conception of science is.

As we noted above, secular humanist Carl Sagan was a cosmologist and wrote numerous popular books on various cosmological topics. In his highly praised television series, *Cosmos*, Sagan famously stated, "The cosmos is all there is, or was, or ever shall be."[56] This is more than a statement. Even though it seems harmless, it is a metaphysical declaration of naturalism, which philosophically amounts to atheism. What do I mean by this? Sagan's statement is basically saying that, metaphysically speaking, God does not exist, only nature does. This assertion flies in the face of all of the natural philosophers we examined in Chapter nine who believed not only that the God of the Bible exists but that He had ordered the world in a way that allowed a natural philosopher to study it scientifically. In fact, the word *cosmos* implies "order" in the same way the word *cosme*tics originates from the Greek root, which implies an "adornment."[57]

To claim that nature is all that exists is to make a metaphysical assumption. Moreover, Sagan *assumes*, right from the start, that God does not exist. This is important because it exemplifies how science functions today. Science operates on the assumption that God either does not exist or, if He does, He does not operate in the natural world, which is considered a *closed system* of natural causes. This is what differentiates how science was conceived pre-Darwin and how science is conceived today.

Over time scientists have erroneously conflated the metaphysical assumption of naturalism (sometimes naturalism is called materialism) with science itself. The result of this type of thinking may be labeled "methodological naturalism." Methodological naturalism means that for a hypothesis or theory to be considered scientific, it must have a naturalistic cause found only in the material universe.[58] Phillip E. Johnson nicely summarizes this conflation of the worldview of naturalism and science: "Scientific materialists genuinely believe that materialism and science are inseparable, that the realm of objective reality belongs entirely to science and that belief in a supernatural Creator is a holdover from the past that has no place in a rational mind."[59]

He goes on to point out that materialists have no problem with religion so long as it stays in its separate compartment, the realm of imagination, and makes no claims on objective reality.[60] As an aside, this is precisely the problem with those liberal theologians who embraced naturalism that we saw in Chapter four. They simply couldn't reconcile miraculous events like the resurrection of Jesus with modern science, so they denied the miraculous events in Christianity while claiming that what they believed could still be called "Christianity" when it could not.

At any rate, *methodological* naturalism proceeds on the assumption that *metaphysical* naturalism is true, whether or not it is.[61] In short, the *method* that scientists use today is not considered scientific unless it comes up with a naturalistic explanation, because many scientists assume that either nature is all there is (God does not exist), or God should play no part in scientific explanations, even if He *does* exist. If there are some holes in scientific theories today, scientists are confident that these holes can be filled in the future with *naturalistic* explanations without the need to appeal to God, who they feel belongs in the realm of religion not science.

Why is this significant? Because it holds implications for how we view our world and our place in it as humans. For example, when hypothesizing about the origin of life, we must question whether God created life, or whether (if God does not exist) we are left with believing that life arose from non-living matter. Are we accountable to God, who created the universe and the first two human beings, or are we simply a product of matter plus time plus chance—a meaningless result of evolution? This is important because if God does *not* exist, then, of course, we are autonomous and accountable to no one. This is secular humanism, which, increasingly, is the default worldview in the culture today.

Contrary to naturalism and secular humanism, we have mounting evidence that suggests that the information of life does indeed point to a Creator. This evidence would fall under the category of the design argument for God's existence, or at least the existence of a Creator. This theory is known as Intelligent Design, which we will look at in the next chapter. But scientists who adhere to metaphysical naturalism claim that allowing God as an explanation of life is really no explanation at all but merely religion disguised as science.

Moreover, for scientific materialists, a strict methodological naturalism must result in a naturalistic explanation, leaving no room for God. As Phillip E. Johnson points out, allowing God a role in the formation of life would force some scientists to admit that there is something outside the boundaries of natural science.[62] In their eyes, this would diminish the role of science. The fact that the universe had a beginning in addition to the evidence for intelligent design holds obvious religious implications that scientific materialists don't want to deal with. They want to maintain a wall of separation between science and religion.[63] Harvard genetics Professor Richard Lewontin is worth quoting at length as he outlines his position:

> We take the side of science *in spite of* the patent absurdity of some of its constructs, *in spite of* its failure to fulfill many of its extravagant promises of health and life, *in spite of* the tolerance of the scientific community for unsubstantiated just-so-stories, because we have a prior commitment, a commitment to materialism. . . . We are forced by our *a priori* adherence to material causes to create an apparatus of investigation and a set of concepts that produce material explanations, no matter how counterintuitive, no matter how

mystifying to the uninitiated. Moreover, that materialism is absolute, for we cannot allow a Divine Foot in the door.[64]

That just about says it all. Lewontin states elsewhere that the problem for scientists is to get the public to stop believing in the supernatural and instead for them to understand that science is "the only begetter of truth."[65]

Of course this raises a question. If scientists are supposed to be objective and follow the evidence wherever it leads, why would it be a problem if the evidence leads to a Creator? Why can't scientists allow a Divine foot in the door? Could it be that many of the scientists we have cited are atheists first and scientists second? Lewontin basically admits as much. Could it be that many of them are atheists who find science appealing because it makes them appear objective and therefore allows them to feel better about their atheism? If not, then why use methodological naturalism alone? Answer: because as applied by atheistic scientists, methodological naturalism always leads to materialism and never to God as a Cause or a Designer.

Of course, this was certainly not the case up until the time of Darwin. But today the conclusions of methodological naturalism as practiced by modern-day scientists always lead to metaphysical naturalism, which is intrinsically atheistic.[66] In other words, the methodology of science today has resulted in a naturalistic worldview in which God plays no part.[67]

A Brief Historical Interlude

Let's get back to history for just a moment. As we saw in the previous chapters on higher education, science came to be the authority during the latter half of the nineteenth century as far as knowledge was concerned. Pre-Darwin the world was considered an *open* system in which design and purpose pointed to God. But Darwin's concept of natural selection provided a naturalistic mechanism for evolution, thus God was no longer needed as the Designer. Slowly but surely, most scientists, and even Christians involved in science, began to accept a naturalistic epistemology (methodological naturalism) under a *closed* system, not realizing that they were witnessing an entire shift from a theistic worldview to a materialistic, and thus atheistic, worldview.[68]

Science became autonomous after that. It was no longer the handmaiden of theology. At the end of the nineteenth and into the twentieth century, science started to gain even more swagger. It became, in Hegel's words, a "Church," which regarded itself as taking the place of the Christian church because it became "the secularization of the originally Christian combination of world design and directions for action."[69]

This bloated image of what science is capable of is known as "scientism" and was predominant during the early years of the twentieth century. Scientism is the belief that 1) science can properly deal with any aspect of existence,[70] 2) science provides us with authoritative knowledge of what is ultimately important in our lives,[71] 3) science alone is able to give us true knowledge,[72] 4) science can "provide us with an unimpeachable source of moral authority,"[73] and finally, 5) science is the source of absolute truth.[74]

As if this scientific hubris wasn't enough, a particularly arrogant mutation of this attitude developed during the years 1925 to 1936 among members of what is known as the Vienna Circle. Circle members proposed what became known as Logical Positivism. In short, from their vantage point, a statement that claimed to be true needed to be verified either empirically (synthetically) or logically (analytically). If a statement or proposition did not pass the verification test, it was considered meaningless. The circle was composed mainly of scientists with a philosophical bent who intended to eradicate metaphysics and religion from the realm of knowledge (science) because metaphysics and religion could not be empirically verified. They purposefully set up requirements for metaphysics and religion that could not possibly be met.[75] Thus, for example, the statement "the God of the Bible exists" is rendered meaningless by their criteria because the statement cannot be verified empirically nor is it tautological. A.J. Ayer's 1936 book, *Language, Truth and Logic*, popularized the views of the Vienna Circle.[76]

Although this particular overbearing and arrogant notion of science has been discredited, it should give the reader an example of how science became authoritative regarding knowledge in our culture after the turn of the nineteenth century.

Science's Epistemological Problems

Fast-forward to today. I think it is fair to say that most scientists give little thought to what science really is. Nor do they give thought to the philosophical issues involved in an examination of science. Moreover, the real issues involve not just science itself, but the *philosophy of science*, which is the interaction of science and philosophy—or in other words, a critical examination of science.

Most people today, including scientists, are totally unaware of the issues involved in the philosophy of science because they simply take it for granted that "science works." This seems obvious to everyone because of the ubiquitous technological advances. But, quite frankly, technology is not science. Technology is "applied science." Neither science nor technology address the issues involved *within* science itself. Because science has gained such authority in our culture, I think it is important to understand how science has been allowed, or encouraged, to overstep its bounds. With this in mind, let's flesh out some of science's epistemological problems.

As we saw above, a commonly held assumption is that for science to be truly scientific, all knowledge gained from science must come from the empirical realm—the realm that can be ascertained by the five senses. This seems all well and good . . . except for one problem. The notion that *all scientific knowledge must come from the empirical realm* did not come from the empirical realm. In other words, *that* notion is a philosophical claim *about* science, not a scientific claim. In other words, by its own definition, the notion that *all scientific knowledge must come from the empirical realm* is not true because it is obvious that the notion itself *did not come from the empirical realm.* The very idea that all knowledge comes only from the empirical realm contradicts itself and is therefore false. If it is false, then all knowledge does not come from the empirical realm and may come from other areas as well. So the belief, still held in the modern mind-set today, that science alone is the be-all and end-all for attaining knowledge is false. Science cannot meet its own criterion.

The verification principle of the Logical Positivists failed for the same reason—the verification principle could not be verified by the empirical realm and neither was it a logical necessity. When asked about the failure of Logical Positivism many years later, Ayer responded: "Well, I suppose the most important of the defects was that nearly all of it was false."[77]

The problem of induction poses another difficulty for science. Science uses the inductive method by which data are gathered from the world around us and then hypotheses, theories, and laws are formed by drawing inferences from that set of data. So, for example, let's use the example of white swans. If a scientist was to observe white swans, and then over a number of years found that in every instance swans were always white, he might conclude from his observations that all swans are white. Basically he looks at the data he has collected from the *past*, and then draws an inference based on that data and concludes that all swans he might come across in the *future* will be white. But one day he comes across a black swan. His hypothesis implodes. The problem of inductive reasoning is that a scientist can never be sure that what occurred in the past will always occur in the future.

In other words, to be sure that one's future prediction will be true, one would have to make an infinite number of observations. This is impossible. Therefore, the inductive method used by scientists rests on something other than *certainty*. The most the inductive method can offer is *probability*. This has been proved again and again as scientists modify their theories and laws. I would also point out that though the inductive method is the modus operandi for conducting science, the inductive method is not scientific, because it is not found in the empirical realm. It is a tool formed by *reason* in the human *mind* for conducting science.

It should be apparent, then, that science cannot operate on its own. This should give pause to those who uphold science as a worldview (scientism) and then claim that science can make accurate pronouncements in every area of life. Science cannot do without philosophy—in this case metaphysics—because science makes certain assumptions *before* the scientific endeavor can even begin. Metaphysics, which is concerned with reality, is indispensable before the scientific enterprise can even get off the ground.[78]

For example, concerning metaphysical reality, science presupposes that 1) nature is uniform, 2) the uniformity in nature is rational and can be apprehended by our senses when "reading" the data of nature, and 3) our use of reason is capable of interpreting the data correctly and coming to valid hypotheses and theories.[79] When I say that "science presupposes" these three things, it is really another way of saying that scientists have "faith" that the universe is structured the way it is and our minds are structured to make sense of the data of experience. Science cannot prove those things; it must *assume* them to even get started. If reality was unstructured and chaotic, science could not even begin.[80] Science needs philosophy and rests on metaphysics. It cannot operate on its own. Science rests on a metaphysical assumption that the universe is structured, rational, and uniform. In short, science is not the epistemological be-all and end-all that most in our society think it is. Science is based on faith.

Summary

The early natural philosophers we looked at in the previous chapter did indeed believe that the universe was ordered in a certain way, which made the scientific pursuit possible. Another way of saying this is that the natural philosophers were epistemically justified in their pursuits because they believed God exists and therefore it did not take a leap of faith to presuppose that the universe was ordered (rather than chaotic or unstructured). Scientists today, however, want to have it both ways. They practice methodological naturalism which leaves God totally out of the picture while *assuming* that the universe is comprehensible without God as the foundation. God and science are put into two separate compartments, or God is dispensed with altogether by scientists who lean toward atheism.

Pre-Darwin the Christian worldview provided a foundation for all areas of human existence. The same God who had designed the universe had also written the moral law on human hearts. Scientific pursuit was called natural philosophy, which endeavored to better understand the purpose and design of nature and even God Himself. All areas of scientific pursuit were integrated under the umbrella of the Christian worldview or at least a theistic worldview.

But after Darwin the complementary nature of Christianity and science started to fall apart. As we pointed out, Darwinism not only damaged the special creation of Adam and Eve as found in Scripture, it opened the way for the denial of God in any activities of His creation. Because natural selection supposedly provided a "natural" mechanism for the evolution of the species, scientists decided that God was no longer to be a part of any scientific endeavors. The method of doing science henceforth (methodological naturalism) allowed only natural causes for understanding science. God was no longer allowed in His own universe. Since that time, methodological naturalism has conflated science with naturalism so that theistic assumptions and conclusions regarding the universe are out of bounds and have been replaced with philosophical naturalism, which assumes that nature is all there is.[81]

For those who embrace scientism, like some of the scientists noted previously, science is capable of answering any and all questions, even philosophical questions regarding life and our place in it. But scientists cannot have it both ways. It is hard to see how science can answer all questions about reality when most scientists practice methodological naturalism, which limits the conclusions of science to the material realm. Certainly the advances in applied science, which provide us with technology and makes most of our lives easier, is a good thing to come out of science. But are non-quantifiable notions like truth, justice, suffering, love, morality, etc., somehow less real because they cannot be found in the empirical realm by methodological naturalism? Is science really capable of informing us about what life is all about, why we are here, why we die, and tell us about eternity?

These are the most important questions we all must address at some point in our lives. Most people think these questions are real and worthy of contemplation. But these questions and their answers cannot be found by science. They involve abstractions and the spiritual realm and cannot be found in the empirical realm. Just because things like numbers, truth, love, angels, goodness, etc., cannot be found in the empirical realm does not mean that they do not exist or are somehow any less real than things that are quantifiable. Moreover, if those things do exist, then naturalism is false.[82] There is more to reality than metaphysical materialism (philosophical atheism).

In addition, why should we be obliged to give precedence to a naturalistic explanation over a nonnaturalistic explanation, especially in light of the problems I pointed out earlier regarding science not meeting its own criterion?[83] If scientists want to maintain a strict adherence to methodological naturalism, then by definition it would seem that they would have nothing to offer about the nonmaterial realm of life and values. But as we will see when we revisit the naturalistic evolutionary worldview in the next chapter, and more specifically the origins of life debate, this is not the case. Naturalism indeed is a worldview that is antithetical to the Christian worldview. There is most definitely a conflict here.

Some scientists like Gould and Eldredge get around this. They see science and religion as occupying two separate compartments. From this point of view, Christianity and science do not inhabit the same realm of human experience. Instead, they both have "non-overlapping magisteria," according to Gould,[84] meaning each is authoritative in its own realm but not in each other's realm. This seems at first glance to be advantageous to both sides because no conflict would exist between science and religion. Religion would be cordoned off into the realm of belief while science would occupy the realm of knowledge and facts. The problem here is that while the so-called knowledge of science would apply to everyone, beliefs would apply only to believers. This makes it look as if the beliefs of Christians, for example, are subjective and hold secondary status when compared with knowledge that only science can give us.[85] Those like Gould might say, "Don't worry, your religious beliefs are important to you and they carry authority for you. But please, don't try to persuade us objective scientists or the rest of society of their validity because we cannot confirm them by methodological naturalism. We concede that we can neither confirm nor deny God's existence, but you Christians can't either, so in return don't push your religion on the rest of us."

The problem with compartmentalizing Christianity and science in this way is that they both deal with the real world and cover many of the same subjects.[86] This is contrary to the popular mind-set that seems to think religion in general, and Christianity in particular, is no longer about the real world.[87] It should go without saying that if the origin of the universe points to a Creator who lives outside the boundaries of science, then this is something we should know about. The question of God's existence cannot simply be cordoned off because those practicing methodological naturalism say so. If the God of the Bible exists, we are accountable to Him. This affects our morals and our way of life and applies to everyone, whether or not they are believers.

Methodological naturalism is doing no one a service when it incorrectly reduces everything to the natural/material realm if this is not the case in real life. Even the great philosopher and atheist Bertrand Russell admitted that many people have adopted materialism as a worldview, not so much out of conviction of its truth, but rather as "a system of dogma," which is set up to attack religious dogma and superstition.[88]

The problems associated with methodological naturalism also arise along with questions about origins of life issues and what it means to be human. Pulling a Kantian gambit by separating the Christian worldview and science does not solve anything. The Christian worldview ends up being marginalized and relegated to second-class status while science is seen as The Authority on everything.

One example of how this plays out in real life involves the late actor Christopher Reeve, who was paralyzed in a horse riding accident. Reeve apparently took issue with what he perceived as religious groups and social organizations intervening with policy on stem cell research. Reeve argued that in matters of public policy debate, "no religions should have a seat at the table." He made it clear that he was not against anyone's religion per se, and went on to say, "I am a Unitarian myself. We're talking about the promise of science, the ethics of science, not religion."[89]

Reeve's attitude toward religion and science is typical of the average American. For Reeve, religion should have no say in anything where science has any input in the discussion. Religion should stay in its own compartment as far as Reeve is concerned. Sure, religion is important. Reeve even pointed to his own religious inclination. But science is the authority for Reeve and many others in our society when it comes to ultimate concerns or especially when science and Christianity are seen in conflict. This also demonstrates my contention that science and religion do indeed overlap on the important issues of life, otherwise Reeve would not have perceived the supposed conflict between religion and science in the first place.

Let us turn now to our final chapter on science, where we will look at an issue where science and Christianity truly conflict—over the question of the origin of life.

Chapter 11

Origin of Life: Abiogenesis or Intelligent Design?

Before we move on to the question of the origin of life, understand that methodological naturalism as practiced by scientists today has stacked the deck in favor of those who want to keep God out of His own universe. In essence, God does not matter as far as the practice of science is concerned because the method for doing science excludes God's existence *a priori*. However, those who believe methodological naturalism has unnecessarily reduced science to materialism (naturalism) have challenged it in recent years. The debate over the origin of life is evidence of this.

Historical Impact of Darwin's Theory

The origin of life issue is important because it demonstrates that two creation stories are competing for viability in our society today. Naturalistic evolution holds that life arose from non-life as a product of matter plus time plus chance as part of an undirected, purposeless process. This theory of how life started is known as abiogenesis.

On the other hand, the Christian worldview, or even a more modest theistic or deistic worldview, holds that God created life and designed the universe. Therefore, the things that God created have a purpose and, more especially, you and I have worth and a purpose to our lives. All the natural philosophers and natural theologians we learned about previously could see the Divine handiwork in the empirical evidence they observed. For them it was natural to infer design from what they saw. Historically then, natural philosophers inferred purpose (teleology) from what they observed in their study of nature, and this was a "source of a knowledge about God."[1]

But Darwin's mechanism of natural selection undermined the notion of purpose that had prevailed until the latter half of the nineteenth century. Darwin's theory provided what increasingly came to be seen as a plausible explanation for the complexity of organisms without the need of a Designer. It wasn't a giant leap after this to suppose that life arose naturalistically, which even Darwin hinted at. This is significant because it is not so much the gradualism or the descent by modification proposed in Darwin's theory that is as important as the fact that the evolutionary worldview has substituted a non-purposeful material initiator of life in place of the Creator.[2] This amounts to atheism. Richard Dawkins's well-known quote points to this: "Darwin made it possible to be an intellectually fulfilled atheist."[3]

The evolutionary worldview as it is understood by most scientists today holds profound implications for humanity as it has trickled down and embedded itself in society today through the media, public schools, and universities. Sir Julian Huxley, the evolutionary biologist and eugenicist who was the grandson of T.H. Huxley and brother of Aldous Huxley (author of *Brave New World*), argued for the importance of evolution: "It is essential for evolution to become the central core of any educational system, because it is evolution, in the broad sense, that links inorganic nature with life, and the stars with the earth, and matter with mind, and animals with man."[4]

Elites, like Huxley, want children to be inculcated with the naturalistic evolutionary worldview, which is one reason it is so dangerous. When asked why he embraced Darwin's theory, Huxley replied, "I suppose that the reason that we leapt at the *Origin* was that the idea of God interfered with our sexual mores."[5]

Men like Huxley and Dawkins are atheists who do not want to acknowledge God as Creator. Evolution provides cover for them under the guise of science as support for their atheism and moral autonomy. But when you remove the Creator, the purpose and worth of humankind also disappears. When we connect the dots between Huxley's worldview and the fact that he was a eugenicist in addition to his coining the term *transhumanism*, it doesn't take an overactive imagination to see where some of this is headed—toward a world in which other species' genes will be mixed with human's genes and humans will no longer be human but some type of hybrid/beast. This will be sold as humankind's "evolution." We will examine transhumanism more closely in Chapter nineteen.

After the final quarter of the nineteenth century, Darwinism became so well-established in scientific circles that methodological naturalism soon followed as a concomitant result and thus became entrenched as the quintessence of science. Methodological naturalism meant that the scientific inference to a Designer (God) was off limits, because there was no precise method for determining whether intelligence or something unintelligent (nature) caused something.[6] Moreover, the practice of methodological naturalism allowed no room for design and thus no room for a Creator.

The Scopes Trial

After the beginning of the twentieth century, the authority of science became even more embedded as a result of the much publicized Scopes Trial (1925). Some facts most people today are unaware of about the trial are worth noting.

John Scopes, a biology teacher, was prosecuted in Tennessee for teaching evolution. The trial epitomized the conflict that had been going on in the beginning of the century between the modernists, who thought that reason and science were authoritative, and their opponents, the fundamentalists who favored biblical literalism. The cultural and scientific elites, with their ever increasing agnosticism dating back to the latter part of the nineteenth century, exacerbated this divide.[7] Because of its national and worldwide publicity, the trial did more than any other modern event to embed in the popular mind-set the notion that Christianity and science have always been at war; that Christians are narrow-minded and backward in their thinking; and regarding any clash of worldviews, science has authority over Christianity.

Most people today, however, are unaware of what the textbook (*A Civic Biology*) Scopes used really taught. As John G. West points out, there is no way *A Civic Biology* would be allowed in today's classroom and not simply because the science is outdated. The textbook used evolutionary theory to promote white supremacy while promoting eugenics. The textbook lamented that the "unfit" of society were often cared for instead of allowing natural selection to run its course. Caring for the unfit meant that their genes would be allowed to pass down to future generations. The author of the textbook, George William Hunter, explained that these unfit "parasites" on society, if they were lower animals, would probably have been killed off "to prevent them from spreading."[8]

A few years later, a college biology textbook came out entitled *Fundamentals of Biology* (1928) in which the author, Arthur Haupt, likewise bemoaned that educational, religious, and charitable organizations attempted to improve the environmental conditions for "defectives" as a method of improving society. Haupt argued that though these attempts were "indispensable," they could improve only the individual but not society, because these defectives would pass down their heredity. Haupt explicitly drew the connection between Darwin's natural selection and eugenics while maintaining that, in the long run, promoting charity could have only an "adverse effect upon the race."[9] People today are totally unaware of the eugenic mind-set that found footing in Darwinism.

Creation Science and the Intelligence Design Project

Henry Morris, a professor of engineering, wrote *The Genesis Flood* (1961), which supported a young earth (created in the last 10,000 years) and a literal six-day creation. He argued that biblical evidence and science supported this. The science supporting his arguments initiated a movement within fundamentalism known as "creation science" or "scientific creationism," the latter of which became the title of another of Morris's books. Emboldened by scientific creationism and their own foray into politics in the 1970s, the religious right fought for the right of creation science to be taught alongside evolution in the public schools. This worked until the Supreme Court ruled in 1987 that Louisiana's Balanced Treatment Act was nothing more than religion masquerading as science.[10]

Today, another movement is trying to gain a fair hearing for design as an alternative to methodological naturalism and evolutionary abiogenesis. Led by a group of people who are highly credentialed in various fields, the Intelligent Design (ID) movement has proposed an alternative to the story that life arose from matter alone (abiogenesis) by sheer chance.

What distinguishes ID from creation science? The point of departure for ID is not Scripture as it was for creation science. Rather, ID starts with the data of nature and proceeds to infer design from that data by using commonly held scientific principles and mathematics to distinguish intelligent causes from natural causes.[11] The ID movement is distinct from creation science in that it holds none of creation science's prior religious commitments as starting points, such as a literal interpretation of Genesis with its diverse array of opinions concerning the creation account.[12]

ID's concern is not to identify the intelligent cause behind the biological information of life. Its project is much more modest than that. Negatively, ID wants to demonstrate the utter improbability that the information of life was the result of undirected chance processes found only in nature. Positively, ID's fundamental claim is that only intelligence is capable of causing the information and the complexity contained in biological structures in addition to showing that intelligence is detectable empirically.[13] Therefore, ID directly challenges both naturalistic evolution and methodological naturalism, which allow only naturalistic/material causes for the origin and evolution of life.[14]

As I have stated previously, methodological naturalism has made it impossible for the design inference to gain any footing post-Darwin. It's not only that scientists leaning toward atheism don't want to let a divine foot in the door. It's because even scientists of good faith are afraid that if they hypothesize design and then it turns out that there is a natural explanation instead of a supernatural one, they will look foolish and their stature as scientists will diminish. This is exacerbated by the fact that until recently no stringent methods for distinguishing intelligent causes from natural ones existed.[15]

The media has played a role in public opinion by portraying advocates of ID as attempting to smuggle in their religious agenda under the guise of science. This is the same charge brought against Creation Science. This media portrayal is accepted as gospel by a public that has been taught that science and religion have nothing to do with each other.[16]

To cite one example, in a *Time* magazine article (2005) entitled "Let's Have No More Monkey Trials," Charles Krauthammer bemoans that evolution, which he describes as "one of the most powerful and elegant theories in all of human science," is being challenged once again in the classroom by ID, which he calls "a tarted-up version of creationism." His article is typical of the misconceptions ingrained in the public mind-set.

He wrote, "Science begins not with first principles but with observation and experimentation." But as we have shown, science would not even get off the ground without presupposing (faith) that the natural world is ordered in a rational, intelligible way, which *is* a "first principle." He goes on to say, "This conflict between faith and science had mercifully abated over the past four centuries as each grew to permit the other its own independent sphere." But as we have shown, there was no overarching conflict between religion and science, at least not until Darwin's *Origin* gained hegemony in the last quarter of the nineteenth century. This is precisely *when* the conflict between science and Christianity began in some respects. Krauthammer likewise maintains that science and faith should have their own separate compartments. But as we have demonstrated, science and Christianity both deal with many of the same worldview issues. They cannot possibly be held in separate compartments.[17] To maintain that they should occupy separate compartments is pulling a Kantian gambit.

It is important to challenge Krauthammer's misrepresentation of this issue. He fails to realize that evolutionary theory carries its own religious worldview, namely naturalism, especially concerning life's origin. We have already seen that some scientists hold to naturalism (which amounts to atheism) as tenaciously as any religious person holds to his or her beliefs. Stephen C. Meyer summarizes the problem with viewing science as neutral: "Contrary to the popular 'just the facts' stereotype of science, many scientific theories have larger ideological, metaphysical, or religious implications. Origins theories in particular have such implications since they make claims about the causes that brought life or humankind or the universe into existence."[18]

Krauthammer finishes his article by admonishing us not to teach "faith" as science because it encourages "the supercilious caricature of America as a nation in the thrall of religious authority."[19] Krauthammer is afraid that outsiders will look down their noses at our country because we are in the "thrall of religious authority," and he believes this would diminish our stature as a country. But this is precisely the thesis of *America's Post-Christian Apocalypse*—that Christianity *has* lost its authority in all areas of our culture. Krauthammer is inadvertently supporting my thesis.

Unfortunately, for Krauthammer, as we will see below, ID is not some "tarted-up version of creationism." It is science. It is certainly not religion or faith, as he would have it, masquerading as science. Indeed, as we will see, if the same demarcation criteria are applied to evolution as they are to ID, Krauthammer's glorious evolutionary theory will come crashing down as well. His article is part and parcel of the misconceptions the public has regarding science and faith. It is an example of how science is perceived as The Authority in our culture and how opposing worldviews in any conflict with science are marginalized.

Other misconceptions and misrepresentations abound as well, especially as proponents of ID attempt to give it a fair hearing in the classroom. Because a greater percentage of biologists are atheists when compared with most others practicing science, it should come as no surprise that in 1995, the National Association of Biology Teachers (NABT) in an official statement of how biology should be taught in secondary schools and college level stated, "Evolutionary theory . . . neither refutes nor supports the existence of a deity or deities." It went on to say that evolution is an "unsupervised, impersonal, unpredictable and natural process."[20]

How does the NABT know this? One wonders if the NABT is trying to slip one past us. As John G. West points out, if evolution by their own definition takes no position on God, then how do they know that evolution is "unsupervised" or "impersonal," and why do they assert this?[21] If the NABT doesn't want religion pretending to be science pushed on young folks, why are they pushing naturalism (atheism) on them?

In 2003, an article published by the *American Biology Teacher* propagated the myth that science and religion have a history of being at war with each other. The article urged teachers that "When young children are indoctrinated into believing that for which there is no evidence (God, Heaven, Hell, etc.) a habit of mind is being developed that is inconsistent with the open, inquiring mind needed for scientific study." It went on to say that the story of evolution must include "the history of the struggle between religion and science, not just the facts of evolutionary science."[22]

Contrary to the quote, we saw in the previous chapter that evolution is not a fact. Many seriously credentialed individuals in the evolutionary camp have raised many thoughtful questions about evolution. But what is more troubling about the quote above is that the author does not want students "indoctrinated" with notions about the supernatural but has no problem indoctrinating them with naturalistic atheism disguised under the auspices of evolution. If the author wants to teach students to be open-minded, why is the supernatural realm closed off to them *a priori*? The bias here is palpable. Furthermore, as we have learned, historically there was no war going on between science and Christianity.

The bias in science against the supernatural is so entrenched that court rulings concerning whether ID can be taught alongside evolution have been affected by it. In 2005 a judge ruled that a Pennsylvania school district could not even tell its biology students about a book in the library that set forth the argument for ID. The judge reasoned that if ID was not science, it must be religion. It turned out the judge lifted 90 percent of his opinion directly from a brief he had received from the ACLU, which sourced the testimony of their own witnesses. In addition, the judge used an outmoded demarcation criterion (which we will look at below) that basically states that ID fails the qualification of science because it violates methodological naturalism. But as Stephen C.

Meyer points out, methodological naturalism in this case amounts to nothing more than prohibiting ID in scientific theories. Because of his preconceived ideas about ID, the judge used circular logic and basically defined ID out of scientific bounds without looking at the evidence.[23]

It seems more than a bit hypocritical that in 2000 an article in the *American Biology Teacher* noted three science professors who argued that "biological literacy" should include the notion that homosexuality is genetically predetermined. The professors' thoughts on this subject were embedded in the context of "taking Darwin seriously," meaning that naturalism should be relied upon more than it already is regarding human behavior.[24] The professors sourced a book by Daniel Dennett, *Darwin's Dangerous Idea* (1995), in which Dennett recommends quarantining parents who don't want their children to be taught evolutionary theory.[25] We can expect more of this Gestapo type bullying as our increasingly post-Christian nation heads into the end of the age.

If educators think it is wrong to introduce religion in the science classroom, why is it acceptable to smuggle in ideas such as "homosexuality is natural" under the guise of Darwinian naturalism? This is promoting anti-Christian morals under the guise of so-called science (evolution). We saw in the previous chapter that many leading evolutionary proponents admit that evolution is the religion of atheism based on faith, which reduces the universe to materialism without the need for a Designer.[26] So if evolution is really a religion, why is it allowed to be taught in the classroom while promoting its atheistic morals?

William A. Dembski, probably the leading figure in the ID movement, explains why: "What many Darwinists yearn for is not just more talented communicators to promote Darwinism in America's biology classroom but an enforced educational and cultural policy for total worldview reprogramming that is sufficiently aggressive to capture and convert to Darwinism even the most recalcitrant among 'religiously programmed' youth."[27] You know, those "programmed youth" who might want to believe in God and hold to traditional values.

Thus, when you get right down to it, the reason in many cases that ID is not welcomed in the classroom or among many scientists today is not so much about methodological naturalism, which is just an excuse to disregard ID. Rather, it is because the debate between ID and abiogenesis is a worldview issue. Many scientists and educators want to maintain their atheism under the auspices of the naturalistic evolutionary worldview. They don't want to deal with the implications of a supernatural intelligence behind the origin of life.[28] When these same scientists attempt to accuse ID of not being science, it is a vacuous charge. ID is every bit as much a "science" as Darwinian theory.

Let's explore this issue now.

How Intelligent Design Works

As we saw earlier, Darwin never directly addressed the origin of life. But his mechanism of natural selection certainly set the stage for believing that life evolved without God's creative decision. The nineteenth century saw the first experimental attempts at trying to create organic matter from inorganic matter. Huxley and Haeckel were emboldened during this time and maintained that no qualitative difference existed between life and non-living matter. They proposed the first theories of how life formed from non-living chemicals.[29] Most biologists after this time believed that what appeared to be design in living organisms was just an illusion.

However, when Watson and Crick discovered the structure of DNA, they also realized that DNA stored information. They found that chemicals called nucleotide bases were ordered in a very specific pattern, and these bases stored and transmitted what amounted to assembly instructions (information) to build proteins and tiny machines that all cells needed for survival.[30]

But this raised a question. Where did the information come from? Did the information contained in the DNA arise from nature alone? Did information merely seem to imitate a designing intelligence? It was clear then, at least to one origin of life researcher at that time, that the question of the origin of life equated to the origin of biological information.[31]

Michael Polanyi, who held a Chair of Physical Chemistry at the University of Manchester, wrote an article in 1968 in which he argued that living organisms behaved like machines. However, the processes that produced those machines could not be reduced to physics and chemistry. Why? Because physics and chemistry cannot determine the arrangement of the characters that relay the information that built the machines in the first place. To say that the information contained in DNA is reducible to the matter that conveys the information is the same category mistake as claiming that the information contained in a book is reducible to the paper and ink.[32] In short, the medium (matter) is not the message.

In the same manner, as John C. Lennox points out, after discovering a mechanism that accounted for planetary motions, Newton didn't suddenly declare that there was no Lawgiver behind that mechanism. Rather, his admiration of God increased because Newton understood that God had designed it that way. Newton did not conflate the agent (God) with the mechanism (gravity).[33]

That the sequencing bases in the DNA do not *have* to be ordered that way by some law of nature demonstrates *contingency*, which is the first criterion in William A. Dembski's explanatory filter for determining ID. Dembski, who holds two PhDs, one in mathematics and one in philosophy, uses the example of a Scrabble board to explain contingency. Because the letters on a Scrabble board cannot be reduced to any law governing the sequencing of the letters demonstrates the sequence is contingent.[34]

Dembski invented his "explanatory filter" to test the probability that some event could have been caused by nature alone. The second criterion involves *complexity*. The complexity criterion demonstrates that the sequences of events is very unlikely, in fact extremely unlikely, to have been caused by chance and are not caused by a prior natural law either.

Finally, the *specificity* criterion, which works in conjunction with the complexity criterion, is the recognition of a match between an observed event and another pattern we know exists independently of the observed event.[35]

All of this is not as complicated as it sounds. Meyer uses the example of Mt. Rushmore. The shapes on that cliff rock are certainly unusual and irregularly shaped compared with the rest of the cliff; therefore, it demonstrates complexity, because to have exhibited those shapes by chance is improbable (complexity criterion).

In addition, the shapes also exhibit a pattern we know exists independently from the shapes on the cliff rock. The shapes resemble the faces of ex-presidents we know from pictures or paintings of them. There is a match between the specific pattern on the cliff rock and what we know in the real world (specificity criterion).[36] Thus, the pattern on the cliff rock demonstrates "specified complexity."

What does all of this mean? It means that from our experience of the world, we know that events that are complex and specified occur not by chance but by intelligent design.[37] If you were flying over a beach and you looked down and saw the word *help* etched in the sand, would you think that the water rushing in and out caused it? No. You would rightly assume that the chance of water causing the word *help* to be spelled out was extremely improbable. In addition, the letters are arranged in a specific order, which makes it likely that someone had a purpose in mind: to convey information.

In the same way, the origin of specified information encoded in DNA leads one to believe that it performs a function or a goal and therefore an intelligent source is behind it.[38] Dembski summarizes his thoughts on ID: "There are natural systems that cannot be adequately explained in terms of undirected natural forces and that exhibit features which in any other circumstance we would attribute to intelligence."[39] Our experience tells us that minds produce specified information. Matter does not have this capacity.[40]

Michael Behe, another pioneer in the ID movement, supports Dembski's contention. Behe's *Darwin's Black Box* (1996) argued that on the molecular level, systems are in place that couldn't possibly have arisen through the evolutionary process. Why? Because some of the tiny systems—machines really—could not have come to exist through successive serendipitous additions to their structure. For example, bacterial flagellum has around forty protein parts: a rotor, bushings, a drive shaft, and a stator, among other parts, that allows it to swim.[41] To take away *any* one of those parts renders the motor completely nonfunctional, thus the flagellum could not have arisen through tiny changes in its structure. This motor is what Behe calls "irreducibly complex."[42]

Darwin had stated that "if it could be demonstrated that any complex organ existed which could not possibly have been formed by numerous successive, slight modifications, my theory would absolutely break down."[43] His disciple today, Richard Dawkins, also believes that if gradualism didn't occur, then evolution has lost its explanatory power.[44] The problem here for evolutionary theory is that Behe's work shows that there could not have been evolutionary gradualism as purported by Darwin because *all* of the parts of these molecular machines are necessary for them to function. It should be noted that Behe *does* believe in Darwin's descent by modification from a common ancestor.[45] He does not believe, however, that Darwinism explains how these tiny molecular machines like the flagellum came into existence.

The case for abiogenesis gets worse. Even though it was popular in the past to propose self-organization theories of chemical evolution to explain abiogenesis, these theories were subsequently questioned by prominent non-Christian scientists. For many it seemed improbable that chemicals could self-organize simply by chance to form life. To cite one famous example, distinguished cosmologist Sir Fred Hoyle in 1983 calculated the odds of constructing the proteins needed to form even a one-celled organism by chance alone is extremely tiny—around one in ten with 40,000 zeros after it.[46] To put it another way, he said that the chance of life arising spontaneously from non-life is the same chance that a tornado blowing through a junkyard would construct a Boeing 747.[47] To give it another perspective, the odds of finding a single marked atom out of all the atoms in our galaxy by chance on the first try is about a billion times more probable than the odds of producing even a small protein by blind chance.[48]

Another problem that confronts those who want to believe life arose by chance is that there was simply not enough time for chance to produce life. According to science today, the universe is around 13.7 billion years old. To form a functioning protein by chance would take, as we saw above, one in ten to the 40,000th power. The universe is nowhere near old enough to support all the possible occurrences it would take by chance to construct a protein. Hoyle contends that the improbability of life forming from inanimate matter is so huge that "It is big enough to bury Darwin and the whole theory of evolution. There was no primeval soup, neither on this planet nor on any other, and if the beginnings of life were not random, they must therefore have been the product of purposeful intelligence."[49] Hoyle, who was an atheist most of his life, became agnostic after examining the evidence.

In spite of the evidence against the evolutionary worldview and abiogenesis, many scientists (especially biologists) and educators would rather hold to this position rather than admit that the evidence points against evolution and in favor of an Intelligent Designer. Dawkins, who to my mind is not just an atheist but an anti-theist, admits, "Even if there were no actual evidence in favor of the Darwinian theory . . . we should still be justified in preferring it over all rival theories."[50] For Dawkins and many others, this is not about science; it is a worldview issue. If it was about science, Dawkins should be able to see that the evidence points to a Designer. Even one of the premiere atheists of the last century, Anthony Flew, admitted, after a lifetime of looking at the evidence, that there had to be a Designer. This was no small admission.

Dawkins leaves one believing that he is blinded to the evidence because of his commitment to atheism. People like Dawkins want atheism to be true because they don't want to be accountable to the living God. They think they can hide behind evolution, but they can't.

Covering oneself with fig leaves has already been tried and found wanting.

Because folks like Dawkins have no way of dealing with the evidence that is insurmountably stacked against them, they have to resort to defining ID out of existence. Their modus operandi is to assert that ID is not science. This is stated over and over until by sheer fiat it becomes a fact. So, for example, the reason the courts have ruled that ID cannot be taught as an alternative hypothesis in the classroom is because it is supposedly not science. This assertion is incorrect.

Science and the Demarcation Problem

The problem of distinguishing what science is from what it is not is known among philosophers of science as the "demarcation problem." In other words, scientists use demarcation criteria to make a distinction (demarcation) between what may be deemed science and what may not. The problem is that scientists themselves cannot agree on how science should be defined. In fact, it is widely understood today that demarcation arguments do not work, because the notion that science can be defined by a particular method is illusory.[51] Unfortunately, although demarcation arguments are outmoded, they are still used in court cases to exclude ID from even being mentioned as an alternative hypothesis to abiogenesis in the classroom.

Part of the problem with demarcation arguments stems from the fact that scientists in different fields use different methods for doing their work. Some scientists do laboratory experiments while others don't. Some methods involve direct investigation, while other methods use more indirect testing.[52] Some fields, for example, such as historical science, infer an event in the past from what can be observed in the present. Thus, in the case of ID, we know from experience that every time we find evidence of specified complexity, an intelligence is behind it.

Those wishing to claim that ID is not science should realize that evolutionary theory would also be excluded under the same criteria, because those in the evolutionary camp likewise use evidence in the present (fossils, etc.) to infer a cause in the past (natural selection).[53] Therefore, philosophers of science are coming to the realization that it is not whether a theory can be defined as "science" that is important, but whether the theory is true or not as supported by the evidence.[54]

Finally, ID uses the same methodology as other scientific fields. No one questions whether forensic science, archaeology, or cryptography are scientific endeavors. These fields certainly work under the premise that intelligence is empirically detectable. So, for example, if archaeologists saw scratches that formed a pattern (specified complexity) on the walls of a cave, they wouldn't simply attribute it to chance. They would correctly infer that something with a mind created the pattern of scratches.

This raises a question. If some patterned scratches in a cave points to intelligence, why wouldn't a 3.5 billion letter sequence in the human genome point to intelligence?[55] If the odds of non-living matter forming life are less than one in ten to the 40,000th power, why would specified complex information not point to life and thus intelligence behind it? If secular humanist and cosmologist Carl Sagan can search for extraterrestrial life by empirically detecting for intelligence, why can't ID proponents do the same thing?[56]

Dan Peterson provides an answer:

> It is precisely because intelligent design relies upon scientific methods and evidence that it is regarded by the materialists as so extraordinarily dangerous. It threatens to allow religion to escape from the ghetto assigned to it by the dominant 19th and 20th century materialism. It actually claims to be true, on the same level that all science claims to be true.…It might change the assumptions on which we conduct our public discourse and education. It might change conceptions about whether there is an objective moral order. It might help open minds that would otherwise be closed.[57]

Summary of the Three Science Chapters

The question we asked two chapters ago is whether Christianity and science are at war. We saw that at least up until the time of Darwin the answer is a decided no. Many of the early natural philosophers considered themselves Christians, or at the very least theists. Science was considered the handmaiden of theology because it was utilized to support the notion that God was the Creator and Designer of the universe.

The purpose of the early science was twofold. First, it was meant to enhance an understanding of God and the purpose of different facets of His creation. Second, the early scientists wanted to gain some control over nature, which mankind had lost at the Fall of Adam and Eve. In this respect, their goal was to improve the human condition. But mostly, science was about contemplating God's creation, because understanding its design and purpose could augment human understanding of God Himself. In short, the early science known as natural philosophy worked hand in hand with theology. There was no conflict.

The common misperception that science and Christianity have always been at war is reinforced in the popular mind-set by the Galileo trial. We saw that much of the supposed conflict between science and Christianity at that time was really a result of natural philosophers like Galileo rejecting the Aristotelian worldview, which the Catholic Church was trying to defend. The real conflict at the time of Galileo was between the upstart Protestants and the Roman Catholic Church. Galileo was simply trying to do science. He wanted to help the Catholic Church come to terms with the Copernican worldview. Unfortunately, his obstinate nature was in part responsible for the controversy.

There was little if any true conflict between science and Christianity up until Darwin. After the publication of *Origin* however, the conflict kicked into gear over the theory of evolution. This did not happen immediately.

Recall that even many Christians embraced Darwin's theory at the outset. This was part of the accommodation process we have seen over and over in this book. Combine this with agnostics like Huxley who actively promoted naturalism under the auspices of evolution, and by the late nineteenth century, science marginalized Christianity because science was considered the authority in more and more aspects of life. But Christians, especially in the universities, did not see the monumental epistemological and metaphysical shift taking place. They did not see soon enough that a theory that offered its own creation account, and was the polar opposite of the Bible, was a threat to the Christian worldview.

Moreover, Darwin's mechanism of natural selection dealt what many considered a death blow to the creation account of Genesis because God was no longer needed as a Designer. This is important because after Darwin, scientists became increasingly convinced that they should look for only naturalistic causes in nature, even though one of the original reasons for practicing science was to understand God more fully through His creation.

As we saw, the epistemological decision to search for only naturalistic causes in nature and to treat the universe as a closed system is known as methodological naturalism. Scientists began to think that all science should be practiced this way. The result is that the universe that had previously been an open system, became a closed system under the auspices of methodological naturalism. God ended up being closed off from His own universe. Scientists began to deny His existence. God was no longer needed as the Cause of creation or the first two human beings. Nature had taken care of it all. There was no need to look anywhere else.

So, in essence, the epistemological shift that took place at the end of the nineteenth century resulted in a metaphysical shift as well. Scientists no longer needed or cared about God. If God existed, that was a question to be left for a field like theology, philosophy, or religious studies. I don't think it is a coincidence that science dispensed with God at the very same time as did the universities in the latter half of the nineteenth century. I am not saying that one caused the other, but I think a synergistic effect was occurring. Dispensing with God in scientific practice (methodological naturalism) certainly reinforced the notion that God might not even exist (metaphysical naturalism). Metaphysical naturalism, which amounts to atheism, turned right around and reinforced the notion that God should no longer be a part of the epistemological equation when doing science.

One result of methodological naturalism is that many began to see Christianity and science as occupying two separate realms. We saw in Chapter nine that Kant was responsible in part for this compartmentalization. Today, science is embedded in the popular mind-set as dealing with facts. Religion supposedly deals only in the realm of faith or beliefs or values. Today, religious beliefs have been demoted to secondary status as mere "opinion" compared with science, which is considered objective and authoritative. As we pointed out in Chapter seven, this was not the case in universities pre-Darwin when Christianity was the centerpiece of education and all other study was integrated around it. But today it is widely held that keeping science and religion in two separate compartments is a workable compromise that avoids warfare between the two.

Some problems arise with all of this, however. One problem is that science has its own faith commitment. In other words, a scientist must have faith that the world is ordered in a rational manner that can be ascertained by our senses. If scientists did not have faith in an ordered world, then science could not even get started. The early natural philosophers understood this. They had no problem believing that the God of the Bible had ordered the world in a certain way, and they wanted to learn something about God's creation and the purpose behind it. Because these natural philosophers believed in God, they were epistemically justified in believing that science could work.

However, scientists today who don't believe in God cannot claim the same epistemic justification. By dispensing with God, they have no *a priori* reasons to believe that the world is rational and ordered. Scientists practicing methodological naturalism have to smuggle in a theistic worldview in which there is order to the cosmos, otherwise they have to take it on faith that science works.

Moreover, science is not the authority everyone thinks it is for the simple reason that it cannot stand alone. Put philosophically, science needs metaphysics. To even get off the ground, science must rest on a foundation of which the universe (metaphysics) is assumed to be ordered. So science does not simply reside in the realm of facts. It makes a faith commitment as well.

With this in mind, it is worth recalling that science has some serious epistemological problems. Because it deals only in the empirical realm, science cannot address questions of value, goodness, justice, love, suffering, and so forth, because these are not found in the empirical realm. Furthermore, the assertion that "only true knowledge can be found in the empirical realm of science" did not come from the empirical realm. Therefore, that assertion is internally inconsistent, which, in essence, means that science cannot meet its own criterion.

Finally, we saw that the problem of induction means that science can lead only to probability, not certainty. The point here is that while not diminishing the efficacy of science as an epistemological tool, the myth in our society that science is The Authority on everything is misplaced.

So from what we just noted above, it should be clear that science involves a faith commitment and cannot provide the *certainty* of knowledge that we were led to believe. Christian beliefs do not have to play second fiddle to scientific beliefs, because science itself is based on a faith commitment.

But let's get back to the question of whether science and Christianity should be kept in separate compartments. Science and Christianity cannot be separated into two realms because they both make truth claims that affect how we view ourselves as humans and how we live our lives. In other words, the worldviews of both Christianity and science overlap in their concerns, making it impossible to compartmentalize them.

When the findings of science contradict what we know from Scripture, then, yes, there will be a conflict. The Christian worldview is in direct contradiction to both metaphysical naturalism and methodological naturalism. Metaphysical naturalism (atheism) holds that God does not exist, only nature does. Against metaphysical naturalism, such as naturalistic evolution, the Christian worldview maintains that God *does* exist and has created everything in the universe. The universe with all of its suns, moons, stars, and planets are there because God created them. The first two human beings, Adam and Eve, are made in the image of God and He directly made them. They and their descendants are not the result of a purposeless mechanism of natural selection that did not have them in mind. God *did* have them in mind and He created them male and female. So the theory of naturalistic evolution, which is inextricably intertwined with science, is a creation story that directly opposes the Christian account of who we are and how we got here.[58]

Likewise, the Christian worldview is in direct contradiction to methodological naturalism, which by definition, excludes God from His creation. If science was truly a neutral endeavor, it would follow the evidence wherever it leads. But methodological naturalism *a priori* excludes God as a Cause, Designer, or Intervener in nature. This is not being neutral. Instead, methodological naturalism by definition always excludes God by reducing the conclusions of the scientific method to nature alone. This has unnecessarily stacked the deck in favor of metaphysical naturalism, which amounts to atheism. Unfortunately, this is the case even if the evidence points to God or at least to an Intelligent Designer.

The result of this is that the method for doing science (methodological naturalism) that grew out of Darwin's theory of evolution has resulted in a built-in bias in science today that points away from God instead of *to* God. This is dangerous because science carries so much authority in our culture as a result of all the wonders of technology. Because science is so authoritative in our culture and because it is considered neutral when it really is not, the atheistic evolutionary worldview is allowed to be taught in our public schools under the guise of science. This points our children away from the God of the Bible while leaving them with the impression that science is authoritative when really it is just an epistemological tool.

Thus, an atheistic worldview (naturalistic evolution), with its own creation story, has taken Christianity's place as part of the secularization process, whether in our schools or in society as a whole. In light of the fact that some leading evolutionists believe that the entire edifice of evolutionary theory is based on faith, it is surely reasonable to question why this creation story is accepted as fact and allowed to be taught in our schools while ID is not.

Technology is awesome and without a doubt has played the primary role in giving science its esteemed cultural authority. This will continue unabated in the future. I think as each generation emerges and technology continues to validate itself and the scientific enterprise, God and Christianity will continue to recede in our minds and hearts. Look at how much time we spend with God each day as compared with our gadgets. If this path we are on continues, and I believe it will, I promise that disaster lies ahead. What I see in the coming years may be represented by a simple formula: Secularism + Technology = Armageddon.

When you combine humans who have left God behind, lost their moral compass, and continue to produce technology that has no moral underpinnings, you will end up with Armageddon. One of the founders of modern science, Francis Bacon, whom we looked at in Chapter nine, wrote, "The root cause of nearly all evils in the sciences [is that] we falsely admire and extol the powers of the human mind."[59]

Technology in the hands of godless men like the global elites (which we will look at in Chapter sixteen) is not going to help humanity. It will enslave humanity. If I am right, then we may expect a real conflict between Christians and applied science (technology) at some point in the future if those in control of the technology attempt to force Christians to compromise their allegiance to the living God of the Bible. More on this in the final chapters.

Chapter 12

Our Public School System Then and Now

When the first colonists came to this land, the parents directly controlled their children's education. They had no regulatory boards and no teacher certification. Eventually they established privately funded common schools, though some were sustained through local taxes. Naturally, these schools were essentially Christian because the early settlers were Christians. In many cases, the colonists arrived in the New World to escape religious persecution, and once on new soil they were free to set up local governments, churches, and schools.[1]

The colonists were adamant about teaching the children to read. In fact, in Massachusetts, the citizens of Boston passed the "Old Deluder Act" in 1647 to defeat Satan, who had used illiteracy in the Old World to keep people from reading the Word of God.[2] The colonists set up schools because they wanted their children to learn how to read the Bible so they would know how to live their lives and gain eternal salvation.[3]

Recall from Chapter seven that in 1643, Harvard College had stated in its Laws and Statutes: "Let every student be plainly instructed and earnestly pressed to consider well the main end of his life and studies is to know God and Jesus Christ which is eternal life" (see John 17:3).[4] It is interesting that this statement was issued just four years prior to the Old Deluder Act of 1647 in Boston. Apparently the early colonists in Massachusetts felt it was important to uphold God, Jesus Christ, and the Bible as central to education. How times have changed.

By the 1830s, a push began for tax-supported public schools that would be open to all social classes. Horace Mann led the common school movement, which aided in preserving republican institutions and provided a solid foundation for morality without which the new nation might fall into tyranny and devastation. Although officially nonsectarian, the schools in practice were very much non-denominational Protestant. This moral underpinning produced a civic function by preventing disorder and promoting virtue and progress.[5]

Generally speaking, the values taught in the schools in the mid-nineteenth century were meant to reflect the values of the growing middle class: Protestantism, capitalism, and American patriotism.[6] One of the main ways the Christian worldview became part and parcel of the children's learning back then was through the grade school textbook known as *McGuffey's Eclectic Reader*. Some 122 million copies of these textbooks were sold between 1826 and 1920.[7] These books read more like a basic theology textbook than a children's textbook because they openly taught a biblical account of the world, which included God's providence, God's ordering of nature, Adam and Eve, sin and damnation, and America's special destiny as chosen by God. This was supplemented by devotional practice, which included reading straight from the Bible without commentary.[8]

Here is an unabashedly Christian excerpt from one of the *McGuffey Readers* as cited in John Westerhoff's *McGuffey and His Readers*:

> The Scriptures are especially designed to make us wise unto salvation through faith in Christ Jesus; to reveal to us the mercy of the Lord in him; to form our minds after the likeness of God our Savior; to build up our souls in wisdom and faith, in love and holiness; to make us thoroughly furnished unto good works, enabling us to glorify God on earth; and, to lead us to an imperishable inheritance among the spirits of just men made perfect, and finally to be glorified with Christ in heaven.[9]

The next excerpt, also found in the *McGuffey Readers*, is the antidote to secularism if there ever was one:

> In this world our friends and our parents die; they go away from us, and we see them no more. And here we all suffer much pain and trouble. But there is a land where there is no affliction. There no one is sick or dies. Our best friend—the Lord Jesus—who died for us on the cross, lives there. He is the Lord and ruler of that happy land. He will send his holy angels to bring all those who love him, to live with him forever.[10]

Can you imagine children reading this in class today? Over and against our current secular worldly mind-set, McGuffey wanted to convey an eternal perspective to his young readers. It's not all about the here and now, which is secular and fleeting. It is about the Lord of heaven—Jesus, who died on the cross for our sins so we could live forever with Him in heaven.

Interestingly enough, schooling in the nineteenth century was so theist centered that educators went out of their way to avoid books that might mislead the children. Thus, they accepted *The Adventures of Huckleberry Finn* by Mark Twain with some reluctance.[11]

By the latter half of the nineteenth century, the call for nonsectarianism in the public schools became more pronounced. Remember that this is exactly what was then taking place in the universities as well. By the end of the century, the religious content in the schools and the universities had been watered down and diminished considerably. The idea that children should be taught to be moral citizens still remained, but nonsectarian Protestantism was no longer the heart of education.[12]

The Reformers and Big Money's Effect on Education

One catalyst for the diminishing of Christianity in the public schools was the same as it was for the universities: progressive reformers wanted to transform education. Education became more about preparing children to fit into the modern industrialized society rather than with preparing children to learn reading and writing and to develop Christian character. The reformers used science (the new authority) and its stepchild psychology to teach that morality was relative to social life. Children were taught to reason about morality based on their own experiences rather than simply accepting traditional (Christian) values.[13] The reformers proposed maintaining the study of the Bible but only as literature.[14] Reformers foisted other anti-Christian tenets on the children that are still entrenched in education today, which we will look at in a moment.

With the advent of science and the rise of the modern industrial society, the big-moneyed interests also had a hand in molding public schooling. These big-money elites, represented by business, government, and the universities in the Northeast, saw that machines driven by coal opened up limitless potential for production. This, of course, was especially evident in the railroad industry. They were also enamored with new inventions like the telegraph.[15] In short, the moneyed elites were giddy just thinking about the potential profits they could make with technology. So, what does this have to do with the children?

Basically, these elites envisioned children as commodities. From their perspective, children needed to be indoctrinated at a young age so that they could be molded into a "human resource" that would lead to an organized scientific society. This attitude can be seen in a speech made by Woodrow Wilson to a group of businessmen just prior to World War I: "We want one class to have a liberal education. We want another class, a very much larger class of necessity, to forgo the privilege of a liberal education and fit themselves to perform specific difficult manual tasks."[16] Frighteningly, this sounds like an adumbration of Aldous Huxley's *Brave New World*.

By 1917, the Education Trust, which consisted of representatives from Rockefeller, Carnegie, Harvard, Stanford, the University of Chicago, and the National Education Association, agreed that children should learn to view themselves, as John Taylor Gatto puts it, "as *employees* competing for the favor of management."[17] Gatto sums up the corporate takeover of public education:

> From the beginning, there was purpose behind forced schooling, purpose which had nothing to do with what parents, kids, or communities wanted; but instead was forged out of what a highly centralized corporate economy and system of finance bent on internationalizing itself was thought to need. . . . School was looked upon from the first decade of the twentieth century as a branch of industry and a tool of governance.[18]

The corporate power elites wanted a dumbed-down population who had a low level of discontent and would be ready to work in the factory system. As one observer pointed out, this was already the modus operandi in England, France, and Germany. Not so coincidentally, these countries were also three major coal producers which had already reduced the common people to industrial workers long before the elites in the United States attempted to implement the same agenda.

Moreover, the power brokers in the United States didn't want children becoming inventors or entrepreneurs who could end up competing with them. Therefore, full-time schooling through grade twelve became the norm and would keep potential would-be entrepreneurs tied up in school and stave off their creative energies. On the other hand, children increasingly learned less and less about farm life and agrarian concerns for the same reason—they were at school all the time. This increased the lack of farming skills and apprenticeships being passed down from generation to generation. This, in turn, prepared the children for the possibility of doing production work of some sort off the farm.[19]

Psychology's Influence on Education

The new field of psychology also played a role in transforming public school education. It offered an independent way of assessing children by using scientific measurements and inventing categories, thus professionalizing education and simultaneously legitimizing the progressive agenda.[20]

Wilhelm Wundt (1832–1920), founder of experimental psychology, wrote the first book on psychology. Wundt wanted to show that humans were neurochemical machines that are the sum total of their experiences (stimuli). As a professor of psychology, he set up the first experimental laboratory at the University of Leipzig in 1879.[21] In the historical context of German scientism, Wundt saw the new psychology in terms of physiology. Wundt made this move because true psychology, which literally should deal with the soul, couldn't be quantified. So Wundt proposed that henceforth psychology should deal only with experience; in other words, with what could be measured and demonstrated scientifically.[22]

As the reader knows by now, science was the be-all and end-all at the end of the nineteenth century and into the twentieth century, which is why Wundt went in this direction. This is important because Wundt made many disciples, and his ideas spread into the American educational system where it has had a profound impact.

Wundt's ideas provided the foundation for the principles of conditioning which B. F. Skinner and Pavlov implemented. Pavlov studied in Leipzig in 1884 just after Wundt had set up his laboratories. Pavlov later expanded upon the principles of conditioning.[23] Wundt helped redefine education as *adaptation* of children to specific behavior so that each child could get along in his or her own group.[24] Instead of viewing the teacher as *educator*, Wundt changed the perception of the teacher to that of a *guide* or a *facilitator* in the socialization of the child.

Wundt's ideas were not totally new. Rather they were a reinforcing agent in the continuation of the government-controlled school system that King Frederick William I had already set up in Prussia starting in 1717. "Government-controlled" meant that everything about the school was geared toward the state, which was seen as the real parent of the children. In the Prussian system, teachers had to be indoctrinated first.[25] Then the teachers performed their duties as bureaucrats molding the young children into obedient citizens who would view the collective life as an ideal.[26]

Wundt viewed humans as animals entirely dependent on external stimuli. If animals could be studied in the laboratory, why couldn't a person's behavior be studied as well? After all, humans had a common ancestry with animals.[27] Of course, Wundt got this idea from Darwin. Wundt, and many psychologists who followed, believed humans were merely social animals that must learn to adapt to their environment and attempt to fit into society. Thus, the education system downplayed individualism in favor of conformity and the "well-adjusted (conditioned) child."[28]

Wundt had an indirect yet profound impact on our public educational system. He taught many students from America who received a PhD from him directly. These students brought his ideas to the States, where administrators implemented them in the public schools. By the end of the nineteenth century, the emphasis in public schools was on teaching children how to fit into democracy and the American way.[29] This resembled the Prussian-German emphasis on children conforming to the state's wishes. Christianity was no longer a central focus. Darwinism also aided and abetted this marginalization of the Christian worldview in the classroom because it viewed humans as animals. Children were no longer a gift from God but were subjects to be studied and conditioned to fit into a particular societal mold the government determined.

One of Wundt's students was G. Stanley Hall (1844–1924), who joined Johns Hopkins University in 1883. The reader will recall from Chapter seven that Johns Hopkins University was considered to be the first secular university. Hall started both the first psychology laboratory in the Unites States at Johns Hopkins and also inaugurated the *American Journal of Psychology*.[30]

Darwin's evolutionary theory influenced Hall, just as it did Wundt. As a true atheist and secular humanist, Hall proclaimed the following:

> Nature and Man—there is nothing else outside, above, or beyond these in the universe. . . . Only now is man beginning to realize that he is truly supreme in all the universe we know and that there is nothing above or beyond him. . . . Science is both his organ of apprehension and his tool by which he must make his sovereignty complete, come fully into his kingdom, and make his reign supreme.[31]

Men like Hall always conceive science as being the tool to get them to their desired heights. In his naïveté, Hall could not foresee that technology in the hands of fallen men doesn't always lead to utopia. It often leads to something less idyllic. In addition, ignoring God's existence and then declaring yourself sovereign, as Hall did, is the height of folly. It is God who reigns over the entire universe, and it is God who will set up His kingdom here on earth in the not too distant future, not men like Hall.

John Dewey: The Father of Modern Education

Hall mentored John Dewey for one year at Johns Hopkins, where Dewey subsequently received his doctorate in 1884.[32] Dewey was in the process of losing his Christian faith (if he had not already lost it), and Hall certainly did nothing to point Dewey in the right direction. In the fashion of Rousseau, Dewey believed in the perfectibility of man.[33] He was not primarily concerned that children learn reading, writing, and facts about history or geography. He was more concerned that children learn how to service modern society.[34] This notion not only mirrored the Prussian model but also fell in line with the desires of the big-money elites. Dewey viewed the public school system as the "new established church" in which democratic values could be engendered. He wanted to divorce children from what he saw as the unreasonable religious influence of their parents.[35] He saw science as a unifying force in fostering communitarian values while helping to discard superstition and sectarian distinctions.[36]

In 1905, Dewey, always a busy man, founded the Intercollegiate Socialist Society, which changed its name in 1921 to the more euphemistic League for Industrial Democracy, whose purpose was to build education for a "new social order."[37] Along with many other progressives, Dewey toured Russia in the 1930s and returned starry-eyed with Marxism and all that Lenin and Stalin had done for the Soviet citizens. It was during this time that the Carnegie Foundation financed a grant on the study of American education, which concluded, among other things, that "the age of individualism is closing and a new age of collectivism is emerging."[38] One can see the beginning of the New World Order trying to emerge during this time.

Over a period of time, Dewey's ideology came full circle—democracy and capitalism gave way to socialism. Instead of fostering individualism, Dewey felt that children should be taught to act "cooperatively and collectively." This Marxist ideal also fell in line with the elites who didn't want any push-back from the unwashed masses. Henceforth, public education should attempt to raise "state consciousness."[39] Dewey's antipathy toward Christianity also fit well with his Marxist socialism. The following decades witnessed the systematic removal of any remnant of the Christian worldview in public schools. Today, psycho-engineered narcissism has replaced morals and character, which traditionally had been grounded in the divinely created human.[40] Samuel L. Blumenfeld sums up Dewey's impact:

> It was thus Dewey who began to fashion a new materialist religion in which humanity was venerated instead of God. This is basically the religion of Secular Humanism, and this is what has become the official religion of the United States, for it is the only religion permitted in its public schools and totally supported by government funds. The Constitution of the United States forbids the government from establishing a national religion. But we have one, whether the people know it or not.[41]

Blumenfeld confirms my thesis that secularism, in many ways, has become the default worldview in our society as well as pointing out that it is the established religion in our classrooms.

It is worth remembering that Dewey coauthored the *Humanist Manifesto* in 1933. This manifesto was born out of the American Humanist Association (AHA), which wanted to eradicate theism from culture.[42] Other humanists shared Dewey's views on education and his antipathy toward Christianity. In 1930, Charles E. Potter stated: "Education is thus a most powerful ally of Humanism . . . What can the theistic Sunday-schools, meeting for an hour once a week, and teaching only a fraction of the children, do to stem the tide of a five-day program of humanistic teaching?"[43]

Fifty years later we see the same sentiment expressed by John J. Dunphy, who wrote in the *Humanist* magazine in 1983: "I am convinced that the battle for humankind's future must be waged and won in the public school classroom by teachers who correctly perceive their role as the proselytizers of a new faith . . . The classroom must and will become an arena of conflict between the old and the new—the rotting corpse of Christianity, together with all its adjacent evils and misery, and the new faith of humanism."[44]

While I strongly disagree with the atheistic worldview of both men, what they were hoping for has come to pass. Is it any wonder our society has become unhinged on all levels now that secular humanism is the religion of our schools and has had a few generations or so to gain a foothold in our culture?

Two other notable figures also held the opinion that schools are an important battleground for winning the propaganda war. Lenin stated, "Give me four years to teach the children and the seed I have sown will never be uprooted."[45] Hitler told parents that the children belonged to the Reich. In one speech he said, "This new Reich will give its youth to no one, but will itself take youth and give to youth its own education and its own upbringing."[46] Abraham Lincoln predicted, "The philosophy of the schoolroom in one generation will be the philosophy of the government in the next."[47] These are important things to keep in mind as the power elites gain more control over the education of our children every day.

Antonio Gramsci and the Global Elites' Agenda

I should also make mention of Antonio Gramsci (1891–1937), a Marxist and leader of the Italian Communist Party, who has had an impact on our educational system as well. Gramsci recognized that Marxism would never gain a foothold in America because its citizens and government reflected a biblical worldview in which each individual was accountable to God. For an ideological revolution to occur in America, the biblical worldview and its emphasis on individual accountability would have to be displaced.[48]

Gramsci, like other atheistic humanists, believed that the way to change culture was to change its educational system, which he referred to as "transformational education." He believed that students should be taught in groups so they would envision themselves as part of a group rather than as individuals. He maintained that math, history, language, and other disciplines were not about truth but were merely constructs that those in power used to subdue the vulnerable masses. These so-called constructs, like Christianity, needed to be deconstructed. In this way he foreshadowed postmodern thought of men like Derrida.

According to Gramsci, education should be used for utilitarian purposes; that is, for the benefit of the society. Unfortunately, Gramsci believed that the ruling elite should determine the good of the society. As citizens, we should be concerned that much of Gramsci's Marxist ideology and postmodern thought has found favor with the academic elites and has made its way into our public schools by way of federal education policies that advocate a "new world order" and other transformational education ideology.[49] Unfortunately, most parents today are unaware of the history, ideology, and agenda of the elites in the public school system.

223

In fact, for at least the last one hundred years, elites have pushed for a "New World Order," which amounts to some type of one world government. This is evident in some of the more formal proposals in the League of Nations (1919), which then morphed into the United Nations (1942). Out of the UN came UNESCO (United Nations Educational, Scientific and Cultural Organization), whose first Director-General was none other than the secular humanist Julian Huxley. UNESCO is important for our purposes because one of the primary goals of its educational program is to promote political unity of the world through dismantling national sovereignties and forging some type of world government.[50]

Globalists view the United States as a major obstacle to world government. The global elites intend to overcome this by educating young children so they become accustomed to the idea of supporting a New World Order and a one world government. It's called indoctrination.[51] In fact, in his book entitled *UNESCO: Its Purpose and Philosophy*, Julian Huxley saw ideologies from the East and West opposing each other and resulting in a final "world unification" as Hegel's historical dialectic played itself out.[52] In fact, teacher-facilitators have used Hegel's dialectic to guide children toward collectivism, as we will see below.

The logical question to ask here is how organizations like the UN or UNESCO can have any influence on *our* educational system in light of the fact that the Tenth Amendment of the US Constitution states that the states, local governments, and people are in charge of education, not our government or any other entity like the UN. The Founders set up our government this way because they were concerned that too much power in one place, like a central government, would be deleterious to the country.[53]

So how is UNESCO able to influence our public school system? The answer is twofold. First, many elites in our country want a New World Order. Allen Quist, a college professor and former legislator wrote, "The U.S. Department of Education is largely run by the same world government crowd that governs the UN."[54] Second, the elites, like those in the Department of Education, can promote the agenda of UNESCO by side-stepping the Constitution. How? They do it by adhering to "policy agreements" that come out of the World Education Forum, which is sponsored by the UN. This is accomplished when the Department of Education sets national curriculum standards that are in line with policy initiatives, like Education for All, that come out of

UNESCO. Both the public and lawmakers are totally in the dark because they do not realize that often our public school curricula are based on government standards that meet the international curriculum standards. The World Declaration on Education for All devised these international curriculum standards, which is an educational initiative under the auspices of UNESCO.[55]

Notice that the World Declaration on Education for All is just that: a "declaration." As Allen Quist pointed out, after being signed by one of our presidents, "declarations," "agreements," or "protocols" that come out of the UN have the effect of being "soft laws." In other words, for all intents and purposes, these documents have the same effect as real laws in our country. Declarations, protocols, and agreements have replaced treaties in many instances, the latter of which must be ratified by two-thirds vote in the Senate to become law. But these declarations, etc., simply need to be signed by a president and, though they are not officially law in our country, in essence have the same effect. In this way, the executive branch can subject the citizens of our country to policies and initiatives that were not voted on but, worse, were proposed by the UN globalists.[56]

So, for example, both President George H. W. Bush and Bill Clinton committed the United States to international agreements on education and later placed the substance of those agreements in the form of a bill entitled Goals 2000, which President George W. Bush later revised and relabeled No Child Left Behind (NCLB). But another bill was passed along with Goals 2000. HR6 was hidden in its 1350 pages, a provision that if a state didn't comply with Goals 2000, it would lose all of its federal education money. So although Goals 2000 was supposedly "voluntary" for all fifty states, in essence, it was not.

This "voluntary" policy continued with NCLB.[57] Quist calls this a *coup d'etat* by a "small group of radicals within the U.S. Department of Education" who have taken over the curriculum in the public school system.[58] This is how the federal government and the global elitists have surreptitiously taken over education curriculum that rightly belongs to the states. It is all part of the global agenda. Bertrand Russell, one of the premiere philosophical atheists of the last century and a UNESCO adviser, put it this way: "Every government that has been in control of education for a generation will be able to control its subjects securely without the need of armies or policemen."[59]

Much of Gramsci's "transformational education" can be found in the federal curriculum like President Bush's NCLB and President

Obama's Common Core, both of which expanded government control of education.[60] The purpose of transformational education is to transform children's traditional values and beliefs into those that conform to the global agenda. A radical change in institutions, government, and culture is the goal of transformational education. Thus many of the children's textbooks promote postmodernism, radical multiculturalism, Marxism, secular humanism, and a world government. Our national sovereignty is undermined along with Christianity, because these are obstacles to the globalist agenda of the elites.[61]

Postmodern thought is promulgated in the school system under the auspices of transformational education. Therefore knowledge is considered to be only a construct. Values and morals are relative to individuals and different cultures. Marriage, for example, is just a construct. The institution of traditional marriage, while good and true for a group of individuals at a certain time in history, may be on the way out according to secular-postmodern ideology. Ideas and values need to evolve. Marriage, though traditionally between a man and a woman, is redefined to include gay marriage. Constructs like traditional marriage that are based on the Bible are out of touch with our modern way of life and should be deconstructed and discarded, according to the elites.[62]

Because a New World Order is the ultimate goal of the global elitists, world government and world citizenship is emphasized over and against national citizenship and national sovereignty. Global elitists view the UN's Declaration of Human Rights as superior to our US Bill of Rights. They believe the founding principles as expressed in the Constitution are outmoded and need to evolve. The upshot of this is that the elites view our God-given inalienable rights, which should be protected by our government, as subordinate to the UN Declaration of Human Rights. In fact, it says in the UN declaration, "These rights and freedoms may in no case be exercised contrary to the purposes and principles of the United Nations."[63]

Under the UN declaration, our rights are not God-given, because God does not exist for these people. From the globalists' perspective, human rights, and states' rights for that matter, are always subservient to the goals of the government or the UN, just like they are in a totalitarian Communist regime.[64] Quist summarizes the globalists' postmodern perspective: "The principles of national sovereignty, natural law and the natural rights of life, liberty and property may have been useful for the culture that embraced them 200 years ago, but that does not mean these principles are appropriate for us today."[65]

This New World Order agenda, whereby the US Constitution and national sovereignty is pooh-poohed, was published in a school textbook entitled *We the People: The Citizen and the Constitution.* The textbook is the federal (national) curriculum for civics and government. In this textbook the "global village" is upheld as an ideal in which a one world government will one day replace national sovereignty.[66]

Paul Vitz has shown that over the past thirty years public school textbooks have, in general, made negative references toward Christianity in addition to excluding our traditional values and American heritage.[67] For example, after reviewing over forty social studies texts for first to fourth graders, Vitz found that there was no mention of "marriage," "husband," or "wife." The word *family* simply referred to a group of people. It was clear, as far as he was concerned, that the notion of family was depicted apart from the institution of marriage, or it was depicted without a father or mother.[68]

From another perspective, Warren A. Nord thinks it is not so much that there is a deliberate intention in all cases to marginalize religious alternatives in the textbooks and classrooms; rather, it is that the secularization process renders religious alternatives in our society increasingly irrelevant. Combine this with many teachers' patronizing attitude toward religion, and the result is that children are making their way through their academic lives without being exposed in any real way to religion at all. Or when they *are* exposed to it, Christianity is portrayed in a negative light. As Nord points out, this has a powerful "cumulative effect" in that children end up thinking and acting in "secular ways."[69]

Molding the Children's Values

From the start, the aim of progressive educators and globalists has been the indoctrination of children, with the emphasis on shaping the children's feelings and morals. Book learning and knowledge acquisition, like history, mathematics, reading, and writing, have always taken a back seat to the molding of the child to the agenda of the elites.

One way this has been accomplished is through the Hegelian dialectic. Back in Chapter three, recall that the philosopher Hegel's dialectical paradigm involved the "thesis," which is confronted by the "antithesis" and then resolved in the "synthesis." Although Hegel's paradigm was meant to describe the flow of history, the educational progressives have employed this dialectical thinking to facilitate the desired values in children.

It works something like this. The *thesis* represents the original values the child brings to the classroom. The *antithesis* are the values the educational elites want instilled in the child, and since these values are often at odds with what the child has learned in the home or church, a conflict exists. The child experiences cognitive dissonance. During this period of confusion, the child's resistance to the new set of values must be broken. This is the job of the teacher-facilitator. Once the child capitulates, we have the *synthesis*. In this case, the *synthesis* is confirmed when the child accepts the intelligentsia's predetermined values and morals. These values would include everything that falls under the ideology of secular humanism.[70]

"Values clarification" began a couple of generations ago with the goal of instilling values in school children. Values clarification is meant to do just that: clarify one's values. The authors define the word *value* on page ten of their book *Values Clarification* as having three components: emotional, cognitive, and behavioral.[71] The word *moral* is noticeable by its absence in their definition of *value*. Apparently, the authors believe morals and values have nothing to do with each other. At any rate, the authors credit this method for clarifying values to the work of Louis Raths, who based his work on none other than John Dewey.[72]

The premise of values clarification is that children come to school with a preconceived set of values from their parents, church, and peers. These values must be dispensed with so children are free to choose their own values. When this method is placed in the hands of the teacher-facilitator, the children "choose" values that are often the polar opposite of those taught by the parents or the church. This is perfectly fine from the intelligentsia's perspective, because children should be taught that they have a right to choose their own values, which are just as good as anyone else's. After all, there are no moral absolutes. Everything is an individual preference.[73]

For example, a teacher who had employed values clarification methodology to a group of underachieving eighth graders found that after the students had worked through the required steps, they subsequently reported that their most valued activities were "sex, drugs, drinking, and skipping school." The teacher, of course, was left with no way to persuade the students that those activities were not something to be valued.[74] As I pointed out in a previous chapter, this is the problem with relativism of any sort. It always slits its own throat.

Thomas Sowell notes that these "brainwashing" techniques, as he calls them, are the same ones used in any totalitarian countries.[75] The elites, whether progressive or global, know that Christianity poses a threat to the implementation of their secular value system which upholds ideals such as atheism, evolution, moral relativism, and socialism.[76] Using the Hegelian dialectic and values clarification successfully contradicts traditional morals and values, thereby undermining them. For the progressives, no one has a right to tell children what their values should be unless it's the UN, our government, or the global elites. Larry Grathwohl argues what the end result is:

> We have a tremendous number of young people who are unable to read or write, or add and subtract. They are, however, very capable of protesting when they think that their individual rights have been imposed upon [and] feel that they are being punished if they have to do homework and learn the basic precepts of our country and our government. In many cases they don't even know that the constitution exists, and if they do, they are taught that this is a document written by old white men 200 years ago and that it is meaningless in today's world.[77]

The indoctrination process goes more smoothly if the children are convinced the teachers know better than their parents what can be taught. One parent, for example, noticed her kindergartner started snapping at her every time she tried to correct her. At one point the child started crying while informing her that she was "a mommy, not a teacher." The mother asked her if someone told her this at school. The child replied, "Yes, I'm only allowed to learn from my teacher."[78]

Court Decisions That Marginalized Christianity
Of course, if removing the God of the Bible from the public schools is the goal, our judicial system did much of the heavy lifting. As recently as 1952, Justice William Douglas stated in a Supreme Court decision, "We are a religious people" and our "institutions presuppose a Supreme Being."[79] Apparently, though, we were not a religious people ten years later (1962–63) when a series of decisions by the Supreme Court removed Bible readings and state-sponsored prayer from the public schools. The *Engel* decision in 1962 banned corporate prayer in schools, even though the justices acknowledged that this practice was essentially the same as that of the Supreme Court justices, who asked for God's blessing at the beginning of each day. The prayer had been

voluntary for parents who could opt out their children from the prayer. It had also been voluntary for the local school boards, yet the decision to ban state-sponsored prayer stood.

Even the media at that time were against the decision by a two-to-one margin. Senators and members of Congress were aghast. One senator claimed, "The Supreme Court has set up atheism as the new religion."[80] Steward, one of the dissenting justices, argued that prohibiting religious expression did not produce "the realization of state neutrality, but rather . . . the establishment of a religion of secularism."[81]

Hats off to Supreme Court Justice Steward for getting it exactly correct. In fact, he summed up one of the sub-theses of this book when he argued that there is no such thing as "neutrality" in instances like this. Once God, the Bible, and prayer are removed, something must logically fill the worldview void in the classroom. That something is secularism. Justice Steward is right on target with his assertion. The myth of neutrality is just that, a myth. Something will always fill the vacuum.

The Supreme Court decisions of 1962–63 seemed to be a watershed moment that opened the floodgates for more anti-Christian attitudes and court decisions. I will mention just a few that are listed in John Taylor Gatto's *The Underground History of American Education*.

- It is unconstitutional for the word *God* to be used in any of the official writings of the Board of Education (1976).
- It is unconstitutional for a prayer to be offered in the opening or closing ceremony of a school graduation (this is found in two court decisions, one in 1985 and the other in 1986).
- Students in Alaska were told that they could not use the word *Christmas*, because it contained the word *Christ* (1987).
- A federal court ruled in Virginia that homosexual newspapers could be handed out on a high school campus but religious newspapers could not (1987).
- In Denver, an elementary school principal removed the Bible from the school library (1988).[82]

Likewise, William Jeynes points out a case in which a six-year-old was placed on in-school suspension because he prayed before he ate at school (2002). The child must have been moving his lips to get in this kind of trouble. You see, a Michigan Supreme Court case in 1965 stated that it was lawful to say grace over your lunch as long as it was done without moving your lips.[83] This court decision is just as juvenile as the children it is trying to deal with.

Jeynes points out another case of a teacher throwing the Bibles of two Texas middle school girls into the trash while stating, "This is garbage!" The school condoned the action because they said the Bible contains "hate speech."[84] So let me understand this. The teacher spewing "This is garbage!" isn't hate speech? Do you think this teacher would have done the same thing with the Koran?

I will make a prediction: In less than a generation and a half from now, throwing out Bibles and claiming that Christianity is unlawful will be the norm, not the exception. Making exclusive truth claims like "Christ is the only way to salvation" will be labeled "extremist," "oppressive," "intolerant" or "hate speech." This is already happening. The progressives and global elites will try, and probably succeed at some point, to outlaw proclaiming the gospel in our country. If we in this country can tolerate school teachers throwing out Bibles while calling them "garbage," then we are only a generation or so away from rounding up Christians as extremists for being intolerant. It will happen. You will see. Remember that the same children who are seeing Bibles thrown out and Christianity maligned and marginalized at every turn will be the same brainwashed children who will be running our country in the not so distant future.

Practical atheists (nominal Christians) who give superficial lip service to belief in God but don't give Him a lick of thought during the course of their lives are not going to provide any resistance to the militant advance of the secular-progressive-globalist agenda. Practical atheists may sit in front of their TVs and bemoan that the country is going to hell in a handbasket when they see examples like those above, but they will not have the intestinal fortitude to do anything about it.

If practical atheists make up as large a share of our demographic pie as I think they do, this would explain why we are in full retreat regarding issues like God getting booted out of schools. There is simply little if any resistance. As each generation passes, a greater percentage of practical atheists and agnostics arise in our country, which means the chances for resisting the secular trend will decrease significantly. Each inroad the secular elites make gains them more of a foothold and further desensitizes the society to their globalist and godless ideology. This just leads to more accommodation and retreat. Wash, rinse, repeat.

Today's School Children

It should come as no surprise that juvenile delinquent behavior increased dramatically beginning in 1963.[85] Some of it may be attributed to the beginnings of the countercultural revolution. But it seems undeniable that a causal relationship exists between the court decisions that expunged prayer and Bible reading from the schools and the rise in delinquent behavior.[86] Look how far we have come. In the 1940s and '50s the biggest disciplinary problems public school teachers had with students were "talking, chewing gum, making noise, running in the halls, getting out of turn in line, dress code infractions, and not putting paper in the waste basket."[87] In 1993, the same survey was given to teachers and the problems were much more serious: "drug abuse, alcohol abuse, pregnancy, suicide, rape, robbery, and assault."[88] The moral decadence is palpable.

After reviewing the adverse influences coming from the progressives, global elitists, and the courts, we should not be surprised to find the public schools today totally devoid of anything resembling a Christian influence. Approximately 47 percent of all high school students have had sex. One out of every four of our teenage girls has a sexually transmitted disease. The United States has the highest teen pregnancy rate on the planet, and for women under thirty years of age, more than half give birth out of wedlock.[89] A Heritage Foundation study showed that sexually active teens are more prone to depression and suicide compared with those who practice abstinence.[90]

But this doesn't stop the educators from passing out condoms. As David Limbaugh points out, apparently the educational establishment is more concerned with avoiding the promotion of values considered religious than with the health and safety of the children. He sardonically questions whether educators should be allowed to continue teaching children not to steal or murder, since those are part of the Ten Commandments.[91]

Of course, Limbaugh makes a good point. But, really, teachers today have no moral justification for teaching against murder or stealing—not simply because the Ten Commandments are no longer allowed in the schools. Rather, it is because children today are encouraged to come up with their own set of values. Having sex, drinking, doing drugs, etc., are what many school students find most valuable. Perhaps most troubling is that 91 percent of so-called born-again teenagers believe that there are no moral absolutes.[92] The brainwashing of these younger generations with postmodern values increases the probability that our republic will give way to the globalist one-world agenda some day.

Because knowledge and learning have taken a backseat to feelings and self-esteem,[93] we have encouraged an unprecedented narcissism in our school children. We've brought up two to three generations or so of children who think it's all about them and how they feel. No wonder the fruit of autonomy is becoming so prevalent in our culture. Every emerging generation is producing men and women who think values are autonomous. Whatever they say and think must be right because no external moral absolutes exist outside of themselves.

Our school children continually score poorly on math and science[94] when compared with other countries but that's perfectly acceptable because the kids still think highly of themselves. Every child is a "winner" in today's coddled fairy-tale land. Progressive educators can't stand competitive games because they create losers, and losing might damage the fragile self-esteem of the children. In some states dodgeball is discouraged or banned because it promotes too much stress and anxiety in those who are eliminated.[95] In addition, progressive educators associate competitive games with capitalism— where there is a need to compete—and these educators question capitalism and its need for competitive behavior.[96] Remember, the global elites, want socialism indoctrinated into the children, not free-market capitalism.

So what we end up with is the need for noncompetitive games that affirm the children's self-esteem. What games, you might ask? Well, some physical education professionals suggest juggling. Yes, juggling. After all, there is no threat of elimination. But not just any old juggling, like with balls or something. No, that may prove too frustrating. There-fore, the President's Council on Youth Fitness and Sports had a former member suggest to the *Los Angeles Times* that "scarves" would work because they "float down slowly" and therefore "lessen performance anxiety and boosts self-esteem."[97] Really? One critic sarcastically suggested that perhaps each child playing musical chairs should be guaranteed a seat so that they can just sit there and talk to one another about how positive they all feel about being included.[98]

The powers that be don't want competitive children. They want docile little lambs that will learn their places in society right from the get-go. How else can the global elitists implement neo-feudalism unless they have dumbed-down compliant worker bees? John D. Rockefeller Sr. said a long time ago, "I don't want a nation of thinkers, I want a nation of workers."[99] We're creating a nation of compliant, unassuming children who are ready to join the elites' traveling circus show and who can't read, write, or spell. But that's okay, because they still feel good about themselves.

The Problems with Drugging the Children

One of the cardinal sins in the public schools today is, well, just being a kid. In other words, if a child (especially a boy) is caught fidgeting, not paying attention, running around, squirming, or is restless, impatient, frequently losing or forgetting things, and a host of other normal, kid-like behaviors, the kid is labeled with a "disability" called ADHD (attention-deficit/hyperactive disorder). As psychiatrist Peter Breggin has pointed out in his book *Toxic Psychiatry*, it is not so much that children are different today. It is more a function of psychologists' and psychiatrists' attempt to give what used to be considered normal childlike behavior a medical diagnosis now.[100]

Of course, this over-psychologizing has been going on for quite some time in our culture. Notice, for example, that in 1952 the American Psychiatric Association listed 106 mental disorders. But by 1994 the list of defined disorders had burgeoned to 374.[101] So either psychiatrists "recognize" many more mental health disorders and, therefore, society is filled with a lot more individuals who are struggling with these issues than had been previously thought, or psychiatrists have gotten completely carried away with "diagnosing" these mental health "diseases." In many cases it appears to be the latter.

Breggin provides us with evidence of this in another of his books: *Talking Back to Ritalin*. He notes that in the early 1970s, psychiatry was floundering, and those in the industry were having trouble filling their practices. Competition from nonmedical helping professions, such as psychologists, family therapists, and social workers, were putting a dent in the psychiatrists' practices because the nonmedical helping professions charged less per visit while still providing good service as "talking therapists." To get themselves out of this quandary, psychiatrists began to convince the public that mental health issues should remain under the control of physicians and psychiatrists, because psychological suffering was grounded in genetics and biology. These mental health problems, they asserted, required drugs, electroshock, and various other medical interventions that could be prescribed only by psychiatrists and medical doctors.

By the 1980s, psychiatrists created what Breggin describes as "an economic and political partnership with the drug companies" in which the medical model and authority of psychiatry were promoted to the public by using drug company funds.[102] In this way, psychiatry removed the threat of the nonmedical professionals, regained market share, and came to exert a powerful political influence in our country.[103]

Another important change took place during this time as well. To ensure that children with real physical handicaps, like hearing loss or sight impairment, could receive a public education, Congress passed the Education for all Handicapped Children Act in 1975. The law was reinstated in 1990, but with a subtle difference. They changed the word *handicapped* to *disabilities*, and a year later the US Department of Education Office of Special Education and Rehabilitative Services determined that a child diagnosed with ADHD could qualify for special education.[104]

Why is this word change important? Because every student labeled with ADHD may be put in a special-education class. Then the school is qualified to receive anywhere from $10,000 to $90,000 per year in extra tax funds. So schools can profit simply by having students diagnosed with the "disability" ADHD. As Joel Turtel claims in his book *Public Schools, Public Menace*, "By joining the ADHD bandwagon, public schools have literally hit the jackpot for federal funds."[105]

What does all of this mean? Well, many groups can benefit by diagnosing children with the ADHD. Schools can benefit because they can alleviate some of the responsibility that teachers have for successfully educating children by blaming kids who (supposedly) have ADHD and often disrupt their classes. In addition, schools also benefit from federal funds that are funneled into the schools where the ADHD children reside. Turtel summarizes it this way:

> Who else profits from ADHD? Of course, pharmaceutical companies make millions of dollars selling drugs used to treat this alleged disease. . . . School authorities can use the law to threaten and pressure parents to give their children these drugs for years while the kids are in school. . . . Then we have the medical and psychiatric professions. Pediatricians, general physicians, and child psychiatric professions all get more business when the ADHD diagnosis is promoted in the public schools. Five million children with alleged ADHD translates into a lot of office visits.[106]

The global elites also win because children are controlled by a system that has children drugged up and compliant to any demands of the "authorities," like the local psychiatrist, school psychologist, or teacher-facilitator.

To date there is no known objective, biological, or neurological abnormality found in the brain or elsewhere in the body that demonstrates or confirms the existence of the supposed ADHD.[107] The National Institutes of Health Consensus Development Conference met in 1998 and discussed ADHD and its treatments. Their stated conclusion: "Finally after years of clinical research and experience with ADHD, our knowledge about the cause or causes of ADHD remains speculative."[108] So these "experts," after years and years of administering the mind-altering drug Ritalin to kids, don't even know what causes the supposed disability in the first place? Life-threatening drugs are allowed to be dispensed on mere speculation? Do these so-called experts have no common sense? Every human being alive knows that kids are antsy. That's part of what makes children, well, children.

Samuel Blumenfeld, who has written eight books on education and public schools, tells how he went to Beijing, China, and was able to observe 500 children during their morning exercises. He asked his host how many of the kids were on Ritalin. His host had never even heard of Ritalin. The children in China don't have ADHD, and the schoolchildren are not drugged.[109]

This leaves one wondering if the vast majority of cases of ADHD diagnoses are contrived. Joel Turtel, who in his book *Public School, Public Menace* cited the anecdote above by Blumenfeld, rightly asks what the war on drugs in our country really means. He wonders aloud how it is possible that police can search a kid's locker for marijuana or cocaine while school employees are allowed to dispense a mind-altering drug like Ritalin to children "like it was aspirin."[110]

The push for diagnosing ADHD and drugging the children certainly seems to coincide with the original intention of the global elites who want compliant little worker bees who know their places in life and won't cause trouble. Drugging children for a manufactured disability is certainly a way to keep the kids docile while they are being indoctrinated with the progressive elites' agenda.

As we noted above, it's also about money. Dr. Lawrence Diller, a pediatrician and author of two books, gave his testimony before a panel of his peers and the families he had sworn to safeguard: "The money, power and influence of the pharmaceutical industry corrupt all. The pervasive control that the drug companies have over medical research, publications, professional organizations, doctors' practices, Congress and yes, even agencies like the FDA is the American equivalent of a drug cartel."[111]

The worst part of this is that in some cases psychotropic drugs may be literally killing our children. One report listed thirty-one school shootings or school-related acts of violence dating back to 1988, which were committed by a person who was either on psychiatric drugs or was withdrawing from them.[112] While acknowledging that correlation is not causation, it seems probable that the drugs these kids were on played some part in the shootings. As Jim Marrs puts it, "The sheer totality of evidence pointing to psychiatric drugs as the culprit behind most school shootings, teen suicides, and other violent behavior is most compelling, if not overwhelming."[113]

We are not just talking statistics. We have to remember that real kids are being affected by the administration of mind-altering drugs. For example, Mark Taylor, a student who survived the deadly Columbine school shooting, even though he took numerous bullets to the heart area, questioned a committee on the administering of these drugs to children:

> How are we supposed to feel safe at school, at home, on the street, at church or elsewhere if we cannot trust the FDA to do what we are paying you to do? Where were you when I got shot? You say that these antidepressants are effective. So, why did they not help Eric Harris? These drugs help increase the rage in people and cause them to do things they would not do anyway. So why didn't these so-called antidepressants not make him better? I will tell you why. It is because they don't work. We should consider antidepressants to be accomplices to the murder.[114]

It's frustrating that the correlation between mind-altering drugs and school shootings is totally ignored by the press, politicians, and government officials. It's as if they don't see the connection because *they don't want to see the connection.* Why not? Because the progressives would rather blame the school shootings on the guns rather than on the true source of the problem, which is the psychotropic drugs these kids are on. In this way the liberal progressives carry out, wittingly or unwittingly, one of the primary goals of the globalists, which is to remove guns from the citizenry.

The Global Agenda Enters the Classroom

Unfortunately, we have more evidence that the globalist agenda has entered the classroom. For example, while teaching about the Constitution, a teacher made the following statement and then asked the children to write it down: "I am willing to give up some of my Constitutional rights in order to be safer or more secure."[115]

The progressive elites and globalists are clearly behind this anti-constitutional thinking. Why is a teacher allowed to teach this rubbish in our country? In contradiction to this anticonstitutional thinking, Ben Franklin wrote, "Those who desire to give up freedom in order to gain security will not have, nor do they deserve, either one."[116] Who are we going to side with—the so-called education experts, or the wisdom of one of our Founders? As noted above, children are taught that the Constitution is an outmoded document. The wisdom of the Founders simply doesn't apply in our fast-paced techno-centered world.

That incident came on the heels of a sixth grade lesson plan that called for the students to create a communist flag of America.[117] You see, the progressives and global elites pushing this agenda want to dismantle the republic our Founding Fathers established. They frown upon national sovereignty so they have the kids think in terms of globalism, such as combining socialist symbols with the American flag.

With this type of globalist agenda in mind, is it any wonder that Christianity, the worldview that underpinned our republic, must be discarded in our public school systems?

So, for example, one CSCOPE lesson plan concerning religion identifies Allah with the God of Abraham.[118] This is absurd. The God of the Bible is a triune God—Father, Son, and Holy Spirit. Three sepa-rate and distinct persons are in the one triune God of the Bible, known as Yahweh. In Islam, one singular person is said to be God: Allah. The God of the Bible and the god of Islam cannot possibly be one and the same. But don't confuse the elites with facts. After all, they have an agenda, and that supersedes truth.

The idea, in this case, is to accustom the children to thinking that the God of the Bible and the god of Islam are the same God. It is the attempt to blend Christianity with the other religions by emptying it of its distinctive theology. It is a form of PC religious pluralism that we discussed in Chapter five. This kind of thinking will become more prolific as the global elites move us toward a one-world government, one-world religion, and one-world currency.

The CSCOPE lesson plan noted above was taught in Texas. It contained some other anti-Christian implications as well. When some of what was taught came to the attention of parents, they held hearings. They learned that the teachers had been forced to sign a contract stating that they would not reveal what was in the curriculum or otherwise face civil or criminal charges. One teacher admitted in tears that he felt he was aiding and abetting a crime.[119]

Why all the secrecy? If teachers are not teaching students anything immoral or illegal, what are the administrators of the curriculum hiding? It seems obvious, at least to me, that the administrators in this particular case don't want parents to know that their children are being taught anti-Christian, anti-Constitution, and anti-America propaganda.

This should come as no surprise. We discovered earlier that Dewey and other secular humanist progressives picked up the ball and ran with it by denigrating Christianity and promoting socialist-globalist propaganda. Moreover, from its very inception, public school education was never solely about reading, writing, and arithmetic. It was about modeling the Prussian school system, which was geared toward worship of the state. So it shouldn't surprise us that global elites want to inculcate our children with globalist ideology and then attempt to hide it from the parents. Look at what Horace Mann said, which dates back to the public school's inception: "We who are engaged in the sacred cause of education are entitled to look upon all parents as having given hostages to our cause."[120]

The elites think they are better than you and smarter than you, and they have an agenda. In fact, this myth that the intelligentsia knows better than parents what is right for the kids can be traced back to progressives like Dewey and has continued unabated until today. For example, in 1946, a Canadian psychiatrist named Brock Chisholm published a paper in *Psychiatry* in which he wrote about making school children "world citizens":

> We have swallowed all manner of poisonous certainties fed us by our parents, or Sunday and day school teachers. . . . The reinterpretation and eventually eradication of the concept of right and wrong, which has been the basis of child training, these are the belated objectives of practically all effective psychotherapy. Psychology and sociology should be taught to all children in primary and secondary schools, while the study of such things as trigonometry, Latin, religions and others of specialist concern

should be left to universities. Only so can we help our children carry their responsibilities as world citizens.[121]

Around thirty years later, in 1973, another psychiatrist, Dr. Chester Pierce, promulgated this notion of "world citizenship" and other global propaganda. While speaking at the Childhood International Education Seminar, Pierce stated that "Every child in America entering school at the age of five is insane because he comes to school with certain allegiances to our founding fathers, toward our elected officials, toward his parents, toward a belief in a supernatural being, toward the sovereignty of this nation as a separate entity. . . . It's up to you teachers to make all these sick children well by creating the international children of the future."[122]

So here are two psychiatrists, both of whom favor some type of globalism, and the latter of which thinks children are insane if they believe in God, listen to their parents, and believe in the Founding Fathers. The view that children are insane if they don't believe the atheistic, anti-republic rhetoric of Mr. Pierce is troubling in light of the fact that psychiatry and psychology carry so much authority in our culture today. I predict this trend will continue as those in power utilize psychiatry and psychology as tools to rid society of those who won't tow the party line, such as Christians, constitutionalists, gun owners, and true libertarians. The folks in these groups will be labeled with some supercilious, polysyllabic epithet contrived by the psychiatric community that will stigmatize them as "unstable" or "a threat to society" by the progressive elites.

So, for example, a Christian in the future may be stuck with a made-up label like "axiological tolerance disorder" because he or she doesn't agree with the politically correct morals and values propagated by the secular humanist elites. That label sounds impressive doesn't it? Anyone can make these things up. It's not that hard. This act of attaching a label to politically incorrect groups is already occurring. Those who practice the homosexual lifestyle label people "homophobes" who disagree with them. Say it often enough and people begin to believe it.

I predict that Christians will be one of the groups that will need to undergo psychiatric "treatment" for speaking out against what was traditionally considered immoral behavior. In the anything goes, PC, morally tolerant society of the future, Christians, constitutionalists, gun-owning conservatives, returning veterans, and other libertarians speaking out against whatever the elites are promoting will be enough to have these people locked up for a while. Are you one of them? Oh, don't worry. A little counseling and rehabilitation will do you good. You know, so that you can be reintegrated back into society with the rest of the sheeple. You will probably be forced to take a pharmaceutical to correct your politically intolerant behavior. Think I'm exaggerating? Wait and see. It's already happening.

Mental Health Screening for School Kids

In 2002, with his President's New Freedom Commission on Mental Health (NFC), Bush 2.0 initiated a push for screening the mental health of *all* Americans. NFC members were to recommend policies that federal, state, and local governments could utilize to enhance psychiatric screening.[123]

The problem, as I pointed out above, is that the number of so-called mental disorders has increased to the point where it seems that every behavior can be labeled a mental disorder of some sort. This is disconcerting because it means that any one of us, by the whim of some "expert" in the field of psychiatry or psychology, can be labeled with a mental disorder we don't really have. Look at what Michael F. Hogan, chairman of the NFC, said about mental disease in our country: "Mental illnesses are shockingly common; they affect almost every American family."[124] This is a truly terrifying statement. It is psychiatric overreach. Perhaps Mr. Hogan himself has one of these common mental disorders. If he does, then, of course, we have no reason to pay attention to his assertions.

Especially troubling is that once again the kids are put in the crossfire with this push for mental health screening. For example, the TeenScreen program is meant to offer a mental health checkup for all youth before they graduate from high school. Kelly Patricia O'Meara lays this out in her book, *Psyched Out.* O'Meara points out that 1) in many cases, the parents don't have to provide consent for the mental health screening to take place, 2) "trained nonprofessionals" are allowed to score the tests, and 3) it is difficult to determine who is ultimately privy to the information gathered on the child during the interview process besides the "trained nonprofessional."[125]

Most troubling is that the creator of TeenScreen, psychiatrist David Shaffer, admitted that the test identifies many suicidal children who really aren't (false positives). In fact, TeenScreen is so comprehensive that, according to Shaffer, "it misses hardly anybody." In other words, no child who has a supposed mental disorder will slip through the cracks. The downside, of course, is that seemingly every child has some mental problem according to how the tests are set up. Thus, in his own 2004 report Shaffer admitted that the positive predictive value was only 16 percent. As O'Meara points out, how does an 84 percent failure rate come to be seen as a successful scientific test?[126]

Again, this means that a plethora of non-suicidal kids are popping up on the tests as if they *were* suicidal and then referred for further evaluation and possible introduction to mind-altering drugs they don't really need. The scary part is that this could become a self-fulfilling prophecy. If the kids who are not suicidal are administered mind-altering drugs, isn't it at least somewhat more likely that they may *become* suicidal while they are on the drugs or attempting to withdraw from them?

This is all the more infuriating when, as O'Meara points out, no known objective, confirmable data demonstrate that psychiatric mental disorders are caused by some sort of abnormality of the brain.[127] And even the FDA warns that a percentage of the population taking mind-altering drugs can experience violent behavior and even harm themselves.[128] But all of this is lost on the intelligentsia as evidenced by the on-site clinicians at the schools who can give their subjective opinion based not on an X-ray, CAT, MRI, PET scan, or blood test, but by the answers provided by the child on the screening test and by briefly talking with the child.[129]

In fact, the children's interviews with the on-site clinician are also a cause of concern for many who see the unintended consequences of what O'Meara describes as the "grand mental health initiative." Why the cause for concern? Because unintended private information may pop up during the course of the child's interview. Are we supposed to trust these mental health professionals not to lead the children to give them answers they want to hear? The executive director of the Association of American Physicians and Surgeons, Jane Orient, MD, puts it this way, as cited by O'Meara:

> Teams of experts are awaiting the infusion of cash. They'll be ensconced in your child's school before you even know it. A bonus is that your little darlings will probably give them quite a bit of information about you also, and then you, too, can receive therapy you didn't know you needed. Do you sometimes raise you voice? Ever spank them? Hug them inappropriately? Have politically incorrect attitudes? Use forbidden words? Own a gun? Smoke

cigarettes, especially indoors? Read extremist literature? Refuse to recycle? Prepare for a knock on the door.[130]

Parents Losing Their Authority

Here is my concern. As we lose more and more of our constitutional rights and as the family unit continues to disintegrate with each successive generation, it will become increasingly easier for our children to be indoctrinated with godlessness, secular humanism, anti-constitutionalism, and a dose of anti-American propaganda thrown in for good measure.

Moreover, the degree to which parents lose their authority—especially one-parent families or those separated through divorce—is the same degree to which the state will fill the vacuum and declare itself The Authority in family matters. I believe the psychiatric/psychological community will work hand in hand with the state to undermine whatever authority the parents once had. And even to take the children away from their parents in more and more cases. Remember, globalists want to own the children.

This is dangerous.

So, for example, a family in New York State, the Carrolls, decided to take their son Kyle off of his medication. Administrators in the school district called the Albany County Child Protective Services, alleging child abuse against the parents. The Carrolls are now attempting to clear their name while trying to keep their child because they have been put on a statewide child abuser list. Michael Carroll, the father, stated that it's beyond the point of whether or not Kyle should be on the drug. It's more about the fact that these so-called authorities can tell him how to raise his own child.

David Lansner, a New York City lawyer, has seen cases similar to the Carrolls, and he calls this kind of thing "so scary. . . . The schools are now using child protective services to enforce their own desires and their own policies. . . . The parent's authority is being undermined when people have to do what some public official wants."[131]

Can you imagine trying to defend yourself in a similar situation if you are a single parent? What if the child happens to mention that you are never at home in the course of an interview? Never mind that you work one or two jobs to keep food on the table and a roof over your heads. Never mind that the child is staying with a relative or a responsible friend while you are at work. What if the clinician decides you are neglecting your child and involves the authorities? Remember, these folks are smarter than you, and they know more than you do concerning what is best for your child. They're progressives. They're on top of it.

As Charles Sykes notes, the educational establishment has taken it upon itself to be in the frontlines of "protective behavior." In fact, curricula have been developed where every child needs to be cautioned about the potential effects of verbal, sexual, or physical abuse. Every child is automatically considered a potential victim, so the responsibility cannot be left to the family, because the family may be the abuser. The children are exposed to this type of message on a regular basis.[132]

Certainly something is disconcerting about allowing outside authorities, whether a counselor, teacher, or clinician, to influence the child regarding what is appropriate or inappropriate behavior like a hug or tickling. It seems to me that children's innocence can be lost just as easily when they are not allowed to trust their God-given instincts and instead are conditioned to question their parents' every move. This is just another example of those in positions of authority taking over more areas of children's lives that were once under the purview of the parents.

With all the trouble and shenanigans going on today in the public school system, it is any wonder that an increasing number of parents homeschool their kids. As I write, Dr. Ron Paul is taking the initiative in the home-schooling movement and has even developed his own curriculum. He is concerned that as our government has taken more and more control over education, the quality of education has declined. Dr. Paul observes that while he was in Congress, he heard "nothing but complaints" from teachers, administrators, children, and parents regarding No Child Left Behind. In addition, the Common Core initiative under the Obama administration has done nothing but exert more government control over the schools, which Dr. Paul finds troubling.[133]

In closing, I should point out that not all the teachers are bad guys. Not every school district propagandizes school children with the UNESCO-type curriculum that has infiltrated our federal curricula. In fact, many teachers are old school. They take their jobs seriously and they really have a heart for the kids. Many of them are pressured into teaching the globalist propaganda against their better judgment.

As I was finishing up this chapter I watched a video of one teacher named Ellie Rubenstein, who quit the teaching profession because, as she states, "Everything I love about teaching is extinct."

Rubenstein's video is her resignation letter. She laments that raising the children's test scores on the standardized tests are the only thing that matter today. From her perspective, the district, state, and federal education boards are concerned only with developing children who would follow the state-sponsored doctrines. The administrators don't trust the teachers and, in essence, micromanage them. As Rubenstein notes, unless you are a yes-man you will eventually have to give up teaching.[134] A sad state of affairs indeed.

Summary

We've certainly come a long way from the days of the McGuffey readers of the 1800s. The children back then were taught a combination of shameless Protestantism and patriotism. Bible reading was allowed and done on a daily basis. But just as the Christian worldview was marginalized in higher education, so too this became the norm in public schools. Many forces played a part in this marginalization process.

We saw in previous chapters how the college reformers imported liberal Protestantism from Germany during the latter half of the nineteenth century. The new psychology was another ideological force brought over from Germany. It reinforced the government-controlled school system that was geared toward worship of the state. Psychologists like Wundt viewed children as social animals. Children were indoctrinated with propaganda that supported the State's wishes.

Wundt's psychological progeny—educators like Dewey—picked up progressive notions that embraced atheism and Marxist socialism. Many of the monied elites viewed those beneath them, especially children, as mere commodities. The elites combined the new psychology with the progressive reformers' ideology and steered children away from embracing a democratic-American ideal and moved them toward a socialist-globalist ideology. Dewey and his ilk were conscious that the public school system was the battleground for the minds of future generations. The Christian worldview, which had held sway in the classroom, gave way to the secular humanist and global agenda, "the new faith" of the progressives and elites.

Federal curriculum under the auspices of UNESCO has furthered the globalist agenda in our public school system. Reading, writing, and arithmetic are not nearly as important as teaching the children anti-Christian, anti-family, and anti-American values while promoting a one-world government. Moreover, the transformational education proposed by Gramsci and implemented by UNESCO has the effect of transforming the traditional values of the children, which they received at home and church, to a new progressive globalist ideology.

The final nail in the coffin as far as Christianity having any influence in the schools came when the Supreme Court decided to expunge state-sponsored prayer and Bible reading in the 1960s. The next decade saw values clarification encourage the children to be their own moral arbiters. This seems logical in retrospect. With God done away with in the '60s, it followed quite naturally that moral autonomy in the form of values clarification would fill the vacuum in the '70s and thereafter. Is it any wonder then that the schools' biggest problems used to be students chewing gum, talking, not putting paper in the wastebasket, and so forth, and now the biggest problems are alcohol, drug abuse, teen pregnancy, rape, etc.?

Psychologists and psychiatrists filled the authoritative vacuum in the schools created by the loss of Christianity. Perhaps most troubling is that mind-altering drugs can be administered to the kids simply by these experts' say-so. As we noted, the real need for these drugs is extremely dubious. Parents may want to question whoever is in charge of administering a drug to their child and make that "expert" provide a cogent explanation as to why that child needs to take it. My concern is that these drugs are making zombies out of the children and literally killing some of them. It's infuriating that as the list of seemingly contrived psychiatric disorders burgeons, more and more children will be administered mind-altering drugs.

It is difficult to believe that a true majority of kids are helped in any way by these medications. In some cases, the kids become violent, as evidenced by the school shootings that are coming at a faster pace now. Certainly the drugs seem to be a causal and contributing factor to the rise in the suicide rate among youngsters. If psychiatrists in the 1970s spent so much time and energy convincing the public that they alone, as medical doctors, should be qualified to diagnose and treat mental disorders, why are nonmedical doctors like the school psychologist allowed to dispense life-threatening drugs now? The experts can't have it both ways.

With the Christian influence safely out of the way, and with many children on medications, the agenda of the progressives and globalists moves forward while it encounters less resistance with each passing year. Parents will continue to lose their authority concerning the well-being of their children. I foresee the government, progressives, and globalists behind this agenda becoming much more intrusive in the children's "welfare" in the years to come.

Under globalist auspices the teacher-facilitator, school psychologist, and psychiatrists, will all recommend what is best for the children. Parents, and especially single parents, will find it increasingly difficult to maintain authority, either legal or moral, over their children. The original Prussian model will be realized as we see the government, and entities like UNESCO, increasingly determine what is best for the children. The educational establishment, psychologists, psychiatrists, and agencies like the Child Protective Services will enforce this model, with its concomitant propaganda. It's part of the globalist agenda and it's coming to a town near you.

I think homeschooling will increase over the next number of years, thereby counteracting the agenda of the global elitists. But I believe this movement will be short-lived. At some point in the future, the government will outlaw homeschooling as subversive. The globalists don't want children who can actually read and write and use critical thinking abilities. They want children who are medicated. They don't want children who have traditional values instilled in them and who might actually hear about God once in a while.

If I am right—that in the future those in power will label Christians "terrorists," "enemies of the state," or at the very least, "subversive elements,"—then it would follow that they will also consider children who are homeschooled potential "terrorists" or participants in subversive activity. This sounds farfetched even as I write it. Nevertheless, I will go on record and say that I firmly believe that history will prove this prediction correct. Homeschooling will be outlawed at some point.

Chapter 13

Fifty Shades of Cultural Decline

The next few chapters will involve a ground-level approach to observing the condition of our culture in the United States. It doesn't take a particularly astute observer to perceive that we are breaking down morally. This is a bleak observation. But anyone with a moral compass can see that the decadence in our culture is not only in progress but accelerating as well.

It should come as no surprise by now that I propose the primary reason we are rotting from the inside out is because we are abandoning the Christian worldview in increasing numbers. In short, we are leaving God behind. When we leave God behind, whether in our individual lives or as a society, we lose our sense of moral direction. In a godless condition we are left to our own devices. We become autonomous, a law unto ourselves.

Today, the fruit of our autonomy is palpable and dangerous. Once the moral foundation is gone, it threatens to bring down our entire republic. Of course, one of the primary causes of the moral disintegration of our culture is the breakdown of the family. As the traditional family unit disintegrates with each passing generation, so too do traditional morals. The loss of traditional morality is due to the Christian worldview not being passed down from generation to generation, which, in turn, reinforces the breakdown of the family. Some, if not most, of this downward spiral accelerated after the countercultural revolution of the late 1960s and early 1970s.

Today, the breakdown of the family and the loss of the Christian worldview result in moral autonomy in which each individual makes up his or her own values. Moral autonomy directly results in moral decay, because moral absolutes are no longer upheld or considered valid. This moral deterioration has affected all levels of society, from the mundane all the way to our laws, politics, and economy. The breakdown of the family combined with the Christian worldview not being passed down both work synergistically to foster moral autonomy and to undermine our republic. With this in mind, the lion's share of this chapter will involve evaluating the evidence (and cause) of this moral breakdown.

The Change in the Father's Role

During the colonial period, the father's role was much different than it is today. The father shared in child-rearing because most fathers worked at home, usually on farms or in small villages, and trained the children to work alongside him. Back then the family looked upon the father as the head of the household. This meant that the father had an authority, a God-ordained "office" or "duty" to represent not only himself but the interests of his entire family.[1] The family dynamic was much different from today because both daily life and labor centered in the home.

With the rise of the Industrial Revolution, fathers left the home to work. The wives increasingly became the child-rearers, when previously they worked alongside their husbands and shared in the responsibility for the economic well-being of the family. With the Industrial Revolution, however, fathers no longer played an integral part in the everyday familial goings-on like he had in the past. Evidence of this is that by the mid-nineteenth century, sermons and pamphlets on child-rearing were solely addressed to the mothers. Previously they were addressed to the father or both parents.[2]

Nancy Pearcey points out that with the rise of the Industrial Revolution, an "atomistic individualism" occurred wherein society perceived men as cogs in the industrial machinery; merely interchangeable parts in competition with one another. In a sense, capitalism came to define the individual rather than the family as the basic unit of society. Capitalism freed men from their traditional responsibilities, from their generational past, and allowed them to compete with other men for their place in the new world of the markets.[3]

Whereas previously a virtuous man was defined by his ability to exercise self-restraint in lieu of the common good, by the end of the nineteenth century, society viewed self-interest as a positive quality that engendered economic success and equality with others. This was totally antithetical to the Puritan ideal, which considered men's passions (personal ambition) a hazard to the order of society.[4] Capitalism became increasingly associated with immediate gratification. Money became "god." These things lured men away from their duty as the author of their families' well-being.

Liberals hoped at the time that a woman could help, in the words of Christopher Lasch, to "transform the potential gambler, spectator, dandy, or confidence man into a conscientious provider."[5] But society no longer viewed the man as a divinely sanctioned authority figure in the home, but simply as a provider. The father's role had changed significantly. As Lasch puts it, "The family was invaded and undermined by the market."[6]

The Family Today

When we look at the family today, in many cases it is nothing short of tragic. Juan Williams wrote a heart wrenching piece in the *Wall St. Journal* in which he pointed out the deleterious effects on young people who don't know their fathers or have no father at home to spend time with them, encourage them, discipline them, and to hold the family together. The kids suffer from uncertainty, not knowing if their fathers are even interested in them. They feel like they have been thrown away.[7] Do you think these kids will go on to start loving homes of their own and espouse the love of Jesus Christ whom many have never been introduced to, so that there won't be another generation of throwaway kids?

As Williams points out, even from a strictly economic standpoint, "Having a dad at home is almost a certain ticket out of poverty; because about 40 percent of single-mother families are in poverty."[8] This is an unassailable statistic and is important because kids who don't have a father at home are far more likely to get involved with drugs and spend time in jail. Their chances for success in life are significantly diminished. A case can be made that children born out of wedlock is the number one social problem facing us today, because it "drives" so many of our other problems, such as poverty, homelessness, crime, drugs, and illiteracy.[9]

Another problem is divorce. One statistic I looked at showed the US divorce rate in 1967 was 26 percent. However eight short years later (1975) it had jumped to 48 percent. This coincides, of course, with the Me generation, counterculture revolution. No-fault divorce became available in the 1970s, which also accounted for the rise in the divorce rate,[10] but it seems far more likely that the self-absorption of the time was the culprit in the rise of divorces and that no-fault divorce followed in its wake.

Regardless, it is hard to escape the conclusion that the narcissism that oozed out of the anti-establishment crowd (remember, marriage is an established institution) was the efficient cause of the parabolic rise in the breakdown of marriages. The level of commitment to others declined as people asserted their own interests as the *sine qua non* of the good life. The prevailing narcissistic attitude of a person's basic right to fulfill him- or herself, even if to do so was damaging to others, is still evident today. The pinnacle of unconcern for others is exemplified in the 1973 *Roe v. Wade* Supreme Court decision, which also emerged during the same years as the sexual/counterculture revolution.

Whether the rate of divorce is the commonly held 50 percent or even something less, it indeed has risen drastically from 5 percent in the 1880s.[11] It is hard, if not impossible, for children whose parents break up to see anything worth trusting or permanent in their lives after that. This leads to more divorces when it is their turn to give marriage a try, because they have learned from their parents that marital commitment is not something permanent, but tenuous. Some young adults don't see marriage as a viable option. The template of a stable family is difficult to emulate when it was not experienced. It is also worth asking how kids are supposed to trust God, whom they *can't* see, when they feel abandoned by their parents, whom they *can* see.

Allan Bloom sums up the tragedy of divorce best:

> Children may be told over and over again that their parents have a right to their own lives, that they will enjoy quality time instead of quantity time, that they are really loved by their parents even after divorce, but children do not believe any of this. They think they have a right to total attention and believe their parents must live for them. . . . To children, the voluntary separation of parents seems worse than their death precisely because it is voluntary.[12]

When I was growing up, it was common to hear that parents were staying together for the sake of the children. But I don't hear this much anymore. Many parents believe they have a right to their own lives and can't bear the pain of suffering their spouse's faults, even for the sake of the children.

In fact, this emancipation—this right to be free—was a common thread running through the countercultural revolution. "The pill," for example, emancipated women from the necessity of having children. Instead, women could pursue higher education or careers if they so desired. Historian Ellen Chesler noted the change in attitude back then: "It was really considered immoral to suggest that women's primary role should not be that of wife and mother, but rather that women should have rights to experience their sexuality free of consequence, just like men have always done."[13]

As the pill became accessible to single women, it freed both men and women from the consequences of sexual intimacy. As the Christian worldview became further marginalized, abstinence increasingly seemed like a nonviable option for single adults. Contraception, instead of abstinence, became equated with being responsible. Promoting abstinence was, and is, considered unrealistic.

One of the God-ordained purposes of men and women coming together after dedicating themselves to each other in marriage is to *have* children, not to avoid having them. In addition, God never meant men and women to share procreative-type intimacy outside of marriage. To do so is selfishness, a way to get what one wants from another person without having to commit to them. It reinforces the attitude that it's all about me and what I need. It supports the notion that one can enjoy sexual intimacy without taking on the responsibility of marriage or children, or to "be free of consequence," as Gloria Steinem put it. But Oswald Spengler noted, "When the ordinary thought of a highly cultivated people begins to regard 'having children' as a question of *pro's* and *con's*, the great turning point has come. . . . When reasons have to be put forward at all in a question of life, life itself has become questionable."[14]

And, yes, life has become questionable today. "Choice" becomes a dangerous tool in the hands of those who are primarily concerned about themselves. This applies to each of us as fallen human beings, who have a natural propensity for self-centeredness. Jesus taught that we are to love others as we love ourselves. He assumed that we love ourselves primarily. Self-centeredness is antithetical to Christ's teachings and thus with Christianity. The problem is that not only are children today subjected to the devastating effects of the parents' choice to divorce but the unborn suffer a far worse fate if the mother chooses to eliminate her baby.

Whichever way one looks at it, marriage, the family, and children are having a tough go of it today. Whether it's a couple who wants to enjoy living together without the responsibility of marriage, or a married couple who divorces, the institution of marriage is not held in as high esteem as it once was, nor is the family unit the stable rock it used to be. But if one's level of dedication can falter in the areas of marriage and commitment to children, what does this say about our relationship to others in our community or our country, where our commitment is not expected to be as high as in marriage, per se? What does it say about our commitment to God? It says that each of us is becoming an island unto himself. It says that we don't care what God or others think.

Single folks are afraid to commit because many of them saw their own parents divorce. It's only a piece of paper anyway, so the thinking goes. Divorcees are afraid to recommit because they have already suffered firsthand the devastating effects of divorce.

All this does not bode well for the concept of community as an ideal. Increasingly, we are living atomized existences regarding others. This atomization, along with other factors, portends the breakdown of our republic as well. The coming societal breakdown will accelerate as the economy continues to deteriorate and then probably suffers a major setback at some point. Perhaps extended families will get together to avoid economic hardship. But, on the other hand, it is possible that more and more families will break up under the stress of money problems or loss of jobs, etc. An increasing number of children may find themselves in foster homes or under some type of state guardianship, on the streets, or in jail if the family breakdown accelerates under the coming economic strain. Everyone who is not part of a functional family will be left to fend for themselves.

The reason much of what I described above is occurring is because we have abandoned God in our daily lives. Once our commitment to God slips, so does our commitment to others, whoever the others may be. How will we be able to turn this around when the family has historically been the institution that passed down the Christian worldview? How will parents today, many of whom don't give God a lick of thought in their daily lives, transmit Christian values and teachings to their children? How will we as a society stop this downward trajectory we have been on for a century or more, which has accelerated since the anti-establishment era of the 1960s and '70s? As Christianity has been marginalized with each passing generation, so too has biblical morality. Anyone who can't see the correlation here is willfully blind. Without a return to biblical morality, it will be impossible to turn our cultural decline around.

Even parents who stay together don't command the same authority in religious matters they once did, because, as Allan Bloom observed a quarter of a century ago, they don't know what they believe and they don't "have the self-confidence to tell their children much more than that they want them to be happy and fulfill whatever potential they may have."[15] Bloom goes on to point out that the schools teaching values clarification attempt to provide a model for how values are passed down to the children. However, these are not really values but propaganda that won't work because these so-called values will change as soon as public opinion changes.[16]

Parents will continue to lose their moral authority because a greater percentage of them in the up-and-coming generations will be practical atheists—Christians in name only. This means that the moral compass will weaken as they place more distance between themselves and God.

The Bible, which once provided the authoritative foundation for the transmission of Christian teaching, is absent in most home life today. The multifaceted tentacles of the media—radio, television, iPhone, Internet, tablets, etc.—demand one's attention in our fast-paced society. The parents simply cannot control the atmosphere of the home like they once could.[17] In a culture that must be entertained on a minute by minute basis, people have no time to read or contemplate the truth and wisdom contained in Scripture.

Summarizing so far then, the breakdown of the family has resulted in the marginalization of Christianity because the Christian worldview with its authoritative teachings and moral guidance is simply not being passed down from generation to generation like it once was.[18] This, in turn, results in a loss of moral authority, because there is no moral foundation for parents to rely on anymore. We also saw that the breakdown of the family means that as time passes, the level of commitment to others decreases as well. People feel less constrained by the duty to any individual other than themselves. The countercultural revolution's ideal of freedom promoted this rampant narcissistic attitude and has led to the autonomy of each individual. Let's flesh this out a bit further as we can now tie in what we learned from Chapters five and six about the fruit of secularization.

Narcissism and Autonomy

One of the slogans of the Me generation was "Do your own thing." The essence of the countercultural revolution consisted of a desire for freedom above everything else. Freedom to do, say, and pursue anything they wanted.

In a sense, I think it is fair to say that the anti-establishment crowd took freedom from religion, which really gained traction back in the Enlightenment era, to its logical conclusion. With God pushed to the periphery of culture or dispensed with altogether, people were free to indulge their own yearnings. Many in the Me generation promoted the ideology that it was all about oneself. The individual was the center of the universe (narcissism) and made up his or her own rules of how to live (autonomy). There was no need to look to God for anything anymore. Autonomous individuals made their own moral choices. They did their own thing.

Narcissism reinforces autonomy (and vice versa), because once people accept that they are the god of their little worlds, it follows that they can also do whatever they want and therefore make up their own moral law. They become a law unto themselves. By the way, this is precisely what children are taught in school—that they can clarify their own *values*. Ethics are situational.

As I pointed out in the previous chapter, *Values Clarification*, the book that provided the foundation for teaching values in schools, mentioned nothing about morals. The problem is that values are not really morals because values can change. Values are relative to an individual or a society. Postmodernism promotes this type of thinking. For the postmodernist, values are constructs. Traditional institutions like marriage, consisting of a two individuals, one of each gender, is now considered a construct.

Values are constructed by individuals or societies to represent what is of worth to them. But this means that values end up being merely the subjective preferences of those holding them. Thus, whatever value a particular individual or society holds is considered righteous or moral. This results in moral relativism.

Doing whatever a person wants to do is not morality.[19] It is moral autonomy. Moral autonomy at its core is really nothing but one's preference. But preference is not morality. True morality is grounded in the character of the God of the Bible.[20] God doesn't change and His character doesn't change. He has revealed Himself and His moral character through His interaction in human history as recorded in the Old Testament, New Testament, the Ten Commandments, and through His Son, Jesus Christ. So we know something about morality and what God expects of us. In addition, because we are made in God's image, we also have a built-in moral compass called a conscience. In fact, Kierkegaard asserted that if God did not exist, a person could never have anything on his conscience.[21]

Unfortunately today, our consciences have been seared with a hot iron; so as a society, our moral compass is broken. We have marginalized the God of the Bible. We simply don't care what God thinks any-more. We are autonomous now and have a right to do whatever we want. Alan Wolfe puts it this way: "Americans are not comfortable be-ing told what to do, even if, perhaps especially if, the teller is a super-natural force whose words are meant as commands."[22]

I don't think it is coincidental that the countercultural movement emerged soon after the courts threw out prayer in public schools in the early '60s. If we don't think God is important enough to be a part of children's lives even for a moment in school, then it seems logical that society has decided to go it alone and leave God behind. Hence, narcissism and autonomy came to center stage during this era.

As each generation passes, and as individuals become more auton-omous, our nation as a whole becomes more culturally decadent. Be-cause we no longer look to the Light of the World to steer us in the right direction, each passing generation increasingly tolerates and then accepts what was once deemed immoral. Immoral behavior is now ac-cepted as normal, because the more we are exposed to what was once considered morally depraved, the more we get used to it. Then we ad-just to it. This cycle occurs because society can assimilate only so much deviant behavior at one time. This phenomenon is known as the "Durkheim constant."[23]

The result is that our nation sees only the goodness of its people and is confident that society will make the right choices going forward. The general consensus, as reported by Wolfe, is that we do not look upon ourselves as godless, and "Relatively few Americans think the world is filled with evil and sin."[24] I would argue that this is because we have become used to our evil and sin.

Fifty or a hundred years ago, kids got into trouble for chewing gum in class. Now in many schools, nurses make condoms available to the students. Homosexuality was considered sin fifty or a hundred years ago. Now, as this book goes to press, the Supreme Court has legalized same-sex marriage in all fifty states, and Barack Obama is the first sitting president to endorse same-sex marriage. People today may not be able or willing to see that we are a godless country. But when we have eliminated 55 million babies in the womb, the vast majority of them because their parent(s) viewed them as an obstacle of some sort, then it is a certainty we have crossed the line into moral decadence. William Bennett says it well: "We have become the kind of society that civilized countries used to send missionaries to."[25] That statement argues for our nation's post-Christian status.

One tenet of secular humanism is that man begins with himself and moves out from there. The anti-establishment crowd reinforced the postmodern mentality and produced many secularists who were concerned only with the here and now. The rejection of authority, especially religious authority, and the celebration of both freedom and the self, which at first blush seems so grand and liberating, soon slides down the slippery slope to nihilism. Why? Because the self, detached from God, is a black hole with nothing to offer but a dark emptiness. Without the living God to provide purpose and meaning to life, freedom soon leads to despair. Freedom in a world without God and a world that doesn't care about you soon degenerates into loneliness and isolation. In short, a price must be paid for our autonomy. That price is nihilism.

The Founders, Morality, God, and Freedom

The freedom for self-determination that emerged from the rebellion of the 1960s is not how society perceived freedom before the modern era. As William A. Nord points out, freedom in the seventeenth and eighteenth centuries meant freedom to do the good and the virtuous. Freedom during that time was tied to religious morality. Nord notes that after the modern era, freedom became more selfish and narcissistic. He goes on to say that "modernity comes at a cost, for it undermines those traditional religious values of duty, self-sacrifice, love, and community that are, arguably essential to our moral well-being."[26] Let's examine the traditional notion of freedom and its relationship with Christianity and morality.

Certainly our Founding Fathers, who have fallen out of favor today especially with the liberal elites, believed the Christian worldview was indispensable for our republic. I am not insisting that all the Founding Fathers were orthodox Christians when we know that many adhered to some form of Deism and some were Freemasons, Unitarians, and so forth. Nevertheless, their eclecticism doesn't negate that the Founders thought it was important to appeal to the God of Christianity, and even to Jesus Christ at times, with regard to guiding the future of the republic. For example, in George Washington's inaugural prayer, he entreats God this way:

> Almighty God, we make our earnest prayer that thou wilt keep the United States in thy holy protection; . . . And finally that thou will most graciously be pleased to dispose us all to do justice, to love

mercy and to demean ourselves with that charity, humility, and pacific temper of mind which were the characteristics of the divine Author of our blessed religion, and without a humble imitation of whose example in these things we can never hope to be a happy nation. Grant our supplication, we beseech thee, through Jesus Christ our Lord, Amen.[27]

James Madison, who wrote the First Amendment, said, "We have staked the whole future of American Civilization, not upon the power of government, far from it. We have staked the future of all of our political institutions . . . upon the capacity of each and all of us to govern ourselves, to control ourselves, to sustain ourselves, according to the Ten Commandments."[28]

If we have indeed "staked the whole future of American Civilization" on the ability to govern and control ourselves according to the Ten Commandments, we have failed miserably, for at least the last fifty years. The Court threw the Ten Commandments out of the public schools, and we have left God behind in our daily lives. Are things so much better now that premarital sex, abortion, and narcissistic hedonism rule the day?

At this point my cultured despisers might point out that the Ten Commandments *should* be absent in public schools under the separation of church and state. However, I think most people are now familiar with the fact that the First Amendment did not mean freedom *from* religion, but freedom *of* religion.

If we look at the historical context, we will see that Thomas Jefferson did not introduce the concept of the "wall of separation between church and state." Rather, a Baptist preacher named Roger Williams did. Williams, along with other Connecticut Baptists, sent a letter to Jefferson expressing fear about a rumor that Jefferson might establish a national denomination—a national religion if you will. Jefferson replied to the Danbury Baptists that the "First Amendment has erected a wall of separation between church and state," assuring them that there would be no national religion.[29] Jefferson borrowed Williams's own expression and used it to make clear that the Danbury Baptist religion would be protected from the government, not the other way around.[30] In fact, as president, Jefferson approved federal funding for the evangelization of Native Americans by different missionary groups.[31] This is a far cry from freedom *from* religion.

Although Jefferson cut portions of the Bible out that didn't suit his fancy, and though he didn't believe in the divinity of Jesus, Jefferson still considered himself a Christian, and he definitely saw the connection between liberty, God, and justice: "Can the liberties of a nation be thought secure, when we have removed their only firm basis, a conviction in the minds of the people, that these liberties are a gift of God? That they are violated but with his wrath? I tremble for my country when I reflect that God is just, and that His justice cannot sleep forever."[32]

Notwithstanding that Jefferson was a slave owner along with other Founders, many of whom belonged to secret societies, he nevertheless understood that true liberty comes from God, not from ourselves. Unlike us, he understood that misusing the freedom that God has given us does not bode well for our country as a whole. Today we certainly don't "tremble" at the thought of what God might think of our consumer-oriented, me-first, morally autonomous, narcissistic, hedonistic society. And the reason we don't fear God is because we have adopted the worldview of secularism by default. Many in our country are practical atheists now. With all of this in mind, let us look at how our definition of freedom today differs from what it meant at the time of the founding of our nation.

Freedom Yesterday and Today

As you are now well aware, freedom today denotes "unrestrained choice," being free from constraints of any kind save where one would infringe on another individual. Freedom, as defined today, also connotes an unbridled moral autonomy where any moral authority outside of the self ceases to exist. In other words, freedom most often today is defined as being liberated *from* something. So, for example, those who advocate for abortion rights or homosexual rights want to be free *from* the constraints that an external moral authority would place on them. "I have the right to my own body" is an example.

As we have seen, this self-centered way of looking at freedom took off after the countercultural revolution. However, freedom was not always defined this way. Freedom is not simply freedom *from*, but freedom *for*. Lord Acton asserted that freedom is "not the power of doing what we like but the right of being able to do what we ought."[33] Thus there is a moral component to freedom. True freedom is grounded in virtue. Os Guinness points out the following in his important book *A Free People's Suicide*:

Freedom thrives on self-restraint and the power to say no. It rests on strong convictions about what is true and on equally strong constraints against what is false. A culture with no claims on its members—or curbs on their desires—would be a culture with no future. . . . When everything is tolerable, nothing will be true; and when nothing is true, no one will be free. . . . The idea that freedom means we can do what we like, so long as we do not hurt anyone else, is a dangerous modern lie.[34]

Actually, this lie is not so modern. It is true that the most recent iteration of this lie can be traced back to the Me generation. But in Chapter three, we also traced the flight from authority back to the Enlightenment. And, as we noted previously, the lie of autonomy and the flight from authority can also be traced all the way back to Adam and Eve's rejection of God's command not to eat of the Tree of the Knowledge of Good and Evil. Therefore, it is evident that humans' exercise of autonomy has been consistent down through the ages. It should be equally evident that rejecting God and the moral virtue that stems from His character will get us into trouble every time.

Guinness is right that true freedom must have virtue as its foundation. This is what the Founders thought as well—that our country would survive only so long as we were a virtuous people. Guinness is also correct in pointing out that if all behavior is tolerated, there is no truth. Jesus said, "You will know the truth, and the truth will set you free" (John 8:32). Freedom requires knowing the truth of how God ordered the world. Therefore, freedom is not only dependent on virtue; freedom depends on truth as well.

Unfortunately, our society increasingly abandons the truth of the Christian worldview. The attendant result is the loss of moral virtue because rejecting godly morals and replacing them with one's autonomy results in a narcissistic hedonism that knows no bounds. But narcissistic hedonism is not morality. It is merely personal preference to seek pleasure at the expense of morality. If everyone is free to do what is right in their own eyes, then we will lose our sense of community. This lack of restraint can lead to anarchy, which in turn threatens our republic. Of course, the unbridled freedom (autonomy) that our government allows itself to exercise over us is another way we can lose our republic, in this case, to totalitarianism. More on this threat in the final chapters.

Reflections on Our Culture: Media and Entertainment

The typical book dealing with cultural criticism written from a Christian perspective would now rehearse example after example of how the media and entertainment industries have purposefully undermined the Christian worldview. But I believe the average informed reader is already well aware of the liberal media and entertainment bias against Christianity. Therefore, we will look at only a few remarkable examples of how the attitude toward Christianity has changed.

Richard W. Flory provides an interesting example in an article entitled "Promoting a Secular Standard" in which he traces the change in editorial content in the *New York Times*. Flory describes what would seem nearly impossible today. Back in the 1870s and 1880s, the *New York Times* not only advocated religion but also promoted a specifically pro-Protestant position. The *Times* urged its readers to resist the "papal influence," which wanted to deny Bible reading in the public schools. The *Times* instead advocated maintaining Bible readings as part of the curriculum.[35]

Likewise of interest is how the *Times* then handled the clash of cultural authorities between Christianity and the new science that was emerging because of Darwin's theory. Amazingly, the *Times* came down squarely on the side of maintaining "traditional religious understandings," as Flory describes it, versus embracing the new modern scientific approach. In December 1875, one editorial dealt with this issue by calling its readers back to the "sacred associations" of the Christmas season rather than being lured by those who attempted to undermine Christianity:

> Men of unquestionable learning and ability are everywhere striving to destroy the foundation of the Christian religion. They insist that God cannot and does not exist, but that the universe is governed by some unknown laws, which are the result of spontaneous evolution. . . . . The belief in a wise and beneficent God, or in Eternal Wisdom ruling all things according to its own immutable decrees, or in any dealings of the Creator with man, or in a life hereafter—all this is summarily rejected by the philosophers. It almost seems at times as though the present aim of science was not so much to enlarge its own boundaries and fields of knowledge, as to convince the world that Christianity is an imposture [*sic*] and that its founder was merely an amiable enthusiast.[36]

Of course, this quote confirms what we learned in a previous chapter in which we saw that science began to challenge the cultural authority of Christianity in the 1870s. So even though Christianity maintained its authority at that point, it wasn't too long after this particular editorial was released that the *Times* began reversing its course slowly but surely. In fact, this is the whole point of Flory's essay—to show that this change in cultural authority that was taking place between science and Christianity was happening with journalism as well.

Moreover, during the first quarter of the twentieth century, the *Times* editorial section had completely reversed its position toward Christianity, evidenced by its coverage of the Scopes Trial (1925). The *Times* was primarily concerned that our nation would look foolish for adhering to Christian fundamentalism rather than the Darwinian position. At that time the paper came down on the side of "science."[37]

The *Times*, however, did not change course entirely because of the Scopes Trial. Other forces had been working behind the scenes as well during that era. The push for professionalization that we witnessed in higher education in the late 1870s also found its way into journalism. Professional journalists felt that improving the status of their field required the adoption of science and rationality. In the long run, this resulted in the displacement of Christianity. It should come as no surprise that with the marginalization of Christianity came a decrease of religious front page stories in the *Times*, from around 20 percent in 1875 down to a mere 3 percent by 1935. Journalists who embraced science as the new cultural authority thereafter viewed themselves as bearers of truth—the moral voice of society with the same status as doctors–dispensing cures for cultural ills.[38]

I offer these examples to show that the media bias wasn't always liberal and anti-Christian. It's amazing to think that newspapers like the *Times* upheld the Christian worldview at one time.

We saw in a previous chapter that *Cosmopolitan* also upheld traditional conservative thinking. Today, of course, the news media for the most part, whether print or television, has embraced secular postmodernism. The result is that the left-leaning liberals, in concert with the global elites who own most of these organizations, portray Christianity in an unfavorable light. The news media considers Christianity not only distasteful but also a clear and present danger to our (post)modern, contemporary way of life.[39]

But the news media today secularizes in another way. Please recall that the word *secular* does not simply mean an absence of religion, but rather it denotes a myopic concern with the here and now. By its very nature, the twenty-four-hour news cycle promotes a worldly, urgent, temporal perspective that keeps us in a perpetual and insatiable "need to know" mind-set. This encourages little rumination or reflection on eternal things, unlike what readers used to find in the *Times*'s editorial articles on Christianity in the late nineteenth century. In other words, the news media today keeps us continually focusing on the secular at the expense of any consideration of eternity.[40]

Gadgets, Technology, and the Culture of Celebrity

The news media is not totally to blame for our focus on the temporal. We are a nation increasingly defined by its distractions, many of which come by way of entertainment and gadgets.

Take the smartphone for example. It has evolved (or devolved) into a gadget that may connect us with other people, but disconnects us from reality. It is a virtual smorgasbord of potential distractions with all of its bells and whistles and games. If ever a gadget lent itself to a narcissistic culture, the smartphone is it. Everywhere you look people are glued to these things like security blankets.

We've all seen people who wield their smartphone to show their domination of their surroundings by interrupting their conversation with you to receive an incoming message of some sort. "Look how important and connected I am" is the perception that is intended to be conveyed by those brandishing these devilish devices. People like this can't go two minutes without fondling or worshiping their smartphones to see if they missed a call or received a text. If so, everything must be put on hold, even if they're at work, so that the oh-so-important call or text (which most of the time is superficial chit-chat) can be returned. This vanity calls to mind the adolescent self-absorbed Valley Girls from a generation or so ago who created a virtual reality of self-importance and dumbed-down behavior that knew no bounds. This type of conduct is quite common in our culture today and it's juvenile. We're becoming a nation of perpetual adolescents.[41]

These gadgets don't connect us. They dis-connect us in so many ways and swallow us whole into the anti-reality they provide. Do two people having dinner together without ever conversing because they are both playing with their smartphones really promote togetherness or intimacy? Will children who have their own PCs, iPads, or smartphones be more prone to share time with their parents or siblings when they are home at night and have some free time? How can parents control the family atmosphere when every child has his or her own PC, tablet, TV, or smartphone? If we really want to get acquainted with someone, why do we communicate by email when we can talk by phone? The answer is that these technological pieces of hardware from hell do not really promote relationships but rather hide people in a virtual reality that allows them to avoid real life. These gadgets cause a loss of community as each person retreats into his or her own little world. A fake world, at that.

So am I saying that everyone should become Luddites and ditch their smartphones? No. They certainly provide a convenient way to communicate with people and obtain information if need be. I also acknowledge that technology is neutral and can be used for good or evil. But my concern is that too many people seem to have gone well beyond using these gadgets to help them communicate with one another. People literally worship these things as evidenced by the fact that they can't stop paying attention to them for more than a few minutes.

Consider the recent advances in technology that seem to have an inverse correlation with family cohesiveness. For example, when the radio first entered the home, everyone sat around it at night as a family and listened to it. The same thing happened when the television first came out.

When the telephone first appeared, it was located in the center of the home. If a young man needed to call his girlfriend, chances are someone could monitor that conversation. The point here is that parents knew what was going on in the home. Not so, today.

During the post-WWII era, advances in technology in combination with the post-war prosperity drove entertainment and consumerism to prominence in everyday lives. The idealization of youth occurred during this time as well. Advertisers began targeting teens for the first time as a gold mine for profits. So as technology and consumerism increased and proliferated, it wasn't long before new products found their way into every room of the home. In the '60s, '70s, and '80s, kids had their own transistor radios, then record players, TVs, and extension phones.[42] Everyone in the family started "doing their own thing," and family togetherness started to wane from the days when everyone sat around one radio or TV.

The family meal is example of the growing isolation of individuals. With every passing generation, the family meal, which once provided cohesiveness to the family unit, has become scarcer as everyone runs on their own schedules. The loss of this important meal may be a reflection of, or even aid in, the breakdown of family togetherness. Studies show that the simple practice of coming together for dinner reduces stress in parents and demonstrates to the children that their parents care about them. It reinforces values in the children, who are less likely to use drugs, smoke, drink, or have behavioral problems.[43] Nowadays, with children and parents running on their own overburdened schedules, the family meal is often bypassed in favor of everyone grabbing their makeshift meals and retreating somewhere alone to adore their gadgets, whether it be the TV, PC, tablet, or smartphone.

The post-WWII era also saw the rise in the "peer group," which began to replace the parents as a means of emotional authority and support. The younger generation began to consider their parents "square." The desire to grow up and take on the responsibility of adulthood diminished during this time as well.[44] Timothy Leary—the "Heisenberg" of chemical emancipation—proclaimed in the late '70s that "pleasure" was the primary industry in the country.[45] Hedonism and the celebration of youth were in. Virtue, delayed gratification, and the Protestant work ethic were out.[46] Of course, Leary's pronouncement coincided with the theme of the Me generation.

It was also during this time that the arts and entertainment industry, which could be used as a conduit for expressing the better side of humanity and the glory of God's creation, was instead exploited to express the vulgar, the decadent, and the trivial. In his autobiography published in 1971, Frank Capra, whose work portrayed the virtuous and redeeming qualities of humanity in films like *It's a Wonderful Life*, summarized the Hollywood mind-set that surfaced in the 1960s:

> The winds of change blew through the dream factories of make-believe . . . The hedonists, the homosexuals, the hemophilic bleeding hearts, the God-haters, the quick-buck artists who substituted shock for talent, all cried: 'Shake 'em! Rattle 'em! God is dead. Long live pleasure! Nudity? Yea! Wife-swapping? Yea! Liberate the world from prudery. Emancipate our films from morality!' . . . To hell with the good in man. Dredge up his evil—shock! shock![47]

The entertainment media may have pushed the envelope, as described by Capra, but our culture seems to have no problem absorbing whatever is put in front of it.

It seems that the current culture of celebrity is just a reflection of the narcissism so prevalent in today's society. What is so fascinating about rich housewives with seemingly nothing but time on their hands, who eat, drink, and backstab one another? What makes us want to watch completely dysfunctional families go through their daily lives of contrived self-importance when they have done absolutely nothing of value for society? I think it is because we wish we were rich and famous and had nothing to do but spend money. So we vicariously live out our fantasies through these celebrities on TV. But what do these people really have to offer? They are the epitome of perpetual adolescents. We should be getting our sense of self-worth from God, not from people on TV who couldn't care less about us. Spending time living our lives vicariously through people we don't know and who seem to be devoid of anything resembling character and virtue leaves little doubt that our culture is lost in a sea of juvenile detritus.

When the governor of New Jersey orders state buildings to fly their flags at half-mast in honor of the death of the man who played the mobster Tony Soprano on TV[48] while real men and women are dying in military service every day, then you know that our values and what we consider virtuous in this country is totally upside down. Why did Governor Christie fly the flags at half-mast for the late Mr. Gandolfini? Because the New Jersey native Gandolfini was, in the words of Christie, an "iconic actor, who left a timeless impact."[49] No disrespect intended toward Mr. Gandolfini, but a "timeless impact" compared with what?

Monsters and Zombies: A Reflection of Our Cultural Selves

Because the horror genre is so popular today, I found it interesting that E. Michael Jones, in his book *Monsters from the Id*, found a connection between the Enlightenment and horror. Since we traced secularism back to the Enlightenment in Chapter three, I thought it would be interesting to see what the horror genre has to say to us today regarding the Enlightenment. Let's briefly flesh out a couple lines of thought from Jones's book.

According to Jones, Mary Shelley's *Frankenstein* (1818), which many consider the first science fiction novel, was a rejection of the Enlightenment project. How so? Recall that the Enlightenment, especially its radical strand, rejected both Christian authority and its moral order. According to La Mettrie (1709–1751), man was just a machine and the only road to happiness was through atheism and hedonism. Thus, according to the Enlightenment mind-set, man as a machine is no longer sacred. He has no soul, no morals, and no responsibilities.

267

According to Jones's analysis, the monster in *Frankenstein* was basically a metaphor for this conception of man as machine taken to its logical conclusion. Horror, in the form of the monster, represents the remorse exhibited by those who opposed the Enlightenment and what it was attempting to create: a soulless man. In other words the monster in *Frankenstein* is remorse personified. Lightning, originally the life-giving force, in the end only illuminates the horror that has been created.[50]

If *Frankenstein* represents the initial stage of the Enlightenment with all of its naïve optimism gone awry, then, according to Jones, Bram Stoker's *Dracula* (1897) symbolizes the end, the disillusionment phase. In historical context, by the end of the nineteenth century, Darwinism provided the metaphysical underpinning in the shift from mechanics to biology, and therefore from electricity (Frankenstein) to blood (Dracula).[51]

Both Christ and the vampire deal with blood and eternal life. But whereas Christ shed His blood so that His followers could have eternal life, Dracula drains his followers' blood so that he can have eternal life.[52] So vampirism is the epitome of autonomy and narcissism. Jones explains it further. "In a satanic way typical of the reversal of Christian order that the vampire creates, man achieves immortality through immorality and by infecting others—that is, through lust. Christianity exalts love; vampirism—Darwin's survival of the fittest pushed to its extreme—exalts the hunger of desire. Man under the thrall of lust as epitomized by this disease, loses his reason and becomes a zombie."[53] Dracula exemplifies the survival of the fittest. He is strong, preys on the weak, and then transfers the life of the weak to himself.[54] Thus, he is a type of anti-Christ.

Today, the zombie continues the theme of the undead. If horror represents remorse over the Enlightenment's attempt to reject the Christian worldview, then the zombie horror genre may also represent something gone astray in our culture today. There is, of course, no definitive interpretation to be made here. But it is difficult to dismiss the metaphor that the zombies represent people having lost their minds to their appetites. As I noted above, we are totally consumed with our mindless pleasures brought about by technology, the entertainment industry, and our sinful natures. Just as the zombies have an insatiable appetite, so too people today have a relentless appetite to fiddle with their gadgets, to consume, and to be entertained. Ethan Cordray supports this line of thinking: "Zombies represent the appetite divorced from everything else. They are incapable of judgment, self-awareness, or self-preservation. Though they still move and act, they are not really alive. They hunger and are never filled."[55]

At rock bottom, our sinful natures are always hungry and never filled. So whether it's lust for money or power, lust for acquiring things, lust for status and recognition, heterosexual or homosexual lust, our zombie-like sinful natures are constantly on the prowl to engage in a feeding frenzy. In fact, the more we feed our sinful natures with worldly lusts the more we lust after these things or behaviors. Just like the zombies, our sinful natures are insatiable and constantly gnawing at us to fulfill ungodly desires.

In his classic micro-doc entitled "The Madness of a Lost Society" Sean Turnbull at SGTreport.com provides a startling glimpse into the living horror show of our collapsing culture. He puts it this way in his video: "This is what we've become—a decadent, mindless, culture who by virtue of this complete and willful ignorance are now officially complicit in the crimes being perpetrated against us."[56]

Summary

So where does this leave us today? The thesis of this book is that Christianity, which once provided the worldview and moral underpinning of our country, has been displaced by secularism. But the secularism that accelerated after the countercultural revolution of the 1960s, with its rampant autonomy, hedonism, narcissism, and ravenous consumerism, has left us empty. With God out of the way, we believed we were liberated. But this Faustian bargain has come at great cost. All the fleeting benefits of consumerism; all the superficial titillation from the cult of celebrity and entertainment; and all the self-absorbed, mind-numbing satisfaction resulting from our adulteress love affair with the latest gadgets cannot distract us from the fact that we now live in a world devoid of meaning because we have left God behind. We wanted an unbridled freedom and received nihilism instead. Nihilism is the rotten fruit that our zombified culture gets to feed on now.

Chapter 14

Homosexuality, Marriage, and Abortion

In this chapter we cover three important issues: homosexuality, marriage, and abortion. The intention here is to see how these matters relate to the climate of PC tolerance and moral relativism, which are fruit of the secularization process. Our society used to consider homosexuality and abortion immoral behaviors, but now they are accepted as a matter of course by a significant portion of the population. These two practices affect marriage and the family, which in turn affect the foundation of society.

These are hot button issues, and I will deal with them in a manner that is respectful of the individuals involved while keeping in mind that all of us are guilty of moral shortcomings, myself included. We've all heard, "No one has a right to judge another's behavior." But if that assertion is correct, there is no need for laws. After all, laws by definition are judgments about moral behavior. And those making the laws are supposedly representing "we the people." Laws are judgments about what society maintains is right and what is wrong. If we cease with all judgments, then there is no need for laws, and we will accelerate into anarchy.

The Change in Attitude Toward Homosexuality

That we are even discussing the moral issues surrounding homosexuality supports my overall thesis that Christianity is losing its cultural authority. Quite frankly, ever since I started the journey of writing this book, our culture is showing signs of moral deterioration so rapidly that it is more apparent with each passing year that Christianity has lost its hegemony. If people a hundred years ago were told that our society today would be discussing the moral pros and cons of homosexuality, they would have been incredulous. Everybody back then knew it was morally wrong; therefore, most people would have considered practicing homosexuality a sin. The laws reflected this. This is not the case today.

As I was putting these notes together, I saw Pope Francis on television stating publicly that he wouldn't judge gay priests. He said, "Who am I to judge a gay person of goodwill who seeks the Lord?" Francis is the first pope to speak out in defense of homosexual priests (who are not sexually active) in the Catholic Church. Commenting on this, Rev. James Bretzke, a theology professor at Boston College, stated, "This isn't a change in the church's teaching, . . . What's important is the change in style and emphasis."[1]

From my perspective, this is a classic case of accommodation. The pope is now accommodating homosexual priests in the Catholic Church. This is brushed over by those who want to assure everyone that it is only window dressing, a mere change "in style and emphasis." But if this is so, why did the *Wall Street Journal* reporter claim that Pope Francis was the first pope to speak in defense of gay priests? Why was it even brought to the public's attention if it is no big deal? You can't have it both ways.

Either Francis was the first pope to defend gays in the priesthood or he wasn't. If he was, then he has accommodated homosexual priests (who ideally and supposedly do not practice their homosexuality), and this accommodation cannot be considered merely window dressing.

This brings up a point about identity. It seems that many people in our society today, including the pope, seem to assume that homosexuality is an identity rather than a choice. But this raises a question: Are homosexuals oriented biologically this way, or is their sexuality simply a preference? This is important, because prima facie it has struck many people that it is unfair of God (or people) to condemn homosexuality if the homosexual has no choice in the matter, because he or she is biologically oriented that way.

I had the opportunity to talk to a couple of Roman Catholics about the pope's accommodation. They both seemed to think it was acceptable. As one of them stated: "As long as they [the homosexuals] don't practice it, who am I to say anything? After all, they are born that way." I pointed out that if homosexuals were "born that way," there wouldn't be any homosexuals left. Moreover, I explained that if homosexuals really had no choice in the matter and simply followed their "identity" and inclinations, there would be no homosexuals left today because homosexuals cannot procreate. They wouldn't be around today because they couldn't have passed the supposed homosexual gene down through their posterity. The reason there are homosexuals today, I told these people, is because choice is involved.

These two folks I talked with demonstrate what I contended in Chapter six, namely, the premiere value in our country right now is tolerance, and more specifically PC tolerance. My two interlocutors' default mind-set was to follow the lead of the pope and the rest of our society not to judge a person involved in homosexual behavior, even if that person is a practicing priest. It's amazing how far we've come in our attitudes regarding what is morally acceptable.

Look at the change in the way homosexuality has been defined historically. As Mark Steyn explains, first it was defined as an "act." That is, sodomy was an act that took place between two people of the same sex (usually males). Then in the late nineteenth century, it was a condition described as "homosexuality." Now it has become an identity, *who* a person is. As Steyn notes: "Each formulation raises the stakes: One can object to and even criminalize an act: one is obligated to be sympathetic toward a condition; but once it's a fully-fledged identity, like being Hispanic or Inuit, anything less than wholehearted acceptance gets you marked down as a bigot."[2] The way our society has regarded homosexuality through its history reinforces my thesis about the accommodation process we have evidenced throughout this book.

So is the gay lifestyle really a reflection of one's identity? Are those who practice homosexuality born that way? The answer to both questions is no. Scientific data today suggests that both a person's genes *and* environmental factors play a part. Michael Ruse, a professor who has written much on the interface between religion and Darwinism, puts it this way: "Modern genetic thinking—specifically, genetic thinking about homosexuality—emphasizes that it is not the genes alone that cause physical characteristics, including social behavioral characteristics. Rather, the genes *in conjunction with the environment* cause these characteristics."[3] A few paragraphs above in the same article, he wrote, "That the genes do play some role in homosexuality seems to be almost certain, that the environment plays some role in homosexuality seems just as certain, but we are a long way from sorting out the respective components."[4] But note what Ruse says next. "It is clear today that something like homosexuality is not a sin."[5] Sin, for Ruse, who is an atheist, is ruled out *a priori*. This same PC attitude regarding homosexuality goes for a growing number of practical atheists and supposed Bible believers in our culture today.

Other studies have corroborated that homosexuality is not strictly genetic. Dr. Dean Hamer of the National Cancer Institute, who identifies himself as gay, concludes for example that "Homosexuality is not purely genetic. . . . There is not a single master gene that makes people gay."[6] Even Dr. Camille Paglia, an admitted lesbian, corroborates this position:

> There may indeed be a genetic component predisposing some people toward homosexuality, but social factors in childhood play an enormous role in determining whether that tendency manifests itself or not . . . the family matrix is central to the sexual story. No one is 'born gay.' The idea is ridiculous, but it is symptomatic of our overpoliticized climate that such assertions are given instant credence by gay activists and their media partisans.[7]

Nevertheless, an ever growing percentage of people in our society accept the myth that homosexuals are born that way.

How Many Homosexuals Are There Really?

Another datum that seems to support the "born that way" misconception is the myth that homosexuals comprise 10 percent of the population. This is not true. Ten percent is a pretty large chunk of people. The more the public is led to believe that homosexuality is more prevalent than it is, the more normal it seems.

The 10 percent figure came out of a study conducted in the 1940s and 1950s by an entomologist named Alfred Kinsey.[8] Kinsey turned his sights from insects to human sexuality with a famous study funded in large part by the Rockefeller Foundation.[9] Kinsey reported a range of homosexuality from one to six, with six being "exclusively homosexual." One of Kinsey's findings reported that "10 per cent of the males are *more or less exclusively homosexual* (i.e., rate 5 or 6) for at least three years between the ages of 16 and 55. This is one male in ten in the white male population."[10] This is the origin of the 10 percent figure. One difficulty, of course, is how the 10 percent figure, which referred only to white males, extrapolated out to females as well, which is how the public perceives the 10 percent figure.

There are other problems with Kinsey's findings as well. Edward Laumann put together a landmark study in which he pointed out that Kinsey did not use probability sampling. Instead, Laumann reported the following:

> Kinsey roamed far and wide in selecting his subjects. He was not adverse to using institutional settings, including prisons and reform schools, from which to recruit his subjects. Kinsey also purposely

recruited subjects for his research from homosexual friendships and acquaintance networks in big cities. . . . These devices would all tend to bias Kinsey's results toward higher estimates of homosexuality.[11]

Laumann argues that the "widely held notion" that 10 percent of the population is homosexual is erroneous and that his own study and others point to a much lower rate.[12]

Kinsey not only over sampled prison inmates, but he looked for those in prison who had been involved as sex offenders—sodomy, child molestation, and rape. The fact that he specifically cited three years of "exclusive" homosexual activity as the criterion for defining someone as a homosexual (rating of 5 or 6) seems to coincide with men who spent at least three years in prison. As Stanton Jones and Mark Yarhouse point out, "What other options are there for men in prison?"[13]

So the entire notion that 10 percent of the population is homosexual is built on a faulty foundation. In reality, prevalence rates of those who identify themselves as homosexuals range from 2 to 4 percent. Laumann's findings suggested that 2.0 percent of males and 0.9 percent of females identified themselves as homosexuals, with an additional fraction of a percent of both males and females defining themselves as bisexual.[14] When men and women are combined, less than 3 percent of the population can be characterized as homosexual, and it may even be lower than 2 percent.[15]

As an art teacher of twenty-three years, Dr. Camille Paglia, whom we quoted above, says she was taken aback not at the frequency with which she saw homosexuality but the rarity of it. As a lesbian, you would think she would have a bias toward supporting the 10 percent myth. Instead, she emphatically states, "Homosexuality is not 'normal.' On the contrary, it is a challenge to the norm; therein rests its eternally revolutionary character. . . . Nature exists, whether academics like it or not. And in nature, procreation is the single, relentless rule. That is the norm. Our sexual bodies were designed for reproduction. Penis fits vagina: no fancy linguistic game-playing can change that biological fact."[16] Paglia calls the 10 percent figure "pure propaganda" and rails against the gay activists for their purposeful avoidance of the truth and the servile media that have continuously supported this myth.[17]

Bruce Voller, the former chairman of the National Gay Task Force, admits that he picked up the 10 percent figure in the late 1970s in order to convince the public that gays "are everywhere." Apparently gay organizations know the 10 percent figure is a farce but use it because "it proves helpful in advocacy efforts," as lesbian activist Jill Harris admits.[18] Gay activist organizations want the public to perceive the homosexual lifestyle as "perfectly normal." As Glenn Stanton and Bill Maier point out in their book *Marriage on Trial,* the media supports this effort with TV programs like *Will & Grace, Queer Eye for the Straight Guy,* and *Boy Meets Boy,* as well as films that give the impression that the number of homosexuals in society is much greater than it is.

Apparently this effort is succeeding. A Gallup poll in 2002 showed that Americans believe one in five people in the United States are homosexuals.[19] An important statistic the gay activists and media don't let the public know, however, is that homosexuals are more likely than their heterosexual counterparts to suffer from mental illness, alcohol and drug abuse, suicide, domestic violence at the hands of their partners, and a host of life-threatening diseases like AIDS, cancer, and hepatitis.[20]

Regardless of their efforts to convince the public otherwise, homosexuality is not normal. Until relatively recently this was not even an issue. In fact, in 1952 the American Psychiatric Association's DSM (*Diagnostic and Statistical Manual of Mental Disorders*) listed homosexuality as a "sociopathic personality disturbance." In the 1968 DSM, homosexuality was softened to "sexual deviancy." By 1973, under tremendous pressure from gay activists, APA removed homosexuality from the DSM.

But even Dr. Ronald Bayer, who is sympathetic to the gay movement and a member of the APA, stated that the removal of homosexuality violated the dictates of science and was based purely on politics. Even four years after the 1973 decision, 69 percent of the psychiatrists in the APA still regarded homosexuality as a "pathological adaptation."[21]

It goes without saying that we have gotten away from the traditional Christian perspective on homosexual behavior. From a Christian perspective, it really doesn't matter if the homosexual population is 2 percent or 10 percent or 80 percent. What we need to know is what God thinks about homosexuality. And to do this we need to look at Scripture.

What the Bible Says about Homosexuality

It is quite plain when looking in the Old Testament that the practice of homosexual behavior did not please God: "You shall not lie with a male as with a woman; it is an abomination. And you shall not lie with any animal and so make yourself unclean with it, neither shall any woman give herself to an animal to lie with it: it is perversion" (Lev. 18:22–23). I included the verse about not having sex with animals because after homosexual marriage becomes commonplace in our culture, it will only be a matter of time before some poor soul in our country wants to marry his or her pet. After all, we are descendants of the same ancestor in the past, and Darwinists consider humans as animals, so what does it matter if one animal has sex with another animal? If you think I am exaggerating, please remember that in the early twentieth-century people would have thought same-sex marriage crazy, even impossible. The point is that all of us, as fallen humans, are subject to moral decadence which always slides down the slippery slope once it gets started. We find the way back to God only by the light of His grace.

Other verses in the Old Testament show God's disapproval of homosexuality, such as Genesis 19, where God incinerated Sodom and Gomorrah. But since Jesus Christ came to earth, we need to see what the New Testament says about homosexual behavior under the New Covenant. Is the practice of homosexual behavior still condemned as it was in the Old Testament? Let's look at a few verses from the New Testament.

"For this reason God gave them up to dishonorable passions. For their women exchanged natural relations for those that are contrary to nature; and the men likewise gave up natural relations with women and were consumed with passion for one another, men committing shameless acts with men and receiving in themselves the due penalty for their error" (Rom. 1:26–27).

"For if God did not spare angels when they sinned, but cast them into hell . . . if he did not spare the ancient world, but preserved Noah, a herald of righteousness, with seven others, when he brought a flood upon the world of the ungodly, if by turning the cities of Sodom and Gomorrah to ashes he condemned them to extinction, making them an example of what is going to happen to the ungodly" (2 Peter 2: 4–6).

"Just as Sodom and Gomorrah and the surrounding cities, which likewise indulged in sexual immorality and pursued unnatural desire, serve as an example by undergoing a punishment of eternal fire" (Jude 7).

We need not go any further, even though there are more verses. We can see that some New Testament writers referred back to Sodom and Gomorrah as examples of sexual immorality and God's condemnation of this type of sin. As Robert A. J. Gagnon explains, "The authors of Jude and 2 Peter undoubtedly understood a key offense of Sodom to be men desiring to have sex with males."[22] We saw in the Romans verse, same-sex intimacy is described as "dishonorable passion."

But what about Jesus? Wasn't He always promoting love and tolerance? As Gagnon points out, you cannot *equate* love with tolerance, or love with nonjudgmental acceptance of ungodly lifestyles or behaviors.[23] Jesus had stern words concerning divorce and adultery (Matt. 5:31–32). He didn't gloss over these things willy-nilly. He forgave the woman caught in the act of adultery but told her in no uncertain terms to "sin no more" (John 8:11).

Jesus's forgiveness did not mean a license to keep on sinning. When Jesus talked about not judging (Matt. 7:1–2), He did not mean to avoid all judgment (otherwise there could be no laws). He meant that no one should act as a person's *final* judge; as if anyone of us fallen humans has a right to judge someone's final condemnation. The final judgment will be left to Jesus when everyone of us stands before Him on judgment day.

Jesus railed against the scribes and Pharisees of His day. He was not tolerant of their attitudes and behavior (Matt. 23). This does not mean that Jesus did not love all of these people, as well as you and me. It means He wants all of us to live godly lives in all our endeavors and behaviors. This is something we should be striving for even if we fall short of it. Unfortunately, our postmodern PC society takes the easy (autonomous) way out and simply lowers the moral bar. This is what happens when we leave God out of our lives.

Advocates of the gay lifestyle and those practicing homosexuality think everyone should have to accept their behavior on moral and legal grounds. In the court of public opinion, the gay community is certainly winning in their attempts to silence their adversaries. They ward off criticism by calling their opponents "homophobes." I want to say that I am not afraid of homosexuals, nor do I bear any animosity toward those practicing the gay lifestyle. Every one of us has sinned. However, if all behavior today must be deemed acceptable under the guise of PC tolerance, our country will continue on its current path of moral decay and destruction with regard to traditional Judeo-Christian ethics.

I don't think we are many years away from being completely muzzled as far as standing against homosexual immorality. People in the near future will be considered extremists for opposing homosexuality. PC tolerance will reign because PC tolerance is the First Commandment in our country. Thou shalt be tolerant.

Finally, on the everyday level, John Corvino, a self-professed liberal and gay man, makes the case for homosexuality: "The positive case for homosexuality, is at one level, strikingly simple; *Same-sex relationships make some people happy.*"[24]

This raises a question: What if having sex with one's pet or with one's child makes someone happy? What if a father decides he "loves" his fourteen-year-old daughter and wants to marry her and divorce his wife? Moreover, the only thing holding us back from these types of behaviors and the inevitable slide down this slippery slope is traditional moral values that are based on Scripture. And since we have discarded the Bible as an archaic book, it will only be a matter of time before personal preference trumps any traditional morals. The apostle Paul asked the Corinthian church to temporarily remove the man who had relations with his father's wife, whether they loved each other or not (1 Cor. 5:1–13). So just because an immoral sexual relationship makes someone happy does not mean it should be condoned.[25]

The simple fact is that we all have fallen human natures and therefore have a propensity toward selfishness and godlessness. We all have different genetic predispositions toward particular behaviors or attitudes, whether it's drinking, gambling, lust, the love of money, anger, envy, etc., which are all ungodly. We all have our weak spots. Does the way our genes are arranged combined with temptations in our environment alleviate us from moral guilt for our sin? No. Jones and Yarhouse wrote: "At the broadest level all humans are heirs to a predisposition that we have not chosen and that propels us toward self-destruction and evil—our sinful nature. The plight of the homosexual who has desires and passions that he or she did not choose is in fact the common plight of humanity."[26]

We are all made in the image of God: the *imago Dei*. This means we have intellect, emotion, will, self-consciousness, a moral compass, the ability to create art, music, etc., and the ability to form relationships with each other and with God. The image of God separates us from the animals and the rest of creation and gives us worth as the pinnacle of God's creation. The person who practices homosexual behavior has just as much worth in God's eyes as I do, because he or she is also made in the image of God just like I am. When I sin or the person practicing homosexual behavior sins, we are both marring the image of

God we were made in. When we sin, in that moment we are not reflecting God's character as human beings made in His image.

The Institution of Marriage

You'll notice that after God created Adam, He then created Eve, who was a different gender from Adam. I don't think we need to rehearse Dr. Paglia's blunt summation of the sexual differences to make this point. The natural love that Adam and Eve shared for each other reflected the love the three persons in the Trinity had for one another before the universe came into existence. The wonderful part is that Adam and Eve's love resulted in the creation of a child, another human being. Their act of procreation was another reflection of being made in God's image, because just as God created them out of love, so too they were given the ability to create a human being out of love who likewise bore the image of God. To put it in the most respectful terms possible, homosexuals do not have this ability to *naturally* create another human being. Therefore, they are not reflecting God's image when they share same-sex intimacy.

All of this, of course, holds implications for the institution of marriage, which is why it is important to discuss this issue. The joining together of Adam and Eve to form "one flesh" is a reflection of the three persons in the Trinity, which constitute "one God." Jesus himself re-authorized the institution of marriage: "But from the beginning of the creation, 'God made them male and female.' Therefore a man shall leave his father and mother and hold fast to his wife, and they shall become one flesh. So they are no longer two but one flesh" (Mark 10:6–8).

Just as the three persons in the triune God have separate functions yet are all equal, so too a man and a woman joined in marriage have separate functions but are both equal, because they are both human (*adam*). A man and a woman fit together and complement each other in a God-ordained way that two humans of the same gender cannot.[27] So from a Judeo-Christian perspective, marriage, as a God-ordained institution, by definition can only be between a man and a woman.

Marriage is not only about the man and the woman but also about the larger society as well. Most couples don't run to the justice of the peace to get married; instead, they hold a public ceremony, because their commitment to each other is also a commitment to family, friends, community, and God. This is why everyone, including civil authorities and churches, get involved. In addition, marriage is also about the next generation.[28] James Q. Wilson argues that marriage is the ceremony that legitimizes the family and so "pretending that anything we call a marriage can create a family is misleading."[29]

Today, traditional marriage is under attack by those whose behavior a hundred years ago was deemed a sin and later a "sickness." Now, in many cases, homosexuality is increasingly accepted unconditionally. Is it any wonder I am predicting that people will demand to have legal intimate relations with their pets or even their own children as we continue down the slippery slope?

In the end, the current debate about traditional marriage is about morality and what we are willing to tolerate regarding the definition of marriage, as John Corvino in the gay camp even admits.[30] Gay activists want to redefine marriage. They have already made unbelievable inroads, considering they are only a tiny fraction of the population. But it is God who defines marriage, not the gay community or the Supreme Court. Gay activists have in many ways shut down their opposition by throwing around emotive invectives like "homophobe" or accusing those who want to uphold traditional sexual mores as using "hate speech." The liberal media is often complicit in this effort.

Gay Activists Pushing the Envelope

We already saw in a previous chapter that the breakdown of the family is one of the greatest societal problems facing us today and literally exacerbates the breakdown of our republic. Redefining marriage to include those of the same sex will only move us further in this direction. Read what prominent gay activist Michelangelo Signorile stated in *OUT* magazine, as quoted by Stanton and Yarhouse:

> The trick is, gay leaders and pundits must stop watering the issue down—"this is simply about equality for gay couples"—and offer same sex marriage for what it is: an opportunity to reconstruct a traditionally homophobic institution by bringing it to our more equitable queer value system, . . . Our gay leaders must acknowledge that gay marriage is just as radical and transformative as the religious Right contends it is.[31]

Signorile went on to admit that the gay community picked up the "equal rights" or "freedom to marry" argument on the recommendation of a Los Angeles firm's PR department who thought it would play well with the public.[32]

Paula Ettelbrick, a law scholar who teaches at both Columbia and New York universities, agrees with the gay activists: "Being queer is more than setting up house, sleeping with a person of the same gender, and seeking state approval for doing so. . . . Being queer means pushing the parameters of sex, sexuality and family, and in the process transforming the very fabric of society."[33]

Gay proponents like these are paving the way for a redefinition of marriage that would include polygamy and group marriage (three or more persons). This would totally destroy the traditional and legal definition of a "family" as well as marriage.[34] Just because a friend loves another friend, or a mom loves her child doesn't give them the God-ordained right to be married. Otherwise we will get to the point where anyone who publicly declares their love for another would have a right to marry, totally destroying the institution of marriage.[35]

At rock bottom, this is not about equality but redefining marriage and family however one sees fit. How does a miniscule fraction of the population get so much pull in determining a new definition of marriage while the traditional notion of marriage as defined by the Judeo-Christian worldview get brushed aside as an increasingly outmoded institution? If we are going to allow/accommodate this type of thinking, it just provides more evidence for the fact that we are rapidly becoming a post-Christian nation.

It is troubling that in the very near future I predict no one will be able to publicly criticize homosexual behavior or any other politically correct behaviors. If Christians, who are already marginalized in the public arena, cannot point to the immorality of homosexual behavior and the gay agenda, what will stop the redefinition of marriage and family, along with the concomitant breakdown of our culture and our republic? (As this book goes to press, we now have the answer: nothing will stop it. The Supreme Court has just legalized same-sex marriage in all fifty states.)

Officials in the Department of Children and Families (DFC) in Massachusetts are "weeding out" foster and adoptive parents who would not fully endorse the LGBT (lesbian, gay, bisexual, transgender) self-identification in a child in their care. The DFC is offering mentoring programs (read: propaganda) for prospective foster and adoptive parents to make sure they are on board with dealing with nontraditional sexual identities so they will be "supportive."[36] This is just another example of the Christian worldview being discarded in favor of PC values.

So today, in that particular state (and I'm sure it will be just a matter of time before all states follow suit), foster kids will not have the benefit of hearing a traditional Christian perspective on sexual identity. Do you think perhaps the reason many of these poor kids are confused about their sexual identity is because they have no parental role models for them to follow? If 20 percent of the kids in foster care in Massachusetts are "gender confused"[37] when only 3 percent or less of the general population identifies themselves as homosexual or lesbian, wouldn't this lend evidence to the fact that these children are not born this way but rather have not "learned" their proper identities? How will they be afforded this opportunity when traditional Christian values are not allowed to be demonstrated?

We are in deep trouble in this country if Christianity, which once represented the moral foundation of our society, is marginalized to the point where Christians are not even allowed to oppose moral decadence, and only those who support politically correct attitudes are allowed a voice. We are accelerating toward this eventuality at breakneck speed. Worse is that we in the Christian community are not helping ourselves when an increasing number of churches and denominations are accommodating homosexuality by allowing homosexuals to serve as pastors and priests. Nevertheless, we grasp some hope as many parishioners are leaving these accommodative churches.

Abortion

If narcissism and an incipient rebellion were motivating factors behind the countercultural revolution, it should come as no surprise that the right to abortion occurred during this time as well. Many women believed an unwanted pregnancy held them back; therefore, they embraced the lie that abortion was a ticket to equality with men. So just as we see the push for equality emerge in the homosexual community regarding gay marriage today, back then women wanted equality with men, which was one of the major factors behind the abortion debate. In short, women felt that they had been cheated out of their freedom or identity in some way. Many women of the feminist persuasion frowned upon motherhood as a constraint that the establishment and tradition used against them to keep them subservient, which thwarted their liberation.

The overarching desire for equality and the idea of having been robbed of something occurred somewhere else in history as well. The

Serpent (Devil) told Eve that God was denying her and Adam's freedom by not allowing them to eat of the Tree of Knowledge because God knew if they ate of it they would be "as gods." This lie caused Eve to take her eyes off God and His commands, just like our country has done. When this happens, things necessarily go wrong. Eve saw that the fruit of the tree was desirable. In her mind, God perhaps had lied to her and Adam, so why should she deny herself the freedom to eat the fruit? Of course, we all know the results. The Fall ended up not only in the spiritual deaths of both Adam and Eve but their physical deaths as well, just as God foretold would happen.

Today we see that the wages of sin is still death. Women's "freedom" to liberate themselves from their pregnancies has caused the death of 55 million unwanted babies. Moreover, disobeying God's moral commands and distancing oneself from God's moral character while exercising one's freedom will always result in death. In short, believing the Devil's lies ends in death. On the other hand, believing God's promises leads to life. Unfortunately our fallen natures beguile us toward believing whatever lie will suit our narcissistic autonomy.

Abortion in Historical Context

Betty Friedan, the first president of the National Organization for Women (NOW), wrote *The Feminine Mystique* in 1960. She made no mention of abortion in the book. Feminism and the right to abortion were not yet connected. Larry Lader, an abortion rights activist, convinced Friedan that abortion rights was important for the organization. Lader was an activist who worked on repealing antiabortion laws, one reason of which was to decrease population growth. Lader teamed up with gynecologist Bernard Nathanson to found NARAL (National Association for the Repeal of Abortion Laws) and convinced Friedan that abortion was a civil rights issue and that all feminist aspirations (education, equal pay, jobs) depended on their ability to control their own bodies. In 1966 abortion was included in NOW's list of goals,[38] which coincided with the sexual/countercultural revolution. The transformation of abortion from a moral question to a political issue continued from the late '60s until the Supreme Court in 1973 upheld the right of a woman to have an abortion.

Abortion rights activists talked about having a world in which there would be no "unplanned" children and all children would be "wanted." They talked about how the illegitimacy rate would go down. They found encouragement in the fact that women with an unwanted pregnancy could abort the baby and continue with their work or schooling. They implied that the need for social services and welfare for unplanned children and their mothers would decrease. And finally, Paul Ehrlich's best seller, *The Population Bomb* (1968), added to the abortion argument by warning that the human population was increasing so rapidly that mass starvation and societal upheavals were a certainty in the very near future. (I might suggest that those concerned about over-population should lead by example.) At any rate, Candace C. Crandall has pointed out that all of these assertions were "empty promises."[39]

We have seen throughout this book that autonomy is a major thread running through the secular mind-set. It is the notion that "I did it my way." Each person becomes their own moral arbiter. This attitude became especially pronounced during the Me generation counter-culture, the very years in which *Roe v. Wade* was embedded. Doing things our way (autonomy) instead of God's way will always end in death sooner or later. This held true for the first two human beings and it still holds true for us today.

Roe v. Wade

The Court decision stemming from *Roe* legally sanctioned moral autonomy to the extreme. It allowed for the taking of the baby's life simply by the decision of the baby's mother. Supreme Court Justice Blackmun admitted that nothing in the Constitution mentioned any "right to privacy" but argued that the idea was broad enough to allow a woman to decide whether or not to end her pregnancy. Blackmun stated that unborn babies had never been "recognized in the law as persons in the whole sense."[40] But this line of thought is nothing more than authorizing radical autonomy hiding behind the cloak of privacy. If Blackmun happened to be one of the unfortunate babies whose brain was sucked out and then had his body dismembered before seeing the light of day, we would not have had to suffer his argumentation. If you think that suggesting this counterfactual is gratuitous and disgusting, you may want to side with those who believe the abortion procedure, at whatever stage it occurs, is gratuitous and disgusting and would like to see a way for this to come to an end.

In retrospect, this decision was nothing more that legislating from the bench. The Supreme Court rather than having constitutional precedent for their decision instead supported the narcissism that was prevalent at the time. Blackmun argued in the majority opinion that abortion had to be considered in the context of "population growth, pollution, poverty, and racial" issues.[41] Citing those issues has nothing whatsoever to do with the Constitution. But no one seems to want to follow the Constitution these days anyway.

Twenty years later, three justices formed a majority in helping to uphold most of *Roe* in *Planned Parenthood v. Casey* (1992), in which Planned Parenthood appealed to another constitutional right that no one had heard of before—the right to "dignity and autonomy," in what is known as "the mystery passage." The justices explained part of their decision this way: "These matters, involving the most intimate and personal choices a person may make in a lifetime, choices central to personal dignity and *autonomy*, are central to the liberty protected by the Fourteenth Amendment. At the heart of liberty is the right to define one's own concept of existence, of meaning, of the universe, and of the mystery of human life."[42] (Emphasis mine.)

Political philosopher Hadley Arkes comments on the Court's explanation: "This is the kind of sentiment that would ordinarily find its place within the better class of fortune cookies."[43] Robert Bork also chimes in: "What this judicial grandiloquence means, aside from a right to have an abortion, nobody knows."[44] One thing is obvious: the justices upheld women's "autonomy." I would argue that when one's autonomy extends to the point of taking another human life merely by fiat, our republic is in serious trouble.

The rationale in *Roe* was that the baby was merely a "potential human life," and the mother's autonomy overrides it. The Court decided an unborn baby was not a person, which before *Roe* would have equated to a "unique human life." This was not possible after the *Roe* decision, because if the baby was considered a unique human life and thus a person, the baby would have had inalienable rights, which the Court necessarily would protect. By divorcing the baby's human life from its personhood, the Court ruled that humans are no longer *intrinsic* right holders at the moment of conception. Rather, humans are *"extrinsic* right *recipients"* whenever the Court somehow decides our personhood begins.[45]

This set an extremely dangerous precedent. The Court has now opened the door to allowing an arbitrary authority other than God to decide the value of human life. This holds dangerous consequences for us as individuals. As we will see in Chapter sixteen, global elites think most of us are useless cattle. What will stop people like these from defining you and me out of existence (just like the unborn) as they continue to gain power in our world? What if those in our own government begin labeling citizens who disagree with them as "terrorists" or "hate mongers" or "traitors" or "extremists" and strip them of their inalienable rights? If you think this is outlandish, let me point out that Hitler began in the early 1920s to define Jews as less than human. This continued on until extermination became the logical conclusion. In fact, this process of classifying people our government deems enemies of the state (gun owners, former military, Christians, etc.) has already begun in our country.

As I pointed out earlier, all of us are made in the image of God, which is what gives us our worth. Our worth doesn't come from some court. Our worth comes from being made in God's image at the moment of conception. Our worth, and therefore our rights, comes from God. Our rights are therefore *intrinsic*, because we are human beings. God declares that humans, as the pinnacle of His creation, have worth. Furthermore, God told the prophet Jeremiah, "Before I formed you in the womb I knew you" (Jer. 1:5a). God considered Jeremiah a person before he was even formed in the womb. This, of course, flies in the face of the Supreme Court decision in *Roe*. If God considered Jeremiah a person before he was formed in the womb, then it follows that Jeremiah was a person while he was *in* the womb.

A critic at this point may argue that we can't have the Court taking sides on these issues, that the Court needs to be "neutral." In addition, people are fond of saying that morality shouldn't be legislated. After all, we have to abide by the separation of church and state—thus, religion shouldn't inform any court decisions or public decision making.

This is shallow thinking. *All* morality is legislated. The problem with the argument about not legislating morality is that there is no possible way to be neutral in moral decision making. Somebody's morality will be legislated and become law. So, for example, when the Court says it is up to the woman and her doctor if the baby should live, that is not taking a neutral stance. It is denying the intrinsic rights of the baby as a human being and handing those rights over to the mother and her doctor. This is supposedly neutral because neither God nor religion nor anything but the mother and her doctor are considered at all in the Court's decision. Dispensing with God is not being neutral; it is embracing secular humanism by default. We should expect things to go morally awry when we ignore the living God. The elimination of 55 million babies is evidence of this.

The Court went about its decision in *Roe* as if the baby's right as a human being did not exist. In addition, the Court made no attempt to

287

consider the woman's decision in relation to the rest of society. It did not take into account the possibly that those in the woman's community could help her bring a new life into the world, even if she decided not to keep the baby. Instead, the Court treated the woman as an isolated individual in charge of her autonomous decision regarding her baby. One can't help but wonder in historical context if part of the reason for the Court's decision is because many women during the countercultural revolution actually wanted to go it alone. They wanted their freedom from anything they perceived as holding them back in their pursuit of self-actualization and equality with men. They wanted decisions to be theirs alone. Abortion promised to be part of the answer to women's liberation.

It was a lie.

Consequences of Abortion

Rather than liberation, abortion causes isolation, guilt, and loneliness. It also exacerbates fracture in the family and the community. Women straining after this ideal of autonomous freedom and then proceeding with an abortion more often than not find themselves detached from everything—their boyfriends, their husbands, their babies, and themselves.

Start with an unmarried couple. Whether the boyfriend pressures the woman to have an abortion she doesn't want, or whether the woman wants an abortion but the boyfriend-father wants to have the baby, the result is the same: a fracture in the relationship. Unmarried couples rarely survive an abortion and usually break up before or immediately after the abortion.[46] Even if both wanted the abortion, the result is the same.

Another fracture occurs in families. If a young girl's parents pressure her to abort her baby, she ends up suffering from guilt for the abortion and resentment toward her parents if she wanted to keep the baby. If an abortion occurs with a married couple, the same scenario plays out as with the unmarried couple. If one wanted the baby, then the one who "lost the argument" resents the spouse.

Another break that occurs over abortion is that the mother is pitted against her own baby. Elective abortion simply is not natural. Mothers have a natural tendency to want to nurture their babies, not kill them. This is all the more tragic for the woman who truly agonizes over whether to abort the child. The research arm of Planned Parenthood reports the two primary reasons to abort are lack of finances and lack of emotional support.[47] Many of these women are in their early twenties and account for the highest abortion rate.[48] Many are unmarried and don't want to be single parents for lack of emotional support or even losing their boyfriends. Others don't feel they have the financial wherewithal to support a child on their own. This would also apply to women who are still in their teens.

For some women, the emotional "support" they receive comes in the form of parents pressuring their daughters to abort the baby so they "can get on with their life" and not suffer the stigma of illegitimacy. In this instance, not only is the teenage girl pitted against her baby, but she is in conflict with herself as well. If she really doesn't want an abortion and succumbs to the pressure, she will suffer guilt and have a difficult time forgiving herself and getting on with her life.

The same goes for women who get pregnant outside of marriage and want to continue unhindered with their careers or schooling. They also find that they are in conflict with themselves. They view the baby in an adversarial role. The baby becomes an obstacle to the woman's achieving her dreams and continuing on with her life. The woman must decide whether it is really worth discarding her baby to advance a career or education. She is conflicted against her natural tendency to have the baby.

So we see a fracturing of relationships over the abortion: women in conflict with men, women pitted against their babies, and women conflicted with themselves. Just as we saw with gay marriage, so too abortion results in a tearing in the fabric of society regarding the relationships that make up society. Life and family are tossed aside in favor of freedom and autonomy however difficult and agonizing the decision to abort comes about. But can life just go on as if nothing has happened after the woman has eliminated her baby? Reality tells a different story.

Women: The Second Victims of Abortion

I would challenge anyone who thinks a woman can simply have an abortion, and then get on with her life, to go online and spend a few hours reading story after story of women who are in anguish over their abortions. The women whose stories I read indicate it simply was not worth it, though it may have seemed so at the time. The vast majority of these women never get over what they have done.

Some didn't come to the reality of what the abortion meant until they brought a child into the world and then realized that another child of theirs should be in this world already. Every woman is affected by abortion differently. But the thread that runs consistently through all the abortion stories is the profound guilt, denial, remorse, despair, alienation, depression, and lack of desire to carry on with any purpose. These women are truly the second victims of abortion.[49]

I have heard nothing reported on this via the mainstream media, whether television or supposedly reputable magazines. This is probably one of the most underreported tragedies in our country in the last fifty years. It cannot be overstated.

If we could somehow muster up a little honesty in this country, maybe bringing to light the wreckage that abortion leaves in women's lives could steer us back to reality. In this case, reality means that a woman can't just gratuitously kill another human being and think it won't affect her. Talking about terminating a pregnancy as a "procedure" may sound clinical and seduces society into believing that a moral decision is not being made, but an ultrasound showing a little baby moving around forces reality upon us—that to remove that baby from the womb is the taking of a human life.

If places like Planned Parenthood, which supposedly are in existence to truly help women with unplanned pregnancies, would share the entire story of what it means to have an abortion, the abortion rate would decrease dramatically and we could get on with a viable solution to unwanted pregnancies (adoption) that uphold the dignity of both the mother and baby. But what may be a viable solution for the unborn baby may not be a viable solution for an organization that in 2006 brought in at least a third of its total income from performing abortions. So it is not surprising that in this same year Planned Parenthood "reported only one adoption referral for every 180 abortions."[50] Combine this with Planned Parenthood's opposition to laws requiring ultrasounds before abortions, parental notification, a waiting period before abortions, and bans on late-term abortions, and at some point one must question if this organization is really about helping women plan for parenthood, or if it is simply about eliminating babies at every turn. With 180 abortions per 1 adoption referral, I think we have our answer. Apparently not enough money is made from adoption referrals.

When you think about it, abortion is a measure of what we are willing to tolerate in this country. I argued in Chapter six that PC tolerance has become the premiere virtue in our culture. The fact that we are willing to tolerate the mother's intentional killing of her baby in the womb demonstrates the accuracy of this assertion. One of the abortion advocates' favorite arguments is "If you don't want to have an abortion, don't have one." The implication here, of course, is that just because abortion opponents don't believe in abortion does not give them the right to deny abortion advocates the right to an abortion. In other words, abortion opponents need to be tolerant.

But this argument doesn't get too far. Should we be tolerant of those who want to own slaves? After all, slave owners could say, "If you don't want a slave, don't own one."[51] Should we be tolerant of those who might want to destroy an abortion clinic? What if some folks said, "Personally we are opposed to destroying abortion clinics, but who are we to deny someone that 'choice'? We don't want to impose our morality on anyone else." If this seems absurd, then think about how absurd it seems for a woman to have the "choice" to take the life of the baby in her womb. If the destruction of property is illegal, why isn't the destruction of a human life illegal?[52] Ronald Reagan was right when he said, "I've noticed that all those in favor of abortion are already born."[53]

One argument that comes up frequently is why the woman shouldn't have a right to an abortion in the case of rape or incest. The problem with this argument is that statistics show that women give this as a reason for having an abortion less than 1 percent of the time. The reasons women give for having an abortion, such as the lack of finances or being unmarried, etc., far outweigh cases of incest and rape as reasons for an abortion.[54] As Robert Bork has pointed out, childbearing and rearing a child can certainly be burdensome. But in light of the fact that a mother has two options—adoption or abortion—if she chooses the latter, then abortion "really is for convenience." It really is just another form of birth control.[55]

Does nine months of inconvenience justify killing a baby? And if women were truly concerned about having a right to an abortion because of rape or incest, do you think they would agree to outlaw all abortions except in those cases? The simple fact is that if abortion was outlawed, 75 percent of women who had an abortion said they would not seek one if it were illegal. This indicates that abortion is done mainly for convenience and is confirmed by the abortion rate skyrocketing after abortion became legal.[56] Moreover, if abortion became illegal, people would have to start acting more responsibly, and the killing of the unborn as a means of contraception and convenience would drop abruptly.

Weren't we told by the liberal elites that sex education and offering contraceptives at school would solve the problem of unwanted pregnancies? Liberal progressives have never understood human nature. Handing out condoms in schools has done nothing but lower the moral bar under the mistaken notion of being "realistic." Young adults still don't take contraceptive measures seriously like they should, and this combined with having sex outside of marriage, which the young folks see the educational elites condoning, results in unwanted pregnancies that still end in abortion today.

There is no doubt that in the vast majority of cases today abortion is done as a matter of convenience. This certainly tells us where we are morally as a society, that killing an unborn baby can come so cheap. At this point, abortion advocates often ask if we want to go back to the days of back-alley abortions. But this is a straw man argument. In 1960 former medical director of Planned Parenthood Dr. Mary Calderone, estimated that *licensed* physicians performed nine out of ten illegal abortions. Most of the mothers' deaths due to illegal abortion were not because of back-alley butchers but because of infection. These deaths fell precipitously after World War II, when antibiotics became available. In fact, in 1966 only 159 deaths occurred in the United States as a result of illegal abortions, and this number fell to forty-one the year before *Roe*.[57]

This is a far cry from the supposedly 5,000 to 10,000 deaths per year from illegal abortions that abortion advocates trotted out. In turns out that this figure can be traced to Bernard Nathanson, the cofounder of NARAL, who confessed in 1979 that this number was "totally false" but was used nonetheless as a "useful figure" to prop up the argument for abortion on demand.[58] Another lie.

Reaping What We Sow
So where do all these lies about exercising our autonomy leave us? Well, we live in a world today where we couldn't care less about what God thinks about anything. We are on our own now. Over the last fifty years or so, we've used up all the moral capital deposited from previous generations. It is all gone now. Believing the lies that emanate from our culture of narcissism and radical moral autonomy has resulted in a surreal world that makes no sense.

We live in a world where unborn eagles are protected by the law but unborn babies are not. We live in a world where in many states a public school needs parents' permission to give a girl an aspirin, but the girl doesn't need permission from her parents to get an abortion. We live in a world where a corporation is considered a "person" and protected by the Fourteenth Amendment, but the unborn baby is not considered a person and therefore is not protected by the same amendment.[59] This is insanity.

There is a way to stop all this nonsense and reduce the abortion rate significantly. How? By reconnecting sexual intimacy with commitment, love, duty, and responsibility, which come only with marriage. Yes, that's right. Stop having sex outside of marriage. I can already hear the gnashing of teeth. "How can you be so stupid?" "How can you expect kids and young adults in this day and age not to have sex?" "Are you naïve?" No, I am not naïve. And, no, I do not think many people will follow my suggestion in this day and age. But when you consider that 85 percent of abortions come from unmarried women,[60] abstinence is still the right thing, the responsible thing, and the godly thing to do. It is the only way to stop the continuing tragedy of abortion from occurring.

Let's look at it another way. If you think abstaining from sex outside of marriage is absolutely out of the question because it is unrealistic, then you must agree that the thesis of my book is correct: we are a nation of practical atheists that give lip service to belief in God but don't really care what He thinks about how we live our daily lives. In other words, the more ridiculous it seems to propose abstaining from sex outside of marriage, the more probable my thesis is correct, that the Christian worldview has been marginalized in our culture. This shows how far we've really come, that abstinence isn't even a viable option for solving the problem of abortion. But it gets worse.

If it's completely unrealistic to expect people in our society to abstain from sex outside of marriage and that terminating a pregnancy is the answer—a convenient way to practice the missed opportunity of contraception—then I have some news for you. *It is totally unrealistic to expect our republic as we know it to survive much longer.* Our killing of the unborn for the sake of convenience will come full circle, and those in power will someday soon discard us just as we have discarded the unborn. Just as we have decided the unborn baby has no rights, so too the powers that be will someday soon enforce laws that take away *our* rights as citizens. This is already taking place.

What are we going to do when those in power take away our rights and we find ourselves moving inexorably toward a Hitler-type police state? Are we going to call on God like we did after 9/11? Importune

God with signs like "God Bless America" or "In God We Trust"? What a joke. Do you think God will answer our prayers when we have stood by and watched the slaughter of 55 million unborn babies in this great "God-fearing" country of ours? When *your* rights are systematically taken away by those in power until you become a non-person (like the unborn), who will defend *you* when you didn't defend those whom Jesus called "the least of these" (the poor and defenseless)?

Our refusal to uphold the inalienable rights of the unborn will come back to haunt us, and those who have the power to decide our fate will ignore our own inalienable rights—just as we had the power to decide the fate of the unborn. Mother Teresa said, "Any country that accepts abortion is not teaching its people to love, but to use any violence to get what they want."[61]

The same rationale we are using to condone abortion will be the same rationale the elites will use (and *are* using) to dispense with you and me. To the global elites (which we will look at in Chapter sixteen), we simply are not convenient to have around, and they will use both power and violence to enslave us or eliminate us if need be. Moreover, God will allow our deeds toward the unborn to be heaped right back upon us. This will be our judgment. We will sow what we have reaped.

A Note of Hope

Before leaving this issue, I would like to offer a word of encouragement in an otherwise dour topic. Sooner or later this book will find its way into the hands of a woman who has had an abortion and is still agonizing over it. I want to speak to that woman. I want to tell you that you are not without hope. The fact that you can't get over your abortion is not a bad thing. It means your conscience is still intact. All of us have sinned, not just you. There is a way out. Let's look at two people who found that Way.

Norma Corvey was the woman behind Roe in the *Roe v. Wade* Supreme Court case. In 1995 she admitted that the whole abortion case that was brought forth on her behalf was built on the lie that she had been gang raped. She thought this would improve her chances of getting an abortion. She never did get the abortion and ended up giving birth to a baby girl.

After working in an abortion clinic, she was haunted by what she saw, including second-trimester abortions. Noticing that the doctor she worked with often lied to the women, she realized that abortion was just a "racket" (her word) for making money. This, in part, led her to abandon the pro-choice movement and to embrace Jesus Christ, in whom she will tell you her sins have been forgiven. She has converted to Christianity and has involved herself in the pro-life movement since August 1995.[62]

Surprisingly enough, the other person I would like to introduce—or perhaps re-introduce would be a better way of putting it—is Dr. Bernard Nathanson. This is the man who lied about the number of back-alley abortions performed and who cofounded the National Association of the Repeal of Abortion Laws (NARAL). When Nathanson was a medical student at McGill University, he got his girlfriend pregnant and subsequently paid for her to have the abortion. In his own words, this episode was the "introductory excursion into the satanic world of abortion." By his own estimation he performed over 60,000 abortions. Over time he became persuaded by those who witnessed to the truth, and Nathanson subsequently became pro-life and was later received into the Catholic Church. After that he spread the gospel and spoke out on the evils of abortion.[63]

These two examples clearly demonstrate that the whole abortion issue, as it was framed at the time, was based on lies.

But even more important, these two people are examples for all of us. It is never too late to turn from our sin and embrace Jesus Christ, who is ready, willing, and able to forgive us. If the sins of these two can be forgiven, and if my sins can be forgiven because I have embraced Jesus, then certainly women who have had an abortion can likewise be forgiven.

Someone who is struggling with a homosexual inclination can also embrace Christ and be forgiven, and with the Holy Spirit's power repent and turn away from a lifestyle that God did not intend for us to practice.

In short, walking in the light of Jesus Christ is the only way we will get this country turned around. It is the only way we will get our moral compass back. There is no other way. Absent repentance, our republic will continue to stumble around in the darkness of narcissism and autonomy. Without repentance, the cracks in the foundation will widen until our republic ultimately crumbles into rubble and we find ourselves enslaved by those in power who mean us harm.

Chapter 15

The Therapeutic Culture, Functional Zombies, and Brave New World Redux

Both psychology and psychiatry have impacted the marginalization of Christianity and reinforced the modern/secular mind-set. The humanistic psychologies that were concurrent with the Me generation counterculture enhanced the priority of "self." The promotion of the narcissistic self is still evident today. Meanwhile, sin has been redefined as a sickness or disease. The purpose of this chapter is to unpack some of this. But before we do, let's go back for just a moment and look at how psychology emerged at the beginning of the twentieth century.

Psychology as a Promoter of Humanism and Secularism
It is not difficult to see why so many people turned to psychology after the late '60s and early '70s when viewed in its historical context. The young adults involved in the countercultural revolution rejected religion because it represented authority.[1] But when those involved in the anti-establishment revolution looked inside themselves (narcissism) to find answers, nothing was readily available. As they got a little older, they thought that perhaps the psychologists could coax some meaning out of life. In addition, many in the middle and upper-middle class who weren't quite so serious or introspective during the '70s and '80s simply thought it was trendy to have therapy sessions. Either way, going to see your local clergyman about a personal problem was out. Going to see your personal "shrink" was in.

I find it interesting the striking similarity in attitudes between those like Wundt and his disciples who founded psychology and the mind-set of those a hundred years later who were turning *to* the very psychology Wundt founded. Just as those during and after the Me generation counterculture rejected the Christian worldview of their parents, so too a century earlier, American psychologists, like the secularist G. Stanley Hall, rejected the faith of their parents as unsustainable after Darwin.

Moreover, atheists like Wundt believed the new psychology replaced the authority of theology, because psychology was supposedly empirical and therefore "scientific."[2] Psychology could provide a more authoritative framework for understanding and enhancing humankind's evolutionary progress. Science was in. Christianity as an authority was out. Much of this same outlook became more common after the late 1960s.

World-renowned Sigmund Freud (1856–1939), the father of psychoanalysis, helped advance this antitheistic mind-set. He constructed his psychology in "opposition to religion" and therefore, according to Keith G. Meador, was "an agent of secularization."[3] As transhumanist advocate Simon Young contends: "Psychoanalysis was the secularization of Original Sin—the last vestiges of an old religion." Interestingly, Young also notes: "It was not the French 'deconstructionists' who were the true founders of postmodern nihilism, but Freud—and his secret mentor, Nietzsche."[4]

Hall brought Freud (and Jung) over to the United States for their first and only visit in 1909.[5] Apparently the liberal Protestants warmly received Freud in spite of his declaring that God didn't exist and that God was only a worldwide authority figure.[6] In fact, in his book *The Future of an Illusion* (1927), which cultural critic Harold Bloom calls "one of the greatest failures of religious criticism," Freud declared that religious doctrines were basically "illusions" or "delusions."[7]

Freud not only denied God's existence, he also did not have a particularly high view of his fellow man. In 1918 he penned, "I have found little that is good about human beings on the whole. In my experience most of them are trash no matter whether they publicly subscribe to this or that ethical doctrine or to none at all."[8]

An elitist, Freud founded psychoanalysis as a branch of psychology that those thereafter in the psychoanalytic community employed to help people. D. H. Lawrence, certainly no friend of Christianity, said of the psychoanalysts of his time, "They have crept in among us as healers and physicians; growing bolder, they have asserted their authority as scientists; two more minutes and they will appear as apostles."[9] B. K. Eakman, summarized Freud's career: "It is difficult to see how this man's work became an integral part of any profession at all; how, despite the appalling lack of scientific foundation, his theories came to have such an enormous impact in America, especially among an intelligentsia that prided itself on reason."[10] Whatever one's perspective of Freud's work, his worldview was certainly antithetical to Christianity.

In contrast to Freud's antireligious sentiments, William James (1842–1910), who considered himself "a Methodist minus a Saviour,"[11] foreshadowed much of the individualist, consumer-oriented, privatized attitude toward religion, which we see today in our culture. James was a "functionalist" (pragmatist). His famous book *The Varieties of Religious Experience* (1902) was an attempt at studying religion from a psychological perspective in addition to presenting it as a pluralistic smorgasbord. James is credited with constructing the first truly American psychology.

James's pragmatism can be seen not only in how people view the notion of truth today but also how they choose a religion. By his own admission, James was intensely individualistic and believed that people must choose the religion that is right for them. He believed as a pragmatist that a true belief is whatever is useful or "works" for a particular individual. Thus James held to a pragmatic view of truth that is ubiquitous today in our society. (We dismantled this erroneous view of truth in Chapter six.) His psychology foreshadowed the rampant individualism, narcissism, and relativity of truth, as well as the politically correct religious pluralism that is embedded in the culture today. James had a major influence on John Dewey.[12]

The humanistic psychology of Abraham Maslow (1908–1970) and Carl Rogers (1902–1987) took the place of Freud's psychoanalytic movement because those in the field of psychology questioned the efficacy of Freud's theories. While working toward my BA in psychology in the late '70s, I studied Maslow and his hierarchy of human needs leading up to "self-actualization." Though Maslow was popular, Rogers wasn't as much. And though I studied Freud, it was more in the context of a historical icon that one couldn't overlook when studying psychology. His ideas were important, but they were no longer accepted as gospel.

At any rate, whereas Freud focused on individuals' psychopathologies, Rogers and Maslow emphasized the healthy side of people's psyche. Both Maslow and Rogers believed that people are inherently good. This, of course, flies in the face of the Christian worldview, which states that man is born a sinner because of the Fall of Adam and Eve. Rogers promoted the "total acceptance" of each individual as the way to finding one's ideal self that may have gotten buried because of an uncaring and unforgiving society. This idea of total acceptance fit well with the counterculturalists who needed someone's imprimatur on their hedonistic and autonomous behavior.[13]

The Therapeutic Culture and PC Tolerance

Humanistic psychology helped to underpin the human potential movement during the '60s and '70s which splintered into various components. Those looking to actualize themselves and find meaning to life attended newly formed encounter groups. One faction broke off into the New Age movement (NAM), which deified the narcissism of the time and combined it with both the human potential movement and secular humanism to form what Douglas Groothuis calls a "cosmic humanism."[14] Holding her arms out before the ocean and proclaiming, "I am God," Shirley MacLaine epitomized the deification of the self.

Some of the therapeutic culture, can be traced back to the Maslow-Rogers paradigm and the human potential movement. The success of these various models may be attributed to the appeal of nonjudgmentalism, tolerance, acceptance of others, and the promotion of self-esteem.[15]

The problem, as I see it, is that much of the humanistic psychology that emerged out of the 1960s and 1970s was built on a foundation that not only rejected God implicitly (and sometimes explicitly) but reinforced the narcissistic tendencies that ran contemporaneous with it and are still in evidence today.

In addition, the humanistic approach sanctioned moral relativism. As people are encouraged to totally accept themselves, the concept of "sin" soon disappears. As Allan Bloom has pointed out, "Psychologists are the sworn enemies of guilt."[16] This means that what was once considered sin is now considered a sickness or disease. What used to be a character flaw or a weakness of the will is now a malady, syndrome, disorder, or pathology of some sort.[17] This has become sacrosanct in our society.

This highlights the difference between then and now. The assertion today that everything is a "disease" underestimates the amount of self-control one can muster to fight his or her problem and instead abrogates people of responsibility for their actions.[18] My aim is not to disparage those who are genuinely struggling with a problem. The point is that the burgeoning psychotherapeutic and humanistic psychologies that ran alongside the countercultural revolution reinforced narcissism and redefined sin, replacing the Christian worldview. The extent to which those two branches of psychology have accomplished this is the extent to which they both have contributed to secularism, the marginalization of Christianity, and moral relativism in our society.

Today, people have grown accustomed to practicing various behaviors that were once considered sin. According to Stanley L. Jaki, when "a statistically significant number of people" in society exhibit a certain behavior, sooner or later that behavior is considered socially acceptable.[19] Moreover, the gospel of self-acceptance, as promoted by humanistic psychology, has won the day,[20] and society now accepts as normal what used to be considered sin. The word *sin* is hardly heard anymore. We are too intellectually sophisticated to believe in old-fashioned notions like that.

With God safely out of the way, Western/modern man no longer feels a sense of moral guilt. Sin seems like an ancient concept, and no authority exists outside the self to say otherwise.[21] As Philip Rieff notes in his classic work *The Triumph of the Therapeutic*, "Religious man was born to be saved; psychological man was born to be pleased."[22] As long as it is viewed as not hurting someone else, any type of behavior is acceptable in our self-absorbed, PC tolerant society. The therapeutic culture, in many ways, reinforces the narcissism and moral relativism that is so prevalent in our culture today.

That psychology has replaced the clergymen in many cases is evidence of the secularizing trend in our society. Whereas in times past people called upon a pastor or priest to help with a personal problem, this is no longer the case today. Psychologists have displaced clergymen because our society has bought into the notion that psychologists and psychiatrists have authority in these matters because they are professionals and practice science. This is another example of Christianity losing its authority in our culture. As noted above, taking your personal problem to God or a clergyman is out. Taking your problem to a psychologist or psychiatrist is in.

I am not saying that it is always wrong to see a psychologist or a psychiatrist. I am also not attempting to diminish the severity of mental health issues that some struggle with. I am simply arguing that, in general, we may want to consider rekindling a relationship with God and with His Son, Jesus Christ. I believe giving God a chance to help work out our problems will resolve many of our mental health concerns.

Much of our mental anguish ultimately results from a lack of relationship with God, which leads to ungodly, unbalanced, and hurtful relationships with others. This, in turn, results in a lot of sorrow and guilt. Unfortunately, we live in a culture that increasingly ignores God and, therefore, is left with no choice but to acquiesce to the authority of the therapeutic professionals. Many of these professionals may be able to diagnose a problem, but are not capable of offering an efficacious solution. Maintaining an active relationship with God would help us avoid mental health issues and a trip to the psychotherapist.

Christians Accommodate Psychology and Humanism

Even Christians have accommodated modern secular psychology. For many Christians, the Bible, which in spiritual matters used to have all the answers people needed to understand their place in the cosmos and to deal with the difficulties of life, has been found wanting. Christian colleges and seminaries now have psychology departments to supplement what can be found in the Bible on these matters. Apparently, sifting through psychological theories proposed by men who rejected God and therefore had no clue about what human existence is all about seems worth it to find a few grains of truth in their theories. I wonder, however, if the ability to *describe* a mental condition (or invent one) necessarily means that one can *treat* it properly with secular theorizing.

The apostle Peter long ago proclaimed that God's power and the knowledge of Jesus Christ equips us *in every way* to deal with life's problems. Apparently, many Christians no longer believe this. Peter offers encouragement regarding what God can do for Christians who are growing in Him:

> His divine power has granted to us *all things that pertain to life and godliness*, through the knowledge of him who called us to his own glory and excellence, by which he has granted to us his precious and very great promises, so that through them you may become partakers of the divine nature, having escaped from the corruption that is in the world because of sinful desire. For this very reason, make every effort to supplement your faith with virtue, and virtue with knowledge, and knowledge with self-control, and self-control with steadfastness, and steadfastness with godliness, and godliness with brotherly affection, and brotherly affection with love. For if these qualities are yours and are increasing, they keep you from being ineffective or unfruitful in the knowledge of our Lord Jesus Christ. For whoever lacks these qualities is so nearsighted that he is blind, having forgotten that he was cleansed from his former sins. Therefore, brothers, be all the more diligent to make your calling and election sure, for if you practice these qualities you will never fall. (2 Peter 1:3-10)

It would do us well as Christians to exercise the things Peter mentioned so that our faith and knowledge of Jesus Christ will increase, and the power of God can permeate our lives to such an extent that we will be able to overcome the trials and difficulties of life with God's help. Non-Christians should acknowledge and repent of their sin and then invite Jesus into their lives so that with His help they can overcome their problems as well.

Instead of taking to heart what the apostle Peter stated above, many of our churches over the last twenty or thirty years have mirrored the ideas that were part and parcel of humanistic psychology and the human potential movement. Church leaders subsequently used these psychologies as a template for how to help fellow Christians and also to attract new congregants. The casualty in all of this is the gospel and the Christian worldview.

For the most part, the days when pastors stood behind the pulpit and preached repentance is becoming a thing of the past. Now that everything is tolerated, there is not much to repent of anymore. Besides, many pastors don't want to preach repentance because it may scare off newcomers who are giving their church a try.

We can trace back a major thread of the psychologized/neutered version of Christianity to Norman Vincent Peale and his famous book *The Power of Positive Thinking*. Robert Schuller, whom Peale influenced, likewise felt it was necessary to "positivize religion."[23] Schuller polled people in the neighborhood to learn what they wanted in a church which foreshadowed, if not set the template for, the seeker-sensitive church. In this way, the focus shifted to what man wants instead of what God wants for a church and a church service.

In 1984, Schuller wrote in *Christianity Today*, "I don't think anything has been done in the name of Christ and under the banner of Christianity that has proven more destructive to human personality and, hence, counterproductive to the evangelism enterprise than the often crude, uncouth, and unchristian strategy of attempting to make people aware of their lost and sinful condition."[24] This statement, not so coincidentally, occurred roughly a decade after the countercultural erosion of Christian cultural authority. It also reflects the impact of the gospel of tolerance preached by the humanistic psychologists and the subsequent human potential movement.

But Schuller's assertion raises a question. If an individual is not made aware of his sinful condition, what does he need to be saved from? If a person does not need to be saved, what is the gospel for?

Why did Jesus Christ come to die for our sins if we don't need to be saved from our sin?

Rick Warren, who is monumentally famous, has been referred to as "America's Pastor." His megachurch, while not the first, has provided a model for how to do church today. Robert Schuller mentored Warren. While Warren retains much of Christian orthodoxy, in recent years he has begun to stray over into the gospel of ecumenism and PC tolerance.

Another man who heavily influenced Warren is Peter Drucker. As Michael D. LeMay points out, "Rick Warren was mentored by Peter Drucker, the man most responsible for turning churches into corporations instead of houses of truth and worship."[25] Drucker wanted above all for the megachurches to be seeker-friendly. He was not really concerned with the doctrinal beliefs of each church as such.[26]

Why bring up Mr. Warren? Because his idea of how to do church reflects the humanistic psychologizing of Robert Schuller and Norman Vincent Peale. Moreover, whether consciously or not, an ever increasing number of our churches in the evangelical community have become primarily concerned with attracting newcomers. Church leaders seem to think that if the unsaved seeker does not feel totally accepted (Rogers), they may run away.

I am not saying that these churches are not preaching the gospel anymore. What I *am* saying is there has already been a slight, perhaps unnoticeable, shift in toning down certain doctrinal rhetoric in many of these churches. Evangelicalism is starting to resemble the accommodative churches, for example, because the words *repentance* and *holiness* are not used much anymore. Newcomers might be turned off.

Because God's holiness is not preached much today, there is no need to repent. Preaching repentance is too judgmental. It doesn't sit well in a society saturated with political correctness. Repentance is "so yesterday." People don't want to hear it. They don't have time for it. It's not tolerant. Seekers may decide to go to another church if they feel they are being judged. It's all about grace and love, love, love today, not holiness. The secular gospel of total acceptance is the new business model.

On the contrary, Jesus called His followers to deny themselves and take up their crosses daily. This is a tough road to hoe for postmodern man. So instead, some preachers proclaim that God has the best for them in the here and now, seemingly without any need for repentance. One wonders how the gospel of "your best life now" is working out for fellow Christians in other parts of the world where they are naked, hungry, cold, tortured, and in some cases beheaded for their refusal to deny Christ. It may seem to work now, but it is only a matter of time until the gospel of "your best life now" doesn't work here in our country either. Why? Because I believe persecution is on the way for Christians as we approach the apocalypse.

Summarizing, the fundamental problem of modern/postmodern man in America today is not the difficulties or hardships of everyday life that lead to an unhealthy mental life. The major problem today is our true moral guilt before a holy God. Secular atheistic psychology and the gospel of "positive thinking" are both powerless to deal with this. Quite frankly, attempting to deal with psychological problems without addressing one's true moral guilt before a holy God is like putting a Band-Aid on a severed carotid artery. It is akin to rearranging deck chairs on the *Titanic*.

If individuals would turn back to God, they would find that many of their psychological problems could be worked out in due time with the Lord's help. Turning to God results in repaired relationships with others and a restoration of mental health. This is what we all need to be striving for. Instead Christians, by and large, have embraced psychology as an authority where it has no authority. The Word of God is the authority when it comes to man's condition and conduct, not psychology. Psychology cannot fix man's moral guilt before a holy God.

Psychiatry, Psychopharmacology, and Functional Zombies

I want to revisit the pharmaceutical approach to psychiatry, which we looked at in the chapter on public schools, because it is important to see where this psychiatric worldview is taking us.

My concerns are twofold. First, the pharmaceutical way of thinking is moving us further in the direction of a culture of what I label "functional zombies." That label is not meant as a pejorative. It is meant as a bleak observation of what a growing number of people look like in our increasingly drugged-up society. Second, I think the government in the future, or whatever power structure is in charge at that time, will use psychiatry (and psychology) to bypass our rights as citizens. In other words, instead of directly taking away people's rights, those in power will use the psychiatric professionals to "evaluate" and then cordon off those who oppose the elitist's agenda. Let's flesh out some of this.

It is worth questioning the psychiatrists' contention that the need for administering unbelievably powerful drugs is because the diagnosed problem is biological or physical in nature. Recall from Chapter twelve that a primary reason psychiatrists pushed the idea that mental illness is biological and genetic was because they were losing market share to the psychologists, who charged less per visit. Therefore, psychiatrists began promoting the idea that only *they* could treat mental illnesses through the use of drugs, electroshock, and other various medical interventions because only *they* (and physicians) were medical professionals. The psychiatrists teamed up with the pharmaceutical companies that put up the money to advance the notion that "mental illness is biological in nature" to the public at large.

So we can see why psychiatrists were motivated to move in this direction. They needed to recapture market share (money). But is the myth they tried to sell to the public true? Is mental illness biological in nature? Daniel J. Carlat, a psychiatrist, sheds some light on this question and others in his book *Unhinged*. While appreciating the candor that Carlat demonstrated in his straightforward approach, I found his explanation of how the psychiatric world works extremely disconcerting. I will rely heavily on Carlat's assessment of the field throughout this section, because he is an insider, and he corroborates some of the fears I have about how psychiatry is practiced today.

Here are some of Carlat's comments from *Unhinged* concerning what psychiatrists know about mental illness and its supposed biological nature:

> We know almost nothing definitive about the pathophysiology of mental illness. (6)

> It would be nice if we had a biological gold standard, which you could correlate with the number of symptoms, but that doesn't exist, because we don't understand the neurobiology of depression. (54)

> Unfortunately, we know a good bit less about what we are doing than you might think. (68)

> In virtually all of the psychiatric disorders—including depression, schizophrenia, bipolar disorder, and anxiety disorders—the shadow of our ignorance overwhelms the few dim lights of our knowledge. (80)[27]

These comments certainly don't engender a lot of confidence that these folks know much about what they are doing. And yet we have been trained from kindergarten forward to always and everywhere acquiesce to the "professionals" on any given subject, especially if it's "scientific." In light of Carlat's assertions, I would suggest that our culture may want to reconsider this knee-jerk deference to the psychiatric field.

We noted, for example, in Chapter twelve that there is no objective, confirmable data to show that mental disorders are caused by a biological abnormality of the brain.[28] But this doesn't stop the psychiatric community from passing out antidepressants like they were candy. The guesswork behind their theory is that a chemical imbalance is caused by a deficiency in serotonin or norepinephrine in the brain. Yet there is no direct evidence of this, even though numerous studies have been done in an effort to demonstrate this deficiency. In fact, the most recent authoritative review in the *New England Journal of Medicine* makes clear that antidepressant research has yet to identify these deficiencies.[29]

But lack of evidence hasn't halted the "chemical imbalance" theory. Dr. Carlat explains the reasoning behind this theory: "We have come to the theory through a process of deduction, reasoning backwards from the effects antidepressants have on neurotransmitters. Antidepressants increase levels of neurotransmitters in the synapses, and they treat depression. Ergo, depression must be caused by a *deficiency* of such neurotransmitters."[30]

It is hard to understand how "reasoning backwards" may be called "deduction." It appears, instead, that Dr. Carlat is employing "abductive" reasoning, not deductive reasoning. Abductive reasoning while useful, can lead to a formal fallacy—assuming what is to be proved. Abductive reasoning might lead us to find, for example, that drinking coffee may increase the levels of neurotransmitters and thus seem to treat depression. Does this mean that some people's brains suffer from caffeine deficiency? Does this mean that caffeine may be as effective at treating depression as antidepressants? If I offered someone a joint to treat his or her anxiety and he or she relaxed, does that mean the person's THC level may have been deficient? If I prescribed taking a swig of liquor every time a person felt hyperanxious and this seemed to calm him or her, does this mean the person was suffering from alcohol deficiency? This seems to be the reasoning used to condone prescribing dangerous mind-altering drugs. Maybe drinking coffee or smoking pot or taking a swig of liquor is just as efficacious in treating various mental illnesses. The list of possible "cures" would be endless. These home remedies would all be accessible without a doctor's prescription, but that would take market share away from the psychiatrists.

Of course, what I am proposing is ridiculous. But is it any more ridiculous than treating something the cause of which psychiatrists are not even sure resides in the physical/biological realm, and have offered no definitive evidence that it does? What if the cause of mental illness is really spiritual or emotional in most cases? What if curing people spiritually/psychologically also restored them emotionally, which then stopped triggering their mental illness?

Even Carlat wonders whether drugs piled upon more drugs to counteract the side effects of the originally prescribed drugs really amounts to dealing with the underlying problem. He questions the efficacy of the new drugs: "Many of my patients seem tentatively held together by a patchwork of new medications whose mechanisms of action are mysterious and whose side effects are still being discovered . . . In treating emotional problems with medications, I worry that we are discouraging patients from learning life skills that they could use to truly solve their problems."[31]

The fragility with which Carlat depicts those who are "tentatively held together" by a "patchwork" of psychotropic drugs is rather frightening. With all due respect, I don't see much difference between those patients Carlat describes above and what I label "functional zombies." In other words, these psychotropic drugs might get people through their day, or give the appearance that they are helping people get on with their lives. But these poor souls are not given the chance to overcome their problems in a sober manner. It's hard to see how anyone could get to the root of his or her problems this way unless the problems indeed are truly biological. Perhaps in some cases they are. But there is no definitive evidence that this is the case.

Whenever I watch a commercial on TV for antidepressants, I am always waiting for someone from *Saturday Night Live* to come on, because these commercials seem more like a parody rather than a sincere appeal to sell these drugs. If these drugs are so great, why do the TV commercials spend a mere five seconds outlining the benefit of the drug and then a twenty-five-second disclaimer describing the multitude of things that can go wrong when taking them? Answer: they are dangerous.

Am I the only one who sees the irony in taking something that is supposed to help you overcome a mental illness, not aid and abet the mental illness? Why would people want to take a chance with these drugs when the one thing they all seem to have in common is that they can cause people to entertain suicidal thoughts?[32] With all due respect, is it really worth the chance that you may want to commit suicide to be "cured" of your mental illness?

But it's business as usual for Carlat, who had one of his patients, for example, on five separate medications at the same time. Regarding this particular client, Carlat says that "everything clicked" and he could just "sit back and admire the results, as one might admire a fine work of art."[33] Is creating a functional zombie to be equated with a fine work of art? Carlat stated that this is the type of patient who "makes psychiatrists love to prescribe drugs." He soon added, however, that he (Carlat) had some reservations about how this patient's "emotions are cobbled together by medications," and he noted the patient's "fragile appearance."[34] Carlat summarizes things this way: "Such is modern psychopharmacology. Guided purely by symptoms, we try different drugs, with no real conception of what we are trying to fix, or of how the drugs are working."[35] Unbelievable.

If psychiatrists do not know what they are trying to fix, why do they administer these drugs at all? Why use this unproven methodology for treating (I use the *treating* in the loosest possible sense of the definition) folks with mental illness? Maybe because psychiatrists can fit in four patients per hour rather than only one per hour if they actually talk to them like human beings rather than treating them like lab rats. Carlat provides some insight on this. He says that using the "chemical imbalance" rhetoric delivers an implicit message to the patient that their illness is biological and therefore it's not their fault.[36] Remember, psychiatrists and psychologists are sworn enemies of guilt. Psychiatrists seem to be making an unspoken deal with their patients. Patients are encouraged to keep coming back, and in return the psychiatrists promise to tell the patients that nothing is their fault. Their problems are biological. And they'll even prescribe the patient some happy pills.

"Happy pills" is the description a coworker of mine years ago used to describe these psychotropic drugs as he gobbled a handful every morning at work. Instead of helping this individual deal with his struggle, his doctor simply prescribed various psychotropic drugs. In other words, the underlying cause of this person's sorrow and struggle was ignored and covered up with drugs. But if a person has to constantly gobble a handful of pharmaceuticals to be happy, then we are not helping people. We are creating functional zombies who will never be truly happy in a sober way.

As noted above, these pills don't always make you happy. They can give a person "suicidal ideation." I knew a woman in another workplace who divulged to many of us that her husband was dealing with depression. But it was worse than this. The medication he was on gave him suicidal thoughts, and his attempt to get off the medication didn't help this problem. We tried to encourage her, but things seemed pretty bad. Her husband came to work for us for a month or so but he committed suicide soon after.

I could share other stories of people I know firsthand who were on these drugs. I think they are dangerous. Psychiatrists don't consider the possibility that the real cause of most of the mental anguish these people deal with stems from living in a world where things go wrong constantly, not because of a chemical imbalance in the brain. Often we are our own worst enemies, and at other times we hurt other people or they hurt us in some way. More important, in the big picture, people in this country have left God out of their lives. They get hurt in some way and then instead of turning to God for help, they turn to the psychiatrists. Though many, if not most psychiatrists truly want to help their patients, it seems as though they are often incapable of offering any assistance other than a cover-up-the-problem remedy of psychotropic drugs.

Am I saying that psychiatrists are incapable of helping people? No. Am I saying that in every last instance it is wrong to take medication that, for example, may help stabilize a person until he (or she) can get back on his feet? Again, no. But I believe pharmacological therapy should be used in only the most extreme cases, not as a matter of course like it is in our country right now. I believe that turning our lives over to God should be the *first* resort (not the last) when attempting to overcome mental health issues. Maintaining an active relationship with God and leading a godly life will go a long way to maintaining psychological health and avoiding mental health problems.

In conclusion, the chemical imbalance theory is the "convenient myth," as Carlat calls it, used to justify administering these dangerous drugs to patients, because, in his own words, "no doctor wants to admit ignorance about the very problems he or she is trained to manage."[37] This is quite an admission. Are doctors ignorant about how to deal with people's mental health issues because they mistakenly believe the problems are thought to initiate only in the brain? Isn't this too reductionistic? Does mental illness always initiate in the brain? Why do psychiatrists think this way?

As we noted above, one line of thinking is that the chemical imbalance theory allows them to recapture market share in their field. But another reason psychiatrists believe mental illness resides only in the natural/physical realm of the brain might have more to do with how "science" is practiced. Let's see why.

Psychology, Psychiatry, and Methodological Naturalism

It is important to reconsider what we learned in Chapter eleven on how science works. Recall that all fields of knowledge after the 1870s became professionalized. Professionalization in conjunction with evolutionary theory resulted in a method of doing science that searched for causes only in the realm of nature (methodological naturalism = science). This is where things still stand today. Because science has been reduced to methodological naturalism, psychiatrists look for mental illness only in the natural realm (the brain) rather than the spiritual realm.

People in the bygone era went to a family member, pastor, or priest for counsel because they understood that problems of daily life were spiritual/psychological in nature. This is not the case today. Why? Because fewer and fewer people know any members of the clergy they can talk to. Another problem is that we've been taught that mental illness is something that needs to be handled by the "experts." People used to give their problems to God to help them get through. But talking to God and trusting Him, for most people today, is not even a consideration. This would seem to be particularly true of practical atheists.

The trouble is that psychiatrists were never trained to uncover spiritual difficulties that may cause mental illness. Methodological naturalism won't allow for it. If psychiatrists can offer no definitive evidence that mental illness is biological in nature, is it possible that they are doing many of their patients a disservice? What if the cause of mental illness is not biological in nature?

Most psychiatrists are trained only to write prescriptions and come up with the right "cocktail" based on what can be gleaned from asking questions about a person's symptoms, not what may be *causing* the symptoms.[38] As Carlat confesses, "Like many psychiatrists, I *don't* do psychotherapy because I *can't* do psychotherapy."[39] He admits that psychiatry has become "unhinged" because it now treats only the symptoms of mental illness rather than the causes.[40]

Peter Breggin MD, an internationally renowned psychiatrist, lends his voice on this issue:

> Modern biological psychiatry is a materialistic religion masquerading as a science. How can I say that my profession of psychiatry is a materialistic religion? Because modern psychiatry makes believe that psychological and spiritual problems, such as anxiety and depression, are caused by mechanical failures in the physical brain, and because psychiatry then attempts to correct these psychological and spiritual problems with physical interventions such as drugs and electroshock.[41]

One psychiatric patient relates her story this way: "The thing I remember, looking back, is that I was not really that sick early on. I was really just confused. I had all these issues, but nobody talked to me about that. I wish I could go off meds even now, but there is nobody to help me do it." Regarding the antipsychotics she is taking, she laments, "you lose your soul and you never get it back."[42]

DSM: The Bible of Psychiatry

The *Diagnostic and Statistical Manual of Mental Disorders* (DSM-5) has recently been released. This manual is the bible from which psychiatrists diagnose mental illnesses and clients can make insurance claims. Using the manual as a guide, psychiatrists ask clients a series of questions then proceed to prescribe drugs based on the answers to those questions. This is how psychiatry is done now. As Dr. Keith Ablow notes, "It was under APA's leadership and the commands of third-party insurers that the professional lives of thousands of psychiatrists were reduced to writing prescriptions for six patients every hour rather than talking to patients about their life stories."[43]

Fifteen new diagnoses have recently been added to the DSM-5. Some of these new disorders include caffeine withdrawal, hoarding disorder, cannabis withdrawal, binge eating disorder, and Internet gaming disorder,[44] the latter of which Senator John McCain apparently suffers from.[45] According to a nationwide diagnostic census, a majority of Americans have suffered from some type of mental illness at one time or another. This has resulted in an "appalling number" of both school children and college students being prescribed medications.[46]

As one can see from some of the disorders listed above, much of this is simply contrived nonsense. The myth that everyone suffers from some type of mental illness in their lifetime stems from psychiatrists labeling more and more behaviors as mental disorders when they are not. But, from psychiatrists' point of view, more and more mental disorders translates into more patients. And more patients equal more money for them and the drug companies.

So, for example, caffeine withdrawal is now supposedly a mental disorder. Can you imagine going to your local shrink and claiming that you are suffering from caffeine withdrawal symptoms? What is he or she going to do, offer you pharmaceuticals to overcome your caffeine hangover? Why isn't alcohol withdrawal listed as a mental disorder? If withdrawing from caffeine is a mental disorder, isn't having a hangover a mental disorder? This is the theater of the absurd.

Dr. Allen Frances, a psychiatrist who chaired the task force for the creation of the previous DSM for the American Psychiatric Association, calls the DSM-5 "deeply flawed" and "clearly unsafe and scientifically unsound." He is concerned that the new DSM will lead to "massive over-diagnosis" and "harmful over-medication."[47]

Regarding over-medicating people, is it a coincidence that in one case (binge eating diagnosis) 50 percent of the DSM-5 task force had ties to the pharmaceutical companies?[48] Probably not. The more mental disorders that can be created, the more drugs psychiatrists can prescribe. This is done in spite of the fact that, according to Columbia university psychiatrist Allen Frances who chaired the DSM-4 committee, not even one biological test was ready for inclusion in a set of criteria for the DSM-5.[49] If this isn't bad enough, the FDA doesn't even conduct their own tests on pending drugs for approval but instead relies on the honesty of the data the drug companies provide.[50] I'm sure there is no bias there.

The real problem, of course, is that a whole host of people with no psychological problems will now be diagnosed with a mental disorder they don't really have (false positives). This trivializes genuine mental health problems.[51] This constant doling out of drugs, with absolutely no empirical evidence of what these drugs are supposedly treating, has resulted in 20 percent of Americans taking at least one psychotropic drugs to treat one or more supposed psychiatric disorders. In fact, use of antidepressant drugs increased 400 percent between 2005 and 2008. Extrapolated out to the early 2020s, this would mean that two in five people would be taking antidepressants.[52] All of this in spite of the chemical imbalance theory being mere speculation. According to Breggin, the chemical imbalance theory "is actually a drug company marketing campaign to sell drugs."[53]

Drug companies are literally money-making machines. For example, the drug reps know before they visit a particular psychiatrist what brand of drugs that particular psychiatrist is prescribing, because pharmacies often sell that information to the drug companies that then pass along that information to the reps.[54] So a rep selling a particular drug may target those psychiatrists who are prescribing a low percentage of the drug, all in an effort to increase their sales. Reps may charm a doctor by bringing him and his staff their favorite coffee and food, for example. In fact, Carlat found himself prescribing a drug that one of his reps sold him that day over those he normally prescribed, though he may not have been consciously aware he was returning a favor. According to Carlat, salesmanship and gifts are a large part of how the drug marketing industry works.[55] This doesn't sound very scientific to me.

Robert Whitaker summarizes our thoughts about all of this:

> Such is the story of the psychiatric drug business. The industry has excelled at expanding the market for its drugs, and this generates a great deal of wealth for many. However, this enterprise has depended on the telling of a false story to the American public, and the hiding of results that reveal the poor long-term outcomes with this paradigm of care. It also is exacting a horrible toll on our society. The number of people disabled by mental illness during the past twenty years has soared, and now this epidemic has spread to our children. Indeed, millions of children and adolescents are being groomed to be lifelong users of these drugs.[56]

Is it possible that there really is no mental illness epidemic going on? Is it possible that the psychiatric community, with the help of the burgeoning DSM, has created an exponential increase of false positives, which makes it look like an epidemic of mental illness? If, on the other hand, there truly is an epidemic of mental illness, then the psychiatric profession has been a colossal failure. In either case, Whitaker is correct, the children are the losers in much of this because they are being conditioned to be lifelong users of these drugs.

Summary

We are truly on our way to becoming a nation of functional zombies. This is *Brave New World* redux. If we continue on this current path, it is not outlandish to predict that sometime in the not too distant future a majority of people in this country will be on some type of drug to help them with their mental illnesses, many of which seem to be contrived by the psychiatric community.

I foresee another problem as well. The global elites will team up with psychiatry and the mental health profession to marginalize anyone who opposes them. This is a terrifying prospect. It will be a way for the ruling elite to totally circumvent the constitutional rights of individuals they want to incarcerate. I think this will be the wave of the future. In fact, it is already happening.

Award-winning singer Lauren Hill became a Christian after being immersed in the dark underworld of the music industry. She subsequently began warning about how real musical talent was being ignored in favor promoting mindless drivel. Hill stated that the media, protected by the military-industrial complex, manipulated the music industry. She was in court over her failure to pay a tax bill after she had withdrawn from the public because of threats on her family.[57] Though she had won a Grammy and obviously knew firsthand about the music industry, a judge ordered her to submit to counseling (read: brainwashing/re-education) because of her conspiracy theories.[58]

In another incident, former marine Brandon Raub was held in a VA psych ward against his will because he accused the government of lying about 9/11. He also called for the arrest of government officials and talked about starting a revolution. He posted all of this on his Facebook page, and some concerned citizens (read: busybodies) reported this. Instead of allowing Raub to exercise his First Amendment rights, the FBI, Secret Service, and Chesterfield County Police in Virginia, in what amounts to overkill, all showed up to "interview" Raub. Why all this needless waste of taxpayer money when they could have sent one or two officers to ask Raub a few questions? Answer: because they want to intimidate.

But this is the truly frightening part: The local PD contacted Mental Health Crisis Intervention officials, who recommended bringing Raub in for "evaluation." Due process of the law was overridden simply by the "recommendation" of a mental health professional. When Raub began to resist, he was handcuffed and taken into custody, though the officials claim he wasn't arrested. So apparently in this Kafkaesque world it is possible to be taken into custody with handcuffs and at the same time not to be considered under arrest. All because of a mental health professional's say-so. This is the type of thing I see happening with much more frequency in the future.

Because of their military experience, former military personnel are considered a problem. John W. Whitehead, a lawyer who defends these type of cases puts it this way: "For government officials to not only arrest Brandon Raub for doing nothing more than exercising his First Amendment rights but to actually force him to undergo psychological evaluations and detain him against his will goes against every constitutional principle this country was founded upon. This should be a wake-up call to Americans that the police state is here."[59]

As an aside, more evidence that the police state is here occurred in 2011 when President Obama signed the National Defense Authorization Act (NDAA), which gives the military the ability to detain U.S. citizens without charge or trial if those in power merely suspect U.S. citizens of ties to terrorism. Simply put, U.S. citizens may now be held indefinitely without due process.[60] President Obama signed this bill on New Year's Eve 2011, when no one was paying attention, in concordance with his promise that his administration would be completely transparent.

Think U.S. citizens can't be unreasonably detained? You may recall that the Japanese in this country lost their rights during WWII and were rounded up and placed in detention camps. The Brandon Raub case provides a recent example. The public, at the present moment, seems blissfully unaware of the mission creep of the police state.

Of course, throwing people into detention camps willy-nilly will probably not sit well with the American people if they were to get wind of it. This is why I am predicting that those in power will increasingly sidestep this direct way of taking away people's rights and will bypass the Constitution by using the mental health professionals.

Imagine the governing powers forcing everyone at some point to take some sort of mental checkup. Well, this is exactly what I am predicting will take place. Of course this will be required under the guise that it will help keep society "safe." It may be euphemistically referred to as a "preventative measure." Your primary medical doctor asks a few routine questions. You mention in passing that you are a bit depressed over losing your job or perhaps the death of a loved one. Or you mention that you are aggravated at the government for cutting your Social Security check in half, or you are angry because your

Medicare was reduced. Your doctor might be required to refer you (red flag you) to a psychologist or psychiatrist for further evaluation.

The results of this evaluation will become part of your permanent record. I believe the government in the future will have access to all of your health care records, which used to be private. (What is private anymore now that we know that the government is spying on all of us?) But what if you fail the subsequent test with a psychologist or psychiatrist? You may have to attend mandatory re-education courses to adjust your mind-set. You may have to take a mandatory anger management course to overcome your "oppositional defiance disorder" regarding your attitude toward the government. You may even be lucky enough to be prescribed (forced to take) some psychotropics to help adjust your attitude or to help with your depression. For really subversive elements like practicing Christians, gun owners, and former military, an all-expenses paid vacation to the nearest FEMA camp may be in order. Books like *America's Post-Christian Apocalypse* won't be allowed, by that time, so I'll probably see you there. (More on the elites and the totalitarian state in the following chapters).

We saw in the chapter on public schools that school children are already being screened for mental illness. This sets up future generations of children who today are being desensitized and then acclimated toward this type of police state behavior by those in authority. These children will be more likely as adults to acquiesce to those wielding power who want to infringe on their rights. The children have been trained at a young age that submission to authority, even if it means giving up one's privacy and constitutional rights, is normal. They are being taught early on that this is what it might take to keep us all safe.

Future generations probably won't offer much resistance to the emerging police state, because they may not even realize their constitutional rights are being taken away from them (if the Constitution lasts that long). The younger generations will be used to having their rights curbed. Many will already be functional zombies on some type of psychotropic drugs. Others simply won't care. Many will be oblivious to what is happening to them, because they will be mesmerized by the latest gadget that enslaves them in the black hole of anti-reality.

With this type of probable government intrusion, is it that difficult to foresee Christians, who are already marginalized, being targeted in the future at some point? Why Christians, you ask? Because Christians have this crazy idea that God exists and that Jesus is going to return someday to this planet to set up His kingdom. More problematic for Christians in the future, however, will be when the Antichrist requires all people to have an RFID chip, bio-stamp, or digital tattoo of some sort implanted in their right hands or their foreheads (Rev. 13:16-17) in order to be able to buy or sell. People at that time probably won't be able to conduct any business at all without the mark. True Christians, in the near future, will begin to resist those in power who attempt to force the precursors of these types of identification on them. Because of this insolent behavior, Christians will be told that they have a mental illness such as paranoia.

I can already foresee the mainstream media in the future, which today, in many cases, has simply become a propaganda piece for the global elites, leading the charge against Christians, whom they already disdain. It will go something like this. "Who needs these people gumming up the works? They are obviously out of their minds. Everyone is getting chipped. What's the big deal? Everyone in our advanced technological society knows that God doesn't exist anyway. We just made Him up to get us through. But our technology will save us now. We are so enlightened. We must progress toward our evolutionary destiny. Christians need to be reeducated. Send them to the camps."

I foresee this occurring in the brave new world, which combines the poisonous cocktail of psychology, psychiatry, and psychopharmacology, with the ever intrusive arm of the emergent surveillance/police state. The power elites won't take all your rights away directly. Rather, they will use a middleman, a psychiatrist or someone in the mental health profession, who will do it for them. The powers that be will thus be able to deflect the responsibility for taking your rights away onto the psychiatrists and psychologists. It's more "scientific" that way. And you know how scientific we are today.

Speaking of *Brave New World*, the author of that book, Aldous Huxley, while speaking at the California Medical School in San Francisco in 1961, predicted the following scenario, which lends credence to my concerns:

> There will be in the next generation or so a pharmacological method of making people love their servitude and producing dictatorship without tears so to speak. Producing a kind of painless concentration camp for entire societies so that people will in fact have their liberties taken away from them but will rather enjoy it, because they will be distracted from any desire to rebel by

propaganda, or brainwashing, enhanced by pharmacological methods.[61]

The Bible also confirms that at the end of the age people will be on drugs. The book of Revelation (9:21) states that people in the end time will not repent of their "sorceries." What does sorceries have to do with pharmaceuticals? Quite a bit. The word *sorcery* comes from the Greek word *pharmakeia*, which is where we get our English word *pharmacy* or *medication*. It is probable that at the end of the age, which looms a bit closer every day, an increasing number of people will be gobbling mind-altering medications. This is what Huxley alluded to above and what he wrote in his book *Brave New World*.

One can only wonder what kind of mind-altering drugs a good portion of our population will be on at that time. It will certainly provide a means of escape for those who have abandoned God, found life meaningless, and attempted to distract themselves with something a little more powerful than the latest gadget. Worse than this though, the ruling elite may force political dissidents to take their medications so that they will be able to fit into society. It will certainly make people's servitude to the New World Order go a lot smoother. But taking mind-altering drugs unfortunately will also make it much easier for the population to be deceived into believing that the New World Order is some kind of utopia. Of course, nothing will be further from the truth.

What exactly is the New World Order I am alluding to, and who are the people behind it? We will address this question and provide answers in the next chapter.

Chapter 16

The Global Elites and the New World Order

We began this book by studying how Christianity became marginalized in our society. We looked at how secularism filled the void that Christianity left after being pushed to the periphery of culture. We learned how modernism has affected institutions like the universities and the public schools in our country. In addition, we noticed that (post)modern secularism has borne its fruit: moral relativism, PC pluralism, PC tolerance, autonomy, narcissism, and a lack of understanding of what truth is. This fruit has become more commonplace after the countercultural revolution of the 1960s and 1970s.

Now that we've put all this together, our next step is to determine where it is taking us. As I argued, an ever increasing number of people in our country are practical atheists who ignore God's existence. Therefore we are now ripe for disaster. Our republic is in serious trouble. As we will see, this is not some overly melodramatic jeremiad. Rather, the loss of truth, moral decadence, narcissism, and other secular fruit that has become part and parcel of our society has blinded us to the reality of the consequences that await us because of our folly of ignoring God.

The Founders warned that our type of government would work only if we continued to be a moral and religious people. That warning was prescient. Because secular modernism eroded the moral underpinnings of the Christian worldview, we no longer have anything to stand on. This places us in peril with those who are up to no good. From my view, the next economic collapse our country is headed toward, and which will most likely be worldwide as well, will serve to accelerate the agenda of a group of movers and shakers who want to impose their will on the rest of humanity. Their ultimate goal is some type of one-world government and one-world economic system. This, of course, would affect our republic adversely, to say the least. Individuals who want this type of arrangement may be labeled "global elites" or simply "globalists."

Most of these global elites consider themselves the cream of the crop. Their lust for power and control fuels them. They are secularists through and through, concerned only with the here and now, giving no thought to eternity or their place in it. They exemplify the corrupt side of human nature, because the worst of this lot couldn't care less about their fellow man. Therefore, it is important to take a closer look at who these elites are and what they have in store for us as we near the end of the age and the biblical apocalypse.

Be aware that because we have abandoned the God of the Bible and the Christian worldview in this country, we have made ourselves vulnerable to the deception, lies, and ultimate power grab of these elites who wish to ultimately enslave us. Re-embracing the truth of Christianity is the only thing that can save us in the long run.

Elites in the Superclass: The Flexians

Some of the global elites are part of a superclass involved mainly in business, finance, and politics. What separates these superclass elites from the rest of humanity are their disproportionate influence, power, and wealth. While the lower half of the world's population owns only 1 percent of the world's wealth, the top 1 percent of the superclass elites own 40 percent of the world's wealth.[1] Many of today's superclass elites run transnational corporations and financial institutions which know no borders. Their loyalties do not necessarily lie with their own countries. Because the size and wealth of the corporations they run often rival, if not eclipse, those of entire countries, these elites wield an immeasurable amount of power and influence around the world.

Senator Jeff Sessions describes some of the global elites this way:

> These super-elites in Washington and Wall Street dream of a world without borders, a paradise where things like laws and rules and national boundaries don't get in the way of their grand chimera. The only challenge these great global citizens face are these pesky people called voters, who cling to the old-fashioned idea of a nation as a home and a border as something real and worth protecting. These elites, you see, know better.[2]

Janine Wedel defines many elites in the superclass as "flexians," a term she coined in her book *Shadow Elite*.[3] Flexians wield power and influence through "flex nets" (informal and interconnected networks), which promote their self-interests and ideologies. Flexians may not necessarily be wealthy like others in the superclass, but what they lack

322

in wealth they make up in influence. Flexians may operate outside or inside governments, using their elastic and overlapping roles to negotiate themselves between the public and the private sectors, often promoting one another into influential and mutually beneficial positions.[4] It cannot be overemphasized that those in the superclass are solely concerned with their own interests. They couldn't care less about you. Quite frankly, they think they are better and smarter than you.

One example of the shifting roles these elite flexians use to further their own agenda is Robert Rubin, the former treasury secretary under Bill Clinton. Rubin played a major role in the financial deregulation of Wall Street, which in turn played a large part in the economic meltdown of 2008–2009 whereby taxpayer money was used to bail out the big banks and Wall Street firms.

In the late 1990s, Rubin and a few cohorts like Alan Greenspan and Larry Summers accomplished financial deregulation through the repeal of the Glass-Steagall Act of 1933,[5] which had prohibited banks from gambling with depositors' money. After the deregulation was in place, Rubin coincidentally stepped down as treasury secretary and became a chairman of Citigroup's executive committee. Citi was a major beneficiary of the deregulation. During the 2000s, Citi leveraged itself up with massive derivative bets on the subprime housing market. When the housing bubble burst, so did the subprime loans on Citi's books, along with the derivatives and other financial products. Rubin saw firsthand the result of his handiwork during the 2008–2009 financial debacle. Nevertheless, he received an annual compensation somewhere between $20 million and $40 million after joining Citigroup but before everything blew up.[6]

Like Rubin, Hank Paulson was an alumnus of Goldman Sachs. In a reversal of roles of sorts, Paulson, who had been the CEO of Goldman, resigned that position and accepted George W. Bush's appointment to treasury secretary in 2006. At least one insider thought Paulson took the job as treasury secretary because he and his cronies foresaw the potential problems in the markets, and they wanted someone at the "tiller" to oversee any "market disruptions"[7] that might take place. Well, what occurred wasn't only a market disruption, it was a liquidity crunch with a stock market freefall. Right on cue, Paulson came to the rescue.

When Lehman Brothers collapsed and the massive economic meltdown was imminent, Paulson authorized an $85 billion bailout for the insurance giant AIG. Coincidentally, AIG owed Goldman Sachs

(Paulson's old buddies) $13 billion, which AIG promptly repaid. But Paulson wasn't done. He approved the U.S. Treasury to buy up to $700 billion in "troubled assets" to keep the big banks afloat and the economy from totally imploding.[8] This was nothing more than "survival of the unfittest" (to borrow a line from Gordon Gekko),[9]— crony capitalism at its best, which is not capitalism at all. Bush admitted as much when in December 2008 he uttered the following non sequitur: "I have abandoned free-market principles to save the free-market system."[10] This is akin to saying, "I have abandoned Jesus Christ so I could become a Christian."

The economic intelligentsia and financial pundits sold the bailout to the public as something necessary so the banks could continue to lend money to the little guy on the street. But this was a lie. The too-big-to-fail banksters don't make their big money from loaning to the man on the street; they make it by gambling in the unregulated derivative markets that Rubin helped create, and by playing the spread in interest rates. At any rate, AIG, even after receiving TARP, paid out $165 million in bonuses using this taxpayer bailout money. It said that paying out big bonuses was necessary so that AIG and other firms could continue to attract "the best and the brightest,"[11] notwithstanding that the best and the brightest caused the financial meltdown in the first place. But facts don't matter to the elites, because they think they are better and smarter than you.

I chose Rubin and Paulson as examples to show how seamlessly these elites move between the public and the private sectors while positioning themselves to further their own interests and their friends' interests as well. I highlighted big banks because we are heading toward another financial meltdown. Instead of fixing the problem, the bailout propped up the big banks and Wall Street firms. This allowed them to continue their risky behavior with impunity.

In my opinion, they should have been allowed to go bust and then be broken up so that we could have started out with a clean slate and had a real recovery. Instead, today we are fed the lie that the economy is recovering when, in reality, we are witnessing the greatest transfer of wealth in history—from the middle class to the financial elites. The Fed printed money to prop everything up to make the economy look good, but this is not a real recovery.

The up-and-coming financial meltdown will be orders of magnitude worse than that of 2008–2009, because these big banks are now much larger and have taken on more risk than ever. One can read about the disreputable behavior of institutions like J.P. Morgan Chase, Goldman Sachs, and other large banks seemingly on a daily basis, yet they never have to admit to criminality after litigation, and they pay fines of only pennies on the dollar for their misconduct. Paying tiny fines is just part of doing business for these folks. It does absolutely nothing to deter them from their morally egregious behavior which will cost the middle class even more than it already has in the not too distant future.

Therefore, it should come as no surprise that the head of Goldman Sachs at the time of this writing, Lloyd Blankfein, unabashedly claims to be doing "God's work," even though a Senate panel investigation found "a financial snake pit rife with greed, conflicts of interest, and wrongdoing in a case where Goldman bet against the very same investments it recommended to its clients."[12] Meanwhile, CEO of J.P. Morgan Chase, Jamie "I'm richer than you"[13] Dimon is high-fived by people when he is out in public, even though that bank has been fined over $25 billion as of this writing for accusations of misconduct.[14] By the time this book finds its way into your hands, I'm sure that number will increase to over $30 billion.

Greg Hunter of USAwatchdog.com rightly asks why Jamie Dimon still has a job. Hunter points out that while J.P. Morgan paid a $2.5 billion fine for its involvement in the Bernie Madoff ponzi scandal, Madoff is still in jail because he isn't allowed to pull out his checkbook and pay a fine for his criminality.[15]

Why are the big banks never convicted of their crimes? Because they write the laws and make campaign contributions to presidents, congressmen, and other politicians, and because they own everything. Therefore, instead of being forced to step down for their part in the financial collapse of 2008–2009, with all of the legally questionable and morally dubious activities since then, the CEOs of these banks are allowed to continue business as usual, making obscene amounts of money in bonuses while they orchestrate an even larger financial crisis that is on the way. In fact, on December 11, 2014, the U.S. House of Representatives repealed part of the Dodd-Frank bill which means if derivative bets of the big banks fail (again), taxpayers' deposits and pensions will be exposed.[16] The public will be on the hook once again just as we were in the 2008–2009 financial debacle. This is more evidence that the banks own the politicians (and everything else).

You'd think that the populace would point their pitchforks at the CEOs of these large financial institutions and guide them *away* from their nefarious activities and *to* the closest jail. But no, as long as people can play with the latest smartphone, fool around with the latest gadget, consume themselves to death, watch sports, and medicate themselves, nothing will rouse our sleeping citizens from their blissful slumbers. Well, at least not until the banks have stolen everything from them and they are out on the street with no food or shelter.

Think I'm exaggerating? Then ask yourself why those in power want to take guns away from its citizens. Why did the Department of Homeland Security buy over 2 billion rounds of ammo? Answer: because the elites know we are headed for another financial collapse thanks to the too-big-to-jail bankers, and they don't want an armed and angry public. They want to arm themselves instead.

The Global Elites

Out of these troubled times, our objective—a New World Order—can emerge. Today, that new world is struggling to be born, a world quite different from the one we have known.[17]

George H.W. Bush

Now that we have broadly defined the elites in the superclass and given a few examples of how they operate, I want to focus a little more narrowly on the global elites. I should point out that elites of any variety—whether wealthy, academic, corporate, or global—are not bound to any strict category.

The elites we are describing now (global elites and those in the rich superclass) are a slippery bunch. They possess many of the characteristics of other garden-variety elites. But what distinguishes the global elites from other elites is that they are motivated by an *ideology* of globalism, which drives the rest of their agenda. The crème de la crème of these elites gather together annually at the Economic Forum in Davos, or the super-secretive Bilderberg meetings, where they do not publish the record of who attends and bar media access. The people attending these meetings literally shape the future of the world. If these people have humanity's best interests at heart, why all the secrecy?

It may be helpful to envision a series of concentric circles when trying to define the global elites. The global elites, at least the extremely wealthy ones who are represented by "old money," mostly occupy the innermost circle. Global elites in the inner circle are "in the know" and at the controls of world affairs in many ways. Many of them are heads of multinational corporations, others are oil tycoons like the Rockefellers, and some are international bankers epitomized by the Rothschilds. Some are influential politicians, and others are involved in the military industrial complex or in academia.

Former Harvard professor Carroll Quigley, the foremost authority on this subject, explains what separates the global elites from other garden-variety elites: "Their aim is nothing less than to create a *world system* of financial control in private hands able to dominate the political system of each country and the economy of the world as a whole. The system was to be controlled in a feudalistic fashion by the *central banks of the world acting in concert*, by secret agreements arrived at in frequent private meetings and conferences."[18]

Some elites occupying the outer circles may have come across globalist ideology and may even agree with some of it, but they are not driven by a need for a one-world government and one-world economic system like the hardcore globalists. As we will see below, the global elites who occupy the innermost circle do not have the best interests of humankind at heart. In short, they are up to no good.

The rise of transnational corporations, in many cases, are run by globalists and often wield more influence than entire countries. In fact, this massive sphere of influence goes hand in hand with their globalist agenda. Global elites would just as soon see the dissolution of separate countries. In fact, they view nation-states as unnecessary relics from the past. Moreover, nation-states are good only to the extent that the global elites can manipulate them to further their agenda.[19]

These elites feel they have legitimate entitlement to power and authority. Therefore, eradicating democratic nation-states and the consent of the people is part of their plan. It follows, then, that one of their primary areas of concern is foreign policy and international relations.[20] So, for example, in 1931, professor and historian Arnold Toynbee wrote in the journal of the Royal Institute for International Affairs (RIIA): "We are at present working discreetly with all our might to wrest this mysterious force called sovereignty out of the clutches of the local nation states of the world. And all the time we are denying with our lips what we are doing with our hands."[21] The RIIA is just one arm of the globalists.

The deception and cloak of secrecy we noted above can be traced back before the nineteenth century in the form of secret societies and various clubs and organizations. Unfortunately, space will permit mentioning only a few examples like the one above, concerning the global elites' secrecy, power, influence, and agenda. Let's look at a few of these now.

In 1906, Teddy Roosevelt spoke about "an invisible government…acknowledging no responsibility to the people."[22] Just a few years later in 1912, Woodrow Wilson confirmed what Roosevelt was alluding to regarding this "invisible government." In one of his campaign speeches Wilson stated:

> Since I entered politics, I have chiefly had men's views confided to me privately. Some of the biggest men in the United States in the field of commerce and manufacture, are afraid of somebody, are afraid of something. They know that there is a power somewhere so organized, so subtle, so watchful, so interlocked, so complete, so pervasive, that they had better not speak above their breath when they speak in condemnation of it.[23]

The same unseen "power" he described above put Woodrow Wilson, a relative unknown at the time (like Jimmy Carter and Barack Obama), into office. International financiers like J.P. Morgan poured cash into Teddy Roosevelt's campaign to split the Republican vote. Wilson, a Democrat, won the election. After Wilson took over the presidency, he appointed Bernard Baruch, another wealthy banker who had influenced Wilson, to the head of the War Industries Board in 1918, where he and the Rockefellers made over $200 million during WWI.[24]

International financiers don't care about those who die in wars. They couldn't care less about nations or people. In fact, they encourage war as a means of making profit and to keep nations in perpetual debt. This is known as the Rothschild Formula.[25] And, of course, they can use war as an excuse for their ultimate goal, which is described by Robert Gates Sr.: "Several years before the outbreak of World War I, the Carnegie trustees were planning to involve the U.S. in a general war, to set the stage for world government."[26]

Woodrow Wilson was a mere puppet for globalists who put him in office. Colonel Edward Mandell House, a career intelligence officer, worked for the Wall Street bankers and helped control Wilson. Under House's influence, entities such as the Federal Reserve, the League of Nations (a forerunner of the United Nations), and "charitable" foundations came into existence.[27] House thought the Constitution should "be scrapped and rewritten."[28] Wilson advocated interpreting the Constitution "according to the Darwinian principle," which meant that it

328

should evolve (change) with the times.[29] This is the same Wilson who, previously as president of Princeton, eliminated Bible classes while ensuring that students were all indoctrinated with Darwinism.[30]

Not everyone at that time was oblivious to the reprehensible workings of the big-moneyed elites. On March 27, 1922, the *New York Times* quoted New York City Mayor John F. Hylan, who summed up what we have been describing:

> The warning of Theodore Roosevelt has much timeliness today, for the real menace of our republic is this invisible government which like a giant octopus sprawls its slimy length over city, state and nation. . . . It seizes in its long and powerful tentacles our executive officers, our legislative bodies, our schools, our courts, our newspapers and every agency created for the public protection . . . let me say that at the head of this octopus are the Rockefeller–Standard Oil interests and a small group of powerful banking houses generally referred to as the international bankers. The little coterie of powerful international bankers virtually run the United States government for their own selfish purposes. They practically control both political parties.[31]

The power of Rockefeller's Standard Oil was obvious during WWII. The Secretary of Treasury under Executive Order allowed Rockefeller's company to sell oil to the Nazis and Nazi collaborators before and after Pearl Harbor. Of course, Roosevelt kept the amount of oil exports hidden from the public. Meanwhile, gas lines were forming in America while the Germans and Japanese "had all the gas they needed," according to Charles Higham in his book *Trading with the Enemy.*

Further "morally indefensible" behavior occurred when Standard Oil fueled U-boats (before a formal declaration of war), some of which sank American ships. And in 1939, when Americans were severely short on rubber for wheels, planes, and tanks, Standard Oil cut a deal with Hitler to provide artificial rubber, while Americans got nothing. This deal continued after Pearl Harbor.[32] This is one example that the big-moneyed global elites have no loyalty to any country, and care only about increasing their wealth and extending their influence.

Fast-forward to 1975. Congressman Larry P. McDonald in the "Introduction" to Gary Allen's book *The Rockefeller File* offers further evidence concerning the disreputable intentions of the global elites:

Money alone is not enough to quench the thirst and lusts of the super-rich. Instead, many of them use their vast wealth, and the influence such riches give them, to achieve even more power. . . . Power on a world wide scale . . . the drive of the Rockefellers and their allies to create a one-world government, combining super-capitalism and Communism under the same tent, all under their control. . . . I am convinced there is such a plot, international in scope, generations old in planning, and incredibly evil in intent.[33]

Look at what David Rockefeller said at one of the secretive Bilderberg meetings back in 1991, which ostensibly two French reporters leaked:

We are grateful to the *Washington Post*, the *New York Times*, *Time Magazine* [*sic*], and other great publications whose directors have attended our meetings and respected their promises of discretion for almost forty years. It would have been impossible for us to develop our plan for the world if we had been subjected to the lights of publicity during those years. But the world is now more sophisticated and prepared to march towards a world government.[34]

He continued, "The supranational sovereignty of an intellectual elite and world bankers is surely preferable to the national auto-determination practiced in past centuries."[35] Translation: the elites like Rockefeller should have all the power and make all the decisions. The rest of us should just be content with being worker bees in their neo-feudal system. The hubris of these people knows no bounds.

The late Hollywood producer Aaron Russo became friends with Nick Rockefeller, a member of the Council on Foreign Relations. Russo corroborated the reprehensible agenda of the elites in an interview with Alex Jones. Russo paraphrased what Nick Rockefeller confided to him about how the global elites want to turn the population into serfs and slaves:

The ultimate goal that these people have in mind is the goal to create a one-world government run by the banking industry, run by the bankers. . . . The whole agenda is to create a one-world government where everybody has an RFID chip implanted in them. All money is to be in those chips. Right—there'll be no more cash. And this is given me straight from Rockefeller himself. This is what they want to accomplish.[36]

The CFR, CIA, and the Trilateral Commission

Organizations like the Royal Institute for International Affairs and the Council on Foreign Relations, which were part of England and the United States, respectively, provide a platform for the globalists' influence. Both organizations were "fronts" for a secret society known as the Round Table, which uber-wealthy international financiers like J.P. Morgan and then later the Rockefellers funded. Colonel House reorganized the American branch of the Round Table in 1921 into what is now known as the Council on Foreign Relations (CFR).[37] The CFR was a by-product of the failure of various leaders around the world at that time to acknowledge the League of Nations as a legitimate world government.[38] Like other globalists, CFR members want to dissolve nation-states and set up a one-world government.

The CFR functions as a kind of intermediary between our government and the wealthy elites, many of whom are globalists. Because the CFR is so powerful and its tentacles seem to reach far and wide, in essence it *is* the government.[39] Servando Gonzales sums up the CFR better than I can:

> The Council on Foreign relations [*sic*] has infiltrated the United States government to the point that currently for all purposes the American government has become a branch of the CFR. In the past forty years, most of American presidents, vice-presidents, Secretaries of State, CIA Directors, Supreme Court judges, and high rank Pentagon officers, not to mention Federal Reserve Bank and IRS directors belong to this group of CFR executors.[40]

The servile media also serves as a branch of the CFR. We saw above where David Rockefeller paid homage to the *New York Times*, *Time* magazine, and the *Washington Post* for keeping silent about the globalist agenda. According to Gonzales, another alphabet agency, the CIA, has co-opted many media outlets such as CBS, NBC, ABC, CNN, *Time*, *Newsweek*, the *Miami Herald*, the *Washington Post*, the *Los Angeles Times*, and the *Wall St. Journal*, to name just a few, as well as news agencies like AP, UPI, Reuters, and others.

If this sounds fantastic, please note that in 1949 the CIA started a secret campaign to spread CFR-created disinformation under the guise of fighting Communism. This was labeled "Operation Mockingbird." The CIA has admitted to recruiting over 400 prominent journalists who secretly carried out various assignments in at least twenty-five organizations in the mainstream media.[41] This goes a long way to explaining why very little hard-hitting reporting is going on except in the alternative media. The mainstream media, in large part, is permitted to feed the public only what coincides with the globalist propaganda.

Formed in 1947, the CIA has never been solely about collecting "intelligence" or protecting the American people. In many cases, it is about carrying out covert operations ordered by the president or his foreign policy advisors who are often part of the invisible government made up of globalists or the power elite. The concept of "plausible deniability," for example, was meant to protect the president politically, but in essence allows elements in the alphabet agencies to "go rogue" in some cases regarding foreign policy, because they can circumvent the president without his knowledge. Fighting Communism back in the Cold War days or stopping the "terrorists" today are just disinformation campaigns often directed by the CFR in order to carry out the globalists' foreign policy agenda.[42]

David Rockefeller and Zbigniew Brzezinski started the Trilateral Commission, a spin-off of the CFR, in 1973. Brzezinski helped groom an unknown peanut farmer named Jimmy Carter for the presidency in 1976.[43] Brzezinski was also Obama's chief foreign policy advisor during the 2008 campaign. In his book of memoirs, *With No Apologies*, Senator Barry Goldwater described the Trilateral Commission: "The trilateral organization created by David Rockefeller was a surrogate—its members selected by Rockefeller, its purposes defined by Rockefeller, its funding supplied by Rockefeller."[44] A few pages later he explained their purpose. "What the Trilaterals truly intend is the creation of a worldwide economic power superior to the political governments of the nation-states involved. They believe the abundant materialism they propose to create will overwhelm existing differences. As managers and creators of the system they will rule the future."[45]

Read what David Rockefeller admitted in his book, *Memoirs* (2002):

> For more than a century ideological extremists at either end of the political spectrum have seized upon well-publicized incidents such as my encounter with Castro to attack the Rockefeller family for the inordinate influence we wield over American political and economic institutions. Some even believe we are part of a secret cabal working against the best interests of the United States, characterizing my family and me as 'internationalists' and of conspiring with others around the world to build a more integrated political and economic structure—one world, if you will. If that's the charge, I stand guilty, and I am proud of it.[46]

Now that we have an idea of who the globalists are and what they want, it is time to look at how they will attempt to carry out their agenda.

The Globalists' Strategy for a New World Order

The globalists want nothing less than to establish a totalitarian dictatorship called the New World Order (NWO), which they—the inner-circle international power elites—will run. Their rule and reign would be established through socialism. Their takeover will be triggered by some type of crisis, whether economic or otherwise. They ultimately want to reduce the population by 85 percent or more, because the little people (you and me) are using up their resources. They want to establish some type of neo-feudal system in which the common folk live as serfs and slaves. Let's look at some possible ways the global elites intend to carry out their agenda.

You might be wondering what it means for the globalists to use socialism as a means to establish their dictatorship. Essentially, they want to use some type of Communo-Fascist economic-political system as a template for instituting their ultimate rule. As Thomas Sowell has pointed out, Communism and Fascism have a lot more in common than most people think. Communism and Fascism are both forms of socialism. Communism is a form of socialism with an *international* focus, while Fascism is also a type of socialism but with a *national* focus. This is why Benito Mussolini defined Fascism as "national socialism."[47] When you begin to see the government, the big banks, and large corporations in bed with one another, you are witnessing creeping Fascism, because Fascism allows corporations to stay intact as long as the government has control of them. We are witnessing this already in our country, especially since the 2008–2009 economic meltdown.

As far as Communism goes, when we envision Marxist Communism, we normally imagine the proletariat (the property-less labor class) rising up to overthrow the bourgeoisie (middle class) and redistributing the wealth so that everything is fair and everyone has what they need. But this is not how the global elites view Communism. In their hands, Communism would involve a redistribution of wealth. But it would mean that the ruling elite would end up taking all of the goods and services for themselves and basically enslaving the rest of us through totalitarian rule.

Whereas Communism as envisioned by Marx involved a *temporary* dictatorship after the proletariat took over,[48] in the hands of the global elites the dictatorship would be anything but temporary. Rather, a dictatorship would be a permanent part of their global totalitarian conquest.[49] We, the people, would be at the bottom of the pecking order as serfs and slaves. In both Communism and Fascism, the state becomes god. If they have their way, even the nation-states would be dissolved so that the globalists could rule the New World Order.

In short, all power and authority would be handed over to the global elites or even one single man. Robert Gates Sr. describes their agenda this way: "Men must be divided into two classes: the omnipotent godlike dictator on the one hand and the masses which must surrender freedom of choice and reasoning in order to become mere slaves in the plans of the dictator."[50] The biblical implications of a single totalitarian dictator ruling over the New World Order will be explored in the final chapters.

One can get a pretty good idea of what the globalists want to accomplish by reading Marx's *The Communist Manifesto*. Among other things, Marx called for an abolition of private property, centralization of credit in the hands of the state, a national bank, and free education for all children in public schools. He also desired the abolishment of all countries and nationalities. In addition, Marx saw Communism eradicating "eternal truths" as well doing away with "all religion, and all morality."[51] He saw the bourgeois family vanishing as a matter of course with the vanishing of capital.[52]

As we have seen through the course of this book, many of these things have already occurred in our country. Christianity has been marginalized, the family is breaking down, a central bank (the Federal Reserve) is debauching our currency, morals are decaying on a daily basis, and the public school system is propagandizing our kids. The global elites are well on their way to accomplishing their agenda; meanwhile, the people of our country are asleep at the wheel.

The left-wing liberal progressives, who have always prided themselves on looking out for the common person and for being a watchdog for the kind of agenda described above, have been noticeable by their absence in the fight against the corporate power elite. This is especially true of the media. Chris Hedges, in his incisive book *Death of the Liberal Class*, laments that the liberal class as represented by the universities, the media, the arts, and the Democratic Party have been "bought off with corporate money" that enriches "a tiny elite."[53] Hedges wrote, "The media, like the academy, hold up the false ideals of impartiality and objectivity to mask their complicity with power. . . . This pernicious reduction of the public to the role of spectators denies the media, and the public they serve, a political role."[54]

Hedges is right, of course. We *are* merely spectators in the media circus that no longer reports real news, or at least not much of it. This was clearly seen in an interview by MSNBC's Andrea Mitchell with Congresswoman Jane Harman concerning the legality of NSA spying. The NSA spying scandal is a genuinely important issue because it involves our right to privacy as citizens. But right in mid-sentence, Andrea Mitchell cut off Harman because of breaking news—Justin Bieber's live court appearance. This was considered "real" news.

Moreover, we have been disengaged from the real issues, such as our loss of rights, and instead have become spectators of the dog and pony show the media feeds us. Is it any wonder that from November 2012 to November 2013 MSNBC lost 45 percent of its viewers while CNN during the same time period lost 48 percent of its audience? Concerning the Bieber coverage, Paul Joseph Watson said, "Just who does MSNBC think its audience is? Fourteen-year-old school girls? The fact that mainstream networks across the board had Bieber as their top story proves that such organizations are no longer in the business of covering real news and are quickly beginning to resemble irrelevant imitations of vapid entertainment cable channels."[55] With the compliant media safely in their pockets, those in power continue to mold public opinion with their own talking points.

The ultimate weapon the globalists intend to employ to set up a totalitarian regime is a "crisis." If they can instigate a crisis and convince the public that big brother will be there to save them, the people will agree to give up even more of their rights. In essence, our blissfully asleep citizens will trade their rights for "security." This is precisely what the power elites are counting on. It has already happened since 9/11.

Bezmenov and the Subversion Strategy

I think this is a good time to share some of the thoughts of former Russian KGB officer Yuri Bezmenov, who defected to the United States in 1970. In 1984 Bezmenov gave a lecture in which he described subversion tactics the Russians planned on using on the United States to destroy it. This ideological subversion can be divided into four stages: 1) demoralization, 2) destabilization, 3) crisis, 4) normalization.[56] I find it interesting that two of the stages in particular have an eerie parallel to what is occurring in the United States at this moment. Am I suggesting that the Russians are still up to their old tricks? No. Am I suggesting that the global elites are aware of the Russian subversion tactics and using them to undermine the United States? No, although some of the globalists might be aware of them.

Nevertheless, it is important to look at the Russian subversion tactics because two of these stages so closely parallel what is happening right now and what I believe will occur in the near future. For example, the demoralization phase has been happening for some time now. In addition, the elites are hoping to instigate a crisis at some point in the future. How do we know this? Because, as we saw above, this is part of the plan they adopted from *The Communist Manifesto*. The crisis phase is most important, because it will be used to usher in some type of totalitarian regime, which would mean the total control of each individual with no opposition. Let's briefly look at all four stages a bit more closely.

Bezmenov describes the first stage of subversion—the "demoralization" phase—which lasts fifteen to twenty years. This is the time it takes to educate (read: propagandize) a generation of children. The media begins to shape public opinion, and the entertainment industry keeps everyone distracted. Bezmenov notes that religion is to be ridiculed and destroyed during this time. The distinction between good and evil is done away with. Morals are to be relativized so that everyone is equal. A criminal will not be considered a criminal anymore. Responsibility will be taken away from the people and bureaucracies put in their place.[57]

The demoralization phase is of particular importance to us because the parallels between Bezmenov's scenario and where our country is right now are obvious. I believe we are in the very late stages of the demoralization phase, which accelerated after the counterculture revolution. We have experienced two generations with which our country has been demoralized. Postmodern secularism is relativizing our morals. Our kids are fed moral relativism at school and told our Constitution and our country is nothing special and never was. We have abortion on demand and same-sex marriage, both of which represent a lowering of the moral bar. Christianity has been marginalized while we have been distracted by both our gadgets and the entertainment industry. The latter ridicules the Christian worldview every chance it gets. The press disparages Christianity and offers no check to the globalist agenda, as we noted above.

Once the work of demoralization is complete, stage two, "destabilization," occurs. Once a country is destabilized, it is ripe for a crisis. This is what the global elites are aiming for.

Stage three is significant because, as Bezmenov points out, the "crisis" stage is where the traditional social structures collapse. Artificial structures (like nonelected committees) take their place. Society can no longer function productively. Bezmenov puts it this way: "The population at large is looking for a savior. The religious groups are expecting a 'Messiah.'" There could be civil war, which could lead to a foreign nation coming in (invading) as a "savior." According to Bezmenov, people are looking for a strong government or a leader who can put them back to work because they have families to feed.[58] This reminds one of what Thomas Jefferson warned, "A government big enough to give you everything you want is strong enough to take everything you have."[59]

Because crisis is such a crucial strategy for the globalists, it is worth pointing out what David Rockefeller said at a United Nations Ambassador's dinner on September 23, 1994: "This present window of opportunity, during which a truly peaceful and interdependent world order might be built, will not be open for too long . . . We are on the verge of a global transformation. All we need is the right *major crisis*, and the nations will accept the New World Order."[60] (Emphasis mine.) This leaves little doubt that the globalists will use a crisis as a trigger for the move to a New World Order and attempt the implementation of a totalitarian dictatorship of some sort.

According to Bezmenov, stage four results in "normalization," which occurs after the country has been stabilized "by force." The self-appointed rulers don't need revolution or radicalism any longer. The new totalitarian leader(s) need stabilization so they can exploit their subjects. Ironically, the people who either knowingly or unwittingly aided in the subversion that lead to the overthrow may suddenly find themselves dispensable by the new ruling elite. Bezmenov explains it this way: "All the sleepers and activists, social workers and liberals and homosexuals and professors and Marxists and Leninists are being eliminated, physically sometimes. They've done their job already. They're not needed anymore."[61]

I found Bezmenov's description of the four-stage subversion process highly relevant to our discussion, because I think we are heading into the crisis stage in the not too distant future. The money printing ("quantitative easing") by the Federal Reserve temporarily averted the financial crisis of 2008–2009, but some type of crisis, probably another financial one or perhaps a pandemic or even war, is surely on the way.

Bezmenov finished his lecture by suggesting that the most important way to avoid the crisis stage is for society to maintain its religious foundation and moral superiority. This is noteworthy coming from a former Communist. The Founders of this country also believed the nation would survive only if it kept its moral foundation. Foreign observer Alexis de Tocqueville likewise confirmed that America's uniqueness was tied to its religious underpinning, which he discovered in his extensive travels around our country in the early nineteenth century.

Bezmenov concluded by advising that the population should exercise self-restraint with regard to consumerism. Finally, he stated that the way to stop a "savior" from taking over is to avoid allowing the crisis phase to evolve into a civil war or an invasion by a foreign entity.[62] I found his advice all the more remarkable considering that it was offered three decades ago.

"Crisis" as a Subversion Strategy

I have the word *crisis* in quotes (above) because the crisis could be contrived to further the globalists' sinister agenda. If the globalists do indeed use crisis as a stratagem for accelerating their agenda, it could go down any number of ways. Look at what has happened since 9/11. The surveillance apparatus that was supposed to catch the "terrorists" has subsequently been pointed at the American people instead. The government is now spying on its own citizens. Our rights are slowly but surely taken away in the name of "security."

Or look what has happened as a result of the school shootings. The local, state, and federal governments are often using these incidents as an opportunity to try to sway public opinion against gun ownership, thus nullifying the Second Amendment. The Founding Fathers put gun rights in place not so we can shoot turkeys but as a line of defense against a government that has gotten too big for its britches. This is precisely what we have today. While this same government is trying to take away our guns, it is arming itself with over 2 billion rounds of ammunition.

There is a growing awareness in the alternative/independent media that events like 9/11, the Boston Marathon bombing, the Sandy Hook school shootings, and other "crises" may have been "false flags" (contrived crises). At the very least, the veracity of these events as depicted by the officials has been called into question. Even a cursory examination of the official record of these tragedies reveals disquieting anomalies combined with a complete lack of coherence regarding how these crises supposedly occurred. Without mincing words, some of these events (and others) may have been contrived, in whole or in part, by those who want to use these events as an excuse to further curb our rights as part of their plan to usher in some type of totalitarian regime and New World Order. This should not come as a surprise, considering what some of the globalists have stated themselves (as quoted earlier).

The power elites could use any number of ways to orchestrate some type of crisis to trigger the hastening of a nondemocratic dictatorship. But it seems probable that the crisis will probably be a financial one, because we already saw in 2008–2009 how easy it would be for this to happen. Moreover, we've seen (and felt) a major wealth transfer from the middle class to the wealthy power elite since that financial crisis. Now that the big bankers have transferred a good portion of our wealth into their pockets, why not have a big financial collapse like the previous one, except on a much larger scale so that a Bezmenov-type crisis scenario could take place with violence, rioting in the streets, food shortages, etc., which would allow the government to step in with bank "holidays" and martial law? This would permit a "savior" to show up on the scene, some type of dictator or even a foreign entity entering our country to restore order while buying up everything we own at discount prices because our government defaulted on its debt obligations. Of course, war could be used to trigger a worldwide economic collapse. War is a favorite method of the globalists for generating a crisis.

Until the crisis occurs, we can expect the globalists and banking elites to continue to confiscate wealth from the citizens of this country drip by drip while lining their pockets. This is part of the enslavement process. One way money is stolen from the people is through what is known as "financial repression."

Financial Repression

Without getting too technical, financial repression is a way for governments to reduce their gargantuan debt by confiscating wealth from the middle class. This is done over time through inflation and negative real interest rates, as well as other things like price controls. When we start talking about price controls and centralization of credit, (which we have in the Federal Reserve), this begins to look eerily similar to some of *The Communist Manifesto*'s game plan. As I pointed out earlier, Communism is the ultimate goal of these elites. But their brand of Communism means they would own everything and the population would live in a neo-feudal system.

People have the mistaken notion that inflation means that the prices of things they need to buy are continually on the rise. But rising prices are merely a *symptom* of inflation. Inflation is really an increase in the money supply and credit. When the Federal Reserve prints money through their "quantitative easing" program, those newly printed dollars are now inflating the money supply and competing with the dollars people have already saved. Those dollars that someone saved in previous years suddenly aren't worth as much, because more dollars are in circulation as a result of the Fed's printing new ones. The effect is that the purchasing power of the dollar goes down and the relative cost of things goes up. Moreover, it takes more of the devalued dollars now to buy the same things that cost far less five or ten or twenty years ago, when the dollar had more value.

This helps the government by allowing it to pay off debt (or at least the interest on the debt) simply by creating new money out of thin air. It's really a form of counterfeiting. Our currency is no longer backed by gold since President Nixon refused to pay France back their gold in 1971. Since then, our currency is backed by nothing but the full faith and credit of the United States and our ever present war machine. But creating currency out of thin air steals the purchasing power of savers, because the money they saved forty or fifty years ago has been stolen through inflation. In short, when the currency is printed *ad infinitum*, it isn't worth as much because it's not as scarce.

In essence, inflation is a nefarious hidden tax on the people that is not passed through legislation. Therefore, the people are unaware of it. They think the symptoms of inflation are just part of life. This is a simple yet effective way the government and banks cheat us out of our hard earned money. Meanwhile, the government pays down the interest on its debt with the phony currency the Fed prints, while the big banks gamble with this same money, which is created by fiat and then handed to them on a silver platter (like it was with TARP). If the banks lose their bets like they did in the 2008–2009 financial crisis, taxpayers bail them out. If they win, they get rich while the savers of the world watch the purchasing power of their money decrease (get stolen) through inflation.

Very briefly, another way financial repression works is by keeping the interest rates artificially low—below the rate of inflation. Keeping interest rates low allows the government to service its gigantic national debt at a cheaper interest rate. But again, this punishes savers and those who are on fixed incomes. How? Because if someone is keeping the money they saved in the bank for a year and earning only .25 percent when the real rate of inflation is, say, 7 percent, they are losing 6.75 percent of their purchasing power for that particular year. This is the price savers have to pay to allow the government to pay down the interest on its debt at an artificially low interest rate.

Artificially low interest rates and inflation are a couple of the tools the government uses to shear the sheeple without a peep out of them. Financial repression avoids both overt taxation and social unrest.[63] Most people don't even know they're getting cheated. As Henry Ford said, "It is well enough that people of the nation do not understand our banking and monetary system, for if they did, I believe there would be a revolution before tomorrow morning."[64]

The Federal Reserve: It's Not Federal and There are No Reserves

The tools of financial repression would not be possible without the Federal Reserve (Fed) central bank. The Fed came into existence as a result of the machinations of the financial elite back in 1913. A lot of lying and deception went into creating the Federal Reserve, which is not federal and has no reserves. The Federal Reserve is not part of our government at all. The bankers concocted this title to make it sound like it is. The Fed is really a cartel of large, privately owned banking interests that deceived the public into thinking a central bank was needed to curb any future banking panics.

The year before Congress passed the Federal Reserve Act (1913), Meyer Nathanial Rothschild said the following to a group of world bankers: "Let me control a peoples' currency and I care not who makes their laws."[65] Twenty-one years later, in 1933, FDR, in a letter to Colonel House, stated, "The real truth of the matter is, as you and I know, that a financial element in the larger centers has owned the Government ever since the days of Andrew Jackson."[66] What we have now in the Federal Reserve is a banking cartel masquerading as part of our government. The Fed is in existence to prop up the gambling expeditions of the big banks in the event their bets fail. This is precisely what we saw in the 2008–2009 financial debacle.

If the Fed was really created to benefit the people, why did the large banking interests construct it in total secrecy? Why did the men who attended the meeting, including J.P. Morgan and Paul Warburg, dispense with using their real names on the way to the supposed "duck hunting" expedition to Jekyll Island, where they and other bankers formed the plans of the Federal Reserve? Why were the usual suspects—the banking conglomerate of William Rockefeller; the J.P. Morgan companies; the Rothschild banks of England and France; the Warburg banks in Germany and the Netherlands; and Kuhn, Loeb and Company—all part of the scheme? Why was the Federal Reserve Act allowed to pass through Congress a couple of days before Christmas, when many senators were on vacation? (More on all of this is explicated in G. Edward Griffin's important work *The Creature from Jekyll Island*.)

The short answer to the questions above is that the government and the politicians are in bed with the banking interests behind the Fed. It goes something like this. The Fed can buy government bonds simply by printing currency for them. Then the government, by way of the politicians, can promise the American people all kinds of things the government wouldn't have been able to afford without the Fed printing currency for it. Of course, the government can't afford all the promises they make anyway, which is why our U.S. government debt is on the way to $20 trillion. Unfortunately for us, the money printing (inflation) used by the Fed to pay for the things the politicians promise causes financial repression, which steals people's purchasing power. Meanwhile, the Fed, the government, and the big banks all get to collect interest on the new currency the Fed prints which is backed by absolutely nothing.

If printing monopoly money and then charging interest on it sounds like a scam, that's because it *is* a scam. Why do you think the banking elite created the Fed in the first place? Since the time the Fed was created over a hundred years ago, the dollar has lost more than 95 percent of its value.[67] In other words, what cost five cents in 1913 now costs a dollar. This is how the power elites steal money over time without the citizens' awareness.

Communists like Lenin certainly understood this. Read what John Maynard Keynes had to say about Lenin's thoughts on this: "Lenin is said to have declared that the best way to destroy the capitalist system was to debauch the currency. By a continuing process of inflation, governments can confiscate, secretly and unobserved, an important part of the wealth of their citizens. There is no subtler, no surer means of overturning the existing basis of society than to debauch the currency . . . which not one man in a million is able to diagnose."[68] And as Ron Paul has stated, "Tyranny always goes hand in hand with government's wrecking of the money system."[69] As we noted, tyranny is the global elite's ultimate goal.

Keeping in mind that a private coalition of banking elites own the Fed, Thomas Jefferson warned about this type of scenario long ago. "If the American people ever allow private banks to control the issue of their currency, first by inflation and then by deflation, the banks and corporations that will grow around them will deprive the people of all property until their children will wake up homeless on the continent their fathers conquered."[70]

The financial repression that has been inflicted on our citizens over the years is made all the more odious by the fact that the same year the Fed came into existence (1913), Congress passed the Sixteenth Amendment, which allowed for a federal income tax. The IRS, a private institution (like the Fed), collects income tax on the currency the Fed prints. But the federal income tax doesn't go to the U.S. Treasury. It goes to the Federal Reserve. Basically, citizens are paying (through interest and taxes) for the ability to use the phony currency the Federal Reserve prints.[71]

At some point the Fed may lose control of their fairy-tale approach to economics they've employed since the financial debacle of 2008–2009. If enough entities around the world lose faith in the dollar all at once, the flight from the dollar could crash the bond market and the Fed's fairy tale will come to an end. If enough people begin all at once to spend dollars in an attempt to get rid of them while those dollars can still purchase something, hyperinflation would be a probability.

Would the Fed and other world banks be able to step in and have a worldwide currency reset before hyperinflation occurs? Only time will tell. As of right now however, hyperinflation in the future seems probable. If hyperinflation were to occur (or even a deflationary implosion) and spread to other countries, this would be another way financial crisis could result in nation-states being destroyed and the attempt to put a one-world government in place.

The Cloward-Piven Crisis Strategy

Another way the financial crisis could come about is through what is known as the "Cloward-Piven strategy," also known as the "crisis strategy." Cloward and Piven were two Columbia University political scientists who in 1966 wrote an article in *The Nation* entitled "The Weight of the Poor: A Strategy to End Poverty." Notice that the article coincided with the time of the countercultural revolution. The Cloward-Piven "crisis strategy" involves expediting the collapse of capitalism by overloading the system with impossible demands.[72]

In their article, Cloward and Piven asserted that there is a "discrepancy" between what people on welfare are receiving and what they are really entitled to. Citing Saul Alinsky (author of *Rules for Radicals*) as the inspiration for their proposal, the two authors argued, "The discrepancy is not an accident stemming from bureaucratic inefficiency; rather, it is an integral feature of the welfare system, which, if challenged, would precipitate a profound financial crisis."[73] The authors went on to say that they want to put more people *on* the welfare system, not take them off. This is pure unadulterated socialism.

In 1960, New York City had around 150,000 welfare cases, but four years after the Cloward-Piven article was published, New York City welfare cases swelled to 1.5 million. By 1975 New York City was bankrupt. Rudy Giuliani named Cloward and Piven responsible for what he described as "an effort at economic sabotage." The National Welfare Reform Organization implemented their strategy at that time. Giuliani charged Cloward and Piven with changing the attitude toward welfare from being temporary to a lifetime entitlement.[74]

Combine this welfare-state entitlement attitude with the bailouts of the big banks and auto industry after the 2008–2009 financial debacle and it is no surprise that the cover of *Newsweek* dated February 16, 2009, announced, "We Are All Socialists Now."[75]

Presently, Obamacare is another example of the transition to socialism. The government is allowed by law to force people to buy healthcare coverage. It would be fair to ask whether this Affordable Health Care plan is really meant to succeed. Allowing those with pre-existing conditions to enter the risk pool ex post facto makes the whole thing seem ridiculous. It is akin to allowing people to forego buying fire insurance until their houses burn down and then allowing them to purchase fire insurance to pay for everything. That is not how insurance works in the real world; therefore, it seems more likely that this is just another use of the Cloward-Piven strategy meant to overload the system and wreck the economy through financial crisis.

Of course, many will claim that every person in our country, including the poor, should have some type of health-care coverage. Perhaps then some type of catastrophic coverage would have been the answer. I wonder how many people who end up in the Medicaid program and are over age fifty-five realize that they aren't getting a free ride. Do they know that they may be subject to "estate recovery," meaning that after they die many of the states can go in and attempt to recover the cost that the person on Medicaid incurred while they were living? In short, states that receive Medicaid funding are required (under a 1993 federal statute) to seek recovery from the estates of those deceased who had been on Medicaid by confiscation of property that would have been passed on to their heirs. This is how the government will "help" poor people by giving them "free" health care and then like true Communists, take their property away after they die.[76]

More Government "Help"

A new IRA, labeled the *my*RA, is supposedly another way for the government to "help" the poor and middle class by making it easy for them to save for retirement. But even a cursory glance proves this to be another lie. *My*RA is just another example of the yoke of financial repression put upon those who think it is meant to help them. It is just another way to seize assets from the citizenry.

Because there are no tax deductions (like some IRA and 401-type plans), the government gets to collect up front *all* the taxes from the *my*RAs every year. Not only does this provide the government with a source of funds it can spend immediately, but the government doesn't have to pay interest on the *my*RA until it is cashed out. In addition, the government pays a rate of interest that is less than the real rate of inflation, which, as we previously pointed out, is a textbook example of financial repression, because the dollars in this type of account will lose purchasing power each and every year as long as inflation continues.[77] This makes it easy for the investors in a *my*RA to lose their money because the government takes the dollars that are still worth something today and pays the person in the future with dollars that have lost their purchasing power. This is simply another way for the government to confiscate the wealth of its populace.

It will be just a matter of time before this type of financial "help" from the government becomes mandatory like Obamacare. I predict that after the economy begins to collapse again and everyone is losing money in their 401ks and other investment vehicles, the government will come to the rescue by forcing people to buy government bonds, which are "guaranteed" and "safe." Government mouthpieces will say that these bonds will help stabilize people's retirement accounts so they won't lose all their money in the stock market again. But what happens if the government defaults on its debt? How much will the government bonds be worth then? What happens if we have hyperinflation and the dollar loses most of its value? How much would the bonds be worth? The government won't care because it will already have taken your money and given you a worthless piece of paper in its place.

Adding insult to injury, at the time of this writing, Jon Corzine, former governor of New Jersey who went to M.F. Global and blew that company up with massive losing bets, is now in charge of *my*Ra. Corzine, a former CEO of Goldman Sachs (a true flexian), "lost," "misplaced," "borrowed," well, you can fill in the blank, $1.6 billion of investors' private segregated accounts, which by law are untouchable. But Corzine still walks around a free man. How else would he have been able to hold expensive fund-raising dinners at his home for President Obama?

Summary

We have brought to light who the global elites are and what their agenda involves. As we noted, the elites in the superclass are those wielding power because of their disproportionate wealth. Some of these super-class elites (flexians) glide seamlessly from one sphere of influence to another. The global elites represent a small number of flexians who have an extraordinary amount of influence in shaping world events. Global elites like the Rockefellers and the Rothschilds are old money, and their reprehensible influence on world affairs can be traced back at least a century or more.

The global elites exercise an inordinate amount of influence around the world because they hold key positions in important institutions and organizations. Some are owners of multinational corporations, some are international bankers, and others sit on the boards of various influential organizations around the globe. The CFR, the Trilateral Commission, and our own Federal Reserve are institutions that support a globalist strategy. The globalists attend meetings like the Economic Forum in Davos and the secret Bilderberg meetings once a year to map out their plans.

Many, if not most of these people, are secularists who are concerned only with the here and now. They couldn't care less about God or eternity. That is why these folks are so dangerous. Ignoring God's existence allows them full autonomy. They are a law unto themselves. They look at the rest of humanity as cattle who are consuming all of their resources. Thus they want to eliminate the vast majority of the human population.

To accomplish this goal, globalists want to set up a New World Order. This would allow them to consolidate their power into one Communist totalitarian system. Their modus operandi is to use a crisis, whether real or contrived, which would allow those in power under them to step in and "help" keep law and order, probably by declaring martial law. A crisis, however, is really a means to take away more of the citizens' rights so the elites can implement a totalitarian regime. The elites want very badly to take away the guns in our country because they need to have this accomplished before a crisis occurs so the citizens cannot defend themselves. Once they take the guns away, it is game over for our population. We will have no viable means left to resist the totalitarian takeover.

A Communist totalitarian state would not mean that goods and services would be evenly distributed. That is a myth. Rather, the elite would institute a neo-feudal system in which they would own everything, including all property rights, and they would enslave the rest of us as worker bees. Well, at least the rest of us who aren't eliminated in the extermination process they hope to implement.

It is probable that the crisis they use will be a financial one, because nothing was solved in the 2008–2009 economic debacle, except that the Fed printed a lot of money to paper over the financial problems. War could also be used to trigger an economic crisis. The next financial catastrophe will be orders of magnitude worse than 2008–2009. Remember, the global elites want to do away with nation-states, and what better way to do that than to bring a country to its knees with a financial crisis. A pandemic could be another crisis used by the global elites.

In the meantime, financial repression is used to steal the wealth from the populace and destroy the middle class. The Fed has already stolen much of the wealth of our country's citizens through inflation. Many asset classes at the time of this writing are in a bubble because of the massive money printing expedition by the Fed. One of these bubbles is going to find a pin, and the whole economic system will come crashing back down.

The Cloward-Piven strategy is being used to overload the entitlement system and crash the welfare state with policies like Obamacare. In addition, it won't be long before banks start charging their customers interest for holding their money. This is already happening overseas. If things get bad enough, I also think it is possible people will lose much of their pension funds through some type of government program. I foresee a day, for example, when the government will offer (force) those with retirement accounts to trade them in for government bonds so that the government has liquidity to pay off its debt obligations.

If those in power right now don't act like adults and take fiscally responsible measures instead of printing monopoly money and then spending it, the economic crisis will be a certainty. Of course, history has shown that going to war is a way to distract the citizenry from the government's irresponsibility while at the same time providing a straw man with which to blame the government's malfeasance. Therefore, war is also probable.

As we move toward the end of the age, Jesus told His disciples that there would be wars and rumors of wars. A worldwide conflict might aid the globalists' strategy. People will clamor for "peace and security." It is not difficult to see that the globalists' solution to this problem would be a one-world government with a one-world economic system that purportedly would avoid both wars and another economic apocalypse. We will continue to look at the NWO and the scenarios surrounding it in the final chapters.

Chapter 17

Nazi Germany 2.0: America's Vulnerability to Totalitarianism

In this chapter I provide evidence for our country's move toward a totalitarian political system. A totalitarian regime means that a government, oligarch, or dictator takes total control over every aspect of people's lives. This has been slowly but surely occurring in our country for some time now. It was not supposed to happen. The Founders established our government precisely so that any totalitarian inclinations by an elite would have a rough time of it.

Our republic is in serious trouble. The government has gotten too big and too intrusive. It has become an end in itself. And a government that becomes an end in itself is already on the road to becoming totalitarian.

Totalitarianism: What It Might Look Like and How It Could Happen

By its very nature, a democracy is vulnerable. On the other hand, Communist totalitarianism is better equipped to defend itself. Anything that threatens a totalitarian regime's existence may be labeled "subversive." Opposition can be squelched immediately. But in a democracy, an internal enemy has a legal right to oppose the system. A leader in a democracy with totalitarian inclinations, for example, could come into power with the surreptitious intent to take total control. This could be implemented slowly through legal channels. Jean-Francois Revel describes this vulnerability of a democracy: "Democracy tends to ignore, even deny, threats to its existence because it loathes doing what is needed to counter them. It awakens only when the danger becomes deadly, imminent, evident. By then, either there is too little time left for it to save itself, or the price of survival has become crushingly high."[1]

Right now in our country we are witnessing creeping Fascism. Fascism allows corporations to exist as private institutions under government influence and control. The bailouts of GM, insurance giant AIG, Fannie and Freddie, and the big banks are examples of Fascism at work. One must remember that Fascism is still socialism. It is "National Socialism," which is what the Nazis practiced politically. Fascism's focus is on what is best for the state at the expense of the individual. Mussolini said that a more proper name for Fascism would be "corporatism," because Fascism is really a merger of state and corporate power.[2]

We are experiencing creeping Communism in our country as well. As we pointed out in the previous chapter, Communism is not really a redistribution of wealth enforced through socialist programs like Obamacare. Communism's true goal is the total takeover of every facet of society and each individual's life through a totalitarian dictatorship or oligarchy of some sort.

Is it really possible to implement a totalitarian regime in the United States? The answer is yes. It could happen incrementally so that all of our institutions seem to be functioning properly but are weakened so seriously that they offer no resistance to the coming tyranny.[3] People start to lose their right to free speech. They lose their right to assemble. Those in power could subdue the press from reporting anything but state-sponsored propaganda. The government could take away citizens' guns, in which case it would be game over for the populace. Small farms could be shut down with obscure and strict regulations. The legislative process could be bypassed with executive orders signed by the president.

I have stated all of the examples above as hypotheticals. But they are all happening now. We have the appearance of a democratic constitutional republic, but we are advancing toward totalitarianism fairly rapidly now. As pointed out, the problem with citizens in a democracy is that they wait until it is too late to do anything about the totalitarian takeover. Now is the time for the citizens of our country to wake up.

Crisis as the Modus Operandi for a Totalitarian Takeover

Although the move toward totalitarianism is speeding up right now, it could happen all at once in the future. How? Through a "crisis." As we saw in the previous chapter, a crisis of some sort is the method of choice for a totalitarian takeover.

Hitler consolidated his power through just such a crisis. In 1933, after the Reichstag building was set on fire, Goering fomented fear in the German people by claiming that the fire was part of a larger plot by Communist terrorists to start a revolution. Goering declared that Germany was on "war footing," and, therefore, parts of the German constitution needed to be restricted. Restricted rights included freedom of the press, freedom to assemble, privacy of postal and telephone communications, and freedom of opinion. The Nazis could search houses without warrants and confiscate property as they saw fit. The Nazis suspended habeas corpus, which allowed them to detain so-called terrorists or revolutionaries at will. Many Communists and social democrats at that time could not vote because they were detained by the Nazis. A month after the Reichstag fire, the lack of voting opposition allowed the Enabling Act to pass, which in turn permitted Hitler to bypass the constitution and rule by decree. Hitler later said, "I am not a dictator, I have only simplified democracy."[4]

The Reichstag fire was probably a "false flag," meaning that the Nazis most likely started the fire to instigate a crisis. A false flag is a contrived crisis. Compare the Reichstag incident with 9/11. The World Trade Center attacks were probably allowed to occur by a rogue/shadow element in our government in order to further an agenda.[5] You might be wondering about what or whose agenda. To answer that, let's consider the results of the attacks.

The government began to take away our rights, just as they were taken away from the Germans after the Reichstag fire. Congress passed the Patriot Act one month after 9/11, with hardly any legislators reading it. Apparently a copy of the legislation was difficult to get a hold of because the bill wasn't printed until *after* the vote was taken that made it law.[6] Notice the propaganda in the wording "Patriot Act." It would have been "unpatriotic" not to sign it, even if one didn't read it. The end result is that the Patriot Act disintegrated the Bill of Rights. Those in power can label anyone who opposes them a potential "terrorist" now.

Just as Goering told the Germans that they were on "war footing," likewise Bush 2.0 told the American people that we are engaged in a "war on terror" after the 9/11 attacks. This is the kind of fear mongering that global elites use to get people to acquiesce to the state's authority and power. In reality, the "terror threat" in many cases is invented by the globalists to spy on the citizenry and to curb their rights.

For example, in the immediate aftermath of 9/11, the TSA began exposing passengers to radiation-emitting scanners and invaded their privacy at the airports. Today, domestic groups that want to practice nonviolent civil disobedience can be labeled as "domestic terrorists" along with religious or political institutions the government regards as subversive. These groups are targeted and spied on. Secret searches and wiretaps are carried out without probable cause, as well as monitoring citizens' email and Internet activity.[7] In this way we are beginning to resemble a totalitarian regime rather than a constitutional republic that upholds individuals' rights. The coming crisis, which a financial collapse, nuclear attack, or perhaps a pandemic will activate, will be used to further control every aspect of people's lives under the guise of maintaining national security.

For example, the latest version of the National Defense Authorization Act (NDAA) signed in 2014 gives the president the ability to indefinitely detain U.S. citizens on American soil without a trial.[8] The present administration and the left-leaning media are already using pejorative labels like "tea-partiers," "religious extremists," and "gun owners" to refer to those who oppose the Communo-fascism agenda. In some cases those who opposed Obamacare were labeled "racists" just because they didn't want to see more socialism forced upon all of us.

It is not difficult to predict that in a crisis, when all hell breaks loose, those who wield power will apply a broad brush to the kinds of groups that oppose them. They will label them "enemies of the state," "spies," "domestic terrorists," "constitutionalists," "traitors," "subversive elements," or "enemies of the people."[9]

If and when a crisis occurs at some point in the future and things deteriorate enough so that the president declares martial law, he or she will then have *carte blanche* to do whatever he or she wishes. Under martial law, some of the aforementioned "subversive elements" may be carted off to secret prisons, indefinitely detained, and possibly worse. Those considered less subversive may simply find themselves in FEMA camps along with those who can no longer feed themselves and have no roof over their heads. If this all seems a little too far-fetched, remember that the U.S. government interned Americans of Japanese descent in camps during WWII.

The Emerging Police State

If you don't think the authorities can pick up people for any reason in our country, I would remind you of former Marine veteran Brandon Raub, whom FBI agents and the local police forcibly removed from his home in 2012 simply because somebody complained that his Facebook page had antigovernment political views and song lyrics posted on it. A Special Justice sentenced Raub to undergo psychiatric evaluation for thirty days until a circuit court judge dismissed the government's case against Raub. Although that's bad enough, what really scared Raub was that he claimed that the evaluating psychiatrist threatened to "brain-wash" him and make him take medication against his will.[10] The Ruth-erford Institute, that defended Raub, commented on his case by warn-ing that "the First Amendment is hanging by a thread in America."[11] Former military veterans will be at the top of the list of groups the to-talitarian regime is afraid of, because former veterans have guns and tactical experience.

Here's another example. Michael Salman was fined $12,000 and incarcerated for sixty days for holding a weekly Bible study on his own property. A neighbor's complaint set the bureaucratic machine in mo-tion. City officials got involved, even though everyone was parked on Salman's 1.5-acre property and the prayer meeting was held in a build-ing he constructed.[12] It was exactly this type of spying by one's neigh-bors, friends, and relatives that brought the Gestapo to the German citizens' doors.

I can already see this type of scenario happening in the future with increasing frequency. For example, an out of control government might force PC incorrect Christian churches to shut down. These churches might be considered a terrorist threat because of their "radical fundamentalist" beliefs. Parishioners would have to adopt a bunker mentality and begin having old-fashioned home Bible studies. In this case, all it would take is a person who doesn't like Christians to inform the police that questionable activity is going on in their neighbor's home, and there will be a knock at the door.

I have no doubt that Christians will be primary targets the closer we get to the end of the age. True Christians believe that Jesus alone is the way to salvation and heaven. Christians will be considered extrem-ists and hated for their perceived intolerance. Remember, PC tolerance is the most prized value in our society today, not truth. Truth is one of the first casualties in a totalitarian regime. Everyone must tow the party line or face the consequences.

At any rate, eventually in the future the cops won't have to knock. They will just point their handy-dandy gadget at your home, which will allow them to see right in. Or maybe they'll send in an insect-drone to spy on you. You know, the drones that are smaller than the size of a quarter. Wonder why that mosquito didn't die when you smacked it on your arm? Wonder no more.

So, for example, if the police see a group of people with their Bi-bles cracked open and that number of people surpasses some new arbi-trary legal limit, you might just get a bit more than a knock at your door. Can't have Christian extremist-haters all congregating in one place, can we? After all, Christians are armed with that dangerous weapon—the Bible.

Think the police state isn't here? Think this won't happen? Then you might want to peruse John W. Whitehead's book *A Government of Wolves*, which provides example after example of government intrusion into our lives and the loss of our rights. Whitehead's Rutherford Institute litigated both Raub and Salman's cases and defends those like them.

Recently, Whitehead commented on a ruling by the Supreme Court (8-1) that gives police officers (and government officials) the go-ahead to violate citizens' fourth amendment rights if that right was violated by a "reasonable" mistake about the law by the officer. Whitehead summarizes the ramifications of this case: "This case may have started out with an improper traffic stop, but where it will end—given the turbulence of our age, with its police overreach, military training drills on American soil, domestic surveillance, SWAT team raids, asset forfeiture, wrongful convictions, and corporate corruption—is not hard to predict. This ruling is what I would call a one-way, nonrefundable ticket to the police state."[13]

When Nazi Germany initially detained people, it was often under the guise of "protective custody." At least at first, they supposedly took dissidents in for their own good, to protect them from the public's ire. But soon after, the Gestapo began picking up people for violating the "malicious gossip" decree that was meant to stop verbal attacks against the government. It wasn't long before the Gestapo was picking up people for all kinds of ill-defined political crimes and placing them in concentration camps. The government told the people that the camps were temporary. The media assured people that no one was mistreated and that those in the camps deserved to be there. The detainees needed to be reeducated. The press even played up the fact that the camp in Dachau helped the local business economy.[14]

The Nazis did not initiate the first camps. Rather the camps began through local jurisdictions like the police or state administrations. They instilled the camps because the local jails were overcrowded. Soon after, the Nazis wanted everyone in Germany to know about the concentration camps so that they would provide a deterrent for their political enemies like the Communists and later the Jews. Five months after Himmler announced the opening of Dachau, the press reported that one of the most dangerous Communists had been shot while trying to escape.[15] Translation: the Nazis eliminated the worst of their enemies. This intimidation was not lost on the citizenry.

Tattling As a Form of Surveillance

The German population as a whole did not level much criticism of the camps. In fact, survivors of the concentration camps said they often were placed there because their neighbors "informed" on them.[16] Thus, the myth that the Nazis acted totally on their own in their malicious endeavors is false. The Germans monitored themselves by informing on those who might have helped a Jew or said something derogatory against Hitler.[17]

It's bad enough that with impunity the government surveillance state today is already spying on anyone they choose. The scary part is that in a future totalitarian state it may be your neighbors and associates who tattle on you if they think you are doing something they perceive as suspicious. Or maybe they'll tattle on you just because they don't like you. Others will inform on their fellow citizens because they think they will receive preferential treatment from those in power.

The government is already encouraging citizens to spy on one another. Former Secretary of Homeland Security Janet Napolitano started the campaign "If you see something, say something."[18] In fact, as I was writing this chapter, I saw that particular slogan on a bumper sticker on one of our local fire department vehicles with a phone number to call.

Citizens in Palm Beach County are implementing this tattling out in real life. Their sheriff is encouraging the local citizens through public service announcements to call a 24-hour hotline if they feel someone could cause harm to themselves or others. The sheriff's department is working closely with mental health workers, trained deputies, and case workers. As Sheriff Bradshaw ruminated, "What does it hurt to have somebody knock on a door and ask, 'Hey is everything OK?'"[19]

What does it hurt? Well, I can think of a few things. First, questioning somebody in this manner relies entirely on the subjective opinion of anyone who may have an axe to grind with the individual in question. Second, mental health professionals may be given too much authority in these matters in light of the fact that their opinions are subjective. What if a mental health worker has a bias against particular behaviors and attitudes they don't deem as normal? For example, how long will it be before believing that Jesus will return someday is considered delusional? What if these social workers or mental health professionals have a problem with Christians? What will happen then?

Because psychiatrists, psychologists, and other mental health advocates are considered to be professionals, the public is conditioned to acquiesce to their expertise.

It is extremely dangerous to allow those in the mental health professions to exercise their authority as if they were law enforcement. But I predict that those in the corridors of power, especially in the future, will utilize these professionals as a way to quarantine, detain, incarcerate, or send to FEMA camps those whom the elites view as a threat. By using these professions, the process of eliminating enemies of the state won't look so Gestapo-like. It will be made to look as if it is done to protect the society from "potential domestic terrorists," or "potential enemies of the state." Your doctor will probably be allowed/forced to cough up all of your health records sometime in the future. I am predicting that there will be no rights of confidentiality at some point for those under suspicion, or perhaps for any citizens.

If you are not feeling at least a little squeamish about the potential tattling in the future, consider that your children may also be a source of concern in this regard. The public school system today encourages children to be sensitive to all kinds of "abuse" from their parents. The children are *already* viewed as potential victims of their families.[20] It is not hard to foresee that in the future, children will be taught that parents who are antigovernment or perhaps religious extremists are abusing their children. Children of practicing Christians may, and probably will, be considered victims, because they were psychologically "abused" by the "religious indoctrination" of their parents.

Moreover, the government doesn't want parents teaching children things like Christianity. Power elites want control of your kids. The government and the educated elite will decide what can and cannot be taught, not the parents. In fact, Professor Melissa Harris-Perry stated, "We have to break through our private idea that kids belong to their parents or kids belong to their families."[21] This type of thinking will become more ubiquitous as time moves on. The breakdown of the family will only make it easier for the elites to steal the hearts and souls of our children. Parents will no longer be authority figures if the progressive intelligentsia has its way.

On the other hand, as I was finishing up this chapter, Homeland Security advisor Lisa Monaco is urging parents to watch their kids for "confrontational behavior." Why? Because it could be an early indication that they may become terrorists. In a speech given at Harvard

University, Monaco groused: "The government is rarely in a position to observe these early signals."

This raises a question. Since when did the government think its job is to watch the kids? Monaco is encouraging parents to be watchdogs so that the government can preempt "homegrown extremism."[22] She seems disappointed that the government can't be alongside the parents in their homes, spying on the children who might become future terrorists. This is the kind of government overreach that is a telltale sign that we are on the way to totalitarianism.

If you think that at some point the government is not going to try to grab authority away from the parents, consider what is happening in the United Kingdom. A new "Cinderella Law" makes emotional abuse of children a criminal offense. Every parent there can now become the target of the new behavior police. Of course, in the hands of the state, the list of potential abusive behaviors is all-encompassing. As Professor Frank Furedi of the University of Kent puts it, "These days, parents who smoke or drink alcohol in front of children risk being characterized as child-abusers. . . . Health activists denounce parents of overweight children for the same offence. Mothers and fathers who educate their children to embrace the family's religion have been characterized as child abusers by anti-faith campaigners."[23] The reason I am bringing up an example in the United Kingdom is because what starts in Europe ends up over here sooner or later. Europe, for example, became secularized first, and now it is happening here in America.

Totalitarian regimes want the children, because it ensures that the next generation will be on their side. Hitler stated, "When an opponent says, 'I will not come over to your side.' I calmly say, 'Your child belongs to us already. . . . You will pass on. Your descendants, however, now stand in the new camp. In a short time they will know nothing else but this new community.'"[24] Elsewhere Hitler proclaimed, "This new Reich will give its youth to no one, but will itself take youth and give to youth its own education and its own upbringing."[25] The Nazi regime was hell-bent on intruding into the family, suppressing the rights of the family, redefining the family, and destroying the moral and spiritual values of the family while simultaneously turning it into something that would benefit the state.[26]

The kids involved in the Hitler Youth lend evidence that brainwashing can take place once the state gets a hold of the younger generation. Therefore, it is not implausible to foresee our own youth tattling on their parents in the future, during and after a totalitarian takeover. As we noted above, many left-leaning liberals today are fond of thinking that the kids do not belong to the parents exclusively. These folks will be more than happy to encourage the children to tell about all the "abuse" they have suffered from their parents.

In a broader context, we are living in a society where the parents are not willing or able to pass down the Christian belief system to their children. Practical atheists don't know much about Christianity. Kids and most parents do not even understand what truth really means nowadays. So if your children do not understand what truth is, they will be susceptible to lies. It is easy to predict that institutions aligned with the state—the media, the public school system, colleges and universities, along with psychiatry and psychology—will be only too happy to fill the void left by the marginalization of Christianity. If your children have been taught that truth and morals are relative, then it will be easier for the elites to mold the children's thinking to support the state's immoral values. This will get worse as time goes on.

The Vulnerability of the Liberal Intelligentsia to Totalitarianism

Those who think that educated or so-called intelligentsia (like those mentioned above) can't fall for the lure of totalitarianism are sadly mistaken. History proves they can. As one observer noted, intellectuals are actually more susceptible to the "totalitarian temptation" because they view themselves as the moral conscience of society. They often feel the need to level the playing field for everyone. In this regard, progressive elites see the government as the solution. They want the government to use its coercive power to *make* people more free.[27] Unfortunately, this level-the-playing-field mentality (equality of outcomes) lends itself to socialism, which, as we saw in the previous chapter, is an ideology on the road to Communist totalitarianism.

The history of Nazi Germany also supports the contention that the educated elite are not immune to the lure of totalitarianism. In fact, during the Nazi reign, a majority of doctors, lawyers, judges, and sociologists fervently went along with the policies of Hitler.[28] You would think that of all institutions, the German universities, which were the most highly esteemed and from which our own universities modeled themselves,[29] would have had the wherewithal to stand up to Hitler. But they didn't. This was very disconcerting for American professors who at that time looked up to their German counterparts and saw nothing but cowardly compromise.

Many German professors went along with Hitler because they did not want to make waves. Other professors lost their jobs through civil service reform which purged those who were racially or politically undesirable. Students managed politics on the campuses and could drum dissident professors out of the universities who didn't tow the party line.[30]

Those in the Nazi Student Association held book burnings and gave speeches to commemorate the "cleansing" process while professors donated books to the effort and stood by watching the fires.[31] Historian Robert P. Ericksen asserts that "we search almost in vain for evidence of opposition to the regime within the universities." He adds that there was a "great deal of enthusiasm" for Hitler there.[32] Of course, after 1945 almost every German professor claimed to have been an opponent of Hitler's regime.[33]

The Eugenics Movement: Ridding the World of the Unfit

Francis Galton, a British scientist and a cousin of Charles Darwin, hatched a plan to improve the human race through favorable breeding. He called this plan "eugenics" (meaning "well born"). This, in essence, put man in control of the process of natural selection. Social Darwinists used eugenics as a tool by applying the biological theories of Spencer, Haeckel, and Darwin to humans. Social Darwinism is the idea that different races and social classes compete for survival. Instead of waiting for nature to blindly and arbitrarily take its course, proponents of eugenics encouraged the reproduction of the favored races, especially the Nordic race, through biologically favorable marriages. As Galton suggested, "What Nature does blindly, slowly and ruthlessly, man may do providentially, quickly and kindly."[34] Notice the word *providentially* in the quote. Man was now going to play God.

The eugenics movement emerged at a time when science was becoming authoritative and the Darwinian worldview was emerging as a substitute for the Christian view of man. In fact, Galton stated that he wanted eugenics to be "introduced into the national conscience like a new religion."[35] The eugenic fanatic and playwright George Bernard Shaw stated in a 1905 essay, "Nothing but a eugenic religion can save our civilization."[36]

American eugenicists didn't have the patience to wait for the advantages of positive marital breeding. They wanted to speed things up. So they employed what is known as "negative eugenics," preventing the "unfit" from reproducing at all. The eugenic elites wanted to eliminate the ancestrally unfit whom they labeled "bacteria," "vermin," "mongrels," or "subhuman." The racially inferior included blacks, Asians, Native Americans, and whites from southern and eastern Europe. They also applied a broad brush to those they considered "defectives" in society, which included the feebleminded, the pauper class, the insane, alcoholics, epileptics, those with deformities, the deaf, blind, mute, and juvenile delinquents.[37]

Some of the more notable eugenic advocates included H.G. Wells, Alexander Graham Bell, and Teddy Roosevelt, the latter of whom stated in 1913 in a letter to Charles Davenport (Davenport headed the Carnegie Institution's Station of Experimental Evolution in 1904 and later the Eugenics Record Office in 1910, both located at Cold Springs Harbor), "I agree with you . . . that society has no business to permit degenerates to reproduce their kind."[38] Winston Churchill also was a passionate supporter for eugenics. He reassured a group of eugenicists regarding Britain's feebleminded that these unfit "should, if possible, be segregated under proper conditions so that their curse died with them and was not transmitted to future generations."[39] This plan called for literally thousands of these unfortunates to be placed in colonies to live out the rest of their lives.[40]

American Eugenics

In America, forced sterilization became the primary political objective and modus operandi of the eugenic elites. In 1907, Indiana was the first jurisdiction in the world to allow forced sterilization of poorhouse residents, prisoners, and mentally impaired people.[41] Virginia was another state that practiced forced sterilization. State authorities went up into the rural mountains to drag off welfare recipients to "have it done on them."[42]

The landmark *Buck v. Bell* Supreme Court case in 1927 upheld the constitutionality of Virginia law, whereby the genetically "unfit" could be forcibly sterilized. Justice Oliver Wendell Holmes, a religious skeptic and thoroughgoing Darwinist, wrote for the majority (8–1) in the *Buck v. Bell* case: "It is better for all the world, if instead of waiting to execute degenerate offspring for crime or to let them starve for their imbecility, society can prevent those who are manifestly unfit from continuing their kind. . . . Three generations of imbeciles are enough."[43] Remember, the elites think they are better and smarter than everyone else.

After this Supreme Court decision was passed down, thirty states followed suit, and at least 60,000 Americans were sterilized between 1927 and the 1970s. In fact, the state of Virginia did not overturn its sterilization law until 1974.[44] That's progress for you. Apparently after *Roe v. Wade* (1973), the elites found it easier to go after unborn babies rather than adults, who could to some degree defend themselves.

Circling back for a moment, as early as 1914, forty-four major institutions of higher education in America offered eugenic instruction, and even high schools used eugenic textbooks. One could draw from a voluminous amount of work—books, journal articles, charts, tables, etc.—that flooded both academia and society. However, as Edwin Black asserts, "Little of it made sense, and even less of it was based on genuine science. But there was so much of it that policymakers were often cowed by the sheer volume of it."[45] All of this massive "research" was not lost on a young German corporal who spent time immersing himself in eugenic textbooks while in prison in 1924. That young corporal was Adolf Hitler.[46]

German Eugenics

By the time Hitler got his hands on this material, America was leading the way in eugenics. But Germany also had its own history of "racial science" and "race hygiene" long before Hitler came to power. For example, Ernst Haeckel (1834–1919) contended that killing the "unfit" was simply a logical consequence of the Darwinian worldview. Haeckel, an advocate of Darwinism, wanted to modify the traditional Christian view of human life in light of evolutionary theory.[47] He misrepresented Scripture to support his morally egregious and racist views. He thought he was being clever when he remarked, "Many are called, but few are chosen!"[48] Following the thinking of Malthus and Spencer, Haeckel argued, "Only the chosen minority of the privileged fit ones is in the condition to survive successfully this competition."[49] In 1895, German social theorist Alfred Jost contended that the state had an inherent right to inflict death on the unfit.[50]

Psychiatrists in Germany called their patients "inferior," "degenerate," or "defective," while anthropologists, ethnologists, and scientists appealed to the biological racism inherent in Darwin's theory.[51] Darwin's influence can be seen in *Mein Kampf*, in which Hitler wrote, "Whoever wants to live, must struggle, and whoever will not fight in this world of eternal struggle, does not deserve to live."[52]

Both the academic and scientific communities in Germany embraced the notion of racial inequality and race struggle. This provided Hitler with intellectual cover. It also suggests an explanation as to why ordinary Germans, physicians, and scientists could all participate in the evil machinations of the Nazis.[53]

Just six months after Hitler's rise to power, the Nazi Sterilization Act (July 1933) made sterilization compulsory for those deemed undesirable by the state.[54] Hitler ended up sterilizing hundreds of thousands of non-Aryans in German culture and murdering millions of Jews and others in death camps. Hitler rationalized it this way: "We are obliged to depopulate as part of our mission of preserving the German population. . . . If you ask me what I mean by depopulation, I mean the removal of entire racial units. And that is what I intend to carry out. . . . Nature is cruel, therefore we, too, may be cruel. . . . I have the right to remove millions of an inferior race that breeds like vermin!"[55]

German eugenics was practiced during the first ten years of Hitler's reign, with the approval and admiration of American eugenicists. In fact, the superintendent of Virginia's Western State Hospital groused, "The Germans are beating us at our own game."[56]

Big money for eugenics came from the usual suspects: the Rockefeller Foundation and the Carnegie Institution. The Harriman railroad fortune also provided funding for eugenic research in America while the Rockefeller Foundation supported research in Germany. The vision of the elites was global. The goal of the Rockefellers was to achieve, in part, the creation of a superior race by identifying defective bloodlines, even if it meant funding German institutions under Nazi control.[57] Under the umbrella of science and progress, the elites hoped to create a utopia—a heaven on earth[58]—through positive and negative eugenics. Edwin Black says that the entire project of the eugenic elites can be summarized in one word: "arrogance."[59]

The Global Elites, Social Darwinism, and Democide

Social Darwinism didn't end after WWII, even in light of the concentration camps. In fact, the agenda of the global elites hasn't changed at all. They want to reduce the population of the world by 85 to 90 percent and then use those who are left as good little worker bees who will live (be enslaved) in some type of neo-feudal system.

Julian Huxley, the Director General of UNESCO, which was formed in 1946, outlined the goals of UNESCO in a treatise entitled *UNESCO: Its Purpose and Philosophy.*

In the not very remote future the problem of improving the average quality of human beings is likely to become urgent: and this can only be accomplished by applying the findings of a truly scientific eugenics. Nature Science is one of the fields in which two of Unesco's general principles—of thinking, in global terms and of relieving the darkness of the "dark areas" of the world—are most obviously applicable. . . . the application of scientific knowledge now provides our chief means for raising the level of human welfare.[60]

I'm not so sure that the millions of people who died in the Holocaust a few years before Huxley penned his thesis believed that eugenic science had raised their standard of living. This goes especially for those who came into contact with the eugenic "research" of Dr. Josef Mengele. The atrocities of the Holocaust seem lost on Huxley. A few pages later in his treatise he talks about "optimum population-size" as an "indispensable first step towards that planned control of populations which is necessary if man's blind reproductive urges are not to wreck his ideals and his plans for material and spiritual betterment."[61] Of course, "spiritual betterment" doesn't include acknowledging the God of the Bible, because Huxley and his elite cronies don't believe in God. They're secularists through and through. They are accountable to no one. This is why they think it is perfectly acceptable to eliminate the "unfit" and enslave those who are not as smart as they are.

As we pointed out in Chapter fifteen, Aldous Huxley (Julian's brother) gave a speech at UC Berkeley in 1962 in which he admitted that what he outlined in his dystopian book, *Brave New World*, was not fiction but was based on what the elites were trying to accomplish in real life. According to Aldous, in the future a "scientific dictatorship" or "controlling oligarchy" will attempt to get people to "love their servitude" possibly through pharmacological means, whether coerced or not.[62]

If there was ever a reason to resist the gradual slide to totalitarianism, Huxley's brave new world is it. Once a totalitarian regime or an oligarchy is in place, it will be much easier for the elites to discard the unfit and to enslave those who are left. But don't worry. People will learn to love their servitude as long as they are allowed (or forced) to gobble pharmaceuticals. Of course, in the future, nanobots which swarm through your body will be responsible for dispensing the drugs. This could all be controlled at a distance, by the ruling elites.

Today, social engineering on a massive scale is still on the table as far as leaders in the genetic community are concerned. Those outside the eugenics circle, however, fear that "self-directed evolution," including genetic therapies, embryo screening, human cloning, and designer babies, could reignite the push for the establishment of a master race. As Edwin Black points out, it could cause a "genetic divide that will yield a superior race of species to exercise dominion over an inferior subset of humanity."[63] Of course, this is just what Aldous Huxley described.

Some people in the future might not be able to obtain insurance because of certain genetic predispositions. They could be discriminated against because they belong to a genetic "underclass." Discrimination of this sort will be more likely when the collection of everyone's DNA becomes mandatory and then those DNA databases go global.[64] This would allow the genetic underclass to be tracked and catalogued. Under a totalitarian oligarchy, their fate, and everyone else's, for that matter, would be in the hands of the elite.

In 1991, Jacques Cousteau wrote in UNESCO'S *Courier* magazine, "The United Nations' goal is to reduce population selectively by encouraging abortion, forced sterilization, and control human reproduction, and regards two-thirds of the human population as excess baggage, with 350,000 people to be eliminated per day."[65] If the elites have your DNA and you are considered "excess baggage," it would be very easy to deny health care, food, or anything else that could support your life.

This is all the more terrifying when one considers that governments killing their own citizens was the number one cause of unnatural death in the last century. In his book *Death by Government*, R. J. Rummel estimates that from the beginning of last century up until 1988, governments murdered between 170 million and 360 million people.[66] Rummel calls government mass murder "democide." He summarizes his thesis this way:

> The more power a government has, the more it can act arbitrarily according to the whims and desires of the elite, . . . The more constrained the power of governments, the more power is diffused, checked, and balanced, the less it will aggress on others and commit democide. At the extremes of Power, totalitarian communist governments slaughter their people by the tens of *millions*; in contrast, many democracies can barely bring themselves to execute even serial murderers.[67]

The horror of democide should make it clear why we don't want to let our constitutional republic continue its slide toward totalitarianism, a precursor to democide.

The Accommodating Churches in America

We can't conclude this chapter without briefly mentioning the churches, because if any institutions should have been able to stand against the evils of eugenics and the Nazi atrocities, it should have been Christians. But, unfortunately, we find that the churches, whether in Germany or in America, had a rather abysmal record when standing up to evil.

Let's look at the churches in the United States first. The American liberal Protestants viewed eugenics as part of a secular reform movement they could get on board with. You'll recall that liberal Protestantism, which originated in Germany, attempted to accommodate Christianity to modernism. As promoters of the Social Gospel movement, liberal Protestants were as much concerned with social salvation as they were with personal salvation. In other words, earthly concerns were just as imperative as heavenly ones. In this they were secularists. So from their perspective, if promoting the preservation of the race and curing social ills could be accomplished through eugenics, they believed it was their duty not to impede scientific progress. But, regrettably, as we have seen repeatedly, liberal Protestantism's balancing act always results in capitulation to modernism and results in cultural captivity.[68]

Christine Rosen, in her important work *Preaching Eugenics*, argues that the further liberals and modernists got away from the traditional doctrines of their respective faiths the more they were willing to support the eugenics movement.[69] One might have expected more hesitancy on their part to embrace eugenics, but because of their wishy-washy theology, liberal Protestants allowed the secular eugenicists to set the agenda for them. Fundamentalists and Catholics, on the other hand, offered resistance to the movement.

One way to promote eugenics to the church crowd was to twist Scripture passages. Psychologist and secularist G. Stanley Hall, who apparently still felt some affinity to his own twisted version of Christianity, stated that eugenics was "simply a legitimate new interpretation of our Christianity."[70] Hall went on, "We only need to turn a little larger proportion of the love and service we have directed toward God, who does not need it, to man who does, and we have eugenics."[71]

Hall believed that eugenics should be taught at both weekday school and Sunday school but not by the parents. He thought eugenics education should be left to the teacher and clergyman.[72] Elites always want to leave the parents out of the picture, because parents are not experts or professionals in their eyes. This was the case a hundred years ago, and it is still the case today.

Jesus was always about helping the poor and downtrodden. But the eugenicists turned the traditional social welfare attitude upside down. Helping the poor, unfit, or defectives through charity ran against evolution. Eugenicists considered this injurious to the future of the race.[73] Albert Wiggam's *The New Decalogue of Science* (1922) revised the Ten Commandments to conform to the agenda of the eugenics movement. Moses did not hand down this New Decalogue; rather, it came from the "New Mount Sinai": the laboratory. "Had Jesus been among us," Wiggam wrote, "he would have been president of the first Eugenics Congress."[74] Many churches bought into this propaganda.

The American Eugenics Society (AES) formed a Committee on Cooperation with Clergymen to find common ground with the churches so that they could promote eugenic causes. One noteworthy result was a eugenics sermon contest in 1926, with the topic, "Religions and Eugenics: Does the Church Have Any Responsibility for Improving the Human Stock?" Clergymen had to deliver the sermon to a regular congregation, and the contest was open to all pastors, priests, theology students, and rabbis. AES awarded money prizes.[75] In this way the eugenics propaganda reached a wide audience of churchgoers who were more likely to accept eugenics because of their pastors' imprimatur.

The AES furthered the campaign for eugenics by holding exhibits with flashing light displays at state and local fairs. They also worked with local health officials at some of the state fairs across the country, which were meant to raise racial awareness and responsibility and where they subsidized eugenic competitions for families.[76] These ideas were not new to those in the Social Gospel movement, many of whom proposed forcing couples to present health certificates before marriage.[77] Catholics and evangelicals were the most vociferous opponents of this. Former baseball player turned evangelist Billy Sunday blasted these efforts as "godless social service nonsense." He informed those at his revival gatherings that they needed to "get right with God" through accepting Jesus Christ not by turning into amateur sociologists.[78]

Instead of fighting the eugenicists, liberal Protestants in the Social Gospel movement went right along with them. Social Gospel movement proponents thought they were trying to usher in God's kingdom on earth. On the other hand, the secular eugenicists were trying to usher in a human-made utopia devoid of God and based on science. The irony is that the liberal Protestants in the Social Gospel movement were really helping the eugenicists set up their godless, secular kingdom all the while thinking they were setting up God's kingdom.

This is what happens when those embracing a feeble and erroneous theology blindly bow down to science as The Authority in matters of life and ethics, where science really has no authority. This is important because the liberal/nominal Christians who capitulated to the modern cultural zeitgeist a hundred years ago and then unwittingly aided and abetted the kingdom of darkness do not represent a one-time event. This accommodation to evil is going to happen again in the near future, which we will look at in the next chapter. This prediction is a very serious one and requires grave and thoughtful consideration.

The Accommodating Churches in Germany

What about the German churches in the first half of the twentieth century? One would like to think that the churches in Germany would have done a better job standing up to the Nazi regime when compared with their counterparts in America who gave in to the eugenics movement. Sadly, the German churches, as a whole, succumbed to the Nazis for the same reasons the rest of the populace did, namely, a convergence of crises that racked Germany, starting with the ignominious defeat in WWI, the unfair Versailles Treaty, hyperinflation in the early '20s, and the Great Depression, which spread to Germany by 1930.[79] Remember, a crisis always predisposes a citizenry to a regime change, especially to a totalitarian one. Germany suffered one crisis after another, so they were especially vulnerable.

Both Catholics and Protestants in Germany seemed willing to embrace a new government as long as it was anti-Communist. Neither had much loyalty to the Weimar Republic, nor did they find anything especially offensive about the blatant anti-Semitism that was so much a part of Nazi ideology.[80] The Catholic Center Party cast the deciding votes for the Enabling Act, which allowed Hitler to become a virtual dictator. The Vatican signed a Concordat in the hope that Catholics would be protected from any abuses by the Nazis. The Nazis, however, took the signing by the Vatican as implicit sanction of their regime.[81]

Another example of accommodation can be seen in the German Christians, a subgroup of the liberal mainline Protestants.[82] Much of liberal Protestantism in Germany found it easy to make concessions to the state and culture. The German Christians wanted to combine Christianity with Nazism and unite Protestants under one national Reich church.[83] They went so far as to request that any new applicants who were of Jewish descent be considered ineligible for ministry. The German Christians tried to distance Christianity from its Jewish roots by requiring pastors to offer proof of their Aryan ancestry and by requiring them to give unconditional support to the Nazi regime.[84] A small minority of Protestants, known as the Confessing Church, opposed this move. The German religious liberals labeled those in the Confessing Church unpatriotic and narrow-minded.[85]

This is important, because many churches in America today that represent a nominal Christianity are just as susceptible to succumbing to a totalitarian regime as those in Nazi Germany. In fact, Robert P. Ericksen puts it this way: "Germany in the 1930s almost certainly represented church attendance and a sense of Christian commitment and identity similar to that in America today."[86] Although 97 percent of the German population was registered as Christian, it appears that their commitment level was similar to today's practical atheists in our own country. This may be why the German populace found it so easy to go along with the atrocities committed by the Nazis.[87] Like the practical atheists today in America, they were Christian in name only.

Summary

This chapter demonstrated it is entirely possible that our constitutional republic could turn into or be overshadowed by a totalitarian regime. This is already occurring so rapidly now that it is difficult to stay on top of all the ways those in charge are taking away our rights. Given a big enough crisis, we will end up in a political situation akin to Nazi Germany. This could happen a couple of ways: 1) Our country could continue its slide toward totalitarianism, 2) it could surrender or lose its sovereignty to an institution like the UN that wants to set up a one-world government, or 3) it could lose its sovereignty to a mega-corporation or conglomeration of mega-corporations that end up owning everything.

Comparing our country's current circumstances with Nazi Germany demonstrates to skeptics that this has happened before. A major crisis, like a war, financial collapse, pandemic, or nuclear strike, will lead us on our way to martial law, more executive orders, more loss of rights, and the vulnerability to a totalitarian dictator or oligarchy. All of this will be done in the name of promoting peace and security. But a totalitarian dictatorship or oligarchy will not bring peace and security. It will bring enslavement.

The surveillance apparatus that is squeezing away our rights is becoming ever more intrusive with each passing day. Increasingly, our government is no longer *by* the people. The government is now a law unto itself and exists on behalf of the elites. *We* the people don't count.

We saw that part of the surveillance in Nazi Germany involved citizens spying and tattling on one another. This is being encouraged in our own country today and will accelerate as our republic continues to fall apart. The powers that be will find it easier to have their way with the citizenry if they can isolate individuals from their families, coworkers, neighbors, or anyone else who is encouraged to spy and inform on them. I have no doubt that sometime in the future the right to confidentiality with one's doctor, psychologist, psychiatrist, or lawyer will become a thing of the past. The power elites will want to engender an environment in which an individual can't trust anyone. This will make it much easier for them to dominate us. It will be just as it was in Nazi Germany.

One thing that concerns me greatly is that I foresee a day when children will be taken from their parents, or vice versa, based simply on the say-so of a psychologist, social worker, psychiatrist, or anyone in the helping professions to whom the governmental powers give that authority. I think it will become commonplace. Not only would this break up families, which is what the globalists want, but it will isolate the children and the parents and then allow for the brainwashing of those who are isolated.

I also foresee a day when both children and adults will be forced to take psychotropic drugs just on a psychiatrist's say-so. Those in power right now are trying to push for forced vaccinations. If the government can force you to get vaccinated, then it can force you to take a pharmaceutical so that you can maintain your place in society as a dumbed-down sheep. Terrifyingly, I see the mental health professions having an inordinate amount of authority in the future which will be used on behalf of the powers that be as a "soft" way to subdue enemies of the state.

If all of this seems outrageous, remember that the eugenics program instituted in the United States and Germany involved the attempt to rid the planet of the "unfit" while attempting to create a master race. Many global elites haven't given up on this agenda. Once our DNA is catalogued, the elites will probably start cordoning off people with bad heredity along with those they view as a threat.

Thinking about opting out of this sinister agenda? Think again. A GPS tracking device will be on your identity card or driver's license, which will make it hard to run, just like it was in Nazi Germany. If you think it was hard to run then, consider that unlike today, the Nazis did not have Google robots that could chase you through the woods while military drones fired rockets at you from the sky. Good luck with that.

If you take the chip, bio-stamp, or digital tattoo that the New World Order will offer at some point, you aren't going anywhere. They'll be able to track you 24/7 everywhere you go. But at least you'll be able to eat if you're sent to a FEMA camp . . . assuming they don't "disappear" you first.

What about the so-called Christians this go-around? Will they put up more resistance than their predecessors in America or Nazi Germany? I doubt it. Practical atheists have nothing invested in their Christian beliefs, and, therefore, they can be won over by propaganda. Totalitarian regimes are not worried about practical atheists (nominal Christians). When pressured, they won't make waves.

Practicing Christians, however, pose a problem because if they are walking in the light of Jesus Christ they will discern truth from lies. This does not mean Christians are perfect or always walk in the light. But when push comes to shove, authentic Christians will side with truth and leave the consequences to God. This will be costly, because in the future Christians will be targeted for being "dissenters," "religious extremists," and "intolerant," in light of the power elites' agenda. Christians will be made to appear as ignorant fools. Many will suffer a fate worse than ridicule. True Christians will ultimately clash with the New World Order and many will be martyred when the Antichrist takes control of the world.

Without a biblical perspective, many so-called Christians will acquiesce to the New World Order, just as the German Christians submitted to Hitler. A crisis of some sort will make it easy for everyone to look for a savior, who sooner or later will be the Antichrist himself. The lies and deception that are taking place today will be orders of magnitude more prolific at the end of the age. This is why we must, as individuals and as a country, get back to embracing a Christian worldview and the God of the Bible, and have at least a working understanding of biblical eschatology. This is the purpose of the final chapters.

Chapter 18

Lies, Deceptions, and the Beginning of the End Time

The majority of this book has been devoted to unveiling the seculariza-tion process that marginalized Christianity in our society. Without the Christian worldview to light the way, our country will continue to walk in darkness while being oblivious to the peril ahead.

In Chapter sixteen, I defined those who make up the superclass and outlined the agenda of the global elites. In Chapter seventeen, by showing the similarities between Nazi Germany and our own country, I demonstrated how a totalitarian dictatorship or oligarchy could come about in the United States by the hands of the globalists. The point of that chapter was to warn that we are already on our way to losing our rights and being enslaved in some type of totalitarian regime if we continue on our present path.

But the battle between our citizenry and the global elites/shadow government is small compared with the real war going on between the powers of light and the powers of darkness. The real confrontation is ultimately a celestial war between God and the Devil.[1] The Bible is clear on this. "For we do not wrestle against flesh and blood, but against the rulers, against the authorities, against the cosmic powers over this present darkness, against the spiritual forces of evil in the heavenly places" (Eph. 6:12). Ironically, contrary to their supercilious attitude toward the rest of us, the global elites are mere puppets of the *kosmokratoras*, the fallen angelic rulers of darkness that influence world leaders and events.

With this in mind, the aim of these final chapters is to look at how the war for human souls will play out on planet Earth. We will review what we've learned so far and then look at the present state of our country in light of biblical eschatology (the study of the end time). Our republic is in a very vulnerable position right now. I'm afraid that our country and its citizens are not prepared for the deceptions that will be part and parcel of the apocalypse and the end of the age. In short, by embracing (post)modernism and rejecting God there is nothing to light our way. Absent repentance and a turn back to God, we are heading for a post-Christian apocalypse.

Leaving God Behind: Our Vulnerability to Lies and Deception

As I have argued throughout this book, Christianity has been marginalized to the point that we are rapidly becoming a post-Christian nation. We learned that Christianity, which once offered authority and the indispensable moral underpinning of our country, lost its hegemony over time. With each passing generation an increasing percentage of people in our country are leaving God behind. Many people care only about the here and now and give no thought about eternity. Secularism is replacing Christianity as the default worldview of our nation. A good majority of our citizens are practical atheists who go about their everyday lives as if God does not exist.

As noted above, because we have left God behind, our nation and its citizens are now vulnerable to deception. This is important because the deception in the future will be orders of magnitude worse than it is today. The troubling part is that most people today are already buying into many of the lies that those in power are feeding them. If people can't discern truth from error today, how will they separate truth from lies in the future when the deceitfulness will be far worse?

A Big Lie: The Economy Has Recovered

Let's take a momentary detour and look at the economy for just a moment as an example of a big lie. I followed the economy very closely after the stock market freefall in 2008-2009, so let me give you a thumb-nail sketch of what has happened. The fabrications in this area alone are legion. The "best and brightest" tell us that the economy is recovering. This propaganda has been going on for years since the economic debacle of 2008-2009. What the so-called experts fail to tell the public, however, is that all the phony money the Federal Reserve bank printed (and will continue to print) combined with artificially low interest rates are making the economy appear to be recovering, when in reality it is not recovering at all.

We're told the unemployment rate has come down. Another falsehood. The real reason for the drop in the unemployment number is because people have left the work force. Tens of thousands of the unemployed have given up on finding a job, consequently those folks no longer show up in the phony unemployment statistics.

Go back to the beginning of the economic crisis. "Liar loans" created much of the economic debacle of 2008–2009. Banks encouraged these toxic loans and then sold them to other banks and pension funds. The rating agencies gave these financial instruments their blessing with triple-A ratings, which is why the banks were able to unload them. These loans (CDOs) should have been rated junk, because the people signing up for the liar loans often defaulted on their mortgages. Those people were not qualified for a loan. The whole thing was a lie that eventually blew up in our faces.

To give the impression that the economy was recovering after the meltdown, the financial elites spread more propaganda. The stock market turned around in April 2009 after the Financial Accounting Standards Board (FASB) told the banks that they could henceforth mark their assets (like mortgage-backed securities) as if those assets would be held to maturity (not default). Mark-to-market accounting, which the financial industry traditionally used to value assets, was thrown out the window in favor of mark-to-fantasy accounting. The banks were allowed to grade their own papers, so to speak. This was done to give the appearance of solvency in order to restore confidence in the banking system.

Today, one can read about the lying and fraudulent activities of the big banks on almost a daily basis. We're expected to believe justice is served when the big banks (that we bailed out) pay only pennies on the dollar for their wrongdoings after a court decision. This is justice? No, calling this justice is another falsehood.

Many, if not most, markets today are rigged one way or another (the gold and silver markets especially) to keep the status quo going and provide the façade of normalcy. It's all a lie. And it's all coming back down. In short, this whole economic "recovery" is just an artificially low interest rate/money-printing/derivative bubble looking for a pin. The bond market and stock market are both in bubble territory and are going to suffer severe corrections at some point.

With this in mind, it is probable that the next crisis in our country could be an economic one. If true, it will be monumentally calamitous. The power elites will use the crisis to take away more of our rights and begin to corral us further into their New World Order (NWO). This will be easier to accomplish when all hell breaks loose, martial law is declared with bank holidays and bail-ins, and people lose their homes and can't afford to feed themselves.

The population, for the most part, seems unaware of what is coming. People keep going about their daily lives as if everything is normal. They have bought the propaganda that the economy is all right now. Most people apparently believe this nonsense.

In fairness, I think many people have a sense that something is amiss. But most folks seem to be more comfortable putting their heads in the sand. Others are waylaid with every superficial distraction that comes down the pike. Some simply don't care. These attitudes are problematic. In short, we need to start caring about the future of our country *now* while there is still time. A major economic crisis could bring our republic to its knees.

Regarding our apathy, perhaps Aldous Huxley was right. People will love their servitude to the NWO elites. Whistle past the graveyard, text somebody, and pretend everything is copacetic. I promise you at some point in the future, however, people's indifference and blissfully ignorant attitudes will give way to *real-life* cares and concerns.

The Fruit of Secularism: Pragmatic Truth, Moral Relativism, and PC Tolerance

Our culture has bought into secularism which is a false worldview. To the extent that we adhere to secular (post)modernism and bear the rotten fruit of this philosophy is to the same extent we are living a lie. Let's look at how some of the fruit of the secularization process makes us vulnerable to deception.

One fruit of postmodernism is the relativization of truth. We noted in Chapter six that many people in our society today, especially the younger generations, believe truth is relative or pragmatic. In other words, they think that truth is whatever works for them. They are under the mistaken notion that truth is personal, subjective, and relative. But it is not.

Truth is universal, objective, and absolute. Truth is what corresponds with reality. This is why truth applies to everyone universally and absolutely. A lie, on the other hand, is an attempt to distort reality. It endeavors to claim that reality is one way when it is really another. In fact, a lie is what started the whole downward spiral of humanity. The Serpent (Devil) told Eve a lie. He said that reality was not the way God said it was and therefore God deceived her and Adam. The Devil, whom Jesus called "the father of lies," is constantly trying to steal and distort God's reality.

The secular worldview promotes the lie that God does not exist (atheism) or that He can be ignored (practical atheism). Moreover, secularism is appealing to an increasing number of people in our society. The power elites are particularly susceptible to atheistic secularism. The truth, however, is that God exists and all of us, including the global elites, are accountable to Him. Practical atheists and secularists willingly or unwittingly ignore the fact of God's existence.

With God safely out of the way, practical atheists are free from accountability to God. This leads to producing more secular fruit. People today think they can live autonomously—a law unto themselves—which is another falsehood. And in turn, autonomy leads to moral relativism. By ignoring God's existence, secularists and practical atheists are free to set their own moral standards. They don't want anyone interfering with their lifestyles. But making up one's values by pretending God doesn't exist is simply not true and won't work because God is the source of moral absolutes. Moral absolutes are based on God's character. If an individual ignores the moral absolutes that stem from God's character, then that individual (and those people he or she affects) will sooner or later suffer the consequences as a result.

For example, Emily Letts, an abortion counselor, posted a three-minute video of herself having an abortion. It went viral on the Internet. She posted the video to destigmatize the abortion "procedure." (Calling the killing of a baby a "procedure" is a disingenuous way of alleviating the mother of any moral considerations in the abortion.) At the end of the video, she states, "I knew what I was going to do was right, because it was right for me and no one else."[2] This is the essence of autonomy and moral relativism. With God out of the picture, each individual can do whatever is right for him or her. Morals become relative to each person.

This young lady went on to say, "I don't think guilt is a productive feeling." She told a reporter, "I forgave myself for not using birth control, I corrected it, and I moved forward."[3] She corrected it? By having an abortion? I would kindly inform Ms. Letts that the guilt feelings she mentioned, often, but not always, arise because God has given us a conscience. Unfortunately, most people's consciences today have been seared with a hot iron. Someone should inform Ms. Letts that true moral guilt is something only God can forgive (through Jesus Christ), not by forgiving yourself.

In short, we are living in a country where we think truth is whatever we perceive it to be, want it to be, or whatever works for us. This has spilled over into the moral realm, where now we can no longer discern the difference between right and wrong. We do whatever is right in our own eyes. In a feeble attempt to try to absolve ourselves of true moral guilt, we created an unspoken pact with one another. You don't judge me and I won't judge you. Anything goes. This is PC tolerance—a rotten fruit of the secularization process.

PC tolerance is the most prized moral value in our society today. This cannot be overstated. It has replaced truth and moral absolutes which are based on God's character. PC tolerance reinforces moral autonomy and moral relativism and makes everyone feel accepted in whatever lifestyle they choose. PC tolerance, moral relativism, and moral autonomy are the fruit of secularization and demonstrate a total disregard for God Almighty, who alone defines what is morally right and wrong. In short, there is no fear of the Lord in our land anymore.

Our increasingly post-Christian society has deceived itself by embracing the secular worldview. To repeat: unless we repent and turn back to God, we will be much more susceptible to lies in the future.

The Global Elites Are Not as Smart as They Think They Are

Fear of the Lord is especially lacking among the power brokers and the global elites. These folks are secularists who think only about the here and now. As I've stated numerous times, these people think they are smarter and better than you. But are they? No, they are not. If "the fear of the Lord is the beginning of wisdom"[4] and the elites have no fear of the Lord, then by definition they have no wisdom. By earthly standards and measures they might be regarded as intelligent. They can pat one another on the back and tell each other how great they are, all the while looking down their noses at the rest of us. But so-called intelligence and being wealthy does not equal wisdom. Wisdom is seeing things from God's perspective.

The elites' intransigence toward the reality of God's existence allows them to be autonomous and disregard their accountability to Him. But they are ignorant of judgment day and eternity, which awaits them as well as the rest of us. They are too busy being big shots to give thought to any of this. Their hubris has deceived them into lusting after power and wealth as if this life is all there is. The apostle Paul described these people this way: "They are darkened in their understanding, alienated from the life of God because of the ignorance that is in them, due to their hardness of heart" (Eph. 4:18). These elites care more about the praise of men rather than the praise of God.

It would be bad enough if the elites destroyed only their own lives by ignoring God, but their secular/godless mind-set affects us all. As we pointed out in the two previous chapters, the global elites have an agenda. The great mass of humanity will not fare well if their agenda comes to fruition. We are just "useless eaters" in their eyes. Many globalists are already monetarily affluent, so their next priority involves acquiring *physical* wealth. They want to make sure that the rest of us don't consume all of the earth's resources, which they consider theirs. In short, they're paranoid. When their paranoia combines with their godless hearts, the result is a toxic combination. Instead of using their immeasurable wealth to help people, the globalists instead want to eliminate or enslave the vast majority of the human population.

We must keep an eye on the globalists, because these folks are doing the Devil's work. The globalists use every available lie and deception to slowly but surely carry out their evil agenda. In fact, it is probable that they will aid (unwittingly, or in some cases knowingly) in setting up the kingdom of Antichrist. Is it any wonder that our country is showing marked resemblances to Nazi Germany?

The time to wake up is now. Waiting for a crisis, whether it is another economic meltdown, pandemic, nuclear strike, or war, will be too late. Some type of real crisis or false flag (contrived crisis) will allow the globalists to implement their agenda much more easily under the guise of maintaining law and order (peace and security) once martial law is declared.

Meanwhile, the overwhelming majority of people in our country are so mesmerized by the latest distractions in entertainment and technology that they allow their rights to be taken away from them on a daily basis. They have no idea that a totalitarian regime and then a NWO ultimately headed by the Antichrist lies ahead. A greater part of our population, and those in other countries, will be sucked into this vortex of lies without any realization of what is happening or what is at stake.

The irony is that the global elites, who are in the process of setting up this NWO, don't realize that they too will be deceived. The globalists don't realize that they too will be little pawns used by the future Antichrist to do his bidding. At some point in the future the Antichrist will consolidate his power and rule the world. The globalists, who think they are better and smarter than everyone else, will end up worshiping the Antichrist like everyone else who falls for his deceptions.

In the meantime, the globalists alive today will continue to deceive and be deceived. If they hang around long enough they, and everyone else on this planet, will find out who's really in charge. Spoiler Alert—It's not the global elites, and it's not the future Antichrist. It's the Lord Jesus Christ. And when He comes back for His bride (the church), I promise you that everyone on the planet will know who's really in charge.

Antichrist and the Coming Apocalypse

Let's look at how the globalist's NWO intersects with Bible prophecy. My goal here is modest. I merely want to offer a glimpse as to how future events may play out in light of Scripture. The accuracy (or inaccuracy) of the scenarios I offer in the next few chapters will become clearer as we near the end of the age. The "end of the age" may be defined as a future event when the church (the universal body of believers in Jesus Christ) will be raptured from the planet when Jesus returns (*parousia*). After this, God will pour out His wrath on the planet of unbelievers who follow the Antichrist.

For those unfamiliar with biblical eschatology, the Antichrist will be a human instrument (and perhaps partly machine) of the Devil. The Antichrist will be a pseudo-Christ, a false Christ. As a phony Christ, the Antichrist will be a colossal liar, who may even claim he is Jesus Christ. The Antichrist will either set up or attempt to set up a kingdom—probably a New World Order. Antichrist's kingdom will be a fake, secular, man-made kingdom that people will be forced to join if they want to buy or sell anything.

One of Antichrist's major deceptions will involve deceiving Israel into signing a seven-year covenant with him. He will break that covenant three and a half years later.[5] After breaking the covenant, Antichrist will defile the Jewish temple and claim to be God. This is known as the "abomination of desolation." At that time, the Antichrist will draw a line of delineation, and no middle ground will be available. You or your children or your children's children or grandchildren will be forced to make a choice. There will be no waffling or pretending to believe in God, like the typical practical atheist is allowed to do today. So what is the "choice" the Antichrist will offer?

The Antichrist will force people to take a "mark" on their right hand or on their forehead if they want to be able to buy or sell anything. If they take the mark, they will have chosen to side with Antichrist and to be a part of his kingdom.[6] The Antichrist will deceive most people on the planet into thinking that he is the real Christ.[7] But he will be a false Christ. He may even entice people by claiming that they can be a god just like him.

The Antichrist's kingdom will probably be some type of NWO on steroids. To repeat—the consequence of not siding with Antichrist is that people who don't have his mark won't be able to buy or sell anything. This will make it next to impossible to live, because those people won't have access to the necessities of life.

Many Christians at that time will refuse to side with Antichrist and will be martyred.[8] Many nominal Christians (practical atheists) and even professing Christians during this time will begin to fall away from the orthodox Christian worldview, because adhering to Christianity will be too costly. These poor souls will end up denying the living and true God of the Bible and side with Antichrist instead. This is known as the "apostasy."[9]

The decisions one will be forced to make at that time will have eternal consequences, not just everyday practical consequences. The pressure to side with the Antichrist and his fake secular kingdom will be tremendous. The reason all of this is so important is because we are slowly but surely heading in the direction of the biblical apocalypse and the end of the age. This is a serious matter, which is why the biblical picture must be brought to light now while there is still time to spiritually and emotionally prepare.

We must be willing to unabashedly inform and prepare the generations coming up behind us of the deceptions that lie ahead. This is made all the more difficult because practical atheists don't care about God, and the generations coming up behind us don't believe half the doctrines of the Bible anymore. People today think they are above the Bible. Trying to explain biblical eschatology to those who don't have a firm grasp of the fundamentals of Christianity is a daunting task.

Evangelicals' Apathy and the Pre-Tribulation Rapture

This dire situation is exacerbated by the fact that even many evangelical churches today are not concerned about the end time. Part of the reason for this lackadaisical attitude toward the end of the age may be that most evangelical Protestants don't believe they will be here when the Antichrist comes to power. In fact, most evangelicals think they will be raptured before Daniel's seventieth week, which is otherwise referred to (erroneously) as the seven-year "tribulation." Almost all of us who were brought up in evangelical circles were taught the pre-tribulation rapture. But this is a false end time doctrine. One of the major tenets of this eschatology is that Jesus may return at any moment. But this is not scriptural.

Let's briefly look at what the Bible actually says regarding the rapture of the church. Space will permit only pointing out the most egregious errors with the pre-tribulation position.

One thing to keep in mind, is that most end time scholars agree that the Antichrist will sign a seven-year (peace) agreement with Israel which marks the beginning of the seven-year time frame known as Daniel's seventieth "week." Those holding to the pre-tribulation position don't think they will be here to see that occur because they think the church will be raptured just before the Antichrist signs this covenant. But let's look at what the Bible states.

The primary reason the apostle Paul wrote his second letter to the Thessalonians is because they thought they had missed the rapture. The Thessalonians were being heavily persecuted, and they thought they had entered the tribulation period. The apostle Paul wrote to assure them the day of the Lord had not already occurred and therefore they had not missed the rapture. Keep in mind that the rapture and the day of the Lord are back-to-back events. In order to prove to the Thessalonians that they did not miss the rapture the apostle Paul laid out a chronology of events:

> Now concerning the coming [*parousias*] of our Lord Jesus Christ and our being gathered together to him [the rapture], we ask you, brothers, not to be quickly shaken in mind or alarmed, either by a spirit or a spoken word, or a letter seeming to be from us, to the effect that the day of the Lord has come. *Let no one deceive you in any way. For that day will not come, unless the rebellion [apostasia] comes first, and the man of lawlessness is revealed*, the son of destruction, who opposes and exalts himself against every so-called god or object of worship, so that he takes his seat in the temple of God, proclaiming himself to be God. (2 Thessalonians 2:1–4)

The apostle Paul did not want the Thessalonians to be deceived. He made it clear that the day of the Lord could not occur until the man of lawlessness (Antichrist) defiles the Jewish temple in what is known as the abomination of desolation. So Jesus's return can't be imminent because the abomination of desolation has to take place first. Jesus told his followers to be watching for this event so that they would know His return is near. In fact Jesus told his disciples, "So when you see the abomination of desolation spoken of by the prophet Daniel..." (Matt. 24:15a). Jesus clearly expected his followers in the end time generation to see the abomination of desolation.

So when does the abomination of desolation occur? According to Daniel the prophet, whom Jesus referred to above, this abomination occurs in the middle of Daniel's seventieth week—in other words, in the middle of the seven-year period (Dan. 9:27). This is crucial. The apostle Paul stated that the day of the Lord and the rapture can't take place until *after* the abomination of desolation occurs. And since the abomination of desolation doesn't occur until the *middle* of the seven-year period of Daniel's seventieth week, the rapture cannot occur until at least three and a half years into the seven-year time frame.

Moreover, the rapture *cannot* occur at the beginning of Daniel's seventieth week as pre-tribulationists believe. This means Christians will indeed be here for at least three and a half years of the seven years. In fact, Jesus told his disciples that "they will deliver you up to tribulation and put you to death, and you will be hated by all nations for my name's sake" (Matt. 24:9). The first three and a half years will involve tribulation of the saints by a world which is rejecting God. The saints may also be persecuted by the emerging Antichrist. This tribulation (persecution) increases dramatically after Antichrist claims he is "God" at the abomination of desolation.

In fact, later in Matthew 24, Jesus points this out. He states that after the abomination of desolation occurs there will be "great tribulation" (v. 20). This will be a time when Antichrist's wrath directed at Christians will be turned up exponentially just after the middle of the seven-year period. Multitudes of Christians will be martyred. But Jesus will cut this persecution short when He returns.

In summary, it is "immediately *after* the tribulation of those days" (v. 29) that the day of the Lord and the rapture will occur (v. 31). So though we don't know the exact day or hour of Jesus's return (v. 36), we know one thing. Jesus will return to rapture His church *after* the abomination of desolation and *after* the "great tribulation" of Antichrist both of which are at least three and a half years into Daniel's seventieth week. Christians who think they will be raptured *before* the seven-year period are simply wrong. There is no place where this is found in Scripture. There is also no evidence that Jesus will return in secret. When Jesus returns, everyone on the planet will know (Matt. 24:30-31, Mk. 14:62).

Where those who believe in the pre-tribulation rapture go wrong is that they think the entire seven-year period is God's wrath. Therefore, they believe that Christians won't be here to suffer God's wrath during any part of the seven-year period. I agree with them that Christians will be raptured *before* God's wrath is poured out on Antichrist and his followers in the day of the Lord. But the day of the Lord doesn't begin until *after* the mid-point of Daniel's seventieth week. God's judgment begins when the sixth seal is broken (Rev. 6:12–17; Matt. 24:29) *after* the abomination of desolation and *after* the "great tribulation" of the saints. Both of these events won't occur until at least halfway through the seven-year period.

In short, Christians *will* be around for at least the first three and a half years of Daniel's seventieth week. During the first three and a half years the four horsemen of the Apocalypse will start to wreak havoc on the planet. This is not God's wrath, however. It is a time of natural calamities as a result of God allowing Satan to have his way when the Antichrist comes to power.

Regrettably, most pastors today don't care about any of this. For many church leaders, ignoring or avoiding what the Bible says about the end of the age is conveniently downplayed in favor of "making disciples." Many pastors and church leaders today seem to have a lopsided theology regarding what is involved in making a disciple.

Although bringing people to the Lord is no doubt an imperative, and should be one of Christians' primary concerns, making disciples also involves much more than this. It also involves teaching sound doctrine to those who already belong to the Lord. In other words, there should be some depth to each Christian's faith. It should not remain on the superficial level.

We saw in Chapter two, however, that many Christians today don't believe half the doctrines of Christianity anymore and others are biblical illiterates like their unchurched counterparts in the world. This tragedy ultimately falls at the feet of the pastors who are called to shepherd and teach the flock, not simply to bring in new converts. In short, I think pastors need to stop worrying so much about the size of their churches and start concerning themselves a little more with nurturing the existing flock.

With this in mind, one of the reasons teaching eschatology is so important is because the Bible talks far more about Jesus's coming (*parousia*) than most Christians are aware. For example, the Bible talks about the need to be born again, which is the foundation of the gospel, nine times. It talks about the need for repentance seventy times. But the Bible talks about Jesus's return three hundred eighty times.[10] This fact is lost on church leaders today. There is little if any preaching on Jesus's *parousia*.

We saw above that part of the reason for this may be that evangelicals have embraced the erroneous pre-tribulation rapture eschatology which can lead to indifference regarding the end of the age. But I think it is also due, at least in some way, to what I might label the "Laodicean church model." We think we are rich, comfortable, and in need of nothing in our big, fancy, casual, modern churches. But we are miserable, poor, blind, and naked. In my opinion, the vast majority of our churches are not ready for the persecution that is on the way.

As H. L. Nigro points out in her important work, *Before God's Wrath*: "God has a plan. He gave us the signs of His coming and we are given careful instruction to watch for them so that we can be prepared. Unfortunately, we haven't heeded His warning. As we sit on the edge of the rise of the Antichrist, the greatest natural and spiritual disaster in history, the Church is an army asleep."[11]

The *Left Behind* series popularized the pre-tribulation rapture. Unfortunately, most evangelicals are too apathetic to check the Bible to see if the pre-tribulation doctrine holds water. It doesn't. The insidious part of this false eschatology is that Christians who think they will be raptured before Antichrist's reign obviously find no need to worry about it. These Christians, or more likely their children or grandchildren, will be taken totally by surprise and will not be prepared for the persecution (tribulation) that will arise when Antichrist comes to power.

Christian parents who believe in the pre-tribulation rapture are placing their children, grandchildren, or great grandchildren in peril by teaching them not to worry about the tribulation and the Antichrist. These kids will be confused and disheartened as adults, and will be far more likely to fall away from the faith when things don't unfold as they were taught, and they find themselves facing unimaginable persecution under the Antichrist. Some may even take the mark of the Beast (Antichrist) in the apostasy.

We must begin to demonstrate some urgency in this regard because the move toward totalitarianism is already occurring. This is important because it may be a precursor to the NWO and the rise of Antichrist. As we saw in the previous two chapters, forces are moving right now (the global elites) to control every aspect of our lives until we have no rights left at all. The globalists want to eliminate "surplus population" and put the rest of us to work for them in the NWO. It is probably not a coincidence that both the NWO elites and the future Antichrist want to rule the entire world.

Some may scoff at all of this. If you are one of them, know that two thousand years ago the apostle Peter predicted that people would scoff at Jesus's return.[12] I would like to assure the reader that betting against the Bible is a dubious endeavor. Jesus promised to come back for His true church, the bride of Christ. With the way things are beginning to line up both historically and biblically, I think the evidence points to the fact that we may be approaching the *beginning* of the end of the age in the not-too-distant future. This is why these issues are so important. However, I want to go on record and say that in my opinion we are not quite as close to the end of the age as some Christian writers seem to think.

To cite one example, one author I saw on television asserted that we are as far along as the sixth trumpet judgment. I would humbly point out that if this observation was true we would already be able to identify the Antichrist. But at the time of this writing the Antichrist has not even signed the covenant with Israel so we don't know who he is. In addition, if we are as far along in the Biblical timeline as the sixth trumpet, then the abomination of desolation would already have occurred. But neither of these events has happened therefore that author's observation is impossible.

My concern is that making false predictions or proclamations regarding the *timeline* for the end time apocalypse, by forcing today's events into Scripture, will do more harm than good. If we continually proclaim that the end of the age is upon us when it is not, people won't be open to the signs of the end of the age when it *is* truly imminent. In other words, if we "cry wolf" too often and our observations (or predictions) are incorrect then we desensitize the church and the world to the genuine warning signs that Jesus told us to look for (Matt. 24) when the apocalypse is truly upon us.

My thought is that we may have at least a generation or more to go before the Lord returns. I could certainly be wrong. Perhaps the end of the age is nearer than I suspect. But it seems that every generation sees itself as the one where the world will end. Every generation seems to think "it can't get any worse than this." And yet, every generation making that claim has been wrong. One can't help but recall all the commotion *The Late Great Planet Earth* caused back in the 1970s. Crying wolf does no one any good. The least we can do is try to understand something of the *timing* and *chronology* of the end time events which can be discerned from what we know for *certain* in Scripture. Scripture should always be the template, not today's events.

In short, we should be careful not to confuse or conflate calamitous events, (as severe as they may be), with biblical apocalyptic events. In other words, just because certain events may look really calamitous does not necessarily mean the biblical apocalypse is upon us. Many events may only be garden-variety catastrophes. We need to keep the Scriptural *timeline* as our guide so we know where we are at in the eschatological chronology.

Until the Antichrist signs a treaty with Israel that we can clearly identify, then the most we can say is that we are not at the beginning of the end of the age as of now. A couple of other things that need to occur is the Temple needs to be rebuilt in Jerusalem, and also a city has to emerge that resembles Babylon the great as described in Revelation 17 and 18. At the time of this writing none of these biblical events are in place, therefore we are not at the beginning of Daniel's seventieth week just yet.

In any case, it is imperative that we prepare not only to resist the advances of the NWO (which is probably a precursor to the Antichrist) but to also wait expectantly for the Lord's return because He asked those of us who belong to Him to do so. As the bride of Christ we should purify ourselves and spiritually prepare for the persecution that will come upon us for our unwavering faith in the Lord Jesus Christ.

Just to be clear—even though I am *predicting* that the Lord's return is still a ways off does not mean we should not *prepare* for it now. Does a bride wait until a few days before the wedding day to begin preparing? No. Though the wedding may be some time in the future she begins preparing as if it is imminent. The bride of Christ (the church) should also prepare for the Lord's return as if it is imminent. At the bare minimum we should sound the warning for the generations coming up behind us.

If you don't belong to Jesus, then now is the time to reconsider your stand with Him, because you or your children or your children's children or grandchildren don't want to be deceived and end up on the Antichrist's side when the apocalypse goes down. If your children don't hear about this now from you, who will prepare them for the coming deceptions and the biblical apocalypse?

The Beginning of the End

Let's continue to look at how the beginning of the end of the age might play out. Although we don't know right now what current events may be taking place in the future, we nevertheless can follow a chronology of biblical events from Scripture that will make it easier to see what we should be looking for as Daniel's seventieth week approaches.

Jesus's disciples asked Him point-blank what the sign of His return and the end of the age would be. Instead of sprawling headlong into all the signs of His return, Jesus started with something very sobering. The first thing out of Jesus's mouth was, "See that no one leads you astray. For many will come in my name saying 'I am the Christ,' and they will lead many astray" (Matt. 24:4–5).

This is important. Jesus's first concern was to make it clear to His disciples that they could be deceived. This cannot be overemphasized, which is why we spent so much time above warning about lies and deceptions. Christians today who are waiting for the Lord's return must take Jesus's warning about avoiding deception very seriously.

In the Scripture passage above, Jesus went on to say that some imposters would claim that they are Christ Himself. This is probably what the Antichrist will do and why it is important to be able to discern these false Christs from the real Jesus Christ. Accepting someone in the future who claims to be the Christ when he is not means embracing the Antichrist, or one of the many phony Christs, instead of the real Jesus Christ.

So what might be worth watching as we move step by step closer to the beginning of the seven-year period Jesus outlined in Matthew 24? There will probably be the continual move toward a one-world government/NWO. As far as our own country is concerned I think we will continue to lose our rights as the globalists continue to turn our country into a totalitarian regime. I think at some point a crisis like an economic collapse, pandemic, or a nuclear strike on one or more major cities could expedite the loss of US sovereignty. This would make it easier for our country to be absorbed into the NWO under the auspices of the UN, for example. It is possible that foreign troops could enter our country under the guise of "peace keeping" in order to "help" maintain law and order under a UN jurisdiction. Guns will be confiscated at that time if they haven't been already.

It is also possible that foreign entities may enter (invade) our country because by that time they may own a lot of our assets after an economic collapse in addition to the fact that we would be extremely vulnerable after an economic disintegration. In any case, at some point it is almost a certainty that the United States will cease to enjoy the hegemony and autonomy it has now. Some type of crisis will have a lot to do with expediting the loss of our national sovereignty. This could also be a reason our country is not mentioned in Scripture.

Some would contest this. Many observers think that the United States is "Babylon the great," as described in Revelation. This is extremely improbable. Babylon the great is a city (*polis*) not a nation (*ethnos*). The Bible states this clearly: "Alas! Alas! You great city, (*polis*) you mighty city (*polis*), Babylon! For in a single hour your judgment has come" (Rev. 18:10b). Another verse makes a clear distinction between a city and a nation while at the same time mentioning Babylon the great: "The great city (*polis*) was split into three parts, and the cities (*poleis*) of the nations (*ethnon*) fell, and God remembered Babylon the great to make her drain the cup of the wine of the fury of his wrath" (Rev. 16:19).

The United States cannot be Babylon the great because the United States is a nation, not a city. If the Bible wanted to inform us that Babylon the great is a nation, it would have done so in the verse just cited. But it didn't. That verse made a clear distinction between cities and nations. Babylon the great is a city. Again, we must be careful to make sure our assessments of the end of the age line up with Scripture to the best of our abilities. As Christians we should strive to rightly divide the Word of truth.

This provides another reason why I believe we have some time left before the end of the age. At the time of this writing, there are no cities like Babylon the great, as described in the book of Revelation. We will have a clearer idea of how this will look as we get closer to the beginning of the end of the age.

Those who are familiar with Christian eschatology know that the Antichrist will reveal his true identity when he signs a seven-year covenant with Israel known as their "covenant with death."[13] As noted above, the signing of this treaty starts the seven-year period called Daniel's seventieth week.[14] This will mark the beginning of the end. This is precisely the time Jesus referred to when He warned His disciples not to be deceived. This Antichrist, who is referred to by many other names in Scripture (the Beast, Prince to Come, Son of Perdition, Lawless One, Man of Sin),[15] will be consolidating his power during the first three and a half years. During this time Jesus said there will be wars and rumors of wars, nation rising against nation, earthquakes in diverse places, famines and pestilences.[16] These natural disasters will probably be much more prolific than they are now.

Chapter 6 in the book of Revelation outlines the same events that Jesus talked about in Matthew 24. Interestingly, the apostle John, who wrote the book of Revelation, heard a voice say, "A quart of wheat for a denarius, and three quarts of barley for a denarius, and do not harm the oil and wine!" (Rev. 6:6b). A denarius in Jesus's day was equivalent to a day's wage. If in the future it's going to take a day's wage just to buy a quart of wheat, it is possible that John saw hyperinflation taking place. Hyperinflation is part-and-parcel of an economic collapse. This would be occurring during the first three and a half years of Daniel's seventieth week and could be the result of wars ravaging countries which subsequently collapse their economies and currencies.

The other interesting thing worth noting in Revelation 6 is the final rider of the four horsemen of the Apocalypse, who rode a pale horse, "And the rider's name was Death, and Hades followed him" (v. 8a). The verse goes on: "They were given authority over a fourth of the earth, to kill with the sword and with famine and with pestilence and by wild beasts of the earth" (v. 8b). It appears likely that a lot of people who are living in the quarter of the earth where this authority is given may be killed with some kind of pandemic disease (swine flu, for example) that originated in the wild beasts of the earth. It could also be a technologically bio-engineered plague, maybe even produced by the global elites.

All of the events that occur in the first three and a half years of Daniel's seventieth week as described in the books of Matthew and Revelation are either natural or man-made events; meaning God's wrath does not cause them. God's wrath will come later. When God's fury is poured out, no one will doubt that His wrath is occurring rather than natural event(s). The events Jesus described so far—earthquakes, pestilences, wars, etc., are the beginning of "birth pangs."[17] Jesus made it clear that those events will not mark the end of the age, rather, the *beginning* of the end. God will allow (not cause) these events, which are carried out by the four horsemen of the Apocalypse who are up to no good.

The Antichrist will be coming to power amid all of the chaos caused by the natural disasters and wars taking place during the first three and a half years. He will be a monumental liar who will probably gain military control, and then political control of the world. As noted above, at the middle point of the seven-year period, Antichrist will break his pact with Israel. He will invade the temple in Jerusalem in what is known as the "abomination of desolation" described in Daniel 9:27 and which Jesus refers to in Matthew 24:15. Antichrist will take his seat in the Jewish temple, opposing and exalting himself against every so-called god or object of worship while claiming to be God.[18]

The Antichrist and the Mark of the Beast

How will a man, who will probably be some smooth-talking globalist, pull this off? Well, the conditions at that time will be ripe for him to step into power, just like they were for Hitler. There will be wars, death from pestilences, natural disasters, economies collapsing with hyperinflation, widespread lawlessness, and chaos as a normal state of affairs. People will be clamoring for someone to put an end to all of the strife. Remember what Bezmenov said back in Chapter sixteen? During a crisis people will look for a "savior."

Because the Antichrist will be a fake Christ, he will attempt to set up a kingdom just like people expected Jesus to do when He came to earth two thousand years ago. I think Antichrist will promise some sort of peaceful global utopia. He will deceive the majority of the earth's population into thinking that this is attainable. He will probably be able to put an end to a lot of the wars as he sets up his one-world government.

Let's look at this from a biblical perspective first and then try to ascertain what might happen on the everyday level. Revelation 13 gives us an idea of how this Antichrist, who is referred to as the Beast in this particular chapter, will operate.

And the beast was given a mouth uttering haughty and blasphemous words, and it was allowed to exercise authority for forty-two months. It opened its mouth to utter blasphemies against God, blaspheming his name and his dwelling, that is, those who dwell in heaven. Also it was allowed to make war on the saints and to conquer them. And authority was given it over every tribe and people and language and nation, and all who dwell on earth will worship it, everyone whose name has not been written before the foundation of the world in the book of life of the Lamb that was slain. . . . Also it causes all, both small and great, both rich and poor, both free and slave, to be marked on the right hand or the forehead, so that no one can buy or sell unless he has the mark, that is, the name of the beast or the number of its name. This calls for wisdom: let the one who has understanding calculate the number of the beast, for it is the number of a man, and his number is 666. (Revelation 13:5–8, 16–18)

The Antichrist will bring together many facets of society under a one-world system. There will probably be a one-world government (political), one-world monetary system (economic), and one-world religion (spiritual), which will all coalesce under the umbrella of the NWO.

Once the Antichrist/Beast/Man of Sin declares himself to be God, everything will change. The Bible says that everyone will be saying "peace and security" at some point.[19] It is unclear whether this will happen right after Antichrist signs the covenant with Israel or whether "peace and security" will occur after Antichrist declares he is God in the middle of Daniel's seventieth week. I lean toward the view that this "peace" will occur near the middle of Daniel's seventieth week just after the abomination of desolation. At any rate, bringing about the cessation of war, even for a short time, will be an unbelievable feat to pull off. Everyone will worship the Antichrist as though he were the real Christ, the Prince of Peace.

Let's look at some other things that will be taking place at the end of the age.

It is clear today that we are heading toward a cashless economy. We saw in the verses above that after the Antichrist takes over, no one on the planet will be able to buy or sell without taking his mark. Jesus predicted famines would occur, so we know there will probably be widespread food shortages. People are going to want to eat, so most will give in and take the Antichrist's mark.

The prevalent thinking right now is that the mark will be an RFID (radio-frequency identification) chip of some sort implanted in the person's right hand (Revelation 13 says it could be the forehead as well). It may also be a digital tattoo. Tattoos are increasingly popular, especially among the younger generations. By the time of the Antichrist, technology will be such that the chip, or whatever the "mark" is at that time, will probably contain all of the individual's personal identification and so-called vital information. This will include health records, income, bank accounts, employment record, political affiliation, driving record, criminal record, religious beliefs, and anything else the government or the NWO can get its hands on. Some of this information will probably be obtained from the screening process (read: enslavement procedure) going on in the public school system. According to one observer, "multipurpose identification" may begin as early as birth.[20] The generations coming up behind us will already be conditioned to relinquishing their personal rights. Personal privacy will be a thing of the past. The Antichrist/Beast system will probably be able to track everyone's whereabouts 24/7. You won't be able to go to the bathroom without the beast-system knowing it.

Whether or not the RFID chip ends up being the mark of the Beast, one thing is certain, we are already rapidly moving toward a loss of privacy today. The move toward some sort of RFID chip in licenses has already occurred in four states. It is probable that before long all state licenses will have an RFID chip buried in them because of "the cozy relationship between Homeland Security and the spychip industry," says Katherine Albrecht and Liz McIntyre, authors of *Spychips*.[21] In the coming years we will see the rise of biometric scanning where, for example, a person will place a finger or hand over a scanner that will identify him or her. This will open the way for the next step, when the RFID chip will be embedded in the hand so that people's personal information can be "protected" from theft, etc. The authors of *Spychips* put it this way: "Governments like to assure their citizens that surveillance will make them safer, but surveillance is more likely to ensure the security of the regime in power than to protect the citizens. Once surveillance tools are in place, governments are tempted to use them to identify and hassle people who oppose their rule."[22]

So, for example, an armband, hand implant, or deep organ implant could be used by the government/NWO to do any number of things from a distance. These devices could release a high voltage shock or release drugs into the victim to render the person unconscious (or worse). The powers that be could also track large numbers of the population at a time. Much of this will already be in place by the time Antichrist comes to power. The surveillance at that time will be overwhelming. The tagging programs always start with those who can't refuse them: government employees, the military, school children, and prisoners.[23] At some point, tracking/tagging will be so ubiquitous, people won't think twice about being enslaved by this technology.

Even before Antichrist shows up on the scene, true Christians will begin to resist this invasive technology, because those who are awake will see where this is going. In the future, taking the mark of the Beast will signify that one belongs to Antichrist's NWO. True, awake Christian believers will not take the mark under any circumstances. Therefore, the world will ridicule them for being backward and ignorant. Of course, in our increasingly post-Christian nation, ridicule of Christians is *already* occurring. But the derision and hatred of Christians will be far greater in the future. Jesus said, "If the world hates you, know that it has hated me before it hated you. If you were of the world, the world would love its own" (John 15:18–19a).

In fact, after the great tribulation begins, Christians will be Antichrist's first target. As we noted above, Jesus told His disciples, "They will deliver you up to tribulation and put you to death, and you will be hated by all nations for my name's sake" (Matt. 24:9). Revelation 13:7 confirms this when it says that Antichrist "was allowed to make war on the saints and to conquer them." Many Christians will go into hiding, which will be difficult. Others will be beheaded for their faith in Jesus Christ when the Antichrist's wrath is poured out on believers during the great tribulation.[24]

Christians will be hated so much because they will be the only ones on the planet who will stay true to the living God besides the two witnesses (Rev. 11:3) and the 144,000 Jews who follow the Lamb (Rev. 14:1–4). PC tolerance will be in full force as the whole world cries "peace and security." Antichrist will mesmerize everyone.

PC tolerance will be promoted because it will bring unity. After suffering the devastating chaos of wars, pestilences, and earthquakes, people will not want to hear Christians' warning that the Antichrist and his one-world system are a counterfeit. In a world that is proclaiming tolerance, there will be no tolerance for people who won't toe the party line.

In what's left of our country, many Christians will probably be rounded up and sent off to FEMA camps to suffer their fate, just like Nazi Germany sent the dissidents and Jews to concentration camps. The persecution of Christians will be taking place worldwide as well.

Spying and Psychopharmaceutical Reeducation in the Future

Widespread spying on neighbors, coworkers, parents, etc., will be taking place during the time leading up to and including the great tribulation. This will translate into more persecution of Christians. It is important to note that Jesus corroborated this: "You will be delivered up even by parents and brothers and relatives and friends, and some of you they will put to death" (Luke 21:16). Let's look at how this overwhelming surveillance could occur.

As we mentioned in previous chapters, those in power are trying to undermine the authority of parents today. While I was writing this section I came across an article where a Michigan mother took her seventeen-year-old daughter to the doctor to have the daughter's injured foot looked at. The staff informed the mother that before the doctor could see her daughter, the law required that a nurse have a private, five-minute conversation with her daughter. The mother also learned that children (ages twelve to seventeen) could obtain online access to their medical records and block their parents from viewing those records on the Website. This is the law in Michigan.[25] It won't be long before this is the law in every state. Soon children will be dictating to the parents what the parents can and cannot do with them.

The elites want your children to side with them. As I pointed out in a previous chapter, they think they own your kids. Children will be turning in their parents to the authorities for all kinds of things, even before the great tribulation takes place.

I am also predicting that mental health screening for everyone will be mandatory in our country at some point in the future. This will be another form of spying and tattling. It will give those in charge the ability to weed out nonconformists. Political dissidents, Christians, gun owners (if guns haven't already been confiscated by then), and military veterans, for example, will test positive for some contrived mental illness. Of course, in the not too distant future, opposing the government or the NWO by definition will be considered a mental illness. It will probably be labeled "Oppositional Defiance Disorder," which is the neologism psychiatrists today attach to children who have trouble getting along with others. Of course, the psychotherapeutic community has no proof that such a disorder exists. But if psychotherapy doesn't work, they may offer (force) psychotropics on people to help them "cope" with this "disorder." More on why the psychotropic "remedy" worries me below.

Evidence that more spying and tattling is on the way may be seen in the following examples. Obama nominee for Surgeon General Vivek Hallegere Murthy thinks doctors should be able to ask patients whether they have any guns in the home. This type of private information could be entered into a patient's medical record and would be available to the government under Obamacare.[26]

Meanwhile, senators Dianne Feinstein and Barbara Boxer are proposing a new federal law that would allow family members "and others" to obtain through the court a "warrant that would allow law enforcement to take temporary possession of firearms" if the individual is a threat to themselves or others. The Pause for Safety Act would allow law enforcement access to state and local gun databases in the event they received "a tip" or warning from a family member "or other close associate."

If this isn't enough, the states can receive grant money (read: bribe) by providing "resources for courts and law enforcement" as they try to implement the "preventive measures."[27] So now you could lose your Second Amendment rights just by the subjective tip of anyone who doesn't like you or is against gun rights. Don't worry. You will only lose your guns "temporarily." The elites' are attempting to take our rights away on almost a daily basis now. It is next to impossible to keep up with all their nefarious activities.

The surveillance in the future will be overwhelming, especially during the great tribulation when the Antichrist controls everything. But even before this, I predict there will be no doctor-patient or therapist-patient privilege at some point in the near future. In addition, your kids, spouse, employer, waitress, golf buddies, and everything in your house and your car will be spying on you. If you're not exhibiting a PC attitude, you'll need to be reeducated in a FEMA camp.

Imbibing psychotropics might actually save some a trip to a FEMA camp because I foresee pharmacological "therapy" being used as an alternative method of reeducation in many instances (rather than extermination). By the time of Daniel's seventieth week, I think psychotropic drug use will be omnipresent.

In some cases pharmacological therapy may be mandatory for citizens so that those in power can keep a large portion of the population docile and in line. I believe your local mental health professionals, as mentioned previously, will have a lot of input regarding to whom these drugs will be administered. I also think many people will take these drugs voluntarily just to cope with all the chaos and calamities that will be occurring at that time. The book of Revelation seems to make mention of this where it states that people during Daniel's seventieth week would not repent of their "sorceries."[28] The Greek word for "sorceries" is *pharmakeia*, which is where we get our word *pharmacy*. The word *sorceries* thus primarily refers to "medication" and secondarily to magic, sorcery, or witchcraft.

It is also possible that people in the future may take psychotropic drugs as a way to open themselves up to the spiritual realm. They may be deceived into thinking that taking mind-altering drugs could help them to achieve godhood or nirvana. I don't know if every one of these drugs really open people up to the spiritual realm. But I know this—demons in the spiritual realm are only too happy to encourage you in the wrong direction. Demons, for example, might suggest that you do away with yourself. This is something worth considering in light of the fact that even the drug companies recognize that many of these psychotropics give people "suicidal ideation."

Before we begin summarizing what we've looked at so far, let's turn to the next chapter and look at more deceptions and a big lie that will likely be circulating at the end of the age, and maybe even earlier than that.

Chapter 19

The Lies of Antichrist and the Apostasy

In this chapter we continue to look at the deception(s) that will occur at the end of the age. We will focus on two of the biggest lies Antichrist will probably use to mislead people in the future. The purpose here is not only to become aware of the Antichrist's future deceptions, but also to avoid being drawn in by his lies. We will also look at the apostasy—the "falling away" that will occur when Christians and others turn away from the truth of Christianity and embrace Antichrist's false belief system.

If we do not impart a biblical perspective on the end time to the younger generations, how will they avoid being seduced by the Antichrist and his NWO system?

Lies of the Antichrist

Let's begin by laying out some scripture that pertains to the deception Antichrist and his cohorts will probably use to deceive the world. Remember that the Antichrist will be a counterfeit Christ who will offer a counterfeit kingdom. The Jews will think that Antichrist is the long-awaited Messiah. This is probably why the Jews in the future will fall for Antichrist's deception. They will sign a seven-year covenant with him which will mark the beginning of the end of the age. Muslims may be looking for their messiah at that time as well. The vast majority of people around the world will fall for Antichrist's lies. Let's look at who will be aiding the Antichrist's efforts before we look at the two specific lies he will promote.

There will be an unholy trinity, so to speak, working to deceive those who do not love the truth at that time. We know that the Devil can't create anything, so he attempts to imitate God in some way or pervert what God has already created. Jesus called the Devil the "Father of Lies."[1] Thus, the Devil is the "father" of this unholy trinity.

As we noted previously, the Antichrist is also called the "Son of Perdition." Therefore, Antichrist is acting as the Devil's "son." The

Antichrist will try to imitate Jesus as the savior of the world and usher in a counterfeit kingdom.

The third person of the unholy trinity is the False Prophet, who will lead people to believe that Antichrist is the Christ/God. The False Prophet will do this by performing false signs and wonders. Just as the Holy Spirit, who is the Spirit of truth, leads people *to* Jesus; the False Prophet will lead people *away* from Jesus and the living God. The False Prophet will perform signs on behalf of the Antichrist and will deceive many into taking Antichrist's mark.[2]

In addition, a second beast, will work in concert with the first Beast (Antichrist). The second beast will perform miracles that will make people believe that Antichrist is the real Jesus Christ, or at least some type of messiah. Let's go back to Revelation 13 for a moment, where it talks about the second beast deceiving people into worshiping the Beast (Antichrist):

> It performs great signs, even making fire come down from heaven to earth in front of people, and by the signs that it is allowed to work in the presence of the beast it deceives those who dwell on earth, telling them to make an image for the beast that was wounded by the sword and yet lived. And it was allowed to give breath to the image of the beast, so that the image of the beast might even speak and might cause those who would not worship the image of the beast to be slain. (Revelation 13:13–15)

The second beast will perform miracles that are so convincing that most of humanity will be deceived into worshiping the Antichrist. It is difficult to tell from our present vantage point what the "image" of the Antichrist will be. Perhaps it will be a holographic image of some kind that may be virtually alive. This will become clearer the closer we get to Daniel's seventieth week (a seven-year period). But however this image is portrayed, it calls to remembrance God's command not to have any other gods before Him or to make an "image" or "bow down to them or serve them."[3] Those who do not worship the Antichrist or his image will be killed. Life-and-death decisions will have to be made at that time, which is why all of this is so important to begin looking at now.

During Daniel's seventieth week, the Devil will be working directly with the Antichrist. In 2 Thessalonians 2:9–11, it says of Antichrist, "His presence is according to the operation of Satan with all powers and signs and wonders of a lie and with all deceit of unrighteousness in the ones perishing because they received not the love of the truth for to be saved. And therefore God sends to them an operation of error for them to believe *the lie*."[4] Though the literal translation of this verse is a bit choppy, we can see that the Antichrist will propagate a specific lie. Those who do not love the truth will fall for Antichrist's lie. What could this lie be?

I think it will be the same lie that that caused the Fall of Adam and Eve. Let's look at the text in the book of Genesis where it talks about the Serpent (the Devil) beguiling Eve into disobeying God and partaking of the forbidden fruit. The text says "But the serpent said to the woman, 'You will not surely die. For God knows that when you eat of it your eyes will be opened, and you will be like God, knowing good and evil'" (Gen. 3:4–5).

The lie the Devil told Eve was that she and Adam could become "like God."[5] It is possible that this will be one of the lies that the Antichrist will use to deceive humanity. Antichrist will tell people that they can become "God" just like he (Antichrist) is "God."

Moreover, the Devil believed his own lie at some point and deceived himself into believing that he could become God.[6] As we noted in the previous chapter, the Antichrist will follow the Devil's lead by claiming to be God at the abomination of desolation. The Devil's mission is to get people to focus on themselves instead of the living God. This is why autonomy is so pervasive in our increasingly post-Christian nation today.

The Serpent embedded another lie in his deception that the future Antichrist will probably use. (By the way, we know the Serpent is the Devil, because Revelation states that an angel "seized the dragon, *that ancient serpent, who is the devil* and Satan."[7]) The Serpent told Eve that eating the fruit would mean their "eyes will be opened." From Eve's perspective, eating the fruit would make one wise. So we have two lies and maybe a half-truth going on here. You can become God, you won't die, and you can become wise. Let's shift for a moment to the transhumanist movement which, in some ways, embraces remarkably similar lies the Serpent told Eve.

Transhumanism may be defined as "a class of philosophies that seeks the continued evolution of human life beyond its current human form as a result of science and technology guided by life-promoting principles and values."[8] In short, many transhumanists want to transcend humanity. They believe that humans, with the help of technology, can evolve past the species of "man." The vast majority of transhumanists do not believe in the God of the Bible.[9] They are atheists. Transhumanists are not secularists, per se, because they are not merely concerned with the here and now. Some of them are hoping to live forever.

I think it may be likely that the Antichrist will promote one of the lies of transhumanism—that people can transcend their humanity and live forever. The Antichrist will probably be a transhumanist himself. He will probably end up becoming post-human, and thus a perversion of what it means to be purely human. In other words, he will be made in his own image rather than the image of God. In short, there may be a reason why the Bible refers to the Beast/Antichrist as "it" in the text above (Rev. 13). The Beast may be some hybrid of human genes mixed with animal genes and perhaps robotic/AI technology. Perhaps the Beast will be a super intelligent computer that is downloaded into a human. It may have the military knowledge and physical power that knows no equals.

The exponential advances in technology will make the promises of transhumanism much easier to believe during the end of the age. The technological and genetic manipulation of humans that I expect to see in the future has not yet occurred. This is one of the reasons I think we have some time left before Jesus's return. This is conjecture on my part and I could be wrong. But my guess is that when scientists, transhumanists, and those in the genetic field start tampering with our humanity—such as mixing human genes with animals—*then* Jesus will return and put an end to this agenda lest all of humanity become perverted.

In short, I don't believe God will allow the genetic tinkering of humans made in His image to go on very long. Support for this line of thinking can be found in the Old Testament. Genetic tampering took place during Noah's time, which is probably why God wiped out everyone but Noah and his family from the face of the earth. Unfortunately, unpacking this line of thought will take us too far afield. Suffice it to say that there is evidence to show that God won't allow the pinnacle of His creation to be tampered with to the point where humanity becomes post-human.

At any rate, let's take a closer look at the remarkable similarities between the promises of transhumanism, and the lie Adam and Eve fell for.

Transhumanism's Lies: You Can Be God; You Won't Die

We will want to keep an eye on the transhumanist movement as we move into the future and toward the end of the age. Transhumanists build their worldview on the theory of evolution. From their viewpoint, matter plus time plus chance made humans. Then humans created technology. Technology will advance exponentially in the next thirty years so that by 2045 the "singularity" will occur where "there won't be a distinction between humans and technology," according to a leading transhumanist Ray Kurzweil.[10] In his book *The Singularity Is Near*, Kurzweil argues that it is not so much that humans will become machines but rather machines will progress to be humans such that a machine will possess a record of its own history and be able to reflect on it as well as demonstrate emotions and aspirations.[11]

Kurzweil admits that this technological explosion will call into question our traditional conceptions of what it means to be human, but he is undaunted by this concern. This is just our evolutionary path to godhood. As Kurzweil said in one interview, "So, does God exist, I would say, not yet."[12] In another interview, his tone softened a little: "I don't think we actually ever become God. But we do become more God-like." When asked by the same interviewer if Kurzweil believed in a God that he planned on meeting when he died, Kurzweil replied, "I'm not planning to die."[13] In fact, Kurzweil said, "Our mortality will be in our own hands. We will be able to live as long as we want."[14]

Look at what physicist and human cloning researcher Richard Seed announced. He said that when the "shift" hits the fan, "I will be God." His proclamation continued: "We're going to become gods. Period. If you don't like it get off. You don't have to participate. But if you're gonna interfere with me becoming God, you're gonna have big trouble."[15]

People like Seed and Kurzweil think they can save themselves. Isn't this what secular humanist Paul Kurtz told us in Chapter two—that no God would save us; we must save ourselves? This is a humanistic man-centered salvation, and it won't work. C. S. Lewis pointed out a long time ago that having a planet full of unregenerate humans who can live forever is not a utopia; it is hell.

It is clear that the lies the Devil told Eve in the garden are the very same lies transhumanists like Kurzweil and Seed believe—you can become God and you won't die. Let's take a look at what the implications of transhumanism might look like as we approach the end of the age.

Joel Garreau, in his book *Radical Evolution*, divides humans of the future into three camps. The Enhanced are those who will pay any price to transform/modify their minds, bodies, metabolism, personality, etc., to transcend the original human equipment they were born with. The Naturals will avoid enhancement, even if given the opportunity. They will stick with the original equipment. The Rest are those who for "economic or geographic reasons" will not have access to enhancement technology.[16]

In the NWO, the Antichrist might promise enhancement for those who take his mark. The Naturals, who will include all true Christians, will be looked upon with supercilious derision because they do not want to evolve. The Rest won't have the financial wherewithal to get enhanced.

In one scenario, there could be a class warfare between the Enhanced, who represent the elites, and the Naturals. Chillingly, Theodore Kaczynski proposed one such scenario in *The Unabomber Manifesto*:

> The average man may have control over certain private machines of his own, such as his car or his personal computer, but control over large systems of machines will be in the hands of a tiny elite— just as it is today, but with two differences. Due to improved techniques the elite will have greater control over the masses, and because human work will no longer be necessary the masses will be superfluous, a useless burden on the system. If the elite is ruthless they may simply decide to exterminate the mass of humanity.[17]

This is not that far-fetched. As we have pointed out repeatedly, the global elites want to eliminate 85 to 90 percent of the population, so Kaczynski's prediction is not outrageous. In the future, the globalists could use "white plagues," for example, consisting of genetically engineered pathogens or self-replicating nanobots that target selective groups for extermination.[18] This would be the technological equivalent of sending people to the Nazi concentration camps to die.

Plagues/viruses and the extermination of a large part of the human population (useless eaters) is supported by Scripture. As we noted in the previous chapter, the fourth horseman of the Apocalypse will use plagues and pestilences to destroy a fourth of the earth. These plagues could very well be bio-engineered pandemics. This is noteworthy because it is possible that people will be forced to take Antichrist's mark in order to be entitled to receive a vaccination to counteract a biological contagion. Perhaps an individual will not be able to gain admittance to a grocery store, workplace, sporting event, school or university, or anywhere else for that matter, unless they receive the mark showing they had been vaccinated and thus are not a health threat to society. It would be impossible to conduct one's daily business (which includes buying and selling) without the mark.

All of these things will become clearer the closer we get to the end of the age. I am just suggesting a way this could play out. It is interesting that at the time of this writing, California is attempting to pass legislation to force vaccinations on children apparently with no exemptions for religious or personal reasons.

Jesus said that Antichrist's great tribulation against "the elect" will be so severe that if this period of time was not "cut short, *no human being would be saved*" (Matt. 24:22a). I think there is the likelihood that the Antichrist (being a good globalist), will probably try to kill off the vast majority of humanity as well as all the Christians.

The Antichrist will be a liar working on behalf of Satan. There is nothing Satan wants more than to take humans made in God's image to hell. This is why, given the opportunity, it is possible that sooner or later Antichrist will try to kill even those who will take his mark. They already belong to him. Why not just kill them so they can go to hell straightaway?

Peace, Security, and Ecumenism

It is probable that sometime after Antichrist signs the covenant with Israel and then begins to consolidate his power that there will be a time, however short, of relative peace. Scripture tells us that the world will be crying out "peace and security."[19]

I foresee PC tolerance being in full force at the time of Antichrist, even more so than it is today. As I predicted earlier, Antichrist will probably bring all religions under one umbrella. Unity and ecumenism will be the watchwords, because they engender peace and security.

A call will go out to tolerate one another's religious differences so all the needless wars can stop. Tolerance will be a unifying force. Many will appeal for the world to be as one. PC pluralism could be ubiquitous. People will mimic Kurzweil, that all roads lead to God and different paths lead to the same truth. New Agers and transhumanist elites could encourage individuals to recognize their own godhood. Mysticism, perhaps enhanced by psychotropics, will supersede objective truth as everyone finds their own truth and their own path to becoming a god. Each person will be on his or her own trip, especially if psychotropics enhance the trip.

Many nations will have lost their sovereignty to Antichrist's NWO by this time. The world will be probably be united under one NWO political, economic, and religious system. Perhaps the Antichrist will allow for some flexibility regarding people holding various religious beliefs. For example, he could unify all religions under one umbrella by giving various religions his stamp of approval as long as their adherents worship him.

I think it is probable that at some point we will receive a "visit" by extraterrestrials (read: fallen angels) who proclaim that they are our "creators." This could expedite a new world religion. Everyone would come together. The Antichrist's counterfeit signs and lying wonders would seem to legitimize his claim to be the apex of humankind's evolution. He would seem like a "god." The ETs could insist that the Antichrist is the pinnacle of humankind's evolutionary progress. With all the wars, natural calamities, and general chaos that will be taking place during the first three and a half years of Daniel's seventieth week, people will be ready for a savior. Especially a savior who had the imprimatur of so-called ETs.

At any rate, it is probable that during the time of peace and security, religious ecumenism will be trending. Now combine this religious climate of unity with transhumanism's lie. This is what Kurzweil says about the interface between religion, evolution, spirituality, and the move toward becoming God:

> The different religions of the world have a surprising agreement on what God is. God is an unlimited amount of what: memory, intelligence, creativity and love . . . What happens in evolution, entities like mammals and humans become more intelligent, more creative, more loving, and moving exponentially to become more God-like; never quite reaching God, but moving in that direction. So evolution is a spiritual process to bring us closer to God.[20]

As we can see, Kurzweil believes achieving godlike status isn't merely through technological evolution—it is a *spiritual* process as well. Kurzweil was brought up in a Unitarian church where he was taught that there are many paths to the truth.[21] He learned that tolerance was important because it helped one understand that "seemingly different stories are really speaking the same truth."[22] Kurzweil's thoughts are worth noting, because he ties together both technology and spirituality as valuable components in man's evolutionary quest to transcend his own humanity. I predict in the future, technology and spirituality will work synergistically in deceiving people that all roads lead to God or that people can *become* a god.

The New Age, Evolution, and Transhumanism

The New Age movement, like transhumanism, includes the spirit of ecumenism, tolerance, and occult mysticism and could also play a role in the end time. Let's look at a few examples of how this could happen.

Warren B. Smith, a former New Ager, quotes occultist Alice Bailey, who received her information from a spirit guide she channeled: "Therefore, in the new world order, spirituality will supersede theology; living experience will take the place of theological acceptances."[23] Amazingly, she penned this over a half a century ago, and yet we can see reference to the "new world order" and also the idea that private spirituality will replace theology. We pointed out this move to privatized religious belief in Chapter two. It is also likely that truth will take a backseat to unity and tolerance, because truth is divisive. People today want only their own autonomous/pragmatic "truth." But this is not truth at all, as we saw in Chapter six.

Bailey's spirit guide (demon) told her a few other things. Bailey had this to say about ecumenism: "The expressed aims and efforts of the United Nations will be eventually brought to fruition and a new church of God, gathered out of all religions and spiritual groups, will unitedly bring to an end the great heresy of separateness."[24]

Two things stand out. First, already over a half a century ago, New Age occultists like Bailey were talking about a one-world church/religion. This ecumenical push is something to keep an eye on. Second, New Agers believe "separateness" is a bad thing, because it means that an individual doesn't recognize they are part of God, or that, in fact, they *are* God. According to New Agers, God is not the personal, living God of the Bible but rather everything in the universe. New Agers are pantheists. They believe everything is God (pantheism) and/or God is in everything (panentheism).

Finally, here is what Bailey said about tolerance and panentheism: "This is the challenge which today confronts the Christian Church. The need is for vision, wisdom, and that wide tolerance which will see divinity on every hand and recognize the Christ in every human being."[25]

As I have repeatedly stated, tolerance is king right now, and it will continue to dominate the cultural climate in the future. Why the need to see the "Christ in every human being" as Bailey mentioned? New Ager Barbara Marx Hubbard answers: "The living, resurrected Christ is the evolutionary potential of the human race, drawing us forward toward our fulfillment."[26] In fact, Hubbard's demonic "Christ voice" informed her, "Those who have the seal of the living God will be able to take the next step of evolution."[27]

One thing clearly stands out with regard to transhumanism and the New Age movement: evolution is the thread that runs through both belief systems. Humankind can evolve and become a god, or at least godlike, in both transhumanism and New Age spirituality.

Pierre Teilhard de Chardin, who is often noted as the father of the New Age movement, attempted to bridge the gap between human evolution and Christianity. Basically, he baptized both science and evolution with Christian terminology. This made his esoteric ideas sound "Christian" when they were really some form of pantheism.[28]

Teilhard de Chardin proposed a concept known as the "Omega Point." Like Kurzweil's "Singularity," the Omega Point is something humans can look forward to in the evolutionary paradigm. The Omega Point is the evolutionary process of complexity and consciousness that converge in God. But this "god" de Chardin talks about is not the personal God of the Bible but the impersonal god of pantheism. Christ's second coming (*parousia*), according to de Chardin, initiates this convergence of the material world and human evolution, which is the Omega point.[29]

Marilyn Ferguson, whose book *The Aquarian Conspiracy* is considered the "bible" for New Age thought and aspirations, explains the importance of de Chardin's concept of the Omega Point for the future history of the world: "This new awareness—evolving mind recognizing the evolutionary process . . . will envelop the planet and will crystallize as a species-wide enlightenment."[30]

Summarizing so far, the enlightenment mentality of inevitable progress that started three centuries ago is still very much alive today in both New Age spiritualism and transhumanism. As we noted in Chapter two, "man is the measure" in secular humanism. But while secular humanism is concerned with the here and now, *trans*humanists are looking instead to the future and perhaps even the eternal future. Kurzweil thinks we can *trans*cend humanity, which is why his worldview is labeled "transhumanism."

Transhumanists consider the possibility and maybe even the inevitability that man can live forever. Moreover, the very same lies that Eve fell for in the garden of Eden have resurfaced in the transhumanist worldview. You can become a god. You don't have to die. You can become wise beyond your wildest dreams with the exponential increase in intelligence humans will have access to in the future. That is, assuming future robots don't transcend humanity entirely. I don't believe, however, God will allow for that.

These same aspirations toward divinity are found in New Age mysticism as well. The idea in New Age occult spirituality is that individuals need to see themselves as God, not separate from God. Humanity can be united once people are enlightened enough to see that each individual is a part of this impersonal god of pantheism. This attitude will encourage an ecumenical spirit that Teilhard de Chardin summarized when he proposed, "A general convergence of religions upon a universal Christ who fundamentally satisfies them all: that seems to me the only possible conversion of the world, and the only form in which a religion of the future can be conceived."[31]

Teilhard de Chardin's call for a "general convergence of religions" in the future, although prescient, is dangerous and will end in the apocalypse. His "universal Christ" will likely be the Antichrist masquerading as the real Christ. The Antichrist will be a lying, phony peacemaker forcing everyone to worship him as the pinnacle of evolution. He may also encourage those who are "enlightened" to become a god just as he is. Warren B. Smith summarizes how the New Agers will view all of these things in the future: "Those who awaken to their own divinity, by aligning themselves as one with God and one with each other will evolve. Those who continue to believe in 'fear' and 'separation,' rather than in 'love' and 'oneness,' will not evolve."[32]

PC tolerance will run rampant in order to promote unity, love, and oneness. They will underpin the humanistic efforts to promote ecumenism and the Antichrist's one-world kingdom.

Christian Exclusivism Will Not Be Tolerated

In the future, transhumanists in the NWO will view true Christians as troublemakers, because Christians will refuse to "evolve." Christians won't want their genes mixed with animals in order to become stronger or see better or live longer. They won't want to download their brains into a computer so that they can live forever in some future cyberspace.[33] They won't be part of an ecumenical movement that rejects the real Jesus Christ. True Christians in the future won't believe, even for a moment, that all roads lead to God or that they can become a god. The world will view them as divisive because Christians believe that Jesus alone is the way to obtain eternal life, rather than through evolution, transhumanism, or some New Age mumbo-jumbo. Christians won't take the Antichrist's mark. They will not want to be a part of Antichrist's kingdom in any way, shape, or form.

Christians' gospel message that Jesus's atoning sacrifice on the cross is the only way to have one's sins forgiven and receive eternal life will evoke screams of anger and gnashing of teeth. Who needs to receive Jesus to have eternal life when you can download your brain into a computer and live forever? Who needs Jesus when, as the New Agers claim, we are on the road to becoming gods? We just need to embrace our own divinity. We don't need Jesus's atonement. We just need to realize our "at-one-ment." In fact, Barbara Marx Hubbard claims that she came to the realization "that the man Jesus was a future human, an evolutionary template."[34] Yes, that's right. Jesus was just an example of how evolved we can all become.

Those leading the charge in the future will claim that the old-fashioned gospel message is too backward and too exclusive. Exclusivism will be out. Tolerance and unity will be in. Look at what Hubbard's demonic "Christ voice" told her about this: "The selection process will exclude all who are exclusive. The selection process assures that only the loving will evolve to the stage of co-creator."[35] In other words, all those "loving" people who take the mark and become part of Antichrist's kingdom will evolve. Christians, on the other hand, will be "selected" for extermination. Can't have those narrow-minded, intolerant Christians gumming up the works.

This weeding out of Christians will probably start even before Antichrist is revealed. Actually, it is happening already today. One Pentagon training manual lumped Evangelicals and Catholics in with Al Qaeda, Hamas, and Sunni Muslims as examples of religious extremism.[36] I believe people will increasingly associate the words *radical* or *extremist* with *fundamentalism* in general, which would include biblical Christianity. I think we are already witnessing a conflation of "fundamentalism" with radical Islam. It will be just a matter of time before those who think radical/fundamental Islam is extremist, to likewise think that Christian fundamentalism is also an extremist religion. This will be an efficient way to marginalize Christians who hold to the fundamentals of Christianity because they will be considered dangerous, just like radical Muslims.

If PC tolerance is ubiquitous now, it will be far more entrenched in the future when the younger generations, which are inculcated with PC values, will frown upon those who don't hold ecumenical and PC attitudes toward other religions. Christians will be excoriated for holding their exclusive, *extremist* views about Jesus Christ—His death by crucifixion, His atoning blood, and His resurrection. It is likely that Christians will be incarcerated in FEMA camps the closer we get to the end of the age because of their perceived intolerance. This is why we must proclaim the gospel now while we still have the opportunity.

In the future, the Antichrist will take the targeting of Christians to a whole new level. The book of Revelation states that Christians will be executed "for the word of God and the witness they had borne" (Rev. 6:9b). These martyred saints "loved not their lives even unto death" (12:11b). As noted above, the Antichrist's wrath against the saints of God will be so severe, God will "cut short" this great tribulation period. This is when the day of the Lord (God's wrath) will fall on Antichrist and his kingdom.

The Apostasy: The Falling Away of Nominal Christians

The Bible also talks about an "apostasy" (falling away) that will take place around the time Antichrist desecrates the Jewish temple at the mid-point of Daniel's seventieth week, (after which the great tribulation begins).[37] Once Antichrist declares himself "God" and forces everyone to take his mark in order to be able to buy or sell, many will fall away from the faith. Essentially, falling away refers to turning away from biblical truth, which centers especially on believing that Jesus is Lord, Savior, and Christ, and that He died on the cross for our sin and was resurrected in real life (history). Let's explore this further so we can gain a clearer understanding of how this falling away might occur.

Let's look at the nominal Christians first. Many practical atheists, who consider themselves Christians, will be easily deceived into accepting Antichrist as their savior. Many never give God a thought anyway, so they will be in no position to distinguish between the true Christ and a false Christ. We have seen over and over in this book that nominal Christians, whether they are the liberal theologians and their converts over the last two centuries, or the practical atheists of today, always accommodate their religious beliefs to the spirit of the age. This will go double for the generations coming up behind us. A large percentage will be practical atheists who practice some form of privatized PC religion, or perhaps no religion at all.

After all the earthquakes, famines, wars, hyperinflationary economic collapses, pandemics, and death, people will be ready to accept someone who claims to be God, and can save them. Remember what Bezmenov said in a previous chapter—a crisis always makes people vulnerable for a "savior." The miraculous signs and lying wonders that Antichrist and the False Prophet will perform will be the clincher for most people. I think even atheists will get on board with Antichrist, because they will see in him a technologically sophisticated transhumanist that can show them the way to become godlike and live forever.

Another class of so-called Christians whom I envision falling away are those who would not normally be deceived but will *allow* themselves to buy into Antichrist's lies, simply because they want to feed themselves and their families. Moreover, many self-professing Christians who know in their hearts that they shouldn't take the mark will take it anyway. They will convince themselves that God will forgive them. After all, a man has to feed his family, right? But Jesus said, "Whoever loves father or mother more than me is not worthy of me; and whoever loves son or daughter more than me is not worthy of me. And whoever does not take his cross and follow me is not worthy of me. Whoever finds his life will lose it, and whoever loses his life for my sake will find it" (Matt. 10:37–39).

The claim that God will forgive those who take Antichrist's mark has no basis in Scripture. Yet one very well respected Christian theologian makes just such a claim.[38] Propagating this faulty belief will make people more comfortable with their decision to take the mark during Daniel's seventieth week, especially if respected theologians at that time are condoning it. Unfortunately, this will lead people to being thrown into the lake of fire along with the Antichrist, the Devil, and the fallen angels.

Let's see what the Bible actually says about taking the mark.

And another angel, a third, followed them, saying with a loud voice, 'If anyone worships the beast and its image and receives a mark on his forehead or on his hand, he also will drink the wine of God's wrath poured full strength into the cup of his anger, and he will be tormented with fire and sulfur in the presence of the holy angels and in the presence of the Lamb. And the smoke of their torment goes up forever and ever, and they have no rest, day or night, these worshipers of the beast and its image, and whoever receives the mark of its name. (Revelation 14:9–13)

Claiming that people will be able to take the mark of the Beast and still repent and be saved makes a mockery of those who will stay true to the Lord Jesus Christ even when it will cost them their lives. The apostle John, who wrote the book of Revelation, said that he "saw the souls of those who had been beheaded for the testimony of Jesus and for the word of God, and who had not worshiped the beast or its image and had not received its mark on their foreheads or their hands" (20:4). These overcomers of Satan and his Antichrist "loved not their lives even unto death" (12:11b).

If you are holding this book when the end of the age events are occurring, I want to make it clear that you are not to take the mark of the Beast/Antichrist under any circumstances, no matter how dire your situation is. This Antichrist will be a liar of monumental proportions. Eternity is a lot longer than this little speck of time in the here and now. Your goal should be to spend eternity with the triune God of the Bible in heaven, not with the Antichrist, the Devil, and all the other liars and haters of the living God who will be thrown into the lake of fire.[39] This is serious business.

I cannot overemphasize that the pressure to conform to the Antichrist/Beast's one-world economic, political, and religious system will be overwhelming. That is why it is easy to predict that the two groups mentioned above will fall away and give in to Antichrist's lies. Practical atheists have no depth of biblical knowledge and little substance regarding their personal relationship with the God of the Bible. Others will succumb for pragmatic reasons. Neither of these groups will have the intestinal fortitude to hold on to Jesus Christ when times get tough. They will allow themselves to be deceived. The lies floating around at that time will be prolific. Moreover, with evolution, New Age spirituality, transhumanism, and preachers claiming that a person can still repent after taking the mark, you have a toxic combination.

Will Christian Churches Be Susceptible to the Apostasy?

The accommodation process we have repeatedly reviewed in this book is still occurring in Christian circles today. This is especially noticeable in many churches within evangelicalism in addition to many Protestant churches in general. In my opinion, churches and movements (like the seeker-friendly and emergent church, for example) today that are willing to accommodate themselves to the spirit of the age will be those that are most vulnerable to Antichrist's deceptions in the future. This could lead to apostasy. Let's look at this for a moment.

411

As I have previously pointed out, one of the most omnipresent accommodative moves that has taken place in the last twenty-five years or so is the shift in many, if not most, evangelical churches (and Protestant churches in general) from a traditional approach to the worship service to a contemporary form of worship. The fact that church leaders feel the need to encourage/accept contemporary music and casual dress in the church service reveals something. It tells us that the primary goal of "doing church" today has switched from concerning ourselves about what God thinks of our worship, to what the unchurched think of our worship.

Many church leaders today have embraced the mind-set that perceives non-Christian visitors as "consumers" whose "felt needs" are sovereign.[40] The primary concern of many churches is to accommodate the unbelieving seeker-consumer who has replaced God as the central focus of worship. The danger, of course, is that sooner or later the Christian message simply becomes a means to an end—the end being fulfilling people's needs and even offering them their best life in the here and now (the secular).[41]

The rationale behind this new paradigm is that if the gospel is to be effective in today's postmodern culture, then the *method* for reaching the unsaved must be updated to attract potential parishioners—thus the move to a contemporary form of worship. Church can be more fun if people can bring their coffee and iced lattes into the sanctuary and treat the whole experience more like a college class rather than a church service.

The mentality here is that the unchurched folks really don't have anything against God, they just don't like old-fashioned church services with choirs, hymnals, and organs. That type of worship is boring. Get rid of those things and people will be happy to come to church. Oh, and perhaps, turn down the sin, repentance, and holiness rhetoric, at least a little bit. People today want an upbeat message. Words like "sin" and "repentance" turn them off. It appears that an increasing number of evangelical churches are slowly but surely moving in this direction in order to be "hip" and "relevant" when it comes to attracting the unchurched.

Unfortunately, space does not permit unpacking the traditional versus seeker-friendly debate over how church should be done. Let me briefly suggest, however, that even from a historical-cultural perspective the notion that Christian churches should accommodate contemporary culture is erroneous. It is precisely this mentality that cost mainline churches much of their membership back in the day.

For example, we pointed out in Chapter four that because there was not much difference between the theological message of the mainline churches and the message that congregants were getting from the world, people figured there was no reason to go to those churches anymore. Of course, church leaders today advocating the seeker-friendly mentality will reply that the *message* of evangelicalism hasn't changed only the *method* of presenting it. But as Gary Gilley points out, sooner or later "the message will ultimately be shaped by the method."[42]

I agree with Gilley. It seems to me prima facie that leaders who are willing to accommodate the spirit of the age to bring the unsaved into their churches will also be more likely to compromise/accommodate Christian fundamentals sooner or later. (I foresee this especially occurring in the generations coming up behind us who are much more likely to embrace PC attitudes.) Gilley puts it this way, "If Harry is drawn to the church in order to *get*, in order to satisfy his flesh, he is not likely to stay around when and if he discovers that Christ calls for him to lose his life for Christ's sake (Matt. 16:25). The result is that churches which have been built on the quagmire of the superficial must remain superficial if they hope to retain their Harrys and Marys."[43]

Recall from Chapter two that seekers today often pick and choose the Christian doctrines that "help" them and discard the rest. A narcissistic consumer does not want to be told that he has to take up his cross in order to follow Jesus. Therefore, Christian leaders are providing no authentic help to the unchurched if these leaders are not ready, willing, and able to confront them with the gospel. Yes, I said "confront." The true, unadulterated gospel is an affront (a "scandal") to the (post)modern mind-set. The gospel involves repentance, which is anathema to those who want to be autonomous.

In my opinion, the churches in Protestantism (and any so-called Christian churches) that continue to move in the direction of worrying about how it will accommodate culture will be the same churches in the future that will compromise doctrinal verities like sin, the cross, repentance, holiness, Jesus's divinity, and the historical resurrection. These doctrines will be watered down or become completely absent from the vocabulary of pastors from the pulpit. This will be done under the auspices of being "tolerant" and "ecumenical."

I believe that most churches today are in no way preparing the up-and-coming generations for the apocalypse ahead. The true church of Jesus Christ in the future will need to stand over and against the deceptions and lies that will be ubiquitous. I fear, however, that many churches will be ready to compromise. In fact, I foresee a time, as the end of the age nears, when churches that are willing to accommodate the world will inevitably give up on the exclusivity of Christ altogether and turn to some form of universalism.

For example, I foresee a day when our own government, or a U.N. authority that is running our nation at that time, will force churches to stop proclaiming the exclusivity of Jesus or lose their tax-exempt status. Sooner or later they won't be able to preach the exclusivity of Christ at all. Preaching the exclusivity of Jesus as the only way to salvation will be considered hate speech or intolerant extremism.

I also think there will come a day in the not too distant future when the preacher can no longer identify homosexuality as sin from the pulpit or risk losing the church's tax-exempt status. The powers that be may even shut these churches down.

Perhaps this won't be a problem in light of the fact that some mainline Protestant churches have already accommodated same-sex marriage and allow for homosexuals in positions of leadership. And even evangelical churches are allowing homosexuals to become members. In any case, in the future, only PC state-endorsed propaganda will be allowed from the pulpit for those churches who want to retain their place in society. It will be Nazi Germany 2.0. Many churches will follow the same pattern we have reviewed in this book—accommodate and retreat. The way things are heading, maybe there won't be that many churches that will need to shut down.

I think many preachers today don't believe in the power of the gospel to change people's lives, so they feel the need to use contemporary ways like the business model approach, the latest pop psychology, or contemporary worship to reach the unchurched. I believe that using "the ways of the world" may seem to work now, but as we approach the end of the age, these methodologies will prove superficial and impotent. As I pointed out in the previous chapter, many of our churches today seem to have adopted the "Laodicean church model"—they seem to think they are rich and prosperous and in need of nothing. But Jesus warned that these seemingly successful churches are really "wretched, miserable, poor, blind, and naked" (Rev. 3:17).

As we get closer to the end of the age, we will know which churches are built on the Rock, and which churches are built on the sinking sand of the superficial. I promise you this: when the heat gets turned up as we approach the apocalypse, only the power of God will help Christians stand against the forces of darkness. When the apocalypse begins to unfold, I believe the casual coffee-drinking approach to the church service will give way to an urgent and reverent approach to God for genuine Christians who see what's coming. Many congregants will be kneeling at the altar instead of sipping on their coffee and checking their smartphones for text messages. It is also possible that much of the true church of Jesus Christ will be going underground at that time. Parishioners still sipping on their lattes will probably be those who belong to a church that has accepted Antichrist's NWO religion by default.

How Privatizing Religious Belief Threatens the Exclusivity of Christianity

We learned in Chapter two that people today want to consider themselves spiritual but not religious. People don't want to be accountable to religious doctrine anymore because it is too confining and it make demands on them. Today, it's all about love not holiness. People want to be autonomous. They want to be free to do their own thing. This is why religion has moved toward privatization. If religion is private, then spiritual consumers can make up their own religious views. They can mold their perceptions of God to fit what they are comfortable with.

Following one's subjective views about God as if those views were authoritative does not necessarily mean, however, that those personal/subjective views are true. The privatization of religious belief is a dangerous trend. Pope Francis's statement about following one's own conscience exemplifies the danger: "You ask me if the God of the Christians forgives those who don't believe and who don't seek the faith. . . . God's mercy has no limits if you go to him with a sincere and contrite heart. The issue for those who do not believe in God is to obey their conscience."[44]

I see what the pope is trying to get at. He is saying that those who don't believe in God should follow their consciences. The problem with this thinking is that today many people's consciences may tell them to follow something other than the living God. For example, Michael Novak said, "My obligation is to be faithful to my conscience, and I do not expect that I would hesitate an instant once it was clear to me that atheism is a more consistent human policy."[45]

From this statement, it is clear that following the pope's advice could lead a person to atheism rather than to God. Following one's conscience in this day and age will probably lead to autonomy and narcissism, not the God of the Bible. The unadulterated gospel must be preached so that people know the truth and follow it. The Christian worldview is based on a proper interpretation of the Bible, not one's conscience or subjective experience.

My point is that following one's conscience, subjective experience, or feelings, can often lead one astray. Let's look at another example. Stephen L. Carter wrote a popular book a while back entitled *The Culture of Disbelief.* In it he bemoaned the fact that our culture often trivializes religion in America. Nothing wrong with his thesis there. But under a subheading entitled Christian Exclusivity, he wrote, "Thus, the argument runs, only Christians—people who profess a faith in Jesus Christ as Son of God and Savior—can achieve eternal life. Many Christians do in fact believe this, citing, for example, John 14:6 as authority. (My own view is that exclusivity of this kind betrays a lack of faith in God's charity, but everyone is entitled to choose a religious belief.)"[46]

In John 14:6, the verse Carter refers to, Jesus says that He is the only way to the Father. However, Carter seems to think that his "own view" of God's charity eclipses Jesus's claim that He alone is the way. Carter's "own view" points to the problem with relying on something other than the authority of the Bible. Once people stray from Scripture, they can simply make up their own version of Christianity. Carter seems to think that his "own view" regarding how God's charity works trumps what Jesus said in the Bible. But how would Carter even know that God has charity if it wasn't in the Bible? Carter's view is a classic example of the smorgasbord approach to Christian theology. Just pick and choose what you are comfortable with and discard doctrine that doesn't suit your fancy. Carter implicitly rejects the authority of Scripture in favor of his subjective view on how God works.

Maybe Carter's conscience won't allow him to hold to Jesus's exclusivity. Perhaps Carter doesn't want the world to view him (Carter) as intolerant. Carter's rejection of Jesus's exclusivity regarding salvation supports my contention that those of us who continue to hold to the exclusivity of salvation in Jesus alone will be seen as uncharitable and intolerant. How long will it be before evangelicals begin to cave in and discard this fundamental doctrine of Christianity? Answer: not too long, if the polls are any indication of where evangelicalism is heading.

Some "emergent" Christians seem to have a problem with the exclusivity of Christ as well. They have been accused of "universalism," which in essence means these particular emergents think everyone will make it to heaven at some point, whether or not they accept Jesus as their Savior.

Brian McLaren, a leader in the emergent church movement, seems sympathetic to some type of universalism (like Carter above) when he states: "How should followers of Jesus relate to people of other religions? . . . So we ask: Is Jesus the only way? The only way to what? How can a belief in the uniqueness and universality of Christ be held without implying the religious supremacy and exclusivity of the Christian religion?"[47]

McLaren is worried that the "exclusivity problem" will make Christianity come off as religiously arrogant and superior. I think McLaren has fallen into the PC pluralism trap. He thinks that because many religions exist, they all must somehow be true in some sense. One religion should not be considered superior to another. But the question McLaren should be asking is not whether Christianity comes off as looking superior because of its exclusive truth claims; rather, he should be asking, "Is Christianity true?"

Was Jesus telling the truth when He said that He alone is the way and the truth and the life? This is all that matters. How Christianity appears to the watching world should not concern us as much as the *truth* of Christianity, lest we start accommodating our beliefs to please the world. Unfortunately, as noted above, this is precisely what is taking place now. In answer to McLaren's other question, we should love our neighbors as ourselves regardless of what they believe. We should share the love of God that is found exclusively in Jesus Christ's atoning death for our sin, and we should help those less fortunate than ourselves.

There is no doubt that the exclusivity of Jesus Christ's atoning work regarding salvation will be the biggest problem for true Christians as we move toward the end of the age. Exclusivity flies in the face of PC pluralism and PC tolerance. To be clear, Christianity is *inclusive* in that everyone on this planet is welcome to come to God by receiving Jesus Christ as their Savior from sin. But salvation is *exclusively* through Jesus Christ alone.[48] There is no other way.

Denying the exclusivity of Jesus's atoning sacrifice ties right in with the "all roads lead to God" mentality and the ecumenical push for unity among the religions that we noted. I believe this attitude will become more prolific as we move forward into the future. Tolerance unifies. Exclusivity divides. PC tolerance will be in. Exclusivity will be out.

Ecumenism at What Cost?

Today we are witnessing the drive for unity among different religions. For example, a document entitled "A Common Word between Us and You" is an attempt to find common ground between Muslims and Christians. Rick Warren and one of his mentors (Robert Schuller) along with others from both religions signed this document. The attempt, here, to reconcile Christians and Muslims is based on two supposed fundamental similarities between the religions: "love of the One God, and love of neighbor."[49]

But there is a problem. This document makes it sound as if Christians and Muslims serve the same God. But they do not. Christians serve the living God of the Bible, who is Triune: Father, Son, and Holy Spirit. The Muslims, however, reject the Trinity. How can there be common ground between the two religions when there is no agreement on whose God is really God? They both cannot be right.

Furthermore, Muslims do not believe that Jesus is God (the second person of the Trinity). In addition, Muslims do not believe Jesus is the Son of God. They do not believe God had a son (Quran 19:34–35; 4:171). In contrast, read what 1 John in the Bible states about God's Son, Jesus Christ:

> Who is it that overcomes the world except the one who believes that Jesus is the Son of God? And this is the testimony, that God gave us eternal life, and this life is in his Son. Whoever has the Son has life; whoever does not have the Son of God does not have life. And we know that the Son of God has come and has given us understanding, so that we may know him who is true; and we are in him who is true, in his Son Jesus Christ. He is the true God and eternal life. (5:5, 11–12, 20)

Jesus Christ is not only the Son of God. He is God Almighty, the second person of the triune God of the Bible.

While it may appear commendable on the face of it for Rick Warren to find common ground with Muslims so that he can carry out his PEACE plan to help assist the poor and care for the sick around the world,[50] there can be no true reconciliation or unity between the two religions. Attempting a phony reconciliation can lead to accommodation on the part of Christians.

This accommodation was evident when Warren prayed in Isa's name at Mr. Obama's Inauguration in 2009. Apparently Warren was trying to be inclusive by using Isa as the Muslim equivalent for "Jesus."

But the Muslim "Isa" cannot be the biblical/historical Jesus. This attempt at accommodation by Warren was a grievous error. Quite frankly, it was blasphemy. Joe Schimmel points out the problem of trying to equate the real Jesus of the Bible with the Koran's conception of Isa:

> "Isa" is used in the Koran in reference to an alleged Palestinian prophet who, according to the Koran, is not the Son of God and did not die on the cross for the sins of the world. He is not only antithetical to the biblical, historical Yeshua revealed over a thousand years earlier through the Old Testament prophets but, according to millions of Muslims, he [Isa] will return to renounce Christianity, destroy all crosses, support the mass murder of Jews and forcibly convert the world to Islam. It is believed that Isa will not only destroy Jews and all crosses, but that he will support the coming Muslim Messiah—the 12th Imam or Mahdi—who many Christians believe will be the Antichrist.[51]

So basically, Rick Warren was praying in the name of someone who will destroy crosses, renounce Christianity, kill Jews, and assist the Antichrist (Mahdi). This certainly cannot be Jesus. This demonstrates why the accommodation game is so dangerous.

While we're at it, let's look at this Muslim messianic Mahdi, whom Isa will assist. Joel Richardson and former Muslim Walid Shoebat argue that the Islamic Mahdi will really be the Antichrist.[52] Look at what the founder and chairman of the Supreme Council of Islam in America, Muhammad Hisham Kabbani, said about this coming Muslim messiah:

> We see that the Mahdi, will lead a world revolution that will institute a *new world order* based on the religion of Islam. Mahdi will govern the people and establish Islam on earth and Islam will be victorious over all other religions. The Mahdi will offer the religion of Islam to the Jews and Christians. If they accept it they will be spared. Otherwise they will be killed and our prophet Jesus will be the executioner under our Messiah Mahdi.[53] (Emphasis mine.)

It is remarkable that even a leading Muslim in our own country would claim that the Islamic messiah will set up a New World Order. Particularly noteworthy is what this Muslim leader Kabbani said about how the Muslim "Jesus" will kill those who reject the religion of Islam. Isn't this exactly what we have been saying, that the Antichrist may even pretend to be the real Jesus Christ, set up a one world system

(NWO), and deceive everyone into following him? Isn't this precisely the deception that Rick Warren is falling into by equating the Islamic "Isa" with Jesus?

Many Christians are already opening themselves up to accommodation and deception by this ecumenical push. Keep in mind that people will be proclaiming "peace and security" (1 Thess. 5:3) at some point during Antichrist's reign as he unifies every aspect of life. This is the danger in attempting to promote unity at any cost. Instead, unity must be grounded in truth. The Antichrist will be a liar. His counterfeit kingdom based on a false unity and peace will deceive most people.

The modus operandi for Warren's new PEACE reformation is to downplay the differences between religions so that they can share a common cause in eradicating poverty and disease while educating people. The problem arises, however, when worldly needs become the primary focus. As Warren said, "It is not going to be about what does the church believe, but about what is the church doing."[54] In other words, it's about deeds not creeds. This is precisely what I predicted above, how doctrine would be put on the back burner in the future.

Recall that this is the same thing that happened back when the Social Gospel movement took place a little over a hundred years ago. Doctrine took a backseat to worldly concerns. Back then the Social Gospelers talked about "the Fatherhood of God and the brotherhood of man." In their minds God is the Father of all, and humans need to recognize their brotherhood with one another.

But this doctrine of the "Fatherhood of God and the brotherhood of man" is erroneous. God is only the "Father" of those who accept His Son, Jesus Christ. The Social Gospel adherents got this wrong back then and it is resurfacing in the ecumenical push today. Trying to accommodate Christianity to Islam as if adherents in these two religions were "brothers" serving the same God is falling for the same watered-down Christianity those in the Social Gospel movement deceived themselves into believing a century or so ago.

Ask the Christians in Syria and Iraq and elsewhere who are being martyred for their testimony of Jesus Christ if they think the Muslims who are beheading them are their brothers. Ask radical Muslims if they consider Christians their brothers. Is it merely a coincidence that the book of Revelation talks about those who will be "beheaded" for their testimony of Jesus? Walid Shoebat does not think so. In fact, he has an entire chapter on the history of beheading as endemic to the religion of Islam in his book *God's War on Terror*.[55]

But let's not get too far ahead of ourselves. We don't want to force today's events into Scripture. Perhaps at the end of the age, beheadings will occur at the hands of non-Muslims as well. For example, right now there are 30,000 guillotines being stored in various military bases on our own soil.[56] Why the need for these guillotines? What do the ruling elites have planned for us?

Interestingly enough, Jesus stated that those who behead Christians will think they are serving God: "I [Jesus] have said all these things to you to keep you from falling away. They will put you out of the synagogues. Indeed, the hour is coming when whoever kills you will think he is offering service to God. And they will do these things because they have not known the Father, nor me" (John 16:1–3). Jesus said that those who kill His disciples really don't know Him or His Father. The point is that Muslims who are beheading Christians today, as well as in the future, think they are serving God.

This raises a question. Who is serving the true God? Can Muslims deny that Jesus is the Son of God and really be serving God? No. Jesus is the litmus test to know whether or not you are serving the true and living God. The Bible makes this clear: "This is antichrist, he who denies the Father and the Son. No one who denies the Son has the Father. Whoever confesses the Son has the Father also" (1 John 2:22b–23). Muslims don't believe in the Father and the Son because they don't believe in the Trinity. As the above verse states, this is the spirit of Antichrist. Muslims are not serving the true God. They are serving Allah.

So what do we make of all of this? When the dots are connected between a Muslim Mahdi (Antichrist), who is supposed to set up a NWO, and a "Jesus" (Isa), who will kill (behead) both Christians and Jews who won't accept the religion of Islam, then the sheer number of coincidences is enough to warrant watching the spread of Islam, the Middle East in general, Israel, and the ecumenical push for an NWO very carefully.

We will need to see how events that take place in the future line up with Scripture. If the Islamic Mahdi is indeed the Antichrist, this would provide another piece of the puzzle—a forewarning on how not to be deceived. In other words, if Shoebat and Richardson are correct, then we may be looking for a *Muslim* who will sign a seven-year covenant with Israel. If indeed he signs this particular peace treaty, then this person would be the Antichrist. This may be the time when the world will be joyfully crying "peace and security."

Muslim leaders expect the NWO to consist of Islamic nations only. From what I've read, Richardson and Shoebat also believe the beast system (NWO) will be solely an Islamic Mideast phenomenon, not a global phenomenon. Mr. Shoebat states in his *God's War on Terror*, "This theory of Antichrist controlling the whole world is completely wrong…" (p. 289). Although Richardson describes a "new *globally enforced* Islamic law" at one point in his book *The Islamic Antichrist* (p.182, emphasis mine), he devotes an entire chapter in his more recent *Mideast Beast* (pp. 35-48) arguing for a *limited* dominion of Antichrist.

Let me provide just one quick example of why I believe the Antichrist will bring the *whole world* (not just the Mideast) under his beast system at some point. In Revelation it states that the Beast/Antichrist "was allowed to make war on the saints and to conquer them. And authority was given it over *every tribe and people and language and nation, and all who dwell on earth will worship it,* everyone whose name has not been written before the foundation of the world in the book of life of the lamb that was slain" (13:7-8). A plain reading of Scripture seems to suggest that the authority of Antichrist will extend to the whole world.

Look in the very next chapter, Revelation 14 where it states: "Then I saw another angel flying directly overhead, with an eternal gospel to proclaim *to those who dwell on earth, to every nation, and tribe and language and people*" (v.6). John uses the same phrase here as he did in the passage above to describe those to whom the angel preaches the eternal gospel. Surely we can't interpret this verse to mean that the angel is going to preach the gospel to just a small (local) part of the world. Jesus is giving the *whole world* one last chance to repent. The entire planet— "every nation, and tribe and language and people" will hear the gospel.

Furthermore, in Revelation 5 after Jesus takes the scroll from the Father, the Bible says "they sang a new song, saying 'Worthy are you to take the scroll and to open its seals, for you were slain, and by your blood you ransomed people for God from *every tribe and language and people and nation*'" (v. 9). Did Jesus die for only part of the world? No, he died for every tribe and language and people and nation. In other words, He died for the *whole world* (1John 2:2).

In order to be hermeneutically accurate and render a proper interpretation, we should stay within the context of the book that John (the author) is writing to see if we can discern the meaning of "every tribe and language and people and nation." In other words, the book of Revelation should be the *primary* place to look for a proper interpretation of the phrase in question. As we argued above, it is apparent when compared with other passages in Revelation (which use the same phrase), John is referring to the Antichrist having authority over the whole world.

The globalists, at the time of this writing, are not Muslims and their NWO agenda is global, not local. Therefore, it is difficult to see how the secular global elite's NWO that I have presented since Chapter sixteen, could be the same entity as the Muslim Antichrist NWO. However, I think it is wise to keep an eye on both scenarios and see how this plays out. There are so many moving parts to apocalyptic eschatology that almost all of us who study this will update and refine our positions based on how end time events in the future line up with Scripture. Although I respectfully disagree that the Antichrist's dominion will be local, I commend Richardson and Shoebat for bringing the Muslim Antichrist scenario to everyone's attention at this point in time.

Both the local and global Antichrist/NWO scenarios have merit, and both have difficulties. I will proceed on the assumption that the NWO will be global and that the mark of the beast will affect everyone on the planet, not just Middle Eastern countries. It *is* possible that the two agendas will mesh somehow in the future. For example, the Antichrist could end up being a (secular) Muslim who allows the ecumenical push to culminate in a one-world (non-Islamic) religion and economic system where he is worshiped as "God." This is one way both scenarios could be reconciled. On the other hand, it may be the case that either my scenario or the Shoebat/Richardson scenario is wrong.

However it plays out, the world will love this fake peace-making messiah. His counterfeit man-made, one-world kingdom will be short-lived, however. That you can bank on. More on this in the next chapter.

Ecumenism and the Apostasy

I want to be clear that sharing some goals with other faiths is not always wrong. For example, Catholics and evangelicals both oppose abortion. That is a true and righteous endeavor they have in common. It is admirable. All I am saying is that bending over backward to compromise the fundamentals of the Christian message in order to promote unity or reconciliation with other religions at the cost of truth is wide of the mark. The apostle Paul warned long ago about straying from sound doctrine:

> I charge you in the presence of God and of Christ Jesus, who is to judge the living and the dead, and by his appearing and his king-

dom: preach the word; be ready in season and out of season; reprove, rebuke, and exhort, with complete patience and teaching. *For the time is coming when people will not endure sound teaching*, but having itching ears they will accumulate for themselves teachers to suit their own passions, and will *turn away from listening to the truth* and wander off into myths. (2 Timothy 4:1–4)

In his first letter to Timothy, the apostle Paul wrote, "Now the Spirit expressly says that in later times some will depart from the faith by devoting themselves to deceitful spirits and teachings of demons through the insincerity of liars whose consciences are seared" (1 Tim. 4:1–2). These two verses describe the apostasy we have been addressing.

Thus, it is clear that at some point people will "depart from the faith" and others will "not endure sound teaching." The Antichrist's job of convincing people he is God will be made much easier once Christians fall away from the faith. Warren Smith offers a sobering thought about this: "For a false Christ to come, he's going to have a lot of people calling themselves Christians saying that he's Christ."[57]

If some Christians mistakenly claim that the Antichrist is really the Christ of the Bible, this would provide ammunition for the rest of the world to heap their scorn on those few Christians who resist the Antichrist's claim that he is the Christ. This type of scenario is not that difficult to foresee in light of PC pluralism, PC tolerance, as well as the ecumenical push we reviewed above where adherents of both Islam and Christianity, for example, claim to worship the same God.

Space does not permit reviewing all the ways the ecumenical push and accommodation are occurring today. For example, I have not mentioned that some evangelicals are trying to find common ground with Roman Catholics at the time of this writing. In fact, some of them met with Pope Francis. The desire of both parties is to become a family and work together so that God can "put his arms around the world."[58]

The problem with this is that there are too many doctrinal differences between Roman Catholics and Protestants for them to become a "family." One famous preacher, Joel Osteen, wasn't at that particular meeting, but he has commented in the past on Pope Francis's ecumenical push: "I love the fact that he's made the church more inclusive. Not trying to make it smaller, but trying to make it larger—to take everybody in."[59]

Technically there is nothing wrong with this statement so long as it is clear that everyone must come to God through Jesus Christ. I predict at some point in the future, however, many so-called Christian church-es (of all varieties) will compromise doctrine and ultimately give up the exclusivity of Jesus's atoning sacrifice in order to "to take everybody in." I believe there will be a push for ecumenism at all costs. Those churches that practice PC tolerance and accommodate the spirit of the age will be most susceptible to the ecumenical push.

Is the Vatican concerned only with bringing more people in? Maybe its objectives are a bit more ambitious. In 2011 the Vatican called for a "supranational authority" and a "universal jurisdiction" with a world central bank run by the United Nations that would rule over world financial affairs so as to avoid another financial crisis.[60] A "supranational authority" sounds an awful lot like the NWO to me.

There are just so many ways that religion, economics, politics, and technology are moving toward a one world system that one can hardly keep up with it. It is important to remember that we must address eve-rything that's happening in the light of Scripture. When the biblical apocalypse begins to unfold at the end of the age and things get really bad, it will seem like there is nothing sure to hold on to. This is when Scripture can provide an anchor for those who are truly searching for the truth and for those who belong to the Lord. The Bible alone is the authority to guide us in the perilous times ahead—not technology, sub-jective feelings, mystical New Age experiences, or ecumenical unity at the expense of truth.

Summary

I am concerned that Christians and non-Christians alike are in no way prepared for the coming apocalypse. There are many trends that are converging toward the biblical Apocalypse such as transhumanism, the New Age Movement, the ecumenical push, the exponential increase in technology, and the marginalization of Christianity. People in our soci-ety have no idea how fast these movements can converge, and before they know it, the end time apocalypse will be upon them.

I believe the events of the biblical Apocalypse are still a ways off. Why? Because the Antichrist has not signed his pact with Israel. In ad-dition, there is no city today like Babylon the great as found in the book of Revelation. The Jewish Temple has not been rebuilt. None of these biblical events have taken place at the time of this writing.

I also think that technology at the end of the age will be far more sophisticated than it is now. This is merely my opinion. However, if it turns out to be correct, then I think it is possible that what many theologians consider symbolism in the book of Revelation may, in some cases, be taken much more literally in light of the technology that will be available at that time. That's how far advanced I think the technology and genetic engineering will be at the end of the age.

Regardless of how all of this plays out, we need to be awake and watching historical events lest we be taken unawares. Jesus wants us to be prepared for His return—as if the events of the Apocalypse were going to unfold today.

The most important thing to do in light of all this is to get right with God by repenting of one's sin and embracing Jesus Christ as Lord and Savior. Quite frankly, if you don't get right with God, it will be impossible to avoid the deceptions that are coming. If you try to go it alone without God's help, I promise you that you'll find yourself on the losing end. You will fall prey to deception. This is not melodrama. It is fact.

The next thing to do is to embrace the truth that is found in Scripture. In other words, getting reacquainted with one's Bible would be a good next step. This facilitates the ability to discern truth from lies that are so prevalent now, and will be even more ubiquitous at the end of the age.

Finally, passing down the truth of the Christian worldview to one's children is imperative. Finding a Bible-believing church to become a part of would be a good way to support this effort because one of the generations coming up behind us (if not our own) will be the one that comes face to face with the NWO and the Antichrist.

Chapter 20

The Coming Clash of Kingdoms: Jesus Crushes the NWO

The previous two chapters presented the different ways events are trending and how things may look at the end of the age when Antichrist comes to power and leads some type of NWO. I provided a biblical framework because Scripture offers a prophetic backdrop with which to plug in future historical events. To this point in our eschatological study, it looks as if the Antichrist will get the better of things. But history doesn't end with Antichrist's phony kingdom. At some point after the middle of Daniel's seventieth week, the living God will put an end to Antichrist's martyring of Christians. Jesus will return and the great tribulation of the saints will be cut short. The day of the Lord will begin, and a clash of kingdoms will occur. The result will be "game over" for the Antichrist, his phony kingdom, and anyone who followed him and took his mark.

The "day of the Lord" is an apocalyptic event in the future when God's judgment and wrath will fall on those who reject Jesus's atoning sacrifice on the cross, and instead are deceived into taking the mark of the Beast (Antichrist) and joining his kingdom. These folks will be taken totally by surprise when Jesus returns after the great tribulation. The apostle Paul, who wrote to fellow Christians, put it this way: "For you yourselves are fully aware that the day of the Lord will come like a thief in the night. While people are saying, 'There is peace and security,' then sudden destruction will come upon them as labor pains come upon a pregnant woman, and they will not escape" (1 Thess. 5:2–3). Why does Jesus return at this particular time? Let's look at the chronology of events leading up to His return.

While all the deceptions we looked at in the previous two chapters will be taking place, Christians who stay true to the Lord will continue to preach the gospel while warning people all over the world not to take the Antichrist's mark. God loves the world so much that He is willing to allow His faithful disciples to suffer tribulation, even death, at the hand of the Antichrist so that they can proclaim the gospel to unbelievers right up to the end of the age. The hope, of course, is that people will accept the truth and become followers of the living God instead of the Antichrist. Just as Jesus laid down His life for the world, so too many saints at the end of the age will lay down their lives as they are martyred by Antichrist for staying true to Jesus.

But at some point during the great tribulation, God will have enough of watching His saints being slaughtered. So God will cut short this wholesale carnage by Antichrist. God will prepare to let the world know who is really in charge.

Before God can pour out His judgment and wrath on an unbelieving world at the day of the Lord, He will first remove His church from harm's way. This is when Jesus will return for the saints who have survived the great tribulation. Remember, Jesus promised His disciples that He would return someday. Understanding something of the Jewish marriage customs will help us to gain a better understanding of Jesus's promise to His disciples.

Jewish Marriage Customs and Jesus's *Parousia*

To establish a Jewish marriage covenant, the man goes to the house of the prospective bride's father. The two men agree to a purchase price, thus establishing the marriage covenant. As a symbol of the covenant, the bride and groom drink from a cup of wine. At this point, the bride is considered to be consecrated and therefore set apart exclusively for the bridegroom.

After instituting the marriage covenant, the groom returns to his father's house for a period of twelve months, during which time the bride prepares herself for married life. The groom prepares a place at his father's house for the bride. After the separation period is over, the groom returns to take away his bride, which usually takes place at night.

Although the bride is expecting the groom, she is not aware of the exact time of his arrival; therefore, as the groom draws near, he shouts to give his bride some time to prepare. After he gathers his bride, the entire wedding party returns to the house of the groom's father, where the wedding guests are assembled.[1]

Keeping in mind that the church is the bride of Christ,[2] this is the promise Jesus made to His disciples: "Believe in God; believe also in me. In my Father's house are many rooms. If it were not so, would I have told you that I go to prepare a place for you? And if I go and prepare a place for you, I will come again and will take you to myself, that where I am you may be also" (John 14:1b–3). The parallels between

Jesus's promise to return for His bride (the church) and the Jewish marriage custom are obvious. Let's look at a few of them.

Jesus left His Father's house (heaven) to come to earth for his prospective bride, the church (Christians). Jesus made a covenant, which He paid for with His blood on the cross. His sacrificial death was the purchase price He paid for His bride, the church.[3] He instituted and symbolized this covenant by the Communion cup of wine He shared with His disciples.[4] After He instituted the marriage covenant, the church was "set apart" (sanctified) exclusively for Jesus Christ.[5] Then Jesus returned to His Father's house and was separated from His bride. This period of separation will continue until the day of the Lord. In the meantime, the church, as the bride of Christ, is to make herself ready for Jesus's arrival. She does this by purifying herself until Jesus returns.[6]

Jesus told His disciples that no one will know the day or the hour of His return.[7] But just like the Jewish bridegroom, Jesus will announce His *parousia* with a shout and then snatch away ("rapture" from the Greek word *harpazo*) His bride to Himself in the clouds and return to His Father's house (heaven). This is clearly seen in the rapture passage where the apostle Paul wrote, "For the Lord himself will descend from heaven with a cry of command, with the voice of an archangel, and with the sound of the trumpet of God. And the dead in Christ will rise first. Then we who are alive, who are left, will be caught up together with them in the clouds to meet the Lord in the air, and so we will always be with the Lord" (1 Thess. 4:16–17).

A few verses down in the next chapter, the apostle Paul explains why Christians are raptured. "For God has not destined us for wrath, but to obtain salvation through our Lord Jesus Christ" (5:9). Jesus comes to snatch away his bride (just as a parent would snatch a child out of harm's way) before the wrath of God is poured out on the planet of rebellious unbelievers who follow Antichrist. Jesus's bride will be taken back to His Father's house, where she will enjoy the marriage supper of the Lamb.[8] Back on planet Earth, the false peace and security that Antichrist offered his followers will come crashing down on their heads when sudden destruction comes at the day of the Lord.

The Day of the Lord

Let's look at some Scripture passages to get an idea of what the day of the Lord will involve. There is a wonderful continuity between what the Old Testament prophets had to say about the day of the Lord, what Jesus described to His disciples, and what He later revealed to the apostle John in the book of Revelation. Joel, an Old Testament prophet, described the day of the Lord from God's perspective: "And I will show wonders in the heavens and on the earth, blood and fire and columns of smoke. The sun shall be turned to darkness, and the moon to blood, before the great and awesome day of the Lord comes" (Joel 2:30–31).

Jesus talked about the great tribulation, the day of the Lord, and the rapture. Here is how He described these events to His disciples who asked Him what the sign of his coming (*parousia*) and the end of the age would look like:

> Immediately after the tribulation of those days the sun will be darkened, and the moon will not give its light, and the stars will fall from heaven, and the powers of the heavens will be shaken. Then will appear in heaven the sign of the Son of Man, and then all the tribes of the earth will mourn, and they will see the Son of Man coming on the clouds of heaven with power and great glory. And he will send out his angels with a loud trumpet call, and they will gather his elect from the four winds, from one end of heaven to the other. (Matthew 24:29–31)

The reader will recall the four horsemen of the Apocalypse that were released when the first four seals were opened. A couple of seals later, the sixth seal, marks the beginning of the day of the Lord. Here is how the apostle John describes it:

> When he opened the sixth seal, I looked, and behold, there was a great earthquake, and the sun became black as sackcloth, the full moon became like blood, and the stars of the sky fell to the earth as the fig tree sheds its winter fruit when shaken by a gale. The sky vanished like a scroll that is being rolled up, and every mountain and island was removed from its place. Then the kings of the earth and the great ones and the generals and the rich and the powerful, . and everyone, slave and free, hid themselves in the caves and among the rocks of the mountains, calling to the mountains and rocks, "Fall on us and hide us from the face of him who is seated on the throne, and from the wrath of the Lamb, for the great day of their wrath has come, and who can stand?" (Revelation 6:12–17).

The use of the word *their* (Greek: *auton*) at the end of the verse above makes it clear that everyone left on the planet realizes that it is the *triune* God of the Bible who is behind the day of the Lord. The One seated on the throne is the Father. The Lamb is Jesus Christ. All three of the previous passages refer to the sun going dark and the moon turning to blood. So first there is a great earthquake that seems to level all the mountains. If that didn't get everyone's attention, then God turns the lights down when the sun goes dark and the moon turns to blood. The stars stop shining. It will probably have the same effect of turning the lights out on a three-year-old who is afraid of the dark. People will be terrified. They know God's wrath is on the way.

Jesus's triumphant return in His magnificent glory to gather His bride in the clouds will be made all the more visible because of the semi-darkness. At that point, the day of the Lord will leave no doubt in anyone's mind that the living God of the Bible has perforated human history. All the contrivances of atheistic science that promote the idea that God doesn't exist—methodological naturalism, uniformitarianism, naturalistic evolution with its contention that matter plus time plus chance created man, all the so-called wonders of technology, all the knowledge and riches and all the false religions in the world—all of these things will look miniscule and ridiculously pretentious compared with the power and glory of the living God, the Creator of heaven and earth.

Jesus compared life at the end of the age to the days of Noah. (By the way, this means that Jesus considered Noah's flood a historical event, which flies in the face of uniformitarianism.) Jesus described the time before His return this way:

> But concerning that day and hour no one knows, not even the angels of heaven, not the Son, but the Father only. As were the days of Noah, so will be the coming of the Son of Man. For as in those days before the flood they were eating and drinking, marrying and giving in marriage, until the day when Noah entered the ark, and they were unaware until the flood came and swept them all away, so will be the coming of the Son of Man. Then two men will be in the field; one will be taken and one left. Two women will be grinding at the mill; one will be taken and one left. Therefore stay awake, for you do not know on what day your Lord is coming. (Matthew 24:36–42)

When Jesus said that some people are "taken," He is referring to the rapture, which is paralleled in the Jewish marriage custom. Unfortunately, to the modern ear, the day of the Lord and the rapture, which are back-to-back events, seem too fantastic to be true.

In fact, the apostle Peter predicted over 1,900 years ago that scoffers in the last days would say, "Where is the promise of his coming? For ever since the fathers fell asleep, all things are continuing as they were from the beginning of creation" (2 Peter 3:4). In other words, people will be carrying on their lives just like they always have. If a Christian at the end of the age warns that Jesus is coming back, scoffers will point out that nothing has changed from the beginning of creation.

You will recall that Lyell's doctrine of uniformitarianism, which laid the groundwork for Darwinism, is exactly the mistaken notion that Peter was referring to. It is the atheistic theory that God (who supposedly doesn't exist) can't intervene in His own creation—that everything will carry on as it always has. People will be seduced by this mind-set because of all the knowledge and technological advances that will be occurring at the time of the Lord's return. People will have forgotten about God (just like today) because technology will lull them into thinking that it offers a type of secular salvation. The day of the Lord will come upon these people as a thief in the night.

When God Closes the Door

The day of the Lord will be a monumentally horrific time for those who reject God and serve Antichrist's kingdom. Seven trumpet judgments followed by seven bowls of wrath will be poured out on the planet. Space does not permit going over all of these events. The amazing part when reading over the coming judgments is that people repeatedly refuse to repent, even though they know God's wrath has come.[9] There is one point, however, after the sixth trumpet judgment, when some people finally do give glory to God, although it is not clear whether they truly repent or not. The text says that after the sixth trumpet is sounded, a massive earthquake occurs, apparently in Jerusalem, where a tenth of the city falls and 7,000 perish, and "the rest were terrified and gave glory to the God of heaven."[10]

After the seventh trumpet is sounded, loud voices in heaven are proclaiming, "The kingdom of the world has become the kingdom of our Lord and of his Christ, and he shall reign forever and ever" (Rev. 11:15). At this point, Antichrist's reign will be officially over as his fake kingdom suffers the horrific process of God's obliterating wrath. Even after suffering all the horrendous trumpet judgments heaped on Antichrist and his kingdom, the vast majority of people will still refuse to repent. In fact, I don't see any evidence of repentance after the seventh trumpet is sounded. People's hearts, instead of turning toward God, will become even harder as the seven bowl judgments are subsequently poured out on them.

It is at this time that God shuts the door. Just as God shut the door of Noah's ark, so too will He shut the door on the unrepentant, rebellious followers of Antichrist. Anyone who would repent has done so. The time for repentance is over, and now those who have hardened their hearts against the living God will receive the full cup of His wrath. They knew full well that they should have taken the opportunity to repent, but they refused. The Bible states that Jesus "will tread the winepress of the fury of the wrath of God the Almighty."[11] We don't hear much from today's pulpits about the wrath of God. It is not politically correct.

Nevertheless, after the seven bowls of wrath have been poured out, Jesus will return on a white horse with the armies of heaven to confront the Antichrist at Armageddon. I hesitate to call it the "battle of Armageddon," because it's not going to be much of a battle. In fact, it's not going to be a battle at all. Jesus will crush the Antichrist and his counterfeit kingdom of godless rebels like grapes that are thrown into a winepress and stomped on.

Let's look at the text:

> Then I saw an angel standing in the sun, and with a loud voice he called to all the birds that fly directly overhead. "Come, gather for the great supper of God, to eat the flesh of kings, the flesh of captains, the flesh of mighty men, the flesh of horses and their riders, and the flesh of all men, both free and slave, both small and great." And I saw the beast and the kings of the earth with their armies gathered to make war against him who was sitting on the horse and against his army. And the beast was captured, and with it the false prophet who in its presence had done the signs by which he deceived those who had received the mark of the beast and those who worshiped its image. These two were thrown alive into the lake of fire that burns with sulfur. And the rest were slain by the sword that came from the mouth of him who was sitting on the horse, and all the birds were gorged with their flesh. (Revelation 19:17–21)

If you go back and read about all the judgments and wrath that God pours out on the world of unbelievers, which includes a third of humankind being killed (Revelation chapters 8, 9, and 16), and then you read above about how Antichrist and the kings of the earth assemble themselves to war against Jesus, you are left with one question. How could these people who are getting ready to fight Jesus be so stupid? They will see firsthand the power of God to literally send utter destruction on the planet over and over again. Yet they think they are going to battle Jesus? What with? The latest technology? Like a laser pistol? Maybe a Dick Tracy watch, or a squirt gun? Perhaps they will bring a portable Hadron Collider and point it at Jesus, and try to zap Him out of existence.

The point to take away here is the depth of rebellion a human heart is capable of. Many of these people who get ready to battle Jesus will be big-shots, like the global elites. They think they are the cream of the crop. They consider themselves smarter than everyone else, but they will learn otherwise. Many will be secularists whose only concern will be the here and now. They will never give God a lick of thought until God's wrath wakes them up. The text says some are kings. I'm sure the "best and the brightest" will be there. Most will be just rebellious people who allow themselves to be deceived into taking Antichrist's mark. All of these people will harden their hearts against the living God and get ready to fight.

The rebellion in these haters of God runs so deep they can't see straight. The only thing they can focus on is trying to kill Jesus, because He will trample underfoot their phony, pretentious, hedonistic, narcissistic, godless kingdom. But anyone moronic enough to point a laser gun at Jesus—or whatever the latest technological kid's toy is at that time—after seeing firsthand what the living God is capable of shows you the depth of stupidity that rebellion can take someone.

If you look at the text closely enough, you'll notice it isn't a war at all. Jesus just grabs the Antichrist/Beast and the False Prophet and throws them into the lake of fire. The rest of the kings, global elites, big-shots, and rebellious people become food for the birds. So much for signing on to Antichrist's great utopia. To put it in the parlance of the stock market—these people found themselves on the wrong side of the trade.

The point of this and the previous two chapters is to encourage you to get right with God so that you, your children, or your children's children or grandchildren won't fall for Antichrist's lies and suffer the same fate as these pompous fools.

Judgment Day and Salvation

Judgment day is coming for everyone who ever lived.[12] If you find yourself standing in line on judgment day and you never accepted Jesus as your savior then you will be in trouble, because you will be judged by your works. Doing good works won't get you into heaven. Good works can't pay for your sin. We are all sinners *by nature* because of Adam's sin. That is our *condition*, and good works can't change our condition. Only accepting Jesus's sacrificial death for our sin can change our condition as sinners.

Moreover, if you repent of your sin and accept Jesus's sacrifice on the cross on your behalf, you become "born again" as the Holy Spirit miraculously regenerates your spirit. In essence, you go from death unto life as the triune God abides in you forever. Your *conduct* (being a good person or performing good works) can't change your *condition* as a sinner. Only God can change your condition. Regeneration is a miracle only God can perform. There is a wonderful passage that summarizes all of this:

> But when the goodness and loving kindness of God our Savior appeared, he saved us, not because of works done by us in righteousness, but according to his own mercy, by the washing of regeneration and renewal of the Holy Spirit, whom he poured out on us richly through Jesus Christ our Savior, so that being justified by his grace we might become heirs according to the hope of eternal life. (Titus 3:4-7)

Unfortunately, those who reject God and His Son, either willfully or by neglect, will find themselves thrown into the lake of fire which God originally prepared only for the Devil and his angels.[13] The time to accept Jesus Christ's sacrificial death on the cross for your sins is today, not sometime in the future.

If you find yourself standing in a line where your name is written in the Book of Life, then congratulations are in order. You must have repented, asked forgiveness for your sin, and then accepted Jesus Christ as your Savior at some point in your life. Therefore, you will not be judged for your sin, because judgment for your sin already fell on Jesus at the cross, where He shed His blood so that you could be justified before a holy God, and saved from His wrath.[14] You have been saved by grace, not works, because, as noted above, good works can't save you.[15]

Although I have dealt mainly with Protestantism in this book, before leaving the topic of salvation I would like to take a moment to kindly address those within the Roman Catholic faith because there is nothing more important than salvation. Please take this in the spirit that it is intended, which is to bring people to a saving knowledge of Jesus Christ.

Over the course of my life, I have spoken to countless Catholics regarding salvation. If the opportunity arises I gently, yet directly, ask them how they expect to get to heaven, or how a person can make it into heaven. Only one Catholic in thirty years has ever answered the question correctly. He was a plumber. In answer to my question of how one gets to heaven, he said, "You know what I think? I think you have to accept Jesus Christ as your Savior." He is exactly right.

Invariably, however, I always receive one of the following answers from Catholics. "I'm a good person," or "I've done the best I can," or "I hope I've done enough," or "I'm Catholic." I ask them if they think they can get to heaven through their good works or by being a good person, then why did Jesus have to pay the price He did by dying on the cross for their sins. After all, I say, when Jesus has the power to speak the universe into existence out of nothing and yet humbled Himself and hung on the cross for our sins, why would Jesus suffer and pay that kind of price if someone can get to heaven through his good works or by being a good person? At this point Catholics usually backtrack and say, yes, they know Jesus died on the cross for their sins. I then ask them why they didn't give me that answer in the first place.

I'll tell you why. Most Catholics, by and large, intuitively or unconsciously think they're getting to heaven, at least in part, by their own merit—by something they've done or because they go to Mass or just because they're Catholic. These things are first and foremost in their minds. However one slices it, Jesus's sacrificial death is always secondary in their thinking.

Let me say this as kindly as I can to those of you who are Catholics, and for any others that think they can make it to heaven by their good works. God doesn't grade on a curve. Jesus doesn't need our "help" with good works we might do. Good works do nothing to earn our salvation. Jesus paid the price *in full, once for all time*[16] (not every week at Mass) when He hung on the cross and shed His blood for your sin and mine at Calvary.

As gently as possible, let me say that Catholicism isn't like an organization or club that you are baptized into as a baby that then assures you make it into heaven. I bring this up because Catholics rarely ever identify themselves as Christians. They always identify themselves as "Catholics," as if being a Catholic is like being a member of a club that automatically puts them in good standing with God. I am not saying that Catholicism is a club. I *am* saying that the way many Catholics perceive themselves leaves one with the impression that they think being Catholic carries clout with God.

Let me say this directly and with no disrespect intended: being a member of the Catholic Church does not automatically make one heaven-bound. Being baptized as a newborn baby into the Catholic Church does not put you in good standing with God as an adult. Only the shed blood of Jesus Christ, His death, and His subsequent resurrection assures each of us of salvation when we *willfully* and *consciously* repent of our sins, embrace Jesus, and walk with Him. Good works and *belonging to a church* (even a Protestant church) will not gain anyone entrance into heaven. Belonging to Jesus Christ *will* get you into heaven.

My intention above is to help those who may not be familiar with what the Bible actually says about salvation as noted in the verse quoted previously (Titus 3:4-7). There is nothing wrong with doing good works or trying to be a good person. But good works *follow* salvation, they don't precede it. Working for the Lord and trying to pursue holiness are things we do *after* we are saved. They are not things we do to earn salvation.

For those in other faiths, let me say that the triune God of the Bible is the only God who can offer you eternal life, because the personal, living God of the Bible *is* eternal life. No one else can offer you that. The God of the Bible is the only God who is really there. The other so-called gods don't exist. It doesn't matter that this assertion is politically incorrect. The only thing that matters is that it is the truth. And as we saw in chapter six, truth is universal, objective, and absolute, which means it applies to you whether you think it does or not.

When you embrace Jesus, you have embraced eternal life. Because Jesus *is* eternal life. Look at what the Bible says about Jesus and eternal life: "And this is the testimony, that God gave us eternal life, and this life is in his Son. Whoever has the Son has life; whoever does not have the Son of God does not have life. I write these things to you who believe in the name of the Son of God that you may know that you have eternal life" (1 John 5:11-13). There is no guesswork involved here. Anyone who repents of their sin and embraces Jesus Christ has eternal life.

Jesus always existed and He always will exist. He is eternal, like the other two members of the Trinity—the Father and the Holy Spirit. We should embrace Jesus with the same desperation that Mary Magdalene did when she recognized who He was on resurrection Sunday near His empty tomb. Mary understood that Jesus *is* salvation. That's why she grabbed hold of Him and would not let Him go. Mary Magdalene understood what most in our PC culture do not—there is no other way to heaven but through Jesus. Period.

After a person repents of his sins and embraces Jesus, he becomes a child of God and can spend eternity with the triune God in heaven and the rest of God's family—those of us who have also embraced Jesus Christ. The primary goal in life should be to develop a relationship with the living God of the Bible through Jesus Christ. This goes for everyone. Christianity is not about religion. Religion binds. People get all bound up with doing this and that and then think they are earning favor with God, and maybe, just maybe, they will have done enough good deeds to get into heaven. But that's not how it works. True Christianity is not about *religion*; it's about *relationship*. It's about your personal relationship with Jesus Christ.

It's also about grace. Grace is unmerited favor. God bestowed His favor on humanity (sinners like you and me) by sending Jesus Christ to die on the cross for our sins so that we can be reconciled with a holy (morally pure) God. Jesus's resurrection proved that Jesus was who He said He was—the Son of God (and God the Son). We tap into God's grace by accepting Jesus Christ's sacrificial death on the cross for our sins and believing that God literally in space-time history raised Jesus from the dead.

Jesus is God Almighty in the flesh and He is the only way to salvation. The "good news" is that *everyone* has access into the grace that has been extended to us through Jesus's death on the cross and therefore we can be justified before a holy God because Jesus Christ paid the price for our sin. This gospel (good news) is worth living for, and dying for, because it is the truth. Christians at the end of the age will pay with their lives when they tell an unbelieving world of God's love as demonstrated through Jesus Christ.

With this in mind, if you haven't done so already, repent of your sin, admit that you need Jesus to save you, and embrace what He did on the cross for you when He shed His own blood for your sin. Embrace Jesus today. You will have a whole new life ahead of you.

Is Success Secular or Eternal?

Many in our society have this notion that being a success is about having a good job or lots of money or prestige or power. Of course, there is nothing wrong with having a good job or obtaining wealth. But in the end, are these things really what make an individual a success? Not really, because oftentimes grasping after or ultimately obtaining these things leaves God out of the picture.

If there's one thing we've learned from this book, it's that leaving God behind as we carry on our daily lives is secular thinking. Secular modernism places man in the center of the cosmos, and therefore is an erroneous worldview. It is too this-worldly. It's too short-sighted and myopic. It's too temporal. Secularism is all of these things because it ignores God and eternity. It steals God's glory and sovereignty. As we've seen over and over in this book, when we ignore God, we become narcissistic and autonomous, and things go wrong.

In reality, success is about embracing Jesus Christ and then finding out what His plan for your life is. Then it is about walking in the center of God's will so He can use all of your unique talents (and even idiosyncrasies) for His kingdom. That's what real success is.

It can start with raising a family in which each member knows and has a personal relationship with Jesus Christ. This is success because it bears good fruit for all eternity as your children become adopted into God's family and ultimately make it into heaven. Meanwhile your children are able to pass down the truth of Jesus Christ to their children and so on. A success is ultimately about bringing as many people as possible to a saving knowledge of the Lord Jesus Christ so that they can also have their sins forgiven and spend eternity with the triune God of the Bible.

In fact, it is my hope that this book will, in some small way, help wake people up and warn them of the peril ahead and assist them in becoming members of God's family today through Jesus Christ. We need to get the God of the Bible back into our lives. Repentance and revival would breathe life back into our nation. This is how we can get our country back on track.

Jesus's kingdom is an everlasting kingdom, so what you do for Him will last forever, not just in this lifetime. As the old saying goes—you can't take it with you. It's ultimately about what you store up for eternity (and primarily where you spend eternity) that counts. It's not about personal gain in the here and now which is secular, temporal, and fleeting. You want to store up your rewards and treasures in heaven, where Jesus is. Embracing Jesus with all of your heart and working for His kingdom is the ultimate cure for secularism.

If you want an idea of what it's going to be like in the new heaven and the new earth for those who spend eternity with the triune God of the Bible, read through Revelation chapters 21 and 22. Spoiler Alert—It's going to be awesome. I hope to see you there.

Notes

Chapter 1

1. David Limbaugh, *Persecution: How Liberals Are Waging War Against Christianity* (Washington, D.C.: Regnery Publishing Inc., 2003), 292–93.

2. Robxz, "Obama: We Are No Longer a Christian Nation," *YouTube*, March 9, 2008. https://www.youtube.com/watch?v=tmC31evZiik.

3. James Hitchcock, *What Is Secular Humanism? Why Humanism Became Secular and How It Is Changing Our World* (Ann Arbor: Servant Books, 1982), 10–11.

4. John W. Whitehead, *The End of Man* (Westchester, IL: Crossway Books, 1986), 40.

5. Alister McGrath, *A Passion for Truth: The Intellectual Coherence of Evangelicalism* (Downers Grove: InterVarsity Press, 1996), 16.

6. David F. Wells, *No Place for Truth: Whatever Happened to Evangelical Theology* (Grand Rapids: Eerdmans Publishing Company, 1993), 80.

7. Hans Blumenberg, *The Legitimacy of the Modern Age* (Cambridge: MIT Press, 1999), 3.

8. Harold Netland, *Encountering Religious Pluralism: The Challenge to Faith and Mission* (Downers Grove: InterVarsity Press, 2001), 147.

9. Harvey Cox, *The Secular City* (Toronto: Macmillan Company, 1969), 15.

10. Steve Bruce, *Religion in the Modern World: From Cathedrals to Cults* (Oxford: Oxford University Press, 1996), 26.

11. Peter L. Berger, *The Sacred Canopy: Elements of Sociological Theory of Religion* (New York: Anchor Books, 1990), 106.

12. Ibid., 107.

13. Bruce, *Religion in the Modern World*, 6.

14. Richard John Neuhaus, *The Naked Public Square: Religion and Democracy in America* (Grand Rapids: Eerdmans Publishing Company, 1984), 198.

15. As cited in Richard Middleton and Brian J. Walsh, *Truth Is Stranger Than It Used to Be: Biblical Faith in a Postmodern Age* (Downers Grove: InterVarsity Press, 1995), 14.

16. Peter M. Williams, *Popular Religion in America: Symbolic Change and the Modernization Process In Historical Perspective* (Urbana: University of Illinois Press, 1989), 12.

17. Wells, *No Place for Truth*, 260.

18. J. Richard Middleton and Brian J. Walsh, *Truth Is Stranger Than It Used to Be* (Downers Grove: InterVarsity Press: 1995), 20.

19. Phillip E. Hammond, *Religion and Personal Autonomy: The Third Disestablishment in America* (Columbia, SC: University of South Carolina Press, 1992), 8.

20. Wade Clark Roof, *Spiritual Marketplace: Baby Boomers and the Remaking of American Religion* (Princeton: Princeton University Press, 1999), 90.

21. Christian Smith ed., *The Secular Revolution: Power, Interests, and Conflict in the Secularization of American Public Life* (Berkeley and Los Angeles: University of California Press, 2003), 26.

22. Phillip E. Hammond, *Religion and Personal Autonomy*, xiv (found in the Preface)

23. Ibid., 10.

24. Smith ed., *Secular Revolution*, 28.

25. Ibid.

26. Ibid., 32–33.

27. Ibid., 4.

28. Robert Wuthnow, *The Restructuring of American Religion* (Princeton: Princeton University Press, 1988), 61.

29. Ibid., 55.

30. Ibid., 58.

31. Smith ed., *Secular Revolution*, 28.

32. Wuthnow, *Restructuring of American Religion,* 159.

33. Ibid., 144.

34. Will Herberg, *Protestant-Catholic-Jew* (Garden City, NY: Doubleday & Company Inc., 1960), 5, (found in endnote no. 8).

35. Thomas C. Reeves, *The Empty Church: The Suicide of Liberal Christianity* (NY: Free Press, 1996), 124.

36. Herberg, *Protest-Catholic-Jew*, 2.

37. Reeves, *Empty Church,* 124.

38. Alan Wolfe, *One Nation After All* (New York: Penguin Books, 1999), 40.

39. Herberg, *Protestant-Catholic-Jew*, 3.

40. Wuthnow, *Restructuring of American Religion,* 154–55.

41. Ibid., 152, 156, 168.

42. Ibid., 168.

43. Ibid., 157.

44. Hammond, *Religion and Personal Autonomy*, 168.

45. Ibid., 12–13.

46. Ibid., 11.

47. Wuthnow, *Restructuring of American Religion,* 158.

48. Roof, *Spiritual Marketplace*, 113.

49. Hammond, *Religion and Personal Autonomy*, 10–11.

50. Berger, *Sacred Canopy*, 48, 127.

51. Ibid., 48.

52. Ibid., 46, 49.

53. Limbaugh, *Persecution*, 345.

54. Wells, *No Place for Truth*, 87.

55. The Free Dictionary, s.v. "apocalypse," accessed July 17, 2014, http://www.thefreedictionary.com/apocalypse.

Chapter 2

1. *Pew Research Center*, "America's Changing Religious Landscape," May12, 2015, http://pewforum.org/2015/05/12americas-changing-religious-landscape/.

2. Ibid.

3. Ravi Zacharias, *Jesus Among Other Gods: The Absolute Claims of the Christian Message* (Nashville: Word Publishing, 2000), 50.

4. Nagel has recently questioned Neo-Darwinian materialism in his book *Mind and Cosmos: Why the Materialist Neo-Darwinian Conception of Nature Is Almost Certainly False* (New York: Oxford University Press, 2012). Nagel's book has wrought screams of anguish from those in his camp. Quote is found in footnote on page 12.

5. James Hitchcock, *What Is Secular Humanism* (Ann Arbor: Servant Books, 1982), 46.

6. As quoted in Norman Geisler and Frank Turek, *Legislating Morality* (Eugene, OR: Wipf and Stock Publishers, 1998), 78.

7. Hitchcock, *What Is Secular Humanism*, 14–15.

8. Henry Morris, PhD, "The Evolving Humanist Manifestos," *Institute for Creation Research*, 2003, http://www.icr.org/article/evolving-humanist-manifestos/.

9. Ibid.

10. Paul Kurtz, *In Defense of Secular Humanism* (Buffalo: Prometheus Books, 1983), 41.

11. Ibid., 39.

12. Ibid., 51.

13. Ibid., 42.

14. Ibid., 119.

15. Ibid., 121.

16. Ibid., 19, 21, 112.

17. James Davidson Hunter, *Culture Wars* (New York: Basic Books, 1991), 76.

18. Brad Stetson and Joseph G. Conti, *The Truth About Tolerance: Pluralism, Diversity, and the Culture Wars* (Downers Grove: InterVarsity Press, 2005), 97.

19. Samuel P. Huntington, *Who Are We? The Challenges to National Identity* (New York: Simon and Schuster, 2004), 104–5.

20. Ibid., 104.

21. Stephen L. Carter, *The Culture of Disbelief: How American Law and Politics Trivializes Religious Devotion* (New York: Basic Books, 1993), 51.

22. Robert N. Bellah, *Beyond Belief: Essays on Religion in a Post-Traditional World* (New York: Harper & Row, 1970), 174–76.

23. Nancy Pearcey, *Total Truth: Liberating Christianity from Its Cultural Captivity* (Wheaton: Crossway Books, 2004), 117.

24. Huntington, *Who Are We?*, 82.

25. Bill O'Reilly, *The O'Reilly Factor*, Fox News, October 5, 2005.

26. Huntington, *Who Are We?*, 351.

27. Randall Balmer, *Blessed Assurance: A History of Evangelicalism in America* (Boston: Beacon Press, 1999), 2.

28. Harold Bloom, *The American Religion: The Emergence of the Post-Christian Nation* (New York: Simon & Schuster, 1992), 37.

29. Klaus Bockmuehl, *The Unreal God: Of Modern Theology* (Colorado Springs: Helmers & Howard, 1988), 2.

30. I have used the term previously in the subtitle of a paper submitted as part of my Master's Degree in 1994, "A Portrait of America: Practical Atheism and the Loss of Accountability." I have also used this term in an article, "A Message of Hope," that was published in *Metro Community News*, April 4, 1999.

31. Christian Smith, ed., *Secular Revolution* (Berkeley and Los Angeles: University of California Press, 2003), 7. Thomas C. Reeves, *The Empty Church* (New York: Free Press, 1996), 55.

32. Robert H. Bork, *Slouching Towards Gomorrah: Modern Liberalism and American Decline* (New York: Harper Collins, 1996), 279–80.

33. Keith G. Meador, "My Own Salvation," Christian Smith, ed., *The Secular Revolution*, 270.

34. Huntington, *Who Are We?*, 66.

35. George Barna, *The Second Coming of the Church* (Nashville: Word Publishing, 1998), 22.

36. Pew shows the number of self-identified Christians as seven-in-ten. *Pew Research Center*, "America's Changing Religious Landscape," May 12, 2015, http://www.pewforum.org/2015/05/12americas-changing-religious-landscape/. An ABC news poll showed 83 percent of Americans self-identify as Christians. Gary Langer, "Poll: Most Americans Say They're Christian," *ABC News*, July 18, 2015, http://www.abcnews.go.com/US/story?id=90356. I am using an average of the two numbers which is 76 percent. Other polls have reported this number as an approximation as well.

37. Barna Group, "Americans Have Commitment Issues, New Survey Shows," April 18, 2006, http://barna.org/faith-spirituality/267-americans-have-commitment-issues-new-surveys-shows.

38. Barna Group, "Christianity Is No Longer Americans' Default Faith," January 12, 2009, http://www.barna.org/faith-spirituality/15-christianity-is-no-longer-americans-default-faith.

39. Barna Group, "Barna Study of Religious Change Since 1991 Shows Significant Changes by Faith Group," August 4, 2011, http://www.barna.org/faith-spirituality/514-barna-study-of-religious-change-since-1991-shows-significant-changes-by-faith-group.

40. Barna Group, "What Americans Believe About Universalism and Pluralism," April 18, 2011, http://www.barna.org/faith-spirituality/484-what-americans-believe-about-universalism-and-pluralism.

41. Ibid.

42. Barna, *The Second Coming of the Church*, 25.

43. Ibid.

44. Reeves, *The Empty Church*, 63.

45. Ibid., 66.

46. Robert Wuthnow, *Struggle for America's Soul: Evangelicals, Liberals, and Secularism* (Grand Rapids: William B. Eerdmans, 1989), 47.

47. William J. Bennett, *The Index of Leading Cultural Indicators: Facts and Figures on the State of American Society* (New York: Touchstone, 1994), 116.

48. Alan Wolfe, *One Nation, After All* (New York: Penguin Books, 1998), 253.

49. Steve Bruce, *Religion in the Modern World* (New York: Oxford University Press, 1996), 35.

50. Pearcey, *Total Truth*, 35.

51. Barna Group, "Christianity Is No Longer Americans' Default Faith," January 12, 2009, http://www.barna.org/faith-spirituality/15-christianity-is-no-longer-americans-default-faith.

52. Wade Clark Roof, *Spiritual Marketplace* (Princeton: Princeton University Press, 1999), 145.

53. Wolfe, *One Nation, After All*, 82–83.

54. Barna Group, "Christianity Is No Longer Americans' Default Faith."

55. Harold Netland, *Encountering Religious Pluralism* (Downers Grove: InterVarsity Press, 2001), 152.

56. Roof, *Spiritual Marketplace*, 137.

57. Jerry Adler, "In Search of the Spiritual," *Newsweek*, August 29–September 5, 2005, 48.

58. Robert Bellah, et.al, *Habits of the Heart: Individualism and Commitment in American Life* (Berkeley: University of California Press, 1985), 220–21.

59. Robert Wuthnow, *The Struggle for America's Soul* (Grand Rapids: William B. Eerdmans Publishing Company, 1989), 116.

60. Bellah, *Habits of the Heart*, xlii.

61. David S. Dockery, ed., *The Challenge of Postmodernism* (Grand Rapids: Baker Academic, 2001), 171.

62. Roof, *Spiritual Marketplace*, 9 and 32, respectively.

63. Lisa Takeucho Cullen Mahtomedi, "Stretching for Jesus," *Newsweek*, August 29–September 5, 2005, 75.

64. Tony Schwartz, *What Really Matters: Searching for Wisdom in America* (New York: Bantam Books, 1996), 422.

65. David Brooks, *Bobos in Paradise: The New Upper Class and How They Got There* (New York: Simon and Schuster Paperbacks, 2000), 10–11.

66. Ibid., 228.

67. Ibid., 237.

68. George Barna, *The Second Coming*, 23.

69. Ronald J. Sider, *The Scandal of the Evangelical Conscience: Why Are Christians Living Just Like the Rest of the World?* (Grand Rapids: Baker Books, 2005), 18.

70. Dennis McCallum, ed., *The Death of Truth* (Minneapolis: Bethany House Publishers, 1996), 204.

71. Ronald Nash, *The Word of God and the Mind of Man: The Crisis of Revealed Truth in Contemporary Theology* (Grand Rapids: Zondervan Publishing House, 1982), 121.

72. Reeves, *The Empty Church*, 33.

73. Bork, *Slouching Towards Gomorrah*, 286.

74. S. D. Graede, *When Tolerance Is No Virtue: Political Correctness, Multiculturalism and the Future of Truth and Justice* (Downers Grove: InterVarsity Press, 1993), 45.

75. Barna Group, "How Post-Christian Is U.S. Society?" May 16, 2013, http://www.barna.org/culture-articles/613-how-post-christian-is-us-society.

76. Ibid.

Chapter 3

1. Bryan Magee, *Confessions of a Philosopher: A Journey Through Western Philosophy* (New York: Random House Inc., 1997), 244.

2. Ibid., 245.

3. Kelly James Clark et. al., *101 Key Terms in Philosophy and Their Importance for Theology* (Louisville: John Knox Press, 2004), 6.

4. Ibid., 85–86.

5. Jeremy Campbell, *The Liar's Tale: A History of Falsehood* (New York & London: W.W. Norton & Company, 2001), 84.

6. Michael Allen Gillespie, *Nihilism before Nietzsche* (Chicago: University of Chicago Press, 1996), 22.

7. Garrett Green, *Theology, Hermeneutics, and Imagination: The Crisis of Interpretation at the End of Modernity* (Cambridge: Cambridge University Press, 2000), 73.

8. Campbell, *Liar's Tale*, 82.

9. Colin Brown, *Christianity and Western Thought*, Vol. 1 *A History of Philosophers, Ideas & Movements* (Downers Grove: InterVarsity Press, 1990), 139.

10. Campbell, *The Liar's Tale*, 84.

11. Gillespie, *Nihilism before Nietzsche*, 24.

12. Michael J. Buckley, *At the Origins of Modern Atheism* (New Haven & London: Yale University Press, 1987), 74.

13. Campbell, *The Liar's Tale*, 75.

14. Gillespie, *Nihilism before Nietzsche*, 24.

15. Rene Descartes, *Discourse on Method and Meditations on First Philosophy*, David Weissman, ed. (New Haven & London: Yale University Press, 1996), 123.

16. Stephen Toulmin, *Cosmopolis: The Hidden Agenda of Modernity* (Chicago: University of Chicago Press, 1990), 54–55.

17. Buckley, *At the Origins of Modern Atheism*, 76.

18. Descartes, *Meditations on First Philosophy*, David Weissman, ed., (New Haven & London: Yale University Press, 1996), 49.

19. Jeffrey Stout, *The Flight from Authority: Religion, Morality, and the Quest for Autonomy* (Notre Dame: University of Notre Dame Press, 1981), 109.

20. McGrath, *A Passion for Truth*, 88.

21. Garrett Thomson, *Descartes to Kant: An Introduction to Modern Philosophy* (Prospect Heights: Waveland Press Inc., 1993), 39.

22. Louis Dupre, *Passage to Modernity: An Essay in the Hermeneutics of Nature and Culture* (New Haven & London: Yale University Press, 1993), 116.

23. Roger Trigg, *Philosophy Matters* (Malden & Oxford: Blackwell Publishers, 2002), 139

24. Ernst Cassirer, *The Philosophy of the Enlightenment*, Fritz C. Koelln and James P. Pettegrove, trans. (Princeton: Princeton University Press, 1979), 13.

25. Ibid.

26. Ibid.

27. This is from the title of Stout's book.

28. Stout, *The Flight from Authority*, 41.

29. Ibid., 49–50.

30. James M. Byrne, *Religion and the Enlightenment: From Descartes to Kant* (Louisville: Westminster John Knox Press, 1996), 57.

31. Peter, Gay, *The Enlightenment: The Rise of Modern Paganism* (New York: W.W. Norton & Company, 1995), 4, 10.

32. James Byrne, *Religion and the Enlightenment*, 31.

33. Allan Bloom, *The Closing of the American Mind* (New York: Simon & Schuster, 1987), 374.

34. Three-step analysis by Alister McGrath, *A Passion for Truth*, 91–93.

35. Byrne, *Religion and the Enlightenment*, 100.

36. Ibid.,16.

37. McGrath, *A Passion for Truth*, 88.

38. Byrne, *Religion and the Enlightenment*, 106.

39. Ibid., 105.

40. Carl Becker, *The Heavenly City of the Eighteenth-Century Philosophers*, (New Haven & London: Yale University Press, 1932), 64–65.

41. Byrne, *Religion and the Enlightenment*, 195.

42. Cassirer, *Philosophy of the Enlightenment*, 158.

43. Byrne, *Religion and the Enlightenment*, 201.

44. Ibid., 202.

45. Newbigin, *The Gospel in a Pluralistic Society*, 2–3.

46. Byrne, *Religion and the Enlightenment*, 143.

47. Ibid., 109.

48. Gay, *The Enlightenment*, 379.

49. Byrne, *Religion and the Enlightenment*, 121.

50. Ibid., 123.

51. Alister McGrath, *Science and Religion: An Introduction* (Oxford: Blackwell Publishers, 1999), 18.

52. William E. Hordern, *A Layman's Guide to Protestant Theology* (New York: Macmillan Publishing Company, 1968), 38.

53. Gay, *The Enlightenment*, 122.

54. Carl Becker, *The Heavenly City of the Eighteenth-Century Philosophers*, 68–69.

55. Nash, *The Word of God and the Mind of Man*, 19–20.

56. Colin Brown, *Miracles and the Critical Mind*, 53.

57. Ibid., 86, 92.

58. Byrne, *Religion and the Enlightenment*, 148–49.

59. Nash, *The Word of God and the Mind of Man*, 20.

60. Bill Austin, *Austin's Topical History of Christianity* (Wheaton: Tyndale House Publishing, 1983), 324.

61. Magee, *Confessions of a Philosopher*, 143.

62. Thomson, *Descartes to Kant*, 253–54.

63. Byrne, *Religion and the Enlightenment*, 210.

64. Garrett Thomson, *Descartes to Kant*, 240–241. Kant may be interpreted many ways. I follow what Thomson calls the "weaker" version of Kant's transcendental idealism.

65. Ibid., 240.

66. Byrne, *Religion and the Enlightenment*, 213.

67. Austin, *Austin's Topical History of Christianity*, 325.

68. Nash, *The Word of God and the Mind of Man*, 22.

69. Byrne, *Religion and the Enlightenment*, 214.

70. Austin, *Austin's Topical History of Christianity*, 325–26

71. Pearcey, *Total Truth*, 104. Quote found on pg. 105.

72. Francis Schaeffer, *The Francis Schaeffer Trilogy: He Is There and He Is Not Silent*, (Wheaton: Crossway Books, 1990), 333.

73. Newbigin, *The Gospel in a Pluralistic Society*, 18–19.

74. Byrne, *Religion and the Enlightenment*, 206.

75. Green, *Theology, Hermeneutics, and Imagination*, 50.

76. Netland, *Encountering Religious Pluralism*, 139.

77. Byrne, *Religion and the Enlightenment*, 228.

78. All of the aforementioned points may be found in the following references: Becker, *The Heavenly City of the Eighteenth-Century Philosophers*, 102–103. Byrne, *Religion and the Enlightenment*, 179. Matthew Stewart, *The Truth About Everything: An Irreverent History of Philosophy*, (Amherst, New York: Prometheus Books, 1997), 222–23. Netland, *Encountering Religious Pluralism*, 67.

79. Gay, *The Enlightenment*, 326.

80. Buckley, *At the Origins of Modern Atheism*, 357.

81. Steve Wilkens and Alan G. Padgett, *Christianity and Western Thought*, Vol. 2 (Downers Grove, IL: InterVarsity Press, 2009), 79, 81.

82. Magee, *The Story of Philosophy* (New York: DK Publishing, 1998), 159.

83. Schaeffer, *The Francis Schaeffer Trilogy*, 233.

84. Wilkens and Padgett, *Christianity and Western Thought*, Vol. 2, 85.

85. A. N. Wilson, *God's Funeral* (New York & London: W. W. Norton & Company, 1999), 48.

86. Klaus Bockmuehl, *The Unreal God*, (Colorado Springs: Helmers & Howard, 1988), 97.

87. Wilkens and Padgett, *Christianity and Western Thought*, Vol. 2, 116.

88. Ibid., 116. Quote found on pg. 124.

89. I retrieved this information from a paper, "Liberation Theologians' Use of Marxist Philosophy," which I submitted for "Christianity and Liberation Theology," a course I took as part of my Master's Degree requirements at Denver Seminary 1991.

90. James Sire, *The Universe Next Door* (Downers Grove, IL: InterVarsity Press, 1988), 76.

91. Wilkens and Padgett, *Christianity and Western Thought*, Vol. 2, 133.

92. Ibid., 133–34.

93. Campbell, *The Liar's Tale*, 163.

94. Wilkens and Padgett, *Christianity and Western Thought*, Vol. 2, 172.

95. Ibid., 170.

96. Ibid., 173.

97. Roger Scruton, *Modern Philosophy: An Introduction and Survey* (New York: Allen Lane, The Penguin Press, 1995), 462.

98. Millard Erickson, *Truth or Consequences* (Downers Grove, IL: InterVarsity Press, 2001), 87.

99. Scruton, *Modern Philosophy*, 297. Quote found on 296.

100. Magee, *The Story of Philosophy*, 177.

Chapter 4

1. Stout, *The Flight from Authority*, 50.

2. Randall Balmer, *Blessed Assurance: A History of Evangelicalism in America* (Boston: Beacon Press, 1999), 15.

3. Ibid., 2.

4. Mark Noll, Nathan O. Hatch, and George Marsden, *The Search for Christian America* (Colorado Springs: Helmers & Howard, 1989), 60.

5. Pearcey, *Total Truth*, 269.

6. Noll et. al., *Search for Christian America*, 54–55.

7. Pearcey quoting Harry Stout, *Total Truth*, 268.

8. Noll, et. al., *Search for Christian America*, 54, 60; Balmer, *Blessed Assurance*, 5.

9. Noll et.al., *Search for Christian America*, 65.

10. Sydney Ahlstrom, *A Religious History of the American People* (New Haven and London: Yale University Press, 2004), 362.

11. Noll et. al, *Search for Christian America*, 65.

12. Nathan O. Hatch, *Democratization of American Christianity*, (New Haven and London: Yale University Press, 1989), 3.

13. Ibid., 112.

14. Wuthnow, *Restructuring of American Religion*, 21.

15. Ibid., 21.

16. Pearcey, *Total Truth*, 264.

17. George Marsden, *Understanding Fundamentalism and Evangelicalism* (Grand Rapids: Eerdmans Publishing Company, 1991), 112.

18. Hatch, *Democratization of American Christianity*, 126.

19. Ahlstrom, *Religious History of the American People*, 236.

20. Austin, *Austin's Topical History of Christianity*, 332.

21. Hordern, *A Layman's Guide to Protestant Theology*, 44.

22. Van A. Harvey, "On the Intellectual Marginality of American Theology," *Religion and Twentieth Century American Intellectual Life*, Michael J. Lacey, ed. (Cambridge: Cambridge University Press, 1991), 189.

23. Nancey Murphy, *Beyond Liberalism and Fundamentalism: How Modern and Postmodern Philosophy Set the Theological Agenda* (Valley Forge: Trinity Press International, 1996), 46–47.

24. Hordern, *A Layman's Guide to Protestant Theology*, 45.

25. Ibid.., 46.

26. Berger, *Sacred Canopy*, 159.

27. McGrath, *A Passion for Truth*, 122–123.

28. Hordern, *A Layman's Guide to Protestant Theology*, 84.

29. Ibid., 82–83.

30. Ibid., 76–77.

31. Murphy, *Beyond Liberalism and Fundamentalism*, 71.

32. Berger, *Sacred Canopy*, 160.

33. Douglas Sloan, *Faith and Knowledge*, (Louisville: Westminster John Knox Press, 1994), 6.

34. Hordern, *A Layman's Guide to Protestant Theology*, 85.

35. Austin, *Austin's Topical History of Christianity*, 477.

36. Reeves, *The Empty Church*, 91.

37. McGrath, *A Passion for Truth*, 122.

38. Ernst Troeltsch, "The Dogmatics of the History-of-Religions School," *Religion in History*, James Luther Adams and Walter F. Bense, trans., (Edinburgh: T & T Clark, 1991), 87.

39. Ibid., 95. Quote found on pg. 94.

40. Ibid., 104.

41. Ibid., "Historical and Dogmatic Method in Theology," 16.

42. Hordern, *A Layman's Guide to Protestant Theology*, 42–43.

43. Charlotte Allen, *The Human Christ* (New York: Free Press, 1998), 5.

44. Steve Wilkens and Alan Padget, *Christianity and Western Thought*, Vol. 2 (Downers Grove: InterVarsity Press, 2000) 165.

45. Ibid., 158.

46. Douglas Groothuis, *Truth Decay: Defending Christianity Against the Challenge of Postmodernism*, (Downers Grove: InterVarsity Press, 2000), 276.

47. Hordern, *A Layman's Guide to Protestant Theology*, 117.

48. Ronald Nash, *Christian Faith and Historical Understanding* (Grand Rapids, MI: Zondervan Publishing House, 1984), 56. Nash offers an excellent treatment of Bultmann in this informative and readable little book.

49. As quoted in Nash, *Christian Faith*, 117.

50. Rudolf Bultmann, "New Testament and Mythology," *Kerygma and Myth*, Hans Werner Bartsch, ed., Reginald H. Fuller, trans. (New York: Harper & Row, 1961) 5.

51. Nash, *Christian Faith.*, 49.

52. Ibid., 55.

53. McGrath, *A Passion for Truth*, 61.

54. Richard Wightman Fox, "The Niebuhrs and the Liberal Protestant Heritage," *Religion and Twentieth Century American Intellectual Life*, Michael J. Lacey, ed., 106–7.

55. R. Albert Mohler Jr., "The Integrity of the Evangelical Tradition and the Challenge of the Postmodern Paradigm," *The Challenge of Postmodernism*, David S. Dockery (Grand Rapids, MI: Baker Academic, 2001), 60.

56. Gordon R. Lewis and Bruce A. Demarest, *Integrative Theology*, Vol.1 (Grand Rapids, MI: Zondervan Publishing House, 1987), 98.

57. Klaus Bockmuehl, *The Unreal God* (Colorado Springs: Helmers & Howard, 1988), 78.

58. R. Albert Mohler Jr., "The Integrity of the Evangelical Tradition and the Challenge of the Postmodern Paradigm," *Challenge of Postmodernism*, David S. Dockery, 62.

59. Bockmuehl, *The Unreal God*, 2.

60. Walter Truett Anderson, ed., *The Truth About the Truth: De-confusing and Re-constructing the Postmodern World* (New York: A Jeremy P. Tarcher/Putnam Book, 1995), 222.

61. Marsden, *Understanding Fundamentalism and Evangelicalism*, 1.

62. Ibid., 36.

63. Hatch, *Democratization of Christianity*, 215.

64. Even Harold Bloom, an avowed agnostic who calls fundamentalists "Know-Nothings," admitted his admiration for Machen after reading *Christianity and Liberalism*. He said, "I have just read my way through this, with distaste and discomfort but with reluctant and growing admiration for Machen's mind. I have never seen a stronger case made for the argument that institutional Christianity must regard cultural liberalism as an enemy to faith." Harold Bloom, *The American Religion*, 228.

65. J. Gresham Machen, *Christianity and Liberalism* (Grand Rapids, MI: Eerdmans, 1996), 7–8.

66. Reeves, *The Empty Church*, 114.

67. George Marsden, "Evangelicals and the Scientific Culture," *Religion and Twentieth Century American Intellectual Life*, Michael J. Lacey, ed., 45.

68. Wuthnow, *The Restructuring of the American Religion*, 134.

69. Marsden, *Understanding Fundamentalism and Evangelicalism*, 61.

70. Reeves, *The Empty Church*, 118.

71. Fox, "The Niebuhr Brothers and the Liberal Protestant Heritage," *Religion and Twentieth Century American Intellectual Life*, 96.

72. Ibid., 94–95.

73. Sloan, *Faith and Knowledge*, 13.

74. Hordern, *A Layman's Guide to Protestant Theology*, 153 and 156.

75. Paul Tillich, *Dynamics of Faith* (New York: Harper & Brothers, 1957).

76. Ibid., 46.

77. Francis Schaeffer, *The God Who Is There*, (Downers Grove, IL: InterVarsity Press, 1972), 58.

78. Paul Tillich, *Dynamics of Faith*, 47.

79. Sloan, *Faith and Knowledge*, 129.

80. Ibid., 132.

81. Ibid., 132–33.

82. I am not calling O'Reilly an atheist; however, I don't think he entirely thought through the implications of his assertion that "God is a philosophy." This reduces the living God to a concept.

83. Reeves, *The Empty Church*, 1.

84. Roof, *Spiritual Marketplace*, 65. See also George Marsden, *The Soul of the American University: From Protestant Establishment to Established Nonbelief* (New York: Oxford University Press, 1994), 415.

85. Peter Augustine Lawler, *Aliens in America: The Strange Truth About Our Souls* (Wilmington, DE: ISI Books, 2002), 228.

86. Roof, *Spiritual Marketplace*, 214.

87. Reeves, *The Empty Church*, 118–119.

88. I owe this categorization to Cal Thomas as found in Reeves, *The Empty Church*, 165.

89. Bruce, *Religion in the Modern World*, 89.

90. Blogger and former commercial hedge fund broker Ann Barnhardt is to be credited with the expression "super-fun-rock-band."

91. Allen West, "Christian Persecution in the US: Openly Gay Houston Mayor Demands Pastors Turn Over Sermons," October 15, 2014, Allen B. West Steadfast and Loyal, https://www.allenbwest.com/2014/christian-persecution-us-openly-gay-houston-mayor-demands-pastors-turn-sermons/.

92. Os Guinness, *The Gravedigger File: Papers On the Subversion of the Modern Church* (Downers Grove, IL: InterVarsity press, 1983), especially page 15. See also Craig M. Gay, *The Way of the Modern World Or, Why It's Tempting to Live As If God Doesn't Exist* (Grand Rapids, MI: William B. Eerdmans Publishing Company, 1998), 256.

93. Os Guinness, *The Gravedigger File*, 15.

94. Smith, *Secular Revolution*, 35.

95. Bruce, *Religion in the Modern World*, 144.

Chapter 5

1. Reeves, *The Empty Church*, 71.

2. Gay, *The Way of the Modern World*, 223.

3. Bellah, et. al., *Habits of the Heart*, 221.

4. Ratzinger, *Truth and Tolerance*, 231.

5. Philip J. Lee, *Against the Protestant Gnostics* (Oxford: Oxford University Press, 1987), 146.

6. I attribute this appellation to a former acquaintance of mine Jessie McCissick, who felt that because Deepak charges such exorbitant prices for his seminars, he should instead be labeled "Deep-Pockets."

7. Deepak Chopra, *The Seven Spiritual Laws of Success* (San Rafael, CA: Amber-Allen Publishing, 1994), 3.

8. Ibid., 43.

9. Reeves, *The Empty Church*, 56.

10. Wells, *No Place for Truth*, 141.

11. Lesslie Newbigin, *The Gospel in a Pluralist Society* (Grand Rapids, MI: Eerdmans Publishing Company, 1989), 14.

12. Harold Netland and Keith E. Johnson, "Why Is Religious Pluralism Fun—And Dangerous?" *Telling the Truth*, D.A. Carson, ed. (Grand Rapids, MI: Zondervan Publishing House, 2000), 54.

13. Newbigin, *The Gospel in a Pluralistic Society*, 14.

14. Byrne, *Religion and the Enlightenment*, 123.

15. Netland, *Encountering Religious Pluralism*, 213.

16. Harold A. Netland, *Dissonant Voices: Religious Pluralism and the Question of Truth* (Vancouver: Regent College Publishing, 1997), 32–33.

17. Netland, *Encountering Religious Pluralism*, 53.

18. McGrath, *A Passion for Truth*, 219.

19. Neuhaus, *The Naked Public Square*, 148.

20. McGrath, *A Passion for Truth*, 215–16.

21. Ravi Zacharias, *Jesus Among Other Gods*, 7.

22. Mortimer J. Adler, *Truth in Religion* (New York: Macmillan Publishing Company, 1990), 1–2.

23. Bruce, *Religion in the Modern World*, 36.

24. Newbigin, *The Gospel in a Pluralistic Society,* 242.

25. Ibid., 39.

26. Berger, *The Sacred Canopy*, 151.

27. Newbigin, *The Gospel in a Pluralistic Society*, 40.

28. Berger, *The Sacred Canopy*, 153.

29. Ibid.

30. Netland, *Encountering Religious Pluralism*, 15.

Chapter 6

1. Stanley Grenz, *A Primer on Postmodernism* (Grand Rapids, MI: Eerdmans Publishing Company, 1996), 92–93.

2. Ibid., 89, 91.

3. Ibid., 90.

4. *Wikipedia*, s.v. "Post-structuralism."

5. Grenz, *A Primer on Postmodernism*, 131, 133.

6. *Wikipedia*, s.v. "Post-structuralism."

7. David Harvey, *The Condition of Postmodernity* (Oxford: Blackwell Publishing Ltd., 1990), 49, 51.

8. Honeysett, *Meltdown*, 41.

9. Grenz, *A Primer on Postmodernism*, 43.

10. Honeysett, *Meltdown*, 42.

11. Ibid.

12. Carson, *The Gagging of God*, 21.

13. Harvey, *The Condition of Postmodernity*, 9.

14. Honeysett, *Meltdown*, 44.

15. Jean-Francois Lyotard, *The Postmodern Condition: A Report on Knowledge*, Geoff Bennington and Brian Massumi, trans. (Minneapolis, MN: University of Minnesota Press, 1984), xxiv.

16. Grenz, *A Primer on Postmodernism*, 45.

17. Ibid., 40, 45–46.

18. Carson, *The Gagging of God*, 20.

19. Roger Trigg, *Reason and Commitment* (Cambridge: Cambridge University Press, 1973), 2.

20. McCallum, *The Death of Truth*, 202.

21. D.A. Carson, *The Gagging of God*, 33.

22. McGrath, *A Passion for Truth*, 191.

23. Bloom, *The Closing of the American Mind*, 25.

24. Ben Shapiro, *Brainwashed* (Nashville, TN: WND Books, 2004), 1.

25. Stetson and Conti, *The Truth About Tolerance*, 63.

26. G. K. Chesterton, *Orthodoxy* (New York: Doubleday, 1990), 32.

27. "Truth" that is really "opinion" is described by Mortimer J. Adler as "poetical truth." It is "truth" that is not subject to logical contradiction. See Mortimer J. Adler, *Truth in Religion*, 12.

28. Lewis and Demarest, *Integrative Theology*, Vol.1, 32.

29. Francis A. Schaeffer, *Francis A. Schaeffer Trilogy* (Wheaton, IL: Crossway Books, 1990), 229.

30. For a more thorough discussion of realism, correspondence theory, and other related topics concerning truth in the surrounding paragraphs, see Frederick F. Schmitt, *Truth: A Primer* (Boulder: Westview Press, 1995). See also Mortimer J. Adler, *Truth in Religion*, 116.

31. Steinar Kvale, "Themes of Postmodernity," *The Truth About the Truth*, Walter Truett Anderson, ed. (New York: Jeremy P. Tarcher/Putnam Book, 1995), 19.

32. Newbigin, *The Gospel in a Pluralistic Society*, 18.

33. Wells, *No Place for Truth*, 280.

34. Schwartz, *What Really Matters*, 422.

35. Netland, *Dissonant Voices*, 32.

36. Groothuis, *Truth Decay*, 148.

37. Ibid., 149.

38. Francis A. Schaeffer, *The God Who Is There* (Downers Grove, IL: InterVarsity Press, 1972), 131.

Chapter 7

1. Anthony T. Kronman, *Education's End: Why Our Colleges and Universities Have Given Up on the Meaning of Life* (New Haven and London: Yale University Press, 2007), 47.

2. George M. Marsden, *The Soul of the American University* (New York: Oxford University Press, 1994), 33.

3. Ibid., 40–41.

4. Kronman, *Educations End*, 48.

5. Ibid., 54.

6. George M. Marsden and Bradley J. Longfield, eds., *The Secularization of the Academy* (New York: Oxford University Press, 1992), 199.

7. Marsden, *The Soul of the American University*, 52.

8. Frederick Rudolph, *The American College and University: A History* (Athens and London: The University of Georgia Press, 1990), 10.

9. Warren A. Nord, *Religion and American Education* (Chapel Hill and London: The University of North Carolina Press, 1995), 66.

10. Rudolph, *The American College and University*, 73, 17.

11. Marsden, *The Soul of the American University*, 55.

12. Rudolph, *The American College and University*, 17.

13. Marsden, *The Soul of the American University*, 55

14. Ibid.

15. Rudolph, *The American College and University*, 17.

16. Ibid., 10–11.

17. Rudolph, *The American College and University*, 10–11. Marsden, *The Soul of the American University*, 57.

18. Marsden, *The Soul of the American University*, 82.

19. D.G. Hart, *The University Gets Religion: Religious Studies in American Higher Education* (Baltimore and London: The Johns Hopkins University Press, 1999), 29–30.

20. Marsden, *The Soul of The American University*, 91.

21. Pearcey, *Total Truth*, 298.

22. Henry F. May, *The Enlightenment in America* (New York: Oxford University Press, 1976), 9.

23. Marsden, *The Soul of the American University*, 91.

24. Pearcey, *Total Truth*, 298.

25. Marsden, *The Soul of the American University*, 91.

26. Ibid.

27. Ibid., 90.

28. Rudolph, *The American College and University*, 40.

29. Ibid., 226.

30. Marsden, *The Soul of the American University*, 93.

31. Rudolph, *The American College and University*, 160.

32. Marsden and Longfield, *The Secularization of the Academy*, 4. Nord, *Religion and American Education*, 263.

33. Marsden and Longfield, *The Secularization of the Academy*, 10.

34. Kronman, *Education's End*, 102.

35. Ibid., 80, 116.

36. Nord, *Religion and American Education*, 84.

37. Marsden and Longfield, *The Secularization of the Academy*, 48. Marsden, *The Soul of the American University*, 19.

38. Marsden and Longfield, *The Secularization of the Academy*, 48.

39. Ibid.

40. Rudolph, *The American College and University*, 171.

41. Ibid., 265.

42. Marsden and Longfield, *The Secularization of the Academy*, 46.

43. Ibid., 14.

44. Marsden, *The Soul of the American University*, 102–03.

45. Ibid., 103.

46. Ibid., 104.

47. Wilfred Shaw, *The University of Michigan* (New York: Harcourt Brace and Howe, 1920), 47.

48. Marsden, *The Soul of the American University*, 107.

49. Rudolph, *The American College and University*, 234. Marsden, *The Soul of the American University*, 110.

50. Marsden, *The Soul of the American University*, 107.

51. Shaw, *The University of Michigan*, 54.

52. Rudolph, *The American College and University*, 290–91, 294.

53. Julie A. Reuben, *The Making of the Modern University: Intellectual Transformation and the Marginalization of Morality* (University of Chicago Press: Chicago & London, 1996), 77.

54. Ibid., 79, 82–83.

55. Skip McAfee, "The Intellectual Take on Our National Pastime," Project Muse, accessed November 15, 2014, https://muse.jhu.edu/login?auth=0&type=summary&url=/journals/nine/v013/13.2mcafee.html.

56. Nord, *Religion and American Education*, 263.

57. Allen W. Wood, "Hegel On Education," Stanford University, accessed July 2, 2012, web.stanford.edu/~allenw/webpapers/HegelEd.doc, document.

58. The German *Bildung* Tradition, University of North Carolina at Charlotte, accessed July 2, 2012, http://www.philosophy.uncc.edu/mledrid/SAAP?USC?pbt1.html.

59. Kronman, *Education's End*, 110.

60. Ibid., 109–11

61. Ibid., 112, 113.

62. Rudolph, *The American College and University*, 305.

63. Kronman, *Education's End*, 63.

64. Rudolph, *The American College and University*, 305.

65. Ibid., 269.

66. Reuben, *The Making of the Modern University*, 68.

67. Ibid., 63, 68.

68. *Wikipedia*, s.v. "Daniel Coit Gilman," https://en.wikipedia.org/wiki/Daniel_Coit_Gilman, last modified November 10, 2014.

69. Reuben, *The Making of the Modern University*, 61.

70. See also Marsden and Longfield, *The Secularization of the Academy*, 21, 76.

71. Hart, *The University Gets Religion*, 34.

72. Ibid.

73. Marsden and Longfield, *The Secularization of the Academy*, 110.

74. Rudolph, *The American College and University*, 346.

75. Marsden, *The Soul of the American University*, 155. Hart, *The University Gets Religion*, 11.

76. Marsden and Longfield, *The Secularization of the Academy*, 110.

77. Rudolph, *The American College and University*, 274.

78. Hart, *The University Gets Religion*, 31.

79. Marsden, *The Soul of the American University*, 113.

80. Ibid., 114–5.

81. Hart, *The University Gets Religion*, 22.

82. Marsden, *The Soul of the American University*, 116.

83. Hart, *The University Gets Religion*, 22.

84. Ibid.

85. Reuben, *The Making of the Modern University*, 59.

86. Marsden, *The Soul of the American University*, 119.

87. Reuben, *The Making of the Modern University*, 56.

88. Ibid., 97.

89. Ibid., 60.

90. George M. Marsden, *The Soul of the American University*, 117.

91. Ibid., 207.

92. Reuben, *The Making of the Modern University*, 97.

93. Christian Smith, ed., *The Secular Revolution: Power, Interests, and Conflict in the Secularization of American Public Life* (Los Angeles: University of California Press, 2003), 112.

94. Robert Benne, *Quality with Soul: How Six Premier Colleges and Universities Keep Faith with Their Religious Traditions* (Grand Rapids, MI/Cambridge, UK, Eerdmans Publishing Company, 2001), 26.

95. Reuben, *The Making of the Modern University*, 96.

96. Ibid., 97, 110–11.

97. Ibid., 57.

98. Robert Benne, *Quality with Soul*, 27.

99. Rudolph, *The American College and University*, 348.

100. Van A. Harvey, "On the Intellectual Marginality of American Theology," *Religion and Twentieth Century Intellectual Life*, 181.

101. Marsden, *The Soul of the American University*, 207.

102. Reuben, *The Making of the Modern University*, 112.

103. Ibid., 5.

104. Ibid., 101.

105. Marsden and Longfield, *The Secularization of the Academy*, 201.

106. Benne, *Quality with Soul*, 27.

107. Reuben, *The Making of the Modern University*, 108, 112–3.

108. Ibid., 106.

109. Ibid., 102.

Chapter 8

1. Reuben, *The Making of the Modern University*, 4.

2. Eva Marie Garroutte, "The Positive Attack on Baconian Science and Religious Knowledge in the 1870s," *The Secular Revolution*, 201.

3. Kronman, *Education's End*, 64–65.

4. Hart, *The University Gets Religion*, 66.

5. Marsden, *The Soul of the American University*, 287.

6. Smith, ed., *The Secular Revolution*, 75–76.

7. Marsden, *The Soul of the American University*, 281.

8. Ibid., 282–83.

9. Smith, ed., *The Secular Revolution*, 76.

10. Benne, *Quality with Soul*, 47.

11. Marsden, *The Soul of the American University*, 284–85.

12. Ibid., 285.

13. Ibid., 286.

14. Rudolf, *The American College and University*, 423.

15. Quoted in Marsden, *The Soul of the American University*, 267.

16. Sloan, *Faith and Knowledge*, 20.

17. Smith, ed., *The Secular Revolution*, 36–37.

18. Marsden, "Evangelicals and the Scientific Culture," *Religion and Twentieth Century American Intellectual Life*, 41–42.

19. David A. Hollinger, "Justification by Verification: The Scientific Challenge to the Moral Authority of Christianity in Modern America," Michael J. Lacey, ed., *Religion and Twentieth Century American Intellectual Life*, 135.

20. William McGuire King, "An Enthusiasm for Humanity: The Social Emphasis in Religion and Its Accommodation in Protestant Theology," Van A. Harvey, *Religion and Twentieth Century American Intellectual Life*, 59.

21. Smith, ed., *The Secular Revolution*, 106–7.

22. Ibid., 106.

23. Reuben, *The Making of the Modern University*, 133, 156.

24. Smith, ed., *The Secular Revolution*, 151, 109.

25. Ibid., 111.

26. Reuben, *The Making of the Modern University*, 167.

27. Hollinger, "Justification by Verification Michael," *Religion and Twentieth Century American Intellectual Life*, 123–25.

28. Ibid., 119.

29. Ibid., 128.

30. Benne, *Quality with Soul*, 38.

31. Marsden and Longfield, *The Secularization of the Academy*, 63.

32. Ibid.

33. Benne, *Quality with Soul*, 40.

34. Hollinger, "Justification by Verification," *Religion and Twentieth Century American Intellectual Life*, 132.

35. Marsden, *The Soul of the American University*, 178.

36. Reuben, *The Making of the Modern University*, 174.

37. Ibid., 175.

38. Nord, *Religion and American Education*, 264.

39. Marsden, *The Soul of the American University*, 308.

40. Ibid., 307.

41. Smith, ed., *The Secular Revolution*, 103.

42. Ibid.

43. Marsden, *The Soul of the American University*, 312.

44. Ibid., 306.

45. Rudolf, *The American College and University,* 415.

46. J. Richard Middleton and Brian J. Walsh, *Truth Is Stranger Than It Used to Be,* (Downers Grove, IL: InterVarsity Press, 1995), 14.

47. J. Gresham Machen, *What Is Faith?* (Edinburgh: Banner of Truth Trust, 1991), 17.

48. Marsden, *The Soul of the American University,* 3.

49. Reuben, *The Making of the Modern University,* 125–26.

50. Ibid., 122.

51. Ibid., 120.

52. Marsden and Longfield, *The Secularization of the Academy, 152.*

53. Marsden, *The Soul of the American University,* 21.

54. Benne, *Quality with Soul,* 11.

55. Marsden and Longfield, *The Secularization of the Academy,* 3.

56. Smith, ed., *The Secular Revolution,* 28.

57. Hart, *The University Gets Religion,* 243.

58. Reuben, *Making of the Modern University,* 118.

59. Marsden, *The Soul of the American University,* 341.

60. Hart, *The University Gets Religion,* 243.

61. Ibid., 233.

62. Hart, *The University Gets Religion,* 233. Marsden and Longfield, *The Secularization of the Academy,* 203.

63. Hart, *The University Gets Religion,* 193.

64. Marsden and Longfield, *The Secularization of the Academy,* 35.

65. Hart, *The University Gets Religion,* 129.

66. Ibid., 115.

67. Reuben, *The Making of the Modern University,* 231.

68. Hart, *The University Gets Religion,* 129.

69. Marsden, *The Soul of the American University,* 310–11.

70. Hart, *The University Gets Religion,* 191.

71. Marsden and Longfield, *The Secularization of the Academy,* 34.

72. Hart, *The University Gets Religion,* 105, 109, 111.

73. Marsden and Longfield, *The Secularization of the Academy,* 35.

74. Ibid., 211–12.

75. Hart, *The University Gets Religion,* 246.

76. Ibid., 113.

77. Ibid., 152.

78. Ibid., 244.

79. Ibid.

80. Ibid., 232.

81. Ibid., 173.

82. Nord, *Religion and American Education,* 306. Hart, *The University Gets Religion,* 133, 114.

83. Marsden and Longfield, *The Secularization of the Academy,* 35.

84. Hart, *The University Gets Religion,* 207.

85. Marsden and Longfield, *The Secularization of the Academy, 35.*

86. Sloan, *Faith and Knowledge,* 187. Marsden and Longfield, *The Secularization of the Academy,* 35.

87. Reeves, *The Empty Church,* 152.

88. Marsden, *The Soul of the American University,* 412.

89. D. A. Carson, ed., *Telling the Truth*, (Grand Rapids, MI: Zondervan Publishing House, 2000), 21.

90. Hart, *The University Gets Religion*, 231.

91. Ibid.

92. Bloom, *The Closing of the American Mind*, 374.

93. Thomas C. Reeves, *The Empty Church*, 18.

94. George F. Will, "Liberals Dominate Campuses," *Buffalo News*, November 29, 2004, Opinion Page, A9. Ben Shapiro also notes that the overwhelming majority of professors are Democrats in the university setting. See his *Brainwashed: How Universities Indoctrinate America's Youth*, (Nashville: WND Books, 2004), 5–6.

95. Stetson and Conti, *The Truth about Tolerance*, 147.

96. Ravi Zacharias, *The Real Face of Atheism* (Grand Rapids, MI: Baker Books, 2004), 14. Michael Novak, *Belief and Unbelief: A Philosophy of Self-Knowledge* (New Brunswick: Transaction Publishers, 1994), 35.

97. Carson, *The Gagging of God*, 36.

98. Phillip E. Johnson, *Defeating Darwinism* (Downers Grove, IL: InterVarsity Press, 1997), 88.

99. Shapiro, *Brainwashed*, 97–98.

100. Glenn Loury, "A Professor under Construction," *Finding God at Harvard: Spiritual Journeys of Thinking Christians*, Kelly Monroe, ed. (Grand Rapids, MI: Zondervan Publishing House, 1996), 75.

101. Bill Donohue, *Secular Sabotage: How Liberals Are Destroying Religion and Culture in America* (New York: Faith Words, 2009), 15.

102. Herbert London, *America's Secular Challenge: The Rise of a New National Religion* (New York: Encounter Books, 2008), 73.

103. William F. Buckley Jr., *Nearer My God* (New York: Doubleday, 1997), 31.

104. Novak, *Belief and Unbelief*, 202–3.

105. Shapiro, *Brainwashed*, 62–63.

106. Ibid., 64.

107. Ibid., 64–65.

108. Jeremy Caplan, "Embattled Ivy," *Time*, March 28, 2005, 19.

109. Kronman, *Education's End*, 49.

Chapter 9

1. Margaret J. Osler, "Myth 10: That the Scientific Revolution Liberated Science from Religion," Ronald L. Numbers ed., *Galileo Goes to Jail* (Cambridge: Harvard University Press, 2009), 91–92.

2. Alister E. McGrath, *Science and Religion* (Oxford: Blackwell Publishers Inc., 1999), 2.

3. John Hedley Brooke, *Science and Religion*, (Cambridge: Cambridge University Press, 1991), 60–61.

4. David C. Lindberg, "Medieval Science and Religion," Gary B. Ferngren, ed., *Science and Religion* (Baltimore, MD: Johns Hopkins University Press, 2002), 61.

5. Nancy R. Pearcey and Charles B. Thaxton, *The Soul of Science* (Wheaton, IL: Crossway Books, 1994), 30–31.

6. Ibid., 31.

7. Richard G. Olson, *Science and Religion 1450–1900* (Baltimore, MD: Johns Hopkins University, 2004), 33–34.

8. David C. Lindberg, "The Medieval Church Encounters the Classical Tradition: Saint Augustine, Roger Bacon, and the Handmaiden Metaphor," David C. Lindberg and Ronald L. Numbers, eds., *When Science and Christianity Meet* (Chicago and London: University of Chicago Press, 2003), 23. "Medieval Science and Religion," *Science and Religion*, 65–66.

9. Lindberg. "The Medieval Church Encounters the Classical Tradition," *When Science and Christianity Meet*, 23–24, 32.

10. Michael H. Shank, "Myth 2: That the Medieval Christian Church Suppressed the Growth of Science," *Galileo Goes to Jail*, 24–25.

11. "Medieval Science and Religion," *Science and Religion*, 59.

12. Michael H. Shank op cit, *Galileo Goes to Jail*, 22.

13. Ibid., 21.

14. Cornelius G. Hunter, *Science's Blind Spot* (Grand Rapids, MI: Brazos Press, 2007), 15.

15. Louis Dupre, *Passage to Modernity* (New Haven and London: Yale University Press, 1993), 70.

16. Ibid., 73. Nigel Brush, *The Limitations of Scientific Truth* (Grand Rapids, MI: Kregel Publications, 2005), 53.

17. Peter Harrison, *The Fall of Man and the Foundations of Science* (Cambridge: Cambridge University Press, 2009), 32.

18. Ibid., 181.

19. Ibid., 180–81.

20. Ibid., 158, 183.

21. Dupre, *Passage to Modernity*, 74.

22. Hunter, *Science's Blind Spot*, 15–16.

23. Ibid., 16.

24. Ronald L. Numbers, "Science Without God," *When Science and Christianity Meet*, 267.

25. Ian Hacking, *The Emergence of Probability* (Cambridge: Cambridge University Press, 1999), 20, 22, 26, 41.

26. Herbert Butterfield, *The Origins of Modern Science* (New York: Free Press, 1965), 102.

27. Harrison, *The Fall of Man and the Foundations of Science*, 106.

28. Dava Sobel, *Galileo's Daughter* (New York: Walker Publishing Company, Inc., 1999), 19.

29. Ibid., 44.

30. Pearcey and Thaxton, *The Soul of Science*, 66.

31. Harrison, *The Fall of Man and the Foundations of Science*, 134.

32. Butterfield, *The Origins Modern Science*, 78–79. Sobel, *Galileo's Daughter*, 170.

33. John Hedley Brooke, *Science and Religion*, 101.

34. Dr. Kirsten Birkett, "Galileo: The Real Story," July 10, 2012, http://www.answering-islam.org/science/galileo.html.

35. Ibid.

36. Pearcey and Thaxton, *The Soul of Science*, 39.

37. Harrison, *The Fall of Man and the Foundations of Science*, 110.

38. Owen Gingerich, "The Copernican Revolution," Ferngren ed., *Science and Religion*, 102.

39. Numbers, "Science Without God," *When Science and Christianity Meet*, 267.

40. Harrison, *The Fall of Man and the Foundations of Science*, 112. Dupre, *Passage to Modernity*, 69.

41. David C. Lindberg, "Galileo, The Church, and the Cosmos," *Science and Christianity Meet*, 45.

42. Richard J. Blackwell, "Galileo Galilei," Ferngren ed., *Science and Religion*, 110. Olson, *Science and Religion 1450–1900*, 14.

43. Brooke, *Science and Religion*, 102.

44. Olson, *Science and Religion 1450–1900*, 14–15.

45. Ibid., 17.

46. Ibid., 17–18.

47. Brooke, *Science and Religion*, 99.

48. John C. Lennox, *God's Undertaker* (Oxford: Lion Hudson, 2009), 24–25.

49. Maurice A. Finocchiaro, "Myth 8: That Galileo Was Imprisoned and Tortured for Advocating Copernicanism," *Galileo Goes to Jail*, 74, 76.

50. Olson, *Science and Religion 1450–1900*, 18.

51. Pearcey and Thaxton, *The Soul of Science*, 40.

52. Brooke, *Science and Religion*, 98.

53. Richard J. Blackwell, op cit, *Science and Religion*, 108.

54. Brooke, *Science and Religion*, 117–19.

55. E. A. Burtt, *The Metaphysical Foundations of Modern Science* (Mineola, NY: Dover Publications, 2003), 204.

56. Stephen Gaukroger, *Descartes: An Intellectual Biography* (Oxford: Clarendon Press, 1997), 16.

57. John Henry, "Causation," Ferngren ed., *Science and Religion*, 135. Peter Harrison, "Myth 12: Rene Descartes and the Mind-Body Distinction," *Galileo Goes to Jail*, 112–13.

58. Pearcey and Thaxton, *The Soul of Science*, 26.

59. Thomas H. Broman, "Matter, Force, and the Christian Worldview in the Enlightenment," *When Science and Christianity Meet*. 86.

60. Sobel, *Galileo's Daughter*, 286.

61. Harrison, *The Fall of Man and the Foundations of Science*, 135.

62. Brooke, *Science and Religion*, 128.

63. Ibid., 117.

64. Ibid., 127.

65. Ibid., 126–27.

66. Ibid., 57.

67. Numbers, "Science Without God: Natural Laws and Christian Beliefs," *When Science and Christianity Meet*, 268.

68. Brooke, "Natural Theology," *Science and Religion*, 165.

69. R. Hooykaas, *Religion and the Rise of Modern Science* (Vancouver: Regent College Publishing, 1972), 48.

70. Pearcey and Thaxton, *The Soul of Science*, 129. Brush, *The Limitations of Scientific Truth*, 139.

71. Burtt, *The Metaphysical Foundations of Modern Science,* 210.

72. Brooke, *Science and Religion*, 7.

73. Ibid., 24.

74. Ibid., 137.

75. Richard S. Westfall, "Isaac Newton," Ferngren ed., *Science and Religion*, 156–57.

76. Brooke, *Science and Religion*, 137.

77. Butterfield, *The Origins of Modern Science*, 137.

78. Pearcey and Thaxton, *The Soul of Science*, 73.

79. Ibid., 157.

80. Alister E. McGrath, *The Foundations of Dialogue in Science and Religion* (Oxford: Blackwell Publishers, 1998), 56, 68.

81. Pearcey and Thaxton eds., *The Soul of Science*, 138.

82. Brush, *The Limitations of Scientific Truth*, 59.

83. John Hedley Brooke op cit, *Science and Religion*, 168–69.

84. Ronald H. Nash, *The Word of God and the Mind of Man* (Grand Rapids, MI: Zondervan, 1982), 22.

85. Brooke, *Science and Religion*, 209.

Chapter 10

1. Stephen C. Meyer, *Signature in the Cell: DNA and the Evidence for Intelligent Design* (New York: Harper One, 2009), 160.

2. Brooke, *Science and Religion*, 276.

3. Calvin Smith, "The 'Trojan Horse' of Deep Time," February 25, 2014, *Creation.com*, http://www.creation.com/trojan-horse-deep-time.

4. Nicolaas A. Rupke, "Geology and Paleontology," Ferngren ed., *Science and Religion*, 180–81.

5. Cornelius G. Hunter, *Darwin's God* (Grand Rapids, MI: Brazos Press, 2010), 134.

6. Ibid.

7. Meyer, *Signature in the Cell*, 160.

8. Daniel C. Dennett, *Darwin's Dangerous Idea: Evolution and the Meanings of Life* (New York: Simon & Schuster, 1995), 39.

9. Jeremy Rifkin, *Algeny* (New York: Viking Press, 1983), 79.

10. Peter J. Bowler, "Evolution," Ferngren ed., *Science and Religion*, 223.

11. Rifkin, *Algeny*, 100.

12. Ibid., 99.

13. Ibid., 100–1.

14. Ibid., 64.

15. Ibid., 107.

16. Ibid., 80.

17. Ibid., 105.

18. Ibid., 106–7.

19. Ibid., 108.

20. William A. Dembski, "What Intelligent Design Is Not," *Signs of Intelligence: Understanding Intelligent Design*, William A. Dembski and James M. Kushiner, eds., (Grand Rapids, MI: Brazos Press, 2001), 9.

21. Quoted in John G. West, *Darwin Day in America* (Wilmington: ISI Books, 2007), 37.

22. David N. Livingstone, "Re-Placing Darwin and Christianity," *When Science and Christianity Meet*, 187.

23. James Moore, "Darwin," *Science and Religion*, 216.

24. Quoted in Hunter, *Darwin's God*, 18.

25. Ibid., 126.

26. Pearcey, *Total Truth*, 308–9.

27. David N. Livingstone, *Darwin's Forgotten Defenders: The Encounter Between Evangelical Theology and Evolutionary Thought* (Vancouver: Regent College Publishing, 1997).

28. Numbers, "Science Without God: Natural Laws and Christian Beliefs," *When Science and Christianity Meet*, 280.

29. Ibid.

30. Livingstone, *Darwin's Forgotten Defenders*, 104–5.

31. Ibid., 64.

32. Brooke, *Science and Religion*, 275. David N. Livingston op cit, *When Science and Christianity Meet*, 187.

33. Ronald L. Numbers op cit, *When Science and Christianity Meet*, 281.

34. West, *Darwin Day in America*, 41.

35. Brooke, *Science and Religion*, 194.

36. John G. West, *Darwin Day in America*, 41.

37. Ibid., 244.

38. Henry H. Bauer, *Scientific Literacy and the Myth of the Scientific Method* (Urbana and Chicago: University of Illinois Press, 1994), 65.

39. Quoted in Pearcey, *Total Truth*, 172.

40. Michael J. Behe, *Darwin's Black Box: The Biochemical Challenge to Evolution* (New York: Free Press, 1996), 30. See also the anecdotal evidence provided in Phillip E. Johnson, *The Wedge of Truth: Splitting the Foundations of Naturalism* (Downers Grove, IL: InterVarsity Press, 2000), 72. Michael Denton points out in the Preface of his book *Evolution: A Theory in Crisis* (Chevy Chase, MD: Adler & Adler, 1996), 16, that though evolutionary biologists see serious problems with the traditional Darwinian framework, they think these problems can be explained with only "minor adjustments" to the theory.

41. Thomas Woodward, *Doubts About Darwin: A History of Intelligent Design* (Grand Rapids, MI: Baker Book House, 2003), 41.

42. Hunter, *Darwin's God*, 69.

43. John Horgan, *The End of Science* (Reading, MA: Addison-Wesley Publishing Company, Inc., 1996), 120.

44. Behe, *Darwin's Black Box*, 40.

45. Phillip E. Johnson, *Objections Sustained* (Downers Grove, IL: InterVarsity Press, 1998), 82.

46. Denton, *Evolution*, 355.

47. Woodward, *Doubts About Darwin*, 49.

48. Quoted in John W. Whitehead, *The End of Man* (Westchester: Crossway Books, 1986), 63–64.

49. Ibid., 64.

50. Ibid.

51. McGrath, *The Foundations of Dialogue in Science and Religion*, 1.

52. Stanley L. Jaki, *The Limits of a Limitless Science* (Wilmington, DE: ISI Books, 2000), 5.

53. Bauer, *Scientific Literacy and the Myth of the Scientific Method*, 52.

54. Meyer, *Signature in the Cell*, 139.

55. Bauer, *Scientific Literacy and the Myth of the Scientific Method*, 52.

56. Lennox, *God's Undertaker*, 30.

57. Roger Trigg, *Rationality and Science: Can Science Explain Everything?* (Oxford: Blackwell, 1994), 130.

58. Bruce L. Gordon, "Is Intelligent Design Science?" *Signs of Intelligence: Understanding Intelligent Design*, William A. Dembski and James M. Kushiner, eds., 195.

59. Phillip E. Johnson, *Defeating Darwinism* (Downers Grove, IL: InterVarsity Press, 1997), 86.

60. Ibid., 86.

61. Del Ratzsch, *Science and Its Limits*, (Downers Grove, IL: InterVarsity Press, 2000), 122.

62. Johnson, *Objections Sustained*, 24.

63. Brush, *The Limitations of Scientific Truth*, 224.

64. Quoted in Johnson, *Objections Sustained*, 67, 71–72.

65. Ibid., 70.

66. Lennox, *God's Undertaker*, 29.

67. Pearcey, *Total Truth*, 311.

68. Ibid., 308–9.

69. Quoted in Hans Blumenberg, Robert M. Wallace, trans., *The Legitimacy of the Modern Age* (Cambridge: MIT Press, 1983), 15.

70. Lennox, *God's Undertaker*, 39.

71. Middleton and Walsh, *Truth Is Stranger Than It Used to Be*, 22.

72. Bauer, *Scientific Literacy and the Myth of the Scientific Method*, 144.

73. Neil Postman, *Technopoly* (New York: Vintage Books, 1993), 162.

74. Walter Truett Anderson ed., *The Truth About the Truth* (New York: Jeremy P. Tarcher/Putnam Book, 1995), 179.

75. Ratzsch, *Science and Its Limits*, 29.

76. Trigg, *Rationality and Science*, 15, 31. McGrath, *Science and Religion*, 71–74.

77. Brush, *The Limitations of Scientific Truth*, 67.

78. Trigg, *Rationality and Science*, 225.

79. James W. Sire, *Why Should Anyone Believe Anything At All?* (Downers Grove, IL: InterVarsity Press, 1994), 19.

80. Trigg, *Rationality and Science*, 224.

81. Peter M. Hess "Natural History," Ferngren ed., *Science and Religion*, 206.

82. Francis J. Beckwith and Gregory Koukl, *Relativism* (Grand Rapids, MI: Baker Book House, 2000), 166.

83. Ratzsch, *Science and Its Limits*, 106.

84. Hunter, *Darwin's God*, 149.

85. Johnson, *Objections Sustained*, 28.

86. Ratzsch, *Science and Its Limits*, 132–33.

87. Trigg, *Rationality and Science*, 232.

88. Edward B. Davis and Robin Collins, "Scientific Naturalism," Ferngren ed., *Science and Religion*, 329.

89. Limbaugh, *Persecution: How Liberals Are Waging War Against Christians*, 192–93.

Chapter 11

1. Ratzsch, *Science and Its Limits*, 100.

2. Philip E. Johnson, *Reason in the Balance: The Case Against Naturalism in Science, Law, and Education* (Downers Grove, IL: InterVarsity Press, 1995), 14.

3. William A. Dembski "The Design Argument," Ferngren ed., *Science and Religion*, 339.

4. John W. Whitehead, *The End of Man* (Westchester, IL: Crossway Books, 1986), 63.

5. Limbaugh, *Persecution*, 335.

6. William A. Dembski, *The Design Revolution* (Downers Grove, IL: InterVarsity Press, 2004), 33–34.

7. Edward J. Larson, *Summer for the Gods* (New York: Basic Books, 2006), 268.

8. West, *Darwin Day in America*, 212–13.

9. Ibid., 215.

10. Larson, *Summer for the Gods*, 270–71.

11. Dembski, "The Design Argument," Ferngren ed., *Science and Religion*, 341.

12. Dembski, *The Design Revolution*, 43. Lennox, *God's Undertaker*, 11. Woodward, *Doubts About Darwin*, 27.

13. Dembski, "The Design Argument," Ferngren ed., *Science and Religion*, 341.

14. Dembski, *The Design Revolution*, 33.

15. Ibid., 33–34.

16. Meyer, *Signature in the Cell: DNA and the Evidence for Intelligent Design*, 441.

17. Charles Krauthammer, "Let's have No More Money Trials," *Time*, August 8, 2005, 78.

18. Meyer, *Signature in the Cell*, 444.

19. Krauthammer, "Let's Have No More Monkey Trials," 78.

20. Quoted in West, *Darwin Day in America*, 221.

21. Ibid.

22. Ibid., 224.

23. Meyer, *Signature in the Cell*, 396–97, 434.

24. West, *Darwin Day in America*, 216.

25. Dembski, *The Design Revolution*, 52.

26. Francis J. Beckwith, *Law, Darwinism, and Public Education* (Lanham: Rowman & Littlefield Publishers, 2003), 6.

27. Dembski, *The Design Revolution*, 53–54.

28. Lennox, *God's Undertaker*, 189.

29. Meyer, *Signature in the Cell*, 46.

30. Ibid., 12.

31. Ibid., 12–13.

32. Meyer, *Signature in the Cell*, 238–240. Johnson, *Objections Sustained*, 106.

33. Lennox, *God's Undertaker*, 45.

34. William A. Dembski "Signs of Intelligence," *Signs of Intelligence*, 178.

35. Meyer, *Signature in the Cell*, 352.

36. Ibid., 352–54.

37. Ibid., 354.

38. Ibid., 199, 347.

39. Dembski, *The Design Revolution*, 27.

40. Meyer, *Signature in the Cell*, 394.

41. Lennox, *God's Undertaker*, 124.

42. Behe, *Darwin's Black Box*, 39.

43. Quoted in Behe, *Darwin's Black Box*, 39.

44. Ibid., 40.

45. Ibid., 5.

46. Meyer, *Signature in the Cell*, 213.

47. Ibid., 257.

48. Ibid., 211.

49. Quoted in Lennox, *God's Undertaker*, 164–65. Lennox includes astrophysicist Chandra Wickramasinghe as being part of Hoyle's quote.

50. Pearcey, *Total Truth*, 168.

51. Charles Alan Taylor, *Defining Science: A Rhetoric of Demarcation* (Madison, WI: University of Wisconsin Press, 1996), 39.

52. Meyer, *Signature in the Cell*, 400–1.

53. Ibid., 420.

54. Ibid., 432.

55. Lennox, *God's Undertaker*, 180.

56. Dembski, *The Design Revolution*, 34.

57. Dan Peterson, "The Little Engine That Could . . . Undo Darwinism," *The American Spectator*, June 2005, 43.

58. Theistic evolutionists would probably contest this, but I see no evidence in Scripture that Adam and Eve were simply chosen from pre-existing hominids.

59. Harrison, *The Fall of Man and the Foundations of Science*, 173.

Chapter 12

1. Limbaugh, *Persecution*, 8.

2. Marlin Maddoux, *Public Education Against America* (New Kensington: Whitaker House, 2006), 15. Kent Greenawalt, *Does God Belong in Public Schools?* (Princeton: Princeton University Press, 2005), 13.

3. Limbaugh, *Persecution*, 8.

4. Maddoux, *Public Education Against America*, 15.

5. Nord, *Religion and American Education*, 71. Greenawalt, *Does God Belong in Public Schools?*, 14. Marsden, *Understanding Fundamentalism and Evangelicalism*, 10.

6. Nord, *Religion and American Education*, 75.

7. Marsden, *Understanding Fundamentalism and Evangelicalism*, 10.

8. John H. Westerhoff III, *McGuffey and His Readers* (Michigan: Mott Media, 1982), 103. Greenawalt, *Does God Belong in Public Schools?*, 15.

9. Quoted in Westerhoff, *McGuffey and His Readers*, 138.

10. Ibid., 85.

11. Whitehead, *The End of Man*, 19.

12. Greenawalt, *Does God Belong in Pubic Schools?*, 15–16.

13. George M. Thomas, Lisa R. Peck, and Channin G. De Haan, "Reforming Education, Transforming Religion, 1876–1931," *The Secular Revolution*, Christian Smith, ed., (Berkeley and Los Angeles: University of California Press, 2003), 380.

14. Ibid., 385.

15. John Taylor Gatto, *The Underground History of American Education* (New York: The Oxford Village Press, 2000/2001), 37.

16. Ibid., 38.

17. Ibid.

18. Ibid.

19. Ibid., 39, 288, 322.

20. Thomas, et al, "Reforming Education, Transforming Religion, 1876–1932," *The Secular Revolution*, 356.

21. B. K. Eakman, *The Cloning of the American Mind* (Lafayette, LA: Huntington House Publishers, 1998), 111.

22. Paolo Lionni, *The Leipzig Connection* (Sheridan, OR: Heron Books, 1993), 1–2, 4, 7.

23. Ibid., 9.

24. It is hard not to notice that facilitating the *adaptation* of the child corresponds to the German *Bildung* we saw in Chapter seven. Each child's individual personhood was to be developed, but now only in the context of the betterment of society as a whole.

25. Samuel L. Blumenfeld, *NEA: Trojan Horse in American Education* (Phoenix, AZ: The Paradigm Company, 1984), 15.

26. Joel Turtel, *Public Schools, Public Menace* (New York: Liberty Books, 2004–2005), 24–27.

27. Blumenfeld, *NEA*, 45.
28. Lionni, *The Leipzig Connection*, 19, 35.
29. Nord, *Religion and American Education*, 76.
30. Lionni, *The Leipzig Connection*, 15.
31. Blumenfeld, *NEA*, 47–48.
32. Lionni, *The Leipzig Connection*, 15–16.
33. Charles J. Sykes, *Dumbing Down Our Kids* (New York: St. Martin's Griffin, 1995), 202.
34. Kenneth R. Calvert, "Why Educate," *Christianity, Education, and Modern Society*, William Jeynes and Enedina Martinez, eds., (Charlotte, NC: Information Age Publishing, Inc., 2007), 68.
35. Stephen L. Carter, *The Culture of Disbelief : How American Law and Politics Trivialize Religious Belief* (New York: BasicBooks, 1993), 173.
36. Marsden, *The Soul of the American University*, 251.
37. Maddoux, *Public Education Against America*, 100.
38. Eakman, *The Cloning of the American Mind*, 159.
39. Maddoux, *Public Education Against America*, 98, 101, 103–4.
40. Christian Smith, "Rethinking the Secularization of American Public Life," *The Secular Revolution*, 27.
41. Blumenfeld, NEA, 55.
42. Eakman, *The Cloning of the American Mind*, 131.
43. Limbaugh, *Persecution*, 65.
44. Jonas E. Alexis, *In the Name of Education* (USA: Xulon Press: 2007), 29.
45. Jim Marrs, *The Trillion-Dollar Conspiracy* (New York: HarperCollins, 2011), 11.
46. Erwin W. Lutzer, *Hitler's Cross* (Chicago: Moody Press, 1995), 115.
47. Norman Geisler and Frank Turek, *Legislating Morality* (Eugene, OR: Wipf and Stock Publishers, 1998), 73.
48. Eakman, *The Cloning of the American Mind*, 148.
49. Allen Quist, *America's Schools: The Battleground for Freedom* (Chaska: EdWatch, 2005), 29–30, 32.
50. Ibid., 82.
51. Ibid., 86.
52. Maddox, *Public Education Against America*, 126–7.
53. Quist, *America's Schools*, 80.
54. Ibid., 84.
55. Ibid., 64, 68–69.
56. Ibid., 57.
57. Ibid., 69, 70, 74.
58. Ibid., 73.
59. Michael S. Coffman, *Plundered* (Bangor, ME: Environmental Perspectives Inc., 2012), 197.
60. Ibid., 164.
61. Quist, *America's Schools*, 101, 129.
62. Ibid., 38, 133, 150.
63. Ibid., 112.
64. Ibid., 112, 137–140.
65. Ibid., 92.
66. Ibid., 89, 97–98.

67. William Jeynes, "Do American Students Need Prayer and Moral Education Returned to the Public Schools?" *Christianity, Education, and Modern Society*, 20. James Davidson Hunter, *Culture Wars* (New York: BasicBooks, 1991), 204–5.

68. Turtel, *Public Schools, Public Menace*, 45.

69. Nord, *Religion and American Education*, 158, 161.

70. Maddox, *Public Education Against America*, 80, 129–130, 133.

71. Sidney B. Simon, Leland W. Howe, and Howard Kirschenbaum, *Values Clarification* (New York: Warner Books, 1995), 10.

72. Ibid., 9.

73. Maddox, *Public Education Against America*, 82–83, 87.

74. Pearcey, *Total Truth*, 240.

75. Noted in Marlin Maddox, *Public Education Against America*, 134.

76. Ibid., 131.

77. Daren Jonescu, "American Education: Rotting the Country from the Inside," *American Thinker*, February 20, 2013, http://www.americanthinker.com/article/2013/02/american-education-rotting-the-country-from-the-inside.html.

78. Michael Snyder, "The Zombiefication of America," *End of the American Dream*, December 28, 2014, http://endoftheamericandream.com/archives/the-zombiefication-of-america.

79. Jeynes, "Do American Students Need Prayer and Moral Education Returned to the Public Schools?," *Christianity, Education, and Modern Society*, 9.

80. Ibid., 10, 12.

81. Ibid., 11.

82. Gatto, *The Underground History of American Education*, 294.

83. Jeynes, "Do American Students Need Prayer and Moral Education Returned to the Public Schools?," *Christianity, Education, and Modern Society*, 13.

84. Ibid., 14.

85. Ibid., 27.

86. Ibid.

87. Ibid., 3.

88. Ibid.

89. Michael Snyder, "21 Signs That U.S. Public Schools Have Become Training Centers for Sexual Deviancy," *End of the American Dream*, February 17, 2013, http://endoftheamericandream.com/archives/21-signs-that-u.s.-public-schools-have-become-training-centers-for-sexual-deviancy.

90. Limbaugh, *Persecution*, 89.

91. Ibid., 93–94.

92. *Religion and the Judiciary*, C-SPAN, April 7, 2005.

93. Marrs, *The Trillion-Dollar Conspiracy*, 191.

94. Maddox, *Public Education Against America*, 13.

95. Christina Hoff Summers and Sally Satel, *One Nation Under Therapy* (New York: St. Martin's Press, 2005), 12.

96. Ibid., 27, 29.

97. Ibid., 13.

98. Ibid.

99. Marrs, *The Trillion-Dollar Conspiracy*, 204.

100. Peter R. Breggin, *Toxic Psychiatry* (New York: St. Martin's Press, 1991), 278.

101. Marrs, *The Trillion-Dollar Conspiracy*, 149.

102. Quoted in Turtel, *Public Schools, Public Menace*, 153–4.

103. Ibid., 154–5.

104. Testimony by Patti Johnson, a Colorado State Board of Education member, before the US House of Representatives Subcommittee, quoted in "How Schools Are Making Big Money On 'ADD/ADHD,'" April 1, 2013, http://rense.com/general4/addd.htm.

105. Turtel, *Public Schools, Public Menace*, 152.

106. Ibid., 153.

107. Kelly Patricia O'Meara, *Psyched Out* (Bloomington, IN: AuthorHouse, 2006), 64.

108. Quoted in Ibid., 75.

109. Turtel, *Public School, Public Menace*, 157–8.

110. Ibid., 159.

111. Quoted in O'Meara, *Psyched Out*, 12–13.

112. "Was Sandy Hook Shooter Taking Psychiatric Drugs?," *PRWeb*, March 18, 2013, http://prweb.com/releases/was-sandy-hook-shooter/taking-psychiatric-drugs/prweb10534438htm.

113. Marrs, *The Trillion-Dollar Conspiracy*, 152.

114. Quoted in O'Meara, *Psyched Out*, 12.

115. Mac Slavo, "Fourth Grade Shock: 'I Am Willing to Give Up Some of My Constitutional Rights in Order to Be Safe or More Secure,'" *SHTFplan.com*, April 12, 2013, http://www.shtfplan.com/headline-news/fourth-grade-shock-i-am-willing-to-give-up-some-of-my-constitutional-rights-in-order-to-be-safe-or-more-secure_04122013.

116. Benjamin Franklin, Searchquotes, accessed June 3, 2013, http://www.searchquotes.com/quotations/those_who_desire_to_give_up_freddom_in_order_to_gain_security_will_not_have_nor_do_they_deserve_either_one/32919/.

117. Slavo, "Fourth Grade Shock," *SHTFplan.com*.

118. Michael Snyder, "Texas Public School Curriculum Teaches Students to Design a Socialist Flag and That Christianity Is a Cult," *End of the American Dream*, March 18, 2013, http://www.endoftheamericandream.com/archives/texas-public-students-to-design-a-socialist-flag-and-that-christianity-is-a-cult.

119. Ibid.

120. Turtel, *Public School, Public Menace*, 191.

121. Coffman, *Plundered*, 201.

122. Marrs, *The Trillion-Dollar Conspiracy*, 200.

123. O'Meara, *Psyched Out*, 135-136.

124. Ibid., 137.

125. Ibid., 144–5.

126. Ibid., 157–8.

127. Ibid., 42–44.

128. Ibid., 110.

129. Ibid., 143.

130. Ibid., 142.

131. Mac Slavo, "You Are Crazy: New Psychiatric Guidelines Target Hoarding, Child Temper Tantrums, and a Host of Other 'Illnesses,'" *SHTFplan.com*, accessed May 24, 2013, http://www.shtfplan.com/headline-news/you-are-crazy-new.

132. Charles J. Sykes, *Dumbing Down Our Kids* (New York: St. Martin's Griffin, 1995), 174.

133. Ron Paul, "'Common Core' Nationalizes and Dumbs Down Public School Curriculum," Infowars, May 27, 2013. http://www.infowars.com/common-core-nationalizes-and-dumbs-down-public-school-curriculum.

134. Mac Slavo, "Watch: Former Teacher Speaks Out, 'Everything I Loved About Teaching Is Extinct,'" *SHTFplan.com*, May 31, 2013, http://www.shtfplan.com/headline-news/watch-former-teacher-speaks-out-everything-i-loved-about-teaching-is-extinct_05312013.

Chapter 13

1. Pearcey, *Total Truth*, 327–28. I am relying on Pearcey's informative summation of the interface between men and family life for the beginning of this section and below.

2. Ibid., 331.

3. Ibid., 330–32.

4. Ibid., 332.

5. Christopher Lasch, *The Revolt of the Elites* (New York: W.W. Norton & Company, 1996), 95.

6. Ibid., 96.

7. Juan Williams, "The Tragedy of America's Disappearing Fathers," *Wall St. Journal*, June 14–15, 2008, A 11.

8. Ibid.

9. Bork, *Slouching Towards Gomorrah*, 170.

10. Audrey M. Jones, "Historical Divorce Rates Statistics," *LoveToKnow*, accessed June 8, 2013, http://divorce.lovetoknow.com/Historical_Divorce_Rate_Statistics.

11. Wells, *No Place for Truth*, 44.

12. Bloom, *Closing of the American* Mind, 119.

13. "This Pill Turns 50," *CBSNews*, May 6, 2010, http://www.cbsnews.com/stories/2010/05/06/earlyshow/health/main6465686.shtml.

14. Quoted in B.G. Brander, *Staring into Chaos* (Dallas, TX: Spence Publishing Company, 1998),135.

15. Bloom, *Closing of the American Mind*, 60–61.

16. Ibid., 61.

17. Ibid., 58–59.

18. Mary Eberstadt, *How the West Really Lost God* (West Conshohocken: Templeton Press, 2013), 5–6. Although Eberstadt's argument refers mainly to European Christianity, I think it may also apply to us in the States. Moreover, the breakdown of the family may not simply be the result of the loss of Christian authority. Rather, the loss of religiosity may be a consequence of the breakdown of the family.

19. Beckwith and Koukl, *Relativism*, 31.

20. Schaeffer, *Francis A. Schaeffer Trilogy*, 300–1.

21. Beckwith and Koukl, *Relativism*, 169.

22. Wolfe, *One Nation, After All*, 82.

23. Bork, *Slouching Towards Gomorrah*, 3.

24. Wolfe, *One Nation, After All*, 85.

25. Quoted in Reeves, *The Empty Church*, 66.

26. Nord, *Religion and American Education*, 332.

27. Alexis, *In the Name of Education*, 50.

28. Geisler and Turek, *Legislating Morality*, 90.

29. Coffman, *Plundered*, 249.

30. Geisler and Turek, *Legislating Morality*, 83.

31. Ibid., 84.

32. Os Guinness, *A Free People's Suicide: Sustainable Freedom and the American Future* (Downers Grove, IL: InterVarsity Press, 2012), 117.

33. Ibid., 152.

34. Ibid., 152–53.

35. Richard W. Flory, "Promoting a Secular Standard," *The Secular Revolution*, 400–1.

36. Ibid., 401–2.

37. Ibid., 405–6.

38. Ibid., 399, 414, 428.

39. Bork, *Slouching Towards Gomorrah*, 291.

40. Craig M. Gay, *The Way of the (Modern) World* (Grand Rapids, MI: William B. Eerdmans Publishing, 1998), 201.

41. Credit to Ann Barnhardt, who used this expression either on her old blog or in an interview.

42. Diana West, *The Death of the Grown-Up* (New York: St. Martin's Press, 2007), 29.

43. Jeremy McCarthy, "Family Mealtime: The Hour that Matters Most," *Psychology of Wellbeing*, October 11, 2011, http://psychologyofwellbeing.com/201110/family-mealtime.html. "Why Mealtime Matters," *J.M. Smucker Company*, accessed October 3, 2013, http://poweroffamilymeals.com/resources/about.

44. West, *The Death of the Grown-Up*, 6, 15, 25.

45. Roger Kimball, *The Long March* (San Francisco: Encounter Books, 2000), 209–10.

46. Os Guinness, *A Free People's Suicide*, 104.

47. Robert H. Knight, *The Age of Consent* (Dallas, TX: Spence Publishing Company, 1998), 121–22.

48. Leslie Larson, "James Gandolfini dead at 51: Chris Christie orders flags to fly half-staff in memory of 'Sopranos' star," *Daily News*, June 21, 2013, http://www.nydailynews.com/news/politics/james-gandolfini-dead-at-51-flags-fly-half-staff-memory-james-gandolfini-article-1.1379195.

49. Ibid.

50. E. Michael Jones, *Monsters from the Id* (Dallas, TX: Spence Publishing Company, 2000), 84, 127, 258, 263.

51. Ibid., 96, 97, 101.

52. Ibid., 124.

53. Ibid.

54. Ibid., 128.

55. Ethan Cordray, "Zombies Are Us," *First Things*, August 15, 2011, http://www.firstthings.com/web-exclusives/2011/08/zomies-are-us.

56. Sean Turnbull, "The Madness of a Lost Society," November 27, 2010, *SGTreport.com*, https://www.youtube.com/watch?v=fOshw4kIGR4

Chapter 14

1. Stacy Meichtry, "Pope Signals Openness to Gay Priests" *The Wall Street Journal*, July 30, 2013, www.wsj/article/SB10001424127887324354704578635401320888608.html.

2. Quoted in Glenn T. Stanton and Dr. Bill Maier, *Marriage on Trial: The Case Against Same-Sex Marriage and Parenting* (Downers Grove, IL: InterVarsity Press, 2004), 15.

3. Michael Ruse, "Are there gay genes? Sociobiology and Homosexuality," *Nature and Causes of Homosexuality: A Philosophic and Scientific Inquiry* Volume 6, no. 4, Summer 1981, Journal of Homosexuality, Noretta Koertge, Ph.D ed., 29.

4. Ibid.

5. Michael Ruse, interviewed by Daniel Ansted, *Patheos*, Jan. 4, 2013, www.patheos.com/blogs/scienceonreligion/2013/01/interview-michael-ruse-on-evolution-creationism-and-religion/.

6. Quoted in Stanton and Maier, *Marriage on Trial*, 135.

7. Camille Paglia, *Vamps & Tramps: New Essays* (New York: Vintage Books, 1994), 72.

8. Stanton L. Jones and Mark A. Yarhouse, *Homosexuality: The Use of Scientific Research in the Church's Moral Debate* (Downers Grove, IL: InterVarsity Press, 2000), 35.

9. Alfred C. Kinsey, Wardell B. Pomeroy, and Clyde E. Martin, *Sexual Behavior in the Human Male* (Philadelphia: W.B. Saunders Company, 1948), ix.

10. Ibid., 651.

11. Edward O. Laumann, John H. Gagnon, Robert T. Michael, and Stuart Michaels, *The Social Organization of Sexuality* (Chicago: University of Chicago Press, 1994), 289.

12. Ibid., 286.

13. Jones and Yarhouse, *Homosexuality*, 37.

14. Ibid., 38.

15. Ibid., 44.

16. Paglia, *Vamps & Tramps*, 70–71.

17. Ibid., 74.

18. Stanton and Maier, *Marriage on Trial*, 143.

19. Ibid., 144.

20. Ibid., 142.

21. Ibid., 144–45.

22. Dan O. Via and Robert A. J. Gagnon, *Homosexuality and the Bible: Two Views*, (Minneapolis, MN: Fortress Press, 2003), 59.

23. Ibid., 50–51.

24. John Corvino, *What's Wrong with Homosexuality?* (Oxford: Oxford University Press, 2013), 16.

25. Via. and Gagnon, *Homosexuality and the Bible*, 68.

26. Jones and Yarhouse, *Homosexuality*, 181.

27. Via. and Gagnon, *Homosexuality and the Bible*, 91.

28. Stanton and Maier, *Marriage on Trial*, 12, 54, 62.

29. James Q. Wilson, *The Marriage Problem: How Our Culture Has Weakened Families* (New York: HarperCollins Publishers Inc., 2002), 24.

30. Corvino, *What's Wrong with Homosexuality?*, 150.

31. Quoted in Stanton and Maier, *Marriage on Trial*, 35.

32. Ibid., 36.

33. Ibid., 163–64.

34. Ibid., 164–65.

35. Ibid., 28.

36. Bob Unruh, "State 'Weeding Out' Christian Beliefs," *WND*, September 27, 2013, http://www.wnd.com/2013/09/state-official-weed-out-conservatives-seeking-to-adopt/.

37. Ibid.

38. Serrin M. Foster, "The Feminist Case Against Abortion," *The Cost of "Choice,"* Erika Bachiochi ed., (San Francisco: Encounter Books, 2004), 34–35.

39. Candace C. Crandall, "Three Decades of Empty Promises," *The Cost of "Choice,"* 15.

40. Paige Comstock Cunningham, ESQ., "The Supreme Court and the Creation of the Two-Dimensional Woman," *The Cost of "Choice,"* 104–5.

41. Pearcey, *Total Truth*, 238.

42. Bork, *Slouching Towards Gomorrah*, 111.

43. Beckwith and Koukl, *Relativism*, 110.

44. Bork, *Slouching Towards Gomorrah*, 103.

45. Robert J. Spitzer, S.J., *Healing the Culture* (San Francisco: Ignatius Press, 2000), 288–9.

46. Paige Comstock Cunningham, ESQ., "The Supreme Court and the Creation of the Two-Dimensional Woman," *The Cost of "Choice,"* 118–19.

47. Serrin M. Foster, "The Feminist Case Against Abortion," *The Cost of "Choice,"* 35.

48. "Are You In the Know?" accessed September 1, 2013, http://www.guttmacher.org/in-the-know-/characteristics.html.

49. E. Joanne Angelo, MD, "The Psychological Aftermath of Three Decades of Abortion," *The Cost of "Choice,"* Erika Bachiochi ed., 87–100. Go to StartPage on the Internet and then type in "abortion aftermath" for stories of women who have suffered the psychological aftermath of abortion. One concise and helpful article can be found at www./arlingtondiocese.org/documents/fl_aftermathabortion.pdf.

50. "Why Pro-Life?," accessed September 5, 2013, http://www.whyprolife.com/planned-parenthood/, 1–2.

51. Beckwith and Koukl, *Relativism*, 137.

52. Hunter, *Culture Wars*, 312.

53. Geisler and Turek, *Legislating Morality*, 108.

54. "Abortions in America," *Operation Rescue*, accessed September 2, 2013, www.operationrescue.org/about-abortion/abortions-in-america/.

55. Bork, *Slouching Towards Gomorrah*, 180.

56. Geisler and Turek, *Legislating Morality*, 167, 175–76.

57. Candace C. Crandall, "Three Decades of Empty Promises," *The Cost of "Choice,"* 17.

58. Elizabeth Fox-Genovese, "Abortion: A War on Women," *The Cost of "Choice,"* 54.

59. Geisler and Turek, *Legislating Morality*, 174.

60. Amanda Marcotte, "The Demographics of Abortion: It's Not What You Think," *The American Prospect*, January 22, 2013, http://prospect.org/article/demographics-abortion-its-not-what-you-think.

61. Geisler and Turek, *Legislating Morality*, 177.

62. "An Interview with Norma McCovey, the 'Roe' of Roe vs. Wade," interviewed by Fr. Frank Pavone, Priests for Life, January 1, 1997, http://priestsforlife.org/articles/2737-an-interview-with-norma-mccorvey-the-roe-of-roe-vs-wade. Geisler and Turek, *Legislating Morality*, 166.

63. Robert George, "Bernard Nathanson: A Life Transformed by Truth on Abortion," *LifeNews*, February 28, 2011, http:www.lifenews.com/2011/02/28/Bernard-nathanson-a-life-transformed-by-truth-on-abortion/.

Chapter 15

1. Of course, the civil rights movement should be distinguished from the Me generation/sexual revolution, because civil rights advocates like Martin Luther King Jr. did not reject Christianity but often used it as a point of departure for gaining equal rights.

2. Keith G. Meador, "My Own Salvation," *The Secular Revolution*, 284, 287.

3. Ibid., 289.

4 Simon Young, *Designer Evolution: A Transhumanist Manifesto* (Amherst: Prometheus Books, 2006), 194–195.

5. Meador, "My Own Salvation," *The Secular Revolution.*, 288.

6. Philip Rieff, *The Triumph of the Therapeutic*, (Chicago: University of Chicago Press, 1987), 91. Meador, "My Own Salvation," *The Secular Revolution*, 305.

7. Harold Bloom, *The American Religion* (New York: Simon & Schuster, 1992), 34.

8. Armand Nicholi Jr., "Finding Hope, Health, and Life," *Finding God at Harvard*, Kelly Monroe, ed. (Grand Rapids, MI: Zondervan Publishing House, 1996), 114.

9. David K. Naugle, *Worldview: The History of a Concept* (Grand Rapids, MI: William B. Eerdmans Publishing Company, 2002), 217.

10. Eakman, *Cloning of the American Mind*, 115.

11. Meador, "My Own Salvation," *The Secular Revolution*, 292.

12. Ibid., 275, 282, 291–293.

13. Christina Hoff Sommers and Sally Satel, MD, *One Nation Under Therapy* (New York: St. Martin's Press, 2005), 57, 70, 76.

14. Douglas R. Groothuis, *Unmasking the New Age* (Downers Grove, IL: InterVarsity Press, 1986), 52–53.

15. Sommers and Satel, *One Nation Under Therapy*, 75–76.

16. Bloom, *The Closing of the American Mind*, 121.

17. Sommers and Satel, *One Nation Under Therapy*, 91.

18. Ibid., 100–1.

19. Jaki, *The Limits of a Limitless Science*, 166.

20. William Kilpatrick, "Faith and Therapy," *First Things*, February 1999, 23.

21. Rieff, *The Triumph of the Therapeutic*, 245.

22. Ibid., 24–25.

23. Michael D. LeMay, *The Suicide of American Christianity* (Bloomington, IN: WestBow Press, 2012), 146.

24. Quoted in Dave Hunt and T.A. McMahon, *The Seduction of Christianity* (Eugene, OR: Harvest House Publishers, 1986), 15.

25. LeMay, *The Suicide of American Christianity*, 147.

26. Paul Smith, *New Evangelicalism: The New World Order* (Costa Mesa, CA: Calvary Publishing, 2011), 123.

27. Daniel J. Carlat, MD, *Unhinged: The Trouble with Psychiatry—A Doctor's Revelation About a Profession in Crisis* (New York: Free Press, 2010).

28. O'Meara, *Psyched Out*, 42–44.

29. Carlat, *Unhinged*, 77.

30. Ibid., 76–77.

31. Ibid., 73.

32. Ibid., 94.

33. Ibid., 71.

34. Ibid.

35. Ibid., 86.

36. Ibid., 75.

37. Ibid., 13.

38. Ibid., 34.

39. Ibid., 13.

40. Ibid., 15.

41. O'Meara, *Psyched Out*, 173.

42. Robert Whitaker, *Anatomy of an Epidemic: Magic Bullets, Psychiatric Drugs, and the Astonishing Rise of Mental Illness in America*, (New York: Crown Publishers, 2010), 20.

43. Dr. Keith Ablow, "The New DSM-5 Fails to Accurately Describe Mental Illness," *Fox News*, May 22, 2013, http://www.foxnews.com/health/2013/05/22/american-psychiatry-needs-to-move-beyond-american-psychiatric-association-dsm-5-1643647435/.

44. Jen Wieczner, "15 new mental illnesses in the DSM," *MarketWatch*, May 25, 2013, http://www.marketwatch.com/story/15-new-mental-illnesses-in-the-dsm-5-2013-05-22.

45. I offer this "tongue in cheek" as McCain got caught and admitted to playing online poker during a Senate hearing on Syria in September 2013.

46. Ablow, "The New DSM-5 Fails To Accurately Describe Mental Illness."

47. Ibid.

48. Ibid.

49. Carlat, *Unhinged*, 64.

50. O'Meara, *Psyched Out*, 117.

51. Carlat, *Unhinged*, 65.

52. Prof. James F. Tracey, "From Persuasion to Coercion: PsychoPharma's 'Priesthood of the Mind,'" *Global Research*, October 6, 2012, http://globalresearch.ca/from-persuasion-to-coercion-psychopharmas-priesthood-of-the-mind/.

53. Ibid.

54. Carlat, *Unhinged*, 109.

55. Ibid., 111.

56. Whitaker, *Anatomy of an Epidemic*, 328.

57. Paul Joseph Watson, "Judge Orders Conspiracy Re-education for Lauryn Hill," *Alex Jones' Infowars*, May 8, 2013, http://www.infowars.com/judge-orders-conspiracy-re-education-for-lauryn-hill.

58. Ibid.

59. Michael B. Kelley, "Marine Veteran Brandon Raub Sentenced to Up to 30 Days in Psych Ward Over Facebook Posts," *Business Insider*, August 20, 2012, http://www.businessinsider.com/former-marine-brandon-raub-is-being-held-in-a-psychiatric-ward-over-facebook-posts-about-911-2012-8.

60. "Obama signs NDAA 2013 without objecting to indefinite detention of Americans," *RT*, January 3, 2013, rt.com/usa/Obama-ndaa-detention-president-288/.

61. Servando Gonzalez, *Psychological Warfare and the New World Order* (Oakland, CA: Spooks Books, 2010), 224.

Chapter 16

1. David Rothkopf, *Superclass: The Global Power Elite and the World They Are Making* (New York: Farrar, Straus and Giroux, 2008), 37.

2. CNSNews.com Staff, Senator Sessions: "'Super-Elites in Washington and Wall Street Dream of World Without Borders,'" *CNSNews*, December 13, 2014, http://cnsnews.com/blog/cnsnewscom-staff/sen-sessions-super-elites-washington-and-wall-street-dream-world-without.

3. Janine R. Wedel, *Shadow Elite* (New York: Basic Books, 2009), 5.

4. Ibid., 5, 15, 153.

5. Nomi Prins, *It Takes a Pillage* (Hoboken, NJ: John Wiley & Sons, Inc., 2009), 92.

6. Barry Ritholtz, *Bailout Nation* (Hoboken, NJ: John Wiley & Sons, Inc., 2009), 214. David Rothkopf in his book *Superclass* cites the compensation at $20 million per year on page 31.

7. Rothkopf, *Superclass*, 133.

8. Matt Taibbi, "The Great American Bubble Machine," *Rolling Stone*, July 9–23, 2009, 98–99.

9. West, *Darwin Day in America*, 105.

10. Ron Paul, *End the Fed* (New York: Grand Central Publishing, 2009), 195.

11. Les Leopold, *The Looting of America* (White River Junction, VT: Chelsea Green Publishing), 2009), 128. For more on the bailout money paid to AIG and their subsequent bonuses, see Neil Barofsky, *Bailout* (New York: Free Press, 2012), 138.

12. Phil Mattingly and Clea Benson, "Senate Panel Says Goldman Bet Against Clients, Misled Congress," *Bloomberg*, April 13, 2011, http://www.bloomberg.com/news/2011-04-13/goldman-sachs-cdos-bet-against-clients-misled-congress senate-panel-says.html.

13. Tyler Durden, "Jamie Dimon: That's Why I'm Richer Than You," *Zero Hedge*, February 27, 2013, www.zerohedge.com/news/2013-02-27/jamie-thats-why-i-am-richer-you.

14. Maureen Farrell, "J.P. Morgan Adds $2.6 Billion to Its $25 Billion Plus Tally of Recent Settlements," *The Wall Street Journal*, January 7, 2014. http://blogs.wsj.com/moneybeat/2014/01/07/j-p-morgan-adds-1-7-billion-to-its-25-billion-plus-tally-of recent-settlements/.

15. Greg Hunter, "Weekly News Wrap-Up 1.10.14," *USAWatchdog*, January 10, 2014, usawatchdog.com/weekly-news-wrap-up-1-10-14/.

16. Ellen Brown, "The Global Bankers' Coup Coming to US with Bail-In Bill," *Activist post*, December 13, 2014, http://www.activistpost.com/2014/12/the-global-bankers-coup-bail-in-and.html.

17. Gonzales, *Psychological Warfare and the New World Order*, 20.

18. Tal Brooke, *When the World Will Be As One* (Eugene, OR: Harvest House Publishers, Inc., 1989), 253.

19. Rothkopf, *Superclass*, 33, 275.

20. Sheldon S. Wolin, *Democracy Inc.: Managed Democracy and the Specter of Inverted Totalitarianism* (Princeton and Oxford: Princeton University Press, 2008), 164, 173.

21. Richard Grove, "British Historian Arnold Toynbee Describes How and Why American Sovereignty Should Be Ended," *Tragedy and Hope*, June 18, 2013, http://www.tragedyandhope.com/british-historian-arnold-toynbee-describes-how-and-why-american-sovereignty-should-be-ended/.

22. Robert Gates Sr., *The Conspiracy That Will Not Die* (Oakland: Red Anvil Press, 2011), 43.

23. This quote was from one of Wilson's campaign speeches that comprised "The New Freedom."

24. Gates Sr., *The Conspiracy That Will Not Die*, 185.

25. G. Edward Griffin, *The Creature from Jekyll Island* (Westlake Village, NY: American Media, 2002), 303.

26. Gates Sr., *The Conspiracy That Will Not Die*, 185.

27. Gonzales, *Psychological Warfare and the New* World Order, 56–57.

28. Gates Sr., *The Conspiracy That Will Not Die*, 185.

29. West, *Darwin Day in America*, 366.

30. Marvin Olasky, "Soaping the Slippery Slope," *World*, August 25, 2012, http://www.worldmag.com/2012/08/soaping_the_slippery_slope/page2.

31. Christopher Jon Bjerknes, "The Jewish Problem, Part 1: The Jews in Education," Pragmatic Witness, accessed December 13, 2013, whitewraithe.wordpress.com/the-jewish-problem-new-essay-series-by-christopher-jon-bjerknes/.

32. Charles Higham, *Trading with the Enemy* (New York: Barnes & Noble Books, 1983), 36, 41, 43.

33. Gary Allen, *The Rockefeller File* (Cutchogue: Buccaneer Books, 1998), "Introduction."

34. Smith, *The New Evangelicalism*, 163.

35. Gonzales, *Psychological Warfare and the New World Order*, 294.

36. Aaron Russo, "Nick Rockefeller explained NWO master plan to Aaron Russo," online video clip, *YouTube*, October 24, 2010, http://www.youtube.com/watch?v=K2WLzQ6z3Iw.

37. Terry L. Cook and Thomas R. Horn, *Beast Tech* (Crane, MO: Defender, 2013), 77.

38. Griffin, *The Creature from Jekyll Island*, 273.

39. Ibid., 283.

40. Gonzales, *Psychological Warfare and the New World Order*, 81.

41. Ibid., 84.

42. Ibid., 36, 46–47.

43. Barry M. Goldwater, *With No Apologies* (New York: William Morrow and Company, Inc., 1979), 287.

44. Ibid., 280–1.

45. Ibid., 285.

46. David Rockefeller, *Memoirs* (New York: Random House Trade Paperback, 2003), 405.

47. Thomas Sowell, *Intellectuals and Society* (New York: Basic Books, 2009), 91.

48. Gary Allen, *None Dare Call It Conspiracy* (GSG & Associates, 1972), 25. Rene A. Wormser, *Foundations: Their Influence and Power* (Covenant House Books, 1993), 178.

49. Allen, *None Dare Call It Conspiracy*, 21.

50. Gates Sr., *The Conspiracy That Will Not Die*, 63.

51. Karl Marx and Frederick Engels, *The Communist Manifesto* (New York: International Publishers, 1948), 28–30.

52. Ibid., 27.

53. Chris Hedges, *Death of the Liberal Class* (New York: Nation Books, 2010), 10, 12.

54. Ibid., 131.

55. Paul Joseph Watson, "This Is Why MSNBC Has Lost Half Its Audience," Alex Jones' InfoWars, January 24, 2014, http://www.infowars.com/this-is-why-msnbc-has-lost-half-its-audience/.

56. Smith, *New Evangelicalism*, 22–24.

57. All of the information in this paragraph and below concerning Bezmenov's explication of Russian subversion tactics can be found at www.youtube.com/watch?v=AAYQ-rfj1CI and also www.youtube.com/watch?v=a-6cvuyCKbw, both accessed October 19, 2013.

58. Ibid.

59. Quoted in Janet Tavakoli, *Dear Mr. Buffett* (Hoboken, NJ: John Wiley & Sons, 2009), 207.

60. Quoted in "David Rockefeller New World Order" *Quotes on the New World Order*, accessed January 28, 2014, nwothesis.blogspot.com/2011/04/david-rockefeller-new-world-order.html.

61. MaDmOnkyKungFu, "Yuri Bezmenov: KGB Psychological Warfare and Subversion Strategy Part 1," online video clip, *YouTube*, April 3, 2011, www.youtube.com/watch?v=a-6cvuyCKbw.

62. Ibid.

63. Daniel R. Amerman, "Financial Repression: A Sheep Shearing Instruction Manual," *Daniel Amerman, CFA*, accessed February 6, 2014, danielamerman.com/article/2011RepressionA.htm.

64. "The Federal Reserve Banking System Deception," *Now the End Begins*, accessed February 6, 2014, www.nowtheendbegins.com/the-federal-reserve-bank.htm.

65. NA, "Still don't Believe in the New World Order?," *HardTruth*, accessed February 7, 2014, http://www.theforbiddenknowledge.com/hardtruth/believe_new_world_order.htm.

66. Ibid.

67. Paul, *End the Fed*, 25.

68. Quoted in Ron Paul, *End the Fed*, 171.

69. Ibid., 117.

70. "Hard Cold Facts Concerning the IRS, accessed February 9, 2014, http://reviveamericanow.myfastforum.org/archives/hard-cold-facts-concerning-the-irs-o-t-57.html.

71. The Disciples of Truth, *Inform America!*, 1997, http://www.tax-freedom.com/ta24003.htm, accessed February 9, 2014. "It's Not Even Income Tax & Who Really Gets The So-Called 'Tax' Revenue," *Tax-Freedom.com*, accessed February 9, 2014, http://reviveamericanow.myfastforum.org/archives/hard-cold-facts-concerning-the-irs-o-t-57.html.

72. Information on Cloward-Piven strategy found in "Cloward-Piven is a strategy for forcing political change through orchestrated crisis," *Tea Party in the Hills*, accessed January 20, 2014, http://teapartyinthehills.org/cloward-piven_42.html.

73. Frances Fox Piven and Richard Cloward, "The Weight of the Poor: A Strategy to End Poverty," *The Nation*, May 2, 1966, http://www.thenation.com/article/weight-poor-strategy-end-poverty#.

74. James Simpson, "Barack Obama and the Strategy of Manufactured Crisis," American Thinker, September 28, 2008, http://www.americanthinker.com/articles/2008/09/barack_obama_and_the_strategy.html.

75. Marrs, *The Trillion Dollar Conspiracy*, 13.

76. Paul Craig Roberts, "Obamacare: The Final Payment- Raiding the Assets of Low-Income and Poor Americans," *Paul Craig Roberts IPE*, February 8, 2104, http://paulcraigroberts.org/2014/02/08/obamcare-final-payment-raiding-assets-low-income-poor-americans.

77. Daniel R. Amerman, "Who Benefits Most from MyRAs: Savers Or the US Treasury?" *Daniel Amerman*, accessed February 14, 2014, danielamerman.com/articles/2014/MyrasB.html.

Chapter 17

1. Jean-Francois Revel, *How Democracies Perish*, trans. William Byron, (Garden City, NY: Doubleday & Company, Inc., 1984), 4.

2. Tommy De Seno, "It's Fascism, Stupid. Not Socialism," *Justified Right*, November 19, 2008, http://justifiedright.typepad.com/justified_right/2008/11/its-fascism-stupid-not-socialism.html.

3. Naomi Wolf, *The End of America* (White River Junction: Chelsea Green Publishing Company, 2007), 32–33.

4. J. Llewellyn et al, "The Reichstag fire," *Alpha History*, accessed March 9, 2014, http://alphahistory.com/nazigermany/the-reichstag-fire/. Wolf, *The End of America*, 41, 145.

5. Susan Lindauer's *Extreme Prejudice* and Sibel Edmonds's *Classified Woman—The Sibel Edmonds Story: A Memoir* demonstrate the corruption and cover-ups in the higher echelons of the intelligence agencies and government and their implications for 9/11. Even a cursory glance at

the evidence concerning 9/11 will reveal that this event could not have gone down as reported in the official accounts.

6. Jim Marrs, *The Trillion Dollar Conspiracy* (New York: HarperCollins, 2011), 216.

7. N.a., accessed March 9, 2014, Http://www.nyclu.org/pdfs/eroding_liberty.pdf.

8. Natasha Lennard, "Obama signs NDAA 2014, indefinite detention remains," *Salon*, December 27, 2013, http://www.salon.com/2013/12/27/obama_signs_ndaa_2014_indefinite_detention_remains/.

9. Wolf, *The End of America*, 47.

10. Jason Howerton, "Attorney of Former Marine Detained for Facebook Posts Tells Beck: Psychiatrist Threatened to 'Brainwash' My Client With Meds," *The Blaze*, August 23, 2012, http://www.theblaze.com/stories/2012/08/23/attorney-of-former-marine-detained-for-facebook-posts-to-beck-psychiatrist-threatened-to-brainwash-my-client-with-meds/.

11. "Brandon Raub," *The Rutherford Institute*, accessed April 29, 2014, http://www.rutherford.org/key_cases/key_cases_brandon_raub/.

12. "Michael Salman," *The Rutherford Institute*, accessed April 29, 2014, http://www.rutherford.org/key_cases/.

13. "U.S. Supreme Court Rules 8-1 that Citizens Have No Protection Against Fourth Amendment Violations by Police Officers Ignorant of the Law," *The Rutherford Institute*, December 15, 2014, https://rutherford.org/publications_resources/on_the_front_lines/supreme_court_rules_8_1 _that_citizens_have_no_protecton_against_fourth_ame.

14. Robert Gellately, *Backing Hitler* (New York: Oxford University Press, 2001), 21, 35, 47, 51–53.

15. Ibid., 51, 59.

16. Ibid., 75.

17. Robert P. Ericksen, *Complicity in the Holocaust* (New York: Cambridge University Press, 2012), 19.

18. Marrs, *The Trillion Dollar Conspiracy*, xx.

19. Dara Kam and Stacey Singer, "Palm Beach County sheriff gets $1 million for violence prevention unit amid questions about civil liberties, care for mentally ill," *The Palm Beach Post*, April 29, 2013, http://www.mypalmbeachpost.com/news/state-regional-govt-politics/bradshaw-gets-1-million-for-violence-prevention-un/nXbs4/.

20. Sykes, *Dumbing Down Our Kids*, 174.

21. Kurt Nimmo, "MSNBC Host: Your Kids Belong to the Collective," *Alex Jones' Infowars*, April 6, 2013, http://www.infowars.com/your-kids-belong-to-the-collective.

22. Paul Joseph Watson, "White House Counterterror Chief: 'Confrontational' Children Could Be Terrorists," *Alex Jones' Infowars*, April 18, 2014, http://www.infowars.com/white-house-counterterror-chief-confronational-children-could-be-terrorists.

23. Paul Joseph Watson, "New Law Could Target Parents Who Drink Alcohol in Front of Kids As Child Abusers," *Alex Jones' Infowars*, April 2, 2014, http://www.infowars.com/new-law-could-target-parents-who-drink-alcohol-in-front-of-kids-as-child-abusers/.

24. Lisa Pine, *Nazi Family Policy 1933–1945* (New York: Berg, 1997), 57–58.

25. Erwin Lutzer, *Hitler's Cross* (Chicago: Moody Press, 1995), 115.

26. Lisa Pine, *Nazi Family Policy 1933–1945*, 182–3.

27. Reeves, *The Empty Church*, 79.

28. Ericksen, *Complicity in the Holocaust*, 19.

29. Ibid., 8.

30. Ibid., 83, 144.

31. Ibid., 88.

32. Ibid., 62.

33. Ibid., 103, 227.

34. Christine Rosen, *Preaching Eugenics* (New York: Oxford University Press, 2004), 5. Edwin Black, *War Against the Weak* (New York: Four Walls Eight Windows, 2003), 18.

35. Rosen, *Preaching Eugenics*, 5.

36. Black, *War Against the Weak*, 28.

37. West, *Darwin Day in America*, 149. Black, *War Against the Weak*, 58–59.

38. Black, *War Against the Weak*, 99.

39. Ibid., 215.

40. Ibid.

41. Ibid., 67.

42. West, *Darwin Day in America*, 140.

43. "Eugenics in Virginia: Buck v. Bell and Forced Sterilization," *Eugenics*, University of Virginia, accessed April 3, 2014, http://exhibits.hsl.virginia.edu/eugenics/. West, *Darwin Day in America*, 138.

44. *Encyclopedia Virginia*, s.v. "Buck v. Bell (1927)," accessed April 3, 2014, http://encyclopediavirginia.org/Buck_v_Bell_1927.

45. Black, *War Against the Weak*, 75, 219.

46. Ibid., 259.

47. Richard Weikart, *From Darwin to Hitler* (New York: Palgrave Macmillan, 2006), 76, 146.

48. Ibid., 80.

49. Ibid.

50. Black, *War Against the Weak*, 262.

51. Weikart, *From Darwin to Hitler*, 98, 114.

52. Ibid., 212.

53. Ibid., 225. Black, *War Against the Weak*, 269.

54. Marrs, *The Trillion Dollar Conspiracy*, 155.

55. Black, *War Against the Weak*, 403.

56. Ibid., 315–6. Quote found on 277.

57. Ibid., 61, 364–5, 370.

58. John G. West, *Darwin Day in America*, 132.

59. Black, *War Against the Weak*, xxv.

60. Julian Huxley, *UNESCO: Its Purpose and Philosophy* (London: Euston Grove Press, 1947), 38.

61. Ibid., 45.

62. *Endgame*, produced and directed by Alex Jones (Inforwars.com, 2007), DVD.

63. Black, *The War Against the Weak*, 441–443.

64. Ibid., 430, 434.

65. Gonzalez, *Psychological Warfare and the New World Order* , xiii, 339.

66. R. J. Rummel, *Death by Government* (Piscataway, NJ: Transaction Publishers, 1997), 9.

67. Ibid., 1–2.

68. Rosen, *Preaching Eugenics*, 16, 13.

69. Ibid., 184.

70. Ibid., 38.

71. Ibid., 39.

72. Ibid.

73. West, *Darwin Day in America*, 129.

74. Rosen, *Preaching Eugenics*, 129. Quote on 130.

75. Ibid., 120.

76. Ibid., 113.

77. Ibid., 63–64.

78. Ibid., 66.

79. Ericksen, *Complicity in the Holocaust*, 15–16.

80. Ibid., 59–60.

81. Ibid., 114, 57–58.

82. McGrath, *A Passion for Truth*, 60.

83. Gellately, *Backing Hitler*, 14. Lutzer, *Hitler's Cross*, 122.

84. Lutzer, *Hitler's Cross*, 124.

85. Richard Terrell, *Christ, Faith, and the Holocaust* (Bloomington: WestBow Press, 2011), 144.

86. Ericksen, *Complicity in the Holocaust*, 9.

87. Ibid., 9, 138.

Chapter 18

1. My detractors might argue that they don't believe in a literal Devil; however, Jesus believed in the Devil and demons, the latter of which He cast out of people. The Devil tempted Jesus. If Jesus believed the Devil existed, we today also have an indisputable reason to believe the Devil exists.

2. Karl de Vries, "Abortion advocates, foes draw lines over viral video of woman undergoing procedure," *Fox News*, May 6, 2014, http://www.foxnews.com/us/2014/05/06/abortion-clinic-stands-behind-employee-whose-video-procedure-has-gone-viral/.

3. Ibid.

4. Proverbs 9:10.

5. Daniel 9:27.

6. Revelation 13.

7. Matthew 24:4–5.

8. Revelation 6:9–11.

9. 2 Thessalonians 2:3.

10. H. L. Nigro, *Before God's Wrath: The Bible's Answer to the Timing of the Rapture*, (Bellefonte, PA: Strong Tower Publishing, 2004), 18.

11. Ibid.

12. 2 Peter 3:3–12.

13. Isaiah 28:18; Daniel 9:27.

14. Daniel 9:24–27.

15. In the KJV, Antichrist is called the beast (Rev. 13), the prince to come (Dan. 9:26), the son of perdition (2 Thess. 2:3), the man of sin (2 Thess. 2:3). He is called "the lawless one" in 2 Thess. 2:8 (ESV).

16. Matthew 24:6–7. Also see parallel account in Luke 21:10–11.

17. Matthew 24:8.

18. 2 Thessalonians 2:4.

19. I Thessalonians 5:3.

20. Coffman, *Plundered*, 211.

21. Katherine Albrecht and Liz McIntyre, *Spychips* (Nashville: Nelson Current, 2005), 77, 143.

22. Ibid., 214.

23. Ibid., 171, 188–9.

24. Revelation 20:4

25. Paul Joseph Watson, "New Medical Law Mandates 'Private' Conversation with Child Before Every Doctor Visit," *Alex Jones' Infowars*, June 6, 2014, http://www.infowars.com/new-medical-law-mandates-private-conversation-with-child-before-every-doctor-visit/.

26. Howard Portnoy, "Obama nominee for Surgeon General says banning guns is part of medicine," *Liberty Unyielding*, March 8, 2014, http://libertyunyielding.com/2014/03/08/another-obama-nominee-cabinet-post-another-radical/.

27. "Feinstein Introduces New Federal Bill to Confiscate Guns if Snitch Feels Unsafe," *Activist Post*, June 7, 2014, http://www.activistpost.com/2014/06/the-pause-for-safety-act-gun-bill.html.

28. Revelation 9:21

Chapter 19

1. John 8:44

2. Revelation 19:20

3. Exodus 20:4–5.

4. The translation of these verses is a bit choppy, but the essence of the Greek talks about a lie associated with wonders (v. 9) and then "the lie" specifically mentioned in verse 11. Alfred Marshall, *NASB-NIV Parallel New Testament in Greek and English* (Grand Rapids, MI: Zondervan Publishing House, 1986), 599.

5. Genesis 3:4–5.

6. Isaiah 14:12–14.

7. Revelation 20:2

8. Max More and Natasha Vita-More, eds., *The Transhumanist Reader* (West Sussex, U.K.: Wiley-Blackwell, 2013), 1.

9. Robert M. Geraci, *Apocalyptic AI* (New York: Oxford University Press, 2010), 69.

10. Ray Kurzweil, *The Singularity Is Near* (New York: Penguin Group, 2005), 40, 41, 136.

11. Ibid., 476–7.

12. Ray Kurzweil, "Ray Kurzweil on How We Will Become Like God," *33rd Square*, January 2, 2014, http://www.33rdsquare.com/2014/01/ray-kurzweil-on-how-we-will-become-god.html.

13. Joel Garreau, *Radical Evolution* (New York: Broadway Books, 2005), 128–9.

14. Kurzweil, *The Singularity Is Near*, 9.

15. Alex Jones, "Real Time Total Information Awareness Tracking Grid Is Being Implemented Now," YouTube video, 7:39, posted by Infowars, May 14, 2014, http://youtube.com/watch?v=fMSW9aiZzoU.

16. Garreau, *Radical Evolution*, 157.

17. Ibid., 143–4.

18. Ibid., 139.

19. I Thessalonians 5:3

20. Kurzweil, "Ray Kurzweil on How We Will Become Like God."

21. Kurzweil, *The Singularity Is Near*, 1.

22. Garreau, *Radical Evolution*, 93.

23. Warren B. Smith, *False Christ Coming: Does Anybody Care?* (Magalia: Mountain Stream Press, 2011), 77.

24. Ibid.

25. Ibid., 76.

26. Barbara Marx Hubbard, *The Revelation* (Sonoma: The Foundation for Conscious Evolution, 1993), 75.

27. Ibid., 140.

28. His notion of the "Omega," for example, by his own admission leads ultimately to the "Impersonal." Teilhard de Chardin, *The Phenomenon of Man*, trans. Bernard Wall (New York: Harper Touchbook, 1955), 258.

29. *Encyclopaedia Britannica*, s.v. "Pierre Teilhard de Chardin," accessed June 30, 2014, http://www.britannica.com/EBchecked/topic/585678/Pierre-Teilhard-de-chardin.

30. Marilyn Ferguson, *The Aquarian Conspiracy* (Los Angeles: J.P. Tarcher Inc., 1980), 50.

31. Teilhard de Chardin, *Christianity and Evolution*, trans. Rene Hague (New York: Harvest/HBJ Book, 1969), 130.

32. Warren B. Smith, *False Christ Coming*, 27.

33. Robert M Geraci, *Apocalyptic AI* (New York: Oxford University Press, 2010), 8.

34. Hubbard, *The Revelation*, 58.

35. Ibid., 294.

36. Todd Starnes, "Pentagon Classifies Evangelical Christians, Catholics as 'Extremists,'" *Fox News Radio*, accessed March 2, 2014, http://radio.foxnews.com/toddstarnes/top-stories/pentagon-classifies-evangelical-christians-catholics-as-extremists.html. After some pushback, apparently this part of the presentation is no longer used.

37. 2 Thessalonians 2:3. The original Greek uses the word *apostasia* in this verse.

38. Brannon House and Jimmy DeYoung, "John MacArthur OUTRAGE: Take Mark of Beast, Still Be Saved," YouTube video, 5:00, posted by Ephesians511sBlog, accessed August 8, 2014, http://www.youtube.com/watch?v=yteZw7VMaRU. MacArthur is an extremely well-respected Christian theologian and biblical scholar who has done much work for the kingdom of God. I would kindly point out, however, that Dr. MacArthur believes in the pre-tribulation rapture, and he is also a Calvinist. Both of these are false doctrines the latter of which may have affected his erroneous view on taking the mark of the Beast.

39. Revelation 20:15

40. Gary Gilley, *This Little Church Went to Market* (Webster: Evangelical Press USA, 2005), 42.

41. Ibid., 73.

42. Ibid., 65.

43. Ibid.

44. Michael Day, "Pope Francis assures atheists: You don't have to believe in God to go to heaven," *The Independent*, September 11, 2013, http://www.independent.co.uk/news/world/europe/pope-francis-assures-you-dont-have-to-believe-in-god-to-go-to-heaven-8810062.html.

45. Novak, *Belief and Unbelief*, 12.

46. Carter, *The Culture of Disbelief*, 90.

47. LeMay, *The Suicide of American Christianity*, 89.

48. Salvation is only through Jesus Christ: John 3:16; John 14:6; Acts 4:12; 1Timothy 2:5–6; 1 John 5:11–13, 20.

49. "The ACW Letter," *A Common Word*, accessed July 5, 2014, http://www.acommonword.com/the-acw-document/.

50. LeMay, *The Suicide of American Christianity*, 160–1.

51. Joe Schimmel, "Rick Warren's Ecumenical Idolatry!" *Cup of Joe*, Good Fight Ministry, January 30, http://cupofjoe.goodfight.org/?p=88.

52. Walid Shoebat, *God's War on Terror* (Top Executive Media, 2010). Joel Richardson, *The Islamic Antichrist*, (Washington, D.C.: WND Books, 2012).

53. "Chrislam One World Religion Emerging," YouTube video, 1:38:52, posted by Jerry Whitehurst, September 27, 2011, http://www.youtube.com/watch?v=wPZTmefDpuc.

54. Roger Oakland, *Faith Undone* (Silverton: Lighthouse Trails Publishing, 2008), 147.

55. Shoebat, *God's War on Terror*, 162–8.

56. Dave Hodges, "Why Does the Government Need Guillotines? *The Common Sense Show*, June 29, 2013, http://www.thecommonsenseshow.com/2013/06/29/why-does-the-government-need-guillotines.

57. "Warren Smith: The New Age, Purpose Driven, and Deception in the Church, Part 1," YouTube video, 9:54, posted by Lighthouse Trails Publishing, November 9, 2008, http://www.youtube.com/watch?v=4PStqjTZEGk.

58. I am not trying to pick on James Robison who made this statement. Mr. Robison does honorable work here with a television ministry, and also in other countries where he builds water wells and provides for the physical needs of the poor, the latter of which I have supported for years. I am merely providing this as an example of the ecumenical push. It is something to keep an eye on. Rick Wiles, "Pope Francis Meets Evangelical Delegation," *TruNews*, June 27, 2014, http://www.trunews.com/trunews-exclusive-pope-francis-meets-evangelical-delegation/.

59. "Pope Francis on Frantic Quest to Unite All Religions under Rome," *Now the End Begins*, June 8, 2014, www.nowtheendbegins.com/blog/?p=22485.

60. Kurt Nimmo, "Vatican Calls for 'Central World Bank,'" *Alex Jones' Info Wars*, October 24, 2011, http://infowars.com/vatican-calls-for-central-world-bank/.

Chapter 20

1. Information in the preceding paragraphs provided by Dr. Renald Shower, "Jewish Marriage Customs," *The Friends of Israel Gospel Ministry, Inc.*, accessed July 20, 2014, http://www.biblestudymanuals.net/jewish_marriage_customs.htm.

2. Ephesians 5:23

3. 1 Corinthians 6:19–20

4. 1 Corinthians 11:25–26

5. Ephesians 5:25–27

6. 1 John 3:2–3; Ephesians 5:27

7. Matthew 24:36

8. Revelation 19:6–9

9. Revelation 8:6—9:21, chapters 15—16.

10. Revelation 11:13

11. Revelation 19:15b

12. Hebrews 9:27

13. Revelation 20:11–15. This is the Great White Throne Judgment for the unsaved.

14. Romans 5:9

15. Galatians 2:16; Ephesians 2:8–9; Titus 3:5–7.

16. Hebrews 9:24–28; 10:12, 14.

Bibliography

Adler, Mortimer J. 1990. *Truth in Religion*. New York: Macmillan Publishing Company.

Ahlstrom, Sydney. 2004. *A Religious History of the American People*. New Haven and London: Yale University Press.

Albrecht, Katherine, and Liz McIntyre. 2005. *Spychips*. Nashville: Nelson Current.

Allen, Charlotte. 1998. *The Human Christ*. New York: Free Press.

Allen, Gary. 1972. *None Dare Call It Conspiracy*. GSG & Associates.

—. 1998. *The Rockefeller File*. Cutchogue: Buccaneer Books.

Anderson, Walter Truett. 1995. *The Truth About the Truth: De-confusing and Re-constructing the Postmodern World*. New York: Jeremy P. Tarcher/Putnam Book .

Austin, Bill. 1983. *Austin's Topical History of Christianity*. Wheaton: Tyndale House Publishing.

Balmer, Randall. 1999. *Blessed Assurance: A History of Evangelicalism in America*. Boston: Beacon Press.

Barna, George. 1998. *The Second Coming of the Church*. Nashville: Word Publishing.

Bauer, Henry H. 1994. *Scientific Literacy and the Myth of the Scientific Method*. Urbana and Chicago: Universtiy of Illinois Press.

Becker, Carl. 1932. *The Heavenly City of the Eighteenth Century Philosophers*. New Haven & London: Yale University Press.

Beckwith, Francis J. 2003. *Law, Darwinism, and Public Education*. Lanham: Rowman & Littlefield Publishers.

Beckwith, Francis J., and Gregory Koukl. 2000. *Relativism*. Grand Rapids, MI: Baker Book House.

Behe, Michael J. 1996. *Darwin's Black Box: The Biochemical Challenge to Evolution*. New York: Free Press.

Bellah, Robert et.al. 1985. *Habits of the Heart: Individualism and Commitment in American Life*. Berkeley: University of California.

Bellah, Robert N. 1970. *Beyond Belief: Essays on Religion in a Post-Tradtional World*. New York: Harper & Row.

Benne, Robert. 2001. *Quality with Soul: How Six Premier Colleges and Universities Keep Faith with Their Religious Traditions*. Grand Rapids, MI/Cambridge, UK: Eerdmans Publishing Company.

Bennett, Willliam J. 1994. *The Index of Leading Culture Indicators: Facts and Figures on the State of American Society*. New York: Touchstone.

Berger, Peter L. 1990. *The Sacred Canopy: Elements of Sociological Theory of Religion*. New York: Anchor Books.

Black, Edwin. 2003. *War Against the Weak*. New York: Four Walls Eight Windows.

Bloom, Allan. 1987. *The Closing of the American Mind*. New York: Simon & Schuster.

Bloom, Harold. 1992. *The American Religion: The Emergence of the Post-Christian Nation*. New York: Simon & Schuster.

Blumenberg, Hans. 1999. *The Legitimacy of the Modern Age*. Cambridge: MIT Press.

Blumenfeld, Samuel L. 1984. *NEA: Trojan Horse in American Education*. Phoenix, AZ: The Paradigm Company.

Bockmuehl, Klaus. 1988. *The Unreal God: Of Modern Theology*. Colorado Springs: Helmers & Howard.

Bork, Robert H. 1996. *Slouching Towards Gomorrah: Modern Liberalism and American Decline*. New York: Harper Collins.

Brander, B.G. 1998. *Staring into Chaos*. Dallas, TX: Spence Publishing Company.

Brooke, John Hedley. 1991. *Science and Religion*. Cambridge: Cambridge University Press.

Brooke, Tal. 1989. *When the World Will Be As One*. Eugene, OR: Harvest House Publishers, Inc.

Brooks, David. 2000. *Bobos in Paradise: The New Upper Class and How They Got There*. New York: Simon and Schuster Paperbacks.

Brown, Colin. 1990. *Christianity and Western Thought, Vol 1. A History of Philosophers, Ideas, and Movements*. Downers Grove: InterVarsity Press.

Bruce, Steve. 1996. *Religion in the Modern World: From Cathedrals to Cults*. Oxford: Oxford University Press.

Brush, Nigel. 2005. *The Limitations of Scientific Truth*. Grand Rapids, MI: Kregel Publications.

Buckley, Michael J. 1987. *At the Origins of Modern Atheism*. New Haven & London: Yale University Press.

Buckley, William F. 1997. *Nearer My God*. New York: Doubleday.

Bultmann, Rudolf, Reginald H. Fuller, trans. 1961. *Kerygma and Myth*. New York: Harper & Row.

Burtt, E.A. 2003. *The Metaphysical Foundations of Modern Science*. Mineola, NY: Dover Publications.

Butterfield, Herbert. 1965. *The Origins of Modern Science*. New York: Free Press.

Byrne, James M. 1996. *Religion and the Enlightenment: From Descartes to Kant*. Louisville: Westminster John Knox Press.

Calvert, Kenneth R., William Jeynes and Enedina Martinez, eds. 2007. *Christianity, Education, and Modern Society*. Charlotte, NC: Information Age Publishing, Inc.

Campbell, Jeremy. 2001. *The Liars Tale: A History of Falsehoods*. New York & London: W. W. Norton & Company.

Carlat, Daniel J., M.D. 2010. *Unhinged: The Trouble With Psychiatry*. New York: Free Press.

Carson, D. A., ed. 2000. *Telling the Truth*. Grand Rapids, MI: Zondervan Publishing House.

Carter, Stephen L. 1993. *The Culture of Disbelief: How American Law and Politics Trivialize Religious Devotion*. New York: Basic Books.

Cassirer, Ernst, Fritz C. Koelln and James P. Pettegrove trans. 1979. *The Philosophy of the Enlightenment*. Princeton: Princeton Universtiy Press.

Chesterton, G.K. 1990. *Orthodoxy*. New York: Doubleday.

Chopra, Deepak. 1994. *The Seven Spiritual Laws of Success*. San Rafael, CA: Amber-Allen Publishing.

Clark, Kelly James. 2004. *101 Key Terms in Philosophy and Their Importance for Theology*. Louisville: John Knox Press.

Coffman, Michael S. 2012. *Plundered*. Bangor, ME: Environmental Perspectives Inc.

Corvino, John. 2013. *What's Wrong with Homosexuality?* Oxford: Oxford University Press.

Cox, Harvey. 1969. *The Secular City*. Toronto: Macmillan Company.

de Chardin, Teilhard, trans. Rene Hague. 1969. Christianity and Evolution. New York: Harvest/HBJ Book.

Dembski, William A., and James M. Kushiner eds. 2001. *Signs of Intelligence: Understanding Intelligence*. Grand Rapids, MI: Brazos Press.

Dennett, Daniel C. 1995. *Darwin's Dangerous Idea: Evolution and the Meanings of Life*. New York: Simon & Schuster.

Denton, Michael. 1996. *Evolution: A Theory in Crisis*. Chevy Chase, MD: Adler & Adler.

Descartes, Rene, David Weissman, ed. 1996. *Discourse on Method and Meditations on First Philosophy*. New Haven & London: Yale University Press.

Dockery, David S. ed. 2001. *The Challenge of Postmodernism*. Grand Rapids: Baker Academic.

Donohue, Bill. 2009. *Secular Sabotage: How Liberals Are Destroying Religion and Culture in America*. New York: Faith Words.

Dupre, Lewis. 1993. *Passage To Modernity: An Essay in the Hermeneutics of Nature and Culture*. New Haven & London: Yale University Press.

Eakman, B.K. 1998. *The Cloning of the American Mind.* Lafayette, LA: Huntington House Publishers.

Eberstadt, Mary. 2013. *How the West Really Lost God.* West Conshohocken: Templeton Press.

Edmonds, Sibel. 2012. *Classified Woman: A Memoir.* Alexandria, VA: Sibel Edmonds.

Ericksen, Robert P. 2012. *Complicity in the Holocaust.* New York: Cambridge University Press.

Erickson, Millard. 2001. *Truth or Consequences.* Downers Grove, IL: InterVarsity Press.

Erika Bachiochi, ed. 2004. *The Cost of Choice.* San Francisco: Encounter Books.

Ferguson, Marilyn. 1980. *The Aquarian Conspiracy.* Los Angeles: J.P. Tarcher.

Ferngren, Gary B., ed. 2002. *Science and Religion.* Baltimore, MD: Johns Hopkins University Press.

Garreau, Joel. 2005. *Radical Evolution.* New York: Broadway Books.

Gates Sr., Robert. 2011. *The Conspiracy That Will Not Die.* Oakland: Red Anvil Press.

Gatto, John Taylor. 2000-2001. *The Underground History of American Education.* New York: The Oxford Village Press.

Gay, Craig M. 1998. *The Way of the (Modern) World.* Grand Rapids, MI: William B. Eerdmans Publishing.

Gay, Peter. 1995. *The Enlightenment: The Rise of Modern Paganism.* New York: W.W. Norton & Company.

Geisler, Norman and Frank Turek. 1998. *Legislating Morality.* Eugene, OR: Wipf and Stock Publishers.

Gellately, Robert. 2001. *Backing Hitler.* New York: Oxford University Press.

Geraci, Robert M. 2010. *Apocalyptic AI.* New York: Oxford University Press.

Gillespie, Michael Allen. 1996. *Nihilism Before Nietzsche.* Chicago: University of Chicago Press.

Gilley, Gary. 2005. *This Little Church Went to Market.* Webster: Evangelical Press USA.

Goldwater, Barry M. 1979. *With No Apologies.* New York: William Morrow and Company, Inc.

Gonzalez, Servando. 2010. *Psychological Warfare and the New World Order.* Oakland, CA: Spooks Books.

Graede, S. D. 1993. *When Tolerance Is No Virtue: Political Correctness, Multiculturalism and the Future of Truth and Justice.* Downers Grove: InterVarsity Press.

Graukroger, Stephen. 1997. *Descartes: An Intellectual Biography.* Oxford: Clarendon Press.

Green, Garrett. 2000. *Theology, Hermeneutics, and Imagination: The Crisis of Interpretation at the End of Modernity.* Cambridge: Cambridge University Press.

Greenawalt, Kent. 2005. *Does God Belong in Public Schools.* Princeton: Princeton University Press.

Grenz, Stanley. 1996. *A Primer on Postmodernism.* Grand Rapids, MI: Eerdmans Publishing Company.

Griffin, G. Edward. 2002. *The Creature from Jekyll Island.* Westlake Village, NY: American Media.

Groothuis, Douglas R. 1986. *Unmasking the New Age.* Downers Grove, IL: InterVarsity Press.

Groothuis, Douglas. 2000. *Truth Decay: Defending Christianity Against the Challenge of Postmodernism.* Downers Grove: InterVarsity Press.

Guinness, Os. 2012. *A Free People's Suicide: Sustainable Freedom and the American Future.* Downers Grove, IL: InterVarsity Press.

—. 1983. *The Gravedigger File: Papers On the Subversion of the Modern Church.* Downers Grove, IL: InterVarsity Press.

Hacking, Ian. 1999. *The Emergence of Probability.* Cambridge: Cambridge University Press.

Hammond, Phillip E. 1992. *Religion and Personal Autonomy: The Third Disestablishment in America.* Columbia, SC: University of South Carolina Press.

Harrison, Peter. 2009. *The Fall of Man and the Foundations of Science.* Cambridge: Cambridge University Press.

Hart, D.G. 1999. *The University Gets Religion: Religious Studies in American Higher Education.* Baltimore and London: The Johns Hopkins University Press.

Harvey, David. 1990. *The Condition of Postmodernity.* Oxford: Blackwell Publishing Ltd.

Hatch, Nathan O. 1989. *The Democratization of American Christianity.* New Haven and London: Yale University Press.

Hedges, Chris. 2010. *Death of the Liberal Class.* New York: Nation Books.

Herberg, Will. 1960. *Protestant-Catholic-Jew.* Garden City, New York: Doubleday & Company Inc.

Higham, Charles. 1983. *Trading with the Enemy.* New York: Barnes & Noble Books.

Hitchcock, James. 1982. *What Is Secular Humanism? Why Humanism Became Secular and How It Is Changing Our World.* Ann Arbor: Servant Books.

Hooykaas, R. 1972. *Religion and the Rise of Modern Science.* Vancouver: Regent College Publishing.

Hordern, William E. 1968. *A Layman's Guide to Protestant Theology.* New York: Macmillan Publishing Company.

Horgan, John. 1996. *The End of Science.* Reading, MA: Addison-Wesley Publishing Company Inc.

Hubbard, Barbara Marx. 1993. *The Revelation.* Sonoma: The Foundation for Conscious Evolution.

Hunt, Dave, and T.A. McMahon. 1986. *The Seduction of Christianity.* Eugene, OR: Harvest House Publishers.

Hunter, Cornelius G. 2010. *Darwin's God.* Grand Rapids, MI: Brazos Press.

—. 2007. *Science's Blind Spot.* Grand Rapids, MI: Brazos Press.

Hunter, James Davidson. 1991. *Culture Wars.* New York: Basic Books.

Huntington, Samuel P. 2004. *Who Are we? The Challenges to National Identity.* New York: Simon and Schuster.

Huxley, Julian. 1947. *UNESCO: Its Purpose and Philosophy.* London: Euston Grove Press.

Jaki, Stanley L. 2000. *The Limits of a Limitless Science.* Wilmington, DE: ISI Books.

Johnson, Phillip E. 1997. *Defeating Darwinism.* Downers Grove, IL: InterVarsity Press.

—. 1998. *Objections Sustained.* Downers Grove, IL: InterVarsity Press.

—. 2000. *The Wedge of Truth: Splitting the Foundations of Naturalism.* Downers Grove, IL: InterVarsity Press.

Jones, E. Michael. 2000. *Monsters from the Id.* Dallas, TX: Spence Publishing Company.

Jones, Stanton L., and Mark A. Yarhouse. 2000. *Homosexuality: The Use of Scientific Research in the Church's Moral Debate.* Downers Grove, IL: InterVarsity Press.

Kilpatrick, William. 2012. *Christianity, Islam, and Atheism.* San Francisco: Ignatius Press.

Kimball, Roger. 2000. *The Long March.* San Francisco: Encounter Books.

Kinsey, Alfred C., Wardell B. Pomeroy, and Clyde E. Martin. 1948. *Sexual Behavior in the Human Male.* Philadelphia: W.B. Saunders Company.

Knight, Robert H. 1998. *The Age of Consent.* Dallas, TX: Spence Publishing Company.

Kronman, Anthony T. 2007. *Education's End: Why Our Colleges and Universities Have Given Up on the Meaning of Life.* New Haven and London: Yale University Press.

Kurtz, Paul. 1983. *In Defense of Secular Humanism.* Amherst, NY: Prometheus Books.

Lacey, Michael J., ed. 1991. *Religion and Twentieth Century American Intellectual Life.* Cambridge: Cambridge University Press.

Larson, Edward J. 2006. *Summer for the Gods.* New York: Basic Books.

Lasch, Christopher. 1996. *The Revolt of the Elites.* New York: W.W. Norton & Company.

Laumann, Edward O., John H. Gagnon, Robert T. Michael, and Stewart Michaels. 1994. *The Social Organization of Sexuality.* Chicago: University of Chicago Press.

Lawler, Peter Augustine. 2002. *Aliens in America: The Strange Truth About Our Souls.* Wilmington, DE: ISIS Books.

Lee, Philip J. 1987. *Against the Protestant Gnostics.* Oxford: Oxford University Press.

LeMay, Michael D. 2012. *The Suicide of American Christianity.* Bloomington, IN: WestBow Press.

Lennox, John C. 2009. *God's Undertaker.* Oxford: Lion Hudson.

Leopold, Les. 2009. *The Looting of America.* White River Junction, VT: Chelsea Green Publishing.

Lewis, Gordon R., and Bruce A. Demarest. 1987. *Integrative Theology Vol. 1.* Grand Rapids, MI: Zondervan Publishing House.

Limbaugh, David. 2003. *Persecution: How Liberals Are Waging War Against Chrstianity.* Washington, D.C.: Regnery Publishing Inc.

Lindauer, Susan. 2010. *Extreme Prejudice: The Terrifying Story of the Patriot Act And the Cover Ups of 9/11 and Iraq.* Susan Lindauer.

Lindberg, David C. and Ronald L. Numbers eds. 2003. *When Science and Christianity Meet.* Chicago and London: University of Chicago Press.

Lionni, Paolo. 1993. *The Leipzig Connection.* Sheridan, OR: Heron Books.

Livingstone, David N. 1997. *Darwin's Forgotten Defenders: The Encounter Between Evangelical Theology and Evolutionary Thought.* Vancouver: Regent College Publishing.

London, Herbert. 2008. *America's Secular Challenge: The Rise of a New National Religion.* New York: Encounter Books.

Lutzer, Erwin. 1995. *Hitler's Cross.* Chicago: Moody Press.

Lyotard, Jean-Francois, Geoff Bennington and Brian Massumi, trans. 1984. *The Postmodern Condition: A Report on Knowledge.* Minneapolis, MN: University of Minnesota Press.

Machen, J. Gresham. 1991. *What Is Faith?* Edinburgh: Banner of Truth Trust.

—. 1996. *Christianity and Liberalism.* Grand Rapids, MI: Eerdmans.

Maddoux, Marlin. 2006. *Public Education Against America.* New Kensington: Whitaker House.

Magee, Bryan. 1997. *Confessions of a Philosopher: A Journey Through Western Philosophy.* New York: Random House Inc.

Marrs, Jim. 2011. *The Trillion-Dollar Conspiracy.* New York: Harper Collins.

Marsden, George M., and Bradley J. Longfield eds. 1992. *The Secularization of the Academy.* New York: Oxford University Press.

Marsden, George. 1994. *The Soul of the American University: From Protestant Establishment to Established Nonbelief.* New York: Oxford University Press.

—. 1991. *Understanding Fundamentalism and Evangelicalism.* Grand Rapids: Eerdmans.

Marx, Karl, and Frederick Engels. 1948. *The Communist Manifesto.* New York: International Publishers.

May, Henry F. 1976. *The Enlightenment in America.* New York: Oxford University Press.

McCallum, Dennis ed. 1996. *The Death of Truth.* Minneapolis: Bethany House Publisher.

McGrath, Alister. 1996. *A Passion For Truth: The Intellectual Coherence of Evangelicalism.* Downers Grove: InterVarsity Press.

—. 1999. *Science and Religion: An Introduction.* Oxford: Blackwell Publishers.

—. 1998. *The Foundations of Dialogue in Science and Religion.* Oxford: Blackwell Publishers.

Meyer, Stephen C. 2009. *Signature in the Cell: DNA and the Evidence for Intelligent Design.* New York: Harper One.

Middleton, Richard and Brian J. Walsh. 1995. *Truth is Stranger Than It Used to Be: Biblical Faith in a Postmodern Age.* Downers Grove: InterVarsity Press.

Monroe, Kelly, ed. 1996. *Finding God at Harvard: Spiritual Journies of Thinking Christians.* Grand Rapids, MI: Zondervan Publishing House

More, Max, and Natasha Vita-More. 2013. *The Transhumanist Reader.* West Sussex, UK: Wiley-Blackwell.

Murphy, Nancey. 1996. *Beyond Liberalism and Fundamentalism: How Modern and Postmodern Philosophy Set the Theological Agenda .* Valley Forge: Trinity Press International.

Nagel, Thomas. 2012. *Mind and Cosmos: Why the Materialist Neo-Darwinian Conception of Nature Is Almost Certainly False.* New York: Oxford University Press.

Nash, Ronald. 1984. *Christian Faith and Historical Understanding.* Grand Rapids, MI: Zondervan Publishing House.

—. 1982. *The Word of God and the Mind of Man: The Crisis of Revealed Truth in Contemporary Theology.* Grand Rapids: Zondervan Publishing House.

Naugle, David K. 2002. *Worldview: The History of a Concept.* Grand Rapids, MI: William B. Eerdmans Publishing Company.

Netland, Harold A. 1997. *Dissonant Voices: Religious Pluralism and the Question of Truth.* Vancouver: Regent College Publishing.

—. 2001. *Encountering Religious Pluralism: The Challenge to Faith and Mission.* Downers Grove: InterVarsity Press.

Newbigin, Leslie. 1989. *The Gospel in a Pluralist Society.* Grand Rapids, MI: Eerdmans Publishing Company.

Newhaus, Richard John. 1984. *The Naked Public Square: Religion and Democracy in Amreica.* Grand Rapids: Eerdmans Publishing Company.

Nigro, H.L. 2004. *Before God's Wrath: The Bible's Answer to the Timing of the Rapture.* Belafonte, PA: Strong Tower Publishing.

Noll, Mark, Nathan O. Hatch and George Marsden. 1989. *The Search for Christian America.* Colorado Springs: Helmers & Howard.

Nord, Warren A. 1995. *Religion and American Education.* Chapel Hill and London: University of North Carolina Press.

Novak, Michael. 1994. *Belief and Unbelief: A Philosophy of Self-Knowledge.* New Brunswick: Transaction Publishers.

Numbers, Ronald L., ed. 2009. *Galileo Goes To Jail.* Cambridge: Harvard University Press.

Oakland, Roger. 2008. *Faith Undone.* Silverton: Lighthouse Trails Publishing.

Olson, Richard G. 2004. *Science and Religion 1450-1900.* Baltimore, MD: Johns Hopkins University.

O'Meara, Kelly Patricia. 2006. *Psyched Out.* Bloomington, IN: Author House.

Paglia, Camille. 1994. *Vamps & Tramps: New Essays.* New York: Vintage Books.

Paul, Ron. 2009. *End the Fed.* New York: Grand Central Publishing.

Pearcey, Nancy R. and Charles B. Thaxton. 1994. *The Soul of Science.* Wheaton, IL: Crossway Books.

Pearcey, Nancy. 2004. *Total Truth: Liberating Christianity from Its Cultural Captivity.* Wheaton: Crossway Books.

Pine, Lisa. 1997. *Nazi Family Policy 1933-1945.* New York: Berg.

Postman, Neil. 1993. *Technopoly.* New York: Vintage Books.

Prins, Nomi. 2009. *It Takes a Pillage.* Hoboken, NJ: John Wiley & Sons, Inc.

Quist, Allen. 2005. *America's Schools: The Battleground for Freedom.* Chaska: EdWatch.

Ratzsch, Del. 2000. *Science and Its Limits.* Downers Grove, IL: InterVarsity Press.

Reeves, Thomas C. 1996. *The Empty Church: The Suicide of Liberal Christianity.* New York: Free Press.

Reuben, Julie A. 1996. *The Making of the Modern University: Intellectual Transformation and the Marginalization of Morality.* Chicago & London: University of Chicago Press.

Revel, Jean-Francois, trans. William Byron. 1984. *How Democracies Perish.* Garden City, NY: Doubleday & Company, Inc.

Rieff, Philip. 1987. *The Triumph of the Therapeutic.* Chicago: University of Chicago Press.

Rifkin, Jeremy. 1983. *Algeny.* New York: Viking Press.

Ritholtz, Barry. 2009. *Bailout Nation.* Hoboken, NJ: John Wiley & Sons, Inc.

Rockefeller, David. 2003. *Memoirs.* New York: Random House Trade Paperback.

Roof, Wade Clark. 1999. *Spiritual Marketplace: Baby Boomers and the Remaking of American Religion.* Princeton: Princeton University Press.

Rosen, Christine. 2004. *Preaching Eugenics.* New York: Oxford University Press.

Rothkopf, David. 2008. *Superclass: The Global Power Elite and the World They Are Making.* New York: Farrar, Starus, and Giroux.

Rudolph, Frederick. 1990. *The American College and University: A History.* Athens and London: University of Georgia Press.

Rummel, R.J. 1997. *Death by Government.* Piscataway, NJ: Transaction Publishers.

Schaeffer, Francis. 1990. *The Francis Schaeffer Trilogy: He Is There and He Is Not Silent.* Wheaton: Crossway Books.

—. 1972. *The God Who Is There.* Downers Grove, IL: InterVarsity Press.

Schmitt, Frederick F. 1995. *Truth: A Primer.* Boulder: Westview Press.

Schwartz, Tony. 1996. *What Really Matters: Searching for Wisdom in America.* New York: Bantam Books.

Scruton, Roger. 1995. *Modern Philosophy: An Introduction and Survey.* New York: Allen Lane, The Penguin Press.

Shapiro, Ben. 2004. *Brainwashed.* Nashville, TN: WND Books.

Shaw, Wilfred. 1920. *The University of Michigan.* New York: Harcourt Brace and Howe.

Sider, Ronald J. 2005. *The Scandal of the Evangelical Conscience: Why Are Christians Living Just Like the Rest of the World?* Grand Rapids: Baker Books.

Simon, Sidney B., Leland W. Howe, and Howard Kirschenbaum. 1995. *Values Clarification.* New York: Warner Books.

Sire, James. 1988. *The Universe Next Door.* Downers Grove, IL: InterVarsity Press.

Sloan, Douglas. 1994. *Faith and Knowledge.* Louisville: Westminster John Knox Press.

Smith, Christian ed. 2003. *The Secular Revolution: Power, Interests, and Conflict in the Secularization of American Public Life.* Berkeley and Los Angeles: University of California Press.

Smith, Paul. 2011. *New Evangelicalism: The New World Order.* Costa Mesa, CA: Calvary Publishing.

Smith, Warren B. 2011. *False Christ Coming: Does Anybody Care?* Magalia: Mountain Stream Press.

Sobel, Dava. 1999. *Galileo's Daughter.* New York: Walker Publishing.

Sommers, Christina Hoff, and Sally Satel, M.D. 2005. *One Nation Under Therapy.* New York: St. Martin's Press.

Sowell, Thomas. 2009. *Intellectuals and Society.* New York: Basic Books.

Spitzer, Robert J., S.J. 2000. *Healing the Culture.* San Francisco: Ignatius Press.

Stanton, Glenn T., and Dr. Bill Maier. 2004. *Marriage on Trial: The Case Against Same-Sex Marriage and Parenting.* Downers Grove, IL: InterVarsity Press.

Stetson, Brad and Joseph G. Conti. 2005. *The Truth About Tolerance: Pluralism, Diversity, and the Culture Wars.* Downers Grove: InterVarsity Press.

Stewart, Matthew. 1997. *The Truth About Everything: An Irreverent History of Philosophy.* Amherst, New York: Prometheus Books.

Stout, Jeffrey. 1981. *The Flight From Authority: Religion, Morality, and the Quest for Autonomy.* Notre Dame: Universtiy of Notre Dame Press.

Sykes, Charles J. 1995. *Dumbing Down Our Kids.* New York: St. Martin's Griffin.

Tavakoli, Janet. 2009. *Dear Mr. Buffett.* Hoboken, NJ: John Wiley & Sons.

Taylor, Charles Alan. 1996. *Defining Science: A Rhetoric of Demarcation.* Madison, WI: University of Wisconsin Press.

Terrell, Richard. 2011. *Christ, Faith, and the Holocaust.* Bloomington: WestBow Press.

Thomson, Garrett. 1993. *Descartes to Kant: An Introduction to Modern Philosophy.* Prospect Heights: Waveland Press Inc.

Tillich, Paul. 1957. *Dynamaics of Faith.* New York: Harper Brothers.

Toulmin, Stephen. 1990. *Cosmopolis: The Hidden Agenda of Modernity.* Chicago: University of Chicago Press.

Trigg, Roger. 2002. *Philosophy Matters.* Malden & Oxford: Blackwell Publishers.

—. 1994. *Rationality and Science: Can Science Explain Everything?* Oxford: Blackwell.

—. 1973. *Reason and Commitment.* Cambridge: Cambridge University Press.

Troeltsch, Ernst, James Luther Adams and Walter F. Bense, trans. 1991. *Religion in History.* Edinburgh: T & T Clark.

Turtel, Joel. 2004-2005. *Public Schools, Public Menace.* New York: Liberty Books.

Via, Dan O., and Robert A..J. Gagnon. 2003. *Homosexuality and the Bible: Two Views.* Minneapolis, MN: Fortress Press.

Webster, Richard. 1995. *Why Freud Was Wrong: Sin, Science and Psychoanalysis.* New York: Basic Books.

Weikart, Richard. 2006. *From Darwin to Hitler.* New York: Palgrave Macmillan.

Wells, David F. 1993. *No Place For Truth: Whatever Happened to Evangelical Theology.* Grand Rapids: Eerdmans Publishing Company.

West, Diana. 2007. *The Death of the Grown-Up*. New York: St. Martin's Press.

West, John G. 2007. *Darwin Day in America*. Wilmington: ISI Books.

Westerhoff III, John H. 1982. *McGuffey and His Readers*. Michigan: Mott Media.

Whitaker, Robert. 2010. *Anatomy of an Epidemic: Magic Bullets, Psychiatric Drugs, and the Astonishing Rise of Mental Illness in America*. New York: Crown Publishers.

Whitehead, John W. 1986. *The End of Man*. Westchester, IL: Crossway Books.

Wilkens, Steve, and Alan G. Padgett. 2000. *Christianity and Western Thought, Vol.2*. Downers Grove, IL: InterVarsity Press.

Williams, Peter M. 1989. *Popular Religion in America: Symbolic Change and the Modernization Process In Historical Perspective*. Urbana: University of Illinois Press.

Wilson, A.N. 1999. *God's Funeral*. New York & London: W.W. Norton & Company.

Wilson, James Q. 2002. *The Marriage Problem: How Our Culture Has Weakened Families*. New York: HarperCollins Publishers.

Wolf, Naomi. 2007. *The End of America*. White River Junction: Chelsea Green Publishing Company.

Wolfe, Alan. 1999. *One Nation After All*. New York: Penguin Books.

Wolin, Sheldon S. 2008. *Democracy Inc.: Managed Democracy and the Specter of Inverted Totalitarianism*. Princeton and Oxford: Princeton University Press.

Woodward, Thomas. 2003. *Doubts About Darwin: A History of Intelligent Design*. Grand Rapids, MI: Baker Book House.

Wormser, Rene A. 1993. *Foundations: Their Influence and Power*. Covenant House Books.

Wuthnow, Robert. 1989. *Struggle for America's Soul: Evangelicals, Liberals, and Secularism*. Grand Rapids: William B. Eerdmans.

—. 1988. *The Restructuring of American Religion*. Princeton: Princeton University Press.

Young, Simon. 2006. *Designer Evolution: A Transhumanist Manifesto*. Amherst: Prometheus Books.

Zacharias, Ravi. 2000. *Jesus Among Other Gods: The Absolute Claims of the Christian Message*. Nashville: Word Publishing.

—. 2004. *The Real Face of Atheism*. Grand Rapids, MI: Baker Books.

Index

Made in the USA
Charleston, SC
10 November 2015